COMMUNITY-ORIENTED POLICING

A *Systemic Approach to Policing*

Fourth Edition

Willard M. Oliver
Sam Houston State University

PEARSON

Prentice
Hall

Upper Saddle River, New Jersey 07458

Library of Congress Cataloging-in-Publication Data

Editor-in-Chief: Vernon R. Anthony
Executive Editor: Tim Peyton
Assistant Editor: Mayda Bosco
Managing Editor: Mary Carnis
Production Liaison: Ann Pulido
Production Editor: Jessica Balch,
   Pine Tree Composition
Manufacturing Manager: Ilene Sanford

Manufacturing Buyer: Cathleen Petersen
Senior Design Coordinator: Christopher Weigand
Cover Design: Amy Rosen
Cover Image: The Image Works
Composition: Laserwords Private Limited,
   Chennai, India
Printing and Binding: R.R. Donnelley
Cover Printer: R.R. Donnelley

Pearson Education LTD.
Pearson Education Australia PTY, Limited
Pearson Education Singapore, Pte. Ltd.
Pearson Education North Asia Ltd.
Pearson Education Canada, Ltd.
Pearson Educación de Mexico, S.A. de C.V.
Pearson Education—Japan
Pearson Education Malaysia, Pte. Ltd.
Pearson Education, Upper Saddle River, New Jersey

10 9 8 7 6 5 4 3 2 1
ISBN-13: 978-0-13-158987-2
ISBN-10: 0-13-158987-3

*Dedicated to my beloved wife Judy,
my son James, and my daughter Sarah.*

*A special dedication goes to Paul, who in death,
through God, gave life.*

Contents

Foreword

There is certainly no doubt that the adventure of community policing has been riding a tidal wave of popularity and governmental support for over a decade now. And that momentum has surely not been overlooked in the academic coursework and textbook publishing worlds. Authors eager to jump on the community policing bandwagon have been churning out a proliferation of articles, commentaries, and textbooks. But just as there may be as many different variations of community policing as there are departments implementing it, the quality and impact of writings on this topic vary widely.

It is no exaggeration, in my opinion, to state that Oliver's book continues to stand out among the many community policing publications that presently exist. In more than thirty years of reviewing and editorial advising for Prentice Hall, I have rarely ever seen a textbook surface and survive that measures up to the standards this author set in his first edition back in 1998. Not only is this topic a very timely one, but more importantly, the author addresses the unique significance of community-oriented policing while still acknowledging that the movement truly embraces many commonsense and traditional ingredients. Whereas some advocates have promoted community policing as the virtual panacea for all agency and social ills, Professor Oliver takes a more rational and balanced approach. He teaches, but does not preach, the message and the values. And in such a reader-friendly manner!

Moreover, this author has done a masterful job of explaining community policing's historical evolution, rationale for existence, implementation strategies, pilot projects, focus of responsibility, delivery techniques, ideals to be achieved, cultures to be changed, and even ways to evaluate these ventures in order to determine when and if we are succeeding. Simply put, no other text on this dynamic topic is as ambitious or as comprehensive!

This textbook combines the best of all worlds. For those who require historical perspective, it is precise and factual. For those who want an update on progress and change, it is detailed and illustrative. For those who ask "What else is new?" it firmly speaks to an inventive philosophy that is interwoven into the often-unbending institution that we all have come to know as our modern police organizational structure. Unlike others, this text also seeks to clarify the management goals that are the critical ingredient. Most other texts are somewhat loose on the delicate issues describing managerial changes needed and ways values must be addressed before departments are capable of delivering a better product to the community in terms of public safety services. It is not easy to overstate how integral decentralization and empowerment are to the entire endeavor.

To many of us, police departments are much the same as our young children were as they were maturing. We have cared deeply about them, we have learned to live with their shortcomings, and we have tried hard to grasp the adjustments they have had to make as society influenced them. They, in turn, worked to adapt themselves to outside pressures, changing environments, and higher expectations. This text describes how those adaptations can occur without ever losing sight of the many diverse roles of the police (not to mention the community, which never quite agrees on how its many needs should all be met).

In reviewing many other resources and materials, one often is inclined to observe that the content is fine for a practitioner but lacks the academic rigor or the proper level of referencing to serve as a college textbook. On the other hand, writings heavy with well-documented research citations often can lack realism and relevance. Or, even more frequently, the narrative may lack the thoroughness and breadth to adequately address the subject. None of these limitations are found in this textbook. There are case studies for the practitioner, foreign comparisons for the international scholar, and research findings for everyone concerned.

Of special value to this new edition is the discussion on evaluation and research initiatives. Rarely does a textbook confront the reality of utilizing evaluation in order to determine the current state of the art and help guide the achievement of future goals. Since community policing involves risk-taking, only valid evaluations can really determine if the community is truly better off or if alternative strategies are called for.

Professor Oliver's *Community-Oriented Policing* contains all of the necessary components to enable one to state that this book combines knowledge, understanding, insight, realism, and direction. It provides a virtual encyclopedia of information about a most significant and widely heralded development in law enforcement.

If community policing accomplishes everything that its advocates anticipate, its current wave of popularity may well stabilize to become a solid foundation underlying the transition of American policing in the twenty-first century. And perhaps most significant is the promise it holds for propelling that momentum to raise policing to the status of professionalism that has been so long sought.

James D. Stinchcomb
Director (Retired)
School of Justice and Safety Administration
Miami-Dade Community College and Executive Advisor
Kaplan College

Preface

*Greater than the tread of mighty armies is
an idea whose time has come.*

—Victor Hugo

Community-oriented policing is truly an idea whose time has come. Research and application over the past twenty years have moved the idea from explaining the past failures of team policing, to a method that could avoid these past pitfalls, to a viable but crude method in the 1980s, to the successful and detailed practices of the 1990s, to the institutionalization of community-oriented policing in the twenty-first century. There is little doubt that this paradigm in policing has captured the attention of both citizen and police, mayors and police chiefs, state government and national government officials, and it has worked its way to becoming a household name. In fact, it has become so popular that one of America's leading econometricians, Anthony Downs, has called for more federal funding of community-oriented policing and placed it on his list of several actions intended to address his highest priority, reducing personal insecurity (Downs, 1994). The dilemma of understanding arises in how community-oriented policing is defined and what the paradigm entails. It is to this end that we must now set our sights.

Perhaps one of the first debates over this approach lies in questioning if it is "old wine in a new bottle." Critics of this paradigm have thus argued it is early-twentieth-century policing glorified and that turning back the policing clock would prove detrimental to both the profession and the citizens served. These critics seem to miss the fact that it is more than just making a new case for the methods, practices, and procedures utilized by the police today. It is an argument for changing the way we think about policing, from the perspectives of both the police and the community. Abraham Lincoln perhaps said it best: "As our case is new, so we must think and act anew." We recognize that the current case for promulgating community-oriented policing is new; what we on many occasions have failed to do, from both an academic and practical standpoint, is allow ourselves to think and act anew. Although nostalgia, common in all organizations, may exist in policing, community-oriented policing is not a push backward but rather a rapid movement forward regarding the mission of the police and the ways they perform their duties. Yet, despite this realization, the questions continue to linger as to what specifically constitutes community-oriented policing.

A key debate within the central understanding of the systemic approach to policing is whether community-oriented policing is a philosophy or a program. The argument on the side of a philosophy is rooted in the premise that for the systemic approach to be fully functional, it must grow from a conceptual framework from which all the actors can adhere to mutual principles but retain the freedom to ad-lib. The argument on the programmatic side is rooted in the understanding that methods employed by the actors must be more substantive and should therefore be put forth in a script with written parts for each actor. The argument can be further broken down into whether community-oriented policing is a concept for the way we think about the police or for actions garnering the policing. It is an argument between the theoretical and the practical.

To delineate the importance of the two, it is crucial to reach an age-old method of issue resolution: compromise. Theory, often in its true form, ignores the practical application, thus negating the possible benefits derived from a theory. Practical application, in turn, often ignores theory, thus negating the benefits that can be derived from a guiding theoretical construct. The consensus lies in the commitment for both the theoretical and practical to coalesce into a synthesis that supersedes the ontological perspectives, thus creating a mutually beneficial relationship. The synthesis can then be utilized for the proposition of a conceptual framework from which to guide the systemic application from the theoretical to the practical.

Community-oriented policing, as a systemic approach to policing, is in fact the realization of this synthesis. It incorporates both the theoretical and the practical in the overall framework, thus allowing the maximization of benefits. It must start as a new philosophy, a new way of thinking about the role of the police in society, and it must be enacted through new and various programs that adhere to the philosophical premise. This, then, is the primary emphasis of this book. It is an attempt to weave together both the theoretical and the practical, as well as to combine the various interpretations of the systemic approach, into one concept under the banner of community-oriented policing.

OVERVIEW OF THE BOOK'S CONTENTS

New to the fourth edition of this textbook is the incorporation of over 70 additional references that have been published over the past three years. Since the third edition was published, the amount of research published on community-oriented policing has seemingly increased tenfold. Much of it has continued to support previous findings, other research has confirmed what was theorized a decade ago, and some has raised questions about the assumptions and premises of community-oriented policing. All of this has been included in the new edition, along with updated charts, new boxes, and additional photographs, in order to present the most contemporary portrayal of both theoretical and practical applications of community-oriented policing.

The first chapter is a historical review of police and community relations since the formation of the United States. Although other authors have attempted to analyze the eras of policing from a strict police perspective, in this chapter I analyze the relationship between the two parties and place them into eras indicative of the type of relationship occurring at the time. A review of history from this perspective, Chapter 1 is largely historical, and that is acceptable because it allows the reader a better understanding of the different relationships we are now entering into under the auspices of community-oriented policing.

Chapter 2 is the guiding chapter for the rest of the book in that it attempts to provide a clear understanding of what community-oriented policing is and how it is defined, in both theoretical and practical terms. The construct of the chapter shares a three-pronged process that was assembled to reach a definition of community-oriented policing. It reflects the multitude of definitions and explanations that have surfaced in the academic literature for the past twenty years, which cover both theoretical constructs and research methodologies. It reflects the practical applications covered in various journals and magazines and synthesizes the definitions and actions implemented by police departments across the United States under the auspices of community-oriented policing. And, finally, the third prong is the inclusion of my understanding and definition of the systemic approach based on my experiences as a police officer and the community-oriented policing programs I have had the fortune to witness. The culmination of this three-pronged approach has revealed many consistent themes throughout the academic literature, the practical literature, and my own experiences. Community-oriented policing can then be defined as

> a systemic approach to policing with the paradigm of instilling and fostering a sense of community, within a geographical neighborhood, to improve the quality of life. It achieves this through the decentralization of the police and the implementation of a synthesis of three key components: (1) strategic-oriented policing—the redistribution of traditional police resources; (2) neighborhood-oriented policing—the interaction of police and all community members to reduce crime and the fear of crime through indigenous proactive programs; and (3) problem-oriented policing—a concerted effort to resolve the causes of crime rather than the symptoms.

The next three chapters concentrate on expanding the definition by breaking down each component into its own chapter. Chapter 3 is a more detailed explanation of strategic-oriented policing and all of the potential methods the police can employ to successfully adopt this component. Chapter 4 is an overview of the many types of police and community programs that can promote interaction and communication between the two actors to understand the quality-of-life benefits that can be derived from this cooperation. Chapter 5 defines the component of problem-oriented policing and draws heavily from the works of Herman Goldstein (academic) and John E. Eck and William Spelman (practical). Chapter 6 has been reformatted for this fourth edition by combining the elements of the implementation material (from Chapter 11 of the third edition) with the synthesis material (Chapter 6 of the third edition). Missing from this new Chapter 6 are the three old case studies due to the fact they are no longer useful as a tool for explaining community-oriented policing in a small, mid, and large city police agency. They have been replaced by numerous case studies in box format throughout the textbook. Merging Chapter 11 with Chapter 6 allows a more logical flow of chapters that explains what community-oriented policing is and then how it is implemented. This also reduces some redundancy that occurred in the two chapters, and the 15-chapter format is more conducive to a typical semester in most academic programs.

Chapter 7 provides an understanding of how the systemic approach to policing will mandate systemic changes to both the organization of the police department and the management methods employed. It specifically details how the police department must decentralize by geography, personnel, and structure to achieve the true benefits of community-oriented policing, and it reviews the varying types of management practices that complement the systemic approach, specifically total quality management (TQM).

The next three chapters detail the role of the three key actors involved in ensuring the success of community-oriented policing: the police, the community, and the police chief. Chapter 8, on the role of the police, gives wide coverage to the changes that must be made to transform traditional police officers to community-oriented police officers. Because the police are the street-level implementors of the philosophy and programs under the systemic approach, they are a key link to the overall success of community-oriented policing. However, because the systemic approach is geared toward the community, it is readily apparent that the community's role in community-oriented policing is equally important. Its role is detailed in Chapter 9, which provides an understanding of what is meant by community and how past attitudes of not getting involved in police matters can be overcome. Chapter 10 then provides the key link to the relationship between the police and the community: the role of the police chief in community-oriented policing. This role, as a result of changes in the police, community, and organizational and management structures, must also change to accommodate the synthesis of philosophy and practical applications. It is important that the chief become a dynamic member of the community and that the chief's office provide the impetus for the systemic approach.

Chapter 11 proves to be the most daunting of the chapters, but it highlights the fact that evaluations under community-oriented policing are crucial to the success of this paradigm. The evaluation process must not be limited to one actor but must be made a part of the everyday duties of the police and can include surveys of local citizens, police officers, and local government employees. As the systemic approach is implemented in an incremental fashion, these surveys become part of the evaluation process and provide the necessary information for the police, citizens, and police chief to make the determination as to whether a particular program or policing method should be continued, deleted, or altered in some way.

Chapter 12 explores the ever-expanding federal role in community-oriented policing as a result of the Violent Crime Control and Law Enforcement Act of 1994, which created the Office of Community Oriented Policing Services (COPS) under the U.S. Department of Justice. The chapter reviews the politics behind the "100,000 cops" initiative, the ways it included the concepts of community-oriented policing, and the methods by which the federal government chose to become involved in the systemic approach. It specifically details the various grants for personnel and equipment, describes the training initiatives, and provides a critical assessment of the COPS program to date.

Chapter 13 details the comparative approach to community-oriented policing by first raising the awareness of comparative studies and then articulating the comparative approach as it applies to the systemic approach to policing. The community-oriented policing programs of Canada, Britain, and Japan are explored in depth, followed by a brief review of other community-oriented policing endeavors worldwide.

Chapter 14 covers many of the caveats that go with implementing community-oriented policing. These caveats are based on the various failures of past policing experiments and recent failures with community-oriented policing. This information provides insight into why certain programs have failed in the hopes that these methods will not be repeated in future implementations of the systemic approach. Hence, these are not in actuality problems for the implementation process but rather caveats to make the police department that decides to shift to this new paradigm aware of the many possibilities for failure.

Finally, Chapter 15 speaks of the future benefits that police departments may receive when implementing community-oriented policing, as well as the overall benefits that have already been achieved. It also delves further into the future to discuss many of the potential benefits and provides some discussion of how police departments can plan for the future, today. Finally, it discusses the future of community-oriented policing especially when faced with what has been called an "era of homeland security."

Acknowledgments

The person I must thank the most, as always, is my wife, Judy Ilaria Oliver. Words cannot describe the admiration and love I have for you. I simply must say thank you for all your support, love, and hard work in keeping our family strong.

I also wish to thank my second son, James Patrick Oliver; my third son, Mark Matthew Oliver (deceased) and my daughter, Sarah Elizabeth Oliver.

Special appreciation goes to three Pauls: Paolo Ponzi, who died saving a child trapped in a well, a life of giving cut short; Paul Fellers, another life cut far too short and a man I would have loved to have known; and Paul Thomas Oliver, my firstborn son, who continues to renew my faith in life. Judy, Paul, James, Mark, and Sarah—all of you are simply the sum total of my life. I thank God for each of you every day.

I would also like to thank everyone at Prentice Hall who has made this book and the other two editions a reality. My heartfelt thanks go to Bryce Dodson, whom I absentmindedly queried for a textbook on community-oriented policing—and then ended up writing one. To Robin Balizewski, and Tim Peyton, who have all served as my editors on the four editions, thank you. And a special thank-you is extended to Mayda Bosco, who has been instrumental in the production of this edition. It is because of such wonderful people as you that it has been a pleasure to write for Prentice Hall.

I must also thank all of the individuals who have reviewed this book for Prentice Hall. Their hints, ideas, and constructive criticism have served to make this a far better book than I could have produced on my own. Thank you for your time and effort, and please know that I am indebted to you for your assistance. My appreciation extends to those who reviewed the first and second editions—James D. Stinchcomb, Kaplan College; Lois A. Wims, Salve Regina University; Richard R. Becker, North Harris College; Leslie W. Parks, University of Texas–Brownsville; Karen J. Terry, John Jay College; David A. Kessler, Kent State University; Barry Dineen, California State University—to those who reviewed the third edition—Wayne Coates, Pitt Community College, Winterville, NC; Holly Dersham-Bruce, Dawson Community College, Glendive, MT; Steve Egger, University of Springfield, IL; Bruce T. Smith, Ohio University–Chillicothe, Chillicothe, OH; and Wayne Wolf, South Suburban College, Blue Island, IL—and to those who reviewed the fourth edition—Elizabeth De Valve, Fayetteville State University, Fayetteville, NC; Jon R. Duke, Missouri Valley College, Marshall, MO; James F. Pastor, Calumet College of St. Joseph, Whiting, IN; Joseph Schafer, Southern Illinois University, Carbondale, IL; and Harry D. Ulferts, Sauk Valley Community College, Dixon, IL.

Along the way there have been so many people who have been instrumental in assisting me in the evolution of this book, both directly and indirectly, that it is impossible to thank all of them individually, but they know who they are and I hope my appreciation is known. To all those at Radford University and West Virginia University who assisted me in my education and as well as my colleagues at Glenville State College and Radford University, thank you. And to those I served with as a police officer and to those police officers I have met along the way, to the members of the West Virginia Community Policing Steering Committee and the West Virginia Regional Community Policing Institute, and to those I have met at the Office of Community Oriented Policing Services and the Community Policing Consortium, thank you for all your assistance. I would also like to extend my heartfelt thanks to my colleagues at Sam Houston State University for receiving me so warmly and making me feel welcome in my new home. I would especially like to thank former Dean Richard Ward, and Current Dean Vince Webb as well as Wes Johnson, Jarex mullnags, and all the faculty who have made me part of the C.J. Family at Sam Houston State University.

As I started with family, so I must end with family. I would like to thank my mom, Carol R. Oliver, for giving me her love and support over the years and for always being my biggest fan. I must also thank my dad, Charles J. Oliver. I would also like to thank my "other family," Donald and Ilaria Fellers, whom I love as much as my own parents, and my "sister" Kathy Fellers. Finally, a very special thanks goes to two wonderful people whom I still consider my "guardian angels," my Uncle Gene and Aunt Julia. The two of you have always managed to be there when I needed you most and when it always meant the most.

I thank all of you for your gifts of kindness.

Willard M. Oliver
Huntsville, TX

About the Author

Willard M. Oliver is an Associate Professor of Criminal Justice at Sam Houston State University, Huntsville, Texas. He is the editor of *Community Policing: Classical Readings* (Prentice Hall, 2000), the author of *Homeland Security for Policing* (Prentice Hall, 2007), and the co-author of *The Public Policy of Crime and Criminal Justice* (Prentice Hall, 2006) with Nancy Marion. He has published in many journals, including *American Journal of Criminal Justice, Policing: An International Journal of Police Supervision and Management, Police Practice and Research: An International Journal, Police Quarterly, Journal of Criminal Justice Education*, and *Crime and Justice International*, on the topic of community-oriented policing. He is the former Research and Evaluation Coordinator for the West Virginia Regional Community Policing Institute (RCPI) and is a former police officer.

CHAPTER 1

The Evolution of Community-Oriented Policing

History in illuminating the past illuminates the present and in illuminating the present illuminates the future.

—Benjamin N. Cardozo

CHAPTER OBJECTIVES

- Recognize the current status of community-oriented policing.
- Trace the historical roots of policing.
- Trace the historical roots of community-oriented policing.
- Understand the political era of policing.
- Understand the public relations era of policing.
- Understand the police–community relations era of policing.
- Understand the current era of policing as community-oriented policing.
- Recognize the originators of the concept of community-oriented policing.

Policing in the United States is once again undergoing a period of rapid change in the wake of the terrorist attacks of September 11, 2001. While police departments across the United States have been implementing the principles of community-oriented policing for nearly two decades, the threat of terrorism and the concentrated efforts of Homeland Security have forced the police to rethink their role. What this will mean for policing is too soon to tell, but there are overtures of police agencies moving toward an enhanced security standing. However, this has not negated the necessity of community-oriented policing in America, and many have argued that it has increased the need for this particular approach (Docobo 2005; Doherty 2006). Regardless, community-oriented policing has become a mainstay of American policing, and its tenets will be practiced well into the twenty-first century.

Community-oriented policing is not a new philosophy. Its roots can be traced as far back as the first conceptual model of policing and the first police department in the free world. Historically, it is firmly established in the founding and evolution of a new nation and its expansion westward, the Industrial Revolution, and the more recent transformation into an information age. Community-oriented policing is found in past policy and procedure regarding the police and in past literature from both the practitioner and academic fields. The concept started with a simple premise and through many successes and failures pushed itself into the well-established doctrine we see and recognize today as part of community-oriented policing.

To understand the concept's development from the early 1980s to the present, it is important to examine these past concepts that have developed into community-oriented policing. What has gone before is important for understanding this theoretical framework that has no standard definition and often lacks a standard method of implementation. Although there are varying thoughts as to the history of policing and the eras from which it has progressed, the majority run along consistent themes that provide the clarity necessary to understand the evolution. In other cases, the lineage of today's concept is clearly evident within the past literature regarding the police. The culmination of these historical approaches to the modern doctrine provides many answers to the philosophy we so highly regard today.

A police officer from the Dallas Police Department teaches students at a local elementary school. (*Courtesy of the Dallas Police Department, Dallas, Texas.*)

HISTORICAL ROOTS OF POLICING

Policing dates back to the early days of humans and is usually dated by historians in the pre-2100 B.C. time frame. In the year 2100 B.C., the first record of a "police" force that enforced written laws and their punishments was the Code of Hammurabi in ancient Babylon. The police at this time, as is common throughout most of civilization's history, was the military. Prior to the 2100 B.C. time frame, it is largely believed that the practices of policing were left to the individual tribes, which utilized either the warriors or the elders (Oliver and Hilgenberg 2006).

The first change in policing is found in the Anglo-Saxon period when King Alfred established the Frank-Pledge system in England (Sullivan 1977). The Frank-Pledge system emphasized rudimentary forms of social control. If a crime or serious matter was at hand, the people raised the "hue and cry" and the other members of the community were required to render assistance (Dempsey 1994). The community was divided up along the power of ten, with groups of ten families known as tithings. Each tithing was responsible for the actions of its group members, and any criminal act or order mainte-nance issue was handled within the tithing. The leader of the tithing was known as the tithingman. The next level of responsibility was the ten-tithing, which was the collection of 100 families, who answered to a constable. Collections of several ten-tithings were or-ganized along geographical lines and were under the control of the king. Although the king was in control of the geographical area, he generally placed a man to govern this collection of various ten-tithings. This man was known as the shire-reeve or, in today's terms, the sheriff (Oliver and Hilgenberg 2006).

The system was perhaps the first in the history of policing that fully integrated the policing of a community with the members of the community. Despite the fact that there were appointed individuals such as the tithingman, the constable, or the shire-reeve, no formal police force existed separate from the citizens. This system is then the first rudimentary element of the concept of community-oriented policing. This system remained in effect from its implementation by King Alfred in A.D. 899 until the Duke of Normandy conquered England in the year A.D. 1066, at which time the function of policing returned to the hands of the military (Sullivan 1977).

In 1215, the rebel barons succeeded in forcing King John to sign the Magna Carta, granting certain rights and concessions to the people. The Magna Carta cleared the way for the Statute of Winchester to pass in 1285; this statute essentially revised the majority of policing practices that had been successful in the past. These successful practices in-cluded the "hue and cry" and the use of the "watch and ward," the night and day patrol, respectively, and required all males from fifteen to sixty to retain arms in their residence (Sullivan 1977). These practices remained in effect for the next 500 years and reflected the only other community-oriented philosophy of policing until the first official police department was formed.

At the turn of the eighteenth century, England experienced its Industrial Revolu-tion. During this time period, major social change occurred within every fabric of society, of which crime was no exception. The rising crime rates necessitated a response in the form of an advanced method of social control. Although previously pursued by Patrick Colquhoun, a London magistrate in 1789, the concept of a metropolitan police force was not received well by the citizenry at that time (Gilbert 1986). However, Patrick Colquhoun planted a seed of possibility in the minds of the citizens, and with the new social conditions this seed began to take shape.

In 1829, Sir Robert Peel, utilizing Patrick Colquhoun's ideas, drafted and promoted the Metropolitan Police Act of 1829. It was a hotly contested concept because of the fear that the police would become another of the military forces that had been so frequently used against the citizens in the past. Citizens feared an even greater control over them by government. Despite these concerns, the proposal passed in Parliament and became law. The first large-scale and official police department was now a reality, and Parliament chose Sir Robert Peel to lead the new organization (Sullivan 1977).

The organization was not military in nature, but it was organized along military lines. The police were uniformed with "three-quarter-length royal blue coats, white trousers, and top hats," were armed with a truncheon (nightstick), and walked a beat (Dempsey 1994, 5). They were housed in an old palace that originally housed Scottish royalty, hence the name Scotland Yard, and they were affectionately known as "Bobbies," named in reference to their founder, Sir Robert Peel. Although this was clearly the first formally organized police department, it was also the first formalized method of community policing.

This community approach is clearly evident in the premise of policing by Sir Robert Peel, when he stated that "the police are the public and the public are the police" (Braiden 1992, 108). This was the foundation of Peel's beliefs of what an effective police department should be like, specifically, community oriented. This perspective was also evident when Sir Robert Peel condensed his theory of basic policing principles into Peel's Principles (Sullivan 1977, 11). (See Table 1-1.) These principles, although not definitively aimed at community policing, provide some insight into the fact that the police

TABLE 1-1   *Robert Peel's Twelve Principles*

1. The police must be stable, efficient, and organized along military lines.
2. The police must be under government control.
3. The absence of crime will best prove the efficiency of police.
4. The distribution of crime news is essential.
5. Proper deployment of police strength, by both time and area, is essential.
6. No quality is more indispensable to a policeman than a perfect command of temper. A quiet, determined manner has more effect than violent action.
7. Good appearance commands respect.
8. The selection and training of proper persons are at the root of efficient law enforcement.
9. Public security demands that every police officer be given an identifying number.
10. Police headquarters should be centrally located and easily accessible to people.
11. Policemen should be hired on a probationary basis before permanent assignment.
12. Police crime records are necessary for the best distribution of police strength.

should be responsive to the community's needs. Peel's Principles attempted to take into account that to a large degree the police must be well-trained, committed, and ethical organizations that are under the control of the government and must be accountable to the people. Although there is a strong demand for a centralized police force within Peel's Principles, there is also the demand for community relations, something largely missing throughout most of policing's history.

POLICING IN THE NEW FRONTIER

The development of the police in the new frontier known as America was slow in its evolution. Although the first city, Jamestown, Virginia, was established in 1607, it would be more than 200 years before the first formal police department was established. This period of American history, prior to the signing of the Declaration of Independence and the passage of the Constitution, was largely policed by the sheriff. The sheriff at this time was generally a political appointee who performed multiple tasks in his jurisdiction to include overseeing elections. Night watches were a common method of policing, borrowed from the old country for nighttime security, and were usually staffed by volunteers, but in some areas men were paid meager wages (Oliver and Hilgenberg 2006).

In 1776, the Declaration of Independence was signed and the United States commenced its journey toward the path of freedom, creating a government whose authority was vested in the people. Thomas Jefferson managed to convey multiple theories of the rights of man, the ideology of community, and the institution of government within this document. When Jefferson explained that "All men are created equal" and that they enjoy certain "unalienable rights," he set the stage for the inherent ideology of the American people that still exerts its influence today. He also detailed that these rights included "Life, Liberty, and the pursuit of Happiness," thereby enumerating those particular rights that Americans hold so dear. When Jefferson spoke of government existing to protect those rights and that the government was created by "the consent of the governed," he alluded to the power of the government to protect the people and that the government is made up of those people. The philosophy that the "police are the public and the public are the police" resurfaces into the "government are the people and the people are the government," all very central to the tenets of community-oriented policing.

In the long, hot summer of 1787, the Constitutional Convention convened to determine the organization of a new government, predicated on the beliefs that Jefferson wrote so eloquently of in the Declaration of Independence. Presented on September 17, 1787, the Constitution became the form of government by the people with a system of checks and balances to prevent dictatorial rule and despotism. Although the Constitution addresses little in the way of specifics for the organization of the police, it speaks tenfold of the police in the greatest mission statement ever written.

The preamble to the Constitution of the United States is essentially the mission statement of the country. Within this superbly articulated sentence, the role of the government is dictated and the inferences to the relationship of the police within the community can easily be extracted. Police power is not specifically dictated within the Constitution but rather juxtaposed by those rights reserved to the people and the requirements of due process.

The preamble states:

> We the People of the United States of America, in Order to form a more perfect Union, establish Justice, insure domestic Tranquility, provide for the common defence, promote the general Welfare, and secure the Blessings of Liberty to ourselves and our Posterity, do ordain and establish this Constitution for the United States of America.

Because the preamble commences with the word *We*, there is no distinction along the lines of government and the common person—perhaps the ultimate sense of community. The goal of these people to "form a more perfect Union" provides the purpose for the organization. However, it is the statement "establish Justice" that stands out most clearly for the police. The police do not exist in a vacuum and are an essential part of this clause. The government, via the police, must ensure that justice is served in our society for the purposes of order maintenance. Through this, the American people can "insure domestic Tranquility."

Another clause that gives credence to the power of the police is the goal to "promote the general Welfare." The police services oriented to law enforcement and order maintenance provide for the overall welfare of the American people. The ability of people to live without fear in their communities is important to the overall health of the nation, and the Founding Fathers understood this important concept. The police are often tasked with overseeing the ideology found in this clause and, through past orientation, have not been as successful in its implementation.

And, finally, the emphasis can be placed heavily on the police ability to "secure the Blessings of Liberty to ourselves and our Posterity" for the purpose of their role in society. The ability of the police to maintain order and to reduce crime intrinsically provides for a better America today and tomorrow. The ultimate goal of the police mission should perhaps be focused primarily on providing a better place to live for our "posterity" because all parents dream of providing a better world for their children. The police and the community have the chance to fulfill this goal through the implementation of community-oriented policing, of which the "Blessings of Liberty to ourselves and our Posterity" is the cardinal goal.

Equally important to the citizens was the fact that despite the rhetoric of the Declaration of Independence and the structure of government as delineated by the Constitution of the United States, no express rights were granted to the people. The citizens at the time felt that they were afforded no protection from the new government becoming as despotic as the British government, and there was a call for some form of preservation of rights. This call was answered in the Bill of Rights, which was ratified on December 15, 1791, and provided protection for the people, against government, for freedom of speech, against unreasonable searches and seizures, and against jailing without due process of law. The citizens gained protection from an intrusive government on that day in 1791, and these rights still stand to protect our individual freedoms.

The power of the government was not lost on any of the Founding Fathers, especially Alexander Hamilton. Although there is no statement as to the authority of the police within the Constitution, there is little argument about whether the function of the police is necessary. Hamilton realized the full potential of the system of justice, or in today's terms the criminal justice system, of which policing is an integral part. Hamilton stated succinctly:

> There is one transcendent advantage belonging to the province of the State governments, which alone suffices to place the matter in a clear and satisfactory light—I mean the ordinary administration of criminal and civil justice. This, of all others, is the most powerful, most universal, and most attractive source of popular

obedience and attachment. It is this which, being the immediate and visible guardian of life and property, having its benefits and its terrors in constant activity before the public eye, regulating all those personal interests and familiar concerns to which the sensibility of individuals is more immediately awake, contributes more than any other circumstances to impressing upon the minds of the people affection, esteem, and reverence towards the government. This great cement of society, which will diffuse itself almost wholly through the channels of the particular governments, independent of all other causes of influence, would insure them so decided an empire over their respective citizens as to render them at all times a complete counterpoise . . . to the power of the union. (Rossiter 1961, 120)

Alexander Hamilton could easily have spoken of the one component of the criminal justice system we are concerned with here—the police. The introduction of the American citizen to not only the police but also the criminal justice system and government itself is often wrapped up within that simple contact of the citizen with a police officer. This contact can be as simple as the introduction of the citizen to the officer or as complex as the interaction between a rape victim and the investigating officer. In either case, it is this contact that formulates the public's perception of the police, the criminal justice system, and the government. The weight of this contact is often lost on those who work the street. Through the concepts of community-oriented policing, this concept that Hamilton spoke of over 200 years ago, is an overall focus to this systemic approach to policing.

POLICING IN A YOUNG AMERICA

The nineteenth century was truly the century that witnessed the early formulation of the concepts of modern-day policing. The sheriff remained the primary law enforcement officer throughout the land, although various forms of nightwatchmen remained in effect. It was not until 1838 that the first organized police department was created in Boston, Massachusetts. The department consisted of eight members who patrolled the streets of Boston during daylight hours (Oliver and Hilgenberg 2006). Similar police departments began formulating across the country, with New York City's in 1845 and Philadelphia's in 1854. The growth of police departments was largely seen in the major urban areas, and most of the appointments were entrenched in politics (Walker 1980).

 COP IN ACTION

Police Museums Offer Opportunities to Teach, Recruit

It's difficult to believe that shortly over a decade ago there was no Houston Police Department Museum. Today, the two-storied treasury of historical artifacts is an impressive teaching and recruiting tool. Its director, Officer Denny Hair, displays interesting memorabilia which recounts the days of Houston's growth, both as a city and a police department. Visitors come in droves. Hair said the facility has greeted more than 180,000 people to date, with many of those coming from both public and private schools. "It's a wonderful recruiting tool for the department," Hair said.

The museum is nestled in a corner of the city's police academy. The setting is both operational and architecturally attractive. It is a grouping of several buildings surrounding a display of water fountains and reflection pools. Visitors see cadets walking and visiting as they change classes, enjoying lunch and break times, and crossing to buildings housing the firing range. An interesting aspect of the museum is its ability to teach adults and children about police officers and their jobs.

With the birth of the museum, Hair went out in the community soliciting assistance. Financial aid in the form of donations from area businesses and the 100 Club of Houston, Inc. provided funding for the necessary display cases to begin the massive project. Then Hair began purchasing mat board, glue, and cutting tools with his own money and began preparation of the displays. Items for the exhibits come from a variety of sources. Donations of family memorabilia—pictures, old uniforms, badges, letters, and scrapbooks—are filled with historical interest. Other displays have been begged for and pieced together.

Hair is proud of his efforts with the museum and wants to ensure that the facility is around long after he is gone. "This is a great recruiting tool. I see the positive impact that officers have on the community because of those who come to visit the museum."

Along with the two-hour tours conducted twice weekly, preparations of exhibits, and other job assignments linked directly to the operation of the facility, Hair also teaches classes on the history of the police department to cadets going through the academy. While his job assignment might be out of the ordinary for the normal uniformed officer on patrol, Hair has proven his point that Houston needed a museum.

Source: Adapted with permission from Ann Worrell, "Police Museums Offer Opportunities to Teach, Recruit," *Law and Order*, December 1993, pp. 32–35.

Eventually Congress passed the Pendleton Act of 1883, which established a civil service system for the federal government to prevent political appointments, corruption, and scandals. The states, counties, and cities soon followed suit, and appointments and promotions were eventually based primarily on merit and not politics. This became one of the first movements toward police reform, but it would not reach fruition until well into the twentieth century. It was then, at the turn of the twentieth century, with the advent of the Industrial Revolution, that policing became the established institution that we recognize today.

POLICING IN THE TWENTIETH CENTURY

Policing, like the whole country, was dramatically changed at the start of the twentieth century by the arrival of the Industrial Revolution. The movement toward technology, the increase in urban populations, and a move toward scientific management principles all promoted progressive changes within the police. However, two key events had the most dramatic effect on the police, both curiously occurring within the same year: the Boston police strike of 1919 and the passage of the Volstead Act in 1919.

The Boston police strike was a direct result of the Industrial Revolution, which witnessed the organization of labor unions. The police coexisted with various industries and organizations that were unionizing and obtaining increased salaries, improved working conditions, and various forms of collective bargaining; at the time, the police were losing ground and becoming one of the least respectable institutions in society. A handful of police departments across the country were allowing their officers to unionize; however, in Boston, Massachusetts, the city refused to allow the American Federation of Labor

(AFL) to establish a union (Cole 1995). This conflict came to a head on September 9, 1919, when over 1,000 police officers went on strike. Riots broke out in the community, and the state militia was mobilized by then-governor Calvin Coolidge. The strike kept police officers from unionizing for several decades and launched Calvin Coolidge into the White House (Oliver and Hilgenberg 2006).

The second significant event during this period was the passage of the Volstead Act in 1919, which became law through the Eighteenth Amendment to the Constitution of the United States, outlawing the sale, transportation, and manufacture of liquor. Prohibition saw the rise in both organized crime and street crime before the amendment was repealed in 1933 by the Twenty-First Amendment. This time period was marked by an increased demand on the police as well as an increase in police corruption. President Calvin Coolidge appointed J. Edgar Hoover to the director's position within the Federal Bureau of Investigation (FBI), and the use of federal, state, and local police dramatically increased. These two events helped launch the police into a new era of policing, which allowed for the police to modify their practices and procedures to the familiar aspects we recognize today.

This time period of policing is often recognized as the political era (Kelling and Moore 1988). (See Table 1-2.) The specific dates of 1840 through 1930 are easily recognizable as a period of policing in its rudimentary stages. Politics were largely responsible for the authority of the police, and, as described previously, the police had multiple functions in society. The police were clearly decentralized, were close to the community, and were well entrenched in the politics of the locale, despite the passage of the Pendleton

The author's son, Paul Oliver, having his fingerprints taken by a Huntsville Police Officer (Huntsville, Texas) at an annual Cub Scout function while his sister (Sarah) and mother (Judy) watch. (*Author photo.*)

TABLE 1-2   *Police and Community Relations over Time in the United States*

ERA OF POLICING	PREMISE	YEARS
Political relations	Political	1776–1930
Public relations	Objectivity	1930–1960
Police–community relations	Advocacy	1960–1985
Community-oriented policing	Partnerships	1985–present

Act. However, many problems surfaced with policing during this time period, necessitating an evolutionary change and a period of reform.

Kelling and Moore (1988) describe the period of 1930 through the 1970s and partially into the 1980s as the reform era. This era is clearly marked by the Wickersham Commission's 1931 report on the criminal justice system and the professionalization of policing through great leaders such as August Vollmer and O. W. Wilson, as well as the reform-minded J. Edgar Hoover, who, in his early years, overtook a corrupt organization and changed both the abilities of the agency and the people's perceptions of the agency. The Supreme Court decisions revolving around police standards also contributed to this reformation of the police, as did the Johnson administration's passage of the Omnibus Crime Control and Safe Streets Act of 1968 and the creation of the Law Enforcement Assistance Administration (LEAA), which existed from 1969 to 1980. A dramatic change in the way police perform their duties was then a direct result of a concerted effort by these individuals, Supreme Court decisions, and various public policies. (See Table 1-3.)

The reform era was essentially the professionalization of the police and a concentration of their effectiveness on laws, through laws (Kelling and Moore 1988). The majority of police departments across the country moved toward centralization to establish better

TABLE 1-3   *Recommendations by the President's Commission on Law Enforcement and Administration of Justice in Their Report Titled* The Challenge of Crime in a Free Society

- The police should formally participate in community planning in all cities.
- Police departments in all large communities should have community-relations machinery consisting of a headquarters unit that plans and supervises the department's community-relations programs. It should also have precinct units, responsible to the precinct commander, that carry out the problems. Community relations must be both a staff and a line function. Such machinery is a matter of the greatest importance in any such community that has a substantial minority population.
- In each police precinct in a minority-group neighborhood, there should be a citizens' advisory committee that meets regularly with police officials to work out solutions to problems of conflict between the police and the community. It is crucial that the committees be broadly representative of the community as a whole, including those elements who are critical or aggrieved.

TABLE 1-3   *(Continued)*

- It should be a high-priority objective of all departments in communities with a substantial minority population to recruit minority-group officers and to deploy and promote them fairly. Every officer in such departments should receive thorough grounding in community-relations subjects. His performance in the field of community relations should be periodically reviewed and evaluated.
- Every jurisdiction should provide adequate procedures for full and fair processing of all citizen grievances and complaints about the conduct of any public officer or employee.
- Basic police functions, especially in large and medium-sized urban departments, should be divided among three kinds of officers, here termed the community service officer, the police officer, and the police agent.
- Police departments should recruit far more actively than they now do, with special attention to college campuses and inner-city neighborhoods.
- The ultimate aim of all police departments should be that all personnel with general enforcement powers have baccalaureate degrees.
- All training programs should provide instruction on subjects that prepare recruits to exercise discretion properly, and to understand the community, the role of the police, and what the criminal justice system can and cannot do.
- Police departments should commence experimentation with a team policing concept that envisions those with patrol and investigative duties combining under unified command with flexible assignments to deal with the crime problems in a defined sector.

Source: Adapted from President's Commission on Law Enforcement and Administration of Justice, *The Challenge of Crime in a Free Society.* New York: Avon Books, 1968.

command and control, effectively isolating themselves from the communities, thus functioning in a detached manner. This mode of policing remained the predominant method of providing services to the community for the greater part of the twentieth century.

In a collective sense of determining the role of the police, one author, Malcolm K. Sparrow (1988, 8–9), sees the combination of these two eras as "traditional policing." The police are seen as "principally responsible for law enforcement" and are "highly centralized, governed by rules, regulations, and policy directives" and "accountable to the law" (Sparrow 1988, 8–9). The simplicity of this analysis allows comparison of community policing to the traditional methods of policing and provides clarity on the changing philosophy (see Table 1-4).

The methods of analyzing the eras of policing are conducive to understanding police practices and procedures prevalent within our society. However, the issue focusing on the relationship between the community and the police is often lost in the overview of policing as an institution within our society but not as a part of society. Unfortunately there was a time period in American policing when this was clearly the case. Occurring during the period that Kelling and Moore (1988, 12) discuss as the reform era, the police were described as "impersonal or oriented toward crime solving rather than responsive to the emotional crisis of the victim." Although the police have migrated through these eras associated with their overall institutions, they have also migrated through eras of community relations.

TABLE I-4   *Traditional versus Community Policing: Questions and Answers*

QUESTION	TRADITIONAL	COMMUNITY POLICING
Who are the police?	Government agency principally for law enforcement	Those who are paid to give full-time attention to the duties of every citizen (Police are the public and the public are police)
What is the relationship of the police force to other public service departments?	Priorities often conflicting	Police are one department among many responsible for improving the quality of life
What is the role of the police?	Focus on solving crimes	Broad problem-solving approach
How is police efficiency measured?	By detection and arrest rates	By the absence of crime and disorder
What are the highest priorities?	Crimes that are high value (e.g., bank robberies) and those involving violence	Whatever problems disturb the community most
What specifically do police deal with?	Incidents	Citizens' problems and concerns
What determines the effectiveness of police?	Response times	Public cooperation
What view do police take of service calls?	Deal with them only if there is no real police work to do	Vital function and great opportunity
What is police professionalism?	Swift, effective response to serious crime	Keeping close to the community
What kind of intelligence is most important?	Crime intelligence (study of particular crimes or series of crimes)	Criminal intelligence (information about activities of individuals or groups)
What is the essential nature of police accountability?	Highly centralized; governed by rules, regulations, and policy directives; accountable to the law	Emphasis on local accountability to community needs
What is the role of headquarters?	To provide the necessary rules and policy directives	To preach organizational values
What is the role of the press liaison department?	To keep the "heat" off operational officers so they can get on with the job	To coordinate an essential channel of communication with the community
How do the police regard prosecutions?	As an important goal	As one tool among many

Source: Malcolm K. Sparrow, "Implementing Community Policing," *Perspectives on Policing,* U.S. Department of Justice, November 1988, pp. 8–9.

HISTORICAL ROOTS OF COMMUNITY POLICING

The early history of policing in the United States, dating back to the colonial period, is heavily marked by politics, as previously demonstrated. From the founding of this nation to the early twentieth century, police relations with the community were intertwined with politics. The relationship was solely based on the dominant power within a community, and it was to this power that the police were appointed and beholden. Although the Pendleton Act was intended to provide relief from these political ties, it did not solve the inherent problems of widespread corruption at the time. The period of the Wickersham Commission's investigation into the criminal justice system is perhaps the best time period to show the transition of the relationship between the police and the community. Like the Kelling and Moore analysis, the political era of policing is closely related to the relationship between the police and the community, tied into politics from the founding of the new nation in 1776 through the year 1930.

HISTORICAL ROOTS OF COMMUNITY POLICING

It has been noted that community policing consists of two complementary core components—community partnership and problem solving. Community partnership is the means of knowing the community. Problem solving is the tool for addressing the conditions that threaten the welfare of the community. It has also been noted that community policing is "democracy in action." The two statements do fit perfectly into the historical and driving force in the establishing of police agencies in the United States. We see from the earliest efforts of our Founding Fathers that they called on the government to ensure domestic tranquility, provide for the common defenses, promote general welfare, and secure the blessing of liberty to ourselves and our posterity, as stated in the Constitution.

The intent of those powerful statements is woven through the studies and commission reports dealing with policing over the last 200 years. The most notable report was probably the President's Commission Office Forms on Law Enforcement and Administration of Justice, which was established by President Johnson and issued in "The Challenge of Crime in a Free Society" (1967). In that report, the commission stated that the role of the police is not simply the suppression of crime, but a much broader role including service to citizens and greater involvement in the overall planning and functioning of the community. In addition, the commission report called for an increase in training and the development of skills to handle situations that are often not criminal in nature but are important to maintaining public order and a positive relationship between government and citizen.

As we see in these statements, the concept of community policing is one that has been with the law enforcement community since its founding. But it has not always been put forth in many agencies' strategic plans. These principles should be threaded through all agencies in our mission statements, values, goals, objectives, and daily activities.

Community policing is not just a program but a philosophy that has roots with the words of the Founding Fathers and has relevancy, perhaps more today [than] ever before. As we have sworn to uphold the U.S. Constitution and our state constitution, we have made a solemn oath to accept and promote the community policing philosophy.

Source: Reprinted with permission from James T. Plousis, "The Historical Roots of Community Policing," *Sheriffs Times,* Winter 1999, p. 3.

The new mode of thinking focused on the relationship between the police and the community in terms of public relations. The idea of public relations entailed a separation of the police and community, although the police still remained somewhat beholden to the community they served. As Richard L. Holcomb (1954, 6), described, "the fundamental principle of good public relations can be summed up very briefly. It amounts to doing a good, efficient job in a courteous manner and then letting the public know about the job." The police had little desire to integrate with the public during this time period and distanced themselves from any ties to the community. The public relations era was marked by simply responding to the public's demands only to that degree that satisfied the immediate problems and in turn the community. The police distanced themselves from the public, and an "us versus them" attitude surfaced and marked the police for many decades to come. This period of relationship existed between the years 1930 and 1960.

The movement from public relations to police–community relations has a far more distinct progression than the previous evolution from political relations. This progression is evident in Radelet's (1973) discussion of the National Institute of Police and Community Relations Conference, first held in 1955 at Michigan State University. This five-day conference provided the impetus for police departments across the nation to begin encouraging and fostering a sense of police and community partnership. The predominant method of carrying out this partnership was through the development of special units within police departments often known as "community resources" or "community relations" divisions. The other key component to this philosophy was developing some understanding between the police and the community. The police had to understand the various sociological aspects of the groups they dealt with on a daily basis, and the community had to understand what tasks police officers had to perform and how they carried out these duties. The overall assumption, then, was to provide for a special unit and create an understanding between the police and the community (see Cohn and Viano 1976; Johnson, Misner, and Brown 1981; Radelet 1973; Watson 1966).

Some debate still exists as to the evolution of public relations to police–community relations. Although Radelet points to the 1955 conference, some argue that the call for police–community relations was a direct result of the civil unrest of the 1960s and a response to Supreme Court decisions such as *Mapp* v. *Ohio* (1961), *Escobedo* v. *Illinois* (1964), and *Miranda* v. *Arizona* (1966) reining in police power. Regardless of the catalyst for the movement to police–community relations, this era of relations began taking shape in 1960 and remained the predominant ideology of policing into the 1980s.

A large proportion of the police–community relations programs was conducted for nothing more than public relations purposes and in some cases political purposes. One primary method of delivering police–community relations services was the concept of "team policing" implemented in various communities across the nation in the early 1970s (Greene 1987; Radelet 1973). Although touted as one of the most prominent police–community relations programs, it failed (Greene 1987). The premise of team policing was to make the team of police officers part of the community and in turn make the community they policed more valuable to them on a personal level. According to Lawrence Sherman (1975), team policing failed because management created the teams and controlled them but failed to provide the proper support. Jack R. Greene's (1987, 3) summation of why team policing failed is perhaps most apt: it "required a rethinking of the social and formal organization of policing on a massive scale," something that did not fit with the climate of the times.

Other programs during this era were aimed at various aspects of creating an alliance with the community. The programs were divided into different aspects of the police–community

Baltimore police officers and local youth pausing for a photograph at a local community event sponsored by the Baltimore Police Department and the 7-Eleven convenience store chain. *(Courtesy of the Baltimore Police Department, Baltimore, Maryland.)*

relations ideology. The division consisted of the public relations programs such as "wave at a cop" and "ride-alongs"; crime prevention and safety education programs such as theft prevention lectures and neighborhood watch; youth programs such as community–police service corps and law enforcement explorers; and core police–community relations programs such as community service units and various volunteer committees oriented on key social issues (see Johnson, Misner, and Brown 1981, 329–363). All of these programs combined were a demonstration of the policecommunity relations ideology. (See Table 1-5.)

TABLE 1-5 *Comparison of Community Policing to Police–Community Relations*

COMMUNITY POLICING	POLICE–COMMUNITY RELATIONS
Goal: solve problems—improved relations with citizens is a welcome by-product.	Goal: change attitudes and project positive image—improved relations with citizens is main focus.
Line function: Officer has regular contact with citizens.	Line function: Officer has irregular contact with citizens.
Citizens nominate problems and cooperate in setting police agenda.	"Blue ribbon" committees identify the problems and "preach" to police.
Police accountability is ensured by the citizens receiving the service.	Police accountability is ensured by civilian review boards and formal police supervision.
There is meaningful organizational change and departmental restructuring, ranging from officer selection to training, evaluation, and promotion.	Traditional organization stays intact with new programs periodically added, with no fundamental organizational change.

(Continued)

TABLE 1-5   *(Continued)*

COMMUNITY POLICING	POLICE–COMMUNITY RELATIONS
It is a department-wide philosophy and acceptance.	It is isolated acceptance, often localized to police–community relations unit.
Influence is from the bottom up; citizens receiving service help set priorities and influence police policy.	Influence is from the top down; those who "know best" have input and make decisions.
Officer is continually accessible, in person or by telephone recorder in a decentralized office.	There is intermittent contact with the public because of citywide responsibility; contact is made through central headquarters.
Officer encourages citizens to solve many of their own problems and volunteer to assist neighbors.	Citizens are encouraged to volunteer but are told to request and expect more government (including law enforcement) services.
Success is determined by the reduction in citizen fear, neighborhood disorder, and crime.	Success is determined by traditional measures (e.g., crime rates and citizen satisfaction with the police).

Source: Adapted from Robert C. Trojanowicz, "Community Policing Is Not Police-Community Relations," *FBI Law Enforcement Bulletin,* October 1990, p. 10.

Officer Tom Ceccarelli of the Boca Raton Police Department assists a youngster at a bicycle rodeo. *(Courtesy of the Boca Raton Police Department, Boca Raton, Florida.)*

THREE GENERATIONS OF COMMUNITY-ORIENTED POLICING

While it is clear that policing has moved through three eras of policing—the political, reform, and community eras—what is not clear is how we have moved through the community era itself. Community-oriented policing in the early 1980s was vastly different from the community-oriented policing of the early 2000s. Because of these differences, Oliver (2000) has described the movement from the early 1980s through the present as consisting of three generations of the community-oriented policing era: the innovation (1979–1986), the diffusion (1987–1994), and the institutionalization (1995 to present) generations.

The first generation of community-oriented policing spans the time period 1979 through 1986 and is labeled the innovation generation (Oliver 2000). Although the start date is somewhat arbitrary, it is based on the realization in the 1970s that few of the long-held beliefs in policing actually worked and a search for the answer to "What works in policing?" began. The publication of Herman Goldstein's important article on problem-oriented policing (1979) seems to have started the move toward answering that question. This, coupled with the publication of Wilson and Kelling's (1989) seminal article "Broken Windows," would become the primary theoretical basis for several significant innovations in policing.

The early concepts of community-oriented policing were most often termed *experiments, test sites,* and *demonstration projects.* They were mainly restricted to large metropolitan cities such as Flint, Michigan; Newark, New Jersey; Newport News, Virginia; Baltimore, Maryland; and Houston, Texas. These experiments were typically funded through federal and state grants as well as through funding by various foundations. The style of community-oriented policing that was generally employed during this generation consisted of a single method such as foot patrols, problem solving, or community substations. Finally, the methods of evaluating these early community-oriented policing programs were mostly through the case study method, with some pretest/posttest surveys. (See Table 1-6.)

The second generation of community-oriented policing spans the time period of 1987 through 1994 and is considered the diffusion generation because as community-oriented policing became more widely known, it began to diffuse, or spread, to other police agencies across the country (Oliver 2000). Community-oriented policing during this generation was largely organized through various programs that consisted of newly created units or extensions of previously existing organizational units. Some examples of the newly created units included the Cartographic Oriented Management Program for the Abatement of Street Sales (COMPASS) program in Hartford, Connecticut; the Community Oriented Policing and Problem Solving (COPPS) program in Hayward,

TABLE 1-6 *Three Generations of Community-Oriented Policing*

GENERATION	YEARS
Innovation	1979–1986
Diffusion	1987–1994
Institutionalization	1995–present

Source: Willard M. Oliver, "The Third Generation of Community Policing: Moving through Innovation, Diffusion, and Institutionalization," *Police Quarterly* 3, no. 4 (2000): 367–388.

California; the Community Police Officer Program (CPOP) in New York City; and the Citizen Oriented Police Enforcement (COPE) program in Baltimore County, Maryland. Like the first generation, many of these programs were funded by federal and state grants, but additional police agencies were making the move toward these innovations without external financial assistance. Many agencies simply retooled some of their existing units in order to adapt to the community-era style of policing.

Community-oriented policing during this era was still mainly restricted to large urban metropolitan areas but was working its way into more medium-sized cities. The diffusion to these larger agencies was due to the greater access to information, larger budgets to absorb any additional costs of community-oriented policing (with or without grant funding) and the preexisting structures in these agencies in which community-oriented policing was often placed. Although some small-town and rural agencies did adopt community-oriented policing, they were the exception and not the rule. In addition, many of these new or evolved community-oriented policing programs were no longer relegated to one type of function (e.g., foot patrol, problem solving) but were now incorporating several components for a more expanded community-oriented policing program. Finally, evaluation of community-oriented policing improved in terms of the number of evaluations, but most were still case studies and survey research (of which most were surveys of police rather than citizens).

The third generation of community-oriented policing spans the time period of 1995 to the present and is considered the institutionalization generation (Oliver 2000). The term *institutionalization* is used to denote the fact that community-oriented policing has become so widespread within American policing that a vast majority of agencies lay at least some claim to having implemented community-oriented policing. In fact, recent research by Zhao, Lovrich, and Thurman (1999, 89) has shown that between 1993 and 1996 there "was a significant increase in community policing activities," but they do conclude that "the ultimate and widespread institutionalization of community policing still remains somewhat uncertain." Despite this conclusion, since the passage of the Crime Bill of 1994 (see Chapter 12), the funding by the federal government for state and local agencies adopting or advancing community-oriented policing, from 1995 to the present, has been staggering. Nearly $10 billion has been sent to state and local agencies to assist them in the adoption and implementation of community-oriented policing, which has contributed to the institutionalization of the systemic approach.

As a result of these grants, the institutionalization generation of community-oriented policing is heavily marked by agencies shifting to or further developing their community-oriented policing programs because of the advantages of the federal money. Not only could large and medium-sized cities now implement community-oriented policing more easily, but small-town and rural agencies could implement it as well. While many small-town and rural agencies did in fact adopt community-oriented policing prior to this generation, the vast majority of them made the move because of the availability of federal grants. Thus community-oriented policing now cast a much wider net than it did in the early 1980s when it was in its infancy stage (the innovation generation).

In addition to the widespread use of community-oriented policing, the concepts behind community-oriented policing had become more refined, and agencies adopting community-oriented policing were beginning to employ multiple integrative strategies consisting of such tactics as aggressive and saturation patrols (see Chapter 3), foot patrols and community substations (see Chapter 4), and problem-solving methods (see Chapter 5). Under the institutionalization generation, the adoption of community-oriented policing was no longer seen as the application of a foot patrol or bike patrol officer but had come to entail numerous innovations, all aimed at enhancing the relationship between police and community. Finally, evaluations of community-oriented policing have become more widespread and much more sophisticated, utilizing a multitude of available methods, from case studies to quantitative statistical analysis and from surveys of police and citizens to the analysis of officer contacts with citizens as well as the testing of such theories as broken windows and problem solving.

A study by Zhao, He, and Lovrich (2003) clarifies how the institutionalization of community-oriented policing has impacted policing. Their study, which surveyed police chiefs at three different time points (1993, 1996, and 2000), found that the movement to community-oriented policing did not necessarily change the core principles of policing, such as law enforcement, control of crime, and service provision, all of which remained largely unchanged throughout the decade. Rather, their analysis demonstrated that the implementation of community-oriented policing "can be characterized as a comprehensive effort by local police simultaneously to control crime, to reduce social disorder, and to provide services to the citizenry" (2003, p. 716). In other words, the institutionalization of community-oriented policing has improved policing in the United States.

As the chapter's opening quote alludes to, the future direction of community-oriented policing can only be assessed in terms of its past and present (see Chapter 15). Community-oriented policing as a philosophy of policing has become well entrenched in the vocabulary of policing. Whether the institutionalization generation will continue indefinitely or whether we will move on to a new generation within the community era, only time will tell.

CONCLUSION

The evolution of community-oriented policing is rooted in the relationship between the police and the community throughout the history of the United States. (See Table 1-7.) From the period of 1776, with the founding of a new nation, to the year 1930, the relationship between the police and the community was one of politics. The period from 1930 to 1960 saw a transformation to the public relations era of cooperation, when the police isolated themselves and only interacted when it was necessary to appease the public. The period of 1960 to 1985 saw a transformation in the relationship to what is now known as police–community relations. This era was marked largely by various programs aimed at providing services to the community and at the same time providing some contact between the police and the citizens. In the mid-1980s, the police–community relations concept gave way to community-oriented policing as the main philosophical approach to policing relations with the public. Although community-oriented policing remains the current ideology of policing and has seen widespread implementation across the country, there is a consensus that the term has no concrete definition.

TABLE 1-7   *Sample of Approximate Start Date of Community Policing by Type and Population of the Jurisdiction Served*

	BEGINNINGS OF COMMUNITY-ORIENTED POLICING		
Type and Population	**Early Pioneers 1985–1989**	**Mainstreamers 1990–1994**	**Latecomers 1995–Present**
Cities			
<50,000		Mascoutah	
50,000–150,000		Flint	Pocatello
		Lakeland	Sandy City
		New Bedford	
		North Charleston	
		Oak Park	
		Racine	
150,000–500,000	Fort Worth	Austin	Des Moines
		Buffalo	
		Huntington Beach	
		Miami	
		Newark	
		Oakland	
500,000+	San Diego	Los Angeles	Las Vegas
		Milwaukee	
		Nashville	
Counties			
<200,000			Fresno County
			Sarpy County
200,000+	Maricopa County	Cobb County	San Bernadino County
Other			
	Las Vegas Paiute Tribal Police		San Diego School Police
	Oregon State Police		

Source: Jeffrey A. Roth and Joseph F. Ryan. *National Evaluation of the COPS Program—Title 1 of the 1994 Crime Act.* Washington, D.C.: National Institute of Justice, 2000, p. 185.

COP* ON THE WORLD WIDE WEB

Dr. George L. Kelling, Biography

http://www.manhattan-institute.org/html/kelling.htm

Biography of one of the originators of the broken windows theory, with links to some of his papers.

Dr. James Q. Wilson, Biography

http://www.bookrags.com/biography-james-q-wilson-professor-cri/index.html

Biography of Dr. Wilson, one of the originators of the broken windows theory.

Dr. Robert C. Trojanowicz, Tribute

http://info.detnews.com/weblog/index.cfm?blogid=6118

Tribute to Dr. Trojanowicz, one of the early founders of community-oriented policing.

Houston, Texas, Police Museum

http://www.houstontx.gov/police/museum2.htm

Trenton, New Jersey, Police Museum

http://tpdmuseum.com/

REVIEW QUESTIONS

1. Is community-oriented policing a new philosophy? Why or why not?
2. What are the three eras of policing? Describe each.
3. What are the three generations of policing? Describe each.

---

*COP is an acronym for community-oriented policing

CHAPTER 2

Community-Oriented Policing Defined

*There is nothing more difficult to take in hand, more perilous to
conduct, or more uncertain in its success, than to take the lead in the
introduction of a new order of things.*

—Machiavelli

CHAPTER OBJECTIVES

- Recognize the problem of a standard definition.
- Understand that community-oriented policing is a philosophy.
- Understand that community-oriented policing is a policy.
- Understand that community-oriented policing is a series of programs.
- Differentiate between community-oriented policing and police–community relations.
- Comprehend the common themes of community-oriented policing.
- Understand that community-oriented policing is a systemic approach to policing.
- Define community-oriented policing.

Community-oriented policing has sparked one of the most fundamental changes in the history of American policing. It has been called a new paradigm by some (Oliver and Bartgis 1998) and simply an epicycle by others (Gowri 2003). Regardless, community-oriented policing has had a profound impact on American policing, as the ultimate goal of policing has shifted from controlling crime to improving quality of life and has done so through a focus on reducing citizen fear and addressing the problems of both crime and disorder.

The fear of crime is one of the most pervasive concerns of the American people, and there is a demand to control what has seemingly spiraled out of control (Dietz 1997). The media constantly reminds the American people of the increasing levels of urban violence and the problems of gangs, drugs, juvenile crime, and a host of other social problems causing the epidemic proportions of crime. Community-oriented policing has become the American panacea for crime, supported not only by the public but also by a rapidly growing number of police departments across the country. This is apparent in the fact that "in 1999, nearly two-thirds of county (66%) and municipal (62%) police agencies with 100 or more officers had a formally written community policing plan, as did nearly half of sheriff's departments (46%)," and "nearly all larger county (97%) and municipal (95%) police departments had full-time community policing officers, as did 88% of sheriff's departments" (Reaves and Hart, 2000, 7).

The ideas of community-oriented policing are relatively simplistic. The police take on a role of being more community oriented, and the citizens become more involved by assisting the police with information. Typically, people conjure up images of the police officer walking a beat, greeting people in the neighborhood as they go about their daily routines, and deterring crime by his or her presence. There is generally the overall idea that the police will be able to solve the community's problems, which will reduce crime and restore social order. The ideas seem simple enough, but their implementation can be difficult.

A Fresno, California, community-oriented policing officer demonstrating the joy of riding a police motorcycle to a local youth. (*Courtesy of the City of Fresno Police Department, Fresno, California.*)

The concept of community-oriented policing is essentially a philosophy of policing that is often difficult to transform into policy (Correia 2000). Although foot patrols are an easily implemented policing tool, the concept goes far beyond the police officer walking the beat. Police departments across the United States hold the philosophy in high esteem but wrestle with the task of implementation. This problem is most apparent when discussing the positions of police chiefs who want to implement community-oriented policing but have no framework for actually implementing the systemic approach. It is a frustrating situation for everyone involved in the process.

The most difficult aspect of understanding community-oriented policing is attempting to arrive at a standard definition. Theorists and practitioners both have the same ideas overall; however, when it comes to defining and implementing the concept, they often diverge. While one organization may implement the concept throughout the entire police department, another may place one police officer on foot patrol in an area of high pedestrian traffic. Both can now lay claim to implementing community-oriented policing. This variance results in a multitude of interpretations of what community policing entails. The term, then, when invoked, conjures up just as many ideas and programs as there are people contemplating what community-oriented policing involves. This variety of perspectives is most clearly seen in the call by President Clinton for the community policing bill, which focused on placing 100,000 additional police officers on the streets of America. As one author points out, "Community policing was not intended simply to put more foot patrol officers on the street; and it was not seen as a quick-fix crime reduction strategy. Many of the current advocates of community policing, such as the *Times* and Bill Clinton, have got it all wrong" (Walker 1994, 136). Clarifying the meaning of the term *community-oriented policing*, then, is critical to any discussion about the concept.

The purpose of this chapter is to review the current literature from both theorists and practitioners and analyze it for consistent themes. The goal is to derive an identifiable definition of what has become known as community-oriented policing in order to advance its theoretical aspects as well as determine the methods of implementation. Because the term has no standard definition, *community-oriented policing* will remain the philosophy's term out of reverence for its immediate capture of the ideological advancement of the police.

LAW ENFORCEMENT MANAGEMENT AND ADMINISTRATIVE STATISTICS (LEMAS), 1999 COMMUNITY-ORIENTED POLICING

As of June 30, 1999:

- 9 in 10 local police departments serving a population of 25,000 or more had full-time sworn personnel regularly engaged in community policing activities.
- 112,611 full-time sworn personnel were serving as community policing officers for state and local law enforcement agencies or were otherwise regularly engaged in community policing activities, compared to 21,239 in 1997.

As of June 30, 1999 among municipal police departments employing 100 or more officers:

- 62% had a formally written community policing plan.
- 76% operated 1 or more community substations.
- 73% had full-time school resource officers.

During the 2-year period ending June 30, 1999:

- 92% trained at least some of their in-service officers in community policing.
- 81% trained all their new officer recruits in community policing.

During the 12-month period ending June 30, 1999:

- 77% offered community policing training to citizens.
- 61% formed problem-solving partnerships through written agreements with local groups or agencies.

Source: Reprinted from Bureau of Justice Statistics, *Summary Findings: Law Enforcement Management and Administrative Statistics, 1999.* Washington D.C., Bureau of Justice Statistics. November 2000.

ABSENCE OF A DEFINITION

It is readily apparent that there is no shared definition of community-oriented policing among the theorists and practitioners of law enforcement (see Cordner 1995; Seagrave 1996). This is clear from the research by key proponents of the community-oriented policing philosophy, such as Herman Goldstein (1990, 24), who wrote, "We now make wide use of 'community policing' to categorize these efforts, but the term does not yet have a uniform meaning." Dennis P. Rosenbaum (1994, xii) claims, "At this moment in the history of policing, there is no simple or commonly shared definition of community policing, either in theory or practice." More recently, Nigel Fielding (2005) stated that "community policing is somewhat a chameleon concept . . . [for] it can stand for: (i) an alternative to rapid response, enforcement-oriented policing involving long-term beat assignment so police are closer to the community; (ii) a process by which crime control is shared with the public, as in Neighborhood Watch, or (iii) a means of developing communication with the public, for example, consultation meetings." It is common to find a lack of definition in most of the literature, and although some try, many are resolved to conclude that the term means many different things to many different people (see Bayley 1994, 278; Greene and Mastrofski 1988, 45; Murphy 1988, 49; Oliver 1992, 46).

Community-oriented policing is an intangible concept based on intangible ideas (Oliver 1992). Theorists have attempted to define the term as a precursor to the implementation of the concept. However, there is often disagreement within the proposed definitions (Grinc 1994), and as is often the case, the definition itself becomes contradictory (Weisheit, Wells, and Falcone 1994). The definitions are often unclear and intangible, thereby not allowing for the concept to be implemented. Many practitioners therefore wonder not only how to define community-oriented policing but also how to implement it.

Because the conceptual definitions can offer no standard definition, many researchers look to the organizations that have implemented community-oriented policing to develop a clear and concise definition based on the actual application of these practices and procedures (Police Executive Research Forum 1996). Unfortunately, the theorists fare no better in reviewing what the practitioners have implemented to arrive at a definition. As Herman Goldstein (1994, viii) states, "In many quarters today, 'community policing' is used to encompass practically all innovations in policing, from the most ambitious to the most mundane, from the most carefully thought out through to the most casual." The term has become an interchangeable phrase, utilized to describe nearly any change or upgrade in a police department's services (Goldstein 1987; Goodstein 1991; McElroy, Cosgrove, and Sadd 1993). Although this term and the concept have remained strong within the literature of both theorists and practitioners, there is clearly the need for a standard definition to avoid the debasement of the term *community-oriented policing*.

COMMUNITY-ORIENTED POLICING, NOT POLICE–COMMUNITY RELATIONS

In attempting to define community-oriented policing, it must be clarified that community-oriented policing and police–community relations are two separate entities. Although community-oriented policing was born of the police–community relations theory, the two have become philosophies unto themselves. This is apparent through a

Memphis police officers with local Boy Scout Troop 63. (*Courtesy of the Memphis Police Department, Memphis, Tennessee.*)

 **COP IN ACTION**

Community Policing: A Philosophy—Not a Program

Of the variety of concepts in police science, community policing is perhaps the oldest, most controversial, and least understood. Community policing in its best sense is a philosophy and not just a program. It is a philosophy of police and community cooperating with one another to ascertain the problems and needs of a community and working in harmony to address those needs. In order for the philosophy to work, there must be total immersion of management and rank-and-files; there must be total commitment. An agency cannot compartmentalize a community-policing program. That model is doomed to failure because of its internal divisiveness and lack of career path for the officers involved.

The philosophic approach to community policing encourages, aids, and abets community cooperation. It means motivating citizens to participate in auxiliary police activities, block watching, police-support volunteer units, community crisis-intervention teams, quality-of-life action groups, neighborhood councils, and town meetings. And all of this cannot be the work of one or two officers dedicated to "community affairs." It must be the work of an entire department and each of its subdivisions.

Critics who say that the philosophy of community policing takes away from the enforcement role of the police officer and makes him or her a "social worker" fail to perceive its underlying effectiveness. The true practice of community policing may well save a cop's life. It may well provide solutions that change a community, once written off as too dangerous to patrol, into a productive, safe neighborhood. It may well provide information previously not available on perpetrators of crime, gang members, and drug dealers. And it may well change the quality of life for both the police practitioner and the public. One need not be a social worker, but one should be aware of the social and economic dimensions of crime.

Over the past three decades, we have seen a marked change in the dynamics of street law enforcement. American society, with its variety of cultural, religious, ethnic, and racial groups, is a phenomenon unequalled anywhere on this planet. This diversity makes our nation strong; yet, ironically, it can also divide us. We are all in a learning curve about understanding and accepting one another. This is what the philosophy of community policing is all about. It is understanding, helping, and supporting one another to build communities and programs that will enhance the quality of life for citizens and officers. This philosophy and methodology do not make any officer less of a "cop." But it does provide new ways to be more effective as a law enforcement professional. It does provide training to defuse neighborhood situations before they became crises. And it does make for a breed of officers who can serve as role models for youth.

Some departments still shy away from a community policing model or from total immersion in its philosophy. A successful model will first assess the community to be served by analyzing demographics and neighborhood composition. It would further assess the department's capability to serve the diverse needs of the community. The next steps include identifying missions and goals, training personnel, reaching out to the community, analyzing budget and resources, targeting neighborhoods for concentration, mobilizing the "grass-roots" forces of the community and establishing community participation. Once in place, the department should evaluate the model every six to twelve months for effectiveness. Indications of success include a decrease in the incidence of crime, improved cooperation with police, improved quality of life, and, of course, an improved community image of the police. But no model is absolute or permanently structured. Each model will change as a particular community's needs change. That's the essence of community policing—it's a living, breathing, changing phenomenon.

I am convinced that the community policing model is the most effective method of delivering police services efficiently, cost-effectively, and humanely. I am also convinced that if we are to create greater harmony and understanding in our society and defuse the ugliness brought on by frustration, hate, and ignorance, the philosophy of community policing is a step in that direction. However, it can only be effective if the philosophy pervades the department and if the cynics and nay-sayers give it an opportunity to blossom.

Source: John R. Gentile, "Community Policing: A Philosophy—Not a Program," *Community Policing Exchange,* November/December 1995, p. 2.

---

slow evolutionary process, as detailed in Chapter 1, that has spanned nearly six decades, with slightly altered and advanced ideas.

The 1930s and 1940s were essentially the public relations era, marked by little to no literature in the law enforcement field discussing the relationship between the police and the community (Trojanowicz and Dixon 1974). The concept of police–community relations was explored in 1955 at the National Institute of Police–Community Relations at Michigan State University (Trojanowicz and Dixon 1974). Over the next several decades, the majority of police departments developed special units dealing in community relations programs. However, much akin to the situation today, the theorists and practitioners could not determine a standard definition for the term (Trojanowicz and Dixon 1974).

The problem of defining the police–community relations concept was caused by the enormous amount of literature being published on the philosophy (see Brandstatter and Radelet 1968; Earle 1967; Pomrenke 1966). As Trojanowicz and Dixon (1974, 52) stated, "Police–community relations have been defined in many similar and some quite different ways." A concrete definition of the concept was never found, but many agreed it was predicated on an interwoven trilogy of ideas: efficiency, responsiveness, and representativeness (Trojanowicz and Dixon 1974). The increased efficiency and responsiveness of the police to the community and an increased representation on the part of the community in dealing with the crime problem formed the nexus of police–community relations.

The literature on this philosophy explored the trilogy of ideas and analyzed the police officer's relationship with the community. The police officer's interaction with various groups in society, ranging from the youth to the elderly, the deaf to the mentally ill, and the gangs to the media, was explored. All of these issues were detailed and explored, and policy was derived from the analysis to make the police–community relationships stronger. Community relations sections became well entrenched within the hierarchy of police organizations, and programs such as Neighborhood Watch were implemented.

At the beginning of the 1980s, the concept of police–community relations, still without an agreed-on definition, was beginning to see a divergence from the profound relationship between the police and community. The literature began exploring variations on police–community relations in order to advance the concept (see Johnson, Misner, and Brown 1981). The publication of "Broken Windows: The Police and Neighborhood Safety," by James Q. Wilson and George L. Kelling (1982), caused a shift in the thinking

A Memphis police officer and local youth participating in a GREAT (Gang Resistance Education and Training) summer camp program. *(Courtesy of the Memphis Police Department, Memphis, Tennessee.)*

relative to the role of the police from crime control to order maintenance, specifically focusing on the issue of public fear. Around the same time, Herman Goldstein (1979) was advancing his ideas on problem-oriented policing, an attempt to solve the root cause of crime rather than repetitively responding to the symptoms. It is a combination of these advanced ideas that would collectively become known and touted as community-oriented policing.

Today's literature often blends the two concepts of community-oriented policing and problem-oriented policing together without any distinction between the two philosophies. Several publications still analyze the police–community relations concept and include a chapter discussing the community policing model (see Mayhall, Barker, and Hunter 1995; Radelet and Carter 1994). Other publications lay claim to advancing the community policing philosophy but are repackaged police–community relations texts (see Miller and Hess 1994). Publications on community-oriented policing have expanded at a rapid rate over the past decade in trade magazines, academic journals, and books. As the concept continues this rapid expansion, there is a clear need for a concrete definition.

The attempt to define community-oriented policing must then avoid recapitulating the police–community relations philosophy and instead advance its own ideas. Trojanowicz and Dixon (1974, 53) explained that "Although police–community relations is very different from public relations, public relations is a part of police–community relations programs." Consistent with this statement, community-oriented policing is very different from police–community relations, yet it too is a part of the community-oriented policing concept.

BROKEN WINDOWS

In February 1982, James Q. Wilson and George L. Kelling published an article in the *Atlantic Monthly* known popularly as "Broken Windows." They made three points.

1. Neighborhood disorder—drunks, panhandling, youth gangs, prostitution, and other urban incivilities—creates citizen fear.
2. Just as unrepaired broken windows can signal to people that nobody cares about a building and lead to more serious vandalism, untended disorderly behavior can also signal that nobody cares about the community and lead to more serious disorder and crime. Such signals—untended property, disorderly persons, drunks, obstreperous youth, etc.—both create fear in citizens and attract predators.
3. If police are to deal with disorder to reduce fear and crime, they must rely on citizens for legitimacy and assistance.

"Broken Windows" gave voice to sentiments felt both by citizens and police. It recognized a major change in the focus of the police. For them, it not only suggested changes in the focus of police work (disorder, for example), it also suggested major modifications in the overall strategy of police departments.

The visual representation of the "broken windows" analogy.

Source: George L. Kelling, "Police and Communities: The Quiet Revolution," *Perspectives on Policing,* June 1988.

Beat officers of the Chicago Police Department's CAPS program walking patrol. (*Courtesy of the Chicago Police Department, Chicago, Illinois.*)

COMMON THEMES

As we recognize that the police officer's role within the community he or she serves has evolved from public relations to police–community relations to community-oriented policing, we must come to an understanding of where we are before we analyze where we are heading. Importantly, establishing some groundwork on this conceptual model to understand the foundation from which this concept has evolved can avoid any unnecessary

BROKEN WINDOWS THEORY OR A THEORY FULL OF "BROKEN WINDOWS"?

Since the publication of the article in the *Atlantic Monthly* in 1982, there has been much debate over the validity of the broken windows theory. As originally proposed by Wilson and Kelling, the theory articulates that minor disorders, such as broken windows, can send a signal to people that nobody cares about that particular neighborhood, thereby attracting more disorder and crime. If broken windows are left unrepaired, crime and disorder can be expected. This theory has been well received in the media, by many in policing, and by the average citizen, all of whom, based on conventional wisdom, tend to agree with the theory. Despite the fact that the theory has existed for more than twenty years, surprisingly there has been little testing to assess the validity of its assumptions. Is the broken windows theory a valid theory? Or, another way of putting it, is it right?

Research by one of the two principal authors of the broken windows theory, Kelling, has demonstrated that the theory is valid (Kelling and Coles 1996). However, in conducting his research, he has relied heavily on anecdotal information, personal interviews, and affirmation of other research. In fact, the one study that has consistently been relied on to affirm the broken windows theory was by Skogan (1990) and concluded that social and physical disorder were closely related to perceptions of crime, fear of crime, and vicitimizations and that disorder preceded crime. Other research has indicated that the application of order maintenance policing techniques do reduce disorder and can decrease drug nuisance behavior, but it is not so clear on violent or property crime (Green 1996; Green-Mazzerolle, Kadleck, and Roehl 1998). Finally, most recently the application of broken windows theory has been found to be effective in terms of public moral and physical disorder crimes (Katz, Webb, and Schaefer 2001) and that it even has a traffic-related application, where police regulating minor traffic infractions can decrease traffic fatalities, which they call the "crumpled fenders" equivalent (Giacopassi and Forde 2000).

There has, however, been much in the way of recent research that has demonstrated little support for the broken windows theory. Harcourt (2001) recently reanalyzed Skogan's (1990) data and found no association between disorder and serious crime. Keeping in mind that for nearly a decade Skogan's data has been the basis of the scientific support for the broken windows theory, this does cast the theory in some doubt. Yet Eck and Maguire (2000) reanalyzed the data as well and found that Skogan had left some neighborhoods in the study that diminished the reliability of his findings, and had he eliminated some of the extraneous neighborhoods in his study, his findings would have been even stronger. But again, two other studies (Novak et al. 1999; Sherman 1990a) found that crackdowns on minor liquor offenses did not have any effect on robbery or burglary, suggesting that order maintenance of minor disorders may not reduce serious crime. Sampson and Raudenbush (1999) (like Harcourt 2001) have also raised issue with the broken windows theory and argue that it is not addressing minor crimes that reduces more serious crimes but rather the cohesiveness among neighbors and the influence they represent in terms of social control, what Sampson and Raudenbush call collective efficacy, are what actually reduce crime. Finally, and most recently, Xu, Fielder, and Flaming (2005) conducted a comprehensive analysis of the data and they concluded that the Harcourt (2001) replication of Skogan's (1990) study contained statistical problems and his selection criterion for what to include and exclude was biased. They also found in their reciprocal feedback model, that Sampson and Raudenbush's (1999) study unintentionally demonstrates support for the broken windows theory. Their study found that, controlling for collective efficacy, physical and moral decay of the community does lead to increased criminality, that community-oriented policing is the solution to disorder and crime, that quality of life and citizen fear are influenced by disorder, and that citizen satisfaction with the police is dependent upon citizens' fear of crime and their perceived quality of life in their community.

The debate continues. While some research has demonstrated support for the broken windows theory, other research has raised doubt. Based on media reporting and a general consensus, the broken windows theory seems valid. Yet research raises questions as to its validity. Is the broken windows theory valid? Or is it really something else, something related to the broken windows theory but more in line with the concept of collective efficacy?

anomalies. It is from the current literature in community-oriented policing that we must derive our definition, pulling the common themes together to establish the premise on which all else will be predicated.

The primary theme originating from all definitions, dealing in both theory and practice, is the use of the term *community*. As Buerger argues,

> Nowhere in this scheme is there an articulated substantive role for the community. Little attention has been given to a definition of the community commensurate with the vast promise imbedded in the rhetoric of community policing. Even less has been spared for defining the role that can be reasonably expected of the community; howsoever, it should be defined. (Buerger 1994a, 415)

Because the current philosophy consistently invokes the term *community*, understanding this central tenet is important to the overall definition of community-oriented policing.

A common sociological definition of *community* is "a group of people who share three things: They live in a geographically distinct area; they share cultural characteristics, attitudes, and lifestyles; and they interact with one another on a sustained basis" (Farley 1994, 506). Utilizing this definition with present-day American society, it is easy to see why community is a key component within the new policing philosophy. The interaction of the community and the shared culture, attitudes, and lifestyles have declined and continue to decline. The issues of order maintenance, quality of life, and complexities of crime all call on the community as well as the police for improvement. It is Buerger again who states, "the rhetoric of community policing ascribes to 'the community' a great power to regulate itself, shake off its fear of crime by forming 'partnerships' with the police, and reestablish community norms that regulate behavior and successfully resist the encroachments of the criminal element" (Buerger 1994b, 270). Although it sounds like an unattainable goal, reestablishing community is possible with some directed guidance on the part of the police.

Instilling a sense of community then becomes the police officer's lot. Although a small town may have established customs to deal with order maintenance, many larger towns and cities do not have these mechanisms in place. The juvenile who attempts to spray paint a building may find this difficult in a town where witnesses will call the juvenile's parents. In other aspects, the officer may have the time and leisure to help improve the quality of life of the community, perhaps by rattling doors at night or playing softball with the local children. In many jurisdictions, there is no time or sense of community to conduct these types of events. These events instill a sense of community that "suggests a fundamental paradox of community policing—in many ways it is the formalization of informal customs and the routinization of spontaneous events" (Weisheit, Wells, and Falcone 1994, 565). Community-oriented policing essentially takes the small-town method of handling problems, much like the fictional town of Mayberry from the *Andy Griffith Show*, and makes it formal policy within a police department.

The definition of *community* within community-oriented policing, then, revolves around the citizens. The interaction between the citizens and police must develop and foster the sense of community spirit. The community must open up to the police and assist them in controlling crime, maintaining order within the community, and forming a working partnership. This relationship must also allow police officers to think of themselves as members of the community and not have what is considered the standard police mentality of "us versus them." As former Speaker of the House Tip O'Neill once stated, "All politics are local"—so, too, is all crime. Each community has its own type of criminal

A flyer announcing the opening of the new Central Precinct in Memphis, Tennessee. The new precinct is aimed at decentralizing the police department and moving the agency closer to the neighborhoods. *(Courtesy of the Memphis Police Department, Memphis, Tennessee.)*

element, local problems, and order maintenance issues. The highly affluent area may have problems with burglaries, suspicious solicitors, and vehicles driving over the posted speed limit. The lower-income subsidized housing area may have problems with prostitution, an open-air drug market, and old abandoned cars lining the streets. Both communities perceive their crime problems as high. Each community feels its problems are the most important and deserve the most attention. Both are presumably right. However, each community's inherent problems call for different methods of response.

COMMUNITY POLICING AND THE FEAR OF CRIME

When crimes occur, society's attention is naturally focused on the victims and their material losses. Their wounds, bruises, lost property, and inconvenience can be seen, touched, and counted. These are the concrete signs of criminal victimization. Behind the immediate, concrete losses of crime victims, however, is a different, more abstract crime problem—that of fear. For victims, fear is often the largest and most enduring legacy of their victimization.

Of course, fear is not totally unproductive. It prompts caution among citizens and thereby reduces criminal opportunities. Too, it motivates citizens to shoulder some of the burdens of crime control by buying locks and dogs, thereby adding to general deterrence. And fear kindles enthusiasm for publicly supported crime control measures. Thus, reasonable fears, channeled in constructive directions, prepare society to deal with crime. It is only when fear is unreasonable, or generates counterproductive responses, that it becomes a social problem.

It is possible that fear might be attacked by strategies other than those that directly reduce criminal victimization. Fear might be reduced even without changes in levels of victimization by using the communications within social networks to provide accurate information about risks of criminal victimization and advice about constructive responses to the risk of crime; by eliminating the external signs of physical decay and social disorder; and by more effectively regulating group conflict between young and old, whites and minority groups, rich and poor. The more intriguing possibility, however, is that if fear could be rationalized and constructively channeled, not only would fear and its adverse consequences be ameliorated, but also real levels of victimization reduced. In this sense, the conventional understanding of this problem would be reversed: instead of controlling victimization to control fear, we would manage fear to reduce victimization.

If it is true that fear is a problem in its own right, then it is important to evaluate the effectiveness of police strategies not only in terms of their capacity to control crime, but also in terms of their capacity to reduce fear. And if fear is affected by more factors than just criminal victimization, then there might be some special police strategies other than controlling victimization that could be effective in controlling the fear of crime.

The current police strategy, which relies on motorized patrol, rapid response to calls for service, and retrospective investigations of crime, seems to produce little reassurance to frightened citizens, except in unusual circumstances when the police arrest a violent offender in the middle of a crime spree. Moreover, a focus on controlling crime rather than increasing security (analogous to the medical profession's focus on curing diseases rather than promoting health) leads the police to miss opportunities to take steps that would reduce fear independently of reducing crime. Consequently, the current strategy of policing does not result in reduced fear. Nor does it leave much room for fear reduction programs in the police department.

This is unfortunate, because some fear reduction programs have succeeded in reducing citizens' fears. Two field experiments showed that foot patrol can reduce fear and promote security. Programs that enhance the quantity and quality of police contacts with citizens through neighborhood police stations and through required regular contacts between citizens and police have been successful in reducing fear in Houston and Newark. These examples illustrate the security-enhancing potential of problem-solving and community approaches to policing. By incorporating fear reduction as an important objective of policing, by changing the activities of the police to include more frequent, more sustained contacts with citizens, and by consultation and joint planning, police departments seem to be able not only to reduce fear, but to transform it into something that helps to build strong social institutions. That is the promise of these approaches. (See Figure 2-1.)

Source: Mark H. Moore and Robert C. Trojanowicz, "Policing and the Fear of Crime," *Perspectives on Policing,* June 1988.

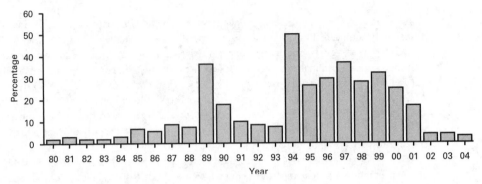

FIGURE 2-1   Percentage of survey respondents indicating crime and drugs as the most important problem facing the country. *Source:* Pastore, Ann L., and Kathleen Maguire, eds. *Sourcebook of Criminal Justice Statistics* [Online]. Available: http://www.albany.edu/sourcebook/ [accessed April 7, 2006].

A variety of authors consistently state that the police and community must work closely together (Breci and Erickson 1998; Brown 1985, 1992; Community Policing Consortium 1994; Eck and Rosenbaum 1994; Grinc 1994; Miller and Hess 1994; Murphy 1988; Roberg 1994; Rosenbaum and Lurigio 1994; Rush 1994; Sadd and Grinc 1994; Skogan 1994; Trojanowicz and Bucqueroux 1990). Through community-oriented policing, one group of authors states, "police will become more connected with and integrated into their communities, which means that police will interact with citizens on a personal level, will be familiar with community sentiments and concerns, and will work with the community to address those concerns" (Weisheit, Wells, and Falcone 1994, 551). Several authors also note that police will work with all members of the community and not just certain selected elements (Brown 1985; Community Policing Consortium 1994; Lurigio and Skogan 1994).

Once the citizens and police start coming together, their first goal is defining those problems indigenous to the community (Capowich and Roehl 1994; Community Policing Consortium 1994; Grinc 1994; Roberg 1994; Wilson and Kelling 1989). Once the problems are identified, developing cooperative solutions becomes the second goal (Capowich and Roehl 1994; Community Policing Consortium 1994; Grinc 1994; Roberg 1994; Wilson and Kelling 1989). The third goal is to develop programs from those solutions that could be implemented by both the police and community and fall within acceptable criteria, such as state law and local norms. And the fourth and final goal is implementation, where "at the operational level, these concepts translate into specific practices that are expected from the police officers engaged in such programs" (Lurigio and Rosenbaum 1994, 147). These programs could include community meetings, neighborhood watch programs, bike patrols, police–youth softball leagues, and police ministations in the community and in the malls. Although individually these programs may not solve the community's problems, collectively they can steer the community in the right direction.

Another consistent theme within community-oriented policing that is also based in this cooperative effort between the police and the community is problem solving. Problem solving is closely associated with the decision-making process described in the cooperative effort between the citizens and the police. The problems indigenous to a

TABLE 2-1   *Attitudes toward Crime Rate in Own Area (1985–2005)*

Question: "In the past year, do you feel the crime rate in your area has been increasing, decreasing, or has it remained the same as it was before?"

YEAR	INCREASING	DECREASING	REMAINED SAME	NOT SURE
1985	40%	17%	42%	1%
1991	55%	5%	39%	1%
1993	54%	5%	39%	2%
1996	46%	24%	25%	5%
1997	46%	32%	20%	2%
1998	31%	48%	16%	5%
2000	34%	46%	15%	5%
2001	26%	52%	18%	4%
2002	37%	34%	24%	5%
2003	40%	39%	19%	2%
2004	37%	37%	22%	4%
2005	47%	33%	18%	2%

Source: Pastore, Ann L., and Kathleen Maguire, eds. *Sourcebook of Criminal Justice Statistics* [Online]. Available: http://www.albany.edu/sourcebook/ [accessed April 7, 2006].

community are defined and solutions are generated to solve the cause of the crime or public disorder rather than the symptoms. This problem-solving process can be a collaborative effort between the citizens and the police, or it can be conducted solely by the police officer in the course of his or her duties. "A problem-oriented approach," as Eck and Rosenbaum (1994, 9) explain, "does not start with a tactical solution to a problem and seek to apply it to all occurrences of the problem. Instead, it begins with the peculiar circumstances that give rise to the problem and then looks for a situational solution."

Although originally put forth as its own individualistic philosophy on policing by founder Herman Goldstein, problem-oriented policing has become an integral part of community-oriented policing (Eck and Spelman 1987; Goldstein 1979, 1987, 1990, 1994; Toch 1995). Problem-oriented policing, as policy, can stand alone; however, "believed it is . . . that in order for community policing to be a truly effective approach the police must do both" (Roberg 1994, 249). Therefore, problem-oriented policing can be implemented without community-oriented policing, but community-oriented policing cannot be implemented without problem-oriented policing. (See Table 2-2.)

An additional aspect of community-oriented policing is the use of standard police tactics, such as patrols and arrests, and the use of specialized units in a slightly different manner. It entails redistributing police sources, directing an excessive amount of resources toward particular problems, and dispersing the criminal element from a particular community. Police Chief Reuben Greenburg utilized this technique in Charleston, South Carolina, with much success, and he coined the term *strategic policing* to describe this innovative use of standard police resources (Greenburg and Gordon 1989). Taking high-quality standard police practices and procedures, the police flood a high-crime area in the hopes of disrupting the entrenched criminal element. The goal is to

TABLE 2-2 *Respondents Reporting Fear of Walking Alone at Night (1989–2005)*

Question: "Is there any area near where you live—that is, within a mile—where you would be afraid to walk alone at night?

Year	Afraid to Walk Alone at Night
1989	43%
1990	40%
1992	44%
1993	43%
1996	39%
1997	38%
2000	34%
2001	30%
2002	35%
2003	36%
2004	32%
2005	38%

Neighborhood get-together sponsored by the Chicago Police Department, the local resident council, and McDonald's as part of the Chicago Alternative Policing Strategy (CAPS) program. *(Courtesy of the Chicago Police Department, Chicago, Illinois.)*

drive out the cause of the crime and replace it with some type of neighborhood program to keep the community free of crime and disorder (Greenburg and Gordon 1989). This type of policing is usually directed at highly visible elements such as open-air drug markets and street prostitutes, but it can be directed toward less visible criminal elements such as crack houses. The federal government has also attempted similar strategies in a program known as "weed and seed" (U.S. Department of Justice 1992).

This program was based on the concept of multiple agencies moving into a community and beginning the process of "weeding"—removing trash, cleaning up the neighborhood, and targeting criminal offenders—and, once cleaned up, utilizing an abundance of social services to "seed" the neighborhood in order to stabilize it and thus prevent crime from returning. There was a great deal of criticism over the federal weed and seed program, including that the federal government forced the program on specific local communities, that all of the resources were not from the local community level but rather from the national government, and that it targeted minorities, who were in fact the "weeds" (see Lyons 1999; Reed 1999). However, these criticisms do not negate the concept if it is conducted at the local level, with local support, utilizing local resources.

The important standard when utilizing strategic policing is putting something in place of the criminal element. Common sense dictates that when the police remove themselves en masse, the criminal element will simply return. This, then, necessitates using neighborhood programs and problem-solving cooperation with the members of the community to determine what will and will not work. These three concepts then become components of an integral web known as community-oriented policing.

However, for any of these concepts to translate into police practices, there is an overwhelming call for the decentralization of the police hierarchy (Cardarelli, McDevitt, and Baum 1998; Geller 1991; Goldstein 1990; Greene, Bergman, and McLaughlin 1994; Rosenbaum and Lurigio 1994; Skogan 1994; Wilkinson and Rosenbaum 1994). For the police to become a part of a community, they must be permanently assigned to that community. Rotating beats and rotating shifts do not foster a sense of community. There is no time to develop ties to the community, to discover the problems indigenous to any segment of the community, or to implement possible solutions because of the organizational commitment to a bureaucracy. The police officers must be given the freedom to interact with the community to develop solutions to problems, and to implement, fail, and discover the benefits of their programs. In the current centralized form of police organization, that capability is not there. "It is an organizational strategy that redefines the goals of policing," Skogan explains, and "community policing relies upon organizational decentralization" to achieve these new goals (Skogan 1994, 167). (See Table 2-3.)

The organizational decentralization, thus called for by the literature, in turn details the fact that community-oriented policing is not a temporary program but a long-term systemic philosophy that must permeate the entire police organization. By decentralizing an entire police department for the components of community-oriented policing to work, all of the fundamentals of policing must change as well. The mission statement, job descriptions, and goals of the police department must change. The role of the police chief, leadership, management style, and management structure must change. The recruitment, training, and requirements of the police officers must change. The expectations, roles, and actions of the community must change.

TABLE 2-3 *High School Seniors Reporting Worry about Crime and Violence (1990–2003)*

Question: "Of all the problems facing the nation today, how often do you worry about . . . crime and violence?"*

CLASS	TOTAL
1990	88.8%
1991	88.1%
1992	91.6%
1993	90.8%
1994	92.7%
1995	90.2%
1996	90.1%
1997	86.5%
1998	84.4%
1999	81.8%
2000	83.5%
2001	81.0%
2002	75.5%
2003	68.9%

*Percentage responding "often" or "sometimes."

Source: Pastore, Ann L., and Kathleen Maguire, eds. *Sourcebook of Criminal Justice Statistics* [Online]. Available: http://www.albany.edu/sourcebook/ [accessed April 7, 2006].

All of these societal structures, collective thoughts, and individuals must change to reflect the community-oriented approach. It is not enough to change one division or to create a new program. The true implementation of community-oriented policing must go from philosophical concept to practical applications throughout the entire police department for its goals and the goals of the community to be achieved.

 ## COP IN ACTION

Community Policing Is Alive and Well

A commander in a big-city department invites the community to help him design an effective drug-gang strategy that avoids the inequity—and the danger—of stigmatizing and harassing minority youth. In a small town in Arizona, the police and the community together launch a curfew incentive program that allows youngsters who play by the rules to earn points toward a bicycle. A chief from the "new" South explores ways to lure other service providers back into the community to work alongside the police in troubled neighborhoods. In an economically depressed New England town, the police open a substation in an experimental school to encourage greater collaboration between public housing residents and their more affluent—and fearful—neighbors. An enterprising captain out West cuts the bureaucratic red tape that had long kept the sidewalks in a poor neighborhood unpaved, thereby ending the corrosive ridicule that the neighborhood's fragile youngsters faced each time they showed up at school with muddy shoes.

With a nod to Mark Twain, these successes, large and small, confirm that reports of the death of community policing are greatly exaggerated. No doubt there will always be the occasional, high-profile casualty—a promising effort that implodes or explodes for a variety of complex reasons. Yet for every widely reported flame-out, there are innumerable unheralded success stories in law enforcement agencies nationwide.

The "No Definition" Myth

Indeed, surveys done by the Police Executive Research Forum and the National Center for Community Policing in conjunction with the FBI confirm that roughly two out of three police agencies in major jurisdictions report that they have adopted some form of community policing or plan to do so in the near future. If that sounds too good to be true, at least in part, it is; the NCCP/FBI research showed that three out of four police agencies that claim to be doing community policing do not allow the community a voice in identifying, prioritizing, and solving problems.

Sadly, some would use that finding to define community policing, insisting that any definition must derive from quantifying what is happening in the field. Yet that ignores the clear and concise definition of community policing in widespread use for more than a decade, which has served as the ideal toward which progressive police have aspired: Community policing is a philosophy based on forging a partnership between the police and the community, so that they can work together on solving problems of crime, and fear of crime and disorder, thereby enhancing the overall quality of life in community neighborhoods.

Its academic underpinnings blend the wisdom of power sharing and decentralized decision-making contained in the ten Principles of Community Policing, as proposed by the late Dr. Robert Trojanowicz, with the effectiveness of strategic thinking in problem-oriented policing (POP), as envisioned by Dr. Herman Goldstein. While each man's vision independently advanced policing far beyond business as usual, combining these powerful approaches together under the rubric of community policing dramatically reinvents the role and function of the police.

Changing the Policing Paradigm

The Trojanowicz legacy underscores the importance of bringing key stakeholders together as equals, since solutions always benefit from including as many perspectives as possible. The police alone cannot make communities safe, and tapping the eyes, ears, minds, and energies of law-abiding citizens increases the likelihood of success. Add to that the Goldstein contribution of the S.A.R.A. (Scanning, Analysis, Response, Assessment) model, which elevates policing from catching the bad guys to exploring the underlying dynamics that allow problems to persist—as profound a shift as from checkers to chess.

Operationalizing the philosophy can differ in terms of specific strategies and tactics, as part of tailoring the approach to local resources and needs, but the major challenge facing police managers lies in harnessing the full power of this potent new paradigm. In this climate, the allegation that community policing has yet to be defined threatens its future. For one thing, it blurs the standards by which we can hold departments accountable, allowing any police agency that jumps on the community policing bandwagon the potential to dilute what it stands for. For another, it allows police a tempting loophole to avoid the hard work of fundamental change, particularly the daunting challenge of engaging the community fully in the following steps: determining the vision, values, and mission of the department; recruiting, selecting, training, evaluating, promoting, and rewarding personnel; and participating directly in problem solving and assessment.

How sad if community policing ends up tagged as a failure without receiving a fair trial on its own merits. *Newsweek* columnist George Will treated community policing as synonymous with "saturation policing," as if the goal is simply to flood neighborhoods with police officers as a visible deterrent to crime. Another challenge now comes from "crime-specific" policing, touted as superior to community policing in reducing target crimes.

The Illusion of "Crime-Specific" Policing

The most famous of the current crime-specific policing sites is Houston, with its 655 Program (which refers to the goal of using overtime to add the equivalent of an additional full-time officer to each of the city's 655 square miles). This approach again narrows the mission of the police to a primary focus on crime, which it addresses by "proactive, aggressive" patrol and investigation, with interaction between the police and the community limited to communication about security concerns.

Conceptually, it differs little from traditional policing, albeit with more sworn personnel and greater fervor for making arrests for minor infractions. In Houston, reports of Part I "suppressible" crimes declined, while arrests for Part II curfew violations and loitering increased.

Mark Twain also warned us about lies, damn lies, and statistics. Even the advocates of crime-specific policing admit that the Houston results are ambiguous, since reductions in crimes such as robberies and burglaries mirrored decreases in neighboring jurisdictions that have not adopted this approach.

Keep in mind as well that only one out of every three crimes is ever reported to the police. By fostering trust, community policing can actually produce an initial increase in crime rates, as people share information about incidents that would otherwise have gone unreported (and surveys confirm that people feel safer). Crime-specific policing, in contrast, may well do a better job of suppressing crime reporting than suppressing crime itself. And if minority communities in particular perceive "aggressive" as "harassing," this approach could elevate the threat of civil unrest, whereas community policing is widely perceived as reducing this risk.

Community policing is about both means and ends. Targeting disorder could be part of a community policing problem-solving initiative, but only as a result of the direct participation and support of the community. It is easy to see the appeal of an alternative strategy that allows police to remain the independent and autonomous experts. Yet crime-specific policing suffers from fostering dependence on government to make communities safe, at a time when there is growing consensus that voters support empowering people to do more for themselves.

The reality is that the choice is not among the four concepts of traditional, community, problem-oriented, or crime-specific policing, but between public and private policing. Community policing did not emerge because it is easy to implement and to do, but because the traditional system is failing. Where a decade ago there were three private security guards for each police officer, there are now four to one. As those who can afford to do so increasingly isolate themselves in high-rise fortresses and walled suburban communities, the public police find themselves left to protect "consumers" who cannot "shop" elsewhere for their safety. What will happen if frustrated taxpayers lose their taste for supporting an unresponsive system that they themselves no longer use?

The question is not whether any new strategy can effect a temporary decline in a handful of selected crime rates, but whether a philosophy of policing helps to inform the use of existing police resources as the catalyst in making troubled neighborhoods safer. As Bob Trojanowicz used to remind us, community policing recognizes that until we are all safe, no one is safe.

Source: Adapted with permission from Bonnie Bucqueroux, "Community Policing Is Alive and Well," *Community Policing Exchange,* May/June 1995, pp. 1–2.

FROM PHILOSOPHY TO STRATEGIC APPLICATION

An extensive part of the literature consistently identifies community-oriented policing as a policing philosophy (Allender 2004; Bennett 1994; Fielding 2005; Geller 1991; Goodstein 1991; Miller and Hess 1994; Rush 1994; Trojanowicz and Bucqueroux 1990). The issue that subsequently arises is whether community-oriented policing can be strategically applied in a real-world setting. Because the definitions of community-oriented policing often specifically detail either the philosophical side or the practical side, there exists much debate on whether these two definitions are truly oriented to the same goal. The debate over practical application of theory has always plagued both the academic and practical worlds. The application of the community-oriented policing philosophy is no different.

As Commissioner Norman D. Inkster of the Royal Canadian Mounted Police stated in the early 1990s, "We have been discussing the concept of community policing for more than ten years; a few of us have actually been practicing it. Some claim to have implemented community policing but—apart from a few discreet programs—their organization continues as before" (Inkster 1992, 28). The disparity over the concept of community-oriented policing has caused much confusion and false promises. Focusing on current and past literature on the community-oriented policing concept helps us move toward a common goal. So, too, does the development of a workable definition of the concept. It is again Norman Inkster who stated, "I think the essence of community-based policing still eludes some of us and many of our efforts do not yield results because we have not properly understood the concept we are trying to apply" (Inkster 1992, 28). The first step to understanding a concept is to understand what is intended by way of the definition.

CONCLUSION

As the review of the literature revealed, a standard definition is lacking for what has become known as community-oriented policing. There are common themes from both the philosophical side and practical side of the concept. The predominant themes consist of the police and community working together, creating solutions to the indigenous problems that plague their community, and implementing programs to solve these problems. It is through this cooperation that communities will be able to actualize the true sense of the term *community*.

To actually implement community-oriented policing, there must be a method of transferring theory and ideas into action and workable programs. In extracting the philosophy's common themes, we can categorize all of the concepts into three components. (See Figure 2-2.)

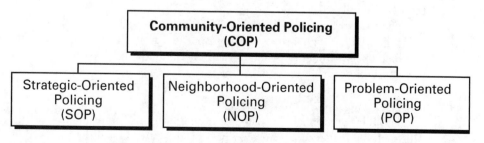

FIGURE 2-2 The three components of community-oriented policing.

A local youth enjoying the festivities during "National Nite Out" sponsored by the Montgomery County Police Department. *(Courtesy of Montgomery County Department of Police, Montgomery County, Maryland)*

The first component of community-oriented policing is strategic-oriented policing (SOP). Here the police utilize traditional police practices and procedures by redistributing their resources toward identified problem areas. The goal of this component is to drive out the criminal element or cause of social disorder in order to allow the community the chance to establish some type of groundwork in reclaiming their community.

The second key component discussed in the literature is neighborhood-oriented policing (NOP). Neighborhood-oriented policing would include any and all programs that help open the lines of communication between the police and the citizens, to work toward fostering a true sense of community. Programs could include police–youth softball leagues being formed, mini police stations being located in the community, or police officers moving into the communities they serve.

The third component revealed in the literature is the problem policing method. This method includes a concerted effort on the part of both the police and the community to determine the cause of crime and social disorder in a community, to create solutions to the problems, and to implement the most viable program. Although this component is predominantly implemented with the cooperation of the community members, it does not preclude the police officer from conducting this type of analysis during a routine shift. This component must be an ongoing process; the success or failure of the programs should be determined and updated or alternative programs then implemented.

This trilogy of components, however, is really an interconnected web of programs that must be implemented together. The strategic policing component clears the way for the neighborhood-oriented and problem-oriented components to be set in motion. Many of the neighborhood-oriented programs that are implemented are determined via the problem-oriented process. And in many cases, to achieve the community's support in problem solving, the communication between the police and the community must be opened up through the neighborhood-oriented policing component. The three components, therefore, depend on each other for the successful implementation of community-oriented policing.

The concept, however, must go further to achieve its end. The true concept must also deal with those common themes found in the literature that detail a department-wide implementation of the philosophy. Community-oriented policing must be a systemic approach to policing, with a decentralized organizational structure, and all members of the police force, including officers, supervisors, and civilians, must be behind the philosophy. And this philosophy, this way of thinking, must be carried over into the programs that complement these ideas.

Therefore, through a consensus of the past and present literature as well as a combination of the philosophical and practical concepts, community-oriented policing can be defined as follows:

> A systemic approach to policing with the paradigm of instilling and fostering a sense of community, within a geographical neighborhood, to improve the quality of life. It achieves this through the decentralization of the police and the implementation of a synthesis of three key components: (1) strategic-oriented policing—the redistribution of traditional police resources, (2) neighborhood-oriented policing—the interaction of police and all community members to reduce crime and the fear of crime through indigenous proactive programs, and (3) problem-oriented policing—the concerted effort to resolve the cause of crime rather than the symptoms.

COP ON THE WORLD WIDE WEB

Dr. Cecil Greek, Community Policing Links

http://www.criminology.fsu.edu/p/cjl-police2.php#community

Dr. James Q. Wilson, Interview, PBS

http://www.pbs.org/fmc/timeline/pwilson.htm

National Center for Community Policing, Michigan State University

http://www.cj.msu.edu/~people/cp/webpubs.html

Web site containing dozens of good solid papers on community-oriented policing.

Shattering "Broken Windows": An Analysis of San Francisco's Alternative Crime Policies, by Khaled Taqi-Eddin and Dan Macallair

http://www.cjcj.org/pubs/windows/windows.html

REVIEW QUESTIONS

1. Compare and contrast police–community relations with community-oriented policing.
2. Define community-oriented policing.
3. Explain community-oriented policing from a philosophical, policy, and programmatic perspective

CHAPTER 3

Strategic-Oriented Policing

Let's take back our streets!

—Reuben Greenberg

CHAPTER OBJECTIVES

- Define the first component of community-oriented policing.
- Understand the concepts behind strategic-oriented policing.
- Define *targeting*.
- Define *directed patrols*.
- Define *aggressive patrols*.
- Define *saturation patrols*.
- Understand the benefits and problems with strategic-oriented policing.

The first component of community-oriented policing, as previously described, is strategic-oriented policing (see Figure 3-1). This method of policing more recently has been called order maintenance policing, broken windows policing, and zero-tolerance policing. While it is clear these names often have a negative connotation for some, the techniques, with proper application, can apply to community-oriented policing. The concept broadens traditional police practices and procedures into a more beneficial model conducive to the goals of establishing all of the tenets of community-oriented policing. It is the catalyst for all of the ideas that eventually will unfold within the community, and it allows for a smooth transition into the other components. Utilizing a slightly altered method of past policing procedures, the police do not have to adapt immediately to a new policing philosophy. Implementing the move from traditional reactive patrolling to community-oriented policing allows this to become the transition stage for not only the police but the community as well.

As Herman Goldstein (1990, 132) stated, "The police always have available to them the option of increasing their enforcement of laws that might bear on a specific problem,

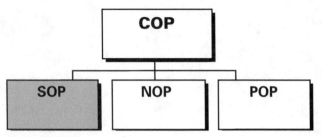

FIGURE 3-1   Strategic-oriented policing.

COP IN ACTION

Operation Ceasefire, Boston, Massachusetts

Operation Ceasefire is a coordinated citywide strategy established in May 1996 to deter youth firearm violence. Ceasefire operates as a system, focusing interventions through the coordination and knowledge of all of the city's law enforcement and criminal justice agencies. The working group devised an overall strategy based on the problem-solving research of the Kennedy School of Government (KSG) at Harvard University and the Bureau of Alcohol, Tobacco, and Firearms (ATF), and the success of tactics that had worked against gangs in the past. The goal was to communicate warnings to gangs that, if violence occurred, there would be a swift, predictable response with weighty consequences.

The strategy began with focused communications. Probation and gang unit police officers who knew the youth, streetworkers, clergy, and community-based organizations met informally and formally with gang youth in schools, homes, neighborhoods, courthouses, and other locations. Probationers were required to attend these meetings. The message was emphatically delivered to them that violence would no longer be tolerated in Boston—it had to stop or the full weight of the law enforcement and criminal justice system would be brought to bear on the perpetrators. The working group wanted youth to realize that this zero tolerance message was not a bluff, but a serious interagency effort. True to its word, when its message was ignored and gang violence erupted, the department's Youth Violence Strike Force (YVSF) used intensive order maintenance and enforcement tactics to quickly suppress flareups of firearm violence in emerging gang hot spots. YVSF targeted noncomplying gangs with aggressive enforcement of public drinking and motor vehicle violations, outstanding warrants, and probation surrenders and made numerous arrests. Street enforcement resulted in two dozen Federal indictments and arrests in August 1996. News of these activities quickly spread to other gangs in Boston whose members saw what could happen if they did not comply.

In addition to the overall targeting of youth firearm violence, Boston Police Department implemented several programs to address the problem from various perspectives. These programs included:

> Boston Gun Project: The Boston P.D. and the ATF worked in concert to flag for investigation every trace that showed guns with a time-to-crime of less than 30 months, more popular gun types, guns with restored serial numbers, those in high-risk neighborhoods, and those associated with gang members or territories. Another tactic was to link the trace data set with the gang membership and turf data, which allowed for identification

of gun owners who were also gang members. The quick enforcement and swift federal prosecution severely disrupted the gun market in Boston.

Operation Night Light: This program pairs one probation officer with two Boston police officers to make unannounced visits to the homes, schools, and workplaces of high-risk youth probationers during the nontraditional hours of 7 P.M. to midnight rather than between 8:30 A.M. and 4:30 P.M., which was previously the norm. The probation officer decides which of 10 to 15 probationers to visit each evening based on which youth were defaulting on compliance. The team wears plain clothes and uses an unmarked car. The terms of probation—which commonly includes curfews, geographic restrictions, and other constraints designed to keep youth from reoffending—are strictly enforced. Probation officers also have been instrumental in convincing judges to impose expanded conditions.

Boston Community Centers' Streetworkers Program: This program operates community centers throughout the city with 30 college educated staff members available 24 hours a day to conduct gang and youth outreach. The streetworkers are ages 25 to 55 and work closely with gang members to mediate disputes and gang truces in schools and throughout the community. The streetworkers also help gang members and their families gain access to much needed social services. Each streetworker is assigned to 5 to 10 gangs, with a caseload of roughly 25 active and 25 less active cases. They work closely with the police department, probation, clergy, courts, and schools.

Youth Services Providers Network (YSPN): The network is a partnership of many of Boston's youth service organizations and city agencies to address teenage runaways, dropout prevention, mentoring, job training, and building leadership skills.

Safe Neighborhood Initiative (SNI): This initiative offers community residents the opportunity to work with law enforcement and government officials to identify and address neighborhood issues through advisory councils.

Since Operation Ceasefire, the Boston Gun Project, Operation Night Light, neighborhood policing, tougher youth offender laws, and expanded prevention and intervention programs went into effect, there has been a dramatic decrease in the number of homicides in the city of Boston. The number of homicides committed by youth under 24 years of age fell from 61 in 1996 to 23 in 1998. This reduction in homicides and youth homicides cannot be directly attributed to any one of these programs but more likely is due to the cumulative impact of this comprehensive multipronged approach.

Source: Shay Bilchik, *Promising Strategies to Reduce Gun Violence.* Washington, D.C.: Office of Juvenile Justice and Delinquency Prevention, 1999.

---

although they may not routinely enforce them because they lack the resources, the problem has low priority, or enforcement is judged to be ineffective." Strategic policing enforces laws oriented on a specific problem, as Goldstein states. However, it realizes and accepts the three problems Goldstein raises.

First, the police throughout history have lacked the necessary resources to accomplish their mission. There is always a need for additional personnel, equipment, and training. The police never have enough staffing manpower due to increased crime rates in specific geographical areas or because too many officers would like their summer vacations at the same time. This is not news to any police administrator. Nor is utilizing

DARE students trying on SWAT equipment during a DARE picnic sponsored by the St. Petersburg Police Department. (*Courtesy of St. Petersburg Police Department, St. Petersburg, Florida.*)

statistical crime data to allocate resources to high-crime areas. However, when these resources are allocated, they are generally limited to only a handful of additional beat cops and perhaps one or two nonuniform officers. The concept of strategic policing recommends the temporary use of multiple officers from various divisions in various ways. This plan may include a single officer assigned to check on a single problem to upward of twenty officers assigned to a specific area for a week or two, of which some may be street officers, tactical officers, detectives, and motor officers, all temporarily assigned for the purposes of a show of force. However, because the police department cannot maintain this extended use of resources for any long duration of time, something else must be put in place of the physical presence of the police. This comes later in the form of neighborhood-oriented policing and problem-oriented policing techniques.

Second, strategic policing recognizes that often many of these "problems" have extremely low priority within the police department. Determining what has priority is often a difficult task. One area may appear to need immediate attention, despite crime statistics for the area that place it in a low-priority category. Another area may not appear to be a high-priority area but may in fact reflect this need in the crime statistics. The goal, then, is to determine which area is in the greatest need, not just by crime statistics but by talking with the officers who work the areas in need and finding out where the members of the local community feel the stepped-up police presence is necessary. This consensus of the allocation of resources will determine exactly what has priority, what necessitates a limited response, and what can wait.

Third, the idea of judging the police presence to be ineffective has generally in the past been based on arrest statistics going up and crime rates going down. In a community sense, this approach can no longer be the sole basis for determining whether the police enforcement was "effective." The quality of living for the community must also be explored, along with the reduced fear and crime perception of the community. This evaluation must be done throughout the various stages of implementing community-oriented policing services in a time series analysis. Determining these elements before the use of strategic policing techniques, after the techniques, and at the commencement of neighborhood- or problem-oriented policing can be helpful. Only then can a true assessment of the community's fear, crime rates, and quality of living be fully understood. Only then can the success rates of community-oriented policing be documented.

There are no limitations to the methods that can be employed under strategic policing. It is only important that "the basic goal remains the effective control of crime" (Moore and Trojanowicz 1988a/6). The techniques, however, can be categorized into the determination of where strategic policing will be implemented and three types of patrols. The determination of where strategic policing is to be implemented is known in the literature as *targeting*, the term used here (e.g., Fleissner et al. 1992; Tien and Rich 1994). The three types of patrols are (1) directed, (2) aggressive, and (3) saturation. These three concepts will be explored further, as will those jurisdictions where particular techniques have been successful and some of the problems that may arise from implementation.

STRATEGIC-ORIENTED POLICING AND VARIOUS DRUG ENFORCEMENT TACTICS

Mail-In Coupons: Police place newspaper advertisements that contain forms for readers to fill in with information on suspected or observed drug activity; readers then mail the form to the department.

Taxi Connection: Undercover police officers ride in taxis and ask the driver to connect them with a drug dealer; if the driver sets up or handles a drug transaction, the undercover officer arrests the driver.

Hotel Managers: Police train managers of hotels and motels to spot signs of drug activity and to call the police.

Package Interdiction: Working with parcel-shipping companies, police in some communities are examining and intercepting packages that may contain drugs.

Clone Beepers: Drug dealers, sellers, runners, and buyers who use beepers may learn that police are tuned to their frequency and can, through new electronic capability, identify telephones from which calls are made; arrests may follow.

Child Abuse and Neglect: Pregnant women who use drugs may be charged with child abuse by police. Parents of juvenile drug offenders may be charged with child neglect.

Traffic Checkpoints: Signs put up by a state highway patrol along interstate highways warn of a drug checkpoint a few miles ahead; motorists who drive off at the next exit, however, learn that the checkpoint is actually on the exit.

Source: National Institute of Justice, *Searching for Answers: Annual Evaluation Report on Drugs and Crime: 1992* Washington, D.C.: National Institute of Justice, 1993.

TARGETING

Targeting is a term often utilized to give credence to the fact the police are not random-ly conducting proactive patrol but are focusing on specific places as well as specific types of crime (National Institute of Justice 1996). Police resources are directed at these tar-gets to alleviate specific problems indigenous to a particular area. There are multiple ways to arrive at what should be targeted, as well as multiple ways to derive a solution for the problems. However, because this is a process to foster a sense of community, the community must be involved.

The determination of what needs to be targeted, what has precedence, and how the strategic policing should be carried out should not be directed in only downward com-munication, but in lateral communication with the police officers who patrol the areas being discussed, other public agencies, community leaders, and citizens who live in the area. It is important to include all of these individuals in a targeting committee, and a majority should be derived from the employees of these agencies and the common citi-zens of the community.

Some may argue that having the employees and common citizens as members of this focal group is pointless because those persons in leadership positions in the agencies and in the community are better equipped to handle the problem analysis and solve the problems through their various administrations. As James Q. Wilson and George L. Kelling (1989, 51) respond, "Forcing them to cooperate by knocking heads together at the top rarely works; what department heads promise the mayor they will do may bear little relationship to what their rank-and-file employees actually do." They then con-clude that "you have to get the neighborhood-level supervisors from each agency together in a 'district cabinet' that meets regularly and addresses common concerns" (Wilson and Kelling 1989, 51). The committee should include not only rank-and-file employees from the various agencies but also a cross-section of the community, from the police to citizens who live in the community.

Inclusion of the police officers is extremely important simply because they are there in the community, day in and day out, dealing with the problems indigenous to a particular community. They have a perspective related to the overall picture of what plagues a particular community, and they can communicate in organizational terms. The patrol officer can provide not only the facts of the problems but also an educated insight into the problems. The key revolves around the fact that officers are members of the community who know the pulse of crime and social problems that plague the community.

Additional public agencies can also provide information on the problems plaguing a community. Any additional police agency that has concurrent jurisdiction is an obvious choice to provide a different interpretation of the crime problems in a specific area. Other public safety organizations such as the fire department and emergency medical services can provide a particularly helpful analysis of the community's problems, including areas of fre-quent drug overdoses, areas prone to multiple assault calls, or areas that could be deemed hazardous to public health, welfare, and safety. The departments of social services or social work can provide input into what specific social problems, ranging from domestic violence to difficulties with area landlords, an area incurs. The housing authority could also provide this insight to housing areas that may be deemed hazardous to the health of its residents or where multiple landlord–tenant disputes occur. Any office of business or economic

A Sacramento police officer demonstrating a field sobriety test to a local citizen during a police department open house. *(Courtesy of the Sacramento Police Department, Sacramento, California.)*

development can provide information on commercial establishments that may be a magnet for various types of crime and social disorders. Finally, the government's public works division can provide a vast amount of knowledge concerning areas that may sustain high crime rates or societal problems from the number of calls received from a specific area or the type of service request received. All of these resources are generally within the reach of the police department, and most can easily provide a representative to attend the meetings regarding the crime, social disorders, and quality of life in a particular community.

One of the most innovative means for targeting has come about through the improvement of technology, namely in the areas of computer technology and satellite global positioning systems. Police departments and citizens now have access to information that was not as easily accessible in the past through what has come to be commonly known as geo-mapping (see O'Connell 1998). The use of geo-mapping software has allowed agencies to combine information from their 911 calls and incident-based reporting databases to interface with computer-generated maps. Calls for service or reports made by the police (e.g., incidents) can thus be located on a map based on their geographical location through either a general location (the address from which the call was received or where the incident took place) or a more precise location by the use of global positioning satellites that allow for the precise location to be downloaded onto the map. By then utilizing the computer-generated maps, the number of incidents or type of incidents can be seen visually and critical targets selected. It is the modern version of using the old wall map and thumbtack method to mark where certain crimes were taking place. This geo-mapping has

Officers from the city of Port St. Lucie, Florida, Police Department's Special Response Team demonstrate equipment to the leadership group of the St. Lucie County Chamber of Commerce. *(Courtesy of Port St. Lucie Police Department, Port St. Lucie, Florida.)*

proven to be highly advantageous not only for the police, who can use the information for targeting certain areas for specific problems, but also for citizens, who can track the types of crimes in their neighborhoods, often via the Internet (which usually rounds the information to the nearest hundred block). Citizens have used this information not only to see how safe their neighborhood is but also to pressure the police to respond.

The community leaders are also important for the roundtable meeting that should be established to determine what will be primary and secondary targets in strategic policing. These leaders can originate from any of the community's established organizations. All organizations could provide some understanding of the crime problems indigenous to a local community. Business leaders or members of the local chamber of commerce are the key personnel to provide information on problems associated with commercial establishments located in a particular neighborhood or area. A member of the local school board, parent–teacher association, or housing association can provide information on problems associated with residential areas located in the community. And finally the various political, social, and religious associations may be able to provide information on specific community problems from their perspectives as members of the community.

It is also extremely important to move away from the governmental and organizational aspect of community members and look to individuals who represent the common man or common woman of a community. The committee should include members of the community who represent the community or area being targeted. A middle-class banker would not be appropriate for discussing quality-of-life problems in the lower-class subsidized housing projects any more than a member from this community would be sitting in on a targeting group for the upper-class neighborhood. The members can be drawn from all walks of life to include the unemployed, family members who stay home during the day, or teenagers who live in the neighborhood. There should be no real criteria for the selection of common citizens, only that they can articulate what they perceive as the crime, social, or quality-of-life problems.

As Wilson and Kelling have stated, the committee should then meet regularly in a roundtable to discuss the various types of problems concerning them. They should develop lists of all the potential problems, brainstorm possible solutions, and prioritize the most serious concerns necessitating immediate action and those that could do with less police response or a different course of action separate from the actions available from the police. The group, in its regular meetings, can assess the success of varying methods in both subjective and objective terms, develop new courses of action, and reprioritize as necessary. New members to the committee, perhaps on a rotating basis or through simple attrition, will be extremely beneficial to the committee, contributing fresh ideas and innovative methods not previously discussed.

The ultimate goal of targeting is the inclusion of the community in making policy decisions as to where police resources will be allocated. Allowing this voice will help target the most real and perceived threats to the community, allow the community to exercise some power in goal setting, and open a direct line of communication with the community, fostering a strong relationship.

 ## COP IN ACTION

High-Profile Program Successfully Drives Prostitutes Out of Town

Some communities seized the cars of "johns" arrested for prostitution. Other cities like Washington, D.C., jacked up fines for soliciting to $1,000. West Palm Beach, Fla., opted for public embarrassment, publicizing the names of johns on billboards and in newspapers, then forcing them to attend group counseling sessions with prostitutes. But perhaps nowhere is the war against prostitution being waged more innovatively than in St. Petersburg, Fla.

The cops there are driving out prostitution with a new high-profile program—one of the most comprehensive in the nation. It's driven not from the top, or by city hall, but by the community police officers on the beat.

Some critics claim that you can't win the war against prostitution—you only drive it across the city line or transform it into a different shape—but St. Petersburg officers strongly disagree. "That's like saying cops can't stamp out crime, so we should give up," said Lieutenant Debbie Prine, one of the key architects of the St. Petersburg anti-prostitution program. She also added, "In St. Petersburg, all of our CPO's (community police officers) make arrests and are actively involved in various investigations. We're not social workers. Our job is to help our neighborhoods solve problems, and from all the feedback I've received, that's being accomplished."

A Community Policing Approach

The anti-prostitution program could not have evolved without St. Petersburg's commitment to community policing, a philosophy that has been vigorously promoted by Police Chief Darrel Stephens. St. Petersburg was one of the first cities in the nation to go city-wide with community policing. The department first identified 48 neighborhoods in the city. Then it assigned community police officers to these areas, along with backup from three to four beat officers.

"We really do believe that our success depends on having a real partnership, where cops work with the people in the community and take a problem-solving approach," Stephens said. "Our conviction is that police do their job better if they empower citizens and work with residents, not against them. This is a perfect example of how officers can focus on preventing crime instead of just arresting criminals."

Doing Their Homework

Prine and her squad members conducted several months of research, which included contacting officers in various police departments to find out what worked and what didn't work. "What we found was that other communities were attacking either the supply or the demand side," Sauer said. "But none of them seemed to be taking a comprehensive approach aimed at the prostitutes, the johns—or what's even more important—the environment that sustains this activity. That means you have to reach the motels, the businesses, and the homeowners who cater to prostitution and allow it to exist.

"We knew we needed a multi-faceted approach," Prine added. "Because doing just one thing wouldn't work. For example, some people don't care if you put their name on television as a convicted john. Maybe they don't live in the area or they just couldn't care less. But they don't want to lose their driver's license. So that would be a way to eliminate that particular group. We reviewed the entire problem, and one by one, discovered ways to deal with each part. That was the key," said Prine.

Spreading the Word

"Dear John" letters are another deterrent developed by the St. Petersburg Police Department. Every person convicted of soliciting a prostitute receives a letter from Chief Stephens. The letter is stamped confidential and mailed to the perpetrator's home address. The letter reminds the individual or family members that the act of patronizing a prostitute is a criminal offense and that there are dangers involved (such as becoming a victim of a serious crime or being exposed to numerous venereal diseases and AIDS).

Mapping Out a Strategy

With the support of the chief judge in Pinellas County, the police department has introduced a "mapping" strategy, in which a prostitute is denied access to the area where she previously worked. It works like this: The arresting officer attaches a map to the arrest papers clearly indicating the street where the prostitute was picked up. When a prostitute is convicted, the judge orders her to stay out of this defined area as a condition of probation. If an officer stops a prostitute for loitering and discovers she is in her mapped area, this is noted in a field interrogation report and forwarded to the probation board. The prostitute can be sent to jail for violating her probation. The St. Petersburg Police Department has found that mapping, along with a seldom-used statute that provides for revocation of a convicted person's driver's license, has been an effective way to keep johns and prostitutes out of their neighborhoods—especially since most johns drive in from other parts of St. Petersburg and other cities.

Tracking Results

As far as measuring its results to date, the anti-prostitution team is now developing statistical measures to assess the impact of the program. "We expect to have one of the best prostitution databases in the nation," Prine said. "The database will list calls, arrests, the names of prostitutes, their pimps, their associates and related drug dealers," Prine said. "This will give us a really superb analytical tool to chart our progress. The data has always been out there but it's scattered. For the first time we'll pull it all together."

"The preliminary system has already paid dividends for officers investigating other crimes. The prostitution core group now gets regular visits from the homicide and robbery units to gather leads and intelligence on their cases. We regularly get requests from other departments to visit St. Petersburg and go along on a decoy operation," Prine said.

Recently Sergeant Butch Barfield and Officer Tony Youngblood from North Charleston (S.C.) spent two days with Lieutenant Prine observing tactics and procedures. Barfield said, "It's always helpful to see another agency's operation firsthand. We observed a lot of good techniques and investigative procedures that can be implemented in our community policing efforts back in South Carolina."

Meanwhile, in St. Petersburg, the cops on the street don't have any illusions. It's not called the world's oldest profession because it won't be around much longer. But they think they're making a difference, especially since only one john has been arrested more than once since they initiated their comprehensive strategy.

Source: Reprinted with permission from Ronald J. Getz, "High-Profile Program Successfully Drives Prostitutes Out of Town," *Community Policing Exchange,* November/December 1996, p. 6.

DIRECTED PATROLS

The first method of strategic-oriented policing is the technique known as directed patrol. This is the easiest of the patrols to conduct because it is easily implemented and has the least drain on police resources. Directed patrols can be implemented for criminal activity and traffic violations. They can be based on officers' discretion, crime analysis, or a specific complaint received by the community or the community committee. The officers are required to simply check on the area involved in their designated assignment in between the calls they receive during a normal tour of duty.

In Arlington County, Virginia, police officers are required to pick one criminal- and one traffic-directed patrol each month. They then record the number of times they check the area and any contacts or arrests they make during their shift. Additional directed patrols are signed out at the beginning of a shift to particular beats where either a crime analysis has shown a high crime or traffic problem or a citizen has complained. The information is recorded on the log sheet and passed along to the next shift if it is a recurring problem not unique to a particular time. Some of the directed patrols may include walks through local parks, patrols of areas where the homeless urinate and defecate, or patrols in the vicinity of known crack houses.

One of the common complaints among officers assigned to directed patrols is being unable to perform the checks or being pulled away from the directed patrol assignment to answer various calls for services and 911 calls and to attend to administrative duties that may tie up the officers for an entire shift. One method that has been implemented is

A field booking station established in concert with a crackdown in response to a Long Beach community's input on decreasing crime, gangs, and drugs. (*Courtesy of Long Beach Police Department, Long Beach, California.*)

a split-force patrol (Tien, Simon, and Larson 1977). This method splits the patrol shift into two segments. One is responsible for responding to calls, and the other is responsible solely for the directed patrols, unless an emergency arises. In this manner, those working the directed patrols have the understanding that they will be able to conduct these patrols without constant interruptions. However, effective management must ensure that the directed patrols are conducted in this method and that the split is rotated daily or weekly to prevent any friction between the officers working the directed patrol split and those tied to a potential backlog of calls in the standard patrol split.

Studies conducted on the success of directed patrols have generally found that crime decreases in the targeted area when this type of patrol is utilized (Cordner 1981; Cordner and Trojanowicz 1992; Roncek and Maier 1991; Warren, Forst, and Estrella 1979). A dedicated patrol, in which the police are continually present, whether at varying intervals or for long periods of time, can clearly be seen as beneficial in stopping criminal activity or in helping solve various social problems.

AGGRESSIVE PATROLS

The second method of strategic-oriented policing utilizes methods that have come to be known as aggressive patrol or aggressive order maintenance. Aggressive patrol is an increased pressure on specific criminal or social order problems, as well as on specific criminal elements, by the police. According to Stephen D. Mastrofski (1988, 53), "aggressive order maintenance strategies include rousing or arresting people thought to cause public disorder, field interrogations and roadblock checks, surveillance of suspicious people, vigorous enforcement of public order and nuisance laws, and, in general, much greater attention to the minor crimes and disturbances thought to disrupt and displease the civil public." The tactics, although aggressive in nature, must be within the legal and societal controls on the police. Aggressive patrols merely increase the quantity of contacts for a particular situation in an attempt to alleviate the problem. The various forms of aggressive patrols may be categorized as follows: field stops, traffic stops, use of plainclothes officers, habitual offender programs, sting operations, and stakeouts.

Field stops, field interviews, or field investigations, regardless of the name used, have always been a method for police to question and record a suspicious person's information. Although the individual may not be committing a crime in violation of a criminal statute, his or her actions may be inappropriate for the surrounding community, which can easily label the individual as "suspicious" or "out of place." The police record their contact with the individual by conducting a pat down, noting personal identification information, and taking a Polaroid photograph, thereby maintaining a record of all individuals encountered in a particular neighborhood. This contact may serve as a deterrent or as a future means of identifying the perpetrator of a crime. An increased use of these field interrogations can have a profound effect on crime and should not necessarily be limited to any particular time, place, or circumstances.

James Q. Wilson (1994) wrote that this particular method could be utilized more often by the police with individuals who are thought to be carrying concealed or unlicensed weapons. He believes this approach would be more effective in reducing crime than the continual passage of new laws attempting to ban these weapons. Additionally, a study conducted in San Diego tested the effects of these field interviews on crime and found field interviews have a substantial effect on area crime rates, specifically as a deterrent for crimes committed by youths in groups (Boydstun 1975). Implementing a common police practice in a more intensified program has a profound effect on crime. These findings are just as clear on the street as they are in the research.

Traffic enforcement has always been a key mission of the police. Their primary function is to maintain the flow of traffic in a safe and expedient manner by monitoring and directing the traffic as well as enforcing all state and local traffic laws. Randomly issuing citations for traffic violations may or may not deter individual drivers from breaking traffic laws, and it is very doubtful that it has any effect on the general population of motorists. However, the use of aggressive patrol techniques at a particular intersection or road subject to either accidents or traffic violations can have this desired overall effect, if the presence and sincerity of the police function in these instances are felt by the public. Essentially the enforcement of traffic laws "contributes to the maintenance of order, educates the public in safe driving habits, and provides a visible community service" (Cole 1995b, 197). Additionally, a significant amount of criminal activity is discovered during traffic stops that may not have been discovered otherwise, and this is further testimony to the successful use of this form of aggressive patrol.

Aggressive patrol used in traffic enforcement is distinctly different from directed patrol used in traffic enforcement. In traffic-directed patrol, officers are encouraged to check on a previously specified area for traffic violations in between their calls or during their tour of a split-force patrol. The use of aggressive patrol is for a dedicated officer, specifically assigned to monitor a particular area, to issue citations to violators without the broad use of discretion. Although the police retain their discretionary abilities in these tours, they should attempt to minimize the overall use.

Despite the fact that this form of aggressive patrol is oriented on traffic, it significantly impacts the criminal element, and not just by reducing traffic problems. The research conducted specifically on the use of aggressive patrol in traffic enforcement has found that areas that utilize this technique have lower crime rates (Wilson and Boland 1978, 1979). Another study on the use of aggressive patrols in traffic enforcement discovered that police departments that implemented this technique had lower robbery rates in their jurisdictions (Sampson and Cohen 1988). The advantage of increasing aggressive patrols in the area of traffic enforcement, then, is not for the sole purpose of reducing traffic problems but for reducing criminal problems as well.

Another method that mixes field stops and traffic stops in a different manner is the use of plainclothes officers. Most jurisdictions have varying names for these types of officers, sometimes called "felony cars" when operating in unmarked vehicles and "tactical teams" or "undercover officers" while on foot in the communities. Regardless of the name, plainclothes officers attempt to blend into the community to observe crimes or order maintenance problems that may not be visible to a uniformed police officer. Wearing street clothes allows officers to follow possible offenders and observe their behavior or follow potential victims unobtrusively. The police are then in a position to either prevent a crime or react to the crime as it occurs. It is also a method of dealing with known criminal problems or a specific area that is suffering an order maintenance problem that would disappear, only to reappear again, if a police officer in uniform was observed. The key, however, as in other strategic policing methods, is to curtail, drive away, or abolish some behavior that is a criminal or order maintenance problem.

Oklahoma City police officers on horse patrol assisting a local child. (*Courtesy of the Oklahoma City Police Department, Oklahoma City, Oklahoma.*)

Another method that has gained popularity over the past decade is the use of habitual offender or repeat offender programs. The habitual offender can be tracked in various ways: by tracking known criminals who are considered by certain factors to be a high risk for future crime; by tracking the number of arrests of an individual by crime type and presenting the history in court; and by a preventive method through cooperation with the district attorney or commonwealth's attorney's office (in which certain individuals can be declared "habitual offenders" and sentenced more harshly if they commit the act again). The key to most habitual offender programs is the relationship between the police and the district attorney or commonwealth's attorney's office, which can reach an agreement as to who is deemed a habitual or repeat offender and can determine the type of sentence the offender will receive for this type of specific violation. Actual programs of habitual or repeat offenders have been utilized for robberies, larcenies from retail establishments, and local prostitutes or drunken offenders.

COP IN ACTION

Integrated Patrol: Combining Aggressive Enforcement and Community Policing

The concentration of police resources on specific groups of people in particular areas or neighborhoods within a community plays well to contemporary political themes, but as an operational philosophy, it falls short of defining a truly encompassing crime control and reduction strategy. Although local political realities often drive a law enforcement agency's response to crime reduction and prevention, the potential benefits of COP make broadening its impact throughout the widest spectrum of the police organization and the community a worthwhile goal. However, this goal should not be considered mutually exclusive of aggressive enforcement. In fact, an operational philosophy that combines community-based policing with aggressive enforcement provides a balanced and comprehensive approach to addressing crime problems throughout an entire jurisdiction rather than merely in targeted areas within a community. In Anne Arundel County, Maryland, an experiment in such integrated patrol has led to dramatically increased productivity in a midnight patrol shift and has contributed to an overall decline in crime throughout the county.

In January 1996, the Anne Arundel County Police Department initiated an experimental integrated patrol strategy in its western patrol district. The demographics of this primarily residential area of suburban Maryland—including a military complex and a number of commercial pockets as well as a steady increase in calls for service—created conditions conducive to a change in deployment strategy. The experiment would be limited to the midnight shift, which was tasked with establishing and refining a model patrol strategy.

Supervisors identified the primary goals of the experiment as increasing officer productivity, expanding organizational responsibility beyond writing incident reports, decreasing reliance on specialized units for case follow-up, and establishing flexibility as an operational norm. To these ends, a new management philosophy quickly emerged that emphasized increased patrol activity—most notably vehicle stops, field interrogations, and building checks. Employing creative closure strategies—including the ability for officers to move throughout the patrol area as they observed crime patterns develop—became an operational hallmark and an important factor in instilling a case-to-fruition mentality among patrol officers.

As part of the patrol strategy, sergeants and lieutenants continually reviewed crime data and brainstormed with patrol officers to determine the best response strategies for particular problems. Cases requiring follow-up were returned to the responding patrol officers before being forwarded to detectives. Individual officers ultimately were held accountable for investigating and resolving crimes that occurred in their patrol areas. If the officer assigned to a particular area identified the need for a stakeout or search warrant, supervisors paired the officer with another patrol officer to assist. In the early days of the experiment, this approach quickly established a standard for what was expected of each patrol officer individually and the squad collectively. As the creativity of patrol officers was allowed to flourish, officers began to demonstrate individualized expertise in such diverse areas as criminal investigations, traffic enforcement, drug suppression, routine patrol, execution of search warrants, stakeouts, and computer support. At the same time, productivity and case-closure rates began to rise. Only months into the experiment, as supervisors saw that the patrol force was capable of assuming much more responsibility for crime clearance, they further refined the integrated patrol strategy. The most productive investigators in the patrol force assumed responsibility for following up on cases that they thought could be resolved quickly. In the interim between such cases, these patrol-investigators worked on cold cases that had fewer solvability factors.

Additionally, in response to an increase in commercial break-ins, each night, a different officer driving an unmarked vehicle was assigned to patrol commercial areas with the sole responsibility of checking buildings for burglaries. Although this revolving assignment did not always prove popular among officers, this preventive patrol approach netted arrests within days of its implementation.

Since its inception, the integrated patrol project has yielded impressive results. Over a fourteen-month period from January 1996 to March 1997, the midnight shift of the western district patrol squad solved 21 breaking-and-entering cases, 23 armed robberies, 27 vehicle thefts, 2 rapes, 20 simple assaults, 34 non-vehicle thefts, 1 carjacking, 1 abduction, and 139 destruction of property cases. In 1996, under the integrated patrol strategy, the squad issued 3,657 traffic citations—compared to 2,010 in 1995—and apprehended 365 drunk drivers—compared to 200 DWI apprehensions in 1995. The increased productivity and enhanced case-clearance rates generated by the integrated patrol approach spurred department administrators to continue the program and to consider expanding it to other shifts and patrol areas.

Although the art of policing has changed a great deal over the last several decades, especially with regard to personnel deployment strategies and new technologies, relatively little attention has been paid to the way in which administrators deal with personnel or define productivity within a structured, paramilitary environment. A management philosophy that sets parameters but encourages solutions by the rank-and-file is infinitely more desirable than a system that discourages, albeit unintentionally, the innovative and creative worker. Together with effective measures that more accurately validate police successes, a new management philosophy can emerge.

The application of community policing programs within this structure, however, is best accomplished through aggressive enforcement, a case-to-fruition mentality, the use of the flexible organizational structure concept, and common sense. The tendency to apply law enforcement resources exclusively to specific communities to the exclusion of others also should be avoided in favor of encouraging individual officers to apply the resources available to them on every call for service. In an integrated patrol approach, shift commanders assume a difficult, but ultimately integral, role. They must know their employees, encourage their employees' activities, measure the results fairly, provide guidance and support, and act to maximize the effectiveness of the team. By combining aggressive enforcement with a comprehensive community-based orientation, law enforcement agencies can unleash officers' full creative power to combat crime.

Source: Adapted from Robert A. Johnson, "Integrated Patrol: Combining Aggressive Enforcement and Community Policing," *FBI Law Enforcement Bulletin,* November 1997, pp. 6–11.

The habitual or repeat offender programs have been very successful where implemented and have seen many of these offenders removed from the street for long periods of time. Following the theory that the police spend most of their time with a small number of the community, by removing this small element from the community the police are freed from this restrictive fact of policing. This form of aggressive patrol, through research, has been found to be an effective method but is also considered to be costly because of the drain on police resources (Martin 1986; Martin and Sherman 1986). Although it may be expensive initially, the goal is for the offenders to receive longer sentences, preventing those officers assigned to this type of enforcement from having to spend too much time in this endeavor.

The final two types of aggressive patrols are old friends to the police: the sting and the stakeout. In the sting, the police establish some type of false front to capture a large portion of a specific criminal element. In many cases, a police officer may pose as a storekeeper who collects fenced property in order to catch those committing larcenies, burglaries, and robberies. The police have established similar fronts in dealing with stolen vehicles, combatting the war on drugs, and attempting to serve warrants. One famous case involved several suspects wanted on outstanding warrants; they were called and told they had won tickets to a baseball game and could meet the local team players for photographs and autographs. The wanted individuals arrived on the day of the baseball game to receive their prizes and were arrested on the outstanding warrants.

The other old friend is the stakeout. Although there is no specific formula for this tactical method, the police essentially establish a hidden position in a store, bank, or crime-prone area, wait for a crime to occur, and then react. Utilizing this technique in an arbitrary manner is generally considered a waste of resources; it should be employed only when there are tips that a crime is to occur or where a pattern of crimes has developed. Either way, this method is a drain on police resources and should be used on a limited basis.

The purpose for raising the awareness of these two common police techniques is to show that there is a use for them in strategic policing. Old techniques are often good techniques and should not be dismissed by the police under the auspices of community-oriented policing. Rather, they should be utilized in new and innovative ways.

SATURATION PATROLS

The third form of patrol under strategic-oriented policing is the use of the saturation patrol. Saturation patrol is the most difficult of the three patrols because it is the largest drain on police resources and the greatest show of force, which can often have a negative effect on the community. However, if implemented with the cooperation of the community, the community will generally support this type of patrol.

Saturation patrol is forming a collection of officers from various shifts, tactical units, traffic units, and investigators, who, all in uniform, saturate a predesignated area in a show of force. The initial action on the part of the police in this form of patrol is to establish their presence in the area, whether the target is an entire neighborhood or a street corner near two or three crack houses. A presence can be established through multiple arrests, investigative stops, or traffic stops of people going into and coming from the designated area. Once the initial impact of the arrests is made, generally over a three-day period, the police must maintain the show of force for an additional period of time, approximately one week to one month. The goal is to drive the criminal element out of the area by temporarily displacing or eliminating the criminal or order maintenance problem.

This technique has multiple applications in the community. Actions against the criminal element are the most obvious, with the ability to drive away users and dealers of drugs from an open-air drug market or to prevent the buyers of prostitution from driving into an area because of the police presence and displacing the prostitutes themselves. Additional applications could involve specific problems such as sexual activity on children's playgrounds or general problems such as communities with extremely high overall crime rates. Saturation patrols can be utilized in order maintenance issues, working in areas known for aggressive panhandlers, homeless people, and drunks whom citizens avoid out of fear created by their presence.

Chief Reuben Greenburg, the police chief of Charleston, South Carolina, has had much success with this technique against drug dealers and prostitutes (Greenburg and Gordon 1989). Research has also proven that this particular type of patrol is an effective method against criminal and order maintenance issues because of its initial deterrent effect (Sherman 1990a, 1990b). Lawrence Sherman (1990a, 1990b) conducted an analysis of eighteen police crackdowns, most of which utilized the police saturation patrol. The study included a drug crackdown in Washington, D.C., against an open-air drug market that utilized 60 police officers assigned to the area each day. In another Washington, D.C., use of the saturation patrol, a project known as "Operation Clean Sweep" used an additional 100 to 200 officers to target 59 drug markets by using various tactics of police presence that netted over 60 arrests a day (Sherman 1990a, 1990b).

Another such operation occurred in New York City, where "Operation Pressure Point" utilized 240 additional police officers to combat a high-drug area (Zimmer 1990). The operation was a success because the result was the reduction of drug trafficking and an increased sense of community (Zimmer 1990). Another success story of the saturation patrol was found in the New York City subway system, where the number of officers patrolling was increased from 1,200 to 3,100 officers, placing essentially one officer per train and station, and the crime rates fell for approximately two years (Sherman 1990a, 1990b).

Use of the saturation patrol is effective for both criminal and order maintenance issues. If implemented with the agreement of the community and targeted at a specific problem, rather than in a shotgun method, it can have a substantial deterrent effect. However, the saturation patrol can lead to displacement—it may drive the criminal activity underground or into another jurisdiction. Not every saturation patrol results in either no displacement or total displacement, but a number of studies have found some level of displacement (e.g., Priest and Carter 2002; Scott 2003).

OPERATION PRESSURE POINT

In early 1984, a newly appointed New York City police commissioner launched "Operation Pressure Point," a two-year crackdown on the Lower East Side drug markets. Prior to the crackdown, the area had offered many blatant drug bazaars, with customers attracted from all over the New York area. Heroin buyers could be seen standing in long lines stretching around street corners.

The crackdown, at a cost of $12 million per year, used more than 150 uniformed officers, most of them rookies. The crackdown began with a high volume of drug arrests—65 per day for the first 6 weeks, then dropping to 20 per day. This rate continued until at least August 1986, by which time the police had made 21,000 drug-related arrests in the target area.

Tactics included observation-of-sale arrests, undercover buys, raids on dealing locations, arrests for unrelated misdemeanors and violations, tips from informers, and a "hotline" phone number.

The initial deterrent effect was a 47 percent reduction in robberies in 1984 compared to 1983, and a 62 percent reduction (from 34 to 13) in homicides during the same period. This initial effect was maintained until at least the first 8 months of 1986, with a 40 percent reduction in robbery and a 9 percent reduction in homicide compared to the first 8 months of 1983. While no displacement to the immediate vicinity was found, other parts of Manhattan experienced a growth in drug markets.

Source: Lawrence Sherman, *Police Crackdowns.* Washington, D.C.: National Institute of Justice Research in Action, March/April 1990.

EXAMPLES OF POLICE CRACKDOWNS

Police crackdowns can target specific neighborhoods or specific offenses, and their duration can range from a few weeks to several years. The following, selected from the eighteen case studies reviewed for this article, illustrate this range. Initial and residual deterrent effects varied, sometimes based on factors outside the scope of the crack-downs themselves.

Drug crackdown, Washington, D.C.   A massive police presence—60 police officers per day and a parked police trailer—in the Hanover Place neighborhood open-air drug market provided an effective initial deterrent.

Lynn, Massachusetts, open-air heroin market.   A four-year crackdown using 4 to 6 police officers led to 140 drug arrests in the first ten months and increased demand for drug treatment.

Operation Clean Sweep, Washington, D.C.   The city allocated 100 to 200 officers—many on overtime—to 59 drug markets, making 60 arrests a day. Tactics included roadblocks, observation of open-air drug markets, "reverse buy" sell-and-bust by undercover officers, and seizure of cars.

Repeat Call Address Policing (REAP) Experiment, Minneapolis, Minnesota.   A special unit of 5 police officers attempted to reduce calls for service from 125 residential addresses by increasing their presence with landlords and tenants.

(continued)

This short-term targeting of resources led to a 15 percent drop in calls from these addresses, compared to 125 control addresses.

Nashville, Tennessee, patrol experiment.   A sharp increase in moving patrol at speeds under twenty miles per hour in four high-crime neighborhoods netted a measurable decrease in Part I Index crime during two short crackdowns (eleven days and fifteen days).

Disorder crackdown in Washington, D.C.   Massive publicity accompanied a crackdown on illegal parking and disorder that were attracting street crime to the Georgetown area of the city. Police raised their weekend manpower 30 percent and installed a trailer at a key intersection to book arrestees.

New York City subway crackdown.   This massive crackdown involved increasing the number of police officers from 1,200 to 3,100, virtually guaranteeing an officer for every train and every station. Crime fell during the first two years of the crackdown but rose again during the following six years.

Source: Lawrence W. Sherman, *Police Crackdowns.* Washington, D.C.: National Institute of Justice Research in Action, March/April 1990.

ASSESSMENT

The current literature on community-oriented policing often cites examples of strategic-oriented policing as being the sole method for implementing this concept. The literature details various implementations of directed, aggressive, and saturation patrols and shows that strategic-oriented policing has a positive result in reducing crime rates, order maintenance problems, and the fear of community members. Whether it has been used to control drug problems (Weisburd and Mazerolle 2000; Younce 1992), gangs (Bassett 1993), or prostitution (Scott 2003), strategic-oriented policing has been found to be a well-regarded policing technique by the police administration, the police officers, and the community. However, despite the immediate benefits of this component of community-oriented policing, several problems must be addressed.

There are essentially three problems with the implementation of strategic-oriented policing: the issue of the duration of success for these programs, the effect strategic-oriented policing has on the community, and the perception that this component in and of itself is community-oriented policing. Although the majority of police crackdowns in the literature demonstrated a strong deterrent effect on crime, it is important to focus in on the fact that this effect has been found to be only temporary (Scott 2003; Sherman 1990a, 1990b). In the New York study, crime rates rose after the initial two-year period and continued to do so for the next six years (Sherman 1990a, 1990b). The research demonstrates that this reduction in the initial effect of strategic policing, especially in the use of saturation patrols, after a certain time period is not uncommon. As Lawrence Sherman pointed out, the effects of the police saturation patrols "began to decay after a short period, sometimes despite continued dosage of police presence or even increased dosage of police sanctions" (Sherman 1990b, 43). This issue must be examined or attitudes toward the effectiveness of these programs will diminish over time and make future implementation highly unlikely.

Another problem that can arise is the effect that these strategic-oriented policing methods can have on the public's attitude toward the police. As Herman Goldstein (1990, 132) explains, "too often they constitute the only response that the police make to a worsening situation—reflecting a narrowly limited concept of what the police can do and, more generally, a lack of imagination and initiative." Resentment or direct hostility toward the police from residents in minority areas can result because they often feel they are the true targets of these forms of patrol tactics, which can spark an unnecessary fire (Scott 2003; Sherman 1986; Siegel 1995). The goal of the patrols utilized in strategic policing would then be negated by this reaction because the overall goal is that of fostering a better relationship with members of the community, not alienating them from the police. As George L. Kelling (1985, 307) summarizes, "these are short-term, unwise, and potentially dangerous approaches. They continue to rely on remote professional and centralized political authority. Moreover, they fail to recognize the inherent normative pluralism of communities and neighborhoods and will likely be perceived as police acting against, rather than on behalf of, localities." What Kelling suggests, then, is that police "agencies continue to explain their crackdowns to 'wannabes' (would-be offenders) and other troubled and troublesome persons . . . such communication develops neighborhood norms, establishes the limits of what can be accomplished, and sets expectations for citizens, neighborhood interests, and authorities" (Kelling 1998, 16). In fact, recent research in two neighborhoods in the Bronx, a borough of New York City (Davis, Mateu-Gelabert, and Miller 2005), found that aggressive policing reduced crime and citizen complaints did not increase but rather declined. The researchers explained that the driving force behind the decrease in citizen complaints was that the precinct commanders demanded that their police officers respect the citizens in the neighborhoods through a program known as CPR: Courtesy, Professionalism, and Respect.

 ## COP IN ACTION

Strategic-Oriented Policing to Target Homicide and Violent Crime

The Department of Justice launched the Strategic Approach to Community Safety Initiative (SACSI) in 1998 to see if the Boston Police Department's collaborative, data-driven problem-solving process could be replicated by ten other cities also fighting high rates of violent crime. Nine of the 10 SACSI sites targeted homicide and other serious violent crime, with a pronounced emphasis on those involving firearms. Memphis was the exception, where the SACSI partnership focused on reducing rape and other sexual assaults. The study found that the SACSI approach, when implemented strongly, is associated with reductions in targeted violent crime in a community, sometimes as much as 50%. Examples include:

Indianapolis

- 53% decrease in gun assaults in target neighborhood vs. 19% decrease citywide
- 44% decrease in armed robberies in target neighborhood vs. 8% decrease citywide
- 32% reduction in homicide citywide during the year after the intervention occurred in the target neighborhood

Memphis

- 49% decrease in forcible rape citywide

New Haven

- 32% decrease in violent gun crimes citywide
- 45% decrease in calls-for-service for "shots fired"

Portland

- 42% decrease in homicide citywide
- 25% decrease in other violent crime citywide

Winston-Salem

- 19% decrease in juvenile incidents in target neighborhoods
- 58% decrease in juvenile robberies in target neighborhoods

Source: Roehl, Jan, Dennis P. Rosenbaum, Sandra K. Costello, James R. "Chip" Coldren, Amie M. Schuck, Laura Kunard, and David R. Forde. *Strategic Approaches to Community Safety Initiatives (SACSI) in 10 U.S. Cities: The Building Blocks for Project Safe Neighborhoods.* Washington, D.C.: U.S. Department of Justice, 2006.

The final problem is the fact that many of these strategic-oriented policing strategies are implemented under the auspices of community-oriented policing. The concept becomes a new method of utilizing police crackdowns on the criminal and order maintenance problems in the community, of which the only difference in regard to past policing methods is that the community at large may support this technique. There is no

A boy touching a Sacramento, California, Police Department robot during a police department open house. (*Courtesy of the Sacramento Police Department, Sacramento, California.*)

regard for the fact that this is a short-term solution to a long-term problem that, it has been shown, is not successful over time.

The community-oriented policing model takes all of these problems into consideration and responds to them when the entire concept is implemented. This model recognizes that these techniques to displace or temporarily eliminate the criminal element or order mainte-nance problems will only work while they are in effect. Once the police scale back, the prob-lem itself creeps back. Remove the police entirely, and the element returns in full force.

 ## COP IN ACTION

The Kansas City Gun Experiment

Increased seizures of illegally carried guns led to a decrease in gun crime, according to a study sponsored by the National Institute of Justice and conducted by a team of researchers headed by a University of Maryland professor. The findings come from an evaluation of the Kansas City Gun Experiment, in which supplemental police patrols focused on gun detection. The Kansas City, Missouri, Police Department reduced gun crimes in one neighborhood by almost 50 per-cent in 6 months by deploying extra patrol teams focused exclusively on detecting guns.

For 29 weeks, from July 7, 1992, to January 27, 1993, police patrols were increased in gun crime "hot spots" in patrol beat 144 of the Central Patrol District. Researchers identified the hot spot locations by computer analysis of all gun crimes in the target area, an eighty-block neighborhood normally covered by one patrol car, and that had a homicide rate twenty times higher than the national average. The population was almost entirely non-white, with more than two-thirds of all residences being owner-occupied, single-family, detached homes. Offi-cers assigned to the target area focused exclusively on gun detection through proactive directed patrol and did not respond to calls for service. Four officers, who worked 6 hours of overtime each night (7 P.M. to 1 A.M.), 7 days a week, for 176 nights, handled the extra patrol, with two officers working an additional 24 nights. A total of 4,512 officer-hours and 2,256 patrol car-hours were logged.

Officers on the directed patrols found guns during frisks and searches and following arrests on other charges. Every search had to conform to legal guidelines for adequate artic-ulable suspicion to ensure the protection of civil liberties, and every arrest for carrying con-cealed weapons had to be approved by a supervisory detective.

To gather information for the study, a University of Maryland evaluator accompanied the officers on 300 hours of directed patrol in the target area. Property room data on guns seized, computerized crime reports, calls-for-service data, and arrest records were analyzed for the 29 weeks before the program began and for the 29 weeks the program was in operation.

Data for the same time period also were collected for a comparison area (patrol beat 242 in the Metro Patrol District), which experienced approximately the same volume of vio-lent crimes and drive-by shootings as the target area. No changes were made in the number or duties of patrol officers in the comparison area.

During the program, officers reported spending 3.27 car-hours of the 12 car-hours per night (or 27 percent of their time) actually patrolling the target area. This resulted in a total of 1,218 officer-hours of potential gun detection and visible patrol presence in the area. The officers thus spent about 70 percent of their time processing arrests and performing other patrol-related duties.

Despite the limited amount of time the officers actually spent on patrol in the target area, the volume of activity was significant. The officers on directed patrol issued 1,090 traffic citations and made 948 car checks, 532 pedestrian checks, 170 state or federal arrests, and 446 city arrests, for an average of 1 intervention every 40 minutes per patrol car.

In the target area, police seized 65 percent more guns from July through December 1992 than in the first 6 months of the year. Gun seizures increased from 46 during January through June 1992 to 76 in the last 6 months of 1992. In the comparison area, gun seizures decreased slightly in the second half of 1992.

Comparison of the data from the first and second halves of 1992 shows that gun crimes declined significantly in the latter part of the year. Eighty-three fewer gun crimes were committed, for a 49 percent decline. In the comparison area, the number of gun crimes increased slightly.

This study shows that a police department can implement a program to increase seizures of illegally carried guns in high gun-crime areas. Police officers can be very productive when given the opportunity to focus on gun detection in identified crime hot spots without being obligated to answer calls for service.

In addition, gun seizures do not appear to require large tactical operations. In the Kansas City high-crime target area, the officers worked in two-officer patrol units, and no gun attacks on officers were reported during the directed patrols. Directed patrols also were shown to be, on the average, about three times more cost-effective than normal uniformed police activity citywide in getting guns off the street.

Significant Findings of the Kansas City Gun Experiment

- Traffic stops were the most productive means of finding illegal guns, yielding an average of 1 gun discovered for every 28 stops.
- The ratio of guns seized to actual time spent on patrol in the target area was 1 gun seized per 84 officer-hours.
- Two-thirds of the persons arrested for carrying guns in the target area resided outside the area.
- After the directed patrol stopped, crimes involving guns gradually increased for the first 5 months of 1993; when the patrols resumed in June 1993, gun crimes decreased again, although not as consistently as in the second half of 1992.
- Drive-by shootings dropped from 7 to 1 in the target area, doubled from 6 to 12 in the comparison area, and showed no displacement to adjacent beats.
- Directed patrols affected only gun crimes; no changes were observed in either the target area or the comparison area regarding the number of calls for service or in the total number of other violent and nonviolent crimes reported.
- The decline in gun crimes in the target area did not appear to cause a displacement of crime to adjoining neighborhoods; gun crimes did not increase significantly in any of the surrounding seven patrol beats.

Source: "The Kansas City Gun Experiment," *National Institute of Justice Update,* U.S. Department of Justice, Office of Justice Programs, November 1994, pp. 12–15.

Under community-oriented policing, the strategic-oriented policing component is only implemented as a short-term solution until long-term solutions, through neighborhood-oriented policing and problem-oriented policing, can be developed. The community can have more freedom for decision making and implementation if the elements the community is to address have been removed from the community or temporarily driven underground. Strategic-oriented policing allows time to get certain programs established in the community, for criminal and civil cases to be heard, and for a sense of community pride to return to those law-abiding members of the community. Once the police presence is reduced by removing the saturation and aggressive patrols, as the criminal element returns, they find a different community than the one they left. In turn, the goal is for the new community and the police to prevent the returning element from thriving again.

CONCLUSION

Strategic-oriented policing (see Figure 3-2) is the catalyst for all other community-oriented policing programs. Implementing the aggressive and saturation patrol tactics in high-crime areas displaces the criminal element through their deterrent effects. The community can then establish innovative programs within the community that will not tolerate the return of the criminal or order maintenance problems. These programs must be put in place for the community to retain its social control of happenings and events. Neighborhood-oriented policing and problem-oriented policing help the community analyze, create, and implement the programs that address the specific needs of the community. These methods are described in the following two chapters, and their relationship with each other is discussed in Chapter 6. It is only with this complete implementation of the three components that community-oriented policing can truly be implemented within a community and subsequently evaluated on these merits.

FIGURE 3-2   The three components of strategic-oriented policing.

COP ON THE WORLD WIDE WEB

National Crime Prevention Council

http://www.ncpc.org

Policing Drug Hot Spots, National Institute of Justice Publication

http://www.ojp.usdoj.gov/nij/pubs-sum/184415.htm

Oxnard, California, Police Department

http://www.oxnardpd.org/Default.htm

Shreveport, Louisiana, Police Department

http://www.ci.shreveport.la.us/dept/police/#Community

Alexandria, Virginia, Police Department

http://ci.alexandria.va.us/police

REVIEW QUESTIONS

1. Explain how police resources relate to strategic-oriented policing.
2. Define *targeting*.
3. What are the three types of patrols under strategic-oriented policing

CHAPTER 4

Neighborhood-Oriented Policing

Crime and bad lives are the measure of a State's failure, all crime in the end is the crime of the community.

—H. G. Wells

CHAPTER OBJECTIVES

- Define *neighborhood-oriented policing*.
- Begin to understand who implements COP.
- Begin to understand the leadership roles of both the police and the community.
- Recognize the five categories of neighborhood-oriented policing programs.
- Define *community patrols*.
- Define *community crime prevention*.
- Define *communication programs*.
- Define *community social control programs*.
- Recognize problem-oriented policing as a type of neighborhood-oriented policing.

The second component of community-oriented policing is neighborhood-oriented policing (see Figure 4-1). This component entails the interaction of police and all community members to reduce crime and the fear of crime through indigenous proactive programs. It is an integration of the police and the community working together, opening up the lines of communication and establishing responses to the criminal and social problems in a community. It is through this cooperative effort that the goals of reducing crime and reducing the fear of crime can be achieved. (Reisig and Parks 2004).

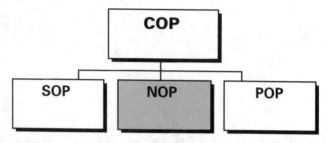

FIGURE 4-1 Neighborhood-oriented policing.

The literature often details this component as the core of community policing or the entire and sole concept of community-oriented policing (e.g., Cole 1995; Moore and Trojanowicz 1988; Schmalleger 1995; Skogan 1994). The practitioners implementing neighborhood-oriented programs often refer to these programs in a general sense as community-oriented policing as well (e.g., Bloom 1992; Fleissner et al. 1992; Hamilton 1993; Perez 1993). However, despite the varying use of the term *neighborhood-oriented policing,* all are focused on the integration of the police and the community. Although this integration is the overall goal of community-oriented policing, when discussing neighborhood-oriented policing the focus should be on the various types of patrols and programs that bring the community and the police together.

Police officers of the Cincinnati, Ohios Police Department presenting a check to the Special Olympics from money raised through the Law Enforcement Torch Run. *(Courtesy of the Cincinnati Police Department, Cincinnati, Ohio.)*

As revealed in Chapter 1, The Evolution of Community-Oriented Policing, the past model of policing known as police–community relations was concerned with establishing police units to address various groups and concerns within the community. A prime example is the importance of children in any community and the establishment under police–community relations of special juvenile or youth units to work with children both in and out of the schools. However, it is imperative to remember that the police officers assigned to these units were dedicated solely to this function.

Under the neighborhood-oriented policing component of community-oriented policing, every police officer should be involved in some form or fashion in establishing relations with the community. The mentality that a police officer not assigned to the juvenile section of the police department should not have to deal with juveniles is a mentality that must be dismissed for neighborhood-oriented policing techniques to be successful.

In the same way, community members must give up the mentality that crime fighting and even order maintenance are a police officer's job and of no concern to them. Police officers know that they have a difficult job because they cannot be everywhere at once. Common citizens recognize this fact as well in the oft-heard statement, "There's never a cop around when you need one." However, this mentality must change. The statement is always heard in a negative sense. However, if citizens recognize that there is never a cop around when you need one because there are so few officers and they legitimately cannot be everywhere at once, then it is citizens' responsibility to assist the police and make them aware of situations that affect the community in both criminal and order maintenance areas.

Changing the mentality of the police and the community and bringing them together to address these issues are the key to a successful neighborhood-oriented policing program. The success also depends largely on the participation of the entire neighborhood or community and not just segments. The institutions found in any community include the family, schools, churches, retail establishments, neighborhood associations, professionals (such as doctors, dentists, and lawyers), and social or community groups (such as the Elks, local historical societies, and the Veterans of Foreign Wars). It is important that all of these institutions pool their resources, participate in the neighborhood-oriented policing programs, and help develop the bonds between the police and the community at large.

To reduce crime and the fear of crime, the neighborhood must create some form of committee or coalition that consists of a cross-section of the neighborhood. The committee should consist of the formal leadership, informal leadership, and the "average" citizen in the neighborhood. This committee must then represent the community and bring to the attention of all the members the criminal and order maintenance problems that exist in the neighborhoods. Committee members must prioritize these concerns and develop courses of action that will abolish the problem or at a minimum alleviate some of the symptoms. These problems must then be brought to the attention of the police, along with the solutions to the problems; viable programs should then be implemented by both the police and the neighborhoods.

COP IN ACTION

Horseplay Brings Officers Closer to Community

Children dream of riding a pony, but many youngsters from urban areas never have the opportunity. In Virginia Beach, Virginia, however, the officers and horses of the Second Precinct's Mounted Unit give children in several targeted neighborhoods the chance to make that dream come true.

As part of its community policing efforts, the department identified a number of low-income neighborhoods experiencing problems with drugs and crime. Reaching out to the children living there was given top priority. Because the Mounted Unit patrols these neighborhoods, the department decided to develop a program that would use the children's natural curiosity about the unit's horses to bridge the gap between the children and the police. The program, named PEP for Police Athletic League (PAL) and Equestrian Program, introduces the children to the officers of the Mounted Unit and their horses. As they learn basic horsemanship skills, participants also get to know the police officers. In turn, the officers can establish positive relationships with the youngsters.

Boys and girls ages eight to fourteen participate in PEP, and all are members of the precinct's PAL program. Divided into groups of ten to twelve participants, they meet once a week for five weeks at the stables. Each session lasts about three hours. The PEP schedule is designed to hold the children's attention without overwhelming them.

During the first meeting, the officers of the Mounted Unit, the grooms, and the training staff introduce themselves to the participants. The children get most excited when they meet the stars of the Mounted Unit, its fourteen horses. Next, they learn about the operation of the barn and how to care for the horses. As part of the program, the children feed, groom, and tack (harness) the horses themselves.

The program participants, like most children, never have been close to a horse and often are reluctant to approach them. Sometimes on the first day, several children even refuse to get off the bus. Yet, the department's nationally recognized equestrian trainer makes the program fun, as well as educational. When the reluctant children see how friendly the horses are and how much fun their friends are having, even the shyest ones become eager to join the group. So far, no one has failed to lead or ride a horse within the first two weeks.

Training games teach the kids basic handling techniques. In one game, for example, the kids line up at opposite ends of the training field and have a relay race where they walk with the horses from one end to the other. This game teaches them how to lead the horses properly. Other games include sitting on the horses while passing beach balls back and forth, jumping on and off the horses (to help alleviate fears of falling), tacking races, and even completing an obstacle course where the children guide the horses over poles, around barrels, and through mazes. During the fourth session, the children go on a trail ride that allows them to control a horse independently, but only under the watchful eye of the trainers and PEP officers. In the fifth week, the PEP officers invite the parents to a riding show put on by the children. The kids compete in games and activities to show off their newly acquired skills. The children receive ribbons noting their riding achievements and a photograph of them riding one of the police horses.

The most important consideration during the development of PEP was the safety of the children. As with any riding situation, the possibility of injury exists. The equestrian trainer who designed the program takes special precautions to minimize the chances of injury, and the department also makes certain that the children are covered by health insurance. In addition to

A Cincinnati, Ohio, police officer introducing a local youth to one of the horses in the police Horse Patrol Unit at an open house event. *(Courtesy of the Cincinnati Police Department, Cincinnati, Ohio.)*

self-insurance provided by the city, all participants receive coverage from the national PAL organization.

To offset the department's expenses for operating the program, the not-for-profit Friends of the Mounted Unit donates funds for refreshments, safety helmets, T-shirts with the PAL and Mounted Unit logos, and photographs of the children. With this assistance, the PEP program does not depend directly on the department for funds, and the burdens of money management are removed from the department's administrators. Members of the Friends of the Mounted Unit also contribute significant time and effort to help administer the program.

In the first summer, the Second Precinct conducted two PEP sessions for children living within its jurisdiction. Other precincts in Virginia Beach have expressed a desire to participate, so the program will expand in the future to include children from targeted neighborhoods citywide.

Strong, positive relationships between children and police officers often grow into similarly positive relationships between adults and police officers. By encouraging and satisfying the children's natural curiosity about horses, PEP officers develop close connections with the communities they serve.

PEP gives neighborhood kids a fun and educational way to get to know the members of the police department who patrol their communities. The Police Athletic League and Equestrian Program provides a unique avenue for the department to pursue its community policing initiatives.

Source: Adapted from W.W. Baker, "Horseplay Brings Officers Closer to Community," *FBI Law Enforcement Bulletin,* January 1995, pp. 6–7.

INITIATION OF NEIGHBORHOOD-ORIENTED POLICING

One subtle issue can have a major impact on the success of not only neighborhood-oriented policing but the overall concept of community-oriented policing as well. The issue arises as to who implements these programs and policies in addressing criminal and order maintenance concerns. If the community does not have a committee in place or some system for addressing the local concerns, the police must initiate neighborhood-oriented policing programs. The police must then do everything possible to draw in the support of the community in assisting them and supporting the programs implemented. The police become the catalyst for a community program and must lead members of the neighborhood down the road to a fully implemented concept of community-oriented policing.

If the community has some form of system in place, then it becomes possible to work together with the police and create programs and policies initiated by both the police and the neighborhood. These programs are generally more oriented to what the community desires of its police and are more in line with the community concept. However, there will always be a problem with power and determining who is in power and who has more power when the community and the police disagree on a course of action.

 ## COP IN ACTION

Mission: Possible

The neighborhood where Quindell Phillips lives is not known for its kindness. All too often, the sounds of gunshots and screeching tires echo through the streets of Plaquemines Parish,* La., a swampy community just south of New Orleans

There, gangs and drugs are part of the social landscape, posing an all-too-real threat for youths with few positive role models to follow.

"Yeah, they got 'Crips' and 'Bloods' down there, but I want to join the Scouts," says Quindell, twelve, who recalls spending several weeks in juvenile detention for a misdemeanor offense. "But I'm staying out of trouble now."

Quindell's friend, James Garrison, agrees that life in Plaquemines Parish is tough for teenagers. "Some of them threaten to rob you if you don't get in their gang," the sixteen-year-old says. "The only way to stay out of trouble is to go fishing early in the morning."

The dream of an outdoor life became a reality for the boys for a week last summer. They joined 196 other youths at Salmen Scout Reservation, near Picayune, Miss., for the New Orleans Area Council's "Mission: Possible" camp for at-risk youth aged eleven through fourteen.

A Chance to Be Boys Again

As the young men entered the 1,600-acre campsite near De Soto National Forest, stately live oaks and magnolia trees provided the first hint of just how different the camp would be from life back home. Within walking distance, a glistening, crystal blue Lake Harvey Peltier beckoned them to hop in.

The sounds of their neighborhood—blaring car horns and booming bass speakers—faded quickly from mind, replaced by a sweeter music of chirping crickets and birds. For one week, they could let down their guards and be boys again, far away from the stress of urban life.

Part of the Scout-Council's crime prevention initiative and urban emphasis program, the Mission: Possible Operation First Class Sheriff's Camp is a collaborative effort of nine area sheriff's departments and the council. Now in its second year, it aims to provide alternatives to gangs and drugs in southeast Louisiana. "We're giving some kids, who otherwise would never have the opportunity, a chance to participate in the Boy Scouts, and that in itself is gratifying," says Jefferson Parish Sheriff Harry Lee, who helped organize the camp. "If you leave them in the neighborhood, they'll gravitate to the bad kids if there is no alternative there."

The camp blends an outdoor experience with educational and instructional skills, career education, leadership, values, and ethics development. The hoped-for result in the young participants will include a greater sense of self-reliance, teamwork, and individual skills ranging from conflict resolution to independent living to outdoor survival.

"They Want to Do the Right Thing"

The new setting is important, Lee says. "You take kids who have never met and put them in the right environment, and they work together. Kids want to do good, healthy, productive things. They want to do the right thing."

Many of the youths were selected to attend the camp by law enforcement officers who got to know them in their neighborhoods. Others had previous brushes with the law, usually for minor offenses, and were referred by Louisiana juvenile probation officers. Each young recruit receives a "Road to Succeed" T-shirt and a "I Will Stay in School" pledge button.

"These are kids who have had some problems, but there's no heavy gang involvement yet," explained Bill Haines, director of field service for the New Orleans Area Council. "They're usually on the borderline of criminal activity."

Each day at camp is packed with activities from 8:30 in the morning to 5:30 in the afternoon. Daily sessions include waterfront (swimming), field sports (archery and rifle ranges), ecology and conservation (nature hikes and a conservation project), handicraft (leatherwork, basketry, metalwork, and pottery), campcraft (knots, first aid, map and compass), and the Project COPE course (personal fitness and teamwork challenges).

Squinting under the blazing noon sun, a group of youths lined up in pairs at the edge of Lake Harvey Peltier, waiting for their cue to hop in for their daily swim. A small part of the lake's edge was cordoned off to separate the more skilled swimmers from the beginners, who splashed around in the shallow water.

The youths laughed and horsed around, but their instructor restored a serious undertone to the activity. Learning to swim, they were reminded, is a valuable lifetime skill that someday could even help to save someone's life. (And by week's end, about half of the 198 campers had passed their swimming test.)

The Skills to Solve Problems

In the campcraft center, Jeff Landry, senior district executive of the New Orleans Area Council, described the camp's program approach. "We may be teaching knot-tying, but we're also teaching goal-setting and problem solving," he explained. "And we're also teaching the skills to create the tools to solve problems."

A group of campers stood around a pile of pine needles and wood, ready to learn how to build a campfire high enough to ignite a piece of string suspended over the pile. They could use only two matches and no lighter fluid or paper.

Mother Nature had another lesson to teach, however, as the wet underbrush from early rains kept the flames from igniting.

Despite the futile attempt, the purpose of the exercise was still fresh in one youth's mind. "Knowing how to light a fire can help you survive," says Eddie Smith, twelve, of Marrero, La.

For some of the youths, the prospect of being away from home and family was too much to handle. A few of them filed into the camp's health center complaining of stomachaches, poison ivy itch, and heat exhaustion. The main complaint, however, was plain old home-sickness.

Camp Director Chris Snyder believes a direct approach is the best way to handle the grumbling. "Going home is not really an option," Snyder informed a sad-faced boy who was wiping a tear from his eye. "This is your home this week," Snyder reassured him. "We want you to be strong and stick it out."

The approach usually works, although it failed to convince at least thirteen youths, who returned home early. "They're tough in the streets, but still cower from bugs, spiders, turkeys, and wild dogs," observed Robert Rotherham, a juvenile detective with the Jefferson Parish Sheriff's Department.

Making Promises to Keep

In the daily Pathfinder sessions, the boys begin the week by organizing their patrols and memorizing the Scout Oath and Law, motto, and slogan. Then they learn to use wood tools, build a fire, and cook a light meal.

The week ends with sessions on the danger of drugs, alcohol, and tobacco and serious discussion of educational goals, child abuse, and citizenship. Each camper promises to stay in school, learn to read, and avoid gangs and drugs.

The end of camp doesn't mean the end of the budding relationship formed between the boys and the law enforcement officers. Each sheriff's department has its own program for mentoring and motivating the youths after camp.

All of the youths from St. Charles Parish are enrolled in Scout troops in that area that are associated with law enforcement agencies, Haines points out. The Jefferson Parish Sheriff's Office operates a STAR (Survey, Target, Arrest, and Rejuvenate) program in which sheriff's deputies knock on doors to check on families and who serve as extra eyes and ears to cut down on drug and gang activities. (The unique program also helps arrange payments for overdue utility bills as well as assistance in transportation needs.)

Meanwhile, at the St. Charles Parish Sheriff's Department, the troops are handled under the Paternal Order of Police, whose officers meet with the youths on a regular basis to build up positive relationships.

"They Are the Future"

"If you want to make a difference, these are the kids to make it with," says Bill Haines. "And seeing them achieve is really rewarding."

Haines knows firsthand the impact Scouting can have on young lives. His father, James R. Haines Sr., headed Troop 113 in Saraland, Ala., and saw four of his six sons become Eagle Scouts. Today, all of the brothers go out of their way to contribute to their communities, Haines says.

As the juvenile crime rate continues to soar in Louisiana, Scouting's role in combating it is more crucial than ever, Haines notes.

"All kids are at risk today," he explains. "Society has changed, with so many single-parent homes and a movement away from traditional values. If you're going to make a difference, you have to deal with these kids because they are the future of New Orleans and other communities. We want to reach as many kids as possible with a program of values that will impact them for life."

Source: Reprinted with permission from Robert Stanton, "Mission: Possible," *Scouting,* January–February 1998, pp. 27–39.

* The community of Plaquemines Parish, Louisiana, was one of the communities devastated by Hurricane Katrina. The article refers to life in this small parish before the Hurricane struck.

For neighborhood-oriented policing to be fully implemented and operational, it should, in actuality, be initiated by the community or neighborhood. The community should no longer be viewed as simply a political ally or functional partner in fighting crime but rather as the head of an institution for which the police work—namely, the community. The police have powers to enforce laws, use deadly force, and with reasonable suspicion invade citizens' lives; therefore, community supervision must be in place, and ultimately the police

(a)

(b)

Before and after. A former crack house (a) was closed down and refurbished into the Atlantic Gardens Substation for the police and local residents to use as a cooperative community center. The after picture (b) shows the block party celebration of the grand opening of the substation. (*Courtesy of the Delray Beach Police Department, Delray Beach, Florida.*)

should be run by the community. Just as the Founding Fathers placed the U.S. military under civilian control, so should the police be under civilian control. This is not to say that the police have no input into the decisions the neighborhood coalition makes or into the programs they wish to see implemented, only that the programs are initiated primarily by the neighborhood.

Herein lies one fundamental problem with the concept of community-oriented policing. Under the concept of neighborhood-oriented policing, it is the neighborhood that makes the decisions. The same revolves around all of the tenets of community-oriented policing. Once these programs are fully functional and have become a part of the local community's method of policing, the community and the neighborhood make the decisions for what is of concern and what is not of concern on the part of the police. These citizens decide where the police place their resources, which high-crime areas should be targeted, and in many cases how they will be targeted. The citizens essentially become one of the two leaders of the police. The leadership that determines the overall mission of the police and the programs that should be implemented is the community. The leadership that carries out the mission and sees to the day-to-day operations is the police chief. The community serves as the "executive board" or "board of directors," while the police chief or sheriff serves as the "chief executive officer." It is a concept of leadership that works and has worked in large institutions, both public and private.

In the concept of community-oriented policing and predominantly in the area of neighborhood-oriented policing, the community must take on the role of the board of directors. The community and neighborhoods must determine what the job, roles, and responsibilities of the police should be and determine how they could best do their job. Under neighborhood-oriented policing, that may consist of determining if bike patrols or foot patrols would be of any benefit to the area as well as the type of programs that should be implemented to lower crime and create better living conditions for all members of the community.

The police chief is then the chief executive officer and is responsible for the police officers' welfare and instilling a sense of unit cohesion to create a police force that is capable of carrying out the tasks or jobs determined by the community. The police chief, in this same line, ensures that the police are highly trained, well educated, and well equipped for the variety of missions that may be dictated by the instrumental leader. The police chief, however, is not relegated to only following orders but is responsible for challenging those tasks that are not feasible for the department, or police officers, to conduct; he or she is responsible for becoming an advocate not only for the police but for the community as well and must set the example for the police department and, by default, for the entire community.

Through this cooperative effort, the concept of neighborhood-oriented policing can be successful in the areas of both order maintenance and crime reduction. The citizens of the local community have a clear and established role in the policing of the neighborhood by directing where police resources should be dedicated through the concerns of those living in the neighborhoods. This empowerment helps citizens become more concerned for their neighborhoods, causing them to work more closely with the police and assisting them in restoring order and in arresting and prosecuting criminals.

Reducing crime in Norfolk, Virginia   This city has cut homicides by more than 10 percent in each of the last three years and, even more impressive, has reduced overall crime rates citywide by 26 percent and in some neighborhoods by as much as 40 percent. A good share of the credit goes to Police-Assisted Community Enforcement (PACE), a crime prevention initiative that works neighborhood by neighborhood in conjunction with teams of social, health, and family services agencies (the Family Assistance Services Team, or FAST) and public works and environmental agencies (Neighborhood Environmental Assistance Team, or NEAT) to cut through red tape and help residents reclaim their neighborhoods.

Campaigning against youth violence in Minnesota   The Minnesota Crime Prevention Officers' Association enlisted the support of families, public officials, and 45 statewide and local organizations, including schools and churches, to wage a campaign against youth violence. Actions ranged from encouraging children and parents to turn off violent television shows to providing classroom training in violence prevention.

Providing safe havens after school in Trenton, New Jersey   A partnership of schools, parents, city leaders, and others led to a Safe Haven program in which the schools in the neighborhood became multipurpose centers after school hours for youth activities including sports, crafts, and tutoring. Children have flocked to the centers as a positive alternative to being at home alone after school or being at risk on the streets.

Helping parents get drug treatment in Ohio   A congregation was the focus for efforts to reach addicted parents and their children. Tutoring for children courtesy of the local college, courses on black history taught by church members, and recreational activities helped raise the spirits and self-esteem of the children. The addicted parents were counseled and supported by church members both during and after treatment. The majority of the parents are now holding steady jobs and reaching out to help others.

Preventing campus crime in Columbus, Ohio   Crime near a college campus became an opportunity for a partnership formed by the city of Columbus, the state of Ohio, Ohio State University, the Franklin County Sheriff, and the Columbus Police Department. The Community Crime Patrol puts two-person radio-equipped teams of observers into the neighborhoods near the campus during potential high-crime hours. A number of these paid part-time observers are college students interested in careers in law enforcement.

Source: National Crime Prevention Council, *Working as Partners with Community Groups.* Washington, D.C.: Bureau of Justice Assistance, September 1994.

NEIGHBORHOOD-ORIENTED POLICING PROGRAMS

There are four types of neighborhood-oriented policing programs:

1. Community patrols
2. Community crime prevention programs
3. Communication programs
4. Community social control programs

These four programs are the practitioner's method of implementing neighborhood-oriented policing. Each program serves a different purpose in addressing the criminal and order maintenance issues of a particular community. The types of programs are general in what they set out to accomplish, and the list of actual programs is by no means inclusive. As each neighborhood is different, so too should the programs utilized be different. And all of the programs should be community driven, with the assistance of the community coalition and the police.

Community Patrols

Community patrols are those types of police patrols that create a strong police presence and allow the police to be more accessible to the public. Although the police cannot be everywhere at once, community patrols allow them to be in areas of high traffic and where they are generally most needed. They often serve a specific purpose with their presence, or they may be available for any type of citizen request or complaint. Regardless, the main concern for community patrols is high visibility because research continues to demonstrate that increased police visibility results in improved citizen perception of the police (Hawdon and Ryan 2003; Hawdon, Ryan, and Griffin 2003).

Perhaps the most well-known community patrol is the foot patrol. Foot patrols have come to symbolize community-oriented policing and have a long and colorful history in and of themselves. The cop on the beat was an early American icon that had grown out of the early watch system. With the advent of automobiles, the police left the limitations of foot patrols behind for the more efficient and faster response time automobiles afforded. The foot patrol became almost totally extinct by the 1960s but was occasionally brought back by some police departments under special programs. By the 1980s, the foot patrol had come to represent a change in the way police performed their duties and subsequently became the shining star of community-oriented policing.

Although foot patrols are easily recognizable under community-oriented policing, they are not the sole program for determining whether a police department has implemented community-oriented policing. Foot patrols are obviously best established in high-density commercial and residential areas with large populations; they would not be feasible or practical in a rural setting. Again, each neighborhood is unique in its problems and must design programs accordingly.

Cities that not only have implemented foot patrols under the auspices of community-oriented policing but have studied their effects as well have all shown positive signs for this type of patrol (see Greene and Taylor 1988; Skogan 1994; Wycoff 1988). The literature shows strong evidence that the public feels safer when foot patrols are implemented; the level of fear decreases and citizen satisfaction with the police increases (Hawdon and Ryan 2003; Kelling 1987). There is also additional evidence that when the foot patrols are removed from a neighborhood, regardless of the reason, the community refuses to allow them to leave

(Geller 1991). Foot patrols are received well not only by the neighborhoods but also by the police officers who work the patrols. Officers have a greater appreciation of the neighborhoods they patrol, and they show greater job satisfaction and higher morale (Kelling 1987).

The only issue on foot patrols currently debated is whether they are successful at reducing the actual number of crimes. There is little to no dispute that foot patrols reduce fear, even when based solely on anecdotal evidence; however, in some studies, foot patrols show no effect on crime rates (Kelling 1987b). One study showed significant decreases in the crime rates in a variety of areas that were targeted with foot patrols; however, it must be kept in mind that the study was based solely on police department data (Trojanowicz 1986). Some argue, through anecdotal evidence again, that crime rates actually increase because the police are spread far too thin and do not have the fast response times they have in automobiles.

Another form of community patrol similar to the foot patrol, but slightly more mobile, is the bike patrol. Bicycle patrol has increased as a mode of getting police officers out of motor vehicles but allowing them to remain somewhat mobile. Arlington County Police Department in Arlington, Virginia, implemented this program in the early 1990s. The department placed officers assigned to the juvenile division (who work in the schools and essentially have no job during the summer months) on mountain bikes. The officers generally patrol high-density areas, housing projects, and bike paths. The community and police response to these patrols has been very similar to that demonstrated in the studies of foot patrols.

A Kansas City, Missouri, community-oriented policing officer having a one-on-one with a local youth. (*Courtesy of the Kansas City Police Department, Kansas City, Missouri.*)

Additional methods of community patrol include police officers patrolling on horseback, such as those conducted in New Orleans during Mardi Gras. These patrols allow the police to see from above the crowds and allow citizens to be able to quickly pick out the police. Motorcycle patrols have also increased with the advent of community-oriented policing, although they have existed in most police departments for several decades.

Other successful types of community patrols are police ministations or storefronts in a variety of settings. One form of the police substation is to utilize a storefront in a business or retail area or an apartment or community center in a residential area. The police utilize this space as a simple office where the public may make incident reports, report or discuss criminal and order maintenance issues, or gather for meetings and neighborhood programs; it is a place for both adults and children to leave their homes for a short respite in a safe environment. The literature has shown these to be viable types of community patrols because the substations are "associated with reductions in fear of personal victimization, lowered perceptions of the amounts of personal and property crime in the area, and lowered perceptions of the amounts of social disorder in the area" (Brown and Wycoff 1987). Once again, this form of community patrol may or may not reduce the numbers of actual crimes, but it changes the perceptions of crime on the part of the public and increases the accessibility and contact with the police officers.

Another variation of the police substation has begun cropping up in malls across the United States. From Prince William County, Virginia, to the CNN Center in Atlanta to Roswell, New Mexico, police substations located in local malls offer citizens an additional avenue of accessibility to the police. They have also helped decrease the fear of crime on the part of the patrons. Regardless of where the substations have been placed, the

The Skyway Community Resource Center is volunteer staffed and community funded in St. Petersburg. (*Courtesy of St. Petersburg Police Department, St. Petersburg, Florida.*)

🛡 COP IN ACTION

The East Dallas Police Storefront

The East Dallas Storefront is one of five stations in the central patrol division. It covers eight square miles just outside of the central business district in a unique neighborhood—a mixture of Asians, Hispanics, Blacks, and Anglos, who live in everything from a public housing project to rundown apartment buildings to tidy blue-collar homes to mansions worth hundreds of thousands of dollars. The staff of four sworn officers and three civilian employees handles everything from bike patrols to community liaisons to after-school sports programs to traditional law enforcement. It has been a success both in terms of community relations and in reduced crime almost from its inception in 1985.

The officers and civilians assigned to the storefront do not stay in their cars or behind their desks, hidden from the public. They patrol on bikes. They speak in schools. They speak to church groups. They offer the storefront building for community meetings. Several community-oriented functions are assigned to the storefront, including central patrol's crime prevention unit and its liaison to the city's gay and lesbian community. Again, these are outreach programs, where the officers are active among neighborhood residents. In addition, a separate mobile unit, commanded by a sergeant and with its own staff, is based at the storefront.

The storefront doesn't operate on a regular eight-hour shift schedule. It's open from 7 A.M. to 7 P.M., making it easier for neighborhood residents to stop by. Also, there is usually someone at the storefront on duty who can speak one of the neighborhood's languages: English, Spanish, or Cambodian.

Among the nontraditional functions embraced by the storefront:

- Social services. Although this is not as important as it was when the storefront opened, officers and staff still handle requests for food, clothing, translation services, and the like. They also refer requests to the proper agencies.
- Fingerprinting. The storefront may be the only place in the Dallas metropolitan area that still fingerprints immigrants, who need the procedure as part of the naturalization process.
- Meeting rooms. Community groups are welcome at the storefront, even at night. A number of programs, including citizenship classes and after-school tutoring, are held there.
- Youth activities.

Source: Adapted with permission from Jeff Siegel, "The East Dallas Police Storefront," *Law and Order,* May 1995, pp. 53–55.

---

overall concept has demonstrated its success in all of the cities in which it has been implemented (Skogan 1994).

Community Crime Prevention Programs

Community crime prevention programs are an important part of neighborhood-oriented policing; many of the programs have been around since the middle to late 1960s. A large portion of these programs were born out of the police–community relations era and have seen some modifications in the way they are presented, but for all intents and

COP IN ACTION

ROPE: The Resident Officer Program of Elgin

If you can't beat 'em, join 'em.

This phrase could sum up the Resident Officer Program of Elgin (ROPE), a program instituted in Elgin, Illinois, where officers live and work in a problem neighborhood. Together with their neighbors, they are helping the area get back on its feet. The program works proactively to eliminate crime and other local problems at their roots by improving the status of life in a neighborhood to the degree that crime and related problems are not produced.

ROPE officers are unique in that they work and reside in a specific neighborhood, dealing only with problems affecting their neighborhood and its residents. Living in donated or subsidized homes or apartments, ROPE officers normally work an eight-hour day but for all practical purposes are on twenty-four-hour call.

The city provides ROPE officers and their families (many are bachelors) with a residence, utilities (not including long distance phone calls), a bicycle and squad car for patrol, answering machine, and whatever expenses are necessary for special needs in the neighborhood. In return, the officers must meet every resident in their areas, work with tenant and neighborhood groups and attend their meetings, and oversee newsletters that are disseminated to residents regularly, in addition to interacting with the residents to learn their concerns and then working to alleviate them.

The program's effectiveness can be seen by the change in answers to a survey distributed to one area's residents. When ROPE first started in their neighborhood, a questionnaire asked what problems concerned the residents. "Drugs and gangs" were the major problems then. Two years later, the same residents answered another survey with "loud stereos and speeding cars."

Source: Adapted with permission from Sheila Schmitt, "ROPE: The Resident Officer Program of Elgin," *Law and Order,* May 1995, pp. 52, 56–58.

---

purposes they are the same programs. The main goal or focus in community crime prevention is reaching out to those individuals, institutions, and groups that may be targets of crime or future perpetrators of crime and preventing either of these. It also includes the awareness and markings of those objects that are potential targets for crime. In most of the community crime prevention programs, the police become the facilitators of the programs, but the community must at a minimum participate for the programs to remain viable and have any chance at success.

The primary community crime prevention programs are Neighborhood Watch programs (block watch, apartment watch), operation ID, and home security surveys. According to Feins (1983), these programs are known as the "big three." Widespread use of these three programs across the United States by a majority of police departments, positive opinion on the part of the communities, and evidence that demonstrates these programs have reduced crime and assisted in solving crimes have contributed to these three programs being labeled as the most successful in community crime prevention.

Neighborhood Watch programs, depending on where one lives, can have a variety of names. Some of the names used are block watch, crime watch, and community alert.

However, all of these programs have one thing in common: to have neighbors watch out for each other, to be alert to day-to-day happenings in the neighborhood, and to call the police when anything suspicious occurs (Garofalo and McLeod 1988). The programs involve meetings with members of the community, usually once a month or once a quarter, in which local crime problems are addressed, crime prevention strategies are shared, and planning for community patrols or surveillance is arranged (Rosenbaum 1987). The meetings not only allow for a chance to share information and make plans but also allow for community contact and enhance the feelings of community commitment. They provide some feeling of empowerment, thereby fostering a stronger sense of social control.

 ## COP IN ACTION

From Storefronts to Street Smarts: Police Work for Safer Neighborhoods

Community policing was born here in an abandoned firehouse. Since that humble start nearly four years ago, community policing in North Providence has come a long way. To date, there have been thirty-seven programs that the department counts as successful.

The first step was opening two community policing storefronts in this town of 35,000. The first site—an abandoned fire station in the Lymansville neighborhood—was in serious disrepair. But police, working with a citizens' board formed to oversee the storefront, had the place up and running in a month's time. Soon, the storefront was a center of activity with the emergence of the Lymansville Crime Prevention Association, a partnership between police and community residents. The association held regular meetings at the storefront to discuss community needs and plan programs. That first year, the group organized seventeen programs, including a steak-fry fundraiser and the establishment of three crime watch groups. A police officer was designated to work with each crime watch group.

The North Providence Police Department's organizational strategy was to make community policing a departmentwide commitment from everyone—sworn and civilian. Decision-making was decentralized, giving police officers the autonomy to try to find solutions to problems in their assigned areas. Officers worked with the community to identify specific concerns and come up with potential remedies. Supervisors were committed to giving officers the skills, technological support, and motivation for the officers to be effective in their new roles.

The department has strived to be proactive in the way it has applied the community policing philosophy. One example of this has been the department's efforts to involve citizens in crime prevention. The department instituted a ride-along program, giving residents the opportunity to join an officer on his or her rounds. Residents come away with a fuller understanding of the officer's duties as well as tips on how to report crime or suspicious activity. And the residents often pass along information about specific neighborhood problems that can be helpful to police—an important reason for keeping lines of communication open.

To maintain close community ties, the department provides bicycle patrols through neighborhoods and makes available cellular phone and pager numbers so residents may contact individual officers directly. Regular community meetings are held so police can learn what specific problems are most on people's minds. For example, when police learn that a specific street or neighborhood is having a continuous problem, the department responds by patrolling the area more frequently.

"Whistle for Safety" is the department's newest program, launched in response to the attempted abduction of a developmentally disabled woman. Police Officer Darlene Keighley devised a program for reaching out to other developmentally disabled residents in the area. The goal is to teach them "street smarts," such as how to deal with strangers, how to protect themselves, and how to use whistles to call for help. Through role-playing and other activities, the participants learn how to avoid potentially dangerous situations. And in the event they are accosted by someone, they are taught to yell such phrases as "I don't know you!" or "You are a stranger!"

Those who complete the program get whistles on key chains and certificates. But more important is the improved confidence that many also come away with.

By keeping in close contact with the community and by giving officers the tools and the authority to tackle problems in the areas they patrol, the North Providence Police Department is in the best position possible for dealing with crime—a proactive position.

Source: Reprinted with permission from William V. Devine, "From Storefronts to Street Smarts: Police Work for Safer Neighborhoods," *Community Policing Exchange,* September/October 1998, p. 4.

The police generally establish these programs; however, they are primarily community programs and must be run by the community, not dictated by the police. Once they are up and running, however, the police will still be involved. As research has clearly demonstrated, Neighborhood Watch programs occasionally need some guidance and sometimes a structure that is facilitated by the police (Garofalo and McLeod 1988; Rosenbaum 1987; Rosenbaum and Lurigio 1994). As with most community prevention programs, the police may establish the programs, but the community must at least participate in, if not manage, these programs for them to be successful.

The other two programs under the "big three" are operation ID and home security surveys. In operation ID, a citizen's property is engraved for future identification in the event it is stolen. In some police departments, the police officer will actually respond to a requesting citizen's home and perform the engraving with a scribe. In other departments, local citizens can check out the scribe to do their own engraving. The general recommendation is that the owner engrave the state's abbreviation followed by his or her social security number for the easiest identification. This number can then be entered into the local and state computer as well as the National Crime Information Center (NCIC) if the owner's property is stolen. There is some evidence that citizens who utilize this program stand a greater chance of not being victimized and recovering their property if it is stolen (Geller 1991).

The final program of the "big three" is the use of home security surveys. Police departments across the United States often offer this service to the victim of a crime after it is too late. The police should advertise this service or notify citizens through the local government that this service is available free of charge. The police will then dispatch an officer on request with a checklist on crime prevention techniques that can be utilized inside and outside the home to make the home a more difficult target for criminals. The home security survey should be tailored to the needs of the citizen and should be conducted in a positive manner.

Another community crime prevention program that has gained nationwide attention and is viewed as a very favorable program by the public is Drug Abuse Resistance Education (DARE). First conducted under the leadership of Chief Daryl Gates of the Los Angeles Police Department in 1983, the DARE program has become a nationwide

A Phoenix, Arizona, Police Department Neighborhood Patrol officer educates a resident on home security. (*Courtesy of the Phoenix Police Department, Phoenix, Arizona, and Mr. Bob Rink.*)

program attempting to prevent the children of today from becoming the drug users and drug dealers of tomorrow. The DARE program trains veteran police officers to teach a structured sequential curriculum in the schools (Bureau of Justice Assistance 1992). The program is seventeen weeks long and "uses a variety of techniques including lectures, exercises, audiovisual material, and role playing to teach students to say no to drugs" (Bureau of Justice Statistics 1992, 104). It is estimated that, as of 2006, nearly 50,000 police officers had been trained to teach in the DARE program, and an estimated 26 million U.S. students and 10 million internation students participated in the program that year (Drug Abuse Resistance Education Homepage 2006).

Although the program presents an admirable crime prevention technique to young children in a country plagued by drugs, the success of the program has not been proven. A study conducted by Rosenbaum and coworkers found no statistical significance on the use of drugs or on attitudes and beliefs about drugs in a longitudinal study on children who had participated in the DARE program. Despite the overall data, it was possible that the program was effective with specific populations such as females, urban residents, and Hispanic students (Rosenbaum et al. 1994). Regardless of the actual effects, in looking at the intent of neighborhood-oriented policing and the category of community crime prevention, there still exist the unquantifiable elements of social control and order maintenance in which a community can benefit from these programs.

One program with demonstrated benefits to the community is the outreach program. Primarily focused on reducing fear in the community, outreach programs go door-to-door in a selected neighborhood to solicit information on crime, determine the local problems, and attempt to form a neighborhood coalition. The first police department to utilize and study this method of police–citizen contact was the Baltimore Police Department in what it called Citizen-Oriented Police Enforcement (COPE) (Cordner 1988; Greene and Taylor 1988; Skogan 1994). The COPE teams were able to determine what the citizens considered to be local problems; in some cases they discovered problems where they thought none existed, and in other cases they found content communities in places they had perceived as crime-ridden. In the end, with the information obtained from the citizens, the Baltimore Police Department was able to address the problems identified, succeed in reducing the fear of crime, and expand the capabilities of the program at the same time (Cordner 1988).

 ## COP IN ACTION

Operation Blue: Cops Become Bankers to Aid Elderly Citizens

"I had never paid much attention to the elderly," Adrian L. "Windy" Miller admitted. "I was not aware how trusting they are. Many of them go to a nearby store or bank to cash their monthly checks and walk away from the counter holding the cash in plain view." These actions, coupled with the somewhat slowed and helpless nature of the elderly, have made them prey for those in need of quick cash. "We had a ring of crooks preying on the elderly," Miller, a member of the San Antonio Police Officers' Association, said. San Antonio is one of Texas's most attractive tourist cities, providing dining, theme parks, outdoor Mexican markets, and the historic Alamo.

Nearly a decade ago, the officers answered a plea for help from the Alamo Area Council of Government, which operated the city's housing projects. In co-sponsorship with Frost National Bank, they began a program known as Operation Blue. The program is activated once a month, as officers gather to transport a temporary banking facility to the elderly who reside in the city-owned housing projects. The officers cash government checks for the residents and assist in purchasing money orders to pay bills.

While Operation Blue is a great service to San Antonio's senior citizens, Miller is quick to point out that the program is also rewarding to the officers involved. "We have become a form of family to them. They are excited to see us and visit with us. Real friendships have developed over the years. There's lots of teasing, and we have a lot of fun. There's a satisfaction in providing someone a little help," he said. "You're providing a potential victim with a safe environment. It gives me a good feeling."

The bank became a co-sponsor in the program as a public service and to show its commitment to the elderly and community. They have co-sponsored the program from its inception, without any financial benefit. The bank's participation actually bears some expense, with its staff preparing for the event and tallying up the results. After nine years the program works very smoothly. The seniors receive their government checks the third of each month, a date known to many crooks. That fact alone was making the seniors victims as the crooks knew where to look and when. The first working day following the third, the officers receive approximately $66,000 from a special account set up at the bank. Miller, who now coordinates the program, divides the cash up according to the needs of each location served. To that he adds a predetermined number of money orders.

The San Antonio Police Officers' Association guarantees the program and is responsible for any losses. The association makes no monetary profit from the system, but the rewards are great. "It's wonderful to see those smiling faces lined up when we get there," Miller said. "Both the elderly and officers really enjoy the program," Detective Corn said. "Its rewards are too great to count. It helps the elderly, cuts down on crime, and provides us with a feeling of doing something really positive for others."

Source: Adapted with permission from Ann Worrell, "Operation Blue: Cops Become Bankers to Aid Elderly Citizens," *Law and Order,* December 1993, pp. 27–30.

Other police departments that have attempted outreach programs have reported similar results. A fear reduction project, which was evaluated by the Police Foundation and conducted by the Houston Police Department and Newark Police Department, was successful in establishing a strong perception by the residents of restored social order and a more positive evaluation of the police (Brown and Wycoff 1987; Pate et al. 1986; Skogan 1994). A study conducted by the Vera Institute on New York City's implementation of the Community Patrol Officer Program (CPOP) found that opening the lines of communication in this outreach manner resulted in enhanced community relations and problem solving of both order maintenance and criminal issues (see Farrell 1988; McElroy, Cosgrove, and Sadd 1993; Weisburd and McElroy 1988).

Additional community crime prevention programs can include, but are not limited to, various types of programs aimed at educating children on the values of respecting one's community and the law. These programs may include a police–school liaison, often referred to as the School Resource Officer Program, in which one or two police officers are assigned to each school in the jurisdiction and that school becomes the officer's or officers' "community." There are also youth camp outings, wilderness programs, and any sports program that integrates the police and the children. These programs serve to open the lines of communication with the children, teach the children that the police are also members of the community, and allow for a subtle form of social control. Other programs may consist of stolen property prevention, such as a registration drive for children to register their bicycles with the police; a Combat Auto Theft (CAT) program in which citizens sign a form saying they will not drive their cars between the hours of midnight and 6 A.M., and if the car marked by a CAT sticker is seen on the road by the police, it may be stopped; and hot lines and cash rewards for stolen property.

The programs available under community crime prevention are too numerous to list, but they are only limited by the imagination of the police and the community. These programs, whether addressing the prevention of future victims and future criminals or the targets for possible crime, should be an important part of neighborhood-oriented policing as it promotes, assists, and is often the catalyst for a complete community-oriented policing program in a community (see Heininger 1997).

Communication Programs

Communication programs stand out from community patrols and community crime prevention because the main goal in these programs is to directly open the lines of communication between the police and the community. Although in the programs previously described in this chapter there seems to be a consistent theme of communication, their goals are separate. Community patrols attempt to make the police more visible and accessible and community crime prevention programs attempt to do just that—prevent crime—while community social control programs (discussed in the next section) attempt to establish a strong sense of social control within the community. Communication programs are just simple methods of communicating to the citizens who the police are, what they do, and how they can assist. They are what a police officer would consider "feel good" programs.

A large portion of these programs also originated from the police–community relations era but have been updated to fill a community-oriented policing approach. The ride-along program, in which citizens can ride a shift with a police officer, is perhaps the best program to open communications with the public. This is a golden opportunity for the police to demonstrate to citizens what a large part of their job entails and why they need the support of the public. The ride-along can also assist the police by advertising to specific segments of the community that may feel alienated by the police, such as new immigrants, or by requesting ride-alongs that speak another language to assist in translations.

Another communication program that was implemented at one time for the spouses of police officers, and more recently for the local community, is a miniacademy. Fairfax County Police Department, Fairfax, Virginia, created a spouses' academy in the 1980s to create a sense of understanding of the police officer's job. The academy consisted of firearms safety and training, courtroom testimony, and classes on the law and officer safety; it culminated in the ride-along program. This form of communication has been implemented in several police departments across the nation with anecdotal success.

Local police programs on cable television have gained wide acceptance. Many of these programs, such as the ones in Arlington County, Fairfax County, Prince William County, and the cities of Alexandria and Manassas, Virginia, are filmed each week and aired as many as a dozen times during the week. The show explains what the police department is currently doing, details accounts of recent crimes, explains safety and crime prevention tips, and provides an overall method of communicating a plethora of information to the public. Other programs that follow similar lines are brochures, newsletters, and attendance at local community events such as fairs, community meetings, and parades.

Once again, these programs are only limited by the ingenuity of the police and community, which is demonstrated in the DARE card program. Through the sponsorship of the DARE program, trading cards can be printed up and given to children while the police work the street. They feature a police officer from the local police department with his or her picture on the front and a short biography and safety tip on the back. The children can then collect them and trade them like any other trading cards. In the Washington, D.C., metropolitan area, the DARE program sponsors DARE trading cards featuring the members of the Washington Redskins football team. Anecdotal evidence suggests these programs are received extremely well by the children; they often approach officers on the street and ask for a trading card, thereby offering an excellent communication opportunity.

Kansas City, Missouri, police officer handing out police trading cards to local youth. (*Courtesy of the Kansas City Police Department, Kansas City, Missouri.*)

Community Social Control Programs

Community social control programs are programs based on social control theory as articulated by Travis Hirschi and transformed into hands-on programs that allow the police and community to exert influence over various segments that cause criminal activity or commit acts against order maintenance. To understand the community social control programs, one must have a simple understanding of social control theory.

Social control theory was born in the 1969 book *Causes of Delinquency,* written by Travis Hirschi. Hirschi used social control theory to explain not just why criminals commit crime but why most people do not commit crime (for a review of social control theory, see Siegel 1995 and Vold and Bernard 1986). Hirschi believed that generally, if left to our own devices, we would all commit crime, but it is our attachments, commitments, involvements, and beliefs that prevent us from committing these crimes (Hirschi 1969). The attachments to our peers, schools, parents, and spouses all keep us from criminal behavior. Our commitments to our education, careers, and future have an equal impact, as do our involvement in the community through church, sports, and social groups; our beliefs in honesty, morality, and caring for others are also important (Hirschi 1969). If these four factors are in place, then that individual is far less likely to commit a crime than those individuals who are lacking in one or more areas. Although this is a theory on crime causation, we can utilize this concept within neighborhood-oriented policing in the development of community social control programs.

These programs consist of not only utilizing the police but once again integrating the police and the community to establish and exert social control on those groups possibly lacking in one of the four areas. Social control also returns to the broken windows theory, which essentially states that if the community allows a broken window in a building to be tolerated, then the community will also allow for further destruction and eventually allow crime to enter the neighborhood, and will thus lose any form of social control (see Wilson and Kelling 1982). Therefore, it is the goal of the police and the community to maintain, enhance, or restore a strong sense of social control over the entire community. They must do so through strengthening the bonds of those groups in a position to exert social control, and they must work with those groups that fail to abide by the societal norms.

 # COP IN ACTION

Beach Patrol: Keeping Islands Safe from Crime

The St. Lucie County Sheriff's Office is committed to providing citizens with the most innovative crime prevention programs possible—while at the same time exercising budgetary restraint. The sheriff's office firmly believes in problem-oriented policing and in encouraging St. Lucie County citizens to work hand-in-hand with the deputies in solving problems. One initiative that allowed the agency to cover all those bases was the Citizens Observation Park Patrol.

St. Lucie County has more than 25 miles of pristine beaches on two barrier islands, North and South Hutchinson Island. The islands are home to more than 20,000 citizens and hundreds of businesses. During the tourist season, the population of the islands increases to more than 50,000. Many parts of the islands offer isolated beaches and quiet parks that are frequented by residents and tourists alike. Also frequenting these off-the-beaten-path locations, unfortunately, are the criminals who take the opportunity to break into cars and commit assaults with little or no detection. As you can imagine, patrolling these islands can be challenging at best. The goal was to substantially decrease and even prevent the sporadic criminal activity occurring in county parks and beach accesses, but with little or no cost to the county taxpayers.

Since 1994, they have successfully integrated hundreds of volunteers in the sheriff's office's day-to-day operations. One of the most successful volunteer-based programs is the Citizens Observation Patrol. Since its inception, the program has significantly reduced criminal activity in several portions of the community. They wanted to incorporate a similar program utilizing volunteers to patrol the various county parks and beach accesses. Unlike the Citizens Observation Patrol, in which members in a designated area are issued a marked patrol vehicle and are responsible for funding the fuel, the funding for the park patrol's fuel would have to come from a different source. Fortunately, the Division of Leisure Services, which provides lifeguards and maintenance for all county parks, offered to allocate $1,800. The St. Lucie County Board of Commissioners unanimously approved the funding and praised the program's potential benefits. Additional costs, such as for uniforms and equipment, are taken from asset forfeiture proceeds.

When formation of the new Citizens Observation Park Patrol was announced, sixteen community members eagerly stepped forward. The volunteers underwent a background investigation to ensure integrity and also attended a sixteen-hour course covering such topics as department policy, patrol procedures, ways to identify and report suspicious activity, defensive driving, and cardiopulmonary resuscitation (CPR). Upon completion, volunteers are issued uniforms that make them easily recognizable as representatives of the St. Lucie County Sheriff's Office. Three refurbished sheriff's office vehicles are currently being used as patrol vehicles. Each vehicle is equipped with a scanner, cellular telephone (donated by a local cellular telephone company), and safety equipment.

They established three shifts and staggered the hours to provide optimum coverage. The idea was for the patrol to not only deter crimes in progress but also prevent them. Members are trained to recognize crime risks, such as property in plain sight and unlocked doors. Any breaches of security are reported on a criminal opportunity form. A copy of the form, addressing the problem and a solution, is left with the person's vehicle or property as a courtesy.

Citizens who have come in contact with members of the Citizens Observation Park Patrol have said they are happy to see the extra "eyes and ears." Based on the park patrol's efforts, the sheriff's office anticipates a decline in criminal activity in the affected areas and a strengthening of their relationship with the community.

The Citizens Observation Park Patrol demonstrates that it's still possible to find cost-effective solutions to crime problems. And relying on volunteers and building partnerships with citizens are not just cost-effective—they're effective, period.

Source: Reprinted with permission from Frank J. Pellegrini, Jr., "Beach Patrol: Keeping Islands Safe from Crime," *Sheriff's Times* 10, no. 1, Fall 1999.

The police and community can work together in a number of ways to strengthen the bonds with those who can exert their influence on other members of the community but who often need some assistance on the part of the police. In some communities, those who abide by the law and rules are often scared to say something to a juvenile spray painting a building for fear of their personal safety, fear of retribution on their property such as a slashed tire, fear of a civil suit, or fear of just getting involved. If the police can strengthen these law-abiding community members, then the element of fear may be removed and the community would be more likely to get involved.

A program could be created for police officers to live in those crime-ridden communities, such as the one started in Alexandria, Virginia. Several police officers were given the opportunity to buy a home at a reduced price and low interest rate if they would move into a troubled neighborhood. This program assists the neighborhood in a variety of ways. The police officer has a more vested interest in the community he or she patrols, the majority of citizens in these neighborhoods are good hardworking people who suffer from the crimes, and the program provides some feeling of security that may in turn enhance the social control by these neighborhood members. In Charleston, West Virginia, Chief Dallas Staples implemented this program in a retirement home setting by establishing a low-rent apartment in the retirement home for a police officer. This program assisted the police officer in cost of housing and reduced senior citizens' fear and increased their ability to exert some community social control.

Another group the police can work with to exert some forms of community social control is the media. Whether it is through television or print, the media can provide an avenue for communicating the social control measures and reinforce the bonds of the community.

The police must also work with groups that violate both the social control of the community and the order maintenance issues by attempting to create an atmosphere of zero tolerance for certain behaviors that the community finds reprehensible. If the community dictates that gang graffiti is a key concern, then the police must work with the gangs and develop programs to eradicate this problem. If the order maintenance issue is the homeless aggressively panhandling, then programs that prevent aggressive panhandling or that stop citizens from giving money to the homeless in this setting must be implemented. Areas known for drug dealing or individual crack houses can be shut down through various means; once gone, the police and community can prevent crack houses from returning.

One method of exerting community social control has been through the development of code enforcement teams. The city of Fort Lauderdale, Florida, created a code enforcement team that consisted of a member of the police, fire, building, and zoning departments to target these order maintenance issues (Donsi 1992). The team, from 1987 to 1991, tore down 124 crack houses, boarded up 587, and reduced the drug activity by 57 percent (Donsi 1992). Additionally, during this time, the team collected $600,000 in fines and forced landlords to spend nearly $6 million repairing property that did not meet code specifications (Donsi 1992). This is a prime example of how attacking the order maintenance issues and attacking the criminal activity in a variety of ways can restore a sense of social control to the community.

COP IN ACTION

Code Enforcement Teams

Seeking new ways to cope with crime-ridden troubled areas, the Albuquerque Police Department set up an interagency team to enforce city codes against delinquent properties. These properties are often focal points for crime, with the knowledge, connivance, or apathy of their owners.

The Code Enforcement Team is an innovation originally pioneered by the Fort Lauderdale, Florida, Police Department. Albuquerque's adaptation of the concept resulted in a team including a police detective, a housing inspector from Albuquerque Family and Community Services, a zoning inspector, and a fire inspector performing comprehensive inspections for violations in all spheres.

The advantages of a team approach are that a law enforcement presence deters intimidation of inspectors and all necessary inspections on a single property are carried out simultaneously. The team approach results in quicker action against violators, who are often absentee landlords who allow their properties to be used for criminal activities.

Abandoned buildings serve as rendezvous points, not only for squatters but also for people involved in illegal drugs. Because of their neglected condition, abandoned properties often constitute safety hazards. A typical trouble spot might include debris, littering, insufficient fire extinguishers, inoperative smoke alarms, exposed electrical wiring, and inadequate drainage. The location might have had police called to it many times with reports of gunshots.

The team gives the property owner thirty days to begin corrective action and schedules a reinspection at the end of this period to monitor progress. If the owner is cooperative, the team may grant an extension, but lacking this, enforcement action is initiated.

Initially, the emphasis was against motels lining old Route 66 (Central Avenue), long a trouble area. Some motels had holes in walls, plumbing defects such as inoperative toilets, insect infestation, and inadequate fire protection. Route 66 motels catered to prostitutes by renting rooms by the hour. These are often substandard rooms because working prostitutes don't require the amenities that legitimate motel guests expect. One Central Avenue motel, for example, had nine rooms out of forty with no toilets.

Private residences can also become targets for collaborative inspections. One apartment complex was notorious for its violations, and the owner had only nine out of its twenty-one units leased. All apartments were occupied, however, by squatters, drug dealers, and other people.

With private residences, sometimes the owner of record is not immediately available or even visible. In these cases, a title search usually produces a name, and the team serves papers on the responsible individual.

Condemnation of an abandoned building is a further step. The team requires the owner to secure and board up an abandoned building within five to ten days, and failure to comply results in a condemnation resolution from the city council. While final action can take six months, the threat of condemnation usually motivates the owner to comply.

Support from the community's courts was necessary to the team's efforts. Some judges commonly passed lenient sentences on violators, apparently because of their unfamiliarity with the seriousness of the situations surrounding code violations. Code Team personnel conducted a slide show and presentation for judges who regularly deal with code violations, to show them how serious the ramifications can be for related crime in the community. This approach required no new legislation, only stricter and more thorough enforcement of existing laws and regulations, including national housing, construction, electrical, health, and plumbing codes.

With more personnel, code enforcement in Albuquerque will become more intense, making it more difficult for criminal elements to obtain and retain a foothold in the community.

Source: Adapted with permission from Tony Lesce, "Code Enforcement Teams," *Law and Order,* September 1995, pp. 93–95.

Finally, another example of a community social control program has been a partnership between the police and mental health counselors known as "Child-Development–Community Policing" in New Haven, Connecticut (Marans and Berkan 1997). This particular program has been implemented as a collaborative effort between the New Haven Police Department and the Child Study Center at the Yale University School of Medicine to address the psychological impact of chronic exposure to community violence on children and families. The greatest benefit has come about because of the collaboration, which has allowed both police officers and clinicians to increase their knowledge of each other's strategies and practices, thus allowing for improved tracking, services, and methods for dealing with community violence. The program has been replicated in other cities, including Buffalo, New York; Baltimore, Maryland; Framingham, Massachusetts; and Newark, New Jersey (Marans and Berkman 1997).

CONCLUSION

Neighborhood-oriented policing (see Figure 4-2) consists of the programs that the police and community can utilize to address criminal problems as well as order maintenance issues. These programs should be utilized based on the community members' needs and their perceptions of the local problems. Whether implemented on their own or with the assistance of strategic policing techniques, these programs are the core of community-oriented policing. They must be created, implemented, and maintained

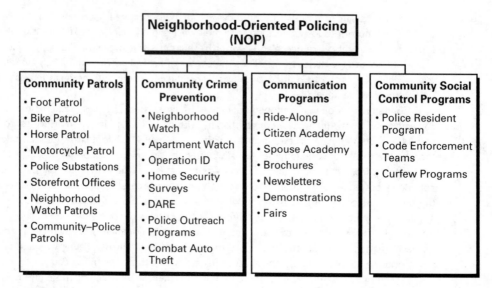

FIGURE 4-2　The components of neighborhood-oriented policing.

with the assistance and cooperation of the community if they are to be viable under the community-oriented policing philosophy. Through the implementation of these four programs—community patrols, community crime prevention programs, communication programs, and community social control programs—and the concepts of problem-oriented policing detailed in the next chapter, community-oriented policing can be achieved.

COP ON THE WORLD WIDE WEB

Austin, Texas, Police Department

http://www.ci.austin.tx.us/police

Boston, Massachusetts, Police Department

http://www.cityofboston.gov/police/default.asp

Chicago, Illinois, Police Department

http://www.ci.chi.il.us/CommunityPolicing

Community Policing Programs Listing

http://faculty.ncwc.edu/toconnor/comlist.htm

U.S. Conference of Mayors—Community Policing

http://www.usmayors.org/uscmcops

Publications with short case studies.

REVIEW QUESTIONS

1. Define *neighborhood-oriented policing* and how it relates to community-oriented policing.
2. Describe the four types of neighborhood-oriented policing programs.
3. Detail what is known about "foot patrol" programs. Are they beneficial? If so, how?

CHAPTER 5

Problem-Oriented Policing

A problem well stated is a problem half solved.

—Charles Kettering

CHAPTER OBJECTIVES

- ■ Identify problem-oriented policing (POP) as its own concept having been developed independently of COP.
- ■ Understand how POP is an integral part of COP.
- ■ Explain POP as created by Herman Goldstein.
- ■ Explain the SARA model as created in Newport News, Virginia.
- ■ Explain the relationship among actors, incidents, and responses.
- ■ List and define the five methods of response under the SARA model.

The third component of community-oriented policing is problem-oriented policing (POP) (see Figure 5-1). This component is a concerted effort on the part of the police and the community to resolve the causes of criminal activity and order maintenance issues rather than the symptoms. Problem-oriented policing addresses a particular problem, analyzes the problem, determines a course of action, implements the program, and then follows up in an evaluative manner. If the problem is resolved, then the police and community must only keep the problem in check. If it is not resolved, alternative solutions are generated and implemented. The goal of problem-oriented policing is for the police and community to work together in solving problems that cannot be solved by traditional police work or that need special attention in the form of developing a tailor-made response for the particular problem and situation.

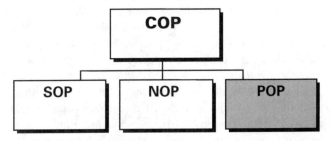

FIGURE 5-1 The third component of community-oriented policing: problem-oriented policing.

The concept of problem-oriented policing was not created within the parameters of community-oriented policing but separately and at relatively the same time. Herman Goldstein, the Evjue-Bascom Professor of Law at the Law School, University of Wisconsin–Madison, studied the police response to various types of crimes in the mid-1970s and developed an alternative to improve the police response. The results were first revealed in his 1979 article in *Crime and Delinquency* entitled "Improving Policing: A Problem-Oriented Approach" (Goldstein 1979). The article detailed Goldstein's concept for creating a more efficient police response to repetitive problems and would later be expounded on in his 1990 book entitled *Problem-Oriented Policing* (Goldstein 1990).

As this new concept of problem-oriented policing began to take shape, another article appeared in 1982 in the *Atlantic Monthly* by James Q. Wilson and George L. Kelling

Two Memphis police officers holding teddy bears donated by local citizens for the purpose of calming children in a time of crisis. (*Courtesy of the Memphis Police Department, Memphis, Tennessee.*)

entitled "Broken Windows: The Police and Neighborhood Safety," which would be the catalyst for the concept of community-oriented policing. Although these two concepts evolved at roughly the same time, the question continues to be raised whether community-oriented policing and problem-oriented policing are the same concept. In much of the literature, the two concepts are presented as consisting of the same philosophy and the same ideas (see Cordner 1988; Goldstein 1987; Lurigio and Rosenbaum 1994; Wilson and Kelling 1989). In other literature, the two concepts are considered different philosophies and therefore translate into two distinct programs (Eck and Spelman 1987a, 1987b; Trojanowicz and Bucqueroux 1989). See Table 5-1. In light of this disparity over the two concepts, it is clear that some relationship exists between the two concepts. John Eck and William Spelman (1987b, 46) stated, "Problem-oriented policing relies on and supports community policing, but it is not synonymous with community policing." Although this is an accurate representation based on the literature, Eck and Spelman should have carried the statement one step further. Problem-oriented policing may not be synonymous with community-oriented policing, but community-oriented policing is synonymous with problem-oriented policing. Problem-oriented policing was designed on its own and can operate and function in a police department on its own without the implementation of community-oriented policing. However, community-oriented policing cannot be implemented

TABLE 5-1   *Comparisons between Problem-Oriented Policing and Community-Oriented Policing Principles*

PRINCIPLE	PROBLEM-ORIENTED POLICING	COMMUNITY-ORIENTED POLICING
Primary emphasis	Substantive social problems within police mandate	Engaging the community in the policing process
When police and community collaborate	Determined on problem-by-problem basis	Always or nearly always
Emphasis on problem analysis	Highest priority given to thorough analysis	Encouraged but less important than community collaboration
Preference for responses	Strong preference that alternatives to criminal law enforcement be explored	Preference for collaborative responses with community
Role for police in organizing and mobilizing community	Advocated only if warranted within the context of specific problem being addressed	Emphasizes strong role for police
Importance of geographical decentralization of police and continuity of officer assignment to community	Preferred, but not essential	Essential
Degree to which police share decision-making authority with community	Strongly encourages input from community while preserving ultimate decision-making authority to police	Emphasizes sharing decision-making authority with community

Emphasis on officer skills	Emphasizes intellectual and analytical skills	Emphasizes interpersonal skills
View of role or mandate of police	Encourages broad but not unlimited role for police; stresses limited capacities of police and guards against creating unrealistic expectations of police	Encourages expansive role for police to achieve ambitious social objectives

Source: Reprinted from Michael S. Scott, *Problem-Oriented Policing: Reflections on the First 20 Years.* Washington, D.C.: U.S. Department of Justice, Office of Community-Oriented Policing Services, 2000.

without the assistance of the problem-oriented policing approach. Therefore, community-oriented policing *is* synonymous with problem-oriented policing.

As the key literature on problem-oriented policing has developed based on its own merits and programs, this chapter will review the evolution of problem-oriented policing, detail the methods of implementation, and review the literature for details of both evaluative and anecdotal evidence of its success and failure.

EVOLUTION OF PROBLEM-ORIENTED POLICING

As previously stated, the evolution of problem-oriented policing commenced with the research of Herman Goldstein. As a result of the policing styles in the 1960s and the demand for changing the way the police conducted their business during that time period, Goldstein raised the issue in an article on public policy formation as it applies to the police (Goldstein 1967). He would eventually expound on the public policy issue and discuss the police and their role in a book entitled *Policing a Free Society* (Goldstein 1977). He then developed his theory, as a result of his extensive research on how police respond to various calls, into his 1979 article entitled "Improving Policing: A Problem-Oriented Approach" (Goldstein 1979). The article successfully showed that police focus on how to deal with the means of a situation rather than the ends. By dealing with the ends, the police would have a better rate of success in the multitude of problems they face on any given shift. This theory became the basis for all the literature that followed on problem solving, and it would be known as problem-oriented policing.

The same problems that existed with problem-oriented policing became readily apparent with community-oriented policing. Many of the police programs attempted to change over to a problem-solving style of policing while some only remotely changed the way they performed their duties, but all of them were utilizing the title "problem-oriented policing" to describe their programs. As Goldstein stated in his 1990 book, "use of the phrase [problem-oriented policing] also creates the great risk that, when the concept is widely broadcast under the abbreviated label, it will be drained of much of its meaning" (Goldstein 1990). He then cites this as one reason for writing the book that expounded further and updated his original policy proposal for the way police carry out their duties.

As Goldstein 1990, 14–15 explained, there were many reasons for the development of problem-oriented policing, but he cites five concerns as strongly influencing its creation:

1. The police field is preoccupied with management, internal procedures, and efficiency to the exclusion of appropriate concern for effectiveness in dealing with problems.
2. The police devote most of their resources to responding to calls from citizens, reserving too small a percentage of their time and energy for acting on their own initiative to prevent or reduce community problems.
3. The community is a major resource with an enormous potential, largely untapped, for reducing the number and magnitude of problems that otherwise become the business of the police.
4. Within their agencies, police have readily available to them another huge resource: their rank-and-file officers, whose time and talent have not been used effectively.
5. Efforts to improve policing have often failed because they have not been adequately related to the overall dynamics and complexity of the police organization. Adjustments in policing and organizational structure are required to accommodate and support change.

The philosophy and implementation of problem-oriented policing across the nation closely followed the concepts as dictated by Herman Goldstein, yet several other programs developed during the 1980s that also influenced the creation of the concept. The first to appear, one evaluated through a pre/postresearch methodology, was the previously mentioned Citizen-Oriented Police Enforcement (COPE) program in Baltimore County, Maryland, which commenced in 1981 (Cordner 1985, 1988). Utilizing many of the problem-solving techniques dictated by Goldstein, the Baltimore County Police Department was able to show that the philosophy, when formed into a program for implementation, was successful. However, the COPE program not only was problem-oriented but also initiated some programs that fell into other categories such as strategic policing and neighborhood-oriented policing styles. It was not until 1986, when the National Institute of Justice studied the feasibility of a problem-oriented approach to policing in its chosen test site of Newport News, Virginia, that a study dedicated specifically to the problem-oriented approach would be conducted.

 ## COP IN ACTION

Underage Drinking: A Community Problem

Ocean City is a resort community located on the Atlantic coast. The seaside community has a base population of 10,000, but that number swells to nearly 300,000 every summer. Tens of thousands of high school and college students converge on the community to enjoy its amenities or work summer jobs. Most students who visit Ocean City are well behaved. But in the summer of 1995, several troubling incidents occurred.

During the 1995 vacation season one teenager under the influence of alcohol jumped to his death from a high-rise condominium. Another intoxicated teen threatened a motel manager and was shot to death. Still another incident involved a drunk teenager who accidentally fell to his death while attempting a handstand from a 12th-floor balcony. Many other youths were arrested that year for committing offenses while under the influence of alcohol.

The resort community is actually very safe, with relatively few violent crimes considering that 8 million tourists visit each year. Despite this reality, the "family" image on which Ocean City built its tourist trade was negatively impacted by the accidental deaths and disruptive youths in '95.

The police department adopted community policing and, to prepare for the up-coming summer season, solicited community involvement to address underage drinking. This effort came to be known as RAAM, or Reducing the Availability of Alcohol to Minors.

The department identified key community stakeholders and asked for their help and also that of the city's hotel, motel, and rental property managers to help stop underage drinking. The police worked closely with both the real estate and hospitality associations to mail informational literature, including new contractual agreements citing underage drinking as cause for eviction, along with rental agreements to visitors and property owners. Hotel and motel managers placed posters prohibiting underage drinking in their lobbies. Additionally, the police department trained the property managers to handle minor disturbances.

The real estate community provided the police department with a database of the city's rental properties and the names of their owners or rental agents. The database enabled the police to quickly notify property owners when disturbances or underage drinking incidents occurred on their properties. When an incident occurred, the property owner or agent was expected to make a reasonable effort to control tenants, using civil remedies when appropriate, or else lose their rental licenses.

The police department also developed a number of new strategies. The chief started by re-training every sworn officer in underage drinking laws and educating each one in the specifics of the RAAM project. In addition, the department prepared a stiffer enforcement strategy involving the use of civil citations for underage drinking. As a final step, the chief sent police officers to high schools and colleges in four neighboring states to warn youths that underage drinking was a danger to them and would bring a stiff response from Ocean City police.

Tactically, police created a special community policing zone comprising both the boardwalk and 25 other city blocks known for their number of disturbance-related calls for service. An increased number of foot, bike, and mounted police units were assigned to the zone, which enabled officers to develop close working relationships with business managers and property owners.

The city's government officials also committed their help and promised to respond within 24 hours to serious safety and quality-of-life code violations identified and forwarded by police officers.

The summer of 1996 was universally hailed by citizens, tourists, local government, and the media as one of Ocean City's most peaceful. No deaths occurred due to underage drinking. The department's calls for service dropped 17 percent, and there was also an accompanying 3 percent drop in serious Part 1 offenses. Every identified problem property showed a decrease of between 40 and 60 percent in police calls for service. Hotel, motel, and rental property owners noted a significant decrease in the consumption of alcohol by minors.

Police officers wrote more than 2,800 civil citations for underage drinking within the zone. In addition, there was a 15 percent increase in total arrests, most for peace and disorder violations that accompanied drinking violations. The public found the community policing zone to be particularly successful because it permitted increased police–citizen interaction and cooperation. Officers also forwarded more than 400 city code referrals to city enforcement agencies, which involved such problems as building safety violations, trash, abandoned autos, damaged street signs, and lighting problems.

The total involvement of the community was critical to making RAAM successful. Many of the concepts and ideas of this project are applicable to other communities that routinely deal with underage drinking and its resulting disorder. Nothing is impossible when government and community act in concert.

Source: Adapted with permission from David C. Massey, "Underage Drinking: A Community Problem," *Community Policing Exchange,* January/February 1997, p. 8.

According to John E. Eck and William Spelman, in their book reviewing the National Institute of Justice study in Newport News, five areas of police research contributed to the formulation and implementation of problem-oriented policing: (1) effectiveness, (2) community, (3) problem studies, (4) discretion, and (5) management (Eck and Spelman 1987a). The effectiveness studies include those on preventive patrol, response time, and investigations revolving around the central question of how effective are the police (Eck and Spelman 1987a). Community studies were largely seen as a result of the policing styles and communication between both the police and community that sparked the implementation of police–community relations. The problem studies Eck and Spelman discuss are predominantly in the area that Goldstein was studying during the 1970s in an attempt to discover how police handle the types of calls they receive. The issue of police discretion has also sparked a complete area of research on its own that attempts to analyze how police officers utilize the wide amount of discretion they have available when handling various complaints and problems (Eck and Spelman 1987a). And finally, they detail the study of police management as it has changed over the past several decades as a growing impetus for the development of problem-oriented policing (Eck and Spelman 1987a). These five reasons, according to Eck and Spelman, were why problem-oriented policing evolved in the manner it did and why it was important to study the potential of this new program.

The National Institute of Justice chose the Police Executive Research Forum to conduct this study in Newport News, and Eck and Spelman became the key authors and proponents of this system (see Eck and Spelman 1987a, 1987b; Spelman and Eck 1987a, 1987b). The Police Executive Research Forum essentially developed its own method of problem-solving policing that allowed it to implement the program on the street. The program's success was lauded, but there were some implementation problems (Eck and Spelman 1987a).

Eventually, many problem-oriented policing programs were implemented across the United States largely based on three methods and philosophies of implementation: Goldstein's model of problem-oriented policing, the Citizen-Oriented Police Enforcement (COPE) programs, and the methodology dictated by Spelman and Eck known as the SARA model, which is detailed later in this chapter. Police departments, such as the San Diego Police Department, with the assistance of the Bureau of Justice Assistance (BJA) and the Police Executive Research Forum (PERF), implemented a problem-oriented policing approach to their drug problems with some success (Capowich and Roehl 1994). In 1986, the New York City Police Department began preparation to implement the Community Patrol Officer Program (CPOP); data collected on problem-oriented policing from December 1986 through February 1988 showed favorable results (McElroy, Cosgrove, and Sadd 1993). In 1990, in Lawrence, Massachusetts, the Lawrence Police Department implemented a problem-solving method of policing that was perceived as a successful program (Cole and Kelley 1993). A Community-Based, Problem-Oriented Policing Program (CBPOP) directed largely at the local drug problem was implemented in Arlington County, Virginia, in 1992 with anecdotal success. And in the Fresno Police Department in Fresno, California, the problem-oriented approach to policing was implemented over a twelve-month period utilizing a POP team with much success (West 1995).

More recent research has found that problem-oriented policing can be extremely beneficial when linked with the assistance of researchers (Baker and Wolfer 2003). Researchers have the capability of bringing their skills into the evaluation process of problem-oriented policing in order to assess the effectiveness of a particular response.

In addition, two other studies (Bichler and Gaines 2005; Rojek 2003) have also found much success when police officers implement problem-oriented policing. The former (Bichler and Gaines 2005), however, noted that police officers tend to identify specific addresses as problems and typically advocated the use of increased officer patrol; while the latter (Rojek 2003), in his assessment of Goldstein Award winners for problem solving, concluded that the "evidence illustrates that police officers are addressing problems with a combination of traditional and alternative responses" (p. 512). Overall, serious police implementation of problem-oriented policing has yielded generally favorable results, but the results were enhanced through the funding provided by the federal government beginning in the mid-1990s.

While police departments across the United States began to implement problem-oriented policing, both as a stand-alone program and part of a larger community-oriented policing program, throughout the 1990s, it was the support of the Office of Community Oriented Policing Services (COPS) that saw problem-oriented policing achieve some of its biggest advances. The COPS office developed a number of grants in the mid- to late 1990s that supported select police departments in their implementation and efforts to advance the concepts of problem-oriented policing (see Chapter 12). However, it was the COPS grant that created the Center for Problem-Oriented Policing, which would contribute greatly to problem-oriented policing moving into the twenty-first century (see www.popcenter.org).

Beginning in 2001, the Center for Problem-Oriented policing focused on the dissemination of information, through a series of problem-specific guides, regarding common problems that most agencies face. These guides draw upon the concepts of problem-oriented policing and attempt to analyze the specific problem in a generic way so as to provide a conceptual understanding of the problems and methods of solving those problems without being too specific (and thus irrelevant to most police departments). Some of these guides include addressing serious crimes, such as "Burglary of Single-Family Houses," "Acquaintance Rape of College Students," and "Robbery at Automated Teller Machines"; and some address disorders, such as the problems of "Cruising," "Loud Car Stereos," and "Panhandling." (These guides are available on-line at www.popcenter.org.) An additional series of publications was developed in 2003 and focused on the different types of police responses (e.g., "The Benefits and Consequences of Police Crackdowns," "Closing Streets and Alleys to Reduce Crime: Should You Go Down This Road?", and "Shifting and Sharing Responsibility for Public Safety Problems"). Finally, a third series of publications was developed that focused on the tools for problem-solving. The titles of these publications include "Research a Problem," "Using Offender Interviews to Inform Police Problem Solving," and "Analyzing Repeat Victimization."

IMPLEMENTATION OF PROBLEM-ORIENTED POLICING

Herman Goldstein, as previously discussed, articulated the concept of problem-oriented policing first in his 1979 article, and then he expounded on it in his 1990 book. The book details the concept of problem-oriented policing, but, more importantly, it provides the framework for a police department to be able to implement the program. Goldstein (1990) carries the progression of steps from identifying the problem to evaluating the problem in a logical and concise order. This process is critical to understanding problem-oriented policing and how it integrates with community-oriented policing.

Goldstein (1990) commences his method with the identification of a problem. He identifies a problem as consisting of three components for the purposes of problem-oriented policing (Goldstein 1990, 66):

1. A cluster of similar, related, or recurring incidents rather than a single incident
2. A substantive community concern
3. A unit of police business

He specifically states that in identifying a problem, it is important to select those clustered recurring problems and identify the sole problem involved (Goldstein 1990). It is often the case that a police officer will respond to a variety of calls at a particular location; although each call may be uniquely different, the calls can be grouped together as a problem focusing on that particular address, as opposed to any one situational "problem."

Goldstein (1990) also discusses a central theme to community-oriented policing: who identifies what is considered a problem. He recognizes that the community should be largely concerned with identifying those things that community members perceive as problems because under his definition of *problem*, it must be of a "substantive community concern," which in reality can only be recognized by members of the community (Goldstein 1990; see also Webster and Connors 1993). Police management should also have a large role in identifying problems because they should be communicating with the community in various settings and be acutely aware of those criminal problems that are ongoing in a particular neighborhood (Goldstein 1990). And, finally, Goldstein (1990) recognizes the contribution of rank-and-file officers, who can identify problems from their perspective as police officers on the street.

One concern shared by the community, police managers, and rank-and-file officers identifying various problems within the community is the resources available to address every problem. Goldstein (1990) articulates that not every problem can be addressed, and therefore the problems must be prioritized through some form of consensus. The decision-making process for determining how the problems should be prioritized is based on a multitude of factors and cannot be reached by one individual or one simple formula. Many things must be considered, and among them Goldstein (1990, 77–78) elaborates on the following:

- The impact of the problem on the community—its size and costs
- The presence of any life-threatening conditions
- The community interest and degree of support likely to exist for both the inquiry and subsequent recommendations
- The potential threat to constitutional rights (as may occur, for example, when citizens take steps to limit the use of the public way, limit access to public facilities, or curtail freedom of speech and assembly)
- The degree to which the problem adversely affects relationships between the police and the community
- The interest of rank-and-file officers in the problem and the degree of support for addressing it
- The concreteness of the problem, given the frustration associated with exploring vague, amorphous complaints
- The potential that exploration is likely to lead to some progress in dealing with the problem

Officers of the Terre Haute, Indiana, Police Department volunteering to roast 6,000 hot dogs at a local church/community event. *(Courtesy of the Terre Haute Police Department, Terre Haute, Indiana.)*

Once the prioritizing decision has been made, the list must also be fluid, subject to change and reranking of those issues, based on the analysis of new information. New concerns should be added to the list and old concerns either removed from the list or moved up and down based on the current status as well as previously mentioned and other factors. From this living and breathing list of problems, those at the top, those that are of the greatest concern to the public, can be addressed.

It is important to remember, as Goldstein (1990) explains, that the substantive problem must be addressed rather than those that are ancillary to the issue. Again, the root of the problem must be addressed—the actual illness rather than the symptoms. Once the root of the problem is determined, whether through holding discussions with the community, surveying the officers working the area to be targeted, or researching the problem, then and only then can a systemic inquiry take place. Otherwise the capability of problem-oriented policing is degraded, and only an effect rather than the cause of the problem is addressed.

The systemic inquiry entails a "systemic collection and analysis of information" regarding the problem (Goldstein 1990, 36). An in-depth probe of the problem requires gathering as much information, from as many varying sources as possible, to acquire the knowledge necessary for determining a course of action to address the problem of concern (Goldstein 1990). Some of this key information should come from police files, rank-and-file police officers, victims, the larger community, direct inquiries of those causing the problems, other agencies in the community, other communities in the area, and possibly department archives (Goldstein 1990). To borrow on an old cliché, no stone should be left unturned. Every piece of evidence or fact must be found and reviewed as if it were a homicide investigation. Although this approach is time-consuming and requires abundant resources, if performed in accordance with all of the tenets of problem-oriented policing, the benefit of this research will be the abolition of the problem.

 ## COP IN ACTION

Graffiti Prevention and Suppression, San Diego Police Department

Scanning

San Diego Police Department's Mid-City Division, which is densely populated and ethnically diverse, comprises four square miles of mixed residential and commercial zones. Thirty-eight languages are spoken in local schools, and the population includes lifelong residents and new immigrants. Housing consists largely of Section 8 apartment complexes and other low-income renters. The business district is primarily made up of churches and small family-owned stores, such as pawnshops, ethnic restaurants, liquor stores, automotive repair shops, and thrift stores. The area has a long history of robberies, drug deals, prostitution, auto theft, and other street crimes. Naturally, the police department concentrated on those crimes.

The division already had adopted wide use of problem-solving techniques, including weekly community meetings. At a community meeting in March 1999, an officer presented crime statistics for robberies, prostitution, and drug offenses in Mid-City. After listening to the litany, a member of the community asked, "What about the graffiti problem?" Several other community members chimed in, "How are you going to stop graffiti in our neighborhoods?" The officer was astonished but had to concede that graffiti, and not other crimes, was the greatest quality-of-life concern for the community. Describing how the increase in graffiti encouraged the increase of crime, one resident said, "Blight creates blight." From this point on, graffiti became a top priority for the police department's Mid-City Division.

A team of officers decided to quantify the extent of the problem. An officer and a detective charted on a map the amount, sites, and types of graffiti in the community. After two days of covering two square miles of the division, their findings were disturbing: Upon reaching 300 instances, the officers discontinued their count. The community's concern, they realized, was well founded. The stakeholders were identified as business owners and merchants, homeowners, local residents, the El Cajon Boulevard Business Improvement Association, shoppers, city government, the school district, and the police department.

Analysis

The community believed that graffiti ranked low on the police department's list of priorities. The community also believed that blight breeds blight: If graffiti were to continue unchecked, property values would plummet, personal safety would be jeopardized, and neighborhoods would decay. A team of two officers and a detective researched the problem. The team calculated the local dollar costs related to graffiti and compared the costs nationwide. In 1998, the San Diego City School District spent $500,000 on paint alone to cover graffiti. The city spent $24,000 to cover walls, curbs, and other city property. Additional money was spent on sandblasting, which is a more common method of graffiti removal. Research also disclosed that the demographic profile of taggers (graffiti writers) in Mid-City roughly matched national findings.

The team analyzed the information from the two-day mapping survey and found the following: (1) Roughly 265 of the 300 instances of graffiti were concentrated on rented multifamily housing that bordered business districts; (2) 35 of the 300 instances of graffiti were at single-family homes; (3) business corridors were tagged on any blank wall and within the first thirty feet of an alley so the tag would be visible to passing traffic and the taggers could see if anyone was coming; (4) alleys, dumpsters, telephone poles, electrical poles, and boxes were prime tagging targets because they rarely got painted over; and (5) school walls were tagged daily.

The officers next studied graffiti-related calls for service, out-of-service time, number of graffiti arrests compared to crime arrests, times of day for tagging, types of graffiti (gang, crew, or solo), age of suspects, and proximity of tagging to suspects' homes. The crime analysis unit of the San Diego Police Department supplied the data. An examination of graffiti-related calls showed (1) calls for service: 218 (1998), 149 (1999); (2) out-of-service time: 264 hours (1998), 227 hours (1999); and (3) arrests: 16 (1998), 18 (1999).

The decrease in calls for service may suggest that the graffiti problem was getting under control. However, based on the intense community concern and the incomplete survey that found more than 300 instances of graffiti, the team concluded that the problem was underreported because of the complacency of residents who felt that the problem couldn't be solved and that there were serious shortfalls in enforcement and arrests. The 300 instances of graffiti were concentrated in two square miles of the division, and only 70 percent of the graffiti tags were reported. Police found the crime cases for graffiti difficult to extract because all vandalism cases were logged under the same penal code section.

Common aspects of graffiti in Mid-City began to emerge as the analysis continued: (1) Tagging is geocentric—that is, it is concentrated near the taggers' homes and along routes to and from school; (2) tagging is a multiple-suspect activity (gangs and crews); (3) time of tagging is most likely from 5 P.M. to 8 P.M. during the week and all hours on the weekend; (4) tagging by scratching (for example, by scraping a sparkplug on Plexiglas) is rapidly growing; and (5) graffiti is prevalent near multifamily housing and adjoining alleys.

The survey disclosed three types of tagging in Mid-City: gang, crew, and solo. The three types form a type of hierarchy, where solo taggers work to form a group, called a tagging crew, that has an identified name. The crew then works to be asked to join a tagging gang, which is the aspiration of most taggers. Gang graffiti and crew graffiti mark the tagger's home territory. The gangs and tagging crews "bomb in packs"—that is, they work in groups to ensure an extensive attack. The crews often cross out tags by rival crews and rewrite their own tag over it. The solo tagger attacks anywhere to promote his tag name. The team identified the sources of most of the graffiti. The top two gang graffitis were identified as the Oriental Boys Society (OBS) and the Holy Blood Gang (HBG). The top two tagging crews were identified as Running the Show (RTS) and Van Dyke Krew (VDK). The top two solo taggers were identified as Clever and Rascal.

Gang and tagger crews comprise 90 percent of the problems in Mid-City, as they all mark territory, bomb in packs, and cross out rivals. The solo tagger causes only 10 percent of the problem, is considered a "lone wolf," and tags everywhere.

After analyzing the graffiti survey, police looked at the social aspect of graffiti. They found that tagging is part of a natural progression to gang activity. Tagging begins at school with children tagging on paper, baseball caps, and backpacks. Tagging is part of social learning through negative behavior. The behavior is learned in small intimate settings with people who have influence. By watching the taggers in focus groups, police found that they exert negative social control, which means that the tagger lacks control and is at the mercy of others who teach criminal behavior.

The team looked at the best solutions adopted by other police departments throughout the nation to control graffiti. The research showed three approaches:

1. Murals. Philadelphia and Reno have painted murals around the city to prevent tagging. Police in both cities discovered that taggers normally leave murals alone. Therefore, taggers on probation paint the murals in highly tagged areas. The murals were left alone because all taggers view the murals as artwork that conveys a sense of ownership.

2. Colorizing. A national study found that a graffiti site covered with paint the same color as the graffiti was ten times less likely to be retagged. Officers in San Diego found, however, that taggers daily hit high-visibility sites (freeway access) even after colorizing. Alleys were slow to be retagged after colorizing.

3. Counseling. Counselors in a graffiti abatement project in Cathedral City, California, identified reasons for tagging and then treated it as an addiction. San Diego police endorsed counseling but asserted that tagging is criminal behavior, not an addiction.

The team developed a survey in conjunction with the San Diego Association of Governments. Police asked juveniles who had been arrested for tagging to explain their motives. Of the 59 juvenile taggers in custody, 25 admitted to tagging. The primary motives given by the taggers were boredom, recognition/popularity, member of a gang, and personal tag identification.

Finally, police analyzed past responses and their effectiveness. The responses included surveillance, citizen paint-outs, random patrol, crime reports and arrests, restorative justice, juvenile court, and probation. None of these responses seemed to deter taggers. The officers at Mid-City knew they had to look for both a different response and new resources.

Response

After in-depth scanning and analysis, officers realized that the best problem-solving approach would be to target both active taggers and potential future taggers. Youth-oriented resources would have to be the primary partners in this effort.

The police department joined with the Community Advisory Board, youth mentoring programs, city schools, the Code Compliance—Graffiti Control Program, juvenile probation, and juvenile court.

Based on the analysis, officers set up six steps to stop graffiti in Mid-City:

1. Counseling. Two social workers volunteered to help in these sessions, which were informative for the police but also designed so the taggers were counseled by the social workers in an attempt to get them to stop tagging. Ten juvenile taggers, who were chosen because they were responsible for 10 percent of the tagging in the area, set goals to stop their tagging. Each week, the taggers would meet with the counselor to discuss methods to prevent tagging. The hours would count toward their community service. Three of the ten juveniles completely stopped tagging. The group was effective, but due to lack of funding, it is no longer being implemented.

2. Paint-outs. Juveniles on probation for tagging clean up graffiti with bimonthly paint-outs at heavily tagged sites. Police and juvenile probation officers, working with Social Advocates for Youth (SAY), supervise the paint-outs. Paint and supplies come from the city's Graffiti Control Program. Community members contact the police department to identify newly tagged sites. Officers drive around the community to identify the tagged areas. The paint-outs colorize the graffiti.

3. Adopt-a-block. Community stakeholders volunteer to keep a block free of graffiti for six months. The Graffiti Control Program provides the paint and supplies.

4. Handler program. Officers are assigned to repeat juvenile offenders. The officers established a list of known chronic taggers by talking to patrol officers and detectives. The list is kept in a secured cabinet but is accessible to all officers dealing with taggers. An

officer, called a "handler," visits weekly with the tagger to monitor his behavior. The handler checks on the juvenile's school, home, and street contacts. The handler updates the juvenile's file after each visit. A zero-tolerance policy is in effect for repeat offenders. If they are not at school or at home when they are supposed to be or if their tag shows up anywhere, they are sent back to the probation officer and are ordered to perform paint-outs in the neighborhood or other community service. The purpose of the program is to let taggers know that the community and police department will no longer tolerate graffiti. The handler program has greatly assisted juvenile probation with its large caseload.

5. Murals. Students at the local junior high school paint murals on heavily tagged walls. The students work with teachers, businesses, and residents to plan and paint murals that reflect positive images of the community. The students have painted seven murals so far. Except for some minor pen marks, the murals have escaped tagging.

6. Joint patrol. Kids in Control, a youth bike team, joins police, also on bikes, to patrol highly tagged sites. The program improves the relationship between youth in the area and police officers. The youth are taught how to work together to solve crime problems, such as graffiti, in their neighborhood. Officer David Tos wrote a grant for Mid-City for Youth to raise money to buy bikes for the youths. Based on the crime statistics for graffiti, the officers concentrated on youth aged thirteen to eighteen.

Assessment

In the past sixteen months, inspections of the neighborhood recorded a 90 percent decrease in tagging. The counseling program was effective, resulting in 30 percent of graffiti taggers in the program ultimately stopping tagging. However, the unbudgeted program ended after the volunteers had finished working with the youths. Juvenile probation continues to work with the police department on the paint-outs. Probation assigns ten juveniles to bimonthly paint-outs in Mid-City.

The handler program has ten chronic graffiti taggers assigned to officers. Police have arrested two of these taggers after visiting the taggers' homes, one for drugs found in his room during a routine visit and the other for curfew violation. The police are adding more handlers to the program.

Seven murals have been painted in the popular graffiti tagging locations. So far, only one mural has been tagged. Additional murals are being planned. The youth in Kids in Control have identified twenty graffiti crews and have identified the neighborhoods in which they tag. The program currently has ten youths involved and is expected to expand to twenty by the end of June 2001. The program is still in its infancy and has yet to be evaluated.

As a result of these newly formed partnerships among existing agencies, the amount of graffiti has been reduced in Mid-City Division. Ongoing efforts and programs will continue to expand. The goal of removing graffiti as the community's biggest concern is closer to being achieved.

Source: National Institute of Justice, *Excellence in Problem-Oriented Policing: The 2000 Herman Goldstein Award Winners.* Washington, D.C.: National Institute of Justice, 2000.

At this point in the process, Goldstein (1990) interjects the issue of analyzing multiple interests. This analysis may reveal a vast amount of beneficial information and should be addressed during the systemic inquiry. A simple crime such as prostitution, which Goldstein (1990) refers to in his book, may have a compounding effect on the community as a result of its presence. Perhaps the best example of this effect returns us to the broken windows theory as articulated by Wilson and Kelling (1982). Once an abandoned building has one window broken, if the window is not repaired, it leads the way to additional broken windows in the building. This may then lead to graffiti painted on the building and the smashing of windshields on cars parked nearby. Eventually the area decays by the community's allowance of one broken window.

Goldstein (1990) articulates that the community should identify and address all of these multiple interests. At the same time, the current police response to the problem must be identified and critiqued, whether it is in the form of a program, a proactive patrol, or merely a reactive patrol (Goldstein 1990). This evaluation is essentially the final stage of the systemic inquiry, as all of the possible research and knowledge have been compiled on the problem and all of the different factors of the problem have been addressed. It is then that the police and the community must work together to create a course of action to address the problem.

The police should work with the community to create solutions to the problem that are acceptable to both. The solutions should also be tailor-made responses for the problem at hand and not a blanket response, as is so often the case in police work (Goldstein 1990). At the same time this community–police coalition is forming a response, they should also be developing alternative solutions to the problem (Goldstein 1990). The possible alternative solutions may become the key alternatives to the problem or may be implemented later if the first solution fails (Goldstein 1990). It is here that the police and community must have free rein to brainstorm various solutions that have no limiting criteria placed on them.

Officer Leake of the Memphis Police Department works with local youth by weeding a local community garden. (*Courtesy of the Memphis Police Department, Memphis, Tennessee.*)

Once a list of possible solutions has been created, the police and community coalition must choose among the possible alternatives (Goldstein 1990). As Goldstein (1990, 141) states, "any single tailor-made response to a problem is likely to consist of a blend of alternatives." Although a single choice may be selected, the integration of various aspects from various alternatives is acceptable. Reaching this decision, however, will often prove difficult, and the choice should be made based on a host of varying considerations. These considerations, according to Goldstein (1990, 143), include the following:

- The potential that the response has to reduce the problem
- The specific impact that the response will have on the most serious aspect of the problem (or those social interests deemed most important)
- The extent to which the response is preventive in nature, thereby reducing recurrence or more acute consequences that are more difficult to handle
- The degree to which the response intrudes into the lives of individuals and depends on legal sanctions and the potential use of force
- The attitude of the different communities most likely to be affected by adoption
- The financial costs
- The availability of police authority and resources
- The legality and civility of the response and the way in which it is likely to affect overall relationships with the police
- The ease with which the response can be implemented

Once the choice has been made, it is important to implement the solution in a timely manner and to not make excessive alterations to the plan because initially people believe it might not work. Instead, the program that is implemented must be evaluated to determine the success or failure, as well as the possible need for one of the alternative responses (Goldstein 1990). The type of evaluation is also left to the devices of the police and community coalition. Each tailor-made response will most likely necessitate a tailor-made evaluation. The evaluation, whether a pre/postanalysis, a survey, or a police data analysis, must be done in a fair and unbiased manner to truly assess the viability of the program.

This process, from identifying the problem to evaluating the tailor-made response to the problem, is the concept of problem-oriented policing as articulated by Herman Goldstein. The steps in the process are similar to those articulated by Eck and Spelman in their SARA model. SARA is an acronym for the problem-solving process consisting of four stages: (1) scanning, (2) analysis, (3) response, and (4) assessment (Eck and Spelman 1987a) (see Figure 5-2). These four stages became the ongoing process for problem-oriented policing during the study at Newport News, Virginia, and later at other police departments adopting the program. However, the SARA model, despite largely being a derivative of the problem-oriented policing model just reviewed, has a simple method for easy application and has been tested in a variety of jurisdictions, allowing it to become a widely accepted model for problem solving.

The National Institute of Justice chose Newport News, Virginia, as its test site for several reasons. The three chief reasons were (1) the police department consisted of 280 employees and was therefore a manageable size; (2) the city was close to Washington, D.C.; and (3) the police chief was already familiar with the background of problem-oriented policing and was committed to the program from the beginning (Eck and Spelman 1987a). The initial stages of the study began with the creation of a task force in 1985.

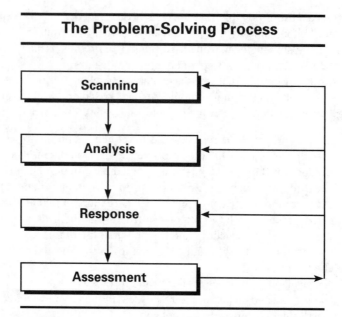

The Problem-Solving Process

FIGURE 5-2   The problem-solving process. *Source:* William
Spelman and John E. Eck, "Problem-Oriented Policing,"
National Institute of Justice: Research in Brief, January 1987.

 COP IN ACTION

Reducing Crime and Disorder on Douglas Promenade Isle of Man Constabulary

Scanning

The problem-oriented policing project by the Isle of Man Constabulary in the Isle of Man, British Isles was names Project Centurion. The problem was the high levels of alcohol related crimes occurring on the Douglas Promenade. The scanning phase was conducted in three separate phases. Phase I consisted of an increased number of public meetings attempting to gather anecdotal regarding the alcohol related crimes. Phase II was to conduct surveys of local citizens/business owners based on some of the information gathered in phase I. Finally, phase III consisted of statistical research with the goal of exploring the causes of the alcohol related crimes based on available information.

Analysis

The analysis of the interviews, surveys, and data revealed three major findings. First, the police found that there was a clear correlation between peaks of assault, criminal damage, and disorder with the times of customers leaving nightclubs at weekends, particularly after "pay day." Second, they found that a lack of late night public transport and limited private transport, such as taxis, created situations that increased crime. And finally, although local youth were not found to be the main cause of the crime, the analysis did reveal that there was little in the way of facilities or activities for young people, thus causing large gatherings of youth with little to do.

Response

Responses included an increase in intelligence led policing, policing that takes action based upon analyses like the one conducted for Project Centurion. Improved cooperation between the police and the public was implemented, and the police worked closer with those agencies that license taxis and youth services. In the Douglas Promenade five new taxi stands were created, along with greater taxi stand management, and, to increase the number of taxi cabs in the area, 12 new licenses were issued. In addition, recognizing the security of the taxi drivers was critical to the response working, improved operating conditions for the taxi drives was implemented through a "Taxiwatch" initiative. Finally, a number of events, activities, and facilities were created, directed at the local youth.

Assessment

An assessment of Project Centurion demonstrated a 33.4% reduction in the crimes of assault, criminal damage, and public order offenses. In addition, improved police–citizen relationships between the project partners were generated. A future public meeting was set to assess the project, identify new problems, and begin problem solving on these new priorities in order to continue to improve the image of the Douglas Promenade and improve the quality of life in that area for all.

Source: Chris Pycroft, "Project Centurion: Reducing Crime and Disorder on Douglas Promenade, Isle of Man, British Isles." Herman Goldstein Award Winner 2005.

The task force had to determine if the problem-solving techniques would work in a police department without altering the organization and if these techniques would be effective (Eck and Spelman 1987a). Perhaps the most difficult step in the process, however, was that "the theory of problem-oriented policing had to be translated into a practice of problem-oriented policing" (Eck and Spelman 1987a, 6). The task force accomplished this task by not only developing practical methods on its own but also soliciting outside counsel, including Herman Goldstein (Eck and Spelman 1987a). The model the task force developed became known as the SARA model (see Figure 5-2).

The scanning stage of the SARA model consists of reviewing the various calls and complaints in a neighborhood and attempting to identify a problem (Eck and Spelman 1987a). It was not the mission of a small group of selected officers to identify these problems but rather the responsibility of every member of the department (Eck and Spelman 1987a). It was also the responsibility of the police officers to utilize every potential source of information to assist them in identifying the problems, ranging from seeking assistance from members of the department such as vice and the crimes analysis unit to seeking information from the community such as the local schools and neighborhood watch groups (Eck and Spelman 1987a). However, the problems had to be identified as legitimate problems with a root cause and not individual incidents with no connection, in the same manner as Goldstein described in his identification phase. The officers were then to list those problems discovered, conduct a limited investigation to verify their legitimacy, and establish a prioritized list of those problems needing further analysis (Eck and Spelman 1987a). Once a list was compiled, a particular problem or, in some cases, multiple problems would be carried into the next stage of the SARA model.

The second stage of the SARA model is the analysis stage. This stage has two objectives that the officer should accomplish before moving on to the third stage of the model.

The first objective is to obtain as much information as possible on the problem and develop a full understanding of the problem (Eck and Spelman 1987a). The officer uses a checklist in this stage to gather information in a methodical manner by addressing "three categories of problem characteristics: actors (victims, offenders, and third parties); incidents (physical setting, social context, sequence of events); and responses (by the community and its institutions)" (Eck and Spelman 1987a, 47) (see Figure 5-3). Once this

Actors
    Victims
        Lifestyle
        Security measures taken
        Victimization history
    Offenders
        Identity and physical description
        Lifestyle, education, employment histor
        Criminal history
    Third parties
        Personal data
        Connection to victimization
Incidents
    Sequence of events
        Events preceding criminal act
        Event itself
        Events following criminal act
    Physical contact
        Time
        Location
        Access control and surveillance
    Social context
        Likelihood and probable actions of
            witnesses
        Apparent attitude of residents toward
            neighborhood
Responses
    Community
        Neighborhood affected by problem
        City as a whole
        People outside the city
    Institutional
        Criminal justice agencies
        Other public agencies
        Mass media
        Business sector

FIGURE 5-3   The problem analysis model. *Source:* William Spelman and John E. Eck, "Problem-Oriented Policing," *National Institute of Justice: Research in Brief, January 1987.*

review of the information on the checklist is completed to the best of the officer's ability, he or she moves on to the second part of the analysis stage—developing the response.

In developing a set of responses to the problem, the options the officer creates must remain consistent with the problem as identified in the information-gathering process (Eck and Spelman 1987a). A variety of responses should be considered for implementation, and they should not be immediately dismissed as impossible or foolish to implement. The solutions to the problem can be derived from the officer, through assistance on the part of the community, or through contact with other members of the police department. Regardless of how the list is created, there should be a variety of possible responses created in order for the officer to move into the third stage of the SARA model.

The third stage of the SARA model is the response stage, and it is here that the officer must meet two objectives: "Select a solution and implement it" (Eck and Spelman 1987a, 48). The necessity of developing multiple responses then becomes clear in this stage, for without a variety of choices, the police officer would be forced to implement only one or two courses of action, which may not be beneficial to solving the problem. It also assists in the final stage of the SARA model if the solution selected does not pan out as a viable solution; an alternative from the list can then be selected.

In selecting the particular response to be utilized, the officer must consider many of the same things Goldstein articulated in his model of problem-oriented policing, such as financial costs and the overall effect on the community. However, once a response has been selected, it must be implemented without reservation and allowed to reach the final stage of the SARA model.

 ## COP IN ACTION

Homeless Men's Shelter, Charlotte-Mecklenburg Police Department, North Carolina

Scanning

The Uptown Men's Shelter at 1210 North Tryon Street provides temporary housing, mental health counseling, substance abuse treatment, and employment and permanent housing assistance to 200 homeless men. The shelter is located near a soup kitchen on a major business corridor adjacent to a residential neighborhood. Calls for service at the Uptown Shelter have increased over the years. Police in the David Three District reported that many responses to the shelter did not require police attention. Area businesses complained of losing business because patrons linked criminal activity with the homeless population. Police found that many of the homeless in the neighborhood were not associated with the shelter.

Analysis

Community Policing Coordinators Nathan King and Ginny Woodlief devised a survey of 911 calls at the shelter to determine whether the shelter's management had taken appropriate action before calling. The survey disclosed that most of the calls concerned matters that should have been resolved by the shelter's management. Police found that managers of the shelter were poorly trained and had little understanding of the appropriate use of 911. Of the 642 calls placed for service to the shelter in 1998, 78 percent required neither an offense report nor an arrest. Police clearly were being used as surrogate shelter managers.

The officers interviewed residents and business owners and found that the respondents assumed that shelter residents caused all the crime in the area. In 1998, 216 suspects listed the shelter as home at the time of their arrest. In truth, only 88 of the suspects were either shelter visitors or residents when they were arrested. Suspects listed the shelter as their home because the address gave them easier access to a state identification card. The cards facilitate the cashing of paychecks from temporary labor services and government subsistence programs.

The officers found that the shelter's few written policies on management were inconsistently applied. For example, some managers would place a resident on probation, others would ban the resident for several hours, and still others invoked permanent bans—all for the same offense. Moreover, the physical appearance of the shelter and its surroundings helped foster crime: An overgrown lot bordering the shelter provided concealment; the shelter parking lot was poorly lit and had two entrances, which hindered efforts to control access; residents walked the railroad next to the shelter to get to the soup kitchen; and high grass along the tracks provided one more concealed area.

Officers King and Woodlief set several goals: (1) Establish a productive working relationship with the shelter staff; (2) improve management of the shelter; (3) reduce the number of calls for service to the shelter; (4) reduce criminal activity at the shelter; and (5) reduce the fear that the facility generated among residents of the neighborhood.

Response

Shelter staffers denied they had a problem, and the shelter director denied any obligation to the community. Officers King and Woodlief then decided to galvanize the community. They suggested to the North Tryon Street Business Coalition and to residents of the Lockwood area that they confront shelter management about their concerns. The officers also spoke with the shelter's board of directors and with a county commissioner. The commissioner reminded the managers that county funds are a critical component of the shelter's budget. The board of directors replaced the site director with the day manager, who had been more cooperative with police.

The survey that police had taken of the 911 calls helped single out shift managers who needed additional training in enforcement of shelter rules. The survey provided examples of improper use of 911, which in turn gave shelter management a clear picture of the problem. Each supervisor now logs the nature and outcome of 911 calls placed during the supervisor's shift. In their training of staff and managers, the officers suggested ways to identify potentially volatile situations so that police could be called before violence broke out. The officers emphasized the distinct roles of police and shelter managers.

The shelter improved the use of ID badges. Police noted that it was difficult to identify shelter residents, which hindered the timely sharing of information between police and management. Officers realized that an identification system and tighter controls at the shelter would help dispel neighborhood fears and prejudice. Shelter managers adopted a written policy, consistently applied across all shifts, that articulates the grounds for banning people from the shelter. The shelter improved lighting on its property and joined in efforts to clean up the immediate area. The shelter posted "No Loitering" signs and closed one of the two entrances to the parking lot. Police expanded their authority in the area by adopting agreements with several businesses and with Norfolk Southern Railroad. The agreements, known as "Authorization to Act as Agent," empower police to enforce the law on private property in the absence of the owner or manager.

Officers set up a method for shelter residents to pass information about criminal activity to an intermediary on the shelter staff, who in turn provides the information to police. This allows residents to share information with police without fear of being intimidated or of becoming known as a snitch. The program is another way that officers hope to gain the trust of a population that traditionally has had an uneasy relationship with police.

Assessment

Police are aware that correcting problems at the shelter is an ongoing effort, not in small part because of the transience of the homeless and the high turnover rate among shelter employees. The most obvious measure of success is the reduction in 911 calls for service to the shelter during 1999. In 1998, calls had reached a high of 642. The next year brought only 282 calls for service to the shelter.

Members of the North Tryon Street Business Coalition and residents of the Lockwood area say they believe that improvements in management procedures and in the physical environment have gone a long way to reduce many of the problems—loitering, assaults, drug dealing—associated with the shelter. Residents and business owners alike have changed their perception of the shelter, believing that the shelter wants to be a part of the solution, not part of the problem.

Source: National Institute of Justice, *Excellence in Problem-Oriented Policing: The 2000 Herman Goldstein Award Winners.* Washington, D.C.: National Institute of Justice, 2000.

Eck and Spelman (1987a) discuss one additional item in the response stage of the SARA model: categorizing the solution selected into one of five groups to assist in not only the overall understanding of what the response is attempting to accomplish but also ways it will be reviewed in the final stage of the SARA model. Accordingly, each response should fit into one of five groups (Eck and Spelman 1987a, 49):

1. Solutions designed to totally eliminate a problem
2. Solutions designed to substantially reduce a problem
3. Solutions designed to reduce the harm created by the problem
4. Solutions designed to deal with a problem better (treat people more humanely, reduce costs, or increase effectiveness)
5. Solutions designed to remove the problem from police consideration

To understand the types of problems that fit into these categories, Eck and Spelman (1987a, 49–50) detail that "group one solutions probably will be most often applied to small, simple problems—problems affecting a small number of people and problems that have only recently arisen," whereas "group two solutions will be applied most often to neighborhood crime and disorder problems." Group three solutions would "be applied most often to problems where it is almost impossible to reduce the number of incidents that they create, but it is possible to alter the characteristics of these incidents," and the fourth group of solutions would only "be applied to problems that are jurisdiction-wide and involve larger social concerns" (Eck and Spelman 1987a, 50). The final group, group five, would essentially be applied to those problems that are created by specific businesses or groups and are the result of the way they do business or those problems that cannot be handled by the police (Eck and Spelman 1987a). These categories of solutions essentially provide the goal of the response selected and in the final stage of the SARA model will "affect how its effectiveness should be judged" (Eck and Spelman 1987a, 50). This brings us to the final stage of the SARA model—the assessment stage.

"Dunk-a-Deputy!" A fund-raiser at a local fair to raise money for a substance
abuse prevention program called Community Outreach Program (COP).
(Courtesy of the Frederick County Sheriff's Department, Frederick, Maryland.)

In the assessment stage, the type of problem and the group of solutions it falls into
will depend on how it is evaluated (Eck and Spelman 1987a). The type of problem and
the type of solution also provide some insight into the type of assessment tool utilized.
Every problem is different, and different styles of evaluation are thus necessary. The
goal or objective in the assessment stage is essentially to provide feedback to the police
department, and it allows the officer to determine if the response selected is working
and whether an alternative response should be implemented (Eck and Spelman 1987a).

The success of the SARA model in Newport News and other police departments
(e.g., Santa Ana, California; see Jesilow et al. 1998) that have implemented the problem-
solving process is perhaps best assessed by the four basic principles of the program that
the police chief of Newport News and the National Institute of Justice insisted on for
the program (Spelman and Eck 1987b). It was determined that the design for the practical model would allow for total participation by everyone in the police department, use
a wide range of information available to the police, encourage a variety of responses not
limited to typical police responses, and, perhaps most important, ensure that the program is reproducible in any police department, regardless of size (Spelman and Eck
1987b). The SARA model was able to accomplish all four principles and has become a
successful model in the practical implementation of problem-oriented policing.

In the late 1990s, two criminal justice professors, Ronald V. Clarke and John E. Eck,
both well entrenched in the development of problem-oriented policing, were given the
opportunity to develop a much more specific manual for problem solving in England.
While this manual was based on the SARA model, it attempted to provide more details on

research methodologies, the use of statistics with regard to comprehensive databases, and the use of geographical mapping software. Because the manual was particularly specific to British policing, through a collaborative effort with the Center for Problem Oriented Policing, Clarke and Eck updated their earlier manual to develop *Crime Analysis for Problem Solving in 60 Small Steps*, which was published in 2005. Their 60 "small steps" walk individuals with an advanced understanding of problem solving through the entire process, from how to prepare themselves for conducting crime analysis through the communication of their findings (see Table 5-2).

TABLE 5-2   *Crime Analysis for Problem Solvers in 60 Small Steps: The 60 Steps*

Prepare Yourself

1. Rethink your job
2. Be the local crime expert
3. Know what is effective (and not) in policing

Learn about Problem-Oriented Policing

4. Become a POP expert
5. Be true to POP
6. Be very crime specific
7. Be guided by SARA—not led astray!

Study Environmental Criminology

8. Use the problem analysis triangle
9. Know that opportunity makes the thief
10. Put yourself in the offender's shoes
11. Expect offenders to react
12. Don't be discouraged by the displacement doomsters
13. Expect diffusion of benefits

Scan for Crime Problems

14. Use the CHEERS test when defining problems (Six required elements of a problem: Community; Harm; Expectation; Events; Recurring; and Similarity)
15. Know what kind of problem you have
16. Study the journey to crime
17. Know how hot spots develop
18. Learn if the 80-20 rule applies (where, in theory, 20 percent of some things are responsible for 80 precent of the outcomes)

Analyze in Depth

19. Research your problem
20. Formulate hypotheses
21. Collect your own data
22. Examine your data distributions
23. Diagnose your hot spot
24. Know when to use high-definition maps
25. Pay attention to daily and weekly rhythms

26. Take account of long-term change
27. Know how to use rates and denominators
28. Identify risky facilities
29. Be ready for repeat victimization
30. Consider repeat offending
31. Know the products that are CRAVED (Concealable, Removable, Available, Valuable, Enjoyable, and Disposable) by thieves
32. Conduct case control studies
33. Measure association
34. Look for crime facilitators
35. Understand the crime from beginning to end
36. Be sure to answer the five "W" (and one "H") questions: Who, What, When, Where, Why, and How
37. Recognize that to err is human

Find a Practical Response

38. Embrace your key role at response
39. Increase the effort of crime
40. Increase the risks of crime
41. Reduce the rewards of crime
42. Reduce provocations
43. Remove excuses for crime
44. Find the owner of the problem
45. Choose responses likely to be implemented

Assess the Impact

46. Conduct a process evaluation
47. Know how to use controls
48. Consider geographical and temporal displacement
49. Examine displacement to other targets, tactics, and crime types
50. Watch for other offenders moving in
51. Be alert to unexpected benefits
52. Expect premature falls in crime
53. Test for significance

Communicate Effectively

54. Tell a clear story
55. Make clear maps
56. Use simple tables
57. Use simple figures
58. Organize powerful presentations
59. Become and effective presenter
60. Contribute to the store of knowledge

Source: Ronald V. Clarke and John E. Eck, *Crime Analysis for Problem Solvers in 60 Small Steps.* Washington, D.C.: Office of Community-Oriented Policing Services, 2005. Also available on-line at http://www.popcenter.org/learning/60steps/index.cfm?page=Welcome

CONCLUSION

Problem-oriented policing, although created separately from community-oriented policing, is the third and final component of the community policing model. Problem-oriented policing can function within a police department based on its own merits and is not synonymous with community-oriented policing; however, it is important to remember that community-oriented policing is synonymous with problem-oriented policing. Without the problem-oriented component, community-oriented policing cannot be fully implemented.

The creation of problem-oriented policing is credited to Herman Goldstein, who has written in detail about the philosophy and concepts surrounding this program. A clear and detailed method of implementing problem-oriented policing can be abstracted from these details; however, it is the SARA model that is most often utilized when a police department uses the concept in a practical setting. The clarity and reproducibility of the SARA model—scanning, analysis, response, and assessment—allow for any police department across the nation to easily implement all of the tenets of problem-oriented policing and in turn the overall concept of community-oriented policing.

Finally, recent research into the success of problem-oriented policing has found that the most successful means of implementing problem-oriented policing is by "giving an officer a specialized community policing job assignment" (Dejong, Mastrofski, and Parks 2001). Moving officers into the community-oriented policing role, allows officers more time to dedicate themselves to engaging in the problem-solving methods, thereby reducing crime and disorder. The importance of implementing community-oriented policing with problem-oriented policing is also becoming very clear because there is a strong consistency in the reported success of problem-oriented policing to control various crimes and disorders, such as burglary and larceny (Eck and Spelman 1987), prostitution (Matthews 1990), and street-level drug dealing (Hope 1994) as well as violent street crime (Braga et al. 1999). In sum, problem-oriented policing appears to work and work well.

COP ON THE WORLD WIDE WEB

Herman Goldstein Award

http://www.ncjrs.org/pdffiles1/nij/182731.pdf

Excellent case studies on POP.

Jane's COP Cases for Problem Solving

http://copcase.janes.com

Note: Full access requires money, but sample cases are provided.

Operation Mantle, a Problem-Oriented Policing Case Study from Australia

http://www.aic.gov.au/publications/tandi/tandi190.html

Problem-Oriented Policing: Reflections on the First Twenty Years

http://www.usdoj.gov/cops/cp_resources/pubs_ppse/default.htm#Problem_Oriented_Policing

San Diego, California, Police Department

http://www.sannet.gov/police

REVIEW QUESTIONS

1. Describe in detail how Herman Goldstein developed problem-oriented policing. What was his reasoning for doing so?
2. Define and describe the four steps in the SARA model.
3. Explain the relationship among actors, incidents, and responses and why this relationship is significant for understanding problem-oriented policing.

CHAPTER 6

Implementing Community-Oriented Policing

The art of progress is to preserve order amid change and to preserve change amid order.

—Alfred North Whitehead

CHAPTER OBJECTIVES

- Understand who initiates COP.
- Understand who should initiate COP.
- Explain how the three components of COP work together.
- Define the term *diffusion* as it relates to the three components.
- Understand how the philosophy of COP is implemented.
- Define Lindbloom's incremental theory.
- Understand how COP is often related to business theory.
- Define *logical incrementalism.*
- Know the eleven leadership actions under incrementalism.
- Recognize that there is no precise method of implementation.
- Understand the five stages of implementation.
- Understand the importance of communication in the implementation process.
- Understand the importance of training in the implementation process.

Community-oriented policing, as previously described, consists of three integral parts: strategic-oriented policing, neighborhood-oriented policing, and problem-oriented policing. These three components, when utilized together in a system to address criminal problems and order maintenance issues, are not only the conceptual framework of community-oriented policing but the practical framework as well. To implement this framework, all three components must be integrated into a continual process that operates on the foundation of mutual dependence. This style of policing does not work in a consecutive manner or cyclical manner, but rather it is a web of interdependence in which each component complements the others. From the initial establishment of the program within a community to the continual process of planning and evaluating, the three components must work in concert to accomplish the goals of reducing fear, alleviating criminal problems indigenous to a community, and addressing the order maintenance issues that affect the sense of community in a specific geographical setting. The integration of these programs is critical to undertaking the community-oriented approach to policing. If one component is not implemented with the concept of community-oriented policing, then the failure of the program is predetermined. Understanding this concept is the key to this chapter.

The most difficult aspect of community-oriented policing is transforming policy into action. How does a police department transform a philosophy into some type of executable program? This implementation process requires extensive research and planning by the police department if it is to succeed. Implementation, then, becomes the most critical aspect of community-oriented policing.

Police administrators must be aware of all the obstacles to the implementation of community-oriented policing. The new policy and programs will affect the line officers, which can add or detract from the implementation process. The environment of the police department and the attitudes of individual officers responsible for implementing and carrying the programs to fruition can impact the success of the policy. Because these factors vary from police department to police department, it is important that the climate of the police department be taken into consideration during the planning stages to maximize the potential for success.

The climate of the police department consists of a wide variety of variables that should be analyzed to assess the current status of the police department. Gaines (1994) describes this status as being the organizational maturity of the police department. These variables consist of two predominant factors: management and the organizational structure. If managers currently have good working relationships with officers and provide leadership, discipline, and control, then the potential for moving the police department to community-oriented policing increases. Equally important is the organizational structure of the police department; if it has a clear chain of command, strong division of labor, unity of command, and reasonable span of control, the potential for implementing community-oriented policing is once again increased. Therefore, the climate of the police department, or its organizational maturity, must be assessed to determine whether the police department can move toward community-oriented policing or whether some areas of the police department need to be addressed prior to implementing the systemic approach.

A study by the RAND Corporation (Wilson 2005) attempted to determine which of these factors needed to exist in order to create the most likely circumstances for the implementation of community-oriented policing. Oddly enough, although supported by other research (Maguire et al. 1997; Zhao 1996), police departments in the West are more likely to implement community-oriented policing than in any other region of the United States. Other influencing factors included organization age (i.e., the older the agency, the more likely it was to implement community-oriented policing because older organizations are more established and thus able to make the changes necessary to implement this systemic approach to policing. Population mobility had a positive influence on the implementation of community-oriented policing, perhaps because mobile populations are more receptive to such programs. In addition, those agencies that received COP funding from the federal government and those that had the formal structural controls of community-oriented policing (e.g., written policies, directives, etc.) were more likely to implement community-oriented policing. It was also noted that the more often an agency faced police chief turnover, the less likely it was to implement community-oriented policing. Finally, the most influential factor for an agency's implementation of community-oriented policing was its past implementation of community-oriented policing. In other words, the implementation of community-oriented policing had lasting effects that an agency could build on to advance its community-oriented policing program.

The ability to move community-oriented policing from policy to program to institutionalization is based in large part on the management's ability to implement change. Any organization will resist change; however, within a police department, that resistance can be a little more stubborn. Effectively changing a police department is essentially changing a subculture and a bureaucracy, two of the most difficult things for even the best of managers to change. To effect change within these institutions, there must be extensive and continual planning as well as goal setting in a long-term scenario, which must factor in institutionalization of community-oriented policing as the ultimate goal.

 ## COP IN ACTION

Who Is the Customer?

Americans are born customers. No other society in history has placed so many diverse products and services before its citizens. Children become ingrained with the basic concepts of consumerism before they learn to tie their shoes. Corporations spend literally billions of dollars a year attempting to determine what their customers want. In general, our culture places a strong emphasis on the bond between the providers of goods and services and their customers. Why, then, do law enforcement agencies have such difficulty identifying what their customers want? Indeed, it seems that the police have lost sight of who the customer really is. This confusion seriously hampers the ability of law enforcement to control crime and protect communities. If we cannot identify who our customers are and what they want, how can we adequately serve them?

In the bygone days of 1950s America, police officers maintained close ties with the citizens they served. In the fictional television town of Mayberry, Sheriff Andy Taylor understood very clearly who his customers were: The citizens of Mayberry. While conditions in the real world may never have been quite so idyllic, individuals who began a policing career in the 1960s and 1970s nonetheless have witnessed a vast change in the way law enforcement does business.

Most important, our perception of the customer changed from citizen to criminal. Granted, many of the forces that led to this shift were external, nurtured by rising crime rates and a simultaneous shift toward leniency within the criminal justice system. By the 1970s, the role of the police in society had shifted from proactive to almost exclusively reactive. As part of this transformation, wrongdoers became the main focus of attention within law enforcement. Criminals, in a sense, became the customers. Law enforcement became preoccupied with criminals, while relegating its true customers—citizens—to second-class.

Any business that subscribed to such thinking would soon be out of business. But, law enforcement internalized this odd view into nearly every facet of its operations. Citizens, once a primary focus of law enforcement, became regarded as outsiders, meddlesome at best, troublesome at worst.

As a profession, law enforcement must rediscover its true customer base. Successful corporations devote a considerable portion of their budgets to this effort and spend a great deal of time determining what their customers want. Of course, individual law enforcement agencies do not possess the resources of major corporations, but that should not stop them from identifying their customers' needs. By taking some small steps, agencies can revitalize their relationship with the citizens they serve.

The first step is to determine what to ask customers. For example, to gauge the crime problem in certain areas, it may be helpful to find out if residents have been victimized or have seen criminal activity in their neighborhoods within a certain time frame. It also is a good idea to elicit citizens' opinions regarding possible solutions to problems cited. Regardless of the specific questions asked, the effort to elicit information from customers should represent a long-term commitment on the part of the agency. Several attempts may be required before sufficient relevant feedback is received. In addition, as law enforcement addresses their needs, citizens' views may change.

Once an agency surveys its customers, the next step is to respond to their needs. In many ways, this process represents an integral component of community-oriented policing (COP). While COP does not replace traditional law enforcement methods, it does provide a proactive mechanism for agencies to satisfy the needs of their customers. COP is a philosophy that involves the entire department, not just a group of select officers. In order for COP to succeed, all personnel within an agency should be trained to see the "big picture." This picture consists of citizens working with the police to address common issues and to solve community problems.

Despite the logic of this arrangement, administrators may find officers reluctant to embrace this seemingly simple concept. To ask officers accustomed to vehicle-based patrolling to get out of their squad cars and talk with citizens door-to-door may be an unpopular request. At the beginning, it may not be easy. However, once officers speak with citizens in positive situations, attitudes change. Instead of constantly being bombarded with negative situations, officers have the opportunity to see firsthand that the majority of citizens support the police and their efforts to control crime. As law enforcement responds to the needs of its customers, citizen–police cooperation becomes the basis of a strong community-oriented policing effort.

To address community crime problems adequately, law enforcement must recognize its true customer base. During the past several decades, the police view in this area has become inverted. We have allowed our enemy—the criminal element—to become our primary focus. Meanwhile, our real customers—the citizens we serve—often are viewed as the enemy. For community-oriented policing to be successful, this distorted view must be corrected. For when it comes to community safety, all of us are customers. Appreciating that we are part of a much larger picture helps us see the value of what we do. The police do not exist for criminals. We are sworn to serve and protect citizens.

Solutions for the problems that face our communities will not come overnight. But we stand a better chance of reaching our goals if we work with citizens rather than against them. The time has come to remember who the customer is, to find out what they want, and to work at finding solutions to community problems together.

Source: Adapted from G. Lynn Nelson, "Who Is the Customer?" *FBI Law Enforcement Bulletin,* March 1995, pp. 24–26.

The Dallas Police Department's mobile community-oriented policing van. (*Courtesy of the Dallas Police Department, Dallas, Texas.*)

The management technique of incrementalism is the key to full implementation over the long term because it assists management in institutionalizing community-oriented policing without being excessively intrusive into the operations of the police and allows for experimentation and alterations to the implementation process along the way. Although police departments implement community-oriented policing in a variety of ways, most implement in stages. Five stages for the implementation of community-oriented policing can be identified, commencing with the planning stage, moving through the micro-community-oriented policing, transitional, and macro-community-oriented policing stages, and culminating in the final stage, the institutionalization of the original policy. Through an understanding of change, incrementalism, and the various stages of implementation, community-oriented policing should find a place in every police department across the nation.

WHO INITIATES?

Who initiates community-oriented policing is a question academics often ponder when they discuss the conceptual feasibility of the program. Inherent within the title, one would assume that the initiating party of community-oriented policing should be the community itself. However, realizing the current state of life in the United States, the community that we look for to implement programs along these lines is often broken, transient, or nonexistent in the sense that members of the "community" desire to remain anonymous and do not want to get involved. Without the sense of community or any established methods of communicating between neighbors, there is little likelihood that the community at large is suddenly going to sign on to a program that brings them together, along with the police and local government, to clean up the neighborhood and solve all of their problems. Living in a high-rise building in the center of a city, despite the close proximity, does not create a better sense of community than living in a preplanned community of single-family dwellings. The lack of community in a society that tends to migrate toward more densely populated areas poses problems on many varying levels.

Extensive research in the field explores the type of people who participate in voluntary organizations and those who do not. The primary group of people who participate in these types of community programs are generally homeowners with a middle-class income who are well educated, are married, and have children (Skogan and Maxfield 1981). Although community-oriented policing is directed at those individuals fitting these characteristics, it is also aimed at every type of community with every type of people and all their varying characteristics.

Directing the efforts of community-oriented policing toward those communities suffering from crime and disorder will always be an issue. This is not to say that those fitting the characteristics described do not have their own set of unique problems or that they should not have their needs addressed, but the severity is generally not as critical an issue in these types of neighborhoods. Therefore, it is probably safe to conclude that those neighborhoods where organized communities exist may more readily initiate a form of community-oriented policing, and those communities that are disorganized and need the assistance and implementation of this style of policing will most likely not initiate the systemic approach. As Cardarelli, McDevitt, and Baum (1998, 413) explain, "residents in neighborhoods at the low-end of the economic spectrum, for example, may have a critical need for police services, but lack the kinds of organizational structures necessary to access these services." In sum, those communities that are in the greatest need of community-oriented policing will, in most cases, not initiate the philosophy.

Recognizing the problems in determining who initiates community-oriented policing, the focus must then shift to one of understanding not necessarily who should implement but who are the actors involved. The key actors in community-oriented policing are the police and the community. The broad definitions of each must be relegated to all-inclusive terms to satisfy the current explanation. The police or the community may initiate community-oriented policing, and either the police or the community may respond to the implementation of community-oriented policing. Utilizing a simple box chart (see Figure 6-1), we can see that the police can initiate and respond (I), the police can initiate and the community respond (II), the community can initiate and the police respond (III), the community can initiate and the community respond (IV), or, ideally, the police and community initiate and the police and community both respond (V). Each of the first four scenarios presents many considerations that weigh on the future success of the systemic approach to policing, while the fifth scenario is presented as ideal community-oriented policing.

It is most likely that for community-oriented policing to be initiated, it must be done on the part of the police. The majority of police departments in the United States that have initiated the systemic approach have had to do so with the police department acting as the catalyst. As Cardarelli, McDevitt, and Baum (1998, 413) explain, "in accepting this responsibility, however, they would do best to coordinate their efforts with those public agencies who are better suited to resolve some of the problems that are detrimental to establishing a sense of social cohesion within the troubled neighborhoods, such as abandoned housing, poor street lighting, non-existent recreational and employment opportunities, and

Who Initiates?

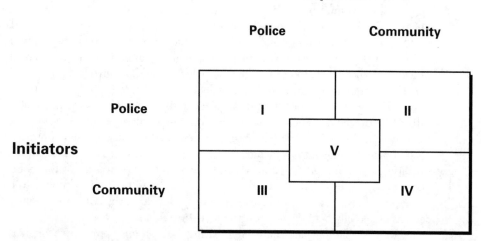

FIGURE 6-1   Who initiates community-oriented policing?

graffiti-laden parks and public buildings." Therefore, what happens after the department has created and implemented the systemic approach can affect the outcome. In some cases the police department may have created the program with the intent of including the community, but as a result of community apathy and perhaps as a result of some initial success without the community, the police may find it easier to exclude the community from any future participation in the systemic approach (see Figure 6-1, I). A second potential drawback is if the police initiate and the community comes to recognize the increased benefits that do not require their assistance, the community members may resign themselves to a form of learned helplessness. They may become so dependent on the police that they abdicate any and all responsibility and authority to the police rather than attempting to achieve a beneficial relationship based on a mutual understanding. A third drawback is the possibility that as the police are attempting to draw the community into the systemic approach, the community may become suspicious, reluctant, and, in extreme cases, militant toward the concept.

It is important to remember, however, that the function of community-oriented policing is the involvement of the community in both fighting crime and addressing order maintenance issues. Therefore, it would be inappropriate and unhealthy for the program if the police implement the concept and ignore the community. Community-oriented policing is not a police-only program. The police department must attempt to integrate the community with the police in the very rudimentary stages of creating community-oriented policing. However, recognizing that community members are often reticent about working with the police, the police frequently have to "sell" the concept to an unwilling public, but they should never stop trying to include the public in every possible way (see Figure 6-1, II).

In rare situations, strong community ties and frustration with criminal problems, order maintenance issues, or both will lead the community to initiate community-oriented policing and to attempt to draw in the police (see Figure 6-1, III). This situation is essentially the reverse of scenario II, in which the police attempt to "sell" the systemic approach to the community; here the community tries to "sell" the new policing approach to the police. Whether the community merely lobbies its local politicians or police department to implement community-oriented policing out of a desire for more effective police or it actually implements many of the programs and concepts under the systemic approach, the community initiates and the police must follow suit. This approach can be healthy for a community because community-oriented policing is largely focused on what the community needs and wants; with the initiation on the part of the community, the message will most likely be very clear. Although community members may also meet police resistance to the idea, they, like the police, should not give up easily.

However, in some cases the police may be so well entrenched in a method and way of conducting their business that the resistance to changing the way they police may be difficult to overcome. The community attempting to initiate community-oriented policing may find itself failing to include the police in its decisions and may venture down the road of taking things into its own hands (see Figure 6-1, IV). This approach can be beneficial if the community's actions do not overstep the boundaries of the police. If the community begins to encroach on what are considered by the local police to be police duties, conflicts can arise. And in the worst-case scenario, the community may either be seen as or actually begin conducting vigilante acts.

Obviously, the fifth alternative of creating the systemic approach through a concerted effort on the part of both the police and the community, with both the police and the community responding to the implementation, would be ideal. This concept of ideal community-oriented policing would then see both of the actors involved in initiating and responding to the systemic approach to policing through planning, creating, implementing, and evaluating the concept.

A good example of this can be found in Chicago's movement toward its Chicago Alternative Policing Strategy (CAPS) (Fung 2001; Skogan and Hartnett 1997). While the police department was searching for alternative solutions to its problems of crime and disorder, two Chicago advocacy groups were also attempting to make policing more community-centered. Leaders from the Chicago Alliance for Neighborhood Safety (CANS) were using their various expertise in community mobilization to bring the police department into its vision of community-oriented policing, while at the same time the police department was moving toward community-oriented policing reforms. As a result, Mayor Richard M. Daley became more interested in moving community-oriented policing along, and "the intersection of professional [police], political [mayor's office], and civic interests [CANS] led quietly to the formulation of a participatory variant of community policing that was piloted in five of the city's twenty-five police districts beginning in 1993 and then expanded to the entire city in 1995" (Fung 2001, 78). What was achieved out of these reforms consists of the creation of opportunities for ordinary citizens to participate continuously and directly in policing, the participation in deliberate decision making at a devolved level (lower than the city governance, police management, etc.), and the empowerment of the local citizenry (Fung 2001). Although the initiation of community-oriented policing does not often work in this manner, it is clear from the success of the CAPS experience that this method, a mutual initiation of community-oriented policing from the beginning, is the most productive and effective means.

The ideal initiation would also see the concept revolve around all three components—strategic-oriented policing, neighborhood-oriented policing, and problem-oriented policing—and eventually the integration of all three. Additionally, both of the actors would fill certain roles within the larger concept to achieve the desired outcome of community-oriented policing—namely, a safer community. These police roles consist of changes to organization and management (Chapter 7) and to the overall role of the police (Chapter 8), but the overall role of the community in addressing criminal and order maintenance problems must change as well (Chapter 9). The link, however, between the police and the community should start with the police chief, who also plays a pivotal role in the systemic approach (Chapter 10). For now, let it suffice to detail specifically how the three components become integrated in the systemic approach.

Neighborhood Development

The issue of who initiates community-oriented policing deals with the willingness of both the police and the community to adopt the tenets of community-oriented policing. Where the community is strong and the police resistant, it is community led, and vice versa. Again, ideally, the implementation of community-oriented policing would be a partnership from the initial stages of planning for community-oriented policing to the final stages of institutionalizing the concept. One very interesting factor, proposed by James J. Nolan III, Norman Conti, and Jack McDevitt (2004), is to consider the level of neighborhood development when considering how specifically to move toward the adoption of community-oriented policing.

Nolan, Conti, and McDevitt's premise is that most of the models for community-oriented policing adoption are driven by the organizational characteristics of the police department. They argue that to be truly "community oriented," the main focus should be on the conditions of each particular neighborhood. Because not all communities are equal, not all should receive the same response by the police under community-oriented policing. Hence, the way that the police go about working with the community should be based upon the type of neighborhood.

The authors identify four different types of neighborhoods: Strong, Vulnerable, Anomic, and Responsive (Nolan, Conti, and McDevitt 2004). The two key variables that generate the four categories are the level of crime and disorder and the level of dependence for dealing with the crime and disorder. The authors identify a strong neighborhood as "one where crime is low and the neighborhood members are either interacting independently on issues of community disorder or they are organizing themselves to do so" (Nolan, Conti, and McDevitt 2004, 110). Vulnerable neighborhoods are those that "have low levels of crime and disorder, but they are also low in terms of neighborhood development" (Nolan, Conti, and McDevitt 2004, 110). An Anomic neighborhood is one that is "high in crime and disorder and low in neighborhood development" (Nolan, Conti, and McDevitt 2004, 110). Finally, a Responsive neighborhood is one that is "high in crime and disorder, but are working together with the police to resolve them" (Nolan, Conti, and McDevitt 2004, 110).

According to the authors, the type of neighborhood a police agency faces when moving to community-oriented policing should determine how the agency works alongside neighborhood residents. Essentially, the type of neighborhood determines the policing style. In response to a Strong neighborhood, the authors state that the policing style should be one of "supporting and recognizing" (Nolan, Conti, and McDevitt 2004). While these neighborhoods need little assistance from the police, they still need to be supported in their efforts and recognized for their achievements in maintaining low levels of both crime and disorder.

The second policing style, "substituting and selling," is in response to a Vulnerable neighborhood (Nolan, Conti, and McDevitt 2004). While these neighborhoods do not have a crime or disorder problem, they could use some assistance in helping them to organize to deal with crime and disorder problems, as well as daily quality-of-life issues. Police should work to build strong communities by "substituting" quality-of-life issues for crime and disorder issues and "sell" the community on working together.

The third policing style was dubbed "securing then organizing" (Nolan, Conti, and McDevitt 2004). This is for neighborhoods that have serious problems with crime and disorder and need to be secured prior to organizing the community to address these problems. This is reflective of the National Institute of Justice program known as "weed and seed," which set out to secure a local neighborhood (weeding) before working with the community to better organize it to deal more effectively with crime and disorder (seeding). This will be discussed more fully in the next section.

The four styles of policing, according to the researchers, involve "systems planning and response" (Nolan, Conti, and McDevitt 2004). Communities are trying to organize to fight against the problems of crime and disorder, but those problems may be so complex that they cannot be resolved by any one entity. In such cases it is the role of the police to begin systems planning, planning that incorporates elements across a wide array of institutions, such as schools, churches, social services, and day-care centers. The idea is that better planning will create a better response.

Although this concept is relatively new and has not seen widespread adoption, the idea has merit. Not every neighborhood faces the same problems or has the same level of organization, and a typical city may have neighborhoods in all four categories. Just as the neighborhoods are different, so too must be the police response. While community-oriented policing has long advocated creating tailor-made responses to a community's needs, the concepts of Nolan, Conti, and McDevitt's situational policing may provide the proper method of determining where a police department should start.

THE THREE COMPONENTS

The ideal initial step in community-oriented policing is to form a coalition that would include a cross-section of the community, both residential and business, as well as a cross-section of the police department. This group would then be responsible for the initial planning of community-oriented policing and would be responsible for directing where the police will establish the first component, strategic-oriented policing, and the types of methods they will utilize. As is often the case, this may be the first step in implementing community-oriented policing where the police enact the program without any assistance from the community. The police are fully capable of determining which areas need to be targeted and the type of strategic-oriented policing methods that should be utilized, largely because these steps are essentially enhanced traditional police tactics. Although it should be recognized that the police will base their selection of areas on objective criteria such as crime statistics and that this method is readily acceptable for addressing criminal issues, it may leave out many unknown variables regarding crime of which the police may not be aware and it may almost completely ignore the issues of social disorder.

Whether it is the community and the police working in concert or solely the police, the first step in the implementation of community-oriented policing should be strategic-oriented policing. The initial decision, regardless of the methodology utilized, must be the selection of a target or multiple targets to determine what area, crime, or order maintenance issue is to be addressed and then the type of strategic policing tactic to be used. If it is the police working with a previously established community group, then some things to consider in the selection of the target would be the consensus of the coalition, anecdotal evidence, or any data the community can provide. If there are no community groups previously formed, the police must work not only to create a community coalition but also to determine what problems or areas to initially target based on police-gathered data, officer experience with the problem or area, and any additional data from other sources such as the fire department, public works, or local government board.

Again the target can be selected based on a single problem such as prostitution, an area or localized problem such as a crack house, or an order maintenance issue such as a city park that is home to the homeless and drug addicts and is in a state of constant disrepair. All of these are common examples of targets that could be addressed through a community-oriented policing approach and could start with the strategic-oriented policing methods. Once the target or targets are selected, the next step is to determine what type of strategic-oriented policing method should be utilized.

As described in Chapter 3, the possibilities are endless but generally revolve around various forms of directed patrols, aggressive patrols, or saturation patrols. The police or coalition should determine which type of patrol to utilize based on what they think will have the most impact on the identified target. While the saturation patrol may work well in the city park, it may be more beneficial to utilize various aggressive patrol tactics on the prostitutes and johns who enter the targeted area, such as a street corner, a particular motel, or a neighborhood residence. The selection should be made on a multitude of criteria ranging from geographical area, police resources, and criminal element to the time available to address the issue.

The goal of implementing the strategic-oriented policing component first is to physically drive out the criminal or order maintenance element or, at a minimum, drive it underground and behind closed doors. Once this element has been removed from the area and the police vacate the location, the criminal element will return. This approach is no different from squeezing a water balloon on one end. All we accomplish is the displacement of water. Once we let go, the water refills the area we were squeezing. Similarly, once we remove the police from their strategic-oriented policing assignments, the elements we removed from the neighborhood will return. The police cannot stay in one place forever; although it would perhaps be comforting to have a police officer on every corner, it is just not feasible based on the resources available. So, once the element is removed from a neighborhood and the police begin to extricate themselves, something must be put in place of the police. This is where neighborhood-oriented policing comes into play.

The removal of the crime and disorder from a specific area, by means of strategic-oriented policing, allows the community a respite from this element and thereby reduces the fear the community has suffered. It also allows time to implement neighborhood-oriented policing programs without the concerns of the element that may have prevented or inhibited the implementation of similar programs earlier. It then provides the time necessary for the program to take hold, allowing it to grow stronger and influence more and more people in the neighborhood. As more people become involved, the police can then remove themselves from the neighborhood, leaving a smaller presence behind (ideally, a community-oriented police officer), and redirect their resources elsewhere.

The type of neighborhood-oriented policing program that should be implemented in the community should also result from the cooperation of the police and the community. The various types of programs, such as community patrols, community crime prevention programs, communication programs, and community social control programs, should all be considered. Some cases may call for an officer to walk a foot patrol of the area, or if it is too large an area for this tactic, bike patrols may be necessary. In other cases, the community may get involved by creating a neighborhood watch program and implementing citizen patrols, by either foot, bike, or automobile. Other possibilities include organized cleanup days, neighborhood block parties with the police, or citizen academies and ride-along programs. Implementing one or several of the community communication programs would help open the lines of communication and may allow for some understanding or revelations of what the community perceives as a problem. All of these options should be considered and implemented based on the needs of the community.

In some cases, the neighborhood-oriented policing programs implemented may have no effect on keeping the criminal element from returning to the area. In this event, the police may have to return to the strategies underlined in the strategic-oriented policing component or utilize some of the methods detailed in the third component, problem-oriented policing. Regardless, the police and community must continue to address these issues and reallocate resources to best suit the needs of the community.

The third component of community-oriented policing, problem-oriented policing, plays a major role in the overall implementation of the concept and is a continual process that should also be conducted on the part of both the police and the community. Problem-oriented policing should commence at the same time as strategic-oriented policing strategies are implemented and should never stop. In some cases, the methods utilized to address a perceived problem may assist in the identification of those targets for strategic-oriented policing. In other cases, the techniques may be utilized to determine the root of the problem in a particular neighborhood and to develop various alternatives that can be implemented under the multiple programs of neighborhood-oriented policing. And in other situations, the concept of problem-oriented policing may be conducted entirely separate from the first two components and later integrated if there exists some connection in the problems discovered and the alternatives selected to address these issues.

This connection is the key revolving around the web effect created from the three components. Each of the components does not operate independently, nor are they mutually exclusive. That is not to say that at times they will not operate without any influence from the other two components, but eventually everything that results from one component will have a direct bearing on the other two. The response that may be derived from a particular method of strategic-oriented policing may dictate what type of neighborhood-oriented policing program is implemented. During this time, a study may be conducted from the problem-oriented policing component, and what is actually causing the problem may be different than what was originally considered. There is then the chance that the alternative selected from the problem-solving process may be a different form of strategic-oriented policing, which may then impact the programs under neighborhood-oriented policing. A continual evaluation of the methods utilized, followed by a reassessment of what may or may not work and then augmented by a change in the methods utilized, will impact and create a web between the three components of community-oriented policing.

A good example of the importance of evaluations in regards to police and community cooperation is found in a study by Mastrofski, Snipes, and Supina (1996) in Richmond, Virginia. After logging 346 observations of citizen compliance during police–citizen contacts, several interesting conclusions were drawn that at least call for further consideration of the police–community partnership. The first was that when officers and citizens were acquainted, citizens often felt that their relationship allowed them more leeway in complying with the officer. As the authors state, "familiarity appears to breed contempt" (Mastrofski, Snipes, and Supina 1996, 296). The other interesting finding was that the commonly held belief that minority officers work better in minority neighborhoods, in regard to police compliance, was found to be false. Citizens of races different from those of police officers were more compliant than those of the same race. Obtaining citizen compliance, at least in relation to calls for service, may raise some issues with the police–community relationship that is desired under community-oriented policing. The authors are quick to identify the need for further analysis, and they articulate many of the successes of the community-oriented policing movement in Richmond, Virginia; however, their research into the relationship raises many important questions.

This interrelationship of the three components then becomes the key to community-oriented policing. All three components must be present for the concept to work in a practical application. The police and community must work in concert and apply all three components to the criminal and order maintenance problems that are both real and perceived. Then and only then can we truly evaluate the community-oriented policing method for what it is, an entirely new and systemic approach to policing.

An excellent example of the adoption of community-oriented policing and the three components working together can be found in the "Bright Leaf Housing Authority," the pseudonym for a large urban public housing area (Walsh et al. 2000). It was there that an initial review of the problems in Bright Leaf indicated that drug trafficking and its related crimes were the biggest problems dealt with by both police and citizens. In order to "take back the neighborhood," the police initially established a strong presence to begin suppressing the drug dealing through the use of strategic-oriented policing methods. The police then began working with local citizens by employing neighborhood-oriented policing strategies such as foot and bike patrols, conducting needs assessment surveys on buildings, meeting with local residents on a regular basis, and implementing citizen patrol programs. Finally, the Bright Leaf police and its citizens adopted the concepts of problem-oriented policing to begin solving the problems in their neighborhood. After the first year, Bright Leaf found that drug dealing was reduced in the housing area, they were able to address fifty-six community problems, and while arrests went up, reported crime and calls for service decreased 15 percent and 14 percent, respectively (Walsh et al. 2000). Finally, it should be noted that after only one year, the residents of Bright Leaf felt their community was safer and they were pleased with the adoption of community-oriented policing.

One final aspect of the integration of the three components under community-oriented policing is the possibility of not only integrating but also diffusing the three components. The components are diffused when strategic-oriented policing, neighborhood-oriented policing, and problem-oriented policing begin to occur simultaneously, by the same community group and police officers in the neighborhoods. In many cases, the problem-oriented team may be deciding what strategic-oriented policing tactics to utilize and how they can be replaced with neighborhood-oriented policing programs. What happens to the three components is a blurring of lines and a loss of clear focus on any of the three distinct components.

Diffusion can occur at any time during the implementation process, but earlier in the process will most likely be detrimental to the implementation. In the later stages of implementation, diffusion may prove beneficial. The reason is simply that the police and the community must understand all the components, their foundations, how they operate individually, and subsequently how they operate together. All of this information should be clear and simplified before the three components are diffused into one system under community-oriented policing. If, in fact, they are diffused in the later stages, it can be beneficial to the systemic approach because it can clearly signify that cooperation between the community and the police is occurring and that all three components are being utilized to implement community-oriented policing.

INCREMENTALISM

In 1959, Charles E. Lindbloom wrote an article entitled "The Science of Muddling Through," wherein he described how a manager "would settle on a limited objective to be achieved by the policy, outline the few options that were immediately available, and make a choice that combined into one 'the choice among values and the choice among instruments for reaching values'" (Denhardt 1993, 95). The incremental method of change is a slow-moving process that allows the manager to implement change on an acceptable level. The overall task of change is brought down to a realistic and operational level by selecting a small area of policy to change. By utilizing only the options that are readily available or easily obtainable, there is not a dramatic change in demands from the department. Personnel adapt more easily to a slow change than to any abrupt changes in policy, and slow change prevents both anarchy and apathy.

Although the incremental method of change seems fairly basic in premise, its simplicity brings with it many safeguards for the manager in implementing policy change. As Lindbloom (1959, 86) stated:

> In the first place, past sequences of policy steps have given him knowledge about the probable consequences of further similar steps. Second, he need not attempt big jumps toward his goals that would require predictions beyond his or anyone else's knowledge, because he never expects his policy to be a final resolution of a problem. His decision is only one step. . . . Third, he is in effect able to test his previous predictions as he moves on to each further step. Lastly, he often can remedy a past error fairly quickly—more quickly than if policy proceeded through more distinct steps widely spaced in time.

The advantages to Lindbloom's presentation of the incremental model are that it exists as an operational method of implementing policy and easily adapts to the bureaucratic nature of a police department. The disadvantages to Lindbloom's presentation are that, in large part, "policy makers generally accept the legitimacy of established programs and tacitly agree to continue previous policies" (Dye 1987, 36). This issue could be of great concern to the policy maker, or police chief, entering a police department that is wrought by corruption or one in which the establishment of past policies has irreparably harmed the police department's functioning.

Because much of the literature on community-oriented policing has shifted to analyzing the application of business management and strategies to the police organization (see Moore and Trojanowicz 1988), it seems only fitting to advance to a more recent study in which incrementalism was utilized as a method of change in several large business organizations to effect this change (Quinn 1980, 1985). James Brian Quinn (1980) advanced the theory of incrementalism in a study of management that analyzed several large organizations attempting to implement change and then subsequently created a method that would allow not only achievement but also acceptance of the implementation process. The theory became known as logical incrementalism, which essentially "describes the process and focuses on the evolution of change as broad goals are more narrowly defined and adapted" (Hersey and Blanchard 1993, 370). The five stages of logical incrementalism are as follows (Hersey and Blanchard 1993, 370):

1. General concerns: a vaguely felt awareness of an issue or opportunity
2. Broadcasting of a general idea without details: the idea is floated for reactions, pro and con, and for refinements
3. Formal development of a change plan
4. Use of a crisis or opportunity to stimulate implementation of the change plan—retirement of a senior manager or a sudden loss of market shares can facilitate rapid acceptance and implementation of the change
5. Adaptation of the plan as implementation progresses

These five stages of logical incrementalism complement the process of implementing community-oriented policing in a traditional police department. Any police chief today can say that with the current status of criminal activity, violence, and public outcry, a growing concern about crime exists. Community-oriented policing has been the essential buzzword in response to this growing concern; with 70 percent of police departments that serve more than 50,000 people having implemented the concept and with that number continuing to grow (Witkin and McGraw 1993), little doubt exists that the opportunity has arrived.

Although the media has projected community-oriented policing into the mainstream, detailing all of the promises and all of the success stories, police departments still need to follow the second stage of logical incrementalism and float the idea to the police department. Doing so allows the line officer to become familiar with the concept and allows for some analysis of what will be seen as positive from this systemic approach and what will be portrayed as negative. The police chief and/or committee tasked with implementing community-oriented policing can make some adjustments to the method of implementation and receive advanced warning on the possible resistance that may be faced. The planning committee can then enter the third stage.

A formal plan that will inaugurate the change from traditional policing to community-oriented policing must be developed. The plan should deal with change from a systemic approach by attempting to implement the change on multiple levels. Again, not everything can be changed at once. Rather, the goal is to implement small amounts of change within the police department at various levels, through various departments, and with a variety of tactics. The plan should also incorporate all three components of community-oriented policing and begin the movement from a centralized to a decentralized structure. Once the initial plan is created, the next stage is actual implementation.

The winners of the Oceanside Police Athletic League's annual surfing contest, pictured with the police officers who work with the youth. *(Courtesy of the Oceanside Police Department, Oceanside, California.)*

Although Quinn speaks from a business perspective in the fourth stage, there is a definite application in the policing field. Today, in many cases, community-oriented policing is actually implemented with the hiring of a new police chief expressly for the purpose of implementing this new systemic approach. Although this is obviously a fitting time to implement change, it is not necessarily the only time. Because the media has made the public aware of community-oriented policing, it stands to reason that any time is a good time to implement this system. However, in some jurisdictions the police may wait for some set date, such as the police department's anniversary, the commencement of the new year, or the election of a new mayor, rather than a new police chief. In other cases, the inauguration date of the systemic approach to policing may actually be set as a result of a citizen call for the program and therefore can be implemented with the completion of the "change plan."

The final stage is then the most crucial within logical incrementalism because adjustments can be made before the policy advances and grows too far beyond the reach of a simple alteration or two. Community-oriented policing provides the long-term values and goals that need to be obtained to achieve the institutionalization of the concept, and incrementalism ensures the success of the program by implementing in small increments, thus avoiding the confusion of an overly extensive policy, reducing conflicts, and maintaining stability and order in the face of change (Dye 1987; Hersey and Blanchard 1993; Quinn 1980). Through the continual focus on the values and goals inherent within community-oriented policing, the use of logical incrementalism will greatly assist the police department and community in achieving this institutionalization. Some additional leadership actions, by both the police and the community, can also facilitate the implementation of the systemic approach. They include the following (Hersey and Blanchard 1993, 370–371):

1. Use multiple information sources to refine and develop broad goals into specific objectives.
2. Build organizational awareness of the change.
3. Create credibility for the change.
4. Legitimize new viewpoints.
5. Use tactical shifts and partial solutions in refining the general ideas.
6. Establish political support and overcome opposition.
7. Maintain flexibility.
8. Use trial balloons and systemic waiting.
9. Create pockets of commitment.
10. Crystallize organizational focus on the changes at the right time.
11. Formalize commitments made to adopt the change.

Through integration of the five stages and the eleven leadership actions, as well as adherence to the values and goals of community-oriented policing, the system can be institutionalized in the long term. However, if one focuses on the long term, the plan of incrementalism can itself be broken down into stages, allowing for incremental goals in the short term. Although the full institutionalization of community-oriented policing may be set for, say, ten years, the short-term goals could be set for every two years, providing a clearer representation of where the organization currently is, where it needs to be in the two years, and what it should achieve along the way. The long-term goal may change with each increment obtained in the short term, but the initial representation of the long-term goal still provides a source of direction.

An example of this type of short-term and long-term goal setting is the scenario of a traditional police department projecting to be fully in line with all the tenets of community-oriented policing in ten years, with five short-term stages, spaced at increments of two years, creating a total of five stages. Although this is not to be interpreted as a steadfast method of implementing community-oriented policing—because every police department will find itself with varying situations, goals, and values—it can serve as a guideline for the establishment of both short-term and long-term plans.

 COP IN ACTION

How to Plan Strategically for Your Community

Yogi Berra once said, "When you come to a fork in the road, take it." His mangled advice could describe how we often plan for the future. Most police chiefs and sheriffs were promoted through the ranks of their organization and still carry with them the old habits that made them good street cops—the ability to size up a situation, act quickly, and resolve the problem. But complex crime problems require police leaders to take a planned, community-based, long-term approach.

Many communities have developed strategic plans and know the problems and benefits associated with that process. Strategic planning can be done in any size agency. While the level of complexity will vary widely with the size and characteristics of each community, the fundamentals that lead to an effective plan are the same. By using some basic planning steps, communities and police organizations can avoid common mistakes and accelerate the benefits of community policing.

What Is Strategic Planning?

A strategic plan is both a document and a process. The document is the map that helps keep both the community and police on track. It is the standard against which budgeting, workplans, hiring, promotion, deployment, organizational structure, and all other implementation elements are tested. The process strengthens the relationship between the community and police, while developing consensus and long-term political support for changes made as a result of strategic planning.

For strategic planning to achieve its potential, the police and community must jointly develop long-term solutions. This requires patience, understanding, and commitment to hearing the various involved groups and individuals, so the plan truly incorporates community ideas.

Making It Happen

The basics of good planning are simple: listen, plan, act, evaluate, then repeat. The challenge comes in listening well, planning appropriately, acting effectively, and evaluating with accuracy.

Key partners in the process include the following participants:

- Chiefs, sheriffs, and elected officials.
  In the hands of a good leader, a strategic plan is a tool for improving the organization. If the leadership doesn't support the plan, it will fail.
- Department personnel.
  The people who will be most responsible for implementation—supervisors, officers, and nonsworn personnel—must be involved.
- Community leaders.
  The process should model the partnerships that are integral to community policing. It is crucial for developing the ongoing support of the community.
- Interagency partners.
  Involve other agencies and keep them informed.

The following pieces are key ingredients of an effective plan:

- Mission and values.
  These elements should be as constant as the northern star. Also, without a strong guiding mission, an organization will be unable to adjust to change.
- Short-term strategies.
  While the document has a long-term vision, it must also define short-term steps. Personnel must clearly see how the mission is translated into action.
- A distinction between goal and process.
  The goal is to reduce crime, fear, and disorder. Don't confuse that with the process; partnership, problem solving, arrest, and investigation are processes that help achieve the goal.
- Required action by units.
  Units should create workplans that address how strategies will be implemented day-to-day. This is crucial for establishing internal ownership of the plan.
- Budget connection.

Unless the plan is used to drive the budget process, it will remain a wish list. Work with the political leaders to develop multiyear budget projections.

Sustaining the Change

Making deep institutional changes requires a long period of time. The following steps will help to ensure that the plan becomes a reality:

- Don't divide the mission.
  Some departments have described the "new" elements (partnerships and problem solving) in ways that suggest the "old" elements (call response, investigation, arrest) are obsolete. Community policing does not throw out existing tools. It adds to them by developing new ways to solve long-standing problems.
- Define new roles for everyone.
  It is essential to define new roles for patrol officers. But without specific roles for supervisors and managers, little can be accomplished. When an officer is given more discretion, the sergeant's role also changes. Each person in the organization must know that his/her role will change. People in the community should also work jointly with police to redefine citizens' roles in community safety.
- Institutionalize.
  To sustain community policing over the long term, each element of the organization and community must incorporate community policing into its behavior. Good ideas falter when they never become part of the daily life of officers, supervisors, or managers. Job descriptions, recruiting and hiring, training, rewards and discipline, promotions, and management practices must all change. Community members must also change from being passive recipients of services to active participants in making neighborhoods safer.
- Focus on organizational culture.
  Sergeants and field training officers, in particular, must be involved. When these "keepers of the culture" adopt the approach, profound change will follow.
- Renew the plan.
  New strategies should be developed to ensure the plan remains pertinent and up-to-date for each new budget cycle.
- Maintain flexibility.
  The mission and values are constant. Goals and objectives are stable for five or even ten years. But strategies evolve and timelines become obsolete. Plans that identify actions by the month for the next five years are unrealistic. Require that unit workplans fill in the short-term detail.
- Disseminate the plan.
  After the plan is complete, distribute it. Make sure community and agency leaders who participated in developing the plan receive a copy. Make familiarity with the plan part of employee evaluations and promotions.
- Don't wait to implement.
  The transition is necessarily incremental—an agency that works twenty-four hours, every day, cannot stop to retool. Some strategies should begin right away.

Policing in America is at a fork in the road. One path leads to business as usual—reacting to individual crimes, but not focusing on solving problems that lead to crime, fear, and disorder. The other path leads to solving chronic problems and uses the resources of whole communities, not just "the thin blue line."

Transforming organizations and creating new community roles require planning, commitment, involvement, patience, and hard work. While community policing is not a panacea, it is an opportunity to make a difference. That's why we got involved. That's why an effective strategic plan matters.

Source: Adapted with permission from Tom Potter and John Campbell, "How to Plan Strategically for Your Community." In *Community Policing Exchange.* Washington, D.C.: Community Policing Consortium, November/December 1995, pp. 1–2.

STAGES

One of the difficulties of defining and understanding community-oriented policing is that the systemic approach to policing is not a predetermined program. No implementation plan exists that police chiefs can follow step-by-step to successfully implement the concept. Community-oriented policing comes in a variety of shapes and forms that are revealed through the changes in the police department, the community, and specifically in those things that change both of these entities in tandem. A wide variety of variables will have either negative or positive impact on the implementation process and in either case may change the basic makeup of the systemic approach.

The variables that cause community-oriented policing to vary from jurisdiction to jurisdiction consist of factors ranging from the large to the small, such as the environment of the community, organizational factors of the police department, various players in the systemic approach, and individuals. The environment of the community is based on such factors as the political, social, economic, and geographical dynamics, any one of which could dramatically alter the makeup of community-oriented policing. Organizational factors may consist of the differences in organizational maturity, leadership, management, and such things as the attitude of the line officers and nonsworn employees. The various players under community-oriented policing also have a dramatic impact on its implementation and hence its makeup once it is implemented. These key players include the police, the community, and the police chief, but also mid-level management, social services, and other governmental service providers. And, finally, the resistance or support of one individual can have a major impact on the outcome of community-oriented policing, in that one citizen or one police officer can effectively block, enhance, or simply alter the final outcome during the implementation of the systemic approach.

Understanding that community-oriented policing will vary from jurisdiction to jurisdiction because the police and the community are different from jurisdiction to jurisdiction is important; however, some consistencies must exist among the wide variety of jurisdictions that have to date implemented community-oriented policing. The majority of police departments that began implementing in the 1980s and early 1990s have all focused on similar policies, methods, and tactics. In the same way that community-oriented policing has been defined in this book, through consensus, so, too, can we then identify a process of implementation that provides a rough outline. Through an analysis of many police departments working under a title of community-oriented policing, varying from small to large police departments, urban to rural settings, and sheriff's departments to police departments, five readily identifiable stages are apparent. The five stages of community-oriented policing are (1) planning, (2) micro-community-oriented policing, (3) transition, (4) macro-community-oriented policing, and (5) community-oriented policing. (See Table 6-1.)

TABLE 6-1   *Implementation Stages of Community-Oriented Policing*

STAGE		ESTIMATED TIMETABLE
I	Planning	6 months to 2 years
II	Micro-community-oriented policing	1 1/2 to 4 years
III	Transition	2 1/2 to 7 years
IV	Macro-community-oriented policing	4 1/2 to 10 years
V	Community-oriented policing	6 1/2 to 14 years

The establishment of a flexible outline and description of each stage for the demonstration of incremental steps in community-oriented policing is then the goal of the rest of this chapter. The concept of creating or reviewing certain stages of implementation is by no means new to the literature (Brown 1989; Bureau of Justice Assistance 1993, 1994b; Fleissner et al. 1992; Ford and Morash 2002; Gaines 1994; Pate and Shtull 1994; U.S. Department of Justice 1992) (see, for instance, Table 6-2). However, by providing this workable framework for implementation, based on a review of community-oriented police departments to date, police chiefs, administrators, managers, officers, and those involved in the study of this evolution of policing will have a better idea of how to turn a traditional police department into a community-oriented policing department.

TABLE 6-2   *Community-Oriented Policing Community Stages*

FOUR-STAGE PROCESS	
Stage 1: Challenging/Venting Stage	Citizens vociferously criticize police methods and instances of abuse of power or fault the police for doing "too little too late." The police, put on the defense, can do little but explain their lack of resources and power. Many of their accusers may abandon the fray once they have vented their anger.
Stage 2: Organizational Stage	Participants agree to "play ball." Community members start to attend meetings regularly, ready to work on specific issues. A stable relationship is developed within which police and community can hammer out a mutual agenda.
Stage 3: Success Stage	Actions are accomplished. Success breeds not only more success but also a trusting relationship. The group is even secure enough to weather turnover and changes in leadership.
Stage 4: Long-Term Stability Stage	The group can mount continuous efforts to resolve problems as well as recruit wider community representation.

Source: Dan Fleissner, Nicholas Fedan, David Klinger, and Ezra Stotland, "Community Policing in Seattle: A Model Partnership between Citizens and Police," *National Institute of Justice: Research in Brief,* August 1992, pp. 8–9.

Stage I: Planning

The first stage is the planning stage. Here, the police department and community should have an established plan for the long-term goals of community-oriented policing, the short-term goals, and how they will begin implementation. Stage I is essentially the policy formation stage, with the end result being a police department and community prepared to commence the incremental changes that will carry them through the second stage of micro-community-oriented policing. This stage, as detailed before, must begin with an assessment of the current relations, foundation, and perceptions of crime between the local police department and the community.

Community-oriented policing must result in a strong collaborative effort between the police and the community, with the community assuming a larger and more powerful role. However, in most instances this is part of the long-term plan rather than the short-term or immediate goals of community-oriented policing. This is generally the case because in most jurisdictions community-oriented policing is planned and implemented without the community's support. In most cases, the police must seek out the community's assistance to move forward with community-oriented policing. In some cases, cooperation with some of the community already exists, and the community can be drawn into stage I; in a very few cases, it is actually the reverse, where the community must draw the police into the action. Regardless of the situation, both parties must eventually be drawn into the concept, and their inclusion in the planning stage must be actively sought. As some authors have noted (Rohe, Adams, and Arcury 2001, 78), "planners and community police officers need to work together to maximize their impacts and to take advantage of the perspectives and skills that each profession brings to the task of improving living conditions in our neighborhoods."

 COP IN ACTION

Salt Lake City Prepares Officers for Transition

The Salt Lake City Police Department published its first formal five-year strategic plan in the summer of 1991. This event marked the department's earnest transition to community policing. The department was just starting to formalize its community policing commitments to officers and citizens when I assumed the chief's position in December 1992.

Most law enforcement leaders are aware that when you're selling change, police officers can be a hard bunch to convince. To counter skepticism, police officers and citizens were brought in at the onset of implementation to learn about community policing's potential. Every officer, regardless of rank or duty assignment, received in-house community policing training, and each learned of the philosophy's goals, objectives, limitations, and envisioned potential for our city.

Initially, we assigned certain officers to high-crime areas in the city and did so without compromising shift strength in the field. These officers focused their attention on community policing efforts when not responding to calls.

Today, Salt Lake City's community policing program has grown to the point that no officer is a "community policing officer" per se. All of our officers are trained in community policing, and all are expected to exemplify the philosophy, regardless of current assignments. These days, it's not uncommon to see off-duty uniformed officers attending city council, community council, and other public meetings. Officers attend these meetings so they can personally hear citizens' concerns; the meetings also give officers the opportunity to educate citizens about police capabilities, available options, and why it is sometimes best for us to divert calls for service to more appropriate public or private sources for resolution.

Our shift to community policing has happened hand-in-hand with the implementation of our Neighborhood Police Offices (NPOs). The department has established eleven NPOs in all of the city council's seven districts in the last four years. Grocery stores, strip malls, regional shopping centers, and shelter facilities are just some of the businesses that have donated office space for the project. The NPOs are not full precincts, and they do not operate around the clock. But they function well as places where officers and department volunteers can meet with citizens, take complaints, and address specific neighborhood issues. Many of the citizen volunteers who staff the NPOs are retired officers drawn back to the neighborhoods they patrolled and loved, who still have a desire to help citizens feel safe in their homes and businesses.

Salt Lake City P.D. established a Mobile Neighborhood Watch program in 1993. Citizen volunteers receive an initial thirty hours of police training and are required to participate in ongoing training to maintain eligibility. Mobile Watch is citizen-regulated and -administered. Shift schedules, field performance policies, internal disciplines, and terminations are all handled by citizens. The initial training class of 25 citizens has grown to 550 in only 2 1/2 years. Citizens have been directly responsible for numerous arrests, lifesaving medical responses, and other on-view field situations through the Mobile Neighborhood Watch program.

A question commonly posed to community policing practitioners is "How do you fund your program?" Salt Lake City P.D. received a Comprehensive Communities Grant that funded additional community policing officers. However, community policing does not require special funding. A law enforcement agency can resolve community concerns with effective and progressive leadership, and good field supervision. Salt Lake City's need for additional staff and funds was not a result of implementing community policing, but of increased population and calls for service. We have found that community policing provides a department with tremendous options and advantages, especially as demands for police services continue to rise and budgets decrease.

Salt Lake City's police department and city administration have fully backed community policing. Our police department has integrated community policing into every aspect of command, training, and administrative operations. As a result, community policing has been a great success in Salt Lake City.

Citizens in Salt Lake City also support community policing. They like being involved, and they like having input in the city's crime-solving initiatives. Citizens have demonstrated their support and appreciation through letters, surveys, and media reports.

Our department will continue to use the community policing philosophy as a focal point in all of our command and administrative decisions. I fully believe community policing will provide scope and purpose for law enforcement agencies, regardless of size and locale, for many years to come.

Source: Adapted with permission from Ruben B. Ortega, "Salt Lake City Prepares Officers for Transition," *Community Policing Exchange,* March/April 1996, p. 6.

Once the climate of the police and community relationship is assessed, it is important to begin moving toward the identification of both police personnel and community participants to begin the planning process. A team or panel of participants should be identified to review the literature, concepts, and practices of community-oriented policing to provide some foundation and mutual understanding. From there, the team or teams can begin working on the overall policy formulation for community-oriented policing.

The policy factors may include determining the long-term and short-term goals of the systemic approach as well as defining some of the overall objectives. The mission statement of the police department, as well as the overall values and goals associated with the concept, should be reviewed. One publication by the Bureau of Justice Assistance (1994a) includes a list of elements for consideration, such as goals, objectives, strategies, activities, roles and responsibilities, resources, potential problems, and proposed solutions. All of these are brought to bear on the overall necessity of the planning stage. More planning accomplished in the first stage will result in a greater chance for successful implementation in the later stages.

Further inclusion of members of the community—both community leaders and average citizens—should also be considered. Greater inclusion of the police must be factored in as well, since they will be an integral part of the overall concept. It is here that the first steps of incrementalism can be utilized, by essentially floating the idea of community-oriented policing. A later assessment of the line officers' reactions, perceptions, and concerns can then be addressed prior to actually implementing any change in police policy, practice, and procedure.

As the planning progresses, other planning concepts need to be addressed and include selecting targets for stage II and, perhaps immediately within this implementation, identifying targets for strategic-oriented policing. Education and training of community and police leaders should be factored in, and the implementation plan for education and training of line officers and community members should also be determined. In many regards, the planning stage may actually incorporate a marketing plan to sell the police and the community on the concept of community-oriented policing, as well as the programs and policies that will follow.

The foundation of the police and community relationship will most likely determine the length of time it takes to achieve the end result of this first stage. Although there must always be a sense of urgency for implementing community-oriented policing, introducing the concept, developing these concepts to reflect the local community, and developing an implementation plan could conceivably take all of two years, as was projected in this framework. Police chiefs must be sensitive to time. Too little time may result in inadequate planning, whereas too much time may result in a lack of interest.

The end result of the first stage should be the establishment of a new mission statement with values and goals that project the community-oriented approach to policing. The long-term goal should be established and the short-term goals should be identified. Potential targets should also be identified, and methods for implementing the three components to address these targets should also be established. The police department, as well as the community, should have some idea of the concepts of community-oriented policing and the proposals to move away from the traditional style of policing toward that of the systemic approach. The community and the police department should then be prepared to begin the practical application of the philosophy, concepts, policies, mission statement, values, and goals of community-oriented policing.

The majority of police departments that have successfully implemented community-oriented policing to date have taken the time to implement stage I as a method of preparing the department and educating the community on this concept. The Spokane,

Washington, Police Department went so far as to develop a mission statement and value statement by soliciting the input of every officer in the police department. In Portland, Oregon, the police bureau saw the community actually drive the move toward community-oriented policing; with the cooperation of many community members, the police bureau, and the local government, a community policing transition plan was put into effect, along with a mission and value statement for the police department to guide them in their implementation efforts. In Lumberton, North Carolina, the police chief implemented community-oriented policing by quickly adopting many of the strategic-oriented policing and neighborhood-oriented policing methods while simultaneously adopting and advancing the strategic plan, mission, and value statements of the police department with police and community input (Communicare 1995e).

Small-town and rural agencies also began making the move to community-oriented policing in the 1990s with more frequency. While some developed strategic plans, such as the Hillsborough County Sheriff's Office (Bromley and Cochran 1999), many of these agencies have not bothered to adopt a community-oriented policing plan but have adopted a more or less changed mission or value statement (Oliver 2001). Whether the catalyst has been the police or the community and whether the police department has planned then implemented, implemented then planned, or conducted both simultaneously, police departments across the United States that have moved to the systemic approach have placed a large emphasis on the factors in stage I.

Stage II: Micro-Community-Oriented Policing

The second stage of the five-stage process is micro-community-oriented policing. Here the police department begins testing some of the concepts, programs, and the synthesis of the three components, without making major changes to the police department and community. Micro-community-oriented policing establishes a test site to determine the potential of the overall systemic approach, to analyze the results, and to determine what to implement on a large scale (in other words, throughout the community) and what not to implement.

The most common form of micro-community-oriented policing is the development of a team or special unit, specifically dedicated full-time to implementing community-oriented policing on a selected target for a set period of time. One such experimentation project, detailed by Pate and Shtull, is the New York City Police Department's Community Patrol Officer Program (CPOP) in 1984, in the 72nd Precinct located in Brooklyn. The implementation and results of this "model precinct" allowed the New York City Police Department to assess the positive and negative aspects of the concept before implementing the concept department-wide and throughout the city, as it did in 1990 (Pate and Shtull 1994). This form of testing allows for an incremental change in the way policing is conducted on a small scale, and the incremental changes made to micro-community-oriented policing can have a fundamental impact on the later stages of implementation.

A target should be selected from those generated in stage I, and the implementation of micro-community-oriented policing should commence with strategic-oriented policing. If, for example, the selected target was a low-income housing/high-drug area, then strategic-oriented policing would target the drug dealing. In the summer of 1991, the Arlington County, Virginia, Police Department targeted an area with the launching of

A Cincinnati police officer showing the utility of a police motor cycle at a community event. (*Courtesy of the Cincinnati Police Department, Cincinnati, Ohio.*)

the Community Based Problem Oriented Policing (CBPOP) team, which was directed at Arna Valley, a low-income housing area with an open-air drug market. The CBPOP team was formed with five officers who directed their efforts at aggressive policing tactics to remove the key drug dealers from the community, then high-visibility patrols drove the drug dealing underground, and finally directed patrols were aimed at specific areas known for a high incidence of drug and drug-related problems such as the local crack houses.

Once the strategic-oriented policing tactics begin to show results, the next step is implementing the neighborhood-oriented policing strategies by developing various

COP IN ACTION

Transitioning Your Community

In rural law enforcement, moving from reactive to proactive responses to meet community needs is neither an automatic nor minor endeavor. To smoothly facilitate such a transition, the law enforcement chief executive officer must fully understand the community policing philosophy and be completely committed to its implementation.

To do it right, the CEO must be accessible to all levels of the changing agency as well as to outside agencies and citizens. Furthermore, the CEO should set the example for change internally. The agency's mission statement, goals, and objectives should reflect a commitment to excellency through community service.

An agency's managers and supervisors must be prepared to address the complaints that are sure to arise from the rank and file reflecting the opinion that community policing is mollycoddling troublemakers. It is difficult to convince many deputies who are accustomed to a traditional policing philosophy that it is more effective to attack the root causes of a problem rather than continue to strike at a problem's results. An effective leader can communicate that community policing techniques enhance rather than diminish conventional enforcement techniques.

Once this groundwork is laid, the next step is the appointment of an officer, committee, or group that coordinates the gradual move into community policing. The person or persons charged with this task must have a clear focus both of the concept of community policing and crime prevention. Not all crime prevention measures lead to, or support, the true concept of community policing. Through skilled coordination, you can avoid duplication of services, runarounds, and "passing the buck" and establish a full-service operation. This coordinating force will monitor the effort, design programs suited to the concept, and guide into the practice of community policing those who have been specially trained and educated about the goals.

It is extremely necessary that the agency transitioning to community policing build strong partnerships with community members and with agencies and organizations representing the community. This can be accomplished through such measures as neighborhood watch programs, citizen law enforcement academy classes, citizen patrol groups, community service officers, and meetings with civic groups. Support for innovative school projects can be mined from community service agencies such as youth clubs, civic groups, church congregations, social service agencies, and other organizations. Private businesses may also be enticed to participate both developmentally and financially in programs that can be shown to benefit youths. To be effective, program coordinators must be skilled in this area of partnership building.

Selling the community on the concept of trust and involvement that is essential to community policing is no easier than persuading officers established in their ways of enforcement to do an about-face. Citizen trust and involvement come one step at a time and become apparent when the calls for service increase in the area community policing is in effect. This is the alert to actively seek citizen participation in programs designed to involve citizens in the policing of their own communities.

A first step is to make officers as much a part of the affected community as possible. When that occurs, recommendations for services police could provide will begin to originate from officers in the field and flow up the chain of command to the CEO. The next step is to develop corrective measures, include the community as much as possible in the process, and implement the new strategies. This concept, for all practical purposes, inverts the traditional power structure of most agencies.

Currently, the majority of law enforcement agencies react to crime by allowing criminals to dictate the placement of officers in the field. The response is for the agency to dispatch officers to react to the call for service. But the activity prompting the call for service will be repeated again and again—without the root cause ever being properly identified, much less attacked. Close community ties can make it possible for the patrol officer to anticipate a developing need for services and address it rather than make a rushed response after the fact to treat the symptoms of the problem. Patterns that lead to crime problems can be seen developing and then dealt with before they are allowed to coalesce into an insurmountable problem.

There is no single best approach to community policing. There are as many different good approaches as there are communities to serve. Each law enforcement executive officer entering into the effort must use cost-effective and valid methods applicable to each segment of the community and program. Programs that work in Cleveland, Ohio, or Fargo, North

Dakota, will not necessarily work or function properly in the Tri-Cities area of Tennessee. But the basic concept of community members policing themselves in partnership with law enforcement is the undisputed wave of the future when it comes to keeping communities safe from crime.

Source: Adapted with permission from Keith Carr, "Transitioning Your Community," *Community Policing Exchange,* September/October 1998, pp. 1–2.

programs that can assist the local community and mobilize community support for resisting the return and proliferation of the problem once the police are removed. This step was accomplished in New York through the implementation of foot patrols, anti-crime operations, crime prevention programs, and the response to special functions (Pate and Shtull 1994). In Arlington County, Virginia, this step was accomplished by working with community patrols and working with the local youth in various capacities, such as coaching a local softball team and sponsoring community activities. Community meetings continued to facilitate many of the programs implemented and became the foundation for problem solving at various stages.

The development of community support and understanding of community-oriented policing is important, as is education on the concepts for both the community and the police. Officers involved in micro-community-oriented policing not only provide training and education to the citizens in the target area, but as they come away with experience of the advantages and disadvantages of community-oriented policing, they can educate the management and line officers of the entire police department as well as members of the local government, local leadership, and citizens in other parts of the community. The collection of data can also be utilized to show what some of these advantages and disadvantages are because there may be differences between the police officer's perception and what actually occurred.

One critical concern with the second stage toward full community-oriented policing returns to the issue of time. The implementation of micro-community-oriented policing must be established as a short-term goal for a certain period of time. If not enough time is allowed for this testing of the larger concept on a small scale, inadequate citizen response, police response, and data collection will create a lack of information available for implementing the next incremental stage. If too much time is allowed for the second stage, the special unit will become stagnant and will come under an excessive amount of scrutiny and criticism from other parts of the police department. Micro-community-oriented policing is not an end to community-oriented policing but only a means to the end. It must not be allowed to become the end result, which may give a false perception of community-oriented policing, as the complete systemic approach would never be able to grow and expand under the microscopic confines of the test site. Therefore, there is a danger if the police department or the community fails to declare the short-term goal of micro-community-oriented policing accomplished and moves on to the next stage.

Moore (1992, 135) also recognizes four additional adverse effects if a police department fails to move beyond micro-community-oriented policing:

1. By isolating the function in a specialized unit, it becomes vulnerable to organizational ridicule.
2. Once a special squad is formed, everyone else in the department is seemingly relieved of responsibility for enhancing the quality of community relations.

3. If the community relations unit should obtain important information about community concerns or ways in which the community might be able to help the department, it is difficult to make those observations heard inside the police department—particularly if what they have to report is bad news or imposes unwelcome demands on the rest of the organization.
4. The organization no longer looks for other ways to improve community relations.

All four of these can be detrimental to community-oriented policing if the police department fails to move forward to stage III after the necessary evaluations have been obtained from the trial run implemented in stage II.

There is value, however, in implementing stage II, and the majority of police departments in the United States that have moved to community-oriented policing have invested much of their time and resources into micro-community-oriented policing, often called demonstration projects or test sites. In the late 1980s, Lieutenant Charles Moose of the Portland, Oregon, Police Bureau, who later became the police chief, participated in a demonstration project known as the IRIS Court Project. This project took a low-income neighborhood riddled with drugs, gangs, and prostitution and, through the three components of community-oriented policing, reduced crime and problems in the neighborhood; this success became the model for citywide implementation (Communicare 1995e).

A good example of a police department finding itself in stage II in the mid-1990s is the Boca Raton Police Department (Boca Raton, Florida, population 61,000). (Communicare 1995b). The Boca Raton Police Department created a community-policing unit that has the primary function of engaging the community and solving problems. It began its micro-community-oriented policing project in a public housing area by permanently assigning a police officer to the community and establishing an office at the local community center. The officer has assisted in cleaning up the neighborhood, creating a new playground for the children, providing services as a liaison between the community and other government services, and, along with the Department of Housing and Urban Development (HUD), purchasing an apartment to become a youth study center with tutors, a library, and computer equipment donated by IBM. Crime rates have dropped dramatically, the community has a sense of pride it previously lacked, and the relationship between the police and the community is at an all-time high.

Two more recent examples of police departments finding themselves in stage II of implementing community-oriented policing are the Helena Police Department (Montana) and the Jackson Police Department (Wyoming) (Giacomazzi and Brody 2004). The Helena Police Department had begun implementing community-oriented policing in the mid-1990s, but due to budget constraints and limited acceptance by mid-level management, implementation lingered into the twenty-first century. However, in 2000, the Western Regional Institute for Community Oriented Public Safety (WRICOPS) provided some training and an assessment of Helena's community-oriented policing program (Giacomazzi and Brody 2004). WRICOPS noted some improvements over the next several years and found that patrol officers were "assigned to districts for several months and given responsibility for problem-solving activity and communicating with members of the community in their district," that there were increased "opportunities for greater input in formulating and changing department policies," and that "greater efforts to reach out to the community, especially children, have occurred" (Giacomazzi and Brody 2004, p. 49).

In terms of the Jackson Police Department in Wyoming, Giacomazzi and Brody (2004) found similar problems in terms of a lack of support for community-oriented policing within the agency itself. Some changes were being made in the wake of the WRICOPS assessment, and these included (1) the department's "mission and values statement [was revised] to be more reflective of the COP philosophy," (2) the community policing coordinator position was eliminated in order to support the department moving toward department-wide implementation, and (3) internal communication was greatly improved (Giacomazzi and Brody 2004). Both of these cases highlight many of the issues that agencies in stage II of implementing community-oriented policing discover: a limited amount of support for adopting community-oriented policing and the difficulties of moving an agency forward through the other stages of COP.

Stage III: Transition

The third stage of implementing community-oriented policing is the transitional stage. In this stage, the police department must begin applying the systemic approach to policing. The transitional stage should commence with all officers in the police department having some knowledge of the community-oriented policing concept: The micro-community-oriented policing stage should have provided feedback on the long-term goal, and the department should now begin addressing the full implementation of community-oriented policing on all fronts. The transitional stage should conclude with every facet of the police department implementing some measure of incremental movement toward the full implementation of community-oriented policing.

It is not possible to detail every facet of the police department that should reveal some change in the transitional stage because every police department is different and

 COP IN ACTION

Community Policing: Department-Wide Task Force Implementation

A prelude to disaster occurs when a police organization adopts a specialized unit approach to community policing as a department-wide philosophy. Regardless of the size of the task force (one, ten, or one hundred people), when officers are singled out to conduct community policing activities with duties and responsibilities that are different from the rest of the organization, that agency has diminished its chances for total philosophical integration and success.

When an organization divides itself into "those who serve the public" and "those who do real police work," barriers of animosity are created. The department will find it difficult, if not impossible, to overcome this rift if the two factions do not believe they share a common goal.

Because police agencies are systemic organizations with each segment relying upon the interaction of the others to achieve common goals, such as the reduction of crime or improvement of quality of life, the entity must work together under one primary philosophy. When community policing is not adopted by the entire organization, it becomes just another program implemented by just another specialized and often resented unit.

To instill a community policing philosophy department-wide, an agency must implement the approach simultaneously throughout the entire department. Each officer must be responsible for engaging in problem-solving activities with the community in his or her area of assignment in addition to normal patrol responsibilities. Small- to medium-size departments will find this easier to accomplish, but it may be logistically difficult for large agencies to implement. The key is that no segment of the organization is excluded from this indoctrination, and that everyone feels as if they are an integral part of the transition.

Source: Adapted with permission from John Matthews, "Community Policing: Department-Wide Versus 'Task Force' Implementation," *Law and Order,* December 1995, pp. 34–37.

---

some are so large that to detail the changes would require a separate book. However, it is possible to detail those central changes that will affect the rest of the police department and subsequently cause some of the transitional change. These changes may include the reorganization of the shift, structure, and beat alignment to allow decentralization of police services. As shifts are redesigned based on consistent time and beat structures for police officers to begin working in "their" community (along with the beat realignment to coincide with the various communities, both residential and business, rather than with some geographical street system), distinct changes will result from this structural change. Ties with the community and community committees for these realigned beats will increase. The potential for altered patrol methods may result. For example, a new beat may exist with a smaller geographical area, such as a business district in a downtown area with only ten blocks to patrol, creating the need for and adaptability of foot patrols. And this realignment also may allow for greater adaptability and implementation of the three components.

In other areas of the department, there should be similar transitional changes to community-oriented policing. Those in charge of hiring can begin implementing changes by drafting, publishing, and hiring under a new job description that complements the new duties of the community-oriented policing officer. The training division can begin department-wide training on the philosophy, three components, and relationship with the community under community-oriented policing. Management can reassess police officer evaluations under the systemic approach and begin the process of incorporating them into the system. The department should coordinate with outside agencies to train them on community-oriented policing, garner their support, and explain their role under the new systemic approach. The foundation of community-oriented policing—the community—should also be largely included in all training, programs, and the three components.

Once again, there should be a time constraint for this stage, which in our model was two years. In some police departments, such as the New York City Police Department, the ability to implement on such a wide scale in two years may be impracticable, whereas implementing the concept in the Wildwood, New Jersey, Police Department may not require the full two years. In either case, the time frame must be balanced with the sense of urgency for understanding the concepts, implementing the changes, and moving forward with the process. The implementation of community-oriented policing must never be allowed to stagnate. As problems arise, changes should be quickly made to the short-term goals, and then the police department should continue moving forward to reach the long-term goals.

Two police departments that have found themselves in stage III of community-oriented policing are the Fort Worth Police Department (Fort Worth, Texas, population

 **COP IN ACTION**

Characteristics of Department-Wide versus Task Force Implementation of Community Policing

Department-Wide Implementation

- The philosophy is embraced by the entire department.
- There is not animosity based on job descriptions; everyone performs community policing initiatives.
- All officers are trained in community policing and problem solving.
- There is a single agenda: to resolve community concerns about crime and disorder by responding to calls for service, mobilizing the community, and building partnerships.
- All officers are responsible for taking action and empowered with authority to make decisions.
- Entrepreneurial problem solving with action and creativity is encouraged.
- Pooling of common resources is encouraged, making them accessible to everyone.
- Community police officers are integrated throughout the organization.
- Officers work on all types and sizes of problems.
- The documentation is shared department-wide.

Task Force Implementation

- Acceptance of the philosophy is isolated to individuals in the community policing unit.
- Employee resentment exists because of job description, "real police" vs. "social worker" mentality.
- Only selected officers are trained in the concept.
- The dual/competing agenda: primary responsibility results in calls for service and other police activities to be neglected.
- Officers are responsible for taking action, but decision-making authority resides with management.
- Bureaucratic entanglements occur due to agency restrictions.
- Specialized resources are permitted strictly for the community policing unit.
- Community-based officers are segregated from others.
- Specific problems are targeted.
- Documentation is limited to isolated special projects.

Source: Adapted with permission from John Matthews, "Community Policing: Department-Wide versus 'Task Force' Implementation," *Law and Order,* December 1995, p. 37.

447,000) and the Lumberton Police Department (Lumberton, North Carolina, population 18,000) (Communicare 1995c and 1995e, respectively). The Fort Worth Police Department, through the cooperation of both the police chief and the city mayor, has successfully moved the police department from stage I, which was conducted in the early 1990s, through stage II in 1992 to its current place in stage III. The police department implemented the concept of neighborhood police officer (NPO) teams in early 1992 by creating a storefront office, creating a working relationship with the community, and problem-solving in specific areas. Although the NPO teams were successful, the police department met resistance from older officers and officers not involved in the implementation of community-oriented policing. In 1994 and 1995, the Fort Worth Police Department brought the entire police department on board with the concept; it is now established citywide through storefront offices, a mobile office that moves from neighborhood to neighborhood on a monthly basis, and community involvement through organizations and volunteers. As a result of the department-wide implementation, the Fort Worth Police Department overcame the resistance on the part of the police and has created advocates out of those who were once detractors. The police department has successfully begun the transition to macro-community-oriented policing by utilizing all three components of community-oriented policing; decentralizing by personnel, structure, and geography through a specific focus on the various communities in the city; and utilizing the storefronts as a focal point for working with the community.

The Lumberton, North Carolina, Police Department, under Chief Harry Dolan, began implementing stage I and stage II of community-oriented policing in 1992 and has successfully moved into stage III. Through the cooperation of the elected officials, business community, media, service agencies, community, and all members of the police department, the Lumberton Police Department moved from testing a substation in southern Lumberton in 1992 as a micro-community-oriented policing project to having a substation in each quadrant of the city. Although each substation is in various stages of development, the decentralization of the police department through geography, personnel, and structure has begun to take hold department-wide. The department has also permanently assigned management, detectives, and line officers to quadrants, thus creating mini–police departments. The methods employed have included first moving into the area utilizing strategic-oriented policing methods, such as increased patrols to drive the criminal element out of the community. The department then successfully established neighborhood-oriented policing tactics such as foot patrols, bike patrols, school resource officer programs, and such programs as DARE and a DARE Band made up of police officers to establish ties with the community. Finally, through contact with the community members, the police have worked with the community to address their local problems and how to solve them through problem-oriented policing. By combining stages I and II, Chief Dolan was able to implement with a sense of urgency and utilize the success and failures, as well as police and community input, to develop a strategic plan for how the police department should continue to move forward with community-oriented policing at a slightly faster rate of implementation.

Stage IV: Macro-Community-Oriented Policing

The fourth stage of the implementation process is macro-community-oriented policing. The fourth stage should begin at the point where the entire police department has seen some implementation of the systemic approach and should end with the full implementation of community-oriented policing. As opposed to its antithesis, micro-community-oriented policing, macro-community-oriented policing should see department-wide implementation. It should no longer apply to one or more target areas, but rather it

Long Beach, California, police officer's working the barbecue for a community celebration. (*Courtesy of the Long Beach Police Department, Long Beach, California.*)

should find its way into every facet of the department, every community, and every target to some degree. Again, because every police department is different, the short-term goals in this stage will be different. However, there are some commonalities regardless of size or location.

The complete decentralization of the police department should be apparent in this stage. Although the office of the chief may feel uncomfortable decentralizing some departments, such as homicide or robbery units, by and large the department should see a flattening of the pyramid. Permanent shifts and permanent beats should be the norm, with little rotation in and out. Training on all aspects of community-oriented policing should be a standard for in-service training as well as for all members of the community, both government workers and average citizens. The three components should be operating on a consistent basis with the support of the community and the community groups. The community should designate strategic-oriented policing targets for their concerns, both real and perceived. Neighborhood-oriented policing programs should be operating, and community committees should evaluate and discuss them. Finally, identifying problems, developing responses, implementing a response in concert, and evaluating the success or failure should be common tasks for the police and the community.

Although it would seem that all of the tenets of community-oriented policing would be satisfied during the macro-community-oriented policing stage, this will most likely not be the case. As the police department begins to see full implementation, the issues that the police chief and the police department as a whole face will be larger in breadth and depth. The earlier example was the complete decentralization of the police department, which entails decentralizing all investigations and transforming specialists into generalists. The police department cannot just decentralize the police on the beat and expect to see the complete application of community-oriented policing; it must decentralize the special units as well. It may prove difficult for a police chief to decentralize the homicide investigation unit in the face of perhaps several critical unsolved cases. The decentralization of the homicide unit at this point may not be feasible and may have to be delayed until the timing is right. Even without several high-publicity unsolved cases, it may still prove difficult to decentralize this unit. This is not to say that community-oriented policing has not been implemented, but, rather, it has not yet been implemented at a macrolevel.

Two current examples of police departments that successfully reached stage IV of implementation include the St. Petersburg Police Department (St. Petersburg, Florida, population 240,000, under Police Chief Darrell Stephens) and the Austin Police Department (Austin, Texas, population 447,000, under Police Chief Elizabeth Watson) (Communicare 1995f and 1995a, respectively). The success of the St. Petersburg Police Department is based on a very positive response on the part of the police chief, citizens, elected officials, business community, and line officers. The police department has been able to move quickly and methodically through the first three stages by soliciting input from all of the members mentioned and receiving their cooperation to move forward with the planning, testing, and transitional stages to macro-community-oriented policing. The St. Petersburg Police Department has decentralized through reassessing where community boundaries lie and permanently assigning officers to these areas. The police department then eliminated rotating shifts; instead, it focused on geographical areas and assigned the responsibility for covering those areas twenty-four hours a day. The police officers have more input as to when they work and what they do to address criminal and order maintenance issues during their shifts. Mid-level managers have also decentralized into geographical areas and are now accountable for everything that occurs in their collection of beat areas. To complement this decentralization by geography, personnel, and structure, both detectives and nonsworn personnel have also been assigned alongside the mid-level managers and are accountable for these geographical areas as well.

The police department has also been heavily engaged in all three components of community-oriented policing. It has utilized strategic policing methods to remove drug and prostitution activity from various neighborhoods to allow for neighborhood-oriented policing methods to be employed. St. Petersburg has utilized a wide range of methods in this second component, such as bike and golf-cart patrols, community events, and community resource centers staffed by citizens who can assist the police and the public at large. Finally, through these specific neighborhoods, the department has been able to solicit the input of the community to determine where problems lie, develop ideas on how to address these problems, and implement and evaluate the department's actions.

The Austin, Texas, Police Department has also managed to achieve stage IV of the implementation process through similar actions. Although the police department began implementing community-oriented policing in 1989, it suffered many of the problems facing a department in stage II by not fully advancing to stage III. When Police Chief Elizabeth Watson (coming from the Houston Police Department, Houston, Texas) was hired in 1992, she immediately began to move the police department into stage III to reduce the resistance of traditional officers and the conflicts arising between traditional officers and community-oriented police officers. The police department immediately reassessed its number of personnel and quickly reduced the layers of bureaucracy in mid-level management; at the same time, it reduced the span of control of sergeants from more than fifteen officers to an average of six. Once this personnel decentralization was complete and a geographical decentralization (in which officers were assigned to a given beat for one to three years) was implemented, the department moved to decentralization by structure. It accomplished this objective by assigning two lieutenants to a specific geographical area for accountability, selecting one to cover patrol and the other to cover community-oriented policing. However, to prevent conflicts between the two sets of officers, all were provided training on community-oriented policing and were directed to work together. Although patrol officers were responsible for responding to calls for service, they were still required to work with the community-oriented police officers on their beat to coordinate many of the projects. Despite the split, this system has worked extremely well for the Austin Police Department.

The department also increased the use of the three components of community-oriented policing by creating crime net teams to handle and conduct various methods of strategic-oriented policing. These teams are made up of officers who move into a preselected area and stay for a length of time to move the criminal element from the area. One additional tactic has been the use of a mobile substation that pulls into a high-crime area for approximately one month and becomes a substation from which officers work to move the criminal element out of the neighborhood. Neighborhood-oriented policing methods have been utilized by working through neighborhood centers, with advisory boards, and hand-in-hand with Citizens on Patrol groups. The department has effectively used such programs as Neighborhood Watch based on the neighborhood centers and advisory boards, graffiti cleanup days, and education programs such as one to educate the community on the use of 911. Additional tactics, such as bike patrols, youth centers for mentoring, and a job fair (that managed to solicit over a hundred businesses to attend and secured over a hundred jobs in one day), have been well received by the community. Finally, the police department anchored the concept of problem-oriented policing in the daily workings of the police and community with much success. For example, a vacant lot where trash and abandoned cars were dumped had become a haven for drug dealers. The police and the community cleaned it up, effectively driving out the dealers from that area.

Under a recent Office of Community-Oriented Policing grant, the Arlington, Texas, Police Department directed its energies toward a neighborhood that had not participated well in the community-oriented policing partnership. The police, through the grant, began addressing the multiethnic neighborhood's perceptions of the police as well as the problems of disorder by developing a police–community problem-solving program, developing cultural awareness programs in the neighborhood, and creating volunteer organizations in the neighborhood for overcoming these cultural barriers. The evaluators of this program found that it was the adoption of community-oriented policing that made the grant and the police–community partnership so successful (Eve et al. 2003).

Stage V: Community-Oriented Policing

The final stage is community-oriented policing itself or, in other terms, the institutionalization of community-oriented policing. The premise for naming it community-oriented policing is that once the entire police department has achieved this decentralization, has implemented the three components, and has shifted much of the power to the community, then and only then can a police department truly call itself a community-oriented policing department. Currently, only a few police departments in the United States have reached this goal. Most police departments are generally in the micro-community-oriented stage or transitional stage; very few have made it to the macro-community-oriented stage. This is not to say that the fifth stage is unobtainable. Rather, the movement toward community-oriented policing has just begun, and it will take the dedication of many forward-thinking police chiefs, motivated line officers, and cooperative community members before the concept will achieve this end.

Two police departments that realized the institutionalization of community-oriented policing are the San Diego Police Department (San Diego, California, population 1,110,000, under Police Chief Jerry Sanders) and the Portland Police Bureau (Portland, Oregon, population 438,000, under Police Chief Charles Moose) (Communicare 1995g and 1995f, respectively). The San Diego Police Department began implementing community-oriented policing in 1988, utilizing mainly the problem-oriented policing methods under the SARA (scanning, analysis, response, and assessment) model, and has since moved through all four stages to reach what is in effect the institutionalization of community-oriented policing. The police department has effectively decentralized by geography, personnel, and structure and has found that as the sixth-largest city in the United States, its communities are diverse. Differences consist of such variables as race, ethnicity, economics, and social and political differences, and the police department realized that its various communities needed a variety of services. Based on this realization, the decentralization of the police department became driven by these communities, and essentially a number of mini–police departments were created, backed by neighborhood-oriented policing teams, management, detectives, and nonsworn personnel.

The community was brought into the concept through the implementation of problem-oriented policing in 1988, and through this pilot program, the department realized the value of citizens assisting the police. Since that time, the police department, with the community's help, has established numerous storefront offices, obtained the help of over 600 volunteers to assist in this endeavor, created a Citizens on Patrol program with an additional 2,500 volunteers, established an eighty-hour academy to provide them training, and established a program known as Retired Seniors Volunteer Patrol (RSVP), in which senior citizens ride in patrol cars in teams of two to assist in traffic accidents, identify problems in the neighborhoods, and take police reports for minor incidents.

The police department has also institutionalized the concepts of strategic-oriented policing, neighborhood-oriented policing, and problem-oriented policing throughout the entire city. One example of this institutionalization can be seen in the methods employed in a drug house area. The police department utilizes a Drug Abatement Response Team (DART) as well as increased patrols to drive the criminal element out of an area with high drug activity. It then works with the community to get it involved in keeping the criminal element from returning once it is driven from the neighborhood by working with community groups, businesses, and individual citizens. Once established, or through the use of preestablished community groups, the department then begins the process of problem-oriented policing to determine what other solutions are available to keep the drug activity from returning. It is clear that San Diego Police Department has been one of the flagships of community-oriented policing with its heavy emphasis on police–community relationships and problem-solving methods. It has made every effort in its shift to the community-oriented policing philosophy to incorporate a systemic approach to policing. As Chief Jerry Sanders (2000, 132) explains, "The shift in philosophy demanded changes in virtually every element of policing. The department has changed its structure, hiring practices, training programs, community-outreach efforts, and mechanisms of accountability."

The catalyst for community-oriented policing in Portland, Oregon, was the rise in the use of crack cocaine and the gang activity associated with its sales. The police department under Chief Tom Potter, driven largely by the community, began the process of determining what methods could be utilized to address the many problems associated with the drug crisis. While a demonstration project was implemented during this time frame to determine the success of community-oriented policing, the citizens of Portland, Oregon, began pushing for a change in policing methods. Through a consensus on the part of the police, the community, and the local government, they defined community-oriented policing, defined the mission of the police, and created a Community Policing Transition Plan, published in 1990, that became the police bureau's guideline for implementing the systemic approach. Despite a change in police chiefs when Chief Charles Moose was elevated to the position, the movement toward institutionalizing community-oriented policing continued.

The Portland Police Bureau, like the San Diego Police Department, decentralized by geography, personnel, and structure and effectively implemented all three components of community-oriented policing. Dividing the police department into precincts allowed managers to be held accountable for what occurred in their areas, and in turn the Neighborhood Liaison Officer Teams were held accountable for what occurred in their specific neighborhoods. This plan was backed by detectives, nonsworn personnel, the district attorney's office, community associations, coalitions, and contact offices as well as the local police union.

Neighborhood kids at a community safety fair sponsored by the Long Beach, California, Police Department. (*Courtesy of the Long Beach Police Department, Long Beach, California.*)

Although it is apparent that both the San Diego Police Department and the Portland Police Bureau have attained the final stage, the institutionalization of community-oriented policing, this achievement is not an end in itself but the creation of a whole new beginning for the advancement of the systemic approach. The move beyond the fifth stage of community-oriented policing in programs that have seen implementation to date is only limited by the creation of new theory, policy, practice, and programs that can be created under this concept. Community-oriented policing could be the foundation for another generation of policing, a link in the evolution process, in similar form and fashion to the way police–community relations provided a stepping-stone to community-oriented policing. However, for now, the goal for the police department moving toward the systemic approach should be this "final" stage.

In 2001, a study on small- to medium-size police departments and their community policing programs was conducted by the National Institute of Justice (Chaiken, 2001). Researchers studied how eight agencies in three different states went about implementing community-oriented policing. These police agencies consisted of Eureka Police Department (California), Humboldt County Sheriff's Office (California), Redding Police Department (California), Shasta County Sheriff's Office (California), Pocatello Police Department (Idaho), Bannock County Sheriff's Office (Idaho), Rapid City Police Department (South Dakota), and Pennington County Sheriff's Office (South Dakota). The researchers identified five progressive stages of community policing, very similar to the five stages previously discussed (see Table 6-3). They found that the key to advancing through these stages appeared to be winning the support of local and state policymakers and civic leaders. These local elected leaders, in turn, demonstrated support for the police department's implementation of community-oriented policing. More specifically, only one jurisdiction in the study was considered

TABLE 6-3   *Progressive Stages of Community Policing*

STAGE	POLICE ACTIVITIES
1	**Establishing a special unit, neighborhood center, or other community policing initiative.** Community policing is handled as special assignments, not part of regular patrol. Departmental priority remains rapid response to citizen requests.
2	**Getting the community more involved.** Outreach and targeted response to reduce high rates of particular crimes in particular neighborhoods are departmental priorities.
3	**Solving problems through coordination and cooperation.** Officers collaborate with residents on short-term projects to address specific local concerns. Problem-solving initiatives are given priority.
4	**Broadening collaboration to prevent crime and delinquency.** Cross-agency/community-wide coalition plans of action include police. High priority is placed on collaboration through long-term programs.
5	**Institutionalizing community policing in city and county strategic planning.** Community policing activities are practiced throughout the department. Priority is given to sustained, community-based approaches.

Source: Marcia R. Chaiken, *COPS: Innovations in Policing in American Heartlands.* Washington, D.C.: National Institute of Justice, 2001.

 **COP IN ACTION**

Longmont Police Department: Community Policing Starts with Communication

In 1993, the Longmont Police Department (LPD) was typical of most police departments in the United States. It consisted of men and women working in a top-down, command-in-control environment. Personnel were managed with excessive policies and procedures.

In early 2000, the LPD developed a long-range strategic plan. The plan called for several initiatives to build better communication and discussion with the community. Police Chief Butler said there was a key concern: "It seemed that unless the police initiated and continued to maintain the community policing efforts, there was a good chance that viable options for dealing with issues would just wither away for lack of interest." Butler went on to say that the information and communication links between police and citizens had traditionally been one-way and not frequent or substantive enough to develop partnerships.

Among the many areas identified that needed to be addressed were training and communication. In regard to training, it was identified that several courses on problem solving, communication skills, and utilizing community resources needed to be added to the police training curriculum. The objectives of these training sessions were to teach employees the concepts of partnership and how to work in partnership with citizens and each other. In regard to communication, the LPD made all meetings open to any employee who wanted to attend. Agendas, to which employees can contribute, were published in advance. Monthly staff meetings, called department-wide "conversations," were implemented.

Among the many programs implemented to address these two concerns included the hiring of community services coordinators, Web site information and homepage, a community messaging system, Spanish immersion training, quarterly newspaper inserts, a weekly cable television show dedicated to crime prevention, community surveys, and "Our Town" conferences.

The Longmont Police Department was found to be very successful in enhancing not only communication between the police and the community, but also among the police themselves.

Source: Adapted from A. Schneider et al., *Community Policing in Action: A Practitioner's Eye View of Organizational Change.* Washington, D.C.: Office of Community Oriented Policing Services, 2003.

---

to have reached the highest stage. Police officials in that city worked closely with local and county officials to incorporate community policing initiatives such as addressing neighborhood blight and introducing youth programs in the jurisdiction's annual strategic plans. This study, then, lends support to the notion that police agencies implementing community policing do tend to go through these five stages and that a key element to achieving full institutionalization of community policing is the support of local elected leaders.

COMMUNICATION AND TRAINING

Two central themes running through the implementation process are the key topics of communication and training. These two topics must be factored into every facet of community-oriented policing and must be included at every stage of the implementation process. Each one becomes a determinate factor in the success of achieving the next stage and implementing all of the policies and programs under community-oriented policing.

Communication is a key ingredient for any successful organization, regardless of whether a police department is traditional or community-oriented. However, as the concepts of community-oriented policing are implemented and the number of people involved in criminal and order maintenance issues grows, there will be a distinct need for better communication. Recent research has highlighted the critical importance of communication in implementing community-oriented policing, especially in terms of police communication with socially disadvantaged neighborhoods (Schneider 1999). In fact, to highlight the importance of the issue of communication in community-oriented policing, a publication by Kidd and Braziel (1999b) titled *COP Talk: Essential Communication Skills for Community Policing* was solely dedicated to teaching officers and students about the importance of communication. Open lines of communication must be maintained between not only management and line officers but also the local government, private organizations, businesses, community groups, and those community committees formed under neighborhood-oriented policing and problem-oriented policing. The decentralization of the police also creates a need for greater communication among all members of the police department as well as every member of the community. Written communication should be generated to keep everyone informed at both the community level and the government level. Written communication can be through such things as the local newspapers; newsletters for individual communities, the police, and the local government; and special publications on the mission, goals, programs, and successes or failures of the implementation process (Bureau of Justice Assistance 1994a). Oral communication must also find its way into the homes of the community and at the highest levels of community leadership under community-oriented policing. Oral communication may be through radio stations, various group meetings, mass community meetings, cable television, local news, in-service training, and various community events, to name a few (Bureau of Justice Assistance 1994a). Telling the community about all of the programs and methods of policing utilized under community-oriented policing not only keeps the public informed and educated but also breaks down many of the barriers between the police and the community.

One additional form of communication that is extremely important under community-oriented policing and throughout the implementation process is feedback from all of the new programs on their successes and failures. This feedback should come not only from the factual data generated through statistical studies of the crime rates but also from the perceptions of crime and order maintenance issues on the part of the police and the community. This feedback becomes critical to the incremental process of implementation because it provides the input for making corrections along the way to implementing new policy and new procedures. The sole focus of the next chapter is thus the evaluation of community-oriented policing.

The other key factor in the successful implementation of community-oriented policing is training (see Birzer and Unnithan 2000; Breci and Erickson 1998; Cardarelli, McDevitt, and Baum 1998; Cornett-DeVito and McGlone 2000; Kerley 2002); Palmiotto and Lab 2000; Ramsey 2002; Quinet, Nunn, and Kincaid, 2003; Williams 1998). In order to adequately prepare for the move to community-oriented policing, training must be provided to every member of the police department, both line officers and management, as well as to the local government, businesses, and members of the community (Dubois and Harnett 2002; King and Lab 2000). Training should not be solely directed toward the police officer on the street, leaving everyone else out of the loop. Managers must receive the same training as well as additional training on their role and function under the systemic approach. At the same time, members of the community outside the police department must also be educated through community seminars, training for other government agencies, and business seminars. Much of the same training should be made available to all of these groups and individuals, but additional tailor-made training should also be provided.

The type of training offered should be created based on the incremental process, by providing training on all of the different aspects of community-oriented policing. An analysis of training needs by Palmiotto, Birzer, and Unnithan generated a suggested curriculum for community policing training. They suggest that officers receive training based on three basic premises (Palmiotto, Birzer, and Unnithan 2000, 13–14): (1) Police officers should possess a sense of social history, (2) police officers should be inculcated with a sense of society and community, and (3) police officers should be equipped with the skills and knowledge for incorporating community policing into their work. In fact, they go so far as to develop a police academy sequence of classes that includes the philosophy of the police department, police history, police culture, police ethics, problem-oriented policing, and crime prevention (Palmiotto, Birzer, and Unnithan 2001). One police department that used a similar approach, the Savannah, Georgia, Police Department, implemented community-oriented policing by using seven training modules to train not only line officers but also management and local government members (Donahue 1993; McLaughlin and Donahue 1995) (see Table 6-4). The seven training modules included training on various aspects of community-oriented policing and integrated much of the literature on community-oriented policing, such as the "Broken Windows" article, by James Q. Wilson and George L. Kelling (1982), and "Problem-Oriented Policing," by William Spelman and John E. Eck (1987b). The modules included one on community-oriented policing as an overview, one on problem-oriented policing, and one on participatory decision making and leadership techniques for management, supervision, and

TABLE 6-4 *Community-Oriented Policing Training Modules*
Savannah, Georgia, Police Department

Module I	Participatory decision making and leadership techniques for management, supervision, and street officers
	• Reviews community-oriented policing (COP) for administrators and managers
	• Reviews overview of all seven modules
Module II	Community-oriented policing
	• Reviews principles and elements of COP
	• Reviews broken windows theory
Module III	Problem-oriented policing
	• Reviews problem-solving methods
	• Reviews problem-oriented policing method (SARA model)
Module IV	Referral system, materials, and city ordinances
	• Reviews resources outside the police department
	• Reviews utilization of city ordinances

Module V	Sources of human information
	• Reviews listening and communication techniques
	• Reviews various types of police–citizen contacts
Module VI	Neighborhood meetings, survey of citizen needs, and tactical crime analysis
	• Reviews methods of soliciting citizen input
	• Reviews methods of crime analysis
Module VII	Crime prevention home and business surveys
	• Reviews methods of crime prevention
	• Summarizes and integrates concepts from all seven modules

street officers (McLaughlin and Donahue 1995). This approach to training was found to be the best method of training in the Savannah Police Department and would be appropriate for most police departments implementing community-oriented policing because of its ability to train the police, local government, and members of the local community with ease (McLaughlin and Donahue 1995). As the members of a traditional police department move forward with the implementation process of community-oriented policing, a good guideline for training would be to emulate the Savannah Police Department method or to utilize the sequence of chapters in this book as an education guide for community-oriented policing, moving from its historical evolution through the basic concepts, the three components, and departmental restructuring to implementation and assessment of the systemic approach to policing.

CONCLUSION

Community-oriented policing consists of three integral components: strategic-oriented policing, neighborhood-oriented policing, and problem-oriented policing. To fully embody the goals of community-oriented policing, all three components must be implemented, thus allowing for the larger concept to succeed. If one component fails to see implementation in cooperation with the other two, the systemic approach to policing is not complete and is therefore destined to fail. Each component depends on the others for the systemic approach to be actualized.

Strategic-oriented policing must be implemented immediately, whether with the involvement of local community groups or by the police department alone. The areas to be targeted must be determined and prioritized, and the various tactics that would work best to address the criminal or order maintenance problem should be implemented. From there the community must be drawn into the program, and planning for the neighborhood-oriented policing programs that would best suit the needs of the target area must be determined. As the sense of urgency of these programs is created and the criminal or order maintenance element is removed from the community temporarily, it allows the community to establish a sense of order and take back its corners, streets, and communities. Problems must be analyzed continuously, and new approaches to addressing these problems must be created. These programs must then be implemented and evaluated based on a variety of factors, and a determination should be made for the program to be abolished, continued, or enhanced. Synthesis of the three components that results in diffusion can only be considered beneficial to the interaction between the community and the police. Then, and only then, can community-oriented policing, a systemic approach to policing, be evaluated as the true paradigm of policing.

Recognizing the various scenarios for the implementation of community-oriented policing and how the three components become integrated under the systemic approach to policing, it is important to turn to the changes that should occur in order to provide an environment in which the framework of community-oriented policing can thrive. This must start with changes in the organization and management of the police (Chapter 7) and changes in the role of the police (Chapter 8). Additionally, changes on the part of the community must be observed (Chapter 9) as well as changes in the role of the police chief (Chapter 10). It is to these changes we must now turn.

The implementation of community-oriented policing is the most difficult aspect of the systemic approach. The application of policy to the practical world is always difficult, and in policing, with its many compounding problems, it can prove to be even more difficult. The implementation of this new approach to policing is largely predicated on policy, and the success of implementation is based on the ability of the police chief and police administration to implement change. This is no easy task, for the obstacles one faces are a natural resistance to change, the police subculture, and the police bureaucracy. Each is difficult to change in its own right, but added together they create a monumental task.

To accomplish this task, police chiefs, with the assistance of their staff, line officers, and the community, should define the long-term goals for achieving community-oriented policing and then define short-term goals that will assist in moving the police department toward this end. By utilizing an incremental method of change, the police department can commence the implementation process in a slow and methodical manner, addressing concerns and dealing with minor issues along the way. Using this approach will create a realistic workload for both management and the line officers, and it will reduce the resistance to change because change will come in a quantity that is acceptable.

A plan for accomplishing this task is drawn from the literature and worked into five stages that create short-term goals for the police department and allow for incremental changes in proceeding from one stage to the next. The first stage is the planning stage, when the ideas and concepts of community-oriented policing are floated throughout the police department and community. Preparations are then made for a department-wide implementation. As the police department moves toward this short-term goal, an interim goal, the second stage, is the implementation of micro-community-oriented policing. By implementing the concept on a small scale, the reactions of the police and community and other factors can be evaluated and changes made to the departmental plan to allow for the correction of what could be bad policy or procedure within a particular police department. Once this reassessment has been made, the police department can enter the third stage, which is the transitional stage. It is here that the police department utilizes the systemic approach to implement at all levels and in all departments within the police department and achieve the next stage, macro-community-oriented policing. In this fourth stage, the majority of the police department should see full implementation, and the police department should move toward full institutionalization of the concept by achieving the fifth and final stage, community-oriented policing.

COP ON THE WORLD WIDE WEB

California COPPS Website, Attorney General

http://caag.state.ca.us/copps/index.htm

Community Policing Index

http://www.ou.edu/oupd/tcpi/tcpi.htm

Links to other community-oriented policing websites.

Fort Collins, Colorado, Police Department

http://www.ci.fort-collins.co.us/police

Police Executive Research Forum

http://www.policeforum.org

Police Foundation

http://www.policefoundation.org

Regional Community Policing Institutes (RCPIs) for Training

http://www.usdoj.gov/cops/gpa/tta/rcpi/rcpi_special.htm

REVIEW QUESTIONS

1. Who typically initiates community-oriented policing. Why?
2. Describe and detail the five stages of implementing community-oriented policing.
3. Why are communications and training so critical to implementing community-oriented policing?

CHAPTER 7

Organization and Management

Order or disorder depends on organization.

—Sun Tzu

CHAPTER OBJECTIVES

- Understand that under COP the organization structure must change.
- Understand that under COP the management style and methods must change.
- Understand how values and goals guide the COP philosophy.
- Comprehend the importance of a sound mission statement.
- Understand the three methods of decentralization.
- Define *total quality management* and understand how this private sector management method is applied in COP.

When a police department moves toward community-oriented policing, it should be understood that for the overall concept to be a viable program, the police department must implement all three components: strategic-oriented policing, neighborhood-oriented policing, and problem-oriented policing. However, the concept of community-oriented policing cannot stop there if it is to be successful. It must change not only the way the product of policing is delivered or what services are offered but also the entire organization and methods of management that provide and deliver these services (Redlinger 1994; Williams 2003). The police department must go far beyond the narrow confines of the three components and the current methods of policing. The police department cannot implement a few new programs, call it community policing, and hope it will become the panacea for all crime and disorder. This kind of thinking—that community-oriented policing is but one more short-term fly-by-night program that the line officers will have to implement on a small scale until management realizes its ineffectiveness and allows the "program" to be folded and labeled a failure—must not be allowed to fester. This method of thought is too narrowly focused and does not comprehend the overall goal of community-oriented policing. Rather, community-oriented policing should be seen as a long-term systemic method of policing that must permeate the entire police department to achieve its goals. Community-oriented policing is in fact about change (Morash and Ford 2002). As Goldstein wrote, "Unlike many of the changes that have occurred in American policing over the years, community policing, if it is to realize its full potential, should not be viewed merely as a new project, method, or procedure that can simply be added, as an appendage of sorts, to an existing police organization. It can better be described as a way of thinking about policing—as an operating philosophy that, in order to succeed, must eventually have a pervasive influence on the operation of the entire agency" (Goldstein 1987, 10–11). This change, beyond the three components of community-oriented policing, is critical to its success.

EMPOWERMENT POLICING

The benefit of empowerment in law enforcement organizations has been the topic of many recent discussions among police managers. Most police executives would agree that employees who are trusted, allowed to make their own choices, and take responsibility for their actions will remain committed to their work and feel that they play an important part in their organizations. Community-oriented policing (COP), today's dominant policing philosophy, is based on concepts of empowerment and teamwork. Nevertheless, organizational structures and other factors, such as individuals who resist change, stand as barriers to achieving the full benefits of empowerment and the COP movement. However, a change in organizational structure and leadership philosophy can remove these barriers to success.

Based on their pyramid-shaped organizational structures, typical paramilitary organizations strictly adhere to the chain of command. They also tend to address problems by growing, becoming more complex, and adding specialized units whenever new problems arise. Those new units typically require additional support personnel and more supervisors—all of which require more sets of rules, more steps for approval, and checks and counterchecks—commonly referred to as red tape. This approach creates new and more complex places to hide problems and place blame.

The need to reduce costs has resulted in a forced flattening of the hierarchy in many paramilitary or bureaucratic organizations. In other words, middle management is shrinking. While removal of organizational layers does not automatically eliminate bureaucracy, this movement to flatten the hierarchy often increases communication by eliminating unnecessary filters of information often found in the middle levels of the organizational pyramid. The flatter a department's hierarchy, the more its leadership must trust and rely on the judgment of line-level officers, who directly provide service to the community and do the bulk of the work. By inverting the organizational pyramid, law enforcement agencies take a bold and symbolic step toward becoming empowered. In a traditional paramilitary law enforcement hierarchy, the chief executive stands alone at the top of the organizational chart with the police officers found toward the base of the pyramid. Inverting the pyramid and placing the chief at the bottom and the police officers at the top symbolizes that the chief serves the organization and is responsible for its leadership. Under such a philosophy, authority comes from within an organization, and its employees become valued because they are a contributing part of the organization, not because of the positions they hold.

Typical leaders of empowered organizations remain unsatisfied with the status quo and never use the phrase "because we have always done it that way." An empowered leader realizes that all else being equal, employees prefer to work in a pleasant environment over an unpleasant one. While a pleasant work environment does not always equal higher performance, employees who view their work as drudgery create a great barrier to sustained performance. However, in every law enforcement agency, times exist when the paramilitary model is the appropriate leadership style. For example, a civil disturbance may require that a force of police officers act together in controlling a crowd. During such an incident, strict control and immediate obedience to orders would prevail over allowing employees to make their own decisions. Commanders should focus on safety, discourage risk-taking, and provide little room for experimentation in such situations.

An empowered organization allows for this departure from the norm in extreme circumstances, but a paramilitary or bureaucratic organization experiences great difficulty switching to an empowered approach when circumstances dictate. Autocratic leaders may interpret empowerment as disloyalty to their departments and consider it the abandonment of the core beliefs of the paramilitary model. Whereas empowerment emphasizes flexibility, an autocratic bureaucracy emphasizes rigid structure and adherence to the rules.

The COP movement is a profession-specific example of empowerment theory. COP embraces many of the concepts of the empowerment model and values people over most other elements in the organization. Empowerment in COP not only allows line officers to solve problems but also gives them the trust and involvement of the entire community. The police and community partnership found in COP is clearly antibureaucratic and should be the focus of every law enforcement leader.

However, the paramilitary organizational design represents a powerful detriment to the COP philosophy. No sets of written rules exist that can systemize and manage what some police departments have accomplished through COP initiatives. Trust and risk are inherent in most of those successful programs. The best achievements from COP initiatives often happen when an officer does something not covered in any written rules and that has never been done before. Practitioners know that "thinking outside the box," a concept that the paramilitary model punishes, remains critical to COP. Many police leaders today remember the old sergeant who illustrated the embodiment of the paramilitary model and believed officers were not paid to think, just to do what they were told.

Trust is the essence of leadership in an empowered organization. Empowered leaders push decision making down to the officer level because they have confidence in their officers' abilities and believe that many decisions are best made at that level. Innovation and creativity normally include some level of risk. Leaders automatically do not punish failures because risk remains inherent, and failures provide valuable learning experiences. All learning involves some failure. This does not suggest that leaders should permit failure in all arenas of policing. In professions such as law enforcement, failure can result in different consequences. For example, an after-school program for at-risk juveniles with low participation can have much different consequences than an unjustified use of deadly force. Creativity, innovation, and experimentation become appropriate in law enforcement only in those areas where the ramifications of failure do not place the safety or welfare of the community or organization at risk. Empowerment philosophy easily adjusts to those narrow areas of policing that require structure and strict rule compliance, providing leaders make the rules and their purpose well known.

Leaders must focus on rewards and not discipline, and they should encourage dissonant information and individual opinions. Additionally, they should consider hiring employees from divergent backgrounds and viewpoints as a strength. Hiring employees with similar backgrounds and experiences encourages organizational inbreeding that hampers creativity and innovation. Above all, law enforcement executives must start by embodying empowerment dynamics in themselves. While empowerment can grow spontaneously, sparked by enlightened leaders at any level of the organization, it must do so covertly if management does not offer full support. In these circumstances, any substantial failure based upon empowerment likely will result in harsh punishment.

Trusting today's educated, independent, and innovative police officers to make the best decisions and take responsibility results in higher performance, greater commitment, and a sense of ownership in the organization. This methodology may be the only way to keep police officers of the future stimulated. Police officers do not want to spend the best days of their lives in a career that denies their abilities and talents. They would like to think of themselves as actors in the system rather than being helplessly acted upon. As a result, empowered police officers make real differences in improving communities.

Law enforcement organizations that value conformity, consistency, and compliance to the rules ignore the changing and unpredictable environment found throughout organizations today. By trying to play by rules designed for past problems, the paramilitary model is simply too inflexible to serve the future to policing. One effective way leaders can make decisions for solving new problems is to trust in the judgment of the police officers who can solve them in a way that no set of rules or rigid command structure can attempt.

Leaders face immense challenges relative to the future of policing. Leaders that implement an organizational design and philosophy that encourage trust and enhance officers' judgment and skills will provide an environment conducive to the type of innovation, commitment, and personal satisfaction necessary to address the problems of the future. The empowerment policing model can help achieve greater successes in the next century of policing.

Source: Adapted from Michael S. Reiter, "Empowerment Policing," *FBI Law Enforcement Bulletin,* February 1999, pp. 7–11.

To fully achieve the implementation of the systemic approach to policing, the organization and management structure must be changed (Morash and Ford 2002; Williams 2003). Police departments must commit to the organizational philosophy and strategy of community-oriented policing (Williams 1998). A police department that continues to utilize a traditional approach to policing but implements the components of community-oriented policing may realize some positive effects. Strategic-oriented policing, through the utilization of directed patrols, aggressive patrols, and saturation patrols, may indeed have some short-term success. However, without any programs to replace the police presence and an organizational structure to support such programs, strategic-oriented policing will fail. Neighborhood-oriented policing, without this structural change, will ultimately fail for lack of community support at the lowest level, and police officers will have no hope of successfully implementing the problem-oriented policing approach to dealing with crime and order maintenance issues. The current organizational structure and styles of management in policing will not allow this systemic approach to grow, and the same people who would give birth to this new idea would also in turn kill the idea through either ignorance, misunderstanding, or unwillingness to change.

At this point in time, with the proliferation of community-oriented policing materials in both the policing and academic worlds, ignorance of the philosophy and its

Sacramento, California, police officers and kids at an Old Sacramento event. (*Courtesy of the Sacramento Police Department, Sacramento, California.*)

programs has become harder to accept. Simply put, information on community-oriented policing is now readily available to those seeking it. Misunderstanding and disagreements are also very common in the area of community-oriented policing, for the literature is sketchy at best in the conceptual arena and generally lacking in the considerations for application. However, the unwillingness to change must be overcome, something that police have traditionally been slow to allow. Resistance to change was a major obstacle of policing throughout the twentieth century and will affect the advent of community-oriented policing. Understanding the problems that cause this unwillingness to change can assist us when implementing the systemic approach to policing, which will be addressed in a later chapter. For now, it is important to understand the type of organizational and management changes that must be made and how they should progress.

    This chapter discusses the process of changing the organization and management structure of a traditional police department to a community-oriented policing police department. It first deals with the police department's ability to communicate the values and goals of community-oriented policing to both the members of the police department and the members of the community. This communication must be accomplished through the creation of a new mission statement for the police department. (See Table 7-1.) Once this reorientation of the mission of the police is complete, then the police department must move toward establishing a decentralized organization, which includes decentralizing by geography, personnel, and structure. Finally, the methods of managing the police department must be altered, utilizing total quality management (TQM) not only to accommodate but also complement the overall process.

TABLE 7-1   *Advantages of Mission-Driven Government*

- Mission-driven organizations are more efficient than rule-driven organizations.
- Mission-driven organizations are more effective than rule-driven organizations and produce better results.
- Mission-driven organizations are more innovative than rule-driven organizations.
- Mission-driven organizations are more flexible than rule-driven organizations.
- Mission-driven organizations have higher morale than rule-driven organizations.

Source: Adapted with permission from David Osborne and Ted Gaebler, *Reinventing Government: How the Entrepreneurial Spirit Is Transforming the Public Sector from Schoolhouse to Statehouse, City Hall to the Pentagon.* Reading, Mass.: Addison-Wesley, 1992.

VALUES AND GOALS

As a police department begins implementing the three components, it must also begin changing the organizational and management structure that will allow for achieving the maximum potential under this concept. Making changes to the way police perform their duties is often difficult, but perhaps the greatest hurdle is changing the way officers think. Because community-oriented policing is concerned with changing the values and goals of a police department to focus on the community, a clear statement about these values and goals can be beneficial to changing the way police officers think (Bureau of Justice Assistance 1994; Wasserman and Moore 1988; Williams 2003; Zhao, Lovrich, and Gray 1995). By expressing these values, the police department can put forth the beliefs of the organization, the standards to be maintained by its members, and the broader mission to be achieved through its activities (Kelling, Wasserman, and Williams 1988). The vehicle for this value statement is the police department's mission statement.

To create a new mission statement, the police department must first reorient the direction of the police department by focusing on the value and goals of community-oriented policing (see Table 7-2). It must determine those key aspects of policing that are most important to the community. The best way to do this is by soliciting the assistance of community members to determine what, overall, is most important to them. The findings should then be reflected within the police department by making the necessary changes to the mission statement.

 COP IN ACTION

Madison, Wisconsin, Police Department's Mission Statement

The mission of the Madison Police Department is to work in partnerships to create safer neighborhoods and preserve our special quality of life.

Source: Madison, Wisconsin, Police Department's Website, available online at http://www.ci.madison.wi.us/police/policy.html . Downloaded June 2002.

TABLE 7-2   *The Most Important Values a Police Department Can Incorporate*

- Preserve and advance the principles of democracy.
- Place the highest value on preserving human life.
- Preventing crime as the number one operational priority.
- Involve the community in delivering police services.
- Believe in accountability to the community served.
- Commitment to professionalism in all aspects of operations.
- Maintain the highest standards of integrity.

Source: U.S. Department of Justice, *Community Relations Service.* Washington, D.C.: U.S. Department of Justice, 1987.

 COP IN ACTION

Department Philosophy of the Boise, Idaho, Police Department

The organization's philosophy is, in essence, those guiding principles and beliefs under which we (the organization) strive to achieve our mission, goals, and objectives.

We believe in equal, fair, and impartial application of laws and ordinances without regard to age, gender, race, creed, color, station in life, or sexual orientation.

We believe in treating all individuals, regardless of their attitude or demeanor, with the courtesy, tolerance, sensitivity, and dignity we would expect if placed in a similar situation.

We believe in the maintenance of individual human dignity and the preservation of human rights under the rule and spirit of law, which dictates that the end does not justify the means and punishment is not the function of police officers.

We believe in providing quality, empathetic, and responsive service to the citizens of our community. The prevention of crime, which is our ultimate goal, can only be achieved through a partnership with the community and active citizen involvement in addressing community problems.

We believe in the empowerment of our people to solve problems, provide service, and satisfy the needs of the community, coupled with accountability and responsibility for actions taken or omitted.

We believe that proactive team management, open communication, and employee input are to be the norm; but once decisions are made, it is critical that everyone work together toward achieving established goals.

We believe that written policy and procedure are necessary to guide individuals in the performance of their duties. However, rules cannot be written to cover all contingencies, and any actions taken must be legal, professional, reasonable, and consistent with the spirit and intent of this philosophy and the law.

Source: Boise, Idaho, Police Department's Web site, available online at http://www.cityofboise.org/police/index.shtml. Downloaded June 2002.

TABLE 7-3   *Newport News, Virginia, Police Department
Motto, Vision, Mission, and Values*

Motto:	Committed to our community.
Vision:	To take a leading role in making Newport News a place where people want to live, work and play.
Mission:	To work in partnership with citizens and government to provide excellence in police services.

Values That Guide Our Actions

Integrity:	We serve with integrity, by determining what is right and acting on that determination, even at personal cost, whether in public or private.
Citizen Participation:	We solicit and accept input from citizens when developing police activities and programs.
Commitment:	We are vigilant in our responsibility to provide effective, efficient and professional police services.
Accountability:	We are an organization of empowered employees, all of whom are responsible for what they say and do.
Communication:	We foster an exchange of thoughts, ideals and information in an open, receptive and positive manner, throughout the organization.
Courtesy:	We perform our duties in a polite and respectful manner.
Teamwork:	We support a team environment that encourages individual contributions and recognizes group accomplishments.
Innovation:	We encourage employees to seek new methods of improving police services.
Our Heritage:	We value and honor all who serve with us. We cherish the memories of those who have served before us, especially those who have given the ultimate sacrifice.

Source: Newport News Police Department, Newport News, Virginia, 2006. Homepage. Available online at *http://www.newport-news.va.us/POLICE/mission.htm.*

The mission statement should reflect the community's expectations of the police and should provide an orientation for every member of the department. It should articulate the values that are important to the community-oriented policing approach and state the overall goal of the police department (see Table 7-3). In turn, everything that the police department then does should reflect the new mission statement and should be conducted in such a manner that it supports these values and goals.

Additionally, new mission statements should be short and simple, and they should be published and readily available to all members of the community. An example of the perfect mission statement is the preamble to the Constitution of the United States, which, in fifty-two words, is capable of orienting and focusing a nation of over 260 million citizens.

One example of a mission statement from a police department that shifted its style of policing to community policing in the latter part of 1992 is found in the Hercules Police Department, Hercules, California, in the San Francisco Bay area. The department shifted its focus and created the following mission statement to reflect such a change:

We, the members of the Hercules Police Department, are committed to the improvement of the quality of life for the citizens of Hercules by working in partnership with them. We will work to maintain safe and secure neighborhoods while treating everyone with respect and dignity. We will be open-minded and consistently improve ourselves professionally in order to serve the community. (Muehleisen 1995, 31)

Another example of reorienting the police department can be found in the Madison, Wisconsin, move to what it termed "quality policing" (Couper 1991; Wycoff and Skogan 1994). Between 1987 and 1990, the Police Foundation, through funding by the National Institute of Justice, studied the implementation of community-oriented policing in Madison, Wisconsin, and its orientation is quickly reflected in the police department's motto: "Closer to the People: Quality from the Inside, Out" (Muehleisen 1995, 77). However, the police department also created a form of a mission statement, its "Twelve Principles of Quality Leadership" (Muehleisen 1995, 76). By doing so, it provided an orientation for the entire police department as well as simultaneously shifting the management philosophy, and in turn the organizational structure, through one quasi mission statement. To understand how this task was achieved, it is important to review the twelve principles (Wycoff and Skogan 1994, 76):

1. Believe in, foster, and support *teamwork*.
2. Be committed to the *problem-solving* process; use it and let *data*, not emotions, drive decisions.
3. Seek employees' *input* before you make decisions.
4. Believe that the best way to improve the quality of work or service is to *ask* and *listen* to employees who are doing work.
5. Strive to develop mutual *respect* and *trust* among employees.
6. Have a *customer* orientation and focus toward employees and citizens.
7. Manage the *behavior* of 95 percent of employees and not the 5 percent who cause problems.
8. *Improve systems* and examine processes before blaming people.
9. Avoid "top-down," *power-oriented* decision making whenever possible.
10. Encourage creativity through *risk taking* and be tolerant of honest *mistakes*.
11. Be a *facilitator* and *coach*. Develop an *open* atmosphere that encourages providing and accepting *feedback*.
12. With teamwork, develop with employees agreed-upon *goals* and a *plan* to achieve them.

As in the case of the Hercules Police Department and the Madison Police Department, to change the organization and management structures from a traditional to community-oriented approach, the values and goals of the police department must be changed. This change should be reflected in the police department's mission statement and communicated to every member of the police force and the community as well. From this reorientation of values and goals, the police department can begin the overall organization and management changes to support and complement community-oriented policing. This is especially apparent when returning to the one key change the police department must undertake if community-oriented policing is to succeed—decentralization.

ORGANIZATION THROUGH DECENTRALIZATION

The concept of decentralization is not new to police departments in the United States. One can trace back through the history of policing in America and find that the police were decentralized for all of the political era and to some degree the public relations era, as described in Chapter 1. The variables of geography, poor administration, management, leadership, and lack of communications and technology all contributed to the decentralization of police departments. Yet the single most important variable was the police department's entrenchment in local politics. Most police departments consisted of specific ethnic groups that reflected the dominant ethnic group in the community, and they were so closely tied to the local politicians that most were considered corrupt (Fogelson 1977; Walker 1977). This corruption prompted many reform-minded individuals, such as August Vollmer and O. W. Wilson, to move the police organization toward a strictly centralized organization utilizing key management concepts such as chain of command, unity of command, and span of control. The centralized organizational form presented itself as the best means for controlling the rampant corruption, political links, and deviant behavior among line officers. During the public relations era, centralization became the commonly accepted form of police management, and by the police–community relations era, it was an institutional norm.

This strict adherence to a centralized command and to standard operating procedures had an additional effect on policing that would not become evident until the late 1960s. The methods employed to prevent corruption involved strict centralized control, demanding scientific and impersonal methods for dealing with crime, and careful recording and documentation of any and all activity to demonstrate what officers were doing during their tours of duty. As James Q. Wilson points out, "this led police managers to treat their departments as if they were production agencies" and "in turn led the officers to emphasize those aspects of their job that were most easily standardized and recorded, that could be directed by radio transmission, and that generated statistics" (Wilson 1989, 170). The emphasis during the public relations era and into the police–community relations era was one of law enforcement because it was easier to document and generate arrest and traffic statistics than to describe how many personal interventions an officer made during a shift. As Wilson sums up, "one part of the police job, order maintenance, was sacrificed to another part, law enforcement" (Wilson 1989, 170). The public, dissatisfied with rampant disorder in communities, called for government to address these growing problems; however, the centralized form of control was not an appropriate method to address these types of problems.

Today, as police departments move toward a philosophy of responsiveness to community needs, there has been an overwhelming call for the decentralization of the police (Geller 1991; Goldstein 1990; Greene, Bergman, and McLaughlin 1994; Rosenbaum and Lurigio 1994; Skogan 1994; Vito and Kunselman 2000; Wilkinson and Rosenbaum 1994). This is because "decentralization empowers officers to use their discretion creatively without having their activities dictated to them by upper-management" (Robinson 2003, 682). Despite the Byzantine effort to centralize the police throughout the twentieth century, the current undertaking across the nation is to decentralize the police. This approach has not been without good reason. Although there is little argument that a centralized police department can more effectively control the problems of corruption and misconduct, it does not allow the police to be responsive to the needs of the community. Additionally, for the three components of community-oriented policing to succeed, the organization and management of a police department must have decentralized authority. Community-oriented policing cannot thrive in a paramilitary, bureaucratic, authoritarian method of organization but rather needs one that is democratic in nature and allows the line officers to participate in the management process. The implementation of neighborhood programs and problem solving must rest in the hands of the line police officer working in partnership with the community. Therefore, the decision-making process and operational methods must be pushed down the chain of command and into the hands of the line officer. All of this can be achieved primarily through the decentralization of the police.

A good example of how far this level of decentralization can carry an agency to successful community-oriented policing is found in the research by Robinson (2003) on the Indianapolis Police Department (IPD) and the St. Petersburg Police Department (SPD). Robinson explained that "in Indianapolis, community policing tasks were decentralized to the district level," which "meant that district commanders were responsible for setting community policing goals and tasks and overseeing community policing projects occurring within their districts" (Robinson 2003, 682). In the St. Petersburg, Florida, Police Department, Robinson found that the agency had "more fully realized decentralization because community policing was decentralized to the officer level," which "meant that individual officers would implement and develop community policing projects with the citizens they encountered on a daily basis" (2003, 682). These officers were more trusted to use their discretion of engage in community-oriented policing. Thus, Robinson concluded that "in terms of designing an organizational structure that facilitated officers engaging in community policing, therefore, SPD was more successful than IPD" (2003, 682). The decentralization of the police department is in actuality a three-part process. There is decentralization by geography, personnel, and structure. Decentralization by geography, often called "physical decentralization" (Radelet and Carter 1994), is concerned with the geographical boundaries of communities within a police department's jurisdiction and how the police service these areas. Decentralization by personnel is concerned with the placement of the line officers within these geographical areas based on shifts, time, and location. And decentralization by structure, often called "decentralization of authority" (Radelet and Carter 1994), is the process by which the police department decentralizes the structure of the department to include the areas of patrol, investigation, and administration. All three forms are extremely critical under community-oriented policing, and the distinction is made for clarity rather than for individual selection. All three must go hand-in-hand during the decentralization process for the overall concept of decentralization to be complete. Decentralization then becomes the glue to our community-oriented policing model. (See Table 7-4.)

TABLE 7-4 *Advantages of Decentralized Institutions*

- Decentralized institutions are far more flexible than centralized institutions; they can respond quickly to changing circumstances and customers' needs.
- Decentralized institutions are more effective than centralized institutions.
- Decentralized institutions are far more innovative than centralized institutions.
- Decentralized institutions generate higher morale, more commitment, and greater productivity.

Source: Adapted with permission from David Osborne and Ted Gaebler, *Reinventing Government: How the Entrepreneurial Spirit Is Transforming the Public Sector from Schoolhouse to Statehouse, City Hall to the Pentagon.* Reading, Mass.: Addison-Wesley, 1992.

Police departments have traditionally organized their police officers along geographical boundaries. Police officers are usually assigned a specific area to patrol during their shift, and these areas tend to rotate on a daily or weekly schedule. The geographical boundaries are often based on logical boundaries where main roads and the size of communities are the deciding factors in the parameters of a particular police beat. Other factors are generally not taken into consideration, and the sole purpose of the boundaries is to tell the officer where he or she can and cannot patrol. Under community-oriented policing, this mentality must change, and the method is through a decentralization of area beats (Saunders 1999).

Police beats or posts are generally the smallest geographical areas that a police officer on duty is responsible for patrolling (Dempsey 1994). *Sector* or *zone* is often the term utilized to distinguish several beats and posts as having a collective area for supervisory responsibility or to distinguish the outer limits of a patrol's responsibility (Dempsey 1994). A precinct is generally the entire collection of beats and sectors established in a particular part of the city or county, such as a county with a north precinct and a south precinct (Dempsey 1994). This division of the police department's jurisdiction is critical in both traditional policing and community-oriented policing. However, the difference lies in how the pie is divided.

As previously stated, most jurisdictions look to physical boundaries and size to determine beats, sectors, and precincts. Under community-oriented policing, the orientation of beats, sectors, and precincts is based on residential and commercial areas, as well as overall communities where the two are integrated. The police should recognize the various neighborhoods and create the beat around these collections of houses, townhomes, or apartments. Neighborhoods can be identified by various methods such as homeowners' associations, preplanned community areas, and various government organizations that divide areas based on community names. In some cases, the beats may be organized along the lines of commercial areas that form their own type of neighborhood but are all a collection of similar businesses and stores. In other cases, the beats can become so small that they may fit the needs of a particular place that creates, in a sense, its own community, such as a school or park.

The larger concentration of beats, known as sectors or zones, should still be established, but they should be a collection of schools, churches, and commercial establishments that service a particular neighborhood or several neighborhoods that are similar in nature. The supervisor can then remain in charge of this area but must work with the community through his or her officers as a quasi police chief for the area. As the officers implement the three components in their particular beats, the supervisor becomes responsible for coordinating and distributing or redistributing resources among the various beats, tracking each officer's progress, and maintaining a larger perspective of how each beat or each problem affects the others identified by his or her officers.

The precincts only become necessary in the case of large jurisdictional areas where the communities that congregate in the various areas are dissimilar in nature. A division by precinct may be made necessary if, for example, returning to the north and south division, one is middle class to upper class with low crime rates while the other is predominantly lower class with high crime rates. The overall emphasis of community-oriented policing will take on different roles in both of these jurisdictional areas and therefore may necessitate the use of precincts. Regardless, when utilizing beats, sectors, and precincts, they must be divided based on how the community sees its neighborhoods and commercial areas rather than logical, visible, physical boundaries.

One method that may assist in the decentralization by geography is the establishment of neighborhood police stations, based on the community's neighborhoods and commercial areas. These are often called ministations, substations, or storefront stations (Bennett 1994; Kelling and Moore 1988; Klockars 1988; Skolnick and Bayley 1986). The police department can create a miniature police department within a particular community in a variety of ways. Establishing a storefront by renting a store or borrowing space within a store to establish a place that members of the community may go to speak with, report crime to, or discuss issues with the police is one possibility. Another possibility is reopening a closed precinct station located in an area accessible to a particular community or several communities whereby several beats may be able to utilize the space.

There is also the possibility that a police department may confiscate a condominium, townhome, or house through asset forfeiture related to drugs or by having one donated to the police department. This becomes an excellent substation because it is already established within the community and is readily accessible to all members of that neighborhood. The Manassas Police Department, Manassas, Virginia, did just that by establishing a substation in a townhome in an area known for high crime rates and drug activity. This substation essentially allowed the police to have a foothold in the community, afforded an opportunity for law-abiding members of the community to report criminal and order maintenance problems, and provided a nearby shelter if needed.

Another possibility is the establishment of substations within the local school system. Every public school, from elementary to high schools, has its own unique problems, ones indigenous to that particular school. By having a police officer permanently assigned to the school as his or her beat, the benefits inherent in community-oriented policing are quickly realized. The Arlington County Police Department in Arlington, Virginia, established this type of program in its county, and crime rates in the schools dropped, order maintenance problems were addressed, and the students and teachers had their own full-time police officer. Eventually, Arlington established a policy that when a student was picked up by another police officer, that student would be brought to his or her school's assigned police officer. Because that police officer was more familiar with the student's background, it provided additional methods of dealing with the youth, and it created a more personal relationship between the officer and the student because the student always had to deal with one particular officer.

There are generally mixed views on the benefits of police substations (Skolnick and Bayley 1986), but much of the discourse is a result of the failed "team policing" project in the early 1970s that utilized a storefront approach without any backing from the respective police departments (Sherman 1975; Sherman, Milton, and Kelly 1973). The storefront or substation design can be of great benefit to the community-oriented policing approach as long as officers do not utilize the substation as a barrier to the public but rather as one method of creating a bridge between the police and the public. These storefronts, substations, and ministations are important because "the purpose behind all of them is to create the possibility of more intensive police–community interaction and heightened identification by police officers with particular areas" (Skolnick and Bayley 1986, 214). This concept can be extremely helpful in assisting police departments decentralize by geography.

Des Moines Police Department's community-oriented policing initiative Neighborhood-Based Service Delivery Unit (NDSD) showing officer assignments for specific neighborhoods. *(Courtesy of the Des Moines Police Department, Des Moines, Iowa.)*

In response to decentralizing by geography, there becomes an even greater need to decentralize by personnel. The decentralization of personnel is based on shifts, time, and location. Because many police departments in the United States utilize rotating shifts, the officers are generally never on the same beat, during the same particular time, for any great length of time. Although this system was desired during the reform era and was regarded as the standard in policing, it is no longer desirable. Over the past several decades, many police departments have moved to establish fixed shifts in which police officers work the same shift the same days of the week. However, in both the rotating and fixed shifts forms of policing, the beat the officer is assigned to is generally not fixed. Beats rotate from day to day, and the officer is at a disadvantage when trying to learn what criminal or order maintenance problems exist in a neighborhood. Even if the officer does ascertain the problems, he or she has no ties to the community and is not around enough to implement any type of program. Under a community-oriented policing approach, the officers must be decentralized to the degree that their shifts, times, and locations, or beats, for which they are responsible remain the same.

This form of decentralization would establish a police officer in a particular beat, enabling him or her to come to know all of the citizens who live in the neighborhood and what they perceive as criminal and order maintenance problems (Saunders 1999). It "enables an officer to get to know the problems of a community, the strengths and weaknesses of existing systems of control, and the various resources that are useful in solving problems" (Goldstein 1990, 160). Even the difference between rotating the times, but not the beats, creates many difficulties for the officer because those problems that need to be addressed during the night are different than those revealed during the day. Therefore, the police officer should be assigned permanently to a shift, time, and location for a period of several years.

Along with the decentralization of personnel, it is inherent within the establishment of a permanent assignment in a specific beat that the decentralization of decision making and authority rest in the hands of the police officer (see Breci and Erickson 1998; Cardarelli, McDevitt, and Baum 1998). The police officer, by being able to work within the community on a regular basis, must have additional authority to work with the community members to establish the three components and have the freedom to implement those that the officer and the community believe would best work to meet the community's needs. The centralized method of authority, top-down management, cannot work in this setting, for the top-level management will not have the vast amount of information and interaction that the community policing officer will have. In fact, one additional benefit to permanent beat assignments is that it has been found to increase officer-initiated investigative activity, thus indicating that community-oriented policing officers are taking greater responsibility for their beats (Kane 2000).

In accordance with this additional authority and decision-making ability, police officers must become more involved in top-level planning and implementation through an increase in the participatory style of management (Kelling and Moore 1988; Wilkinson and Rosenbaum 1994). Officers must be a part of the management process that creates, implements, and evaluates those programs under the three components. They must be involved in the coordinated efforts to respond to all criminal and order maintenance problems within their patrol area. And their contact with the community, their understanding of the real and perceived problems, must be heard and their decisions respected. However, to achieve these varied roles, tasks, and requirements of the police officer under community-oriented policing, it is imperative that the personnel position of police officer change as well.

Every aspect of the position of police officer will change as a result of the adoption of the systemic approach to policing. The mission statement, values, and goals under the community-oriented policing philosophy should be the guiding principles for the department; however, police officers will find their own mission statement in terms of the job description, which must be "comprehensive in terms of duties, responsibilities, working conditions, knowledge, skills, and abilities required for successful performance of the job, and it should indicate the relative importance of the various work behaviors so identified" (Geller 1991, 365–366). These duties will be drastically different from those of traditional policing, and they should be based on the new community-oriented mission statement as well as a job analysis that "consists of describing and evaluating a job in terms of tasks performed, methods or tools used, services provided, and knowledge, skills, and abilities required to perform the tasks successfully" (Geller 1991, 365). These tasks will include traditional aspects of the job, along with such things as public speaking, organizational skills, and problem-solving abilities. It is this job description of the community-oriented policing officer on which all other personnel issues will be based.

COP IN ACTION

Screening for Success in Community Policing

Being selected as a police officer means the candidate has successfully demonstrated he or she has "the right stuff" by most law enforcement agencies' standards. But during the past ten years, traditional policing practices have been challenged, and the police officer's role has been redefined. And yet, even as law enforcement agencies move toward community policing— and get more in-depth into problem-oriented policing, neighborhood-oriented policing, and "strategy-oriented policing," traditional policing practices still have their place in law enforcement. As a result, what it means to have "the right stuff," what it takes to be an effective law enforcement officer, is undergoing a paradigm shift. Therefore, law enforcement agencies would do well to review their selection process.

Police officers undergo one of the most rigorous selection processes, for good or for ill. It is not easy to find the right person for the right job. It is even harder to find the right candidate for a profession that tends to be highly stressful, and that demands a high level of skill and responsibility. According to Timothy Bullock (1995), police departments need individuals who are educated, resilient, resourceful, empathetic, competent, and patient.

The Camden Police Department adopted the community policing philosophy in 1993. Prior to this change, not much attention had been given to the importance of psychological examination or the relationship of an officer's education to actual job performance. The department was only interested in whether the candidate had a past psychological disorder that could affect his or her ability to perform police duties. We can see now that this was a missed opportunity; the lack of input into the process compromised the potential predictive outcomes that could have been yielded by psychological evaluation.

Law enforcement managers today must examine their selection process to ensure it is compatible with the criteria demanded by the type of police services being rendered. Some determinants for consideration should include not only those characteristics that Bullock suggested, but also the qualities of courage, honesty, and intelligence. These underlying traits make a difference when it comes to finding the most suitable candidates.

An industrial psychologist once found that one of the most alarming personality traits found among a pool of candidates for an entry-level position was that a majority of them were motivated by a desire for power and dominance over others (Stanard 1995). That quality would not be desired in a law enforcement officer, but it would take in-depth psychological evaluation to determine whether that quality was present.

Most law enforcement agencies use written personality tests, usually the Minnesota Multiphasic Personality Inventory (Stone 1994). The model selection process for what it takes to be a cop in the twenty-first century needs to include a more comprehensive battery of psychological testing designed to be predictive with some degree of validity.

To develop a selection process, police managers should incorporate a three-step approach.

Step One: Develop a set of desired personality traits to be provided to the psychologist performing the testing. Ideally, the traits should reflect the type of police agency desired by management, city officials, and the community. Regardless of the instrument, the standards or criteria used to screen applicants must be clearly related to the police officer's job, and they should have predictive validity (Stone 1994). Keep in mind we are measuring the police applicant's past behavioral traits in attempting to predict future behavior.

Step Two: Inform the psychologists you want to "screen in" candidates as well as screen them out. Police pre-employment screening is designed to prevent the occurrence of several kinds of problem behavior, such as use of excessive force. Consequently, screening has become focused on identifying characteristics of bad officers. Less is known about the traits of good officers, or how career experiences can buffer personal tendencies (Scrivner 1994). Although clinical information is critical to employment decisions for highly sensitive jobs, the tendency to focus on the negative has influenced the screening process.

Step Three: Utilize risk-assessment models and situational testing. Psychologists have available tests for risk-assessment models, situational testing, or job simulators, which could incorporate a wide range of information on which to base a hiring decision.

The model community policing officer must have the traits of kindness—not to be mistaken for weakness—and desire to serve as a potential mentor for young adults. Our ideal candidate has the ability and desire to deal with matters pertaining to the elderly and children. Today, we find a variety of school programs designed to hold up police officers as potential mentors. The Drug Abuse Resistance Education (DARE) and Gang Resistance Education and Training (GREAT) programs are good examples.

Personality inventory tests assist police managers with the selection process. Longitudinal studies of behavior patterns for practicing police officers also help managers determine if the selected evaluation scales prove effective. Psychologists can put together a battery of tests designed to screen out candidates who do not fit the community policing mold and, at the same time, screen in those candidates who potentially possess the traits that are essential to effective community policing.

Source: Adapted with permission from Charles J. Kocher, "Screening for Success in Community Policing," *Community Policing Exchange,* March/April 1999.

These additional personnel areas will include everything from recruiting and training to performance appraisals and promotion of community-oriented policing officers. The criteria for hiring, from the written test to the interview, should see systemic changes that reflect a community-oriented policing approach, thereby giving the police department an excellent opportunity to hire based on its values and goals (Booth 1995). Once hired, the training of the new recruit will become a concern that must go far beyond the traditional police academy emphasis on law, rules, and procedures (Kelling, Wasserman, and Williams 1988). Although these three areas of training are still critical to the police officer, additional areas, such as community relations, the problem-solving process, and organizational skills for coordinating meetings, activities, and programs, must be emphasized. Additionally, in-service training must be provided on these same skills for officers who worked for the police department prior to the adoption of community-oriented policing. A number of police departments that have implemented the systemic approach have had significant success training officers to identify, analyze, and implement various responses to community concerns (Eck and Spelman 1987a; Goldstein 1990; Higdon and Hubert 1987).

Two additional police personnel issues that come into play include the method of evaluating the officer's performance as a community-oriented policing officer and, based on this evaluation, the promotion process under the systemic approach. The system utilized for performance evaluations must be changed to reflect the goals of community-oriented policing, which, again, may include problem-solving capabilities, community interaction, and community mobilization capabilities (Bureau of Justice Assistance 1994a). These evaluations under the new job descriptions and mission statements will be the impetus for promotions. These promotions to the next higher rank or position should not be based on traditional policing methods such as quota systems but rather on many factors such as the number and effectiveness of neighborhood-oriented policing programs implemented and the ability of the officer to solve problems under the problem-oriented policing approach. There must be some recognition of the community-oriented policing accomplishments that complement the promotion process (Booth 1995; Goldstein 1990) because there are fewer opportunities in a decentralized or flattened pyramid organization when it comes to promotions. Consequently, for the police officer to be able to perform and succeed under this added weight of authority and decision making and reduced room for advancement, the organization itself must be decentralized in such a manner that it will support and encourage the community-oriented policing officer.

 ## COP IN ACTION

Boston Police Department: Same Cops/Same Neighborhood

The department's full-scale commitment to the philosophy of community policing dates back to 1992 with the development of its initial Neighborhood Policing Plan of Action. That plan sought to align and integrate both the service delivery and management models of the organization, with the community policing philosophy being adopted by the total organization. In 1995, a BPD (Boston Police Department) citywide strategic planning initiative paved the way for more extensive implementation of its neighborhood policing efforts. The commitment to community/neighborhood policing was a shift for the whole organization, not the creation of a special unit or program.

A strategic planning team was developed at the district and citywide levels, and the team identified "having the same police officer in the same beat" as an important change needed to support neighborhood-level problem solving and the fuller implementation of community policing in Boston. Although the police and the community set the goal of Same Cops/Same Neighborhood (SC/SN), changing organizational processes and practices was another matter.

The goal was to decentralize the police, but decentralization presented challenges. Chief of Patrol James Claiborne saw his role and responsibility as "changing to be one where I responded to the needs of those working under my command, facilitated change, and attended to process as well as giving people room to make mistakes." A further challenge was that, as in many departments trying to work with a decentralized model, tension between the field and headquarters could make systemic and systematic change difficult. This challenge was exacerbated by the lack of enthusiasm some district commanders felt for the changes that would be required to implement SC/SN.

In the end, Boston PD successfully implemented the difficult organizational change of decentralizing their organizational structure in support of community policing.

Lessons Learned

- It was important to pay attention to "process," listen to those who were working to implement changes, and be willing to change tactics to achieve the intended outcome.
- Resistance to decentralization diminished over time and members remained fluid, flexible, agile, and adaptable.
- Both the organization and the police leaders needed to commit to change and the effort involved.
- It was important to think systemically, because these changes affected the whole organization.

Source: Adapted from A. Schneider et al., *Community Policing in Action: A Practitioner's Eye View of Organizational Change.* Washington, D.C.: Office of Community Oriented Policing Services, 2003.

The final form of decentralization is the decentralization by structure. Traditionally, police departments have organized along the lines of a bureaucracy, as was previously discussed, and therefore established the hierarchy by function. Most police departments see the division along the lines of patrol, administrative, and support services. Within this structure of the police department, the strict chain of command that all members of the department must adhere to generally promulgates multiple layers of mid-level and upper-level management. This standard structure of management and organization must change if community-oriented policing is to remain a viable program. The police department must decentralize the functions and the levels of command by flattening the organizational pyramid (see Cardarelli, McDevitt, and Baum 1998; Saunders 1999).

If we understand the police department as being a pyramid with all of the line officers at the bottom, the police chief at the top, and multiple layers of management in between, we then understand the structure of a typical police department. These orthodox hierarchical structures have been found to create many problems within an organization such as adversarial management–labor relationships, depersonalization of individual members of the organization, centralized decision making, and discouragement of individual initiatives (Russell and MacLachlan 1999; Solar 2001). The goal of community-oriented policing, then, is to flatten this hierarchical pyramid. We must realign the levels of management, integrating various levels of management and then pushing them outward, not upward. By reducing the number of levels, as Kelling and Moore (1988, 20) point out, it creates a paradox because "while the number of managerial levels may decrease, the number of managers may increase." In other words, if we have a police department with the simple ranks of police officer, corporal, sergeant, lieutenant, captain, and chief, we will abolish the ranks of corporal and captain (see Figure 7-1) but create additional sergeant slots and lieutenant slots (see Figure 7-2). Although we are disrupting the rank structure, we succeed in abolishing two levels of management and we create more management responsibility and authority for those existing managers than they previously had under the centralized form of police organization (Kelling and Moore 1988).

Recognizing, however, that there are fewer opportunities in a decentralized organization when it comes to promotions, the community-oriented police department may want to consider alternatives. One possibility is a reorientation of the rank structure that allows police officers room for advancement in both rank and pay yet at the same time remains true to the concept of flattening the pyramid or hierarchical structure of the police

FIGURE 7-1 Traditional centralized organization.

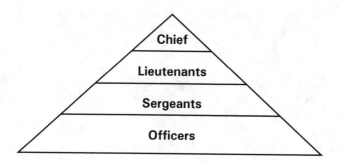

FIGURE 7-2 Community-oriented policing decentralized organization.

department. The police department could establish some other form of promoting police officers into higher ranks without necessarily placing them into management positions. This promotion system could be implemented through the creation of two separate tracks, one for management and one for line officers, in which certain ranks or grade levels can denote level of authority, expertise, or experience.

The areas of function within a police department, specifically the administrative and service operations, must also be decentralized to assist the line officers on the street. This decentralization includes the entire workforce, both sworn and nonsworn personnel, working within the police department. The structure then focuses on the most important asset the police department has in its community relations—the police officer—or, for clarity in relation to the new form of policing, the community-oriented policing officer. This is the ultimate goal for decentralization not only by function but also by geography and personnel.

Two Memphis community-oriented policing officers talking with local youth in an elementary school. (*Courtesy of the Memphis Police Department, Memphis, Tennessee.*)

There are essentially five clear benefits to the decentralization of a police department. First and foremost is the fact that the overall decentralization supports community-oriented policing. Without the decentralized organization and management structure, police officers would not have the support, freedom, or authority to make the decisions and implement the programs at their level. The difficulty in a top-down approach lies in information that is not connected to the concerns of the public but rather the concerns of management. If all of the decisions made on the street with citizen input were required to be processed up the chain of command for approval and then processed back to the line officer, this form of management would be slow, burdensome, and often incompetent. What is then needed is more authority vested in the line officers, the ones working with the citizens, to make the decisions at their level. The decentralized organization and management structure are both complementary to this style of management and allow for a method by which community-oriented policing can be supported for the long term.

The second benefit of decentralization is the fewer layers of management that the line officers must deal with—hence, fewer layers of management that decisions must be administered through before arriving at a resolution (Kelling and Moore 1988). Through a reduction in the multiple echelons of management in the typical police department, the communication flow between line officer and police chief can be greatly improved, the time in which a decision is to be made can be reduced, and many of the problems with the typical bureaucracy can be reduced, if not eliminated.

A third benefit is the opportunity afforded to upper-level management to move away from concentrating on details, or dealing with the "small picture," and move toward the creation of strategies on a macrolevel, or ones that deal with the "big picture" (Geller 1991, 43). Good leadership focuses on the goals and results of an organization rather than the day-in and day-out operations. If high-level administrators and upper-level management must be involved in every decision, they will find themselves locked into micromanaging their organizations—constantly worrying about minor details and losing sight of the overall systemic perspective. Upper-level management should concentrate more on assessing where the organization is and where it should be in the future rather than focusing solely on the means to achieve these goals. Lower levels of management and line officers are then free to concentrate on the issues at hand and to deal with them without interference from managers far removed from life on the street.

A fourth benefit is the creation of better operational decisions because those decisions are being made at the appropriate level (Geller 1991; Wilson and Kelling 1989). Situational imperatives can have a decisive impact on police officers and how they perform their job as they deal with a variety of people, events, and situations each shift. Police officers do not resort to "street justice" in these situations to the degree the media would have one believe, but often they resort to what one author calls "street-level bureaucracy" (Lipsky 1980; see also Vinzant and Crothers 1994). As an organization that deals with the lowest common denominator, the public, the police essentially deliver the end result of a bureaucracy, namely services. However, there are often constraints on the actions that officers take far beyond the reality of the street, and they can be found in centralized decision making, politics, and policy, all of which can have an impact on the officers' ability to make decisions. Although officers should be constrained from misconduct and the excessive use of force, officers should not be constrained by bureaucratic supervision. At the street level, variables change from situation to situation, and second-guessing one's actions based on politics, bureaucracy, and decision makers far removed from the street can be dangerous. Freeing officers from this burden, allowing them to make decisions at the street level, places the decision-making process at the appropriate level.

And, finally, decentralization allows the police department to utilize the full potential of each individual officer, generally creating an atmosphere that fosters higher job satisfaction and allows the individual to grow, whereas standard management practices do not accommodate this type of atmosphere (Denhardt 1993; Geller 1991). Decentralizing the police department and placing the decision-making authority in the hands of the police allow the individual police officer the opportunity to utilize more than a simple ability to apply policies and procedures to life on the street. Community-oriented policing, through the decentralization process, allows each individual police officer to utilize a variety of skills and knowledge that he or she may already have and to learn and develop new ones. It promotes innovative thinking, analytical thought, and the creation of solutions for problems plaguing the community. This demand on the officers in turn allows for continual growth on the part of the employees and the department, prevents boredom in a job that can become very routine, and allows a personal connection to specific problems in "their" neighborhoods. The adherence to doctrine and standardized procedures, under traditional police organization and management, does not allow room for individual officer growth.

A study by Gregory D. Russell and Susan MacLachlan (1999, 48) confirmed many of these findings; the researchers concluded that "the changes in management approach, from a very traditional orthodox hierarchical model to a more open community policing model, generally produced perceived change in the organization."

Graduates of the Junior Police Academy in 2005 pictured with officers of the Terre Haute, Indiana, Police Department. (*Courtesy of the Terre Haute Police Department, Terre Haute, Indiana.*)

The overall decentralization of the police department is critically important to the success of community-oriented policing. This structure essentially requires that supervisors give officers more autonomy by allowing them to handle problems on their level and supporting them in their operations (Wilson and Kelling 1989). The department must decentralize along geographical, personnel, and structural lines, pushing the responsibility and decision-making process down into the hands of the line officer and providing the organizational structure support. Through the combination of decentralization by geography, personnel, and structure, the police department will accomplish the overall concept central to the success of community-oriented policing—decentralized authority. This element, along with the synthesis of the three components, becomes the fundamental basis for community-oriented policing. It becomes the system.

MANAGEMENT THROUGH TOTAL QUALITY MANAGEMENT

To guide a change from the traditional police department to one that adopts the systemic approach to policing, not only the mission statement and organizational structure but also the management style being utilized must change (Sykes 1994). Although there are multiple methods and philosophies on how to manage organizations found in the vast amounts of literature surrounding both public and business administration, managing a police department and police officers is particularly unique, and managing them under community-oriented policing is exceptionally unique. There must be a management style that complements not only the change to decentralization and community orientation but the police professional as well. The management style of total quality management (TQM), created by W. Edwards Deming, rises to this challenge (Stevens 2002).

 # COP IN ACTION

Total Quality Management

The big question facing law enforcement agencies is: How can administrators strike a balance between a shrinking budget and the delivery of quality service? The answer may be found in Total Quality Management (TQM).

Perhaps TQM is just another buzzword or fad, but we can't afford to dismiss it without examination. If police agencies are to be successful today, they must solicit the assistance and cooperation from the community they serve, including the programs and policies its businesses have found successful.

Measuring the quality of service a police department delivers involves determining how residents rate the agency. It goes far beyond crime rate and statistics, which may give insight to effectiveness, but not quality and efficiency.

For example, a department completes a crime clearance rate report at the end of the year and compares it to the state standard. If the rate is equal to or better than the state standard they assume they are doing a good job. However, a state standard is based upon the average clearance rates of other departments within the state, not the victim's perception of the quality service.

A department that solves the crime may be satisfied, but the resident may not experience the same level of satisfaction. Quality service is unique to the individual receiving the service; therefore, what has been satisfactory in the past may require more or less effort in the future. Law enforcement agencies must measure the department's goal as well as the individual's goals.

Before we can apply TQM, we must first know what it is. "Total Quality Management refers to a management process and set of disciplines that are coordinated to ensure that the organization consistently meets and exceeds customer requirements." Total quality management made its debut in Japan as a part of the post-war aid the United States provided to Japan. American management consultants assisted Japanese industry and today we know how successful the Japanese are in business.

In a survey, 250 leading U.S. companies were asked what strategies they were using to address quality and continuous improvement—68 percent were using total quality management. TQM has been successful in the business profit-oriented model; therefore why not attempt to manage our police departments as a business.

Total quality management is not a quick fix or an overnight solution to problems. It is a philosophy that must be adopted and continuously measured by our customers (the community). To be successful in developing loyal customers, through efforts and programs, we will have to take a major step toward keeping our customers and attracting new ones.

Benefits of total quality management as experienced by the private sector are:

1. Reduced cost in bringing high quality through efficiency.
2. Greater retention of customers and attraction of new ones.

3. Improved morale and increased employee participation.
4. Stronger employee loyalty from team productivity and rewards.

How can we implement TQM in the public sector? The process involves strong leadership, evaluation, training, measuring customer satisfaction, and constant re-evaluation, striving for improved quality service.

The first step in implementing a successful program involves strong leadership. An administrator must develop a vision for the quality of service the department can provide the community. This can be accomplished best by gaining the assistance and support of the agency's commanders. The commanders must explore ways to improve services and reward those who are creative in developing innovative approaches to delivering quality service for less.

Administrators must communicate the mission to all employees and unions in an effort to gain support. They must also gain their commitment to providing the highest quality service by empowering employees with the freedom to make decisions in the interest of providing quality and also gaining customer satisfaction. This can be accomplished by holding department-wide meetings, and meeting with the various unions, to communicate what direction the department is taking and the vehicle needed to take it down the road to providing better service.

The feedback from employees should indicate the amount of support that you might receive to accomplish this task. Remember, this information is going to scare and intimidate some because it's new and different. You must be prepared to sell this new concept hard.

Unlike a product-driven environment, there is a difference between products and service, as indicated by K. Albrecht and R. Zemke, of Service America.

1. Service is produced at the instant of delivery and cannot be created in advance and stored in inventory.
2. Service cannot be centrally produced, inspected or stockpiled.
3. Service cannot be demonstrated, nor can a sample be sent in advance for approval.
4. In the absence of tangible product, customers value service on the basis of their own personal experience.
5. Faulty service cannot be recalled.
6. Customers' assessment of service quality tends to decrease in proportion to the number of employees they encounter during the delivery of service.
7. Customers' assessments of service quality are subjective and strongly influenced by expectations.

Although the public sector is a service driven environment, quality may be more difficult to achieve, but not impossible.

The next step to implementing TQM is to evaluate your organization. There should be an ongoing process to evaluate the following areas: Leadership, Information Analysis, Strategic Quality Planning, Human Resource Utilization, Quality Assurance, Quality Results, and Customer Satisfaction.

The internal evaluation process involves conducting a candid assessment to determine how information is captured, analyzed, and applied to the agency's operation. Does this information play a role in the planning of future programs for the department? How are personnel distributed throughout the agency: is it planned or does it just seem to happen?

If the latter is true, the agency must develop staffing plans to meet future challenges. Once the internal systems have been evaluated and modified, the next component of the process is measuring customer satisfaction.

Organizations need to regularly identify and prioritize those needs. Public perception may be indicated by customer dissatisfaction—for example, internal affairs complaints or letters to the local newspaper. If an organization doesn't have the mechanism to capture this information, then before they can proceed they must develop a system and examine the results. Many service oriented businesses use surveys to measure customer satisfaction and make the necessary modification to raise the level of service.

Once the information has been examined and analyzed, a training strategy must be prepared to address the deficiencies. The following training needs must be considered: employees should understand not only TQM principles, but how it works, why it works, and why it fails.

Training should address the skills needed to assist in improving the quality of service delivered. The organization needs to develop the employees so that they work together collectively as a team. This is accomplished by shifting the paradigm from the traditional chain of command to a flatter organizational structure, whereby you remove the barriers for effective communication between divisional personnel.

The members of this new team need to understand its role and the skills needed to meet the change in philosophy. Training must be a continuous flow of information to allow for the improvement of performance.

Employees' efforts must be recognized and rewarded if the organization wants to succeed because the employees are also considered customers and the same philosophies that apply to the external customers also apply to the internal ones. Recognition and rewards mean different things to different people; therefore, it is important to know what motivates your people, whether they are intrinsic or extrinsic.

As alluded to earlier, customers are at the heart of this philosophy. Law enforcement agencies need to build a partnership with their customers. They need to listen and understand the customers' perception of the quality of service they receive. This feedback is vital to measure the success or failure of the organization to meet the needs of its customers.

Quality service surveys are a tool to measure the public's perception of the services it receives. Don't assume you deliver quality service, ask your customers. Surveys can be conducted using a standard questionnaire form.

These surveys not only gauge citizen satisfaction but also act as a deterrent to reduce citizen complaints. The feedback improves morale by forwarding positive comments to the officer from the public. It is also a mechanism to identify and correct deficiencies.

For example, a patrol officer may be unaware that his approach is offensive to drivers when conducting a vehicle stop. The survey would be brought to his attention in an effort to correct the deficiency without of course compromising officer safety.

A broader sampling can be conducted using a broader survey to the community to measure overall satisfaction with the police department. These surveys allow a department to measure its success not by its Uniform Crime Reporting statistic, but by the satisfaction or dissatisfaction felt by its community.

Long Hill Township is a community of 12,500 located at the southern end of Morris County, between two urban centers. The Police Department has twenty-nine sworn police officers with a support staff of seven civilian employees. Some of the programs used to facilitate the delivery of quality service are: Career Development Program, Employee Recognition Program, Five-Year Plans, Quality Control Surveys, and Inspectional Service.

The resulting high morale is a result of career development and employee recognition programs. The high satisfaction rating from the public and a reduction in citizen complaints resulted in a 50 percent reduction in citizen complaints in 1996 as compared to 1990. If the current trend for 1997 continues, we will experience an 80 percent reduction from 1990.

Police departments must change their emphasis from traditional crime fighting to a more progressive proactive model of crime prevention. Programs such as problem-oriented policing and graffiti eradication are considered TQM philosophies because of the satisfaction derived by the community.

For instance, a police department receives numerous calls regarding a vacant building being used by drug dealers. The department would solicit the assistance of the town building inspector, who would work to condemn the building. But it doesn't end there: the owner would be required to repair the building or the city would demolish it.

The result: satisfied residents because the dealers are gone. Police are satisfied because they addressed an ongoing problem that drained resources with poor results in the past. The owner is satisfied because he has his building back. The only loser or dissatisfied group in this hypothetical situation is the dealers, but they are not our customers.

TQM principles may require more effort in the early stage for some departments, but without conducting a self-assessment, you cannot answer the question, "Are you providing quality service to your community?" Only by taking the necessary steps to examine, develop, refine, train, and survey will you be able to provide quality as well as monitor for constant improvement.

Total quality management principles are a viable solution that requires vision on the part of our law enforcement administrators and the willingness to put forth some effort to gain enormous dividends, community satisfaction. Without their satisfaction, we are destined to be run out of business by our competitor, privatization.

Source: Reprinted with permission from Sam Hishmeh, "Total Quality Management," *Law and Order,* April 1998, pp. 92–95.

In the early 1970s, W. Edwards Deming created TQM, which has become the paradigm for good management (Cohen and Brand 1993). Although the concept developed over the past three decades into a working management style, Deming's original concept was oriented toward private business. The ultimate question a variety of authors, from a variety of disciplines, have wrestled with revolves around the issue of TQM's application to the public sector (Bassett 1995; Cole 1993b; Osborne and Gaebler 1992; Simonsen and Arnold 1993; Swiss 1992). Can the public sector, with a basic orientation of serving the public, utilize a management style originally designed for the private sector, whose basic orientation is for profit? The answer in most of the literature has been in the affirmative, with some qualifications by the various authors exploring this possibility.

To understand the concept of TQM, one must understand the definition. However, this is difficult because there is no strict definition (Bassett 1995). Some authors describe TQM as "a management process and set of disciplines that are coordinated to ensure that the organization consistently meets and exceeds customer requirements" (Capezio and Morehouse 1993, 1). Others describe it as "providing the customer with quality products at the right time and at the right place" (Pegels 1995, 5). Deming himself, however, has a different understanding that concentrates more on the quality of the worker, workplace, and product rather than on product quality itself. To achieve this fundamental goal, Deming created fourteen points for TQM (Deming 1986, 17):

1. Create constancy of purpose for improvement of product and service.
2. Adopt the new philosophy.
3. Cease dependence on mass inspection.

4. End the practice of awarding business on the basis of price tag alone.
5. Improve constantly and forever the system of production and services.
6. Institute modern methods of training on the job.
7. Institute modern methods of supervision.
8. Drive fear from the workplace.
9. Break down barriers between staff areas.
10. Eliminate numerical goals for the workforce.
11. Eliminate work standards and numerical quotas.
12. Remove barriers that rob people of pride of workmanship.
13. Institute a vigorous program of education and training.
14. Create a structure that will accomplish the transformation.

Although it is clear that all of these points may not be directly applicable to the public sector, many of the points detail aspects of community-oriented policing in an overall sense. David Couper, former chief of police of the Madison Police Department, Madison, Wisconsin, saw the opportunities under Deming's approach to management and was able to successfully apply them to the department's adoption of community-oriented policing (Osborne and Gaebler 1992; Wycoff and Skogan 1994). Through the application of Deming's fourteen points, Chief Couper was able to create the police department's "Twelve Principles of Quality Leadership," detailed earlier in this chapter, to develop a guiding philosophy. This philosophy not only allowed for the public to be seen as the customer but also for the employees of the department to be seen as internal customers who have their own problems in need of identification and resolution (Wycoff and Skogan 1994a). In this instance, TQM proved very successful and demonstrated that this approach to management was complementary to the systemic approach to policing.

TQM has more recently seen adaptation at the federal level. In Office of Management and Budget, Draft Circular A-132, 1990, the federal government stresses seven methods to integrating TQM (Denhardt 1995, 336–339):

1. Top management needs to give TQM its leadership and support.
2. Quality improvement should be included in the organization's strategic plan.
3. The main focus should be on the customer.
4. A true commitment to training and recognition must be made. Employees are motivated to achieve total quality through trust, respect, and recognition.
5. Employees need to be empowered and work in teams in addressing quality issues.
6. Techniques in measurement and analysis of process and outputs need to be implemented.
7. Quality assurance through meeting customers' needs, standardization, and benchmarking will assure quality.

Additionally, the U.S. Department of Justice and the Federal Bureau of Investigation have also drafted their concept of TQM and have begun implementation to ensure quality and to incorporate the creativity and capabilities of every individual in their employment. To assist in this implementation, they published "What Total Quality Management Is and Is Not" (U.S. Department of Justice and Federal Bureau of Investigation 1990). TQM has truly become the paradigm of public management in the same manner that community-oriented policing has become the paradigm in policing.

TABLE 7-5 *What Total Quality Management Is and Is Not*

It Is	It Is Not
A structured approach to solving problems	"Fighting fires"
A systemic way to improve products and services	A new program
Long term	Short term
Conveyed by management's actions	Conveyed by slogans
Supported by statistical quality control	Driven by statistical quality control
Practiced by everyone	Delegated to subordinates

Source: Federal Bureau of Investigation, Administrative Services Division, *Total Quality Management.* Washington, D.C.: U.S. Department of Justice, October 1990.

It is on the combination of these two paradigms that police management should focus their attention for the improvement of both the community and the police (see Table 7-5).

To focus on the link between community-oriented policing and TQM, there are essentially six areas of concentration that management must explore, the first of which has already been explored in depth. These areas are (1) decentralization, (2) customer orientation, (3) long-term commitment, (4) proactive management, (5) training and education, and (6) evaluation.

The first area is the decentralization of the organizational structure. Using smaller workgroups of personnel, placing the line officers closer to the public geographically, and reducing the layers of management, all concepts of decentralization, are also tenets of TQM (Wycoff and Skogan 1994). The last of Deming's fourteen points brings this reality to fruition in the sense that the decentralized structure will accomplish the transformation of management from past practices to TQM. The creation of a new mission statement, values, and goals and the decentralization of authority allow for the paradigm of TQM to be implemented within the police department.

The second area of focus under both paradigms is the movement to a customer or community orientation. There is also a dual focus that should be maintained in that both the employee of the police department and the public should be seen as customers. If management is customer-oriented and line officers are seen as customers, the department then has an obligation to listen to their concerns and determine how best to address them, in similar fashion to the problem-solving methods employed under problem-oriented policing. The officers should have input into management decisions, they should be responsible for their actions, and they should be afforded more responsibility in the performance of their jobs. Both management and the police officers then also have an obligation to view the public as the customer to the services that they provide and adopt this orientation, which again should be captured in the mission statement, values, and goals of the entire police department. The public should also be afforded the same opportunity for input by incorporating citizens into the decision-making process.

The third area of focus is in understanding that both TQM and community-oriented policing are long-term concepts that cannot be implemented overnight and do not end within any certain time frame. Managers and leaders under TQM and community-oriented policing must look forward to the challenging task ahead, often by determining first what the organization wants to achieve and then working backward to figure out how the organization will get there. As Deming himself stated in the opening of the Federal Bureau of Investigation's manual on TQM, "A big ship, traveling at full speed, requires distance and time to turn" (U.S. Department of Justice and Federal Bureau of Investigation 1990, 1). A department's goals should have this long-term outlook incorporated into a strategic plan and implemented in an incremental fashion.

The fourth area of management focus should be the movement away from mass inspections and the utilization of numerical quotas because they are poor management tools, ignore qualitative issues, and are reactive in nature. Rather, management should focus on methods of incorporating proactive methods of management that focus on outcomes and customer satisfaction. Police supervisors should help officers develop sound judgment, provide feedback on their performance, and help them work on problems in their neighborhoods (see Mastrofski, Parks, and Worden 1998). Even in the area of discipline, where there is much resistance to focusing on outcomes rather than means, proactive methods are available to management. One such method is use of an early warning system that proactively assesses employees' performance and intervenes before misconduct occurs (Moore and Wegener 1996; Oliver 1994a). The early warning system has been described as part of the TQM commitment to personnel development within the police department (Alpert and Dunham 1992).

The fifth area of concentration under TQM should be the emphasis on education and training for all employees. This area includes an emphasis on not only training in the line officer's job position but also training of line officers in TQM and community-oriented policing. Management cannot incorporate TQM and community-oriented policing into the management philosophy and style unless the line officers understand the process and methods utilized under both of the philosophies and practices. Employees must understand their roles and new job descriptions not only under TQM but also under the community-oriented policing department.

And, finally, management must concentrate on utilizing a variety of methods in the evaluation process. As one of the principles of quality management in the Madison Police Department states, "Be committed to the problem-solving process; use it and let

St. Petersburg Police Department DARE vehicle obtained via a drug seizure. (*Courtesy of St. Petersburg Police Department, St. Petersburg, Florida.*)

data, not emotions, drive decisions" (Wycoff and Skogan 1994a, 58). It is important that management under both TQM and community-oriented policing be responsible for evaluating and assisting in the evaluation of various programs to determine if they are truly effective and should be continued or are ineffective and should be abolished. These types of decisions must not be made under the pretenses of either personal influence, misguided perceptions, or political influence. These decisions must be based on the quality of delivery and the honest satisfaction of the customer, the community. Evaluations are a daunting undertaking and one that will prove most difficult to police departments, but they must be considered central to the success of not only TQM but also community-oriented policing. Evaluations are the guide to incremental changes in the implementation process; therefore, they are discussed in greater depth in a later chapter.

 ## COP IN ACTION

Nontraditional Problem Solving

Three years ago, the Lawrence, Massachusetts, Police Department realized that the traditional way of doing things was not always effective in resolving some crime issues. Nor were they dealing with the needs of many of their citizens. Lawrence is an urban city of 70,000 people in seven square miles, twenty-eight miles north of Boston. Its population is 50 percent white and 47 percent Hispanic. It was once a prosperous working class city, but the textile mills closed down and urban decay set in. Lawrence saw crime rates increase as drug use and sales grew, home ownership dropped drastically, and gang activities increased.

From our readings on community policing and talking with agencies that have implemented such programs, we decided three underlying principles would meet the needs of the city: (1) community policing is a philosophy that should be practiced by the whole department. It is not just a program that may be here today and gone tomorrow; (2) community policing uses problem-solving techniques to deal with neighborhood problems; (3) problem solving involves both line officers and the people living in a neighborhood.

Since we were going to make a fundamental change in our operations, we needed a management system that would not only help us implement the community policing philosophy but also support it once it was in place. The Total Quality Management (TQM) philosophy is a structured system focusing on exceeding customer needs. It involves the whole organization in the planning and implementation of break-through operational processes and the continuous improvement of the daily operations of the organization. TQM uses many different management and planning tools and involves customers, managers, and employees in the development of a system that meets the needs of not only the external customers but also the internal customers of an organization. Law enforcement is a service industry; therefore the philosophy, tools, and methods of TQM can effectively focus law enforcement services on the customer (citizen) and involve everyone in the organization with the delivery of those customer-focused services.

TQM and community policing, therefore, have the same underlying concepts: customer focus, problem solving, total organization participation. TQM is not only an excellent customer-focused management philosophy in its own right but is also an excellent management system that will drive the community policing philosophy. The TQM process allowed the Lawrence Police Department to see that what our customers were really concerned with was "feeling safe" and having their neighborhoods free of "disorder problems."

Operating within the community policing and TQM philosophies, the department was able to work with people in the neighborhood and was willing to try nontraditional responses to resolve problems. One nontraditional solution involved the use of barricades and the monitoring of traffic in a neighborhood with an open drug market problem. This limited access to the neighborhood to one entrance, vehicle tag numbers of people cruising the neighborhood were recorded, and letters were sent advising vehicle owners that they were seen in the area.

Any time such an operation is planned, we first ensure that it is within our Value and Mission: (1) protecting individual rights; (2) involving the community in solving their own neighborhood problems; and (3) reducing fear of crime and improving the quality of life through the use of creative problem solving.

The Lawrence Police Department feels that it is important to have residents involved. Meetings are scheduled to address other neighborhood concerns, including poor street lighting, abandoned buildings, speeding cars, and litter-strewn vacant lots. We have assured residents that we will continue to work with them to resolve their problems. We told them that they need to organize and participate in controlling their neighborhood and together we will be able to have a positive impact in their neighborhood.

Source: Adapted with permission from Allen W. Cole, "Non-Traditional Problem Solving," *Law and Order,* August 1993, pp. 59–64.

Because the concepts and philosophical underpinnings of community-oriented policing and TQM are similar in nature, it is only fitting that this style of management is the method of choice and most applicable to the systemic approach to policing. In a recent survey of police leaders across the country, Dennis J. Stevens (2001, 26) found that "police supervisors should blend police managerial techniques with Total Quality Management skills since those managerial skills appear to optimize community policing practices." TQM is focused on the achievement of long-term goals and is complementary to a decentralized organizational structure, clearly meeting all of the needs of the community-oriented policing department. (See Table 7-6.) Therefore, by adopting all three of the components of community-oriented policing, decentralizing the organizational structure, and adopting TQM as the guiding management style, a police department ensures its success in achieving the values and goals set forth in the mission statement, which will foster a better working relationship between the public and the police.

TABLE 7-6 *Organizational Changes to Implement Community-Oriented Policing*

1. Revising mission, vision, and/or values statements
2. Developing a strategic plan for the implementation of community policing
3. Changing policies and procedures to enhance beat integrity and stability, increase community contact, and enhance officers' sense of ownership of their patrol areas, through:
   a. Aligning administrative, patrol, and community beat boundaries to coincide with the level of problems and natural neighborhood boundaries
   b. Assigning officers to beats permanently or for a significant period of time
   c. Switching from a time (watch/shift) imperative to a territorial (beat) imperative, making supervisors and officers responsible for problems in the area on a twenty-four hour basis, not just during the watch

(Continued)

TABLE 7-6   *(Continued)*

---

    d. Flattening the organization to reduce the levels of command, and giving officers discretion to handle problems as they see fit

    e. Providing time for officers to do problem solving and engage in proactive community contact by freeing some officers from answering radio calls or increasing the amount of time officers have

    f. Involving units other than patrol and designated community police officers in community policing activities

4. Providing training to all personnel in the principles and practices of community policing

5. Changing performance criteria to reflect community policing principles

---

Source: Jeffrey A. Roth and Joseph F. Ryan, *National Evaluation of the COPS Program—Title 1 of the 1994 Crime Act.* Washington, D.C.: National Institute of Justice, 2000, p. 226.

CONCLUSION

After an in-depth analysis of community-oriented policing and organizational change, Zhao (1996, 83) concluded that the process is slow and "innovation in policing cannot be achieved within a short period of time." A related study by Zhao and Thurman (1996, 15) also found that "innovations are a direct result of police organizations' responsiveness to their external environment." Still another paper believes that "less formalization, decentralization of *some,* but not all, management functions, and more rather than less complexity . . . of which the reorganization of service delivery around geographic areas requires clinical crime prevention specialists, who in turn require other support specialists, and all of these specialists require coordination, which will place increased needs for more supervision, and thus more vertical complexity," will not lead to the appropriate reforms (Mastrofski and Ritti 2000, 206–207). In fact, they "anticipate that contemporary police organizations cannot and will not take bold steps in these directions" (Mastrofski and Ritti 2000, 207). Taken together, these studies demonstrate that police organizational change has historically been slow, that organizational change under community-oriented policing is also a slow process, that true policing change has come from outside the police department (primarily from citizens), and that decentralization of the organization faces an uphill battle. In sum, the keys to organizational change under community-oriented policing are ensuring that the community is involved and keeping in mind that planning for change incorporates both a systemic and long-term approach. (See Table 7-7.)

To effectively restructure the organization and management of a traditional police department and move it toward a community-oriented policing police department, the police administration must first determine the values and goals of the police department. This determination should be based on the fundamental concepts of community-oriented policing and should allow for some input from the members of the community and the police officers themselves. The police department must then create a new mission statement that will focus the department on the undertaking of this systemic approach to policing. This new mission statement should reflect the values and goals of the community-oriented policing police department and should be based on a new job analysis, the concepts of community-oriented policing, and the community's concept of

TABLE 7-7   *Systemic Considerations*

• Mission statement	• Job description
• Recruiting	• Hiring
• Performance evaluations	• Training
• Promotions	• Awards
• Rank	• Research
• Planning	• Technology
• Reserve officers	• Auxiliary officers
• Seasonal officers	• Volunteers
• Budget	• Media operations
• Criminal investigation	• Police detectives
• Organization	• Management
• Leadership	• Unions
• Police culture	• Dispatch
• 911 response	• Discipline
• Field training	• Counseling
• Accreditation	• Equipment
• Facilities	• Consultants
• Education	• Policy
• Procedures	• Regulations

the role of the police. This mission statement should be communicated to every member of the police department, both sworn and nonsworn personnel, as well as to every member of the community.

Based on the new mission statement, the process of decentralizing the police department and implementing the three components can commence. The foundation for the systemic approach to policing is a decentralized departmental organization, which can be achieved through decentralization by geography, personnel, and structure. Decentralization by geography consists of decentralizing the beats, sectors, and precincts based on neighborhoods, business districts, and the various communities found in the police department's jurisdiction. Decentralization of personnel should be based on shift, time, and location to allow the police officers to work within a neighborhood beat on a regular basis for a period of several years, and it should include a complete and systemic change in the position of police officer. The final form of decentralization is by the structure of the department, which consists of removing multiple layers of mid-level management, flattening the pyramid, and incorporating these systemic changes into every facet of the police department. This structure enables the police department to deal more effectively with the community-oriented policing officer, places management closer to the street level, and provides the authority and decision-making capabilities the officer needs to perform his or her duties. Although recent research has demonstrated that major metropolitan police departments have managed to decentralize their agencies somewhat by decreasing the height of the organizational pyramid, it has also been found to be a laboriously slow process (Maguire 1997; see also Zhao and Thurman 1997).

To accomplish the implementation of community-oriented policing and the decentralization of organization, it also becomes necessary to change past practices of management. TQM, as applied to the public sector, becomes the management style of choice for its adaptability to the systemic approach to policing. In addition to the adoption of the three components, the decentralization of the organization, and the adoption of a new management style, the roles of three key players in community-oriented policing—the police officer, the community, and the police chief—must change. This triangle of players is discussed in depth over the next three chapters.

COP ON THE WORLD WIDE WEB

Charleston, South Carolina, Police Department

http://www.charleston-pd.org

Fort Worth, Texas, Police Department

http://www.fortworthpd.com/communit.htm

Newport News, Virginia, Police Department

http://www.newport-news.va.us/ police/index.htm

Northwestern Report on Chicago's CAPS Program

http://www.northwestern.edu/ipr/news/CAPS99release.html

Program in Criminal Justice Policy and Management, Community Policing

http://www.ksg.harvard.edu/criminaljustice

REVIEW QUESTIONS

1. Why are mission, vision, and value statements important in community-oriented policing?
2. The decentralization of the police consists of three related parts. Name and describe these methods of decentralization.
3. How does total quality management (TQM) complement community-oriented policing?

CHAPTER 8

The Role of the Police

Every society gets the kind of criminal it deserves.
What is equally true is that every community gets the kind
of law enforcement it insists on.

—Robert Kennedy

CHAPTER OBJECTIVES

- Understand the traditional role of the police.
- Understand the traditional functions of the police.
- Explain the change in the role of the police required by community-oriented policing.
- Articulate the role of the community-oriented police officer.
- Explain how new officers should be educated.
- Explain what training all officers should receive.
- Understand the issue of higher education for police officers, specifically pertaining to community-oriented policing.

There is one ultimate determining factor regarding the viability of community-oriented policing: the police officer. The police officer is the foundation of community-oriented policing. Although a jurisdiction may have the support of the community, if the police are not responsive to the changes, community-oriented policing will fail. Equally, if the police chief attempts to force community-oriented policing on the police officers in a top-down approach, the police officers hold the key to success. If they do not support it, it will fail. If they are supportive of the concept, it will succeed. Therefore, if a police department attempts to move away from the traditional style of policing to a community-oriented policing department, the police officers are of critical importance to the overall plan.

It is important to look at the role the police have played under traditional forms of policing and how this role has developed. Only then can we understand some of the differences in the role of the police under community-oriented policing. Defining that role is difficult at best; however, creating that role is perhaps the greatest challenge to the police management, the community, and the police themselves.

To understand the police officer's role in community-oriented policing, it is helpful to look at what bearing this systemic approach to policing will have on the police officer's perceptions of his or her job. Attempting to communicate the benefits of community-oriented policing to the line officer can be difficult, but gaining his or her support, as previously stated, is critical to the success or failure of this new method of doing business. It is also critical that the police be afforded the opportunity to develop the new skills that will be necessary under community-oriented policing prior to taking on the challenge rather than beginning with no understanding of how they should perform according to their new mission.

All of these issues, from the role of the police officer to the attitudes exhibited toward community-oriented policing and the skills necessary under this systemic approach to policing, will be explored in this chapter. The traditional role of the police will be explored, and the debate between the law enforcement role and order maintenance role, as has been previously referenced, will be discussed, followed by a review of the new role the police will assume under community-oriented policing. The attitudes that police officers

Sacramento, California, police officers speaking to the Hmong community during a Hmong Cultural Academy event organized by the Police Department. *(Courtesy of the Sacramento Police Department, Sacramento, California.)*

have had toward community-oriented policing and variations on this theme will be analyzed through past research on officers' perceptions of the programs and their reports of job satisfaction. This chapter will also address all of those skills a community-oriented policing officer will need to be effective and successful in this new environment.

TRADITIONAL ROLE OF THE POLICE

To understand the importance of police officers under community-oriented policing, it is imperative to understand their role in society. For the greater part of the twentieth century, the police, the communities, and academia have wrestled with the question, "What is the role of the police?" To define the role of the police, we cannot look to the individual police officer but rather must look to the system in which that officer works. In most cases, the police style can be categorized into two distinct functions that reflect the overall role of the police. These functions are enforcing laws and maintaining order in society. Whether we utilize various terms such as *crime fighters* and *order maintenance* (Dempsey 1994), *law officers* and *peace officers* (Banton 1964), or *legalistic* and *watchman style* (J. Q. Wilson 1968), we are generally discussing the two key roles of the police. Some researchers have identified other roles of the police, such as the ambiguous role (Dempsey 1994) and the service role (J. Q. Wilson 1968); however, these are ancillary to the greater debate about the traditional role of the police. Therefore, the two roles of the police, under the traditional role of the police, have been the law enforcement and order maintenance functions.

Most people are familiar with the function of law enforcement (see Tables 8-1 to 8-3). It is the image of the police that is most often portrayed in the media, and it is the one most recognizable by the public. It is the adherence to the strict letter of the law and subsequently the arrest of any violator of the law. The goal of the police in the law enforcement function is to make as many "good" arrests as possible and to see the successful prosecution of these criminals, whether adult or juvenile, felony or misdemeanor, criminal or traffic offense. The advantage to this crime-fighting function is that it allows for "real" police work to be conducted, evaluated, and quantified. It is a simple process with immediate identification of the value of the work as well as the level of the officer's own self-worth. If the police officer goes to work and makes an arrest, it was a good day. If the police officer goes to work and cannot even issue a summons or find one good traffic offense in which to issue a summons, it was a bad day. The simplicity of quantifying this crime-fighting model allows supervisors to determine the value of the officer's work, the officer to determine his or her own worth, and the officer's peers to easily recognize whether that officer is a "good cop." In addition, when an officer exhibits such behavior as handling himself or herself well in a high-speed pursuit, taking on a subject who resists arrest, or stopping the commission of a felony before it occurs, he or she is praised and admired by both management and peers.

The second function, order maintenance, is not interested in enforcing the law to such a strict standard or making multiple arrests. Rather, enforcing the law through an arrest is the last course of action to be taken, only after all other courses of action have been exhausted. The goal of the police under this function is to simply maintain social order, or at a minimum, the appearance of social order within the community. The police utilize informal and formal intervention techniques and attempt to intimidate, persuade, and threaten people into

TABLE 8-1   *Reported Confidence in the Police (2005)*

Question: "I am going to read you a list of institutions in American society. Please tell me how much confidence you, yourself, have in each one—a great deal, quite a lot, some, very little, or none: Police?"

	GREAT DEAL/ QUITE A LOT	SOME	VERY LITTLE	NONE
National	63%	29%	7%	1%
Sex				
Male	65%	27%	7%	1%
Female	61%	31%	7%	1%
Race				
White	66%	28%	5%	1%
Nonwhite	53%	31%	14%	2%
Black	49%	37%	14%	0%
Age				
18 to 29 years	52%	31%	14%	3%
30 to 49 years	66%	29%	4%	1%
50 to 64 years	63%	29%	8%	0%

Source: Kathleen Maguire and Ann L. Pastore, *Bureau of Justice Statistics Sourcebook of Criminal Justice Statistics—2005.* Washington, D.C.: Bureau of Justice Statistics, 2006.

TABLE 8-2   *Respondents' Ratings of the Honesty and Ethical Standards of Police (1995–2005)*

Question: "Next, please tell me how you would rate the honesty and ethical standards of people in these different fields—very high, high, average, low, or very low: Police?"

	VERY HIGH	HIGH	AVERAGE	LOW	VERY LOW
1995	8%	33%	44%	11%	3%
1996	10%	39%	38%	8%	3%
1997	10%	39%	40%	8%	2%
1999	9%	43%	38%	8%	2%
2000	12%	43%	34%	8%	3%
2001	23%	45%	26%	5%	1%
2002	13%	46%	33%	6%	2%
2003	14%	45%	35%	4%	2%
2004	17%	43%	31%	7%	2%
2005	13%	48%	31%	5%	3%

Source: Kathleen Maguire and Ann L. Pastore, *Bureau of Justice Statistics Sourcebook of Criminal Justice Statistics—2005.* Washington, D.C.: Bureau of Justice Statistics, 2006.

TABLE 8-3 *High School Seniors Reporting Positive Attitudes toward the Performance of the Police and Other Law Enforcement Agencies (1993–2003)*

Question: "Now we'd like you to make some ratings of how good or bad a job you feel each of the following organizations is doing for the country as a whole. . . . How good or bad a job is being done for the country as a whole by . . . the police and other law enforcement agencies?"

(Percentage responding "good" or "very good")

CLASS OF	TOTAL
1993	27.1%
1994	29.3%
1995	28.7%
1996	27.6%
1997	28.7%
1998	33.0%
1999	33.7%
2000	33.6%
2001	33.2%
2002	38.9%
2003	40.8%

Source: Kathleen Maguire and Ann L. Pastore, *Bureau of Justice Statistics Sourcebook of Criminal Justice Statistics—2005.* Washington, D.C.: Bureau of Justice Statistics, 2006.

compliance to achieve order. In looking at the police officer's function in order maintenance, we have a more difficult time recognizing good police work, and often it is dismissed as nothing more than public relations. Police management has a difficult time recognizing and quantifying order maintenance, the officer does not receive the immediate gratification that is otherwise derived from the crime-fighting role, and the officer's peers criticize the officer for not doing "real" police work. Although an officer may implement a community action program under the order maintenance role, it may take several years for the program to become effective and be deemed a success. In the meantime, the officer may be working hard in his or her role, but there is no recognition or feedback from either management or peers.

In attempting to determine the role of the police in our society, it is important to look at the historical approach to policing in the United States. According to James Q. Wilson (1969), from the founding of the United States to the early part of the twentieth century,

 COP IN ACTION

A COPS Show of Your Own

The three most popular themes on television today are crime, crime, and more crime. Offerings include the likes of *Cops, Law & Order,* and *CSI.* The list goes on and on. Then there's the network and local news that drive their ratings up with a steady stream of mayhem, sensationalism, and celebrity murder trials. But police don't need to settle for thirty seconds on the nightly news to, or try to, explain the significance of the crime bill in twenty-five words or less. They can have a "cops show" of their own—and do it on a shoestring by utilizing government cable access television.

That's what the St. Petersburg, Florida, Police Department elected to do with a television program entitled "Police Report" that has attracted a respectable audience of regular viewers. "Police Report" succeeds by making real cops the stars, focusing cameras on the drama of the streets, and dealing head-on with issues that people care about.

"Never before has it been so crucial for police to communicate effectively with their community residents and to present the facts about crime and law enforcement," St. Petersburg Police Chief Darrell Stephens said. "Today you have to actively market crime awareness and tell your side of the story. That's what we're doing with 'Police Report.'"

Stephens was instrumental in expanding St. Petersburg's highly successful community policing program. It was one of the first cities in the nation to go citywide with community policing, with officers working closely with community leaders and neighborhood organizations to set priorities and solve problems. "Police Report" is consistent with Stephens's belief that everybody has a stake in making law enforcement work.

"Police Report" is currently broadcast to 70,000 households in St. Petersburg (about 60 percent of its population) on government access cable. Cost to the police department is basically staff time. That's primarily the five days a month that is devoted to a sixty-minute program that is seen at least once a day, every day, during the month.

What's the best thing about St. Petersburg's cops show?

"'Police Report' lets us talk directly to the people we serve and gives our officers exposure that's better than almost anything we've been able to do," Stephens said. "That's what I like. It's a chance to enhance our image by making our cops the stars of the show and demonstrate to the community that our officers care."

Source: Adapted with permission from Ronald J. Getz, "A COPS Show of Your Own," *Law and Order,* February 1995, pp. 43–49.

---

the police were largely concerned with order maintenance rather than law enforcement. Wilson describes the shift away from order maintenance to law enforcement as beginning with Prohibition and the Great Depression (Wilson 1969) and ending in the 1960s and 1970s as a response to the crime wave that began in the early part of the 1960s (Wilson and Kelling 1982). It is this shift that Wilson and Kelling found most disturbing and subsequently called for the return of order maintenance in their famous article and theory, "Broken Windows," which would become the impetus for community-oriented policing.

However, even a return to order maintenance is not necessarily the goal of community-oriented policing. Although there is no denying that order maintenance is extremely important under the new approach to policing, it is important not to entirely dismiss the law enforcement function. Rather, there must be a synthesis of these two traditional functions of the police as well as the addition of new functions. This is then the contextual setting for community-oriented policing.

ROLE OF THE COMMUNITY-ORIENTED POLICE OFFICER

If a police department does in fact plan to move from the traditional style of policing to community-oriented policing, it must then answer the following question: What is the role of the police in community-oriented policing? The role of the police in community-oriented policing becomes a synthesis of both the law enforcement and order maintenance roles found in the traditional form of policing. It also includes the service style that J. Q. Wilson

(1968) details as being the third style of policing, in which the servicing of the community is the primary goal of the police. Community-oriented policing does not mean the police have to give up the nature of police work with which they have been enamored. In some cases, community-oriented policing may not mean the officers must arrest less, and in many situations it may entail more arrests. The deciding factor is the situation and, in a sense, the function of police, which under community-oriented policing could be called "situational policing," a form of situational leadership (Hersey and Blanchard 1993). In some cases, the law enforcement approach may be more productive in solving the problems of the community than would the order maintenance or service style of policing. In other cases, community members may desire a service approach to certain problems within their neighborhoods, which may be the applicable approach. Regardless, all three functions of policing play into the role of the community-oriented police officer.

The role of the community-oriented police officer must also be one of leadership within the community he or she serves. The officer must, in many cases, become the de facto leader of the community, while in other cases the role may actually be that of adviser or even follower. In this sense, the police officer abides by the tenets of situational leadership in which, depending on the community and the various situations, the officer may have to be an autocratic, democratic, or laissez-faire leader (Hersey and Blanchard 1993; Holden 1986; Peak 1995). The officer must have the support of the police department to be this type of leader. The department must have a vested interest in what is accomplished through community-oriented policing. (See Table 8-4.)

A Kansas City police officer awarding local youth certificates and fishing poles at the Kansas City Police Department's Adventure Club. Police officers working with youth in summer camp settings has been found to be popular with both police and children and enhances communication. *(Courtesy of the Kansas City Police Department, Kansas City, Missouri.)*

TABLE 8-4   *Full-Time Community Policing Officers in Local Police Departments (by size of population served, United States, 1997 and 2000)*

| Population Served | FULL-TIME COMMUNITY POLICING OFFICERS | | | | | |
| | 1997 | | | 2000 | | |
	Percent of Agencies Using Officers	Number of Officers	Average Number of Officers	Percent of Agencies Using Officers	Number of Officers	Average Number of Officers
All sizes	34	15,978	3	66	102,598	12
$1,000,000 +	75	1,111	93	100	33,214	2,209
500,000 to 999,999	75	726	40	85	8,617	297
250,000 to 499,999	76	1,729	49	95	6,866	180
150,000 to 249,999	82	1,183	22	94	8,580	53
50,000 to 149,999	75	3,171	9	93	7,167	20
25,000 to 49,999	64	2,170	5	83	7,854	12
10,000 to 24,999	54	2,354	2	72	9,184	7
2,500 to 9,999	33	2,000	1	63	12,745	5
<2,500	21	1,535	1	60	8,370	3

Source: Kathleen Maguire and Ann L. Pastore, *Bureau of Justice Statistics Sourcebook of Criminal Justice Statistics—2005.* Washington, D.C.: Bureau of Justice Statistics, 2006.

This vested interest is often articulated in one area of community-oriented policing research in which the police department is conceptualized as being a corporation, and corporate strategies are employed to "define for the organization how the organization will pursue value and what sort of organization it will be" (Moore and Trojanowicz 1988, 2). However, a more accurate representation would be the employee-owned corporation, often called a cooperative or simply an employee-owned business. Here the employees of a business are essentially all in business together, and if the business fails, they all fail. The community-oriented police officer is then considered a partner in the police department and is no longer seen as being at the bottom of the hierarchy.

 COP IN ACTION

Book 'Em: Cops and Libraries Work Together

Where would you rather take your kids—to a police station or a library? Both places are highly educational to visit and can open up whole new worlds of sights and sounds to youngsters.

But do you want impressionable children to experience some of the "colorful" characters and goings-on at the average law enforcement center? Overwhelmingly, of course, parents will choose the library. In Chicago, police officers are choosing the library, too, as the place to reach kids in what may be the country's first police-library cooperative effort.

In this example of intra-city teamwork, Chicago's libraries and police have created a number of fun and educational programs for the city's youth where not only the kids benefit, but the participating organizations as well. Whether it's listening to scary stories in the cemetery at Halloween, fishing at local ponds, or learning how to be a detective while reading mysteries, Chicago's youngsters have a variety of programs available to them, courtesy of the city, its libraries, and the police.

While it may seem that the quiet atmosphere of the library would clash with the clamor of a police station, Elizabeth Hanson, first assistant children's librarian at the library's uptown branch, said that police officers and libraries "work very well" together.

"It helps that we're both city agencies," she said. "Many of our goals overlap. Everyone—especially the children—benefits from fun and meaningful programs, and working together means we can maximize our resources. We provide an audience [for the police] they wouldn't have ordinarily and give them an entrée into the community." Chuck Eberspacher, youth liaison officer for the Chicago Police Department, agreed that the police-library team is a winner. "Everyone I've talked to about the program is shocked that we had collaborated," he said. "We're the only ones with such a partnership that I know of."

Eberspacher said there are numerous advantages to the cooperative programs. "It humanizes the department," he said. "People don't know what all we do, and the kids can be so paranoid they wouldn't think to talk to one of us. With the library programs, we can talk one to one with them and take away the fear, open doors."

Hanson agreed that getting to know the police is an important factor in their efforts. "There are at least forty languages spoken in the Albany Park District (where she worked until a recent promotion) and in many cultures, police are to be feared," she said. "By getting to know the police, the fear is taken away and they learn that the police are their friends."

One of the most popular programs is the Mystery Beat Book Club, a five-week after-school book club where students ages six to twelve read mysteries. "This program is not new, but we brought in other resources," Hanson said. During the course of the program, a K-9 and handler demonstrated their skills, and a detective spoke on crime reporting, taught how to crack codes and write in invisible ink. Students also visited the city's 911 Emergency Center where they all got T-shirts, then were bused to a park where a mounted unit put on a demonstration, then were awarded badges and certificates.

"It had all been done before, we just did it splashier," Hanson laughed. McGruff the Crime Dog and Viola Swamp (an evil substitute teacher who is a popular figure in a children's book series) visited area schools to promote the program before it began. "We projected about 15 kids signing up," Hanson said. "We were blown away."

Much of the funding for the program comes from the Blue Skies for Library Kids program, through a grant from the Chicago Community Trust, which is administered through the Chicago Public Library Foundation. "These funds provide seed money for us to look at new trends, and to survey a needs inventory for kids and families," Hanson said.

Eberspacher got involved by "being at the right place at the right time," he said. Formerly assigned to an "incident car" in the 17th District, which handled specific complaints where traditional policing didn't work, a new administration eliminated the incident cars and absorbed their personnel into the Neighborhood Relations division.

The new District Commander wanted to expand children's programs and wanted input from officers and the community. Eberspacher "ended up at the library to do research on kids' programs" and asked Hanson for her advice. "She went out of her way to help me," he said, "and we decided to join resources and utilize the contacts we both had."

The first program was a fishing program. The Illinois Department of Conservation donated fishing poles to the department, which held a fishing jamboree. The program spread to the library, who, along with the department, promoted it as a "Rods and Reads" program.

"We wanted to be part of a national program," Eberspacher said, "and wanted to use the 'Cops and Bobbers' slogan of the IPA, but didn't get their permission. So, we went through the Future Fishermen's Foundation in Virginia who let us use their 'Get Hooked On Fishing, Not On Drugs' slogan and who have supported it wonderfully."

The FFF conducted a seminar for those involved and Eberspacher learned the program qualified for federal funds as an anti-drug campaign. "Other districts (in the Chicago Police Department) had participated, but we wanted it to grow, involving sponsors and the community," he said. The fishing program currently has about 200 participants.

Probably the most visible program is "Ghosts in the Graveyard," held on Halloween night. "It began about four years ago, when we started 'safe alternative' programs," Hanson said. "Then, two years ago, as part of a program to increase literacy, Chuck and I talked about taking the kids to a cemetery and reading scary stories."

Eberspacher knew an officer who worked security at a local cemetery, who talked to the manager about having a program there. "The manager thought it was great, and so did the cemetery board," Hanson said. "They liked it because it would deter the vandalism that often happens to cemeteries on Halloween."

That is precisely what happened the first year. "A couple of kids, carrying eggs, came over the fence," Eberspacher said. "They didn't know we would be there, and you should've seen their faces when they saw a devil and a wolf-man chasing them."

Pre-registered students ages eight and up meet at the library and are bused to the cemetery, where officers are dressed as monsters and librarians tell spooky stories. "It's great," Hanson laughed, "to see a busload of mainly boys, mainly about age twelve, trying to look cool while screaming."

More than 100 kids plus some parents attend the hour-and-a-half-long program, where "once the buses are in, the gates are locked," Eberspacher said. When they return to the library, participants receive a pumpkin and goodie bags (all donated).

Other cooperative programs included fingerprinting and photographing of children on Safe Kids Day, held at the library instead of a stationhouse because of the open, unthreatening atmosphere; a story hour in which "The Three Little Pigs" learn to call 911; and a special project where teenagers painted a special Chicago Transit Authority bus, named the "Knowledge Express," which runs between two area libraries.

Hanson explained, "The bus was coordinated through officers working in the high school who knew kids who were great artists and mentioned it to us. They painted it over five weekends, and now the bus is like a bridge between the neighborhoods."

Feedback on the programs from parents and residents is overwhelmingly positive. "They love the sense of the programs being not just educational," Hanson said, "but also safe, promoting a unified effort, and presenting positive role models."

Hanson and Eberspacher both look to the future and the continued success of the programs. The future holds "whatever we can cook up," Eberspacher said. "We can do anything."

"It's like reading," Hanson added. "With imagination, you can go anywhere."

Source: Reprinted with permission from Sheila Schmitt, "Book 'Em: Cops and Libraries Work Together," *Law and Order,* May 1997, pp. 47–48.

The community-oriented police officer should be given the authority to act independently when working with the community to plan and implement certain strategic-oriented policing tactics; to organize the community under various neighborhood-oriented policing programs; and to determine the problems within a community, develop alternatives to solving these problems, and implement and assess these solutions. Officers must be allowed to utilize all of their capabilities when performing their function within community-oriented policing and must receive the assistance of the police department. (See Table 8-5.)

TABLE 8-5 *Full-Time Community Policing Officers in Sheriff's Offices (by size of population served, United States, 2000)*

| | FULL-TIME COMMUNITY POLICING SHERIFF'S DEPUTIES | | |
Population Served	Percent of Agencies Using Officers	Number of Officers	Average Number of Officers
All sizes	62	16,545	9
$1,000,000+$	65	3,502	161
500,000 to 999,999	73	1,156	23
250,000 to 499,999	73	2,225	26
100,000 to 249,999	72	2,025	10
50,000 to 99,999	68	1,747	7
25,000 to 49,999	59	2,087	6
10,000 to 24,999	54	2,190	5
<10,000	63	1,614	4

Source: Kathleen Maguire and Ann L. Pastore, *Bureau of Justice Statistics Sourcebook of Criminal Justice Statistics—2005.* Washington, D.C.: Bureau of Justice Statistics, 2006.

The community-oriented police officer, like the traditional police officer, must be "all things to all people," only in a different manner. Under community-oriented policing, the officer becomes a leader of the community as well as a follower of the community. He or she must be an ombudsman to the police department as well as an ombudsman and co-ordinator among varying community groups, business groups, and government institutions. The officer must listen to the community to determine those criminal and order maintenance issues that need to be addressed, address and inform the community of varying concerns, and motivate the community to action when necessary. (See Table 8-6.)

Above all, however, for the community-oriented police officer to function, he or she must change the perception of the community toward the police. Doing so is often one of

TABLE 8-6 *Community Police Officer's Day*

In addition to traditional law enforcement activities, such as patrol and responding to calls for service, the day might include the following:

- Operating neighborhood substations
- Meeting with community groups
- Analyzing and solving neighborhood problems
- Working with citizens on crime prevention programs
- Conducting door-to-door surveys of residents
- Talking with students in school
- Meeting with local merchants
- Making security checks of businesses
- Dealing with disorderly people

Source: Stephen D. Mastrofski, "What Does Community Policing Mean for Daily Police Work?" *National Institute of Justice Journal*, August 1992, p. 24.

COP IN ACTION

Cop Cards

If you run into Police Chief James A. Cost on the streets of Campbell, California, he will hand you a cop card.

The chief decided to steal a play from baseball by printing up the trading cards in October 1991 as part of an effort to improve community relations in a neighborhood dominated by Southeast Asian immigrants.

Twenty police officers volunteered to have their photos taken and to hand out the cards. An initial order of 4,000 cards, 200 per officer, was placed. It turned out to be not nearly enough.

"The kids went crazy," the chief recalled. "Even adults started collecting them."

The department quickly reordered 40,000 cards. Half of this order was packaged and sold to adults for $10 a packet. The kids continued to get them for free from officers. Money received from the sale of the cards to collectors pays for the printing cost of the program— an unexpected windfall.

But the main benefit has come from the kids. "Officers used to drive by and the kids wouldn't make eye contact," Cost said. "Now, they flag down patrol cars and ask for a card. It's been good for the officers, particularly if they're reluctant about approaching a kid."

Cost, not one to let a public relations gesture slip by, sent a packet of the trading cards to President George Bush. Bush's response is framed in the hallway: "I appreciate . . . the outstanding job that you and your law enforcement community are doing. Keep it up."

After an appearance on CNN, the Campbell Police Department was besieged with calls from all over the country from police departments who wanted information on how to create their own cards. "For thirty days our life was trading cards," the chief said.

Source: Adapted with permission from Carolyn V. Leal, "Cop Cards," *Law and Order,* October 1992, pp. 63–64.

the most difficult aspects of community-oriented policing. When the systemic approach is implemented, there is often a resistance to change and a negative perception on the part of the police. If the police themselves do not find satisfaction in their role as community-oriented police officers, then they will not want to fill this new role and may revert back to their old roles. Reverting back to traditional methods can be detrimental to the police department attempting to implement the change from traditional policing to community-oriented policing and necessitates a review of the literature on police departments that have implemented community-oriented programs.

POLICE ATTITUDES TOWARD COMMUNITY-ORIENTED POLICING

It is probably safe to say that the police are generally a very skeptical group of people. The reasons why may range from the theories of the police subculture to a simple reactionary method for dealing with life on the street. Regardless of why police harbor such feelings, we must recognize the skepticism and look to the outcome for the line officer under community-oriented policing. Police officers, like everyone else, often ask what is in it for them when a new program is implemented or management alters the way they perform their mission. Although it is beneficial to provide an explanation of what they can expect under the new program, often we can only explain the concepts of what we believe will occur and why it is to their benefit, due to the lack of a knowledge base on the program.

The conceptual benefits such as more freedom to perform their job, a better commitment by management, and better working conditions may all sound pleasant, but in reality they are hard to comprehend. The more simplistic benefits such as additional pay, better uniforms, and fewer hours are something anyone can quickly grasp and so usually create a more immediate desire within the worker. However, in the overall picture, these benefits are quick-fix solutions and do not solve many of the underlying problems, solutions that would better serve the officer over the span of his or her career. As Herman Goldstein pictures the conceptual benefits, he touches on one of the greatest benefits in the officer's career. Goldstein (1990, 28) states that there are two potential benefits: "the most important is the improvement that this could produce in the quality of the responses that the police make to oft-recurring community problems," and that "such a change would be directly responsive to some critical needs in the police organization—the need to treat rank-and-file police officers as mature men and women; to demonstrate more trust and confidence in them; to give them more responsibility and a stake in the outcome of their efforts; and to give them a greater sense of fulfillment and job satisfaction." It is job satisfaction that is of greatest concern to the line officer.

There is one thing that all workers, including police officers, desire in their job: greater job satisfaction (Hersey and Blanchard 1993; Peak 1995). This has been true through the ages and is readily apparent in various studies, from the Hawthorne Plant studies to Herzberg's motivation-hygiene theory to the ultimate theory of human needs found in Maslow's hierarchy of needs (Hersey and Blanchard 1993; Peak 1995). If we look solely at this last familiar theory, we find that the top of Maslow's hierarchy, self-actualization, requires job-related satisfiers including planning of one's work, freedom to make decisions affecting work, creative work to perform, and opportunities for growth and development (Maslow 1970; Peak 1995). In other words, the ultimate goal is job satisfaction. If the change from a traditional police department to a community-oriented policing police department can improve police officer job satisfaction, then this is inherently officers' greatest benefit for assisting in the successful implementation of this systemic approach to policing.

The ability to communicate whether this change will promote greater job satisfaction is difficult at best. However, through an analysis of studies conducted on police programs that were implemented under the auspices of community-oriented policing, the potential for deriving at least an understanding of the effect these programs had on police officers' job satisfaction is great. With this understanding, the communication of job satisfaction can be greatly enhanced and allow for some of the police skepticism to be dispelled.

One study, conducted by Lurigio and Rosenbaum (1994), reviewed the literature to determine the impact of community-oriented policing on the police. Lurigio and Rosenbaum (1994) explored some programs from the 1970s that were more in line with the police–community relations movement of the time, but some rudimentary concepts of community-oriented policing can still be seen. The study, conducted in 1973 and 1974 in San Diego, was known as Community Profile Development. It revealed that these officers were "more likely to report that their job was interesting and less likely to report that their job was frustrating" (Lurigio and Rosenbaum 1994, 149). In Cincinnati, Ohio,

Delta Police Department police trading cards. *(Courtesy of the Delta Police Department, Delta, British Columbia, Canada.)*

in the early 1970s, the police implemented a program known as Community Sector Team Policing (COMSEC), which reported little evidence that police officers' job satisfaction was enhanced (Lurigio and Rosenbaum 1994). The studies of other team policing projects also seemed to report similar findings during the 1970s (Sherman 1975; Sherman, Milton, and Kelly 1973).

COP IN ACTION

Officers "Love Our Kids"

The Love Our Kids program, sponsored by the Coalition of Ministers Against Crime, pairs a mentor with a school child, chosen by the school, considered at risk for dropping out of school. The mentor works individually with the child several times a week. The police department even allows this time to be spent during working hours. The premise is that one person helping one child to build self-esteem and reinforce positive values, along with tutoring, will help them remain in school. It is estimated that up to 50 percent of the students in the area are at risk of dropping out of school by age sixteen. Students rarely drop out of school because of academic reasons, but rather because of overwhelming personal problems.

While the focus of the program is geared to expanding certain areas of a child's specific needs, it shows the pattern of a two-fold purpose. When many of today's youth show little or no respect for authority figures, these children learn that a police officer is truly a friend.

The Love Our Kids program is headed by Sergeant Dennis Carter in the Houston Police Department's Community Services Division. "We sent out the initial information shortly before the holiday season in December, and I didn't expect the response to be very good," he explained. Carter said thirty-one officers signed up immediately, often working with more than one child each. The program has evolved into five elementary campuses located throughout the inner city. "I did not expect such a response and was pleasantly surprised."

Officers receive training prior to their involvement with the children. They are taught how to tutor and about the rules and regulations necessitated by Texas state law and the Houston Independent School District. They learn about target schools, the neighborhoods, and typical family situations involving the children. Tutors sign a formal commitment with the intent to be involved in the program for at least one year, and make visits with the students from one to three times weekly. They also sign a confidentiality agreement protecting the children's rights.

"The goal of the program is to provide love and caring for the children, without expectations of anything in return," Carter explained. "We are told to never expect any thanks. However, my fellow officers who have been involved have seen the results and received many thank-you's from the children and their families."

Source: Adapted with permission from Ann Worrell, "Officers 'Love Our Kids,'" *Law and Order,* September 1993, pp. 109–110.

In reviewing the programs implemented in the 1980s, there is generally a closer resemblance to the community-oriented policing programs found under the three components. In Flint, Michigan, in the early 1980s, the Neighborhood Foot Patrol Program (NFPP) was implemented, and interviews with the foot patrol officers compared with interviews of motor patrol officers proved quite revealing in the area of job satisfaction (Lurigio and Rosenbaum 1994). The officers in the foot patrol program had much higher job satisfaction than those riding in motor vehicle patrols, and the factors that enhanced job satisfaction were that the "officers were more likely to perceive that they were doing an important job in the department and in their patrol areas, improving police–community relations, performing a job that the police department views as important, and working as part of a police team" (Lurigio and Rosenbaum 1994, 152).

Another study in the early 1980s was the Baltimore County, Maryland, Citizen-Oriented Police Enforcement (COPE) project, which was developed as a community-oriented policing initiative but developed into a problem-oriented policing program, thereby utilizing two of the three components (Cordner 1988; Hayeslip and Cordner 1987; Lurigio and Rosenbaum 1994). It was found that "those officers who participated in COPE had higher levels of reported job satisfaction, more cooperative and service-oriented attitudes about the police role, more positive attitudes toward the community, and more positive evaluations of the COPE project's effects" (Hayeslip and Cordner 1987, 115).

Previously discussed programs such as the Police Foundation's Fear Reduction Study in Houston, Texas, and Newark, New Jersey, utilized mainly neighborhood-oriented policing strategies in the implementation of their programs (see Brown and Wycoff 1987; Lurigio and Rosenbaum 1994; Pate et al. 1986; Williams and Pate 1987; Wycoff 1988). The reports for the purposes of police officers' job satisfaction are anecdotal in nature in both studies, but they are revealing because the same high job satisfaction that is found in these studies is also found in other studies (Wycoff 1988).

In New York City, the Vera Institute implemented a study known as the Community Patrol Officer Program (CPOP) in the latter part of the 1980s; the program utilized neighborhood-oriented policing and problem-oriented policing components (Lurigio and Rosenbaum 1994; McElroy, Cosgrove, and Sadd 1993). Although the study revealed some anecdotal evidence of an increase in job satisfaction, it collected data on those things that inferred job satisfaction with some mixed results (McElroy, Cosgrove, and Sadd 1993). The officers were skeptical at the outset of the program but eventually came to see the importance of CPOP as revolving around such things as working as a unit, having visibility, and addressing problems (McElroy, Cosgrove, and Sadd 1993). And the attitudes of the officers became more positive toward the CPOP program, the community, and their job as police officer; however, their attitudes about the functioning of the police department grew more despondent (McElroy, Cosgrove, and Sadd 1993).

Additional studies conducted during the 1990s almost uniformly reveal a skepticism on the part of the police officers before implementing community-oriented policing, but posttests show an increase in overall job satisfaction. In Madison, Wisconsin, a study on the Quality Policing program showed an increase in police officers' satisfaction with their jobs in a variety of areas to include greater working conditions, more participatory management, and greater community support (Lurigio and Rosenbaum 1994; Wycoff and Skogan 1994b). In Joliet, Illinois, officers reported an increase in job satisfaction the first year for those in the Neighborhood-Oriented Policing (NOP) program; in the second year, officers working in the program and outside the program reported a more positive change in both the characteristics of their job and their level of satisfaction (Rosenbaum, Yeh, and Wilkinson 1994). In Louisville, Kentucky, officers reported higher job satisfaction, and the researchers also found that the results of this higher satisfaction were related to the level of support the officers received from the community, department, and other agencies (Wilson and Bennett 1994). In Kalamazoo, Michigan, a study of officers' attitudes revealed that there was a positive attitude toward community-oriented policing when citizens were involved in the process, when they had job involvement, and when community-oriented police officers were like other officers (Dicker 1998). However, as Dicker points out, what was most interesting about this study was that "neither rank, organizational trust, level of pride in the police department, supervisor trust, nor satisfaction with the amount of control over the work environment predicted support for Community-Oriented Policing" (Dicker 1998, 79). In a sense, it was the officers' opinions of community-oriented policing that mattered the most.

Time and time again, research continues to demonstrate that a department's shift to community-oriented policing has a profound impact on officers' satisfaction with their job. (Engel and Worden 2003; Ford, Weissbein, and Plamondon 2003; Paoline 2004; Pelfrey 2004). Police department studies in urban agencies (Lurigio and Rosenbaum 1994; Novak, Alarid, and Lucas 2002; Sims, Scarborough, and Ahmad 2003; Wilson and Bennett 1994), in Sheriffs' offices (Cochran, Bromley, and Swando 2002), in a public housing police agency in Philadelphia (Greene, Collins, and Kane 2000; Greene et al. 1999), and in small-town rural America (O'Shea 1999) all consistently find that officer satisfaction increases, officers demonstrate higher levels of self-initiated policing (Greene, Collins, and Kane 2000), they receive fewer citizen complaints (Kessler 1999), and essentially community policing officers are more likely to meet the needs of the citizens they police (Mastrofski et al. 2000). As Russell and MacLachlan (1999, 48) concluded in their study on officer satisfaction, "the evidence supports the hypothesis that community policing will improve employee satisfaction in a law enforcement agency." There is, however, an important distinction to recognize in terms of police officer satisfaction with community-oriented policing. When there is a lack of agency support for community-oriented policing, police officers often feel that their status as "real cops" is challenged, whereas in those agencies where community-oriented policing is supported by the department hierarchy, police are satisfied with their positions and do not feel stigmatized (Garcia 2005). In addition, where "those officers who perceive that the sheriffs office has sufficiently prepared itself and its employees for the transition toward community policing are more open to change" (Cochran, Bromley, and Swando 2002, p. 521) and are thus more likely to be satisfied with the implementation of community-oriented policing. It is clear through twenty years of research that a bona fide shift to community-oriented policing enhances officer satisfaction in the long term, which can result in better policing and greater citizen satisfaction.

In some reported studies, it should be noted, however, that community-oriented policing was not so successful. One study in Chicago where the police department implemented the Chicago Alternative Policing Strategy (CAPS), a form of community-oriented policing, found that after implementation in the early 1990s the "officers were very ambivalent about community policing in Chicago" (Lurigio and Skogan 1994). A study in Philadelphia, where another program known as Community-Oriented Police Education (COPE) was implemented in the 1980s, found that officers, when questioned about job satisfaction, reported that they "were less satisfied with their police career and direct assignment, and were less likely to see their job as providing challenges and opportunities for self-initiative" (Lurigio and Rosenbaum 1994). Another study, however, reached the opposite findings, but with some of its own unique problems. The study found that as employees' satisfaction with their job increases, resulting from the shift to community-oriented policing, and because their jobs are more interesting and more challenging than management positions within the department, many officers may choose to remain on the street rather than take the less glamorous role of sergeant (Scarborough et al. 1999). This could create problems for promoting qualified candidates into the mid-level management positions, thus unintentionally creating problems in the long term. Finally, several studies have found that community-oriented policing can induce stress, strain, and frustration in officers because of the organizational change and demands placed on officers (Lord 1996; Yates and Pillai 1996); these difficulties

Officers Patricia Gomez and Gregory Szymanski of the Toledo Police Department receive their t-shirts to commemorate the fifteenth annual family Block Watch Picnic. (*Courtesy of the Toledo Police Department, Toledo, Ohio.*)

may lead to a negative attitude toward the implementation of community-oriented policing. These negative findings, however, seem to be the exception to the rule.

The overall analysis reveals that most of the police officers' responses to the implementation of community-oriented policing are somewhat skeptical at first. Once the officers are involved in the community-oriented policing programs, however, as long as the department offers the support necessary through the decentralization concept and implements a participatory style of management, the officers' attitudes become more positive and job satisfaction increases. The officers in most of the studies show signs that they are challenged more, have more input into their role as police officers, and feel they are truly helping the community deal with its criminal and order maintenance problems. (See Table 8-7.)

TABLE 8-7   *Benefits of Community Policing for the Police.*

1. The police will receive greater community support.
2. The police will be able to share the responsibility for the control of crime and disorder with citizens.
3. Police officers will have greater job satisfaction because they will be able to see the results of their efforts at problem solving.
4. The communication and cooperation among units in the police department will be enhanced.
5. Police departments will have to reexamine their organizational structure and management practices.

Source: Adapted from Lee P. Brown, "Community Policing: A Practical Guide for Police Officials." *Perspectives on Policing.* Washington, D.C.: National Institute of Justice, 1989.

DEVELOPMENT OF COMMUNITY-ORIENTED POLICE OFFICERS

Although community-oriented policing may create an atmosphere in which police officers are more challenged and achieve a higher level of job satisfaction, it is imperative that the police department assist police officers in training to be community-oriented police officers. As Edwin Meese (1993, 5) states, "changes in titles and organization can provide the conditions for improved professionalism, but only human beings can fulfill the potential of the new strategies for police work." If a police chief changes the police department overnight from a traditional orientation to community-oriented policing, he or she cannot expect the police officers to adapt instantaneously. The police officers must be provided the conceptual aspects of the new philosophy as well as the understanding of the managerial changes that will complement this new approach to policing. Then the officers must be instructed in their role in community-oriented policing, provided the skills and training necessary to perform these duties, and given every opportunity to reach their potential.

In a perfect world, it always seems easier to start from scratch when creating an entirely new program. It may seem easier to begin anew with all new police officers hired specifically for community-oriented policing, training them in the academy and on the street for this new approach, and providing them additional training and opportunities to excel as community-oriented police officers. This approach is not only impossible but undesirable as well. The skills and understanding of the community that the police officers have gained in a traditional police department are still necessary and desirable to some degree under community-oriented policing. However, that is not to say that under this approach new officers being hired, trained, and placed into neighborhoods as community-oriented police officers should not receive additional, and often very different, training from the traditional training.

The hiring of new police officers, based on the new job analysis and mission statement of the police department, should be specifically for community-oriented policing (Novak, Alarid, and Lucas 2002). The officers should already possess many of the skills and the education necessary to perform the function and duties of this new style of policing.

An approach has been to go directly to the source—namely, to recruit community residents (Novak, Alarid, and Lucas 2002; Williams 1998). The benefits of this method include that the individual is familiar with the local jurisdiction and is already connected to and interacts with the community on a personal level. Once the officers are hired and enter into the police academy, their instruction should at a minimum be supplemented with some of the training necessary to create officers who can handle many of the new situations they will find themselves in, such as community leader, problem solver, and coordinator among various government agencies. Some possibilities have included creating an entirely new police academy for the community-oriented police officers and sending them solely through this academy or sending them through the community-oriented policing academy and then the traditional police academy. Other possibilities include expanding the length of time spent in the police academy to accommodate all of the additional training necessary. This approach would obviously be extremely cost-prohibitive for most police departments, and there is some doubt as to the potential benefit of this concept. Meese (1993) suggested a split academy in which the officers would obtain traditional police training, enter field training for a designated period of time, and then return to the academy for enhanced community training. However it is conducted, the police officers must be taught the role of the police under community-oriented policing to foster the perception and understanding of this new systemic approach to policing, allowing them to be successful in this new role.

Officers who have previously been hired and have worked under the traditional form of policing must be provided additional training to, first and foremost, alter any negative perceptions they may have of this systemic approach (Lumb and Breazeale 2002). Knowledge is the greatest combatant to fear of change and animosity, and police officers should be taught about community-oriented policing before it is implemented. If possible, simple training on the concept and the three components, as well as some of the literature on community-oriented policing, can assist in breaking down some of the barriers and resistance to change that will no doubt be experienced. These familiarization briefings can go a long way in the preparation for actual training programs the officers will be required to attend to enhance the specific skills they will need under community-oriented policing.

 ## COP IN ACTION

Rock Hill Police Department: Embedding Community Policing in Neighborhoods and Officers' Careers

The Rock Hill Police Department proposed to advance community policing by undertaking cultural change within its organization. Members of the department needed more training to institutionalize community policing to withstand a change in leadership. The following were major goals of Rock Hill's Community Policing initiative:

- Develop a comprehensive reward system that provides incentives for employees who demonstrate support of the change process.
- Provide for and institutionalize organizational readiness for change.
- Institute and maintain an organizational culture that is closely linked to agency goals and objectives.
- Communicate to all employees the importance of an organizational culture that supports departmental goals, objectives, programs and activities.
- Reduce barriers to employee participation in the cultural change process.
- Increase the value placed on education, research, and participatory management.

The Community Policing initiative created a career police officer track that provided for five promotional opportunities for all sworn officers below the rank of sergeant. This program was developed to address concerns about promotion and training opportunities and as a tool to integrate community service into the criteria for promotion.

The program was called the "Career Ladder Program," and a core part of the program was mandated training for community policing. More training accompanies each promotion. In addition, each employee must contribute a minimum of 25 hours of voluntary community service on an annual basis, as a requirement for promotion.

According to Lieutenant Robinson, "The career ladder program has been our biggest retention tool. More money, more recognition, more responsibility, and more training is a winning formula for police officers and increasing the professionalism of our staff."

Source: Adapted from A. Schneider et al. 2003, *Community Policing in Action: A Practitioner's Eye View of Organizational Change.* Washington, D.C.: Office of Community-Oriented Policing Services.

The basic skills police officers will need under community-oriented policing will be reviewed; however, they are by no means all-inclusive because each police department, through specific needs dictated in large part by the community, will develop its own list of required training. The majority of skills necessary under community-oriented policing are communicative in nature. However, they also include many basic skills critical in the officers' new role. The communications skills include enhanced listening skills, public speaking skills, skill in preparation and delivery of communicative briefings, conflict resolution and mediation skills, the ability to organize and preside over formal meetings, possibly instruction on the way other cultures communicate, and, in some cases, language skills (see Kidd and Braziel 1999a). The enhanced listening skills are extremely important because we have little to no training in listening but utilize it more in the workplace than speaking, reading, and writing (Hersey and Blanchard 1993). Learning to listen to not only words but also such things as paralanguage, rate of speech, diction, tone, rhythm, and volume—as well as various forms of nonverbal communication such as gestures, facial expressions, eye contact, body language, and positioning—can greatly assist the officer in various situations within the community (Hersey and Blanchard 1993).

Public speaking skills are a must in community-oriented policing and a form of training most police officers do not receive (Meese 1993). As the community-oriented police officer begins coordinating among various governmental agencies and creates, or helps create, community groups for both neighborhood-oriented policing and problem-oriented policing, he or she will need the skills to communicate effectively to the various participants. Because the majority of problems in the workplace arise out of miscommunications or the failure to communicate, the ability to speak in public, to address many people at one time, is critical to all of the tenets of community-oriented policing.

A community-oriented policing school resource officer of the Berkeley Police Department speaking with students from Berkeley High School. (*Courtesy of the Berkeley Police Department, Berkeley, California.*)

The ability to speak in public also assists the community-oriented police officer in various forms of briefings. The officer may be called on to brief various groups or people such as the police chief, the neighborhood supervisor, other officers, the community, or other government organizations on his or her actions or the actions of the community under community-oriented policing. These briefings may include simple informational briefings, or they may be as complex as a decision briefing in which the officer must detail not only the situation or problem but all of the alternatives to solving the problem and the course of action that was taken or the one that is recommended. Again, these briefings provide a format for communication among the community, management, and other line officers.

Police officers should also be provided a means to develop conflict resolution and mediation skills. Because officers spend a majority of their time getting involved in disputes, there must be a move away from the traditional policing reaction of making an arrest or declaring "it's not a police problem." Community-oriented police officers should be provided with those skills necessary to resolve these types of conflicts and to defuse their situations rather than waiting to be called back to the scene. Also, when working with various segments of the community and deciding on tactics to utilize under the three components, community-oriented police officers often find that community members may disagree on what should be done about a particular problem or how to prioritize these problems. Here, the conflict resolution and mediation skills can provide the officers the tools to reach a valuable conclusion to the disagreement.

In holding these community meetings, police officers also find, at least initially, that the community members look to their authority and position as a simple declaration that they are in charge. Eventually, it is more desirable to have a community member preside over the meetings, but officers should set the standard initially. Therefore, officers must have some understanding of the various types of meetings and the various skills to effectively run a meeting. The meetings of the community should not be complaint sessions directed toward the police or other members of the community, but rather they must be open discussions about issues that affect the entire community.

In some cases, in some communities, various cultures will be represented. Because every culture has different ways of communicating both verbally and nonverbally, it is important that police officers have at least some familiarity with these differences prior to conducting these meetings. It can assist the officers in defusing some uncomfortable situations just through the education on various cultural attitudes, beliefs, and values. It may also be equally important for the police officers to learn at least some basics of the various languages spoken in the community, and the officers should be provided every opportunity to learn a language both inside and outside the police department, with departmental assistance.

The additional skills that community-oriented police officers will need beyond the communication skills include decision-making and problem-solving skills, computer skills, and research skills to obtain information on a community from every aspect possible, beyond just crime information. Decision-making skills are some of the most critical skills necessary under community-oriented policing. The ability to address a problem, create alternatives for solving the problem, and select the alternative for implementation is an integral part of community-oriented policing. Because problem solving is the primary emphasis of the third component, problem-oriented policing, it is easy to demonstrate the need for this skill.

 COP IN ACTION

School Resource Officers: Community Outreach Benefits

Although crime rates in the United States have generally dropped in recent years, the rate of juvenile crime has risen rapidly. Also, a recent survey reported that one in every four students feels that violence has lessened the quality of education in his or her school. One program to combat the increase of juvenile crime is gaining popularity across the country. It involves a partnership between law enforcement and the schools known as the school resource officer.

This program assigns uniformed police officers to schools, usually junior and senior high schools, to perform a variety of functions. The fact that it is not a structured program is often a benefit in that the program can be tailored to the individual needs of the community. The cost of the officers is often split between the city government and the school district, since hopefully each benefits. School resource officer programs, in use since at least the 1970s, have grown rapidly across the country during the past decade as a result of increasing crime and violence problems in the public school systems.

Although the duties of school resource officers are different in every jurisdiction, most programs have set the following goals:

1. Provide safety and security on the campus.
2. Teach students, school staff, and parents about law enforcement.
3. Reduce truancy by enhancing the learning environment.
4. Create goodwill and increase understanding of law enforcement.
5. Strengthen student–police relationships.

School resource officers can benefit law enforcement, school districts, and the community in general. By having the officers in the schools every day, they can open lines of communication between school officials and the law enforcement community. Many times officers and school officials work on the same problems and have to handle the same "bad" kids but are not able to work closely together for various reasons. The school resource officers help break down these barriers.

A school resource officer program is good public relations for the police department and the school system. The public wants governmental agencies to work together to help solve community problems, and this program is a good example of it working. Although a school resource officer program may be of help to many, each jurisdiction must decide what will work best for them. Each community should take into consideration the extent of their juvenile problem, their population demographics, the potential for participation by school officials, and the community's budgetary concerns. What works well in one community may or may not work equally well in a different one.

Source: Adapted with permission from Michael K. Ahrens, "School Resource Officers," *Law and Order,* July 1995, pp. 81–83.

A Sacramento, California, police officer preparing donated Christmas toys for disadvantaged youth during the holiday season. *(Courtesy of the Sacramento Police Department, Sacramento, California.)*

Additionally, it is important that police officers have both typing and computer skills because the use of computers in the criminal justice field is increasing. Many police cruisers are now equipped with mobile data terminals from which police officers can quickly obtain information (Meese 1993). The ability to work with computers can increase the police officers' productivity immensely and provide a huge source of information for the officers about their community. To a large degree, computers will be where the officers will obtain the majority of information on their prospective communities, both criminal- and noncriminal-related. However, in many cases, information cannot be obtained through a computer, and community-oriented police officers must be instructed on the varying locations from which they can obtain information on their communities. This information should not be limited by any means and could include items revealing social, economic, and demographic information. The officers should also have an understanding of what information other governmental agencies can provide, how to contact the other agencies, and what support the agencies can offer.

The ability of community-oriented police officers to adopt all of these skills will be critical in their new role and can mean the difference between success and failure (Lord and Schoeps 2000; Sherwood 2000). To safeguard the community-oriented policing concept and for it to be truly successful when implemented, many believe new officers should have a college degree because a college education provides a police officer with many of these skills already intact (Meese 1993). The reasoning is perhaps best articulated by Riechers and Roberg:

In doing community- and problem-oriented policing, line officers are asked to attempt to alleviate specific problems, which they have helped to identify by orienting themselves to the needs of the community, with *creative* and *innovative* solutions in a fair, just, and legal manner. This requires certain skills, including problem conceptualization, synthesis and analysis of information, action plans, program evaluation, and communication of evaluation results and policy implications. Numerous studies have indicated that skills such as these are enhanced by a college education. . . . Suffice it to say that the sensitivity and demands of the role of community policing require an individual with a high degree of intelligence, open-mindedness, and nonprejudicial attitudes. (Riechers and Roberg 1990, 111)

However, in a survey of police departments in the United States, 97 percent of local police departments had a formal education requirement, but the typical minimum education requirement of 86 percent of the departments was the completion of high school (Chaiken 1995). In total, 12 percent of the local police departments surveyed required some college education, while only 7 percent required a two-year college degree and 1 percent required a four-year college degree (Riechers and Roberg 1990).

Police departments across the nation are slowly encouraging their officers to seek out additional college education, and as seen from the percentages mentioned, police departments are also beginning to require some college prior to the hiring process. However, the debate over college education for police officers has existed for nearly three decades; it was originally pushed to the forefront by the Law Enforcement Assistance Administration in the late 1960s. A storm of debate in both police and academic circles has since arisen. With strong proponents on either side of the issue, there is no simple answer.

The ultimate question for determining the necessity of higher education is, generally, whether it makes a better police officer (Radelet and Carter 1994). For our purposes, the question should be phrased as follows: Does it make a better community-oriented policing officer? Radelet and Carter (1994) answer this question with a qualified "maybe" as a result of the literature; however, they believe it does make for a more effective community-oriented officer. If we sidestep the larger debate and incorporate the idea that the skills necessary for the community-oriented police officer can be obtained through higher education, the question then becomes why college makes the officer more effective.

As we reviewed those skills necessary for the community-oriented police officer, supported by Riechers and Roberg (1990), many of those skills are learned in the higher education environment. Computer classes and public speaking classes are generally required general education classes in most colleges and universities, which immediately provide the college-educated officer with a slight edge. Over the past twenty plus years, we have seen a dramatic increase in the number of colleges and universities with formal programs related to the study of crime, criminology, law enforcement, and the criminal justice system (Oliver 1995). Many of these programs incorporate the utilization of computer skills and public speaking skills as well as decision-making skills and the study of ethics in the criminal justice system, all of which enhance the skills of the community-oriented police officer. Additionally, if the college or university offers a course on community-oriented policing or even police–community relations, it provides a fundamental background for the police officer when he or she enters a community-oriented policing police department.

Some studies have determined that many benefits accrue to police officers obtaining a higher education degree that are not as quantifiable as those listed earlier but are still of critical importance in regard to community-oriented policing. Some of these benefits include more experience and maturity, understanding of both the government and criminal justice systems, greater creativity and innovation, capability of seeing the "big picture," greater tolerance for other lifestyles and ideologies, more effective communications, more ability to work on their own, more professional demeanor, and a developed ability to adapt (Carter and Sapp 1990). Officers with postsecondary education also tend to be less authoritarian and cynical (Carter and Sapp 1990). Some studies have also found that police officers with a higher education degree are more ethical, have fewer complaints filed against them, and have fewer disciplinary problems (Oliver 1995). Additionally, the police departments themselves benefit overall from having police officers with higher education degrees. As Patrick Murphy states in the foreword to *The State of Police Education: Policy Directions for the 21st Century:*

> In general, a police department that has had a four-year college degree as an entry requirement for ten years or more can be quite a different organization from one requiring only a high school diploma. More responsibility can be placed on the officers, and a more collegial style of management can be utilized. The college-educated force sets higher professional standards and goals, which, in turn, command public respect and help shape public opinion. Finally, a college-educated force has the potential to proactively, rather than just reactively, address the crime and drug problems that plague society today. (Murphy 1989, iv)

The benefits of police officers obtaining higher education are demonstrated by the research, and the majority of those benefits detailed are especially useful for a community-oriented police officer. Therefore, it should be an integral part of the requirements for being a police officer under this new systemic approach to policing. There is a potential downside to encouraging higher education standards among police officers, however. One study of four police departments in New Mexico found that officers with higher education levels were less likely to support community-oriented policing because of a strong belief in traditional police activities (Winfree, Bartku, and Seibel 1996). Another study supporting this finding reported that officers found their crime-fighting role to be far more socially significant and personally satisfying than community-oriented policing roles (Perrott and Taylor 1995). Thus, higher levels of education may not be the ultimate answer to getting officers to support community-oriented policing (Sherwood 2000). This is also not to say that police departments that use community-oriented policing should no longer hire those with only a high school diploma. Rather, the police department and the community must set the hiring standard as they see fit. However, the department must also encourage and provide not only the opportunity but also the incentives to ensure their officers receive some higher education classes and potentially a bachelor's, master's, or professional degree.

CONCLUSION

The role of the police officer is dramatically different under community-oriented policing than it was under the traditional approach. Although police officers still retain many of the old functions of policing under community-oriented policing, officers have to practice situational policing to determine which of the three functions—law enforcement, order maintenance, or service—is appropriate under the new circumstances in which they find themselves. Officers also have to practice situational leadership when working with the community to determine not only the style of leadership they should assume (authoritarian, democratic, or laissez-faire) but also whether they should even have a leadership role or assume the role of adviser or follower. Whether leader or follower, police officers must be an integral part of the community in their new role as community-oriented police officers.

The police are a critical asset under community-oriented policing, and their importance must not be ignored. Their perceptions of community-oriented policing when implementing this new systemic approach can be the difference between success and failure. They must be informed of both the conceptual and practical aspects of the system, and they should be afforded every opportunity to participate in the management process. The new officer should be hired and trained with the express purpose of filling the role of community-oriented police officer, and the previously hired officer should be afforded every opportunity to learn and improve on the skills necessary under this new approach.

The department implementing community-oriented policing may face many obstacles when it comes to officer participation. As Mastrofski, Willis, and Snipes (2002, 107) have concluded, when an agency makes the shift to community-oriented policing, "a rapid, wholesale change in patrol officers' behavior is not likely." However, animosity toward community-oriented policing can be overcome through education and revealing the findings of job satisfaction from other police departments that have implemented similar programs. The benefits to the police under community-oriented policing far outweigh any negative aspects they may face. Community-oriented policing is beneficial not only to the community and the police department but also to the police officer.

COP ON THE WORLD WIDE WEB

CopNet

http://police.sas.ab.ca/homepage.html

Domestic Violence Community Policing Resources

http://www.vaw.umn.edu/FinalDocuments/commpoli.asp

Federal Law Enforcement Training Center (FLETC)

http://www.fletc.gov

Juneau, Alaska, Police Department

http://www.juneaupolice.com

Officer.Com

http://www.officer.com

REVIEW QUESTIONS

1. What is meant by the "traditional role of the police"?
2. What is the role of the police in community-oriented policing?
3. Is higher education necessary for police officers in community-oriented policing?

CHAPTER 9

The Role of the Community

Nothing will ruin the country if the people themselves will undertake its safety; and nothing can save it if they leave that safety in any hands but their own.

—Daniel Webster

CHAPTER OBJECTIVES

- ■ Understand the important role of the community in COP.
- ■ Understand the multiple definitions of *community*.
- ■ Recognize the traditional roles of the community.
- ■ Articulate the importance of the leadership role.
- ■ Discuss community involvement in COP.
- ■ Understand the obstacles to community involvement.
- ■ Understand how the obstacles to community involvement can be overcome.

Inherent within the name of community-oriented policing is a role and position for the community in the systemic approach. The role is defined by the position the community holds in our society today and by the relationship necessary to eradicate crime and order maintenance issues that plague our streets and neighborhoods. The role of the community must be a powerful one under community-oriented policing. The community cannot be relegated to the role of silent partner or advisory board; rather, it must, at a minimum, obtain equality with the police, and in the most desired goals of community-oriented policing, community members must become the leaders of the police. This role of the community is perhaps one of the most difficult aspects of community-oriented policing to understand, but at the same time it is one of the most critical for the

The Berkeley Police Department's Citizen's Academy graduating class of spring 1995.
(*Courtesy of the Berkeley Police Department, Berkeley, California.*)

systemic approach to be complete. The community must be an integral component of community-oriented policing for the concept to succeed.

Understanding the critical role of the community as it relates to community-oriented policing has become a focal area of research over the past decade (Bohm, Reynolds, and Holmes 2000; Buerger 1994a; Correia 2000; Duffee, Fluellen, and Renauer 1999; Grinc 1994). More effort has begun to focus on the appropriate means of defining *community* (Correia 2000; Duffee, Fluellen, and Renauer 1999), what the appropriate role of the community is in community-oriented policing (Buerger 1994a; Grinc 1994; Manning 1988; Murphy 1988), what impact community-oriented policing has on citizens (Greene, Collins, and Kane 2000; Kessler 1999), and what the effect is of various police–citizen contacts, such as the citizen police academies (Bumphus, Gaines, and Blakely 1999; Jordan 2000). All of these are important in understanding the critical role of the community within the framework of community-oriented policing, but what must first be understood is *why* the community is necessary for bona fide community-oriented policing to be successful.

 ## COP IN ACTION

Connecting with the Cornerstone of the Community: Family

Community policing comes down to problem solving. When officers arrive at your door and listen to the problem, we should be able to offer both short-term relief and long-term solutions. For the average cop, nothing is more frustrating than having to tell the caller, "There is nothing (or little) we can do."

Law enforcement agencies across the country are experiencing an increasing number of family disturbance calls involving out-of-control children. In the past, we have recommended community organizations, parenting classes, and counseling to parents.

Unfortunately, traditional parenting classes do not deal with gangs, drug use, violent kids, runaways, and other criminal behaviors. These are truly law enforcement issues. Community resources are neither designed nor equipped to confront these behaviors, and most law enforcement agencies do not have concrete answers for these families. However, most agencies are now aware that without structured intervention, the officer soon will be returning for similar calls.

Accordingly, the Thousand Oaks Police Department's Community Oriented Policing Unit now offers a program called the "Parent Project." This program is specifically designed to help parents change destructive adolescent behavior.

The Parent Project was created for parents with difficult or out-of-control adolescent children. Parents learn and practice specific prevention and intervention strategies for destructive behaviors such as truancy, alcohol and other drug use, gangs, practice of the occult, running away, violence, and suicide. Parents facing these crises constantly say to officers, "Just tell me what I should do." In the Parent Project classes, parents receive specific step-by-step plans for intervening in these and other destructive behaviors.

The classes significantly improve police–community relations, bring parents into the problem-solving process, and help reduce juvenile crime. Families now see the officers helping them through some very difficult times. Parents are referred to the classes by officers in the field, juvenile detectives, diversion programs, the juvenile probation department, school officials, and the court system.

Depending on a family's specific needs, the Parent Project can last ten to sixteen weeks. Part I is called "Laying the Foundation for Change" and consists of six activity-based instructional units. Typically, each unit is delivered at a weekly three-hour session. Parents learn identification, prevention, and intervention techniques for the most destructive adolescent behaviors and criminal activity (gangs, violence, etc.).

Part II is called "Changing Behavior and Rebuilding Family Relationships," consisting of ten topic-focused parent support group sessions. Each session is designed to provide parents practical and emotional support as they continue the process of change in their home. These two-hour sessions also include an activity-based parenting skills component.

For many parents, but especially single parents, emotional and practical support is not available to them at home. Using a highly structured, self-help support group model, the Parent Project offers a vehicle for the establishment of ongoing self-help parent support groups throughout the community.

For agencies that want to work with the entire family, there is a teen component as well. "Choosing Success . . . Choosing Life" focuses on the choices children make and helps teens explore positive alternatives to destructive behaviors.

Finally, parents who are actively involved in the program are linked with a community policing officer in their area. The message we want to send to parents is: If you are trying to change these destructive behaviors, we want to support you in every way we can.

The Thousand Oaks Police Department Community Oriented Policing Unit began offering the Parent Project to local parents in April 1998. Initially, the program was designed to run as one ten-week class, four times per year. Because of the demand, a second class was added in Spanish. Now we are running classes four times per year in both English and Spanish. Since its inception, we have trained more than eighty parents. As an officer for more than seventeen years, it is extremely rewarding to finally provide effective long-term solutions to the parents in our community.

We have seen parents of gang members and parents with children who are using hard-core drugs and alcohol. We were told by one parent that her thirteen-year-old son's aspiration in life was to grow up to be a "porn star." After ten weeks of instruction and application of what these parents have learned, the aspiring porn star has changed his career goals and is now participating in positive family activities.

In another case, a mother of a gang member reports that while her son is still a gang member, the confrontations at home with him are no longer violent and are less frequent.

The truth is that parents have the influence and power to help their children and there-by change the communities in which they live. The Parent Project shows them the way.

Source: Adapted with permission from Ed Tumbleson, "Connecting with the Cornerstone of the Community: Family," *Community Policing Exchange,* January/February 1999, p. 3.

According to Wilson and Kelling, in their article "Broken Windows," and as discussed in the last chapter, the police, throughout the early part of the twentieth century, were focused on the role of order maintenance for performing their duties (Wilson and Kelling 1982). As the crime wave of the early 1960s began with the largest population explosion the United States has ever experienced, the police began to focus more on law enforcement than order maintenance. The introduction of the baby boomers and their ascension into those crime-prone teenage years caused the police to rethink their role in society. The order maintenance concept was not working with this new population, and a switch to the role of law enforcement was made. The goal for better policing was then focused on ways "the police could solve more crimes, make more arrests, and gather better evidence" (Wilson and Kelling 1982, 33). Crime fighting became the central focus for all policing, and the social control mechanisms, largely influenced by the community and reinforced by the police, collapsed. Both the community and the police began to change.

The community, which had its own sense of social control over the people, began to disappear from inner-city neighborhoods and eventually from many of the suburbs. People became more engrossed in their work; our society became more mobile; age-old institutions of family, neighborhood, and community crumbled; and government attempted to fill the void. Our societal makeup has changed dramatically since the early 1960s and has not supported the establishment of cohesive neighborhoods, which in turn would foster the sense of community people speak of so often. Citizens drew up within much smaller groups and decided they did not want to get involved or it was not their problem. Society allowed social disorder to reign and turned any semblance of social control over to the police. Crime fighting and social disorder are the job of the police because "that's what we pay them for." Although this evidence is somewhat factual, partly anecdotal, and largely ontological in nature, the changes demonstrated in the police are not.

The police have changed dramatically since the early 1960s, and mostly for the better. Speaking first of that which is better on the part of the police is the move to become more professional in their work, better equipped, and better trained. However, what the police have given up in return has not been worth the price. The police have given up their order maintenance role and their relationship with the community, and they have collectively determined they can handle all criminal problems on their own, and the rest is not their concern. However, there is even doubt the police can handle the crime. As Walinsky (1995, 39) reports, "in the 1960s the United States as a whole had 3.3 police officers for every violent crime reported per year. In 1993 it had 3.47 violent crimes reported for every police officer." Despite the greatest endeavors of the U.S. Congress to add 100,000 police officers on the street via Title I of the 1994 Crime Bill, according to Walinsky (1995, 40), to retain the position the United States had in 1960, "we would have to add not 100,000 new police officers but about five million." This number is impractical and nearly infeasible, so we must look at the way things really are. The police are consistently a small group in any society, whether it is the 5 police officers in Glenville, West Virginia, policing a community of 4,000; the 325 officers in the Arlington County Police Department serving 100,000; or the 38,000 police officers in the New York City Police Department serving 8 million citizens. These three police departments and all of the departments in the United States, however effective they are, cannot hope to truly fight all the crime on their own and deal effectively with the order maintenance issues. As Herman Goldstein (1990, 21) stated, "a community must police itself," and "the police can, at best, only assist in that task."

This, then, demonstrates the need for the community to be an integral part of community-oriented policing. The police need the community, and the community needs the police. To continue effectively fighting crime, the police must elicit the help of the community. To reestablish order out of disorder and to maintain the community through order maintenance, the police and community must work together. To achieve these objectives and to work effectively together, the police and community must implement community-oriented policing and address all of the problems together through the three components. And the desired goal of the concept is to have the community dictate the problems, prioritize their importance, determine means to effectively address them, and then either implement or assist in the implementation of the various solutions. In effect, the community members become the leaders of the police.

To understand this concept better, the term *community* must be effectively defined for the purposes of community-oriented policing. It is also important to analyze what role the community has developed in regards to police relations since the early 1960s and what its practical role would be under community-oriented policing. And, finally, it is important to look to the development of community involvement in this systemic approach because some communities will call for community-oriented policing on their own, whereas others will have no desire to even discuss their involvement in the police function.

COMMUNITY DEFINED

Defining the term *community* is difficult because there are multiple meanings exploring everything from the tangible to the way people organize to a spiritual sense of the word. Exploring the various dictionaries provides a collection of confusing and often conflicting definitions that serve little purpose under our larger definition of community-oriented policing (Buerger 1994b; see also Lynes 1996). Because this larger definition is more concerned with the social behavior and the human aspects of defining community, we must look to the sociological definitions of community for assistance.

Unfortunately, even the field of sociology falls prey to the multiple definitions of community, despite its central focus on human social behavior (Schwab 1992). However, looking to general definitions of community in the field, we find one definition detailing "a spatial or territorial unit of social organization in which people have a sense of identity and a feeling of belonging" (Schaefer and Lamm 1992, 546). Another definition is more analytical in its categorization of community: "the term community refers to a group of people who share three things: They live in a geographically distinct area (such as a city or town); they share cultural characteristics, attitudes, and lifestyles; and they interact with one another on a sustained basis" (Farley 1994, 506). Although these sociological definitions are helpful in perceiving some of the elements present in some communities, they are not as helpful as we would like them to be when analyzing the street from a police officer's perspective.

Some communities may adhere to the concepts of geographical distinction, sharing of culture, and interaction on a regular basis, but then they are most likely communities with low priority for the police. This is not to say that they are not important and deserve no attention under community-oriented policing, but these types of communities will most likely have fewer criminal, order maintenance, and environmental problems than those communities lacking in some area of the sociological definition. Areas that are ridden with crime, where there is no consensus of attitudes or beliefs, and where there is little to no interaction among the residents are still communities for our purpose. These are the communities the police are most familiar with, and these are the communities we must not forget in community-oriented policing. Hiding behind the doors and windows, even in the worst of inner-city deprivation, are good, honest, hardworking citizens who are caught in a situation that they cannot escape but have come to endure.

Trojanowicz and Moore (1988) share a similar understanding of what is meant by the term *community*. Having reviewed the various definitions of the term, as well as the evolution of the term over time, they suggested that there are, in reality, two conceptions of community: "geographic communities" and "communities of interest." A geographic community is a physical area in which people or members interact, whereas a community of interest is one focused on a common interest, such as a professional

Berkeley Police Department DARE officer instructing his elementary school class in the spring of 1995. (*Courtesy of the Berkeley Police Department, Berkeley, California.*)

community, the police community, or a college student community. Prior to the advances of technology and industry, because people were constrained in their abilities to interact with others, both of these communities tended to be one and the same. However, once technology advanced and people began to move about more freely, communities of interest came to dominate people's time, minimizing the importance of the geographic community. Hence another concept that must be considered when defining community is the differences between geographic and interest communities.

Another segment of society that the police recognize as a community, which may or may not be inclusive within the sociological definition of community, is the criminal community. Whether we are discussing the community of crack houses and drug dealers, gangs, or prostitutes, there still exists a community with which the police must interact. As Herman Goldstein (1990, 26) stated, "from a practical standpoint, 'community' is not synonymous with 'law-abiding.'" The relations with this community will be different from those with the law-abiding community; however, many of the central tenets of community-oriented policing will be utilized to maintain order and address the worst of the criminal problems within this criminal element.

To clearly define the term *community* is difficult because of the conceptual ambiguity of the term itself (Correia 2000). The ability to look to one strict analysis and definition of community is of no benefit to community-oriented policing, for there are always communities within communities. As Goldstein (1990, 26) explains, "communities are shifting groups, defined differently depending on the problem that is addressed." We therefore must be content with looking to community as it is defined by multiple parties, including the police, the citizens, and the government. We can look to geography to help us form a conceptualization of community by analyzing the police department's geographical boundaries and the institutionalized conception of geography such as a city, neighborhood, or business district. However, within these confines we can only define community as consisting of a group of people who interact and have some shared attitudes and beliefs, whether they are criminal or law-abiding, residential or business-oriented, socially acceptable or not acceptable.

Community-oriented policing, then, perceives the community as whatever collective group it is dealing with to address a criminal or order maintenance issue. As Mastrofski points out, a minimum standard for community-oriented policing is a "demonstration that a group of people—say a neighborhood—shares a definition of what constitutes right order, threats to it, and appropriate methods for maintaining it" (Mastrofski 1988, 49). He further states that "to the extent that community implies a basis for citizens to work collectively with police to restore and preserve order, it also requires a sense of group identity or attachment—a 'we-ness' derived from shared experience and interaction" (Mastrofski 1988, 49). In a perfect setting, this may already exist, but in a conceptual sense, it may require the creation of community where none exists.

Defining who the community is, is important when exploring the past role of the community in policing, but more importantly in conceptualizing and understanding the community's role within community-oriented policing (See Table 9-1.). Without the community's involvement in this systemic approach to policing, it will cease to exist, and the police will be forced, by default, to return to the isolated form of traditional policing.

TABLE 9-1   *Who Is the Community?*

The following is a list of community members who can provide resources, information, and assistance for strategic-oriented policing; can assist in creating various programs under neighborhood-oriented policing; and should be involved in neighborhood groups assembled to address local problems under problem-oriented policing:

- Families
- Children
- Senior citizens
- Single people
- Transients
- Businesspeople
- Service people
- Homeless people
- Residences
    - Single-family homeowners
    - Apartment dwellers
    - Condominium owners
    - Townhome owners
    - Public housing dwellers
    - Temporary renters
- Churches
- Businesses
    - Service
    - Retail
    - Industrial
- Government
    - Schools
    - Hospitals
    - Libraries
    - Parks
    - Recreation centers
    - Police department
    - Fire department
    - Human services
    - Sheriff's department
    - Mayor/city manager
    - City council
    - Small business administration
    - Public works

- Planning and zoning
- City prosecutor
- Courts
- Charities
    - United Way
- Civic organizations
    - Profit
        - Chamber of commerce
        - Business associations
        - Real estate associations
    - Nonprofit
        - Fraternal lodges
        - Veterans of Foreign Wars
        - Big Brothers/Sisters
        - Advocacy groups
        - Boy/Girl Scouts
        - Neighborhood associations
        - Homeowners' associations
- Unions
- Crime prevention
    - Police athletic leagues
    - Guardian angels
    - Neighborhood watch
    - Crime stoppers
- Utility companies
    - Water
    - Gas
    - Electricity
    - Cable
    - Telephone
- Federal agencies
- Federal law enforcement
- Neighborhood residents
- Private security

TRADITIONAL ROLE OF THE COMMUNITY

Despite the call for greater community integration into policing and essentially the greater institution of government under community-oriented policing, this concept is not new to America. From the founding of the United States to present-day America, citizen participation has been a strong underlying facet of our form of government. Citizen participation is safeguarded within the Constitution, and the United States has a longer history of cherishing this noble endeavor than it does in its dismissal. This reaction of citizen participation in government and, more importantly for our purposes, in policing can be seen as a result of the centralization of local governments after World War II (Johnson, Misner, and Brown 1981), causing them to become "increasingly remote from neighborhood concerns" (Wilson 1975, 40). At the same time, government had to determine a method by which the citizens could be drawn back into the participatory process that was once the foundation of American government.

Johnson, Misner, and Brown (1981) highlighted three distinct stages whereby the government, since World War II, has attempted to draw on citizen participation. The first stage, from 1949 to 1963, emphasized the creation of carefully appointed committees to the government process "that were only advisory in nature" and "had little or no influence on the official policies that were made" (Johnson, Misner, and Brown 1981, 276). In the second stage, from 1964 to 1968, governments selected "indigenous citizens" to participate in the policy-making procedure (Johnson, Misner, and Brown 1981, 276). Those involved largely consisted of citizens from the local communities, specifically oriented to obtaining a cross-section by race, gender, and national origin. The third stage of citizen participation as articulated by Johnson, Misner, and Brown (1981) was said to exist from 1969 to the time of their writing in 1981, and this stage emphasized planning and advisory councils in a regionally decentralized manner.

However, a clear and distinct category of citizen participation has emerged since Johnson, Misner, and Brown's book, and subsequently a fourth stage should be added. In this stage, running from the early 1980s to the present, citizen participation has been decentralized (as in the third stage), but it has commanded more power, moving away from the advisory role to one of authoritative action. In the police field, despite an enormous amount of debate (see, for example, Dudley 1991; Kerstetter 1985), this form of citizen participation increased dramatically through the 1980s in the form of the civilian review board, which generally reviews police misconduct and deadly shooting encounters (see, for example, Geller and Scott 1992; Radelet and Carter 1994).

As Johnson, Misner, and Brown (1981, 276) articulate in their book, the important aspect of this historical interpretation is to understand that citizen participation in the governmental process "has a long history in this country." The role of citizen participation within the role of the police is no different. This interrelationship can be clearly seen when we look to the historical correlation between the two. The role of the police in our society shifted from order maintenance, largely citizen participatory, after World War II and moved to that of law enforcement, which is highly centralized and is not citizen participatory. Despite the shift of the police, along with the rest of government, away from citizen participation, it is important to remember that the citizen still played some role, albeit a minor one at times.

Officer George Roush challenged the Sunday school children at this church to gather teddy bears to fill a police wagon. The bears are later given away at police calls where young children are involved. (*Courtesy of the Toledo Police Department, Toledo, Ohio.*)

The traditional roles of the community in relationship to the police function are perhaps best articulated by Buerger's (1994a, 1994b) categorization of four standard roles. Traditionally, the first and primary role the community has had is acting as the "eyes and ears of the police" (Buerger 1994a, 270). Providing the police information about crime, criminals, and suspicious activity via the phone, personal contact, or clandestine contact (such as informants) has been the key way for citizens to participate in the police function. In the second role of "cheerleader," citizens, in a collective sense, articulate their support for the police (Buerger 1994a, 1994b). The third role the community has is a supportive role, usually in the form of monetary assistance through tax levies aimed at increasing the funding for the police (Buerger 1994a, 1994b). The fourth role is that of "statement making," in which the community makes statements that are "symbolically confrontational" such as "the annual Take Back the Night rallies—or activities with more lasting effects, such as posting 'Drug-Free School Zone' or Neighborhood Watch signs" (Buerger 1994a, 271). All of these roles are indicative of the traditional role the community has had over the past several decades and that remains a part of community-oriented policing. However, the systemic approach to policing allows for a much larger role for the community.

ROLE OF THE COMMUNITY IN COMMUNITY-ORIENTED POLICING

The community must take on a larger role under community-oriented policing for this new approach to be successful. The community, one of the most important factors in both law enforcement and order maintenance, can effectively deal with crime and greatly improve the environmental conditions in which its citizens live if citizens take on a wider role in policing and are provided the opportunity for this role. The community must be allowed to share power with the police, be allowed decision-making capabilities under all three of the components, and effectively lead the police. To accomplish these goals, it is important to look at the community's expanded role and function under community-oriented policing.

Eck and Rosenbaum (1994) identified five ways in which the citizens of a community can effectively deal with the criminal and order maintenance issues that face their neighborhoods. Eck and Rosenbaum (1994) identified the first and primary function, found in the traditional role of the community, which continues in the community-oriented policing role: to be the eyes and ears of the community. The second function is for citizens to form patrols, confront criminal and disorderly individuals, and drive them from the community (Eck and Rosenbaum 1994). Although this function was generally discouraged under the traditional role of the community in policing (Buerger 1994a), some police now encourage such action under community-oriented policing (Eck and Rosenbaum 1994). The third function of the community is to reduce its citizens' chances of victimization, reduce the opportunity for crime, reduce the actual amount of crime, and reduce the fear of crime (Eck and Rosenbaum 1994; Skogan 1987). The fourth function is for citizens to "put pressure on others to act" (Eck and Rosenbaum 1994, 14). As Eck and Rosenbaum (1994, 14–15) articulate,

> They can demand more police resources, they can pressure businesses to change their practices, they can lobby local government agencies to obtain services and get favorable rulings from regulators, and they can threaten property owners and organizations with civil suits to change behaviors and physical conditions.

And the fifth function they discuss is allowing "the police to act on their behalf" (Eck and Rosenbaum 1994, 15). The police, through meetings with the community, can gather the opinions of the community members and authorization from them to extend their capabilities beyond the normal routines of policing. These enforcement capabilities in any other environment may not be acceptable (Eck 1993; Eck and Rosenbaum 1994; Weisburd, McElroy, and Hardyman 1988), but it is a return to pre–World War II America when "the police . . . assisted in that reassertion of authority by acting, sometimes violently, on the behalf of the community" (Wilson and Kelling 1982, 33). Although this is not a call for the community to allow police brutality, it is a call for the police to have greater authorization and capabilities to deal effectively with criminal and order maintenance issues. For example, in a neighborhood with an open-air drug market, obtaining the authorization of all the residents to allow the police to stop all vehicles entering and leaving the neighborhood without a reasonable suspicion can be one way to effectively deal with the drug problems through citizen authorization.

The authors, however, all leave out one important function of the community under community-oriented policing: the leadership role the community must have for the concept to be fully implemented. The community, made up of indigenous citizens from the targeted neighborhood, must be given the authority to determine what the criminal and order maintenance problems are in their neighborhood, their priority, the type of programs that should be implemented, and ways police resources should be allocated. They must be given a leadership role in taking back control of their community. As Friedman

⬟ COP IN ACTION

Beyond Neighborhood Watch: Role of the Community in Community Policing

The bulk of what has been written about implementing community policing addresses what can be done within police agencies to promote community policing initiatives. And although most agencies interested in modifying traditional methods of police service delivery are working hard to establish and extend partnerships with business owners, public and private service providers, community groups, and the media (see Trojanowicz and Bucqueroux 1994), they have given less attention to the specifics of what the average community member's role is, or can be, under a community policing model. It appears, however, that we are at the point in this evolutionary process to further explore the role of the community in community policing.

Citizens have typically assisted the police with the detection and reporting of possible criminal activity in their communities (Buerger 1994a). Members of groups such as Neighborhood Watch or citizen patrols are often defined as "the eyes and ears of the police." Unfortunately, the success of programs such as Neighborhood Watch may contribute to the problems that many agencies experience as they try to get community members involved in more proactive efforts to increase neighborhood safety. Citizens often believe that they have fulfilled their civic duties when they call 911 to report troublesome activity to the police. It is possible that these early crime-prevention efforts have actually created more, not less, of a dependency on the police. It is now time to work toward making community residents more proactive and less dependent.

A variety of obstacles, however, must be overcome in order to make community crime-prevention efforts more proactive. One of the first steps should be to increase citizens' knowledge of police operations, particularly regarding the limited resources police have at their disposal. In most areas of this country, regardless of whether the jurisdiction is urban, suburban, or rural, it is often impossible for the police to address every instance of crime and disorder in a community. Some police fear that if the public gets more involved in crime prevention, they may develop unrealistic expectations of the amount of time that the police can spend attending to their specific concerns. Such unrealistic expectations may lead to decreased levels of citizen satisfaction with police services if those expectations are not met. Police must make concerned citizens aware of the constraints (realities) within which the police must operate and help them understand exactly how these constraints affect police practices.

The second step is to give the public a multitude of very specific suggestions about how they can contribute to neighborhood safety. Community members, possibly organized in neighborhood associations, local schools, or worship groups, can play an important role in several areas including the following: (1) identifying problems (identifying conditions of crime and disorder that threaten citizen safety); (2) prioritizing these problems; (3) identifying potential solutions to these problems (focusing specifically on what community members themselves can do to solve problems); (4) designing, implementing, and evaluating crime-prevention initiatives; and (5) educating and mobilizing other community members, friends, and relatives.

Third, most community groups will probably need some hands-on assistance with initiating and sustaining community involvement in community policing. Given that most police resources are already stretched to capacity, or beyond, police administrators may need to look outside their own organizations for assistance. For example, faculty and students at local and regional colleges and universities may be willing to help inform community groups of the community-policing philosophy. They may also be willing to work with these groups to systemically identify problems that threaten citizen safety and help to develop potential solutions to these problems. In addition to the obvious benefits to the community and the police, this strategy could provide an excellent opportunity for students to acquire a more complete understanding of how problems are viewed and addressed by citizens and the police.

The time is right to seriously explore how concerned citizens can play more active roles in the promotion of public safety in their communities. By providing citizens with an abundance of specific activities in which they can engage, it may be possible to further develop the concept of "community" in community policing.

Source: Adapted with permission from Lynette Lee-Sammons, "Beyond Neighborhood Watch: The Role of the Community in Community Policing," *Community Policing Exchange.* Washington, D.C.: Community Policing Consortium, September/October 1995, p. 3.

(1994, 263) states, "The community must have a voice in the forums that define community policing itself, must be a ready and knowledgeable ally to the forces of reform, and, in the neighborhood, where the benefits are supposed to be delivered, must have a serious part in implementing solutions as well as nominating problems." In fact, recent research has demonstrated that the most effective communities have utilized their community organizations to apply pressure through activism to obtain changes in policing practices that are more in line with the philosophy of community-oriented policing (Bass 2000; Duffee, Fluellen, and Renauer 1999). To accomplish this goal, the community must have a shared form of leadership in both the policy-making and decision-making processes, and like the police, the community's citizens should be held accountable for their actions. When the community works with the police in this shared leadership role, the citizens have not only a vested interest in how the police perform their role but also a responsibility for their role that has not existed since the loss of the order maintenance role around the 1950s.

One method of creating a shared powers role for the community has been through the establishment of citizens' steering committees or councils. Osborne and Gaebler (1992, 320), in their publication *Reinventing Government,* go so far as to call for a system of "Public Safety Coordinating Councils" at the state and local level, which would consist of representatives of the providers (government) and the customers (local citizens). These councils would oversee all of government rather than just the police. However, there is a strong need under the community-oriented policing model to institute this concept specifically for the police. As Guyot (1991a, 297) has pointed out, "listening to the many voices of the community is essential for police officers and police managers in their striving for fairness" and "police departments need structures that can encourage officers to be more attentive to the diversity of views in a neighborhood." If Zhao and Thurman (Zhao 1996; Zhao and Thurman 1996) are accurate in their analysis—that it is the external environment that brings about organizational change among police departments—then it is clear that these types of councils should be a focal point of community-oriented policing. In addition, community-oriented policing should be primarily a means for community empowerment rather than a means for extending the power of police, which is often the case (see Lyons 1999; Reed 1999). Although this issue can be a source of contention for chiefs who do not embrace sharing power with the community (Brown 1985), it is the basic fundamental principle for agencies adopting the systemic approach. However, chiefs should not fear the concept because as Osborne and Gaebler (1992, 320) envision them, these councils "would steer their local systems, but would not row."

Citizens learn the art of fingerprinting at a civilian academy sponsored by the St. Petersburg Police Department. (*Courtesy of the St. Petersburg Police Department, St. Petersburg, Florida.*)

One example of the public safety council concept is the highly successful Charleston Public Safety Council located in Charleston, West Virginia, and overseen by John Chapman. The council is an independent nonprofit foundation formed by an alliance of business, local government, and social agencies to address citywide public safety issues and to help mobilize support for neighborhood organizations (Addesa 1998). The safety council has worked on a variety of projects by identifying the specific problems that plague the community and then exerting pressure on the local government to bring about change. The council members have found that they can bring about change by working with the local police department. Some examples of the projects undertaken by the Charleston Public Safety Council include working on the issue of domestic violence, addressing the problem of false security alarms, dealing with public inebriates, mediating in landlord–tenant disputes, and helping the Charleston Police Department secure computer equipment donated by local businesses. This arrangement has allowed the community to have a means of exerting external pressure on the police and thereby effecting change. It has allowed the community to steer, while the police department and other local government agencies row.

One other role that the community has often been asked to play in overseeing and working with police agencies comes in the form of citizen review boards. These boards existed in various forms prior to the community-oriented policing movement but have taken on a special level of importance under the systemic approach. These boards often consist of a group of local citizens who are tasked with reviewing complaints against police, cases of official misconduct, and allegations of excessive use of force. It is evident from this list why police departments, including both line officers and management, often resist the development of any form of citizen review board. However, when an agency is attempting to adopt the philosophy of community-oriented policing, any attempt to resist the establishment of a citizen review board can be construed as running counter to the

TABLE 9-2   *Benefits of Community Policing to the Community*

1. The police make a commitment to prevent crime rather than just react to it.
2. Public scrutiny of the police is improved because more citizens know what police do and why.
3. Police officers are accountable for their behavior not only to the department but also to citizens.
4. Police services will be tailored to the needs of each neighborhood.
5. As citizens become more involved in police activities, the community will become more organized and therefore more effective in responding to problems.

Source: Adapted from Lee P. Brown, "Community Policing: A Practical Guide for Police Officials." *Perspectives on Policing.* Washington, D.C.: National Institute of Justice, 1989.

philosophical changes being implemented. Hence agencies may be perceived as not being sincere about their community orientation under community-oriented policing.

It has been noted that the three variations on this concept of civilian oversight are (1) civilian review, in which an agency outside the police department accepts complaints, investigates and judges them, and then recommends discipline to the chief; (2) civilian input, in which citizens who are part of the police department undertake the investigation of excessive force complaints while police investigate other complaints; and (3) civilian monitors, in which an outside agency is available to investigate and mediate complaints from those who think that police investigation and outcome were unfair or inadequate (Skolnick and Fyfe 1993). Whichever form is used, however, it is important to note the reason that citizen review boards are developed: because in most instances the police investigate police misconduct and citizens do not always trust the police. The important concept is that the review process, because of its sensitive nature which mandates that it cannot be an open process, must have some form of citizen oversight to ensure that the police department is held accountable for any misconduct and, in the case of a lack of evidence of misconduct, has a legitimate voice to substantiate such findings.

The one major obstacle to this process of fully implementing community-oriented policing is community involvement. The police must not rely solely on "government-backed" citizens (citizens employed by the government) or citizens from preexisting organizations (e.g., members of the local lodges, the Veterans of Foreign Wars, or the various social organizations); rather, they must tap the common citizen who is indigenous to the particular neighborhood because he or she is fully qualified to determine what is wrong with the community. Although the ultimate role for the community under community-oriented policing is one of leadership, involving the community to reach this point is difficult. The way to involve the citizens is then critical to our discussion of community-oriented policing. (See Table 9-2.)

COMMUNITY INVOLVEMENT

Getting the community involved in all three components to address the criminal and order maintenance problems that plague their neighborhoods is critical to the success of community-oriented policing (see Skogan 1998; Williams 1998). There are multiple ways in which to get the community involved in this new systemic approach, but we will break it down into three categories, from the most common to the least common. The three categories of community involvement under community-oriented policing are police-initiated, police and community–initiated, and community-initiated.

The police-initiated community-oriented policing program is the most common of the three (see, for example, Brown and Wycoff 1987; Cordner 1988; Farrell 1988; Kratcoski and Dukes 1995c; Lasley, Vernon, and Dery 1995; Weisburd and McElroy 1988).

Although the ultimate goal of community-oriented policing is to have the community lead the police, often the police first have to motivate the community to action and slowly allow it to acquire the leadership role. In some jurisdictions, the police are at an advantage because they will be able to tap into community organizations, both public and private, to assist them in gaining the community's support in the programs. In other jurisdictions, most likely as a result of those criminal and order maintenance issues that community-oriented policing is designed to address, there are no community support groups, either public or private. In these situations, the police have to create a sense of community where none exists, develop ties within and among the community where none exist, and assist in the creation of public and private community organizations where none exist before the community can take the leadership role. Through strategic-oriented policing, the police can create an environment conducive to this creation of community by allowing the community a respite from the problems that plague the neighborhood. However, the police must then work to create and foster that sense of community in a place where the police are most likely treated with suspicion. Although this is the most difficult of the police-initiated community-oriented policing programs, it can also be the most beneficial to the community at large.

 ## COP IN ACTION

The DARE Program

The DARE program consists of seventeen sessions that demonstrate how the program is administered. Although created without the assistance of community-oriented policing, it has become an integral part of the systemic approach to policing. The following are brief summaries of each lesson:

1. **Practices for personal safety.** The DARE officer reviews common safety practices to protect students from harm at home, on the way to and from school, and in the neighborhood.
2. **Drug use and misuse.** Students learn the harmful effects of drugs if they are misused, as depicted in a film, "Drugs and Your Amazing Mind."
3. **Consequences.** The focus is on the consequences of using or choosing not to use alcohol, marijuana, and other drugs. If students are aware of those consequences, they can make better informed decisions regarding their own behavior.
4. **Resisting pressure to use drugs.** The DARE officer explains different types of pressures that friends and others exert on students to get them to try alcohol or drugs, ranging from friendly persuasion and teasing to threats.
5. **Resistance techniques: Ways to say no.** Students rehearse the many ways of refusing offers to try alcohol or drugs—simply saying "no" and repeating it as often as necessary; changing the subject; walking away or ignoring the person. They learn that they can avoid situations where they might be subjected to such pressure and can "hang around" with nonusers.

6. **Building self-esteem.** Poor self-esteem is one of the factors associated with drug misuse. How the students feel about themselves results from positive and negative feelings and experiences. They learn to see their own positive qualities and discover ways to compliment others.

7. **Assertiveness: a response style**. Students have certain rights—to be themselves, to say what they think, to say "no" to offers of drugs. They must assert those rights confidently without also interfering with others' rights.

8. **Managing stress without taking drugs.** Students learn to recognize sources of stress in their lives and to develop techniques for avoiding or relieving it, including exercise, deep breathing, and talking to others. Using drugs or alcohol to relieve stress causes new problems.

9. **Media influences on drug use.** The DARE officer reviews strategies used in the media to encourage tobacco and alcohol use, including testimonials from celebrities and pressure to conform.

10. **Decision making and risk taking.** Students learn the difference between bad risks and reasonable risks, how to recognize the choices they have, and how to make a decision that promotes their self-interest.

11. **Alternative to drug abuse.** Drug and alcohol use are not the only way to have fun, to be accepted by peers, or to deal with feelings of anger or hurt.

12. **Alternative activities.** Sports or other physical fitness activities are good alternatives. Exercise improves health and relieves emotional distress.

13. **Officer-planned lessons.** The class is spent on a special lesson devised by the DARE officer himself.

14. **Role modeling.** A high school student selected by the DARE officer visits the class, providing students with a positive role model. Students learn that drug users are in the minority.

15. **Project DARE summary.** Students summarize and assess what they have learned.

16. **Taking a stand.** Students compose and read aloud essays on how they can respond when they are pressured to use drugs and alcohol. The essay represents each student's "DARE pledge."

17. **Assembly.** In a schoolwide assembly, planned in concert with school administrators, all students who participated in Project DARE receive certificates of achievement.

Source: William DeJong, "Project DARE: Teaching Kids to Say 'No' to Drugs and Alcohol," *National Institute of Justice: Research in Action,* March 1986.

The second category of community involvement under community-oriented policing is police and community–initiated (see, for example, Greene and Decker 1989; Tien and Rich 1994; Williams and Pate 1987). This form of community involvement is perhaps the most healthy for the implementing of community-oriented policing because the police and the community bring their perspectives of addressing criminal and order maintenance issues together at first, and then the community slowly takes the leadership role. Since the community will have preexisting organizations, both public and private, the effort to mobilize other members of the community is that much easier. And at the same time, it allows the police and community to work together, on the same level, easing some of the suspicions they may have of each other. The process of implementing the three components is usually faster under this form of community involvement and usually more successful. Also, at the first sign of any failure, there is little likelihood that the community and neighborhood coalitions will disband. Instead, they usually remain intact to work through the difficult beginnings.

A good example of a program that was community and police initiated is the Child Development Community Policing (CDCP) program that was begun in 1991 in New Haven, Connecticut (Murphy et al. 2005). The program was developed through a collaboration between the Yale Child Study Center and the New Haven Department of Police Services in response to a problem of police dealing with traumatized youth. The program commenced through a collaborative effort in which police and clinicians partnered to receive 32 hours of training focused on child development and trauma, followed by a 24-hour class on community policing. Police and clinicians would then meet once a week to review specific cases and to develop a tailored response. Clinicians would then meet with other clinicians to determine the proper clinical response. Finally, clinicians received training on how to be first responders in "the immediate aftermath of children's exposure to violence and other trauma" (Murphy et al. 2005, p. 108). After an incident has occurred, police call in the clinician for assistance; then both the officer and the mental health worker continue to work with the child over the following months. A five-year study conducted on this program found that the "receipt of an immediate, direct, community based intervention at the behest of law enforcement first responders suggests that such collaborations may play an important role in extending care to those with greatest needs" (Murphy, et al. 2005, p. 117). The program proved to be a unique and successful collaboration on behalf of traumatized youth, and it highlights the benefits of police–community initiated programs.

COP IN ACTION

Police Academies for Citizens

The department began its CPA (Citizen's Police Academy) program about seven years ago at the suggestion of Richard Overman, now a chief in Delray Beach, Florida. He attended a bobby "night school" on a trip to England and returned with the idea of offering citizens an in-depth education in police procedure. Under then-Chief Danny Wilson, OPD's community relations unit organized the first class, which met at headquarters for three hours every Tuesday evening for ten weeks.

The CPA was an instant success. Word of mouth and referrals from alumni and officers on the street soon filled a second class. Today, there is a waiting list for its twice-a-year sessions. Interested residents fill out a one-page application with two personal references—a safety check for the department since CPA participants ride on patrol and wear photo IDs that give them access to headquarters.

CPA condenses the official Central Florida police academy (minus physical training) into a thirteen-week syllabus. It's a serious undertaking: OPD makes clear that it expects regular attendance, although no one assigns homework. Most presentations take place in a classroom with officers from every unit of the department taking turns to explain their mission and their day-to-day routines. Responding to student demand for more information, OPD expanded the program to thirteen weeks. Otherwise, format has changed little over the years.

The CPA tries to build each week on previous lessons. It covers the following topics:

Week 1: Introduction/selection and training—welcome by the chief and majors, recruiting goals and results, training procedures and evaluations.

Week 2: Laws of arrest, search and seizure, internal affairs, constitutional vs. criminal law, probable cause, the chain of response to complaints.

Week 3: Communications, statistics, planning and evaluation, tour of communications center, meaning of crime tabulations.

Week 4: Patrol operations/organization of patrol, demonstration of arrest, panel of beat officers.

Week 5: Special operations/traffic enforcement, canine demonstration, trip to mounted patrol barn.

Week 6: Violent crimes section/homicides, convenience-store robberies, career criminals.

Week 7: Property section and special investigations/car theft, counterfeiting, photo lineups, child abuse, rape.

Week 8: Special investigations, technical services/polygraph tests, crime-scene protocol.

Week 9: Undercover narcotic operations, vice crimes, uniformed vs. masked enforcement, interagency drug stings.

Week 10: Special teams/SWAT, crisis negotiation.

Week 11: Youth section, community involvement section/officers in the school, DARE, Neighborhood Watch.

Week 12: Special problems in law enforcement, use of force—liability, hot pursuits, "Shoot! Don't Shoot!"

Week 13: Graduation—diplomas, speeches, photographs, cake.

Although optional, field trips always draw a large crowd. Students tour Orange County jail with a deputy and at the range learn to fire the standard-issue 9mm semi-automatic pistol. Students may also ride for an evening on patrol.

By encouraging officers and students to speak freely and frankly, OPD fosters camaraderie between public and police that extends beyond the classroom. Some graduates join the CPA alumni association, which now numbers about seventy-five active members, according to Edwards. Every year the group cooks a Christmas breakfast for officers on duty, and volunteers answer phones, staff booths, and handle paperwork when needed. Recently, the association also chipped in to buy a horse for the mounted patrol.

The CPA alumni association is not the only measure of the program's success. Just as importantly, OPD has seeded the community with people who have walked in the shoes of a cop, if only for three months. When officers look into a crowd, they often see familiar, friendly faces.

Source: Adapted with permission from Sylvia Whitman, "Police Academies for Citizens," *Law and Order,* June 1993, pp. 66–71.

In the third form of community involvement, the most rare, the community wants to implement community-oriented policing, and through the community groups, both public and private, it exerts political pressure on the local government and police department to enact this program (see, for example, Friedman 1994). This obviously creates a situation in which from the very early ruminations of community-oriented policing, the community commands the leadership role. Although this form may be beneficial to the overall implementation of the systemic approach to policing, it can cause animosity on the part of the police, and the community may expect the program to be a quick fix to its ailments. Working through police animosity, although difficult, is feasible. Convincing the community that the program it desires is not a short-term fix but a long-term solution can prove more difficult. However, under this form of community involvement, the community members are serious about the concept and the police will have their full backing, which can mean that if some programs or solutions fail, the community groups will remain intact and will not abandon the program at the first signs of trouble.

The concept of community involvement will no doubt meet many obstacles along the way in any of the three forms. Although there may be fewer obstacles when the community initiates the movement from traditional policing to community-oriented policing, there may be some reservations by some committee members and there may be problems when attempting to draw the common citizen into the planning and decision-making process. The police will no doubt experience multiple problems when attempting to get the community involved; the three most common responses are mistrust, apathy, and no response.

 ## COP IN ACTION

Building Better Civilian Review Boards

A law enforcement agency that takes the initiative to create a review board can have major impact in its design, implementation, and ultimate success. Police executives who do not direct the process allow others—government administrators, elected officials, community activists, etc.—to create a board that serves its own needs, which are not necessarily the needs of law enforcement or the community it serves. When implementing a civilian review board, police executives need to consider several major factors. These include timing; goals, powers, and procedures; audience and stakeholders; and member qualifications.

When law enforcement administrators create civilian review boards in response to community demands following high-profile incidents, the public may view the administrators as reactionary and shortsighted. Worse, police executives' colleagues and subordinates, as well as some community members, may see them as merely yielding under pressure.

In contrast, proactive police executives who take the initiative and propose civilian review boards before their constituents demand them appear confident about their departments and open to dialogue with their communities. Ultimately, they exert greater control over the process and the final product than their reactive colleagues.

The board's goals, powers, and procedures represent the lifeblood of the review board. The goals of the review board determine its powers, which, in turn, affect the procedures it follows. For this reason, law enforcement administrators must consider these factors not only separately but also as a function of one another.

First and foremost, an effective review board must possess clearly stated goals. These objectives may range from broad areas, such as improving communication between the police and the community or increasing police accountability and credibility with the public, to specific purposes, such as reviewing all shooting incidents in a department. Or, the board may serve as a liaison between the community and all public service agencies—not merely *law enforcement* agencies.

A citizen review board can accomplish its goals better when the members know exactly what those goals are. However, clearly defined objectives mean little unless accompanied by the power to attain them.

When public officials form review boards in response to citizen protests, the resulting boards often lack the power to accomplish their goals. Without power, boards serve primarily a ceremonial function. Officials truly committed to improving service to the community establish review boards that are more than mere window dressing.

Although the method used to enact a board does not determine what powers the board will possess, it does dictate how the board's powers are established and modified. More important, it may reflect the seriousness with which the board is viewed by its creators. Four commonly used means to enact civilian review boards are municipal ordinance, city or county code, resolution, and executive appointment; each method has advantages and disadvantages. Establishing a citizen review board by ordinance signals that the government views the board as important enough to constitute it under law. Furthermore, ordinances require public hearings, which allow all interested parties to provide input. Boards instituted by city or county code possess legislative clout. However, as with ordinances, the bureaucratic process may hinder efficiency. Boards founded by resolution can accommodate emerging needs quickly with minimal bureaucratic red tape. However, this flexibility increases the possibility of political manipulation. Quick implementation and a safeguard against political influence ideally characterize executive appointments. However, when boards are formed in this manner, board members may be perceived as tame—representing the established viewpoints of the official who appointed them. A review board's goals form the basis of its power and, ideally, determine the specific tasks it will perform.

The procedures that a board follows depend on its powers. There are three major types of boards based on their methods of investigation. In the first, police officers conduct the investigation and present their findings to the review board, which submits a recommendation to the department head. The second type calls for civilian investigators selected by the board to conduct the inquiry, with the board making the decision. In the third type of review board, the police complete the analysis and make recommendations to the department head, who makes the final decision. In this type, the board functions only as an avenue of appeal for citizens unsatisfied with the final decision.

Members of citizen review boards are exactly that—citizens. Thus, the board should be a microcosm of the community, reflecting the diversity of its residents. In addition to this basic requirement, planners should consider other factors when establishing board member qualifications. These include, but are not limited to:

• Imposing age and/or residency requirements
• Disqualifying convicted criminals, police officers' family members, elected officials, members of the governmental empowering board, and/or plaintiffs in legal actions against any governmental entity
• Requiring current or previous community involvement

Once the stakeholders determine the member profile, they can begin to select individuals for positions, according to a previously established method agreed upon by all stakeholders.

Establishing and empowering a citizen review board, defining its operational goals and procedures, and selecting its members are only the beginning. Now, the members must be trained. Clearly, a properly trained review board will serve the community better. Equally important, board members who undergo a thorough training regimen enhance the board's credibility with the residents and the police.

Today's citizens expect both sensitivity and accountability from law enforcement. Civilian review boards represent a viable option for building a strong police–community relationship, especially when initiated prior to public demand.

Civilian review boards can enable law enforcement agencies and communities to open a dialogue that benefits all the stakeholders. Citizens become involved directly in accountability issues and better understand the nature of police work. At the same time, police officers feel less threatened by what they view as an uninformed public.

Without proper implementation, however, citizen review boards are doomed to failure. Problem analysis and good communication remain the keys for initiating, constructing, and training a review board that is an asset to the police department and to the community.

Source: Adapted from Mitchell Tyre and Susan Braunstein, "Building Better Civilian Review Boards," *FBI Law Enforcement Bulletin,* December 1994, pp. 10–15.

The police, especially under the traditional forms of policing, are often viewed with a sense of mistrust by community members (Grinc 1994; Sadd and Grinc 1994). Although they desire the presence of the police in an emergency, they feel the police serve no other function in their daily lives. Because the precepts of community-oriented policing call for the police and community to work together, the police must dismiss the "us versus them" mentality, and the community must do away with its mistrust of the police. Communication is generally the key because a lack of information on anything tends to trigger a sense of mistrust.

In other cases, the community may respond to community-oriented policing with a sense of apathy or lack of interest in the program (Grinc 1994; Sadd and Grinc 1994). This apathy is most likely in response to the centralized government, in which control of multiple life issues rests in the hands of the local government, and therefore getting involved in policing is seen as not part of the community's responsibilities. People often like the ideas and are very supportive of the issue but lack the desire to get involved or perform any action to support the idea. This form of apathy is prevalent in the United States and is perhaps best represented by the lack of voter turnout for elections. However, the lack of interest is only an obstacle to community involvement, and education about the police role, police resources, and police programs under the three components will most likely alleviate some apathy. Education seems to be a key to getting the community involved. The police must ensure that the community is educated and receives as much information about community-oriented policing as possible so that community members will become actively involved (Webb and Katz 1997).

The third response of community involvement in community-oriented policing is actually no response at all. When implementing any program, there may be no response from anyone to participate. A lack of response does not necessarily mean there is no interest or that the program is not viable. It may only mean that people do not understand their role in the overall concept or they have received no information on the program. In most cases, all three of these responses can be rectified with various forms of communication with the public explaining what is proposed under community-oriented policing and what role the community must take as well as what role the police must take under this new form of policing (see Kidd and Braziel 1999).

The media can offer assistance in this area by publishing and updating information about the movement of a police department from traditional policing to community-oriented policing. Other methods may include meeting with established public organizations (Williams and Pate 1987) and private organizations ranging from social groups to neighborhood associations (Fleissner et al. 1992). In some cases, the police may have to go door-to-door to announce their campaign (Wycoff and Skogan 1994) or distribute a newsletter (Brown and Wycoff 1987) to keep citizens informed of police and community actions under community-oriented policing. And one very innovative way of educating the community on both its role and the role of the police in community-oriented policing is through the use of citizen police academies (Enns 1995; Radelet and Carter 1994). Here citizens can learn about community-oriented policing (e.g., the three components), various aspects of policing (e.g., legal, use of force, court procedures), and technical aspects of policing (e.g., evidence collection, firearms training), and they can participate in a hands-on sense (e.g., shoot/don't shoot scenarios, firearms, ride-alongs). All of these methods and numerous others will have to be utilized to reach all members of the community and to solicit their help and cooperation under community-oriented policing. In several recent studies of citizen police academies, the basic findings have been favorable; "both the police officers and the citizens benefit from the close interaction" (Cohn 1996, 269), and the academies "appear to have substantive value and should be an integral part of the total law enforcement approach" (Grubb and Terry 1999, 28). However, several studies on citizen police academies have raised the question of whether they are truly about enhancing the police–citizen relationship or are a "window dressing to enhance the police image" (Bumphus, Gaines, and Blakely 1999, 78), thus creating a "political agenda" (Jordan 2000, 102).

One additional qualification to community involvement under community-oriented policing is that citizens may actually find more reasons *not* to get involved because of potential success with the systemic approach. If a police department makes the transition to community-oriented policing by demonstrating its resolve, citizens may choose to become less involved because of higher levels of satisfaction (Frank et al. 1996). This argument

Members of VFW Post 2018 show off their latest contribution to the Pomona, California, Police Department—four K-9 officers–which demonstrates their commitment to police and community relations. Shown left to right are Officer Ceasar Rivera and his dog Rudy; Mike Vitelli with Ricky; Mark Shannon with Marko; Doug Wagman with Roy; VFW Post Commander Don Stockwell; Dick Mazzarella; Jerry Lamb; Dave Densmore; Richard Callipi; Bill Portee; Tom Jones; and Henry Alt. (*Reprinted with permission from the March 1996 issue of* VFW *Magazine. Photograph by Jeff Dye.*)

is similar to that made by Mancur Olson (1965), an economist, who explains that as an organization increases in size, it becomes easier for people to benefit from the organization without having to actually contribute to it in any way. For instance, one can freeload and listen to National Public Radio without contributing to its operation. Hence, citizens will not see any reason for their involvement. This same study also found that citizen involvement may come about only when citizens are highly dissatisfied with the police and they feel that their community problems have become very troublesome (Frank et al. 1996). This situation should not change police resolve to work with the community, but, rather, it should serve as an indicator that there may be many complex reasons why citizens choose to either become involved or not become involved.

Two researchers who focused on the community role in community-oriented policing, Jill DuBois and Susan M. Harnett, offer some good advice based on their years of research into Chicago Police Department's community policing program (2002). They offer four key lessons regarding the community's involvement in community policing. First, they state that community support must be won. The police cannot make the assumption that they will automatically get community support when implementing community policing. Rather, they must work toward earning the community's respect and then their involvement. Second, community involvement is largely dependent upon having an organized community. In those communities that are not well organized, the police may be called to play a pivotal role in getting it organized and then soliciting the assistance of the community. Third, the training of the community is imperative to the success of community involvement in community policing. Just like training the police before expecting them to be able to conduct community policing is key to community policing success, the same applies to training the community members. Finally, they caution that there is a real risk of inequitable outcomes. Those communities that are well off and well organized will take to community policing readily; conversely, communities that are not well off and are disorganized may be resistant and less likely to get involved. Police must be dedicated to building partnerships, even with the most difficult of communities (DuBois and Harnett 2002).

 ## COP IN ACTION

K-9 Contributors

If a dog is a man's best friend, what is an expertly trained Belgian Malinois of the highest breeding? Well, that is a policeman's best friend, and something Post 2018 in Pomona, California, knows all about.

Over the past two years, this dedicated Post has donated four of the expensive canines, about $5,000 apiece, to the Pomona Police Department. And the dogs have already justified their hefty price tags.

"They've been responsible for the apprehension of hundreds of violent criminals," said Captain Joe Romero, Jr., of the department's Patrol Services Division. "Each K-9 team saves us time and man-power on area and building searches. More important, though, is the increased safety gained by the use of the dogs."

Post 2018 has also outfitted four police-mounted bikes for the department's Bicycle Patrol Unit. But these generous gifts are just the latest in a long history of community activism by the service-minded Post.

"During the last four years, our Post has donated approximately $40,000 every year toward our community, our local veterans, and the VA hospital in Long Beach," said Post Commander Don Stockwell.

Last September, the Post donated POW/MIA flags to people and businesses to commemorate National POW/MIA Day. For Thanksgiving, it purchased five thousand pounds of food for the Salvation Army and fed five hundred people at a local church. Post 2018 also works closely with the Pomona Fire Department, recently contributing $5,500 for a defibrillator unit.

The police department hosted a luncheon last summer to honor local groups that contributed to the department's Community-Oriented Policing program. Post 2018 received special recognition.

"It is particularly gratifying to know that the members of Post 2018 stand shoulder-to-shoulder with law enforcement and are committed to making a difference in our community," Romero said.

Source: Reprinted with permission from Tim Dyhouse, "K-9 Contributors," *VFW Magazine,* March 1996, p. 24.

COMMUNITY ATTITUDES REGARDING COMMUNITY-ORIENTED POLICING

While the research related to police officer attitudes regarding community-oriented policing has been broadly explored, until more recent years, little was known about community attitudes toward community-oriented policing. Although conventional wisdom articulated that citizens would be in favor of the police and community engaging in partnerships, it was simply that—conventional wisdom. When the issue of community was explored, the starting point tended to be the extensive research related to fear of crime as well as the citizen perception of police literature. A natural extension was to begin looking at these two bodies of research from a community-oriented policing perspective.

In regard to fear of crime, traditional policing did not focus on reducing fear of crime by targeting fear, rather it did so by trying to target crime itself. A variety of studies have demonstrated that actual crime and fear of crime are not necessarily associated with one another. Hence in the late 1970s and early 1980s, police attention began to focus on citizen fear of crime, not just the crime itself. According to Dietz (1997), this concept has been associated with community-oriented policing for the "reduction of fear of crime has been associated with community police programs since their inception" (p. 83). As the community-oriented policing philosophy and its strategies developed, crime reduction, fear reduction, and improved quality of life, all became central tenets of this systemic approach to policing. Today, it is well understood that one of the goals of community-oriented policing is to reduce the fear of crime among citizens.

The past 25 years have yielded an extensive amount of research focused on fear reduction by the police. Zhao and his associates (2002) conducted an analysis of all of the studies available, using quasi-experiments, to determine if police could, in fact, reduce citizen fear of crime. Out of the 50 studies they included in their analysis, they found 31 studies had demonstrated that police were able to reduce the fear of crime, 18 found no changes in the level of fear, and only one study was reported to have found an increase in citizen fear. The study also suggested that simple police presence is not as effective as the proactive interventions and partnerships that are part of community-oriented policing.

The more important question, then, is whether or not community-oriented policing can reduce citizen fear of crime. One study, which analyzed 12 cities in the United States, found that perceptions of community-oriented policing do have a strong positive effect on citizen satisfaction with the police, but that citizen perceptions of community-oriented policing do not directly affect levels of fear (Scheider, Rowell, and Bezdikian 2003). Follow up research, utilizing the same data, advanced on the notion that community-oriented policing did not directly affect levels of fear, but may have somehow indirectly reduced fear among citizens (Roh and Oliver 2005). This research found that community-oriented policing has a direct impact on the perceptions of incivilities by citizens and dissatisfaction with their quality of life. Community-oriented policing works toward reducing incivilities and improving the quality of life, which in turn leads to a reduction in fear. Thus, the study found, like so many others, that community-oriented policing does decrease fear of crime.

Additional research into citizens' perceptions has continued to yield an enormous body of literature that points toward the success of community-oriented policing. For instance, in an analysis conducted across five small cities in North Carolina, citizen awareness of the implementation of community-oriented policing contributed to reduced fear of crime, stronger feelings of community attachment, and citizens engaging in self-protection efforts more often (Adams, Rohe, and Arcury 2005). In addition, programs such as Citizen Police Academies have been found to generate a more positive attitude toward the police, along with the willingness to assist the police in community-oriented policing programs (Brewster, Stoloff, and Sanders 2005). This also creates somewhat of a feedback cycle, making the relationship between police and citizens stronger, for other research has found that those who do volunteer to assist the police in community-oriented policing programs have a higher confidence in their police (Ren et al. 2005). Moreover, other research has found that the positive impact of community-oriented policing is not necessarily limited to affluent or well-off neighborhoods but can apply at all levels on the socioeconomic scale (Reisig and Parks 2004). In fact, the researchers in this last study conclude that "citizens' perceptions of police actions that are consistent with the principles of community policing are associated with individual interpretive processes of local conditions and may enhance quality of life assessments" (p. 163). Another way of saying this is when community-oriented policing is truly implemented, people see the results and their quality of life improves. Citizen perceptions do change when faced with honest community-oriented policing.

One note of caution, however, is related to an interesting line of research that takes the concept of "citizen" a little deeper: Race and ethnicity may play a role in how citizens perceive things (Huebner, Schafer, and Bynum 2004; Schafer, Huebner, and Bynum 2003; Thomas and Burns 2005). While police interaction with the citizens is almost uniformly welcomed by whites, blacks and Latinos do not necessarily perceive this the same way, especially when the methods implemented by the police may consist of crackdowns and other methods of aggressive policing. While demographics were found to matter in these studies, what seemed to be more important was the type of contact citizens had with the police. If it is a positive contact, citizen perceptions of the police and quality of life go up, while fear of crime goes down. However, if those contacts are not perceived as positive, this jeopardizes what community-oriented policing is working toward. As stated previously, community-oriented policing is not a cookie-cutter model of policing, and how it is delivered in one neighborhood may differ in even an adjacent neighborhood. The racial and ethnic makeup of the neighborhood must always be considered when implementing community-oriented policing.

CONCLUSION

The role of the community in community-oriented policing is critical to the overall implementation of this systemic approach to policing. Although the term *community* is often difficult to define and we must rely on a variety of factors, such as geography, similar characteristics, and both the public and police perceptions of community, the community, in whatever shape or form, must be an integral part of the overall concept. The community must take back its streets, corners, and neighborhoods by working with the police to determine the type of programs community members believe would be beneficial to their community and what problems affect their community; they must develop policy, procedures, and programs to address these problems. Community-oriented policing must be implemented so as to make these community groups and coalitions the true leaders of the police.

Community involvement is then critical to this participatory form of policing; regardless of whether it is implemented via a police-initiated, police and community-initiated, or community-initiated style, it must be allowed to exist in the overall plan and be allowed to grow. Despite mistrust, apathy, or no response on the part of the community, the role of the community must become a mainstay of community-oriented policing. As Jiao (1997) has pointed out, we must achieve not only community-oriented policing but, in a sense, policing-oriented communities as well.

To understand the community's role in the movement from a traditional police department to a community-oriented policing department, we can look to the common stages that communities go through on their way to full implementation. Based on a study in Seattle, Washington, and as demonstrated in many other jurisdictions, the four stages are (1) challenge and venting, (2) organizational, (3) success, and (4) long-term stability (Fleissner et al. 1992). In the first stage, the challenge and venting stage, the police will meet the mistrust, apathy, and lack of response on the part of the police. This stage is also "when citizens vociferously criticize police methods and instances of abuse of power or fault the police for doing 'too little, too late'" (Fleissner et al. 1992, 9). The second stage is the organizational stage, in which the community participants agree to attend the meetings and work to address the specific issues (Fleissner et al. 1992). Although the community may remain somewhat mistrustful or apathetic, it will give the program a chance and work toward the common goal of addressing the criminal and order maintenance problems. In the third stage, the success stage, programs are implemented, a trusting relationship develops, and "the group is even secure enough to weather turnover and changes in leadership," moving from either the police or the police and community maintaining the leadership role to the community taking over the leadership role (Fleissner et al. 1992). Finally, the evolution of community-oriented policing achieves the ultimate goal of stage four, which consists of long-term stability of the systemic approach to policing; in this stage "the group can mount continuous efforts to resolve problems as well as recruit wider community representation" (Fleissner et al. 1992, 9).

The progression of community involvement from stage one to stage four is the overall goal of the role of the community in community-oriented policing. Although the issue of community involvement may be difficult at first, as the program is communicated to the public and more citizens participate, the return to the social order of pre–World War II can be achieved. The police and community will be able to, through a cooperative method, take back the streets and neighborhoods, drive out some of the criminal problems, and suppress much of the disorder found in so many communities today.

COP ON THE WORLD WIDE WEB

Boise, Idaho's Police Department's Citizen Police Academy

http://www.cityofboise.org/police/cpa/cpa.shtml

Citizens Committee for New York City

http://ccnyc.neighborhoodlink.com/ccnyc

Community Development Organizing and Activists Connections and Resources

http://trochim.human.cornell.edu/gallery/king/gmk.home.htm

New Haven, Connecticut, Police Department's Checklist for Organizing Community Events

http://www.cityofnewhaven.com/police/events.htm

Washington State's Citizen Police Academies

http://www.mrsc.org/pubsafe/le/le-academy.htm

REVIEW QUESTIONS

1. What is meant by the "traditional role" of the community as it relates to policing?
2. What is the role of the community in community-oriented policing?
3. What are the potential obstacles to community involvement, and how do police departments overcome these obstacles?

CHAPTER 10

The Role
of the Police Chief

*No organization, regardless of its character, can rise higher than the
quality and competency of its supervisory officials.*

—August Vollmer

CHAPTER OBJECTIVES

- Identify the significant contribution of the police chief to community-oriented policing.
- Understand the role of the traditional police chief.
- Explain the changes in police chiefs over time.
- Explain the change in management styles over time.
- Understand the role of the police chief in community-oriented policing.
- Explain the ten principles for an effective police chief in community-oriented policing.

The role of the police chief in today's society is dramatically different from the police leadership of the last generation. This shift is due in large part to an everchanging America; the advancement in all areas of knowledge, especially in the field of management; and the increase in technology. Police chiefs are required to be more educated, more skilled, and more adept at management, decision making, and the disciplinary process. They are much more visible today through advancements in technology and multimedia capabilities, and as a result they are held more accountable for their actions, and particularly the actions of their officers, than they were just a generation ago. They are the pivotal figure of the community in good times and often the easiest to blame in bad times. And amidst all of these responsibilities, trials, and tribulations, the police chiefs of today

Police Chief Darrel Stephens of the Charlotte-Mecklenburg Police Department and McGruff the Crime Dog at a crime watch "National Nite Out" event. *(Courtesy of the St. Petersburg Police Department, St. Petersburg, Florida.)*

are being asked to advance their police departments with all the propositions of community-oriented policing.

In light of the national movement toward community-oriented policing, it is readily apparent that the police chiefs of today are being called on to implement a style of policing that they know very little about. It is often assumed that since they are police chiefs, they will have a complete understanding of the concept. The public often believes that all the chief has to do is implement community-oriented policing overnight and it will be the panacea to all crime and social disorder problems. Police chiefs know that community-oriented policing is not a quick fix, and generally, through a misunderstanding of the concept, they are hesitant to truly implement it. At the same time, many abide by the public's request and "implement" community-oriented policing by utilizing the moniker and driving on with business as usual. This approach is detrimental not only to the concept of community-oriented policing but also to the police department and communities that must bear this new program that understandably is predestined to fail. However, this is not to say that the reasoning behind this decision for failure is beyond comprehension.

 COP IN ACTION

Providing Proper Police Service in the Twenty-First Century

There is value in discussing strategies for policing diverse communities and maintaining positive relations with communities of different cultural and racial backgrounds. But for many years, my perspective, both as chief and throughout my law enforcement career, has been that both functions set up a problematic dichotomy that may likely be the cause—rather than the cure—for prejudicial and unjust application of police authority in minority communities.

Additionally, as our metropolitan communities become more diverse, from an ethnic, racial, and cultural perspective, law enforcement agencies can no longer function in a manner in which our attitudes and activities toward these citizens are an "exception" to our normal rules of operation.

In St. Paul, we believe the department should provide good and proper service to all our residents. However, we also recognize that sometimes certain people must be "policed." To accomplish these often-divergent tasks, our police department has instituted a philosophical foundation and an operational methodology that ensure that police authority is equally and justly applied to all the city's residents. Our police strategies and tactics are directed at behaviors that either are unlawful or threaten the safety, peace of mind, and/or the quality of life of our citizens. By basing our police actions on observed behavior, we greatly reduce the possibility that the actions taken by our police officers are motivated by race, religion, sexual orientation, or other irrelevant factors that would result in prejudiced or unjust application of the law.

The philosophical foundation of our activities is presented in the department's mission statement, which states, "The St. Paul Police Department will be more reflective of and more responsive to the community we serve." By "reflective," we mean that we will do our best to represent the diversity that exists in our community, in as many dimensions as we can, within the sworn and civilian populations of the organization. By "responsive," we mean that we will establish communications with all our communities so that we understand their issues and concerns. We will then structure our department's strategies and tactics to successfully address those issues and concerns.

In conjunction with this philosophical position, we have instituted an operational methodology that has an internal and an external component. Internally, we have put in place a set of guiding values we call the Four P's: Pride, Professionalism, Participation, and Productivity. As they pertain to our department's philosophy, these guiding values mean police action will be based on observed behaviors rather than on profiling or other inappropriate methods.

The external operational component is based on an application of the community policing concept that has been personalized to fit the situations and needs of St. Paul. A major objective for our department, and a measure of the effectiveness of the application of the Four P's, is the degree to which the performance of individual officers, and our department overall, demonstrates a high level of involvement and trust relative to individual citizens and community groups. This includes officer evaluations relating to problem-solving ability, response to calls for service, preventive activities, and general goodwill. We also work diligently with community organizations and individual citizens to help them understand their roles and responsibilities in the overall effort to improve the quality of life in their neighborhoods and to combat crime. They are also given appropriate opportunities to participate in the identification, development, implementation, and evaluation of the strategies and tactics needed to achieve our objectives. We employ such vehicles as district crime prevention councils, Neighborhood Watch groups, and the Police/Civilian Internal Affairs Review Commission. These and other strategies provide opportunities for citizens to have a voice in how the community is to be policed and how it can play an active role.

It is important to note that these strategies and tactics are tailored to meet the needs and expectations of our city's neighborhoods. They are not based on race, religion, culture, or other so-called indicators of diversity. We view our communities as a whole, not as a composite of many segments, and relate to them in a corresponding manner.

The major outcome of this mode of operation is that a bond of trust and cooperation is developed between the police and the community. This bond is of tremendous value in our efforts to prevent and, when necessary, solve crimes.

I hope that these thoughts will stimulate discussion and further consideration of ways to address the increasingly complex issues and situations facing law enforcement agencies as we move into the new millennium.

Source: Reprinted with permission from Chief William K. Finney, "Providing Proper Police Service in the 21st Century," *Community Policing Exchange,* January/February 2000.

Police chiefs in the past generation, many of whom remain in office or whose legacy remains entrenched in the community today, were constantly dealing with the so-called rhetoric of police and community relations. The implementation of this policy was through the police–community relations model, which usually consisted of an organizational addition that was touted as the panacea to the poor relationship between the police and the community during the turbulent 1960s. The programs were generally established as a separate unit, usually understaffed, underbudgeted, and largely ignored by the administration. The programs most often failed to please a large segment of the community and were in many cases not even known to exist. The hands-off attitude by the police chief relegated the program to obscurity in most jurisdictions, keeping the unit and its budget small.

Today, police chiefs are expected to buy into the latest form of police and community relations known as community-oriented policing, and they are skeptical. However, against the backdrop of Rodney King and the Los Angeles riots, faith in the police has waned, and community-oriented policing is often touted as the new panacea for improved relations with the public. Community policing as the panacea for police problems has chartered a difficult course for the police chiefs of today because they are skeptical of the community-oriented policing philosophy; they are afraid it will be another failed program that they will have to implement to appease the local government and the community, and they are receiving little information on the concept. Community-oriented policing is thus at a critical juncture at the beginning of the twenty-first century. The police chiefs of today are the central force in deciding the success or failure of community-oriented policing simply due to the position they now hold.

The police chief has a pivotal role in community-oriented policing. If the chief implements community-oriented policing as a front for community appeasement, it will fail. If the chief implements it without seeing to its direction, the mid-level management and line officers will clearly see this and let the program fade away as a failure. If the mayor or city council desires the new style of policing but the chief resists, it will fail. And without the support of the chief, even in a department in which the line officers desire the change in policing and the community supports it, community-oriented policing will still die a certain death. This should not be a call for chiefs to let the new style of policing die so they can move on to "real police work." Rather, it should be a call to every police department, local government, and community to realize that without the support of the police chief, community-oriented policing will not succeed. In fact, a study of eight police departments implementing community-oriented policing found that the police chief or sheriff must be fully committed to community policing and drive its implementation, or it will not take hold, let along advance (Chaiken, 2001). The future of community-oriented policing looks promising, and the dedication and commitment of the police chiefs can be crucial factors in this future.

To understand the role of the police chief, it is important to understand the past role of the police executive and how it changed and evolved in the twentieth and early twenty-first century. It is equally important to understand the current role the police chief plays in the systemic approach in modern-day America. And, finally, the key responsibilities of police chiefs under community-oriented policing will be explored to assist in defining the role they will play now and in the future in this systemic approach to policing.

TRADITIONAL ROLE OF THE POLICE CHIEF

If we return to the simplistic division of traditional policing and community-oriented policing for the analysis of police leadership in America, there is an interesting evolution of change clearly demonstrated in the people, organization, and management styles of the police. The evolution from the political era of policing to the public relations era was a slow process, taking well over a century to change. However, even the evolution within what we conceived of as traditional policing, the move from the 1930s to the era of community-oriented policing, was slow as well.

The traditional type of leader during the traditional era can be "defined in neutral terms as an efficient, honest, apolitical manager, equipped to implement the professional model of policing" (Goldstein 1990, 152). It is this detachment from the community that has so marked much of the change in policing since the 1930s and continues to mark the current evolution seen today, although in a different direction.

The police chiefs who were instrumental in moving the police from the political era into what we consider the traditional era of policing were August Vollmer and O. W. Wilson (Dempsey 1994; Geller 1991; Peak 1995). These two men were considered pioneers in the field of policing for both their foresight and their ability to reform.

August Vollmer, the chief of police in Berkeley, California, from 1905 to 1932, was largely responsible for professionalizing the police and launching them into the traditional era (Dempsey 1994). He was quick to call for the expansion of the police department to patrol both day and night, he applied the techniques of modus operandi to criminal investigation, and with the assistance of a biologist at the University of California, he was able to apply the sciences as well (Douthit 1991). In 1908, he created the first police academy, he advanced police patrols with bicycles and motor vehicles, and he introduced the polygraph to policing (Douthit 1991). In 1931, he became the first professor of police administration at the University of California and that same year wrote the section entitled The Police included in the Wickersham Report (Douthit 1991). Despite all of these technical advancements, the importance of the police officer was not lost on Vollmer; he wrote in 1931, "After spending nearly a quarter of a century instructing policemen I have come to the conclusion that the mechanics of the profession are of less importance than a knowledge of human beings" (Douthit 1991, 109). The key to Vollmer's success, however, was not so much his modernization of the police department but his application of the science and technology of his time to the police.

The movement in management at the turn of the century was toward scientific management (Hersey and Blanchard 1993). Through the development of technology and the application of various methods to increase productivity in the workplace, science was applied to management, and the result was the scientific management movement (Hersey and Blanchard 1993). Using such things as time-motion studies, organizing for optimum productivity, and making administration more efficient were the emphasis of this new movement that shaped both the organization and the methods of management. Although the founding theorist of the scientific application in management was Frederick Winslow Taylor, it was August Vollmer who first applied these techniques to the police.

A disciple of August Vollmer's, O. W. Wilson was the second police chief to greatly advance the police during the traditional era of policing. Wilson became the police chief of the Wichita, Kansas, Police Department in 1928 and through the use of simple management tools greatly advanced police organization and management (Dempsey 1994). Wilson organized the police department in a very centralized manner with a strict chain of command and applied such principles as communication, span of control, delegation, and accountability (Peak 1995). He later authored two highly acclaimed books that are still the basis for many textbooks today: *Municipal Police Administration* and the International City Management Association's *Police Administration*, which became affectionately known as the "green monster" by later police administrators because it was often the study guide for promotions (Wilson 1941, 1950). These two books simply articulated basic scientific management techniques, applied them to the police, and presented them in a clear and concise manner.

In the early 1930s, studies revolving around the scientific management approach found that another variable was involved in successful management: the employee. In the famous Hawthorne study at the Hawthorne plant of the Western Electric Company, where researchers attempted to manipulate the environment of the workers, they found that whether they made the conditions better or worse, productivity continued to rise. The independent variable for the increase in output was a result of the human interaction between the researchers and the employees. Thus was born the human relations management approach (Hersey and Blanchard 1993). A similar realization in police management did not take hold until the 1940s and 1950s, when "the management structure began to shift toward the more democratic or participatory management that is familiar in law enforcement today" (Lynch 1995, 6). However, it is important to make note that the change to both scientific and human relations management was not immediate in either space or time but varied in application from jurisdiction to jurisdiction and across time.

 ## COP IN ACTION

Operation Bootstrap: Opening Corporate Classrooms to Police Managers

U.S. businesses spend over $30 billion a year to provide about 17 million formal training and career advancement courses for their employees according to some estimates. This investment demonstrates the belief that what is taught in corporate classrooms can sharpen management skills and thus increase a company's competitive edge.

This same investment can also be a resource for the public sector. An infusion of high-quality corporate training into law enforcement agencies, for example, could help those agencies upgrade management skills to better address the increasingly complex and ever-changing demands society places on public safety professionals.

In fact, such a program already exists. Operation Bootstrap, begun in 1985, is an educational clearinghouse that provides tuition-free corporate management training programs to a cross-section of police administrators and officers across the country.

Launched as a pilot program of the International Association of Chiefs of Police (IACP), Operation Bootstrap now reaches into forty states with support from private foundations and the National Institute of Justice. It offers state-of-the-art management training and self-help programs that range in length from one day to one week and cover subjects such as effective supervision, conflict resolution, group problem solving, and stress management.

What Law Enforcement Gains from the Corporate Classroom

1. While these outside training programs are designed for corporate managers and their role in the corporate environment, nearly every law enforcement attendee has cited the usefulness and relevance of the course instruction.
2. Operation Bootstrap offers a smorgasbord of courses, some of which might appear to be of limited value to the law enforcement profession, until the breadth of responsibilities faced by these managers and supervisors is taken into account.
3. Also important are the insights law enforcement officials gain from their brief but intense encounter with the corporate world. Cornelius Behan, chief of the Baltimore County Police Department, noted that "Training such as this enables us to have supervisors who are not only more thoroughly prepared for management roles, but also have a better understanding of the private sector."

How the Community Benefits

Bootstrap participants help combat any negative police stereotypes through their interaction in the classroom with business executives. "Corporate people realize we police officers are people too," commented one Connecticut commander. He added, "They discover we have the same management problems as they have." Moreover, business leaders appear gratified to find so many law enforcement personnel who are interested in learning modern management techniques. Meanwhile, America's future police leaders are gaining a better understanding of the business community and its concern about crime.

Ultimately, of course, society benefits as law enforcement executives improve their own agencies by adapting some of the techniques used successfully by business executives in reaching corporate decisions, managing personnel, and performing their own individual jobs.

Source: Bill Bruns, "Operation Bootstrap: Opening Corporate Classrooms to Police Managers," *National Institute of Justice: Research in Action*, August 1989.

As policing moved into the 1960s, the current trend was toward police–community relations, and many police departments were still applying scientific management principles to this new philosophy of policing. The police administration treated police–community relations as the need for more specialization within the centralized structure. The police could not alter the entire organization and management structure that they had spent decades shaping, but they created a specialized unit to provide the service while retaining centralized control. This technique and others such as quota systems or point systems continued into the 1980s as a method of greater control and greater accountability on the part of the police officer. This approach led both to a greater detachment from the community and to the infamous attitude of "us versus them." Under community-oriented policing, it is not just one specialized unit that must be created, but rather the entire police department, the police organization, and management—most importantly, the chief—must change as well.

As society evolves and people evolve, so too must management. The organizational structure and the style of management are not a single entity etched in stone once the system is said to work. Rather, they are living and breathing concepts that must grow, adapt, and evolve. The realization of these concepts was captured in the management field under the auspices of systems management, which "fused the individual and the organization" and was "designed to help managers use their employees in the most effective way while reaching the desired production goals" (Lynch 1995, 6). Since the incorporation of systems management in the mid-1960s, some police chiefs have been able to recognize this assertion, and many of today's chiefs recognize the need under the auspices of community-oriented policing. The next evolution in policing is to the systemic approach to community-oriented policing, and it is the police chiefs of today who will carry us well into a successful future.

COMMUNITY-ORIENTED POLICING ROLE OF THE POLICE CHIEF

As we move into the community-oriented policing era, an interesting evolution of change already exists that, as with the traditional era, is clearly demonstrated in the people, organization, and management style of policing. The key people in community-oriented policing are too numerous to mention, but many of the names have already been shared. Like the traditional era, the community-oriented policing era has its share of police chiefs and scholars. The police chiefs include Lee Brown (Houston Police Department and New York City Police Department), Willie Williams (Los Angeles Police Department), Reuben Greenburg (Charleston, South Carolina, Police Department), Elizabeth Watson (Houston Police Department and Austin Police Department), Jerry Sanders (San Diego Police Department), Charles Moose (Portland, Oregon, Bureau of Police and Montgomery County, Maryland, Police Department), Harry Dolan (Lumberton, North Carolina, Police Department and Grand Rapids, Michigan, Police Department), and Darrel W. Stephens (St. Petersburg, Florida, Police Department and Charlotte-Mecklenburg, North Carolina, Police Department). All of these chiefs have greatly helped advance community-oriented policing and represent what is clearly a new breed of police leadership. As George Kelling so bluntly states, "Unlike the tendency in the past for chiefs to be local and inbred, chiefs of this generation are urbane and cosmopolitan" (Kelling 1988, 5). He goes on to say that "members of this generation of police leadership are well educated and of diverse backgrounds" and "have sponsored research and experimentation to improve policing" (Kelling 1988, 5). Many others are advancing the research and experimentation in policing or in the academic field, and often in both areas, to provide the latest advancements and innovations that will move the systemic approach well into the twenty-first century.

Because the decentralized organizational structure under community-oriented policing was previously discussed in Chapter 7, it is important to focus solely on the style of

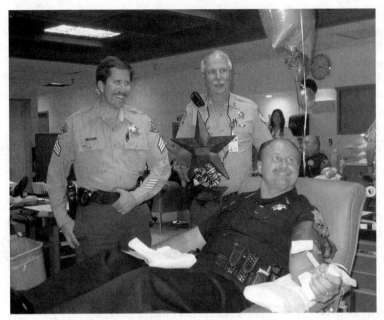

Fresno Police Department's chief of police donating blood in a community blood drive. (*Courtesy of the City of Fresno Police Department, Fresno, California.*)

policing that the chiefs will have to abide by under this systemic approach. The police chiefs of today do not have the luxury of simply managing from atop the centralized administration their predecessors had. Today's generation of police leadership must focus on numerous roles and responsibilities that are inherent within the position. As Oliver (1993, 85) puts it, "today a chief is often the agency's major policy maker, a leader of the community, liaison to the media, negotiator with the unions, disciplinarian, public speaker, quasi-lawyer, quasi-accountant, administrator, and agency leader." The role of police chief is extremely demanding, and under community-oriented policing, it will be even more so. In some cases, it can prove rather costly, as has been demonstrated in numerous cases.

In one cited year, from mid-1991 to mid-1992, eight of the fifteen largest police departments had undergone a change in or were undergoing a change in the police chief position (Witkin 1992). Expanding that time frame to 1991 through 1993, twelve out of the fifteen largest police departments experienced a turnover. The tenure of the average metropolitan police chief has gone from 5 1/2 years to between 3 1/2 and 4 1/2 years (Witkin 1992). The police chiefs of today are under greater public scrutiny than at any other time in our history, and it must be recognized that in many cases, particularly under community-oriented policing, they are not directly to blame for their removal. The police chief is held in check by crime rates, officer misconduct and brutality, unions, the mayor or city manager, governmental policies, political considerations, and a host of additional variables that may prevent him or her from enacting many of the tenets of community-oriented policing. All of these stand as potential roadblocks to enacting the components of the systemic approach; decentralizing the police department by personnel, geography, and structure; or merely organizing the community for its input into both criminal and order maintenance concerns from its perspective. These problems can bring on adversity, they can realistically damage the chief's professional image, and they can also have the highest price—as was demonstrated in the one-year period cited—removal from office.

POLICE CHIEFS AND SHERIFFS SUPPORT COMMUNITY-ORIENTED POLICING

Community Policing

Police chiefs and sheriffs were asked if they had community policing in their departments. Because community policing is a broad category, the survey did not attempt to determine the specific activities that comprised a department's community policing approach. (Indeed, community policing could be the subject of another survey of these agencies.) The survey results show that police chiefs and sheriffs strongly supported community policing. Several offered comments on why their departments decided to embrace community policing and the steps needed to continue it.

Broad Interest in Community Policing

Interest in community policing cut across the entire country in small, medium, and large agencies. Of the 337 responding police chiefs, 278 (82 percent) indicated that they had active community policing in their departments, and virtually all the remaining departments indicated that they wanted community policing. Sheriffs provided a similar result with 172 (65 percent) of the 265 responding sheriffs stating that they had community policing and 61 (25 percent) indicating that they wanted community policing in their departments.

It should be noted, however, that comments from the police chiefs and sheriffs clearly indicated that most community policing efforts were just developing and were confined to a few designated neighborhoods. Most comments mentioned foot beats, special units, and neighborhood substations as primary activities comprising their community policing efforts.

Some of the most interesting comments regarding community policing explained why the departments were interested in changing from a traditional/professional model of policing to community policing. The primary reasons given were to improve quality of life in the neighborhoods, to involve citizens in crime fighting activities (especially against drug problems), and to have a more concerted effort towards crime prevention. With regard to quality of life, one police chief wrote,

> The workload increase for this department stems from neighborhood problems and quality of life issues rather than major crimes. We are adopting community policing in an effort to address these quality of life issues.

Other chiefs wrote comments on using community policing to address drug problems: "We have invested in community policing to better involve the public in solutions to our crack cocaine problems," and "We have been attempting to convince the community that drug problems are a community problem, not just a police problem."

Two chiefs cited broader problems as their reasons for introducing community policing:

> The contributing factors to our workload have been greater availability of guns for juveniles; more sophisticated firearms in possession of criminals; decline in family cohesiveness in inner-city neighborhoods; availability of illegal drugs; and inadequate prison space. We are responding by shifting resources from traditional vehicle patrol to community policing.

> During the past three years, we have experienced a dramatic surge in violent crimes, especially those committed by juveniles. Property crimes have increased as our local drug problem has

come to the forefront as our major contributing factor to criminal activity. Subsequently, our caseload has dramatically increased. We are implementing various forms of community-oriented policing strategies in our neighborhoods deemed "high crime" in an effort to decrease these problems.

Ironically, some police chiefs and sheriffs stated that community policing had increased, rather than decreased, their departments' workloads. One police chief wrote, "The move to community policing and problem solving has also increased workload. As we become more responsive and credibility increases, we achieve more neighborhood involvement and workload increases."

Training and Personnel Needs

A total of 293 police chiefs stated their departments had training programs for community policing, but 83 percent of these chiefs indicated that the training needed improvement. For sheriffs, 189 stated they had training, with 83 percent indicating that the training needed improvement. A total of 39 police chiefs and 44 sheriffs without community policing training would like to see the training develop in their agencies.

Several problems were indicated by the respondents in regard to their training efforts. One problem was simply making time available for the training sessions. Some respondents commented on mandated state and federal training requirements that take precedence over topics such as community policing. Other police chiefs were concerned about "selling" community policing to officers: "Currently, the department is making a transition to community policing. The training challenge is to train and involve sworn members in the understanding and implementation of this process in such a way as to make community policing eagerly embraced." "Problem solving is addressed in our community-oriented policing, and we are striving to get officers to think of themselves as problem solvers."

Police chiefs and sheriffs also commented on the need to have more officers in order to expand their community policing efforts. Typical comments follow:

An effort was made to implement community policing; however, due to manpower shortages, we were unable to continue. (sheriff)

Community policing is being vigorously looked into for further deployment, but due to manpower it is being postponed. (police chief)

We currently have one community-based, problem-oriented police team. We wish to replicate this team's efforts in other neighborhoods because it has been effective in reducing drug crimes, has reduced overall calls for police service, improved citizen perceptions of safety, and has been effective in providing role models for adolescents. If resources become available, we would expand into neighborhoods where there is a large culturally diverse population. (sheriff)

Our citizens are concerned with community policing and seeing officers walking in their neighborhoods. However, our department now has 828 officers, as opposed to 975 officers four years ago. This reduction, coupled with an increase in calls for service, makes it difficult. (police chief)

In summary, police chiefs and sheriffs have been implementing community policing in their agencies and appear to be enthusiastic about its future. The two primary obstacles to expansion have been the need for better training on community policing and for increases in the number of officers to perform community policing activities.

Source: Tom McEwen, *National Assessment Program: 1994 Survey Results.* Washington, D.C.: National Institute of Justice, June 1995.

There are many examples in which police chiefs have endured all of these problems for the sake of community-oriented policing. In Houston, Texas, Police Chief Lee Brown and his successor, Police Chief Elizabeth Watson, implemented neighborhood-oriented policing (NOP) as a pilot program in 1983 and citywide in 1987, when crime rates began to rise in the middle to late 1980s. Budget cutbacks added to these concerns by reducing the force by 655 police officers during this same period. The mid-level managers relinquished little authority to the line officers, and morale for the program on the part of the police was diminished. The public also became disenchanted with the program, and eventually it came to be known as "NOP: Nobody on Patrol" (Witkin and McGraw 1993). Police Chief Brown had since moved on to New York City to serve as its police commissioner, and Elizabeth Watson was replaced in 1992. Watson moved on to the Austin, Texas, Police Department and implemented community-oriented policing with great success, learning from past mistakes. Subsequently, she became a part of the national community-oriented policing movement by going to work for the Office of Community Oriented Policing Services (COPS), U.S. Department of Justice.

There should be little doubt that engaging in anything other than the status quo in a police department can be difficult, but changing, advancing, and integrating the police with the community can have a significant impact. If the performance and satisfaction of officers increase under community-oriented policing and, when implemented with sincerity, public satisfaction increases as well, taking the risks of implementing change should prove well worth the effort. It is important to also note that "experience has shown that when decisions are based on the principles of whether the decision is right, moral, ethical, legal, and in the best interest of the community, and not on what is politically expedient, the chief has little to worry about. Those programs, those requests, and those decisions that do not meet these criteria present predictable sorts of problems for the chief" (Brown 1985, 83). There should be little doubt that community-oriented policing's premise is what is right, moral, ethical, legal, and in the best interests of the community.

It meets the criteria and it will continue to be successful, but it is dependent on police chiefs who are willing to take the risk, are forward thinkers, and are dynamic leaders.

TEN PRINCIPLES FOR POLICE CHIEFS

Although many of the principles of management under community-oriented policing are being practiced by police chiefs today, many of them are new or have a different focus than they have had in previous years, by virtue of the organizational changes and tenets of the systemic approach. Essentially ten principles can be extracted from police chiefs, such as those previously mentioned who have implemented community-oriented policing with great success in their communities (See Table 10-1.). The ten principles community-oriented policing chiefs follow to manage community-oriented police departments are (1) leadership; (2) ombudsman; (3) policy maker; (4) commitment; (5) style; (6) change; (7) power sharing; (8) educator, motivator, and trainer; (9) role model; and (10) disciplinarian. Each of these ten principles is discussed in relation to its application under community-oriented policing.

TABLE 10-1   *Ten Principles of the COP Chief*

1. Leadership
2. Ombudsman
3. Policy maker
4. Commitment
5. Style
6. Change
7. Power sharing
8. Educator, motivator, and trainer
9. Role model
10. Disciplinarian

Leadership is the most important skill a police chief must have to be successful under community-oriented policing. Although some argue that leadership is an innate trait, others argue that it is something that can be cultivated and expanded. There are many success stories of people who were considered born leaders, but an equal amount of literature describes those individuals who were found to be great leaders more because of their environment and situation than because of any innate skills. Some examples include Abraham Lincoln, who was a mediocre senator yet excelled in the role of the presidency, and Dwight D. Eisenhower, who was a great military leader but functioned as only a mediocre president. We must then bypass the argument of nurture versus nature and deal with the relevant fact that leadership is extremely important in any institution, as well as any police department, but it is especially important under community-oriented policing.

It is also important to understand that leadership does not necessarily equate with good management (see Goldstein 1977, 225–231). An individual could be an excellent administrator and run an efficient and effective centralized police department. However, under the community-oriented policing approach, good administration will prove inadequate for the success of the program. Community-oriented policing needs dynamic leadership that can motivate the mid-level management, detectives, unions, and line officers to reevaluate the way they have been policing for so many years. Good administration will assist in the transition from a centralized police department to a decentralized structure, but it will not motivate the department to accomplish this task. Good administration may be able to implement the three components, but it may not succeed in leading the community to action. As Lawrence Sherman (1985, 466) stated, "without . . . leadership, it is unlikely that policing can be substantially improved."

The leadership, however, must also transcend the current expectations of leadership from a police chief. The limitations of the office of the chief, the avoidance of entering into politics, and the watchful eye of the community and media can create a chief who is more interested in maintaining the status quo than venturing into experimentation and possible failures. However, under community-oriented policing, the police chief "must be dynamic and forceful in taking the community and police force toward a goal of community values and community standards" (Oliver 1993, 86). The chief must be able to articulate truthfully where the community is, where it needs to go, and why the components and structural reorganization of community-oriented policing are necessary to achieve these goals. Therefore, the police chief must be more than a good manager, more than a good law enforcer, and more than an assistant to the mayor in the same vein as the director of public works or parks and recreation. Community-oriented policing calls for a police chief who can be not only a dynamic leader but also a statesman.

Lawrence Sherman (1985, 462) argued that the police chief must be a statesman, which he defined as a "leader of a democracy, someone who can transcend the current values of the day and lead both police and the public into accepting a better set of values and strategies for policing." Although many may argue that this role either lies beyond the parameters of the office of the chief or is part of the mayor's responsibilities, under the systemic approach to policing, this argument no longer holds. The chief must be a leader of not only the police but the community as well when it comes to the issues of crime, safety, and order maintenance. These are the chief's obligations and liabilities, and they should not be relegated, or delegated, to anyone else. Even though taking on this role will most likely place the chief in a highly visible and focal position within the community, it is necessary in order to drive the values and goals of community-oriented policing. The allegations of politics and interfering with the mayor's responsibilities will be a rallying cry from the pundits; however, for a chief to effect change, they must be endured.

Research into the importance of leadership on the part of police chiefs in making the move to community-oriented policing has found their role to be critical, especially among the officers they lead (Cheurprakobkit 2001; Stevens 2002). A study of police officers' perceptions of police chiefs found that most officers did not believe their chief possessed the leadership skills necessary to implement community policing (Cheurprakobkit 2001). These negative perceptions were even further exacerbated by those officers who had received community-oriented policing training and had a firm grasp of what the community-oriented policing philosophy entailed. This is why the author of the research believed that in order for chiefs to implement community-oriented policing, they must "fully understand its concept, have a set of values, a clear vision, and a mission statement that are consistent with COP principles, and create an organizational climate that is conducive to change" (Cheurprakobkit 2001). Yet the author also pointed out that while a firm understanding of these concepts of community-oriented policing is important, it is not enough. He explains that "chief executives must also show that they themselves understand and are committed to the COP concept, and create an environment that is conducive to implementing COP programs" and that they "must establish the leadership skills necessary for the success of COP" (Cheurprakobkit 2001, 53). In sum, if police chiefs are not committed to the philosophy of community-oriented policing, their line officers will know, thus creating a profound impediment to the implementation of community-oriented policing.

One question arises in relation to the principle of dynamic leadership: Where do we find such dynamic leaders? Police chiefs, until the latter half of the twentieth century, were largely a product of the police department's hierarchy, where they were cultivated up through the ranks. In the 1970s and 1980s, there was a move to hire police chiefs from outside the police department, a shift that has continued to generate a high degree of controversy. The up-through-the-ranks chief is better equipped to deal with both the informal and formal structure because he or she has personal knowledge via his or her experience with the department. The outsider, a police chief hired from another police

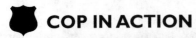

COP IN ACTION

Supervising Officers in the Community Policing Age

As community policing sweeps across the nation, it changes the roles and duties of law enforcement officers. And with this wave of change comes a new challenge for law enforcement supervisors who have to effectively manage the employees in these new roles.

The literature tells us to empower officers and give them greater flexibility, but it says little about how to supervise them as they do this. Confronted with the competing values of traditional and community policing, many law enforcement supervisors are forced to improvise. Unfortunately, they sometimes select management strategies that could jeopardize the future of community policing.

Decentralizing Does Not Mean "Hands Off"

With more law enforcement agencies incorporating the community policing philosophy into their organizational structures, what was once a radical idea is now becoming part of the mainstream. This increasing acceptance comes with some drawbacks. Stability and predictability can lull managers into becoming inattentive. As their attention is drawn to matters they may deem more pressing, managers may give less scrutiny to community policing activities. Law enforcement managers must remain vigilant and stay attuned to the officers and deputies engaged in those activities.

Arguing that traditional management strategies are too restrictive, community policing advocates propose more flexible, participatory structures. But in an effort to be more flexible, some managers have adopted a laissez-faire approach that essentially leaves programs to run themselves. Abdicating management responsibility, however, is unacceptable. Without proper controls, law enforcement officers' personal interests may foster inefficient or inappropriate practices.

Law enforcement supervisors need to find effective management techniques that control without stifling. Management strategies must be flexible enough to allow officers to innovate and adapt to change. Effective management will monitor and control officers yet allow them to function effectively. And effective management will shift performance evaluation from quantitative to more qualitative measures to further reinforce community policing initiatives.

Keeping the Focus on Community

Most supervisors understand that community police officers need to engage in problem solving. However, it is often unclear how problem-solving agendas are developed. What issues have the officers chosen to address? How are problems identified and prioritized?

The community should play a significant role in identifying and solving problems. Initially, maybe an officer will need to identify and solve a problem on his or her own just to demonstrate that problems can be solved. Then the officer can use that success to stir up community interest in taking a more active role in improving the neighborhood's quality of life.

Public input and participation in problem solving should be reflected in subsequent initiatives. If the initiatives selected by community police officers and deputies do not further community interest, the community may not support them. Or, even worse, law enforcement's efforts may alienate the community and jeopardize its support. An officer would not readily recognize he or she was alienating the public unless the public was involved in planning and carrying out the initiative.

TEN PRINCIPLES FOR POLICE CHIEFS

Law enforcement managers need to ensure their community police officers and deputies are working productively and in the community's best interest. The best way to do this is to encourage the officers to see their roles as facilitators of action that empowers and enables residents to work with law enforcement on improving the neighborhood's quality of life. Then the manager needs to monitor the officers to ensure they do not digress from that role.

When the community participates in problem solving, it actually simplifies the manager's role because the community members will be scrutinizing the officers' actions. In effect, the community shoulders a portion of management's monitoring role.

When assessing a community policing initiative or a community police officer's performance, the supervisor should ask two questions: What are the important problems as defined by the community? What are community members doing to solve them? If you cannot identify significant community involvement in answering both questions, you need to refocus your efforts. If the community is not involved, what is driving the process? Personal, organizational, or political interests? The manager must assess whether the initiative is still on track.

Supervising law enforcement officers engaged in community policing means keeping them focused on community needs and aware of their role as facilitators. Such a management strategy is a key ingredient to success in community policing.

Source: Reprinted with permission from DeVere D. Woods, Jr., "Supervising Officers in the Community Policing Age," *Sheriff Times* 1, no. 10 (Fall 1999).

---

department, may be familiar with only the formal structure but not the informal structure of the police department. The insider is at a disadvantage when it comes to change because of the ties to the informal structure, and the outsider is at a disadvantage because of the lack of ties and information. However, to effect change, there must be a police chief who is willing to promulgate change, which can usually only be done by an outsider. When large corporations look for their chief executive officers, they generally do not look from within but look for an effective leader from outside the corporation. In some cases, they look not only for an outsider but for a leader who has no background in what the corporation specifically does; instead, they seek a candidate who simply has strong leadership qualities. Despite the many arguments about the uniqueness of being a police officer, the hiring of a police chief from outside the policing profession is but one additional possibility for implementing the systemic approach to policing. However, community-oriented policing to date, by and large, has had more success with the police chief being an outsider yet still from the policing profession.

Closely tied in with the leadership role the chief must accept is also the role of ombudsman. In the community-oriented policing model, the chief is required to work with multiple agencies, community groups, and organizations that the police have to deal with during the planning, implementation, and maintenance of a community-oriented approach to policing. The greater the ability of the chief to act as the ombudsman, the greater success the programs will have when they are implemented. Success is readily apparent when dealing with organizations within the police department, such as unions, fraternal organizations, and spousal associations; dealing with organizations outside the police department, such as the chamber of commerce, local fraternal organizations, and community associations; dealing with other police agencies, such as local college campus police, the sheriff's department, and state narcotics units; dealing with other government agencies, such as public works, engineering, and planning and zoning committees; and, finally, dealing with the committees specifically established for the purposes of community-oriented policing, such as community groups assisting in the implementation of strategic-oriented policing, committees established to determine what neighborhood-oriented policing programs to implement, and problem-oriented policing committees designed to solve problems indigenous to the specific neighborhoods. All of these committees are important to the success of community-oriented policing, and the office of the chief will become even more important as it becomes the focal contact point for all of these groups when they need to coordinate their activities.

 COP IN ACTION

Charleston Tries Voluntary Program

Chief Reuben M. Greenberg can be heard on the police radio day and night responding to calls. The chief also makes sure he is accessible to Charleston's citizens and often acts as a sounding board. Two years ago, citizens asked Chief Greenberg to help parents keep their kids off the streets late at night.

Greenberg decided that a plan similar to an antitruancy program that he started in April 1991 could possibly help alleviate parents' concerns. The truancy program assists education administrators by picking up unsupervised kids in public areas and returning them to school.

In August 1993, Operation Midnight, a voluntary curfew program, went into effect. Under Operation Midnight, officers pick up juveniles on the streets between midnight and 6 A.M. and return them to their homes. Concerned parents and guardians fill out an Operation Midnight form and mail it to the Charleston Police Department to make their kids eligible. A complete list of registered youths, stored in a centralized database, is available for officers' reference.

The program applies to youths up to age seventeen who are traveling by foot or vehicle. "By 12 A.M., kids who have gone out to a ball game or a movie should be back at home," says Greenberg. "A lot of parents have told us that they want their kids home by midnight. We're doing our best to ensure they are.

"Operation Midnight is not a mandatory curfew program, and it does not require violators to appear in court," comments Greenberg. "It is totally voluntary, and the only way it works is if the parents want it to work." A voluntary program eliminates having to process youths at the station before they go home. "You're not going to lock kids up for being out too late at night, so why not just take them straight home. Also, a mandatory curfew presents problems for youths who work late or whose parents have no objection to them being out late," says Greenberg. "My officers are familiar with the kids working newspaper routes and others who have legitimate reasons for being out between midnight and 6 A.M."

Youths not registered with the program are not taken home if found on the street after midnight. However, the department does not tolerate parents who allow very young children to be out in the early morning hours. "Parents who think it's okay for kids aged eight, nine, and ten to be out late at night are referred to the juvenile courts. We don't see these parents as being responsible, nor do the judges," states Greenberg.

Parents' reactions to Operation Midnight have been overwhelmingly positive. In two years, parents have signed up 650 kids, and to date, 150 have been picked up and returned home. "We've had numerous calls from parents voicing their approval of Operation Midnight," says Chief Greenberg. "So far, our only critic has been a teenager."

Chief Greenberg makes it clear that Operation Midnight is a partnership between parents and the police department. "We need the parents' support to make it work. For our part, if we see kids out on the street, we will stop them. We want to protect our youths from ending up as possible driveby shooting victims. Conversely, we want to ensure that kids aren't out at night committing crimes. Either way you look at it, Operation Midnight is a crime prevention program."

Source: Adapted with permission from Charles E. Francis. "Charleston Tries Voluntary Program," *Community Policing Exchange,* January/February 1996, p. 7.

A third principle the chief must adhere to, which is also closely related to the role of leader and ombudsman, is the role of policy maker. Although the chief is the key policy maker for the police department, under community-oriented policing, this role must expand and grow beyond the confines of the police force. The police chief will no longer serve to dominate the actions of the police officers but will guide the police officers functioning under this systemic approach (Bureau of Justice Assistance 1994a). The police chief will then have to create a strong vision of the values, goals, and strategies of community-oriented policing for the policy to serve as a clear mandate for action. Jurisdictions that have demonstrated this strong vision in their policy have been successful in their implementation of community-oriented policing (Kelling and Bratton 1993). Although there is little debate on whether the chief is the key policy maker within the police department, there has been extensive debate on whether the police chief should be a major municipal policy maker (see Geller 1985, Part 1).

Although this debate is clearly important for any police chief, police department, and community, it is even more important when introducing community-oriented policing. There should be no doubt that the police chief will be a major policy maker in his or her community under this systemic approach. As Richard Brzeczek (1985) articulated, the police chief is a policy initiator, and the role of the chief should not be subordinate to the mayor but rather supportive of the mayor and, in our case, supportive of the tenets of community-oriented policing. Another police chief expressed that the chief is a policy maker for three key reasons: "first, the chief is responsible for controlling the great discretionary power that police exert over the lives of individuals and groups, . . . second, the chief's importance as a community leader stems from the extraordinarily important but rarely discussed role the police play in resolving conflict before the need to suppress it develops," and "third, the chief inevitably attains community prominence by virtue of the fact that the police touch the lives of an extraordinary number of citizens, exerting many different (often unpleasant) influences" (Andrews 1985, 11–12). Andrews (1985, 17) thus concludes that "clearly, the community leadership style [community-oriented policing] [that is called] for is not that of an administrative minion but that of an effective, innovative, and pioneering community leader." The chief must be a policy maker in the area of crime and social order within the police department and the community. The type of policy maker under the systemic approach, however, is just as important.

As James Q. Wilson (1968) explained, policies affect police behavior; however, most policies have focused on the negative or, rather, what not to do instead of what officers should do. Under community-oriented policing, the focus of policy should be on the positive by telling officers what they should be doing. This style of leadership in policy making is more akin to the style of leadership, decentralization, and management necessary under the systemic approach. It takes into consideration that the workers are individuals who can perform their duties in a professional manner and values workers' contributions to the organization and the community rather than treating them as poor ineffectual workers who need constant negative reinforcement.

Lynchburg police get tough on neglected and abandoned buildings under the broken windows theory. Local officials are seen here erecting a sign for people to contact the owners and complain. Within weeks the house was painted and improved. (*Courtesy of the Lynchburg Police Department, Lynchburg, Virginia.*)

TOP 12 LEADERSHIP CHARACTERISTICS FOR COMMUNITY POLICING

Leading Organizational Change

Creative ability

Toughness

Subordinate and public trust

Delegation of responsibility

Decision-maker

Taking action

Communicator

Sharing command

Visionary

Integrity

Commitment

Source: Dennis J. Stevens, "Community Policing and Police Leadership." In *Policing and Community Partnership,* (pp. 163–176), ed. Dennis J. Stevens. Upper Saddle River, N.J.: Prentice Hall, 2002.

Another key aspect of the role of the police chief under community-oriented policing is a commitment to the systemic approach. Commitment is clearly an important aspect of the police chief's role in community-oriented policing (Goldstein 1990; Kelling and Bratton 1993; Reiss 1985b; Skolnick and Bayley 1986). Police chiefs today, as previously discussed, often endure short tenures and move from police department to police department. Herein lies the importance of commitment not only to the position of chief, the community, and the mayor but to community-oriented policing. There must be the understanding that community-oriented policing is a long-term solution to the problem of crime and social disorder. It is not a quick fix for what ails a community. Therefore, it cannot be implemented as a quick, successful program that will turn around the police department and earn the chief high recognition. Under community-oriented policing, the recognition may be slow in coming. If the chief's tenure is short, the full implementation of community-oriented policing may not be revealed prior to his or her vacating the position. Consequently, police chiefs must remain committed to the program.

This commitment must also transcend to another level. The chiefs must demonstrate their commitment to community-oriented policing not only through the sincere implementation of the system but also through personal action. In some cases, the chief provides a forum for both police and citizens to discuss their concerns and he or she is directly involved. Another chief puts on a uniform once a week and works alongside the officers in the implementation of foot patrols, community meetings, and storefront posts, not only placing himself or herself closer to the community and the police but truly demonstrating commitment to the success of community-oriented policing. This approach sends a strong message to both the public and the line officers of the police department.

An example of this importance is revealed in a study that interviewed a number of police personnel, who all consistently pointed to the police executive as the driving force behind the implementation of community-oriented policing (Giacomazzi and Brody 2002). The police chief is the key person who must believe in the principles of community-oriented policing and must promote them. Giacomazzi and Brody (2002) quote one respondent who stated, "people internally have to get in line with COP (Community-Oriented Policing), but this won't happen until the troops perceive that there is commitment from the top" (p. 51). Another study found that "the more that top management was seen as committed to the community-policing philosophy, the more committed the officers were to the strategy and the more likely they were to behave in ways consistent with the goals of community policing" (Ford, Weissbein, and Plamondon 2003, p. 177). It would appear that without the commitment of the police chief or sheriff, community-oriented policing stands poised to fail from the outset.

Another principle adhered to by the community-oriented police chief is the style of leadership and police management. This is a very broad category to analyze because there are multiple styles of both policing and management, but it is important that they are "characterized by receptivity to community involvement" (Reiss 1985, 64). This essentially means that the old autocratic and centralized style of policing and management must be replaced by a style more conducive to the values and goals of community-oriented policing. The two most important styles that can and have been utilized are situational leadership and, as previously discussed in Chapter 7, total quality management (TQM). Both align themselves quite well under the community-oriented approach to policing.

Situational leadership is focused on the environment and the situations that leaders encounter (see Figure 10-1). Thus, as Hersey and Blanchard (1993, 116) explain, "the emphasis is on the behavior of leaders and their group members (followers) and various situations. With this emphasis on behavior and environment, more encouragement is given to the possibility of training individuals in adapting styles of leader behavior to varying situations. Therefore, it is believed that most people can increase their effectiveness in leadership roles through education, training, and development." Although according to style theory, most individuals will adopt one style, either autocratic, democratic, or laissez-faire, situational leadership follows the doctrine that the style utilized is based largely on the situation (Peak 1995). Under community-oriented policing, police chiefs will find themselves in a variety of settings in which one style of management will not lend itself to every situation. Rather, depending on the environment in which they find themselves, such as a community focus group or the overseeing of a strategic-oriented policing program, the style of policing will have to shift. The tenets of situational leadership then lend themselves well to the precepts of community-oriented policing.

The style of management that lends itself well to the values and goals found in community-oriented policing is TQM. This style of management was first articulated by W. Edwards Deming in the 1950s, with the five principles of focusing on results, customers, decentralization, prevention, and a systems approach (Peak 1995). However, David Osborne and Ted Gaebler advanced the propositions that Deming had articulated and found that

> most entrepreneurial governments focused on promoting competition between service providers. They empower citizens by pushing control out of the bureaucracy, into the community. They measure the performance of their agencies, focusing not on inputs but on outcomes. They are driven by their goals—their missions—not by their rules and regulations. They redefine their clients as customers and offer them choices. . . . They prevent problems before they emerge, rather than simply offering services afterward. . . . They decentralize authority, embracing participatory management. They prefer market mechanisms to bureaucratic mechanisms. And they focus not simply on providing public services, but on catalyzing all sectors—public, private, and voluntary—into action to solve their community's problems. (Osborne and Gaebler 1992, 19–20)

It is easy to see how the precepts of TQM complement the precepts of community-oriented policing. Since TQM is focused on the customer, which in the case of the police is the citizen, this style of management should find successful implementation as a style of

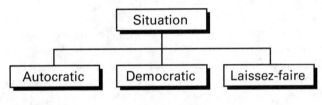

FIGURE 10-1 Situational leadership.

policing under community-oriented policing. Indeed, it already has at least one success story in Madison, Wisconsin, where Police Chief David Couper implemented what he defined as "Quality Policing" (Couper and Lobitz 1991; Wycoff and Skogan 1993, 1994). Couper was able to create a set of twelve principles directly aimed at the police that applied TQM to police management, and he was able to provide a guide to the police department for the style of police management and services, under the auspices of community-oriented policing (see Chapter 7 and Wycoff and Skogan 1994a, 76–77). Similar success was achieved in the Lawrence Police Department, Lawrence, Massachusetts, when it applied TQM methods to policing (Cole 1993b). Although situational leadership and TQM are not the only leadership and management styles of policing under community-oriented policing, the two are conducive to all of the underpinnings of the systemic approach.

Inherent within the entire philosophy of community-oriented policing is the principle that the police chief will have to abide by, that of remaining open to change. A police chief cannot hope to implement the true system of community-oriented policing if he or she is unwilling to change from the traditional methods of policing. As Reiss (1985b, 64) explains, there can be no fixed solutions and the change must come "at all levels of function—from training to operations—and at all levels of staff and command." At the same time there is a willingness to change, there must also be a willingness to fail. The freedom to experiment and fail is part of the advancement to providing better police services. Although we would never want our experiments to jeopardize the safety of the public, we must be willing to attempt new methods of service delivery, whether they are under the strategic-oriented or neighborhood-oriented components.

Utilizing the latest research available and commissioning research on community-oriented policing (see Chapter 12) will be one way in which police chiefs can create change, adapt to change, and anticipate further changes in the future (Toch 1995, 8). As Toch explains, "their role involves integrating what we may learn in the experiments that are conducted, so we can chart new directions and new approaches to policing. Research becomes incremental experience that leads to incremental reform, but ultimately, allows for summated experience that translates into new directions and substantial or revolutionary reform."

Perhaps the best example of both commitment and the concept of remaining open to change can be found in Newark, New Jersey. As Skolnick and Bayley (1986) describe, no U.S. city has experienced more racial tension, more government corruption, less economic strength, or higher crime rates than Newark, New Jersey. Yet, despite these odds, the police department remained committed to change and allowed experimentation with new methods of providing police services to create a more effective police department. The police were able to successfully address corruption; ease racial tensions; conduct strategic-oriented policing tactics, such as street sweeps for loitering, public drinking, drug sales, purse snatching, and street harassment by local groups; establish neighborhood-oriented policing programs, such as substations, home visits, newsletters, and cleanup programs; and address local problems through the adoption of problem-oriented policing (Skogan 1990, 1994; Skolnick and Bayley 1986; Williams and Pate 1987). There are numerous examples of police departments that have successfully implemented change through innovation and experimentation, but one key ingredient in each of their success stories has been the chief's willingness to change.

COMMUNITY-ORIENTED POLICING (COP) SUCCESS INSURANCE STRATEGIES

1. CEOs should do first things first. They should develop a positive organizational culture before implementing COP.

2. CEOs should resist the inclination to have in-house personnel conduct the TQM training. Instead, they should enlist the assistance of instructors from the local community college or other local educators proficient in TQM.

3. CEOs should appoint a team to develop a mission statement, allowing all employees to (1) review the proposals, (2) provide input, and (3) vote for their choice.

4. CEOs must commit completely to the COP endeavor. They should not consider COP a short-term solution to budget woes. Additionally, especially in the early stages of COP, the CEO must remain alert for setbacks in the effort and take immediate corrective action.

5. Upon introducing COP to any target-specific area, CEOs should prepare to have crime displaced to other sections of the community.

6. CEOs eventually should target even those areas experiencing little crime, whose residents want the extra attention community policing delivers. Depending on the pressure exerted by residents in other sections of the city, implementation may need to be expedited.

7. CEOs should not neglect neighborhood business districts. Though they need to be modified somewhat, COP principles work there as well.

8. CEOs should implement COP incrementally and slowly.

9. Community watch groups represent a key component to a successful COP effort. CEOs should ensure that all community policing officers know how to initiate a community watch program. A checklist will aid the process.

10. Community policing officers must survey their assigned neighborhoods to determine their customers' needs and priorities. They should use the KISS principle for survey questions: keep it short and simple.

11. CEOs should establish a leadership council that includes citizens, elected officials, and other key members of the community. The council should meet regularly to set priorities and provide feedback.

12. Beat assignments are important to community policing success. Still, CEOs should give their community policing officers reasonable leeway regarding straying from their assigned neighborhoods. However, officers who take advantage of this wide latitude of personal responsibility should receive an objective evaluation that matches the level of their contribution to the COP effort.

13. COP is labor-intensive. If officers do not have any uncommitted time to conduct COP operations, the department should defer implementing COP until officers can sustain the one-third workload principle.

14. Funding generally emerges as seed money to help an agency develop a foundation for a wide-ranging, comprehensive purpose. Using funding to implement COP in a specific area as a supplement to traditional policing efforts is prudent; however, COP should evolve into a departmentwide and citywide approach, where all officers perform as team players guided by the precepts of the COP philosophy.

15. CEOs must recruit those candidates with the right qualities to work COP. Granted, candidates need to be physically and mentally fit, but they also should be able to solve

problems, communicate with people, and seek out resources in the absence of close supervision. Above all, applicants and newly hired officers must understand the department's allegiance to COP.

16. CEOs should provide all officers and their supervisors at least rudimentary in-service COP training until they can attend a formal police academy course.

17. Officers should receive rewards for their participation in this new philosophy of policing.

18. In addition to the traditional annual or semiannual performance appraisal, the CEO should meet monthly with key personnel to establish and monitor goals. Postponing regular progress reviews may deteriorate any positive achievements or may put the COP effort gravely behind schedule.

19. Overall, the department's performance evaluation system must coincide with the goals of the agency's COP endeavor. Officers who meet their goals should be recognized on their appraisals. Officers who continually falter, assuming they have received proper training (including remedial training), support, resources, and time, should receive ratings commensurate with such marginal performance.

20. Officers who receive the necessary support, training, resources and time, and still fail to attain acceptable COP objectives should receive progressive discipline. However, officers who achieve planned objectives should be recognized and rewarded.

Source: Adapted from Randall Aragon and Richard E. Adams, "Community-Oriented Policing: Success Insurance Strategies," *FBI Law Enforcement Bulletin*, December 1997, pp. 8–18.

The next principle of the police chief's role in community-oriented policing is that he or she share power with the community. Originally articulated by Police Chief Lee Brown (1985, 81), "the concept of power sharing is premised on the assumption that it is difficult for one person to serve another when the 'servant' possesses all the power, which is exactly the case in traditional police work: An inverse power relationship exists between the servants and those served." Although Brown was not calling for the abdication of power on the part of the police chief—the chief is and always will be the final decision maker and authority—he was calling for a larger role for the community.

As stated earlier, the best example is the relationship of power sharing in the instrumental and expressive leader relationship. The community must take on the role of the instrumental leader by determining the job, roles, and responsibilities of the police and how they could best do their job. This is essentially a shared role within the police chief's policy-making role. The chief will not abdicate this role but through a collaborative effort will enhance not only his or her role but also the role of the community. The chief essentially becomes the expressive leader who is responsible for the police officers' welfare and instilling a sense of unit cohesion to create a police force that will carry out the goals and values that are part of community-oriented policing. Currently, under community-oriented policing, there are numerous examples of police–community power sharing, whether it is through the use of a forum with the public, such as the one found in the Portland Police Bureau, Portland, Oregon; through neighborhood advisory committees and one city-wide advisory committee in the Spokane Police Department, Spokane, Washington; or through the implementation of Community Services Council meetings in Fort Wayne, Indiana, under their total concept of community-oriented government.

The police chief, under the systemic approach to policing, also finds himself or herself as the key educator, motivator, and trainer on every facet of this approach to policing. If the police chief fully supports the concepts of community-oriented policing, it will show through these three roles that are distinctly different and at the same time quite similar. The chief must educate not only the police department but also the mayor, community, and various groups and organizations on the concepts of community-oriented policing. The police chief must continue to motivate the police officers to maintain a high level of community interaction, and he or she must be the primary trainer of his or her police officers in community-oriented policing as well as actively participate in the training. To some extent, the police chief should personally provide training to the public, the community groups, the mayor, and other government officials and agencies.

The ninth principle in the role of the chief is that he or she must, at all times, be the role model for both the police department and the community. The police chief has always been the police department's main role model under the traditional form of policing, and this role is strikingly more important under community-oriented policing. The values and goals espoused within the tenets of community-oriented policing must be the guiding philosophy of the chief both on and off duty, inside and outside the public purview, and from the chief's office and among the line officers (Whisenand 2007). At the same time, under the leadership principle of providing leadership not only to the police department but to the community as well, the chief must be the role model for every facet of the community he or she serves. The police chief should reflect the values and goals inherent within community-oriented policing and must never forget that he or she represents the police department, the government, and the community policing philosophy.

The final principle is the role of the disciplinarian as it applies to police accountability. Although numerous instances of police misconduct and police brutality have marked the public eye and damaged the reputation of individual police departments, not to mention the reputation of all police departments nationwide, any such conduct under the community-oriented policing philosophy not only may damage the reputation but also may destroy the community's faith in the systemic approach. The community will easily raise the banner of the police department having failed the community while pretending to be more community-oriented. Community mistrust can have a detrimental effect on the new approach to policing, and it is therefore even more important that the police keep the public trust, become more accountable to the local populace, and administer discipline under circumstances requiring such action. A disciplinary program, in whatever form or shape it takes, must be open to the public and not secreted within the police department under the community-oriented policing philosophy. However, it is important to note that the openness of the disciplinary process may be in opposition to due process procedures, departmental policy, governmental policy, police union rules, civil service policy, bargaining units, and a host of other variables that exist to protect the rights of the employees, perhaps at the expense of police–community relations. Every effort should be made to factor in the community and the impact the misconduct may have had on the community.

In attempting to achieve a disciplinary program under the community-oriented policing approach, Chief Stephens of St. Petersburg, Florida, has implemented a disciplinary process in which all employees are actively involved (see Kappeler, Sluder, and Alpert 1994, 249–252). Although every disciplinary program should be consistent and

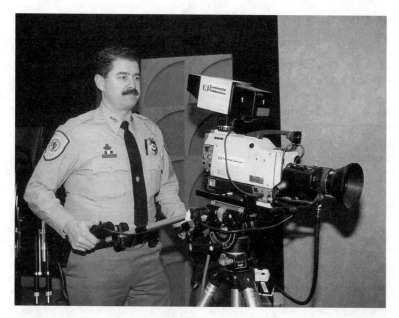

Holland, Michigan, police officer Drew Torres assisting in the Community Access video-taping of "Street Talk," a monthly half-hour production dealing with police and community issues. (*Courtesy of the Holland Police Department, Holland, Michigan.*)

 COP IN ACTION

Chief Sees Local High Schools as Department's Future

When Chief Arturo Venegas came to the Sacramento Police Department in 1993, he began looking around for the ideal recruits. Chief Venegas knew that the shift in emphasis from crime fighting to community policing had placed a heavy burden on law enforcement agencies to recruit candidates of multifarious talents. Some agencies pay big bucks to analyze their recruitment and selection procedures and to come up with incentives. Agencies search nationwide for the ideal recruit. New York state troopers use employee feedback to redesign their recruitment brochures. To qualify for the Largo Police Department in Pinellas County, Florida, recruits must have a four-year college degree. Some agencies, such as the Camden Police Department in New Jersey, have hedged their bets, relying on psychological screenings.

Chief Venegas soon discovered that, for his department, the mostly likely candidates—the elusive "ideal recruits"—are teenagers: teenagers living right there in the city of Sacramento, junior high students, all of thirteen years old. Chief Venegas's budding recruits are students at the city's three criminal justice and community service academies, each associated with a high school. The police department and the Sacramento School Department established the first academy at Kennedy High School in 1990. So, right in his own backyard, the chief had a garden with potential recruits and the tools for cultivation.

Applicants to the academies are screened and interviewed, not unlike the practices at a college admissions office. Parents and students sign a contract, agreeing to the requirements of the four-year program, which include more than fifty hours of community service, exemplary citizenship, and maintenance of academic standards. Students wear uniforms. The college prep courses cover ethics as well as law and criminal justice procedures approved by the California Commission on Peace Officer Standards. Physical fitness training is rigorous enough to prepare the students to ace the Sacramento Police Department's fitness exam. Students also learn conflict management, computer skills, and goal setting.

Chief Venegas realized that he did not have to beat the national "bushes" for ideal candidates. Instead, he committed the Sacramento Police Department to cultivating its own force of intelligent, motivated, physically fit, service-oriented homegrown recruits.

At one point, budget cuts put the future of the first academy in doubt. Chief Venegas successfully fought for the academy's life, rallying the community in 1994 to add two more academies devoted to criminal justice and community service. "I thought," he says, "that the program was essential to maintain a crime prevention program and school partnership and to help the police department in developing our workforce." The three academies are financed with state grants, municipal funds, community foundation grants, fund-raising, and in-kind donations. The police department provides a full-time officer, supervising sergeant, guest speakers, uniforms, and some equipment.

At a 1999 forum of the National Career Academies Coalition, criminal justice executives endorsed the idea of exposing students to law enforcement careers at an early age. They reasoned that agencies stood a better chance of attracting a diverse ethnic group into local law enforcement, and that in turn would better reflect the makeup of the community.

The students at Sacramento's three academies demographically reflect the city's population. "They speak a variety of languages," says Chief Venegas. "It's like a little United Nations." Another dividend, he adds, is that the department now "is able to access a higher percentage of girls."

Academy students are in high demand. Public and private agencies have come to rely on the students' volunteer services. These agencies vie for students to serve as escorts at public events or to lend a helping hand for political campaigns, soup kitchens, graffiti abatement, school beautification, and fund-raisers. "The students are actually a hot commodity around the city since they are highly trusted and respected," says Chief Venegas.

Academy graduates have more training in law enforcement methodology and physical fitness than the average police academy graduate. All of this is music to the chief's ears. Or is it? Most academy students don't consider a career in law enforcement, instead going on to medicine, engineering, finance, and the legal profession. Actually, the chief has no problem with that. The police department needs accountants, investigators, analysts, and people with good business sense. "Thirty percent of our staff is nonsworn staff," Venegas says. "There are lots of opportunities for those students who don't want to become police officers to go into police work." What, then, can Chief Venegas do to encourage more academy graduates to join his staff? He's working to establish more education and pay incentives. He wants to set up an academy at Sacramento's other four public high schools, which would give the city seven academies. Chief Venegas says, "Fifteen young people from the program are now Sacramento Police Department employees. On top of that, they are high-quality personnel. The costs to recruit fifteen staff like this would have been far more excessive than the investment we make in the academies."

Source: Reprinted with permission from Stephanie B. Francis, "Chief Sees Local High Schools as Department's Future," *Community Links,* March 2001.

---

fair, "for the St. Petersburg Police Department consistency is defined as holding everyone equally accountable for unacceptable behavior and fairness is understanding the circumstances that contributed to the behavior while applying the consequences in a way that reflects this understanding" (Kappeler, Sluder, and Alpert 1994, 250–252). To abide by this understanding, the police department looks at multiple factors in each incident, including employee motivation, the degree of harm, employee experience, intentional versus unintentional errors, and employee's past record (Kappeler, Sluder, and Alpert 1994).

 COP IN ACTION

San Jose: Creating a Shared Vision through Leadership Training

The San Jose Police Department started community policing efforts in earnest in 1991 and chose to make community policing every member's responsibility—there were no specialized community policing officers. By the late 1990s, the department's community policing efforts had lost momentum. A number of focus groups revealed that a comprehensive program to address leadership development and the creation of a consistent vision for community policing were needed to reinvigorate the department's effort.

The San Jose Police Department's goals and objectives to reinvigorate their community policing program included:

- Increase the leadership capacity of middle management and line supervisors and develop a core set of attitudes for community-oriented policing
- Increase the decentralization of decision making
- Develop a comprehensive community oriented policing professional development course through site visits and research
- Using leadership simulation gaming, train 300 supervisory and command personnel in practical leadership skills related to community policing issues
- Create a shared vision for the future of community-oriented policing in San Jose
- Institutionalize leadership and professional development training within the department

The San Jose Police Department was able to act on these goals and objectives by:

- Training for lieutenants and captains on how to create and sustain community policing
- A professional development course for sergeants that included community policing skills
- The development and training of peer mentors who would mentor newly promoted supervisors and serve as facilitators for the professional development course
- Site visits to Baltimore and Boston and a visit to the Los Angeles Police Department to study its West Point Leadership Model
- The acquisition and use of technology to support Web-based training
- Training on leadership and community policing including LeadSim (Leadership Simulation) training
- Evaluation of the professional development course
- A retreat for the chief of police and top command staff to create a consistent vision for community policing

The lessons learned by the San Jose Police Department after achieving their goals and objectives included:

- Communicate regularly and in detail about the scope and intent of activities and initiatives

- Convene members of the department on an ongoing basis to discuss progress
- Include community members in any training or discussion about community policing
- Empower individuals to take responsibility for projects
- It is not enough for the chief of police to support community policing; but that support must extend through the chain of command and be demonstrated daily

Source: Adapted from A. Schneider et. al., *Community Policing in Action: A Practitioner's Eye View of Organizational Change.* Washington, D.C.: Office of Community Oriented Policing Services, 2003.

CONCLUSION

The role of the police chief is dramatically different under community-oriented policing than it was under the traditional approach to policing. The chief must become the central figure in this systemic approach to policing because he or she is the key to successful implementation of the concept. It is imperative that the chief abide by the ten principles in order to fulfill his or her role within community-oriented policing (see Table 10-1). The chief must be the key leader and policy maker within both the police department and the community. Although all of these principles are important, none is more important than the principle of leadership. The community-oriented police chief must be a dynamic leader who is skilled at functioning on multiple levels, able to handle a variety of situations, and able to instill the values and goals of community-oriented policing in his or her police department and direct it toward a goal of sustainment for the systemic approach to policing.

The advancement of the police, such as the advancement from the political era to the traditional era of policing, cannot be carried out without the tenacity of the police chief. The police chiefs of today must recognize community-oriented policing as the next step in the evolution of the police much in the manner that August Vollmer saw the evolution from politics to strategic management. The chiefs of today must be willing to implement all of the tenets and all three components of community-oriented policing, and they must face the inquisition of the program by many pundits from many fields. However, the rewards of successful implementation of the program will not be lost on the people who truly count, members of the community who are tired of the high crime rates and the lack of social order. These citizens will be indebted to the police chief for leading the community to a better life, marked by less crime and social disorder, and they will recognize the chief as a member and leader of the community.

COP ON THE WORLD WIDE WEB

Charlotte-Mecklenburg, North Carolina, Police Department, Chief Darrel Stephens

http://www.charmeck.nc.us/cipolice

Chief Paul Walters on the Community Policing Philosophy

http://www.chiefwalters.com/philosophy

Community Policing Guidelines for Police Chiefs

http://www.concentric.net/%7EDwoods/guide.htm

Interview online with Chief Charles Alexander Moose, WTOP Radio

http://www.connectlive.com/events/wtop/moose052902.html

Montgomery County, Maryland, Police Department, Chief Charles Alexander Moose

http://www.co.mo.md.us/services/police

REVIEW QUESTIONS

1. Explain why the police chief's role in community-oriented policing is critical to COP's success.
2. What do you think are the three most important principles of the ten principles for good leadership and management in community-oriented policing? Why?
3. Define *situational leadership*. How does this term apply to community-oriented policing?

CHAPTER 11

Evaluation

That evil is half-cured whose cause we know.

—Shakespeare

CHAPTER OBJECTIVES

- Recognize the importance of evaluations in COP.
- Understand the three eras of developing police evaluations.
- Recognize the significance of the Kansas City Preventive Patrol Experiment.
- Understand the problem of early police evaluations.
- Articulate the five criteria for evaluating COP.
- Identify the two types of program evaluation.
- Explain the various methods of program evaluation.

As police departments across the nation begin moving through the various stages of community-oriented policing, from strategic planning to institutionalization, one necessary tool for success is evaluation (Toch 1995). As the police begin testing the waters with a host of programs, tactics, and methods under the three components, they must be able to adequately assess whether those practices employed are beneficial to both the community and the police. Because community-oriented policing must be tailored to the community the police serve, a sound program in one community may prove to be a failure in another. Therefore, it is of utmost importance that each police department institute its own evaluation process for implementation of community-oriented policing (Masterson and Stevens 2002).

The practice of conducting evaluations in a community-oriented police department is a key aspect of the systemic approach that complements both the preferred style of management, total quality management (TQM), and the concept of incrementalism. TQM is premised on improving the system of production and services and ensuring customer satisfaction, and evaluations are a tool to determining if the delivery of police services is the best it can be and if the citizens are satisfied with their police. In the case of incrementalism, evaluations are the necessary tool to determine if programs or certain practices are beneficial to the implementation of community-oriented policing and if adjustments need to be made midstream. Evaluations allow the police department to make changes while the programs develop rather than allowing the development of a lasting mistake. Combining the need for the evaluation process under both TQM and incrementalism solidifies the need for evaluations under the systemic approach.

Recognizing a need for police departments to utilize evaluations as another tool in their implementation of community-oriented policing is important, but some would argue that police have always utilized various evaluation methods. As in the evolution of police–community relations, we have also seen an evolution in how police utilize evaluations. In the past, the police utilized evaluations to assess how well their officers were doing rather than how well they were delivering their services. It was assumed that if the numbers of arrests, tickets, and calls for service were high and the response time was low, the police officer was performing well. The central question police management asked was, "How many?" Under the systemic approach, police management must ask the question, "How well?" It is no longer adequate to analyze the success of the police based on quantitative and objective criteria; rather, an assessment must be based on qualitative and subjective criteria as well. In such an evaluation, as described under the precepts of TQM, the focus must be on the system for delivering services and customer satisfaction rather than the individual police officer. Evaluations must be utilized to assess programs, environment, and citizen satisfaction under community-oriented policing and not the number of parking tickets a police officer can write during a given shift.

Two officers of the Dallas Police Department work with local youth at a community fair. (*Courtesy of the Dallas Police Department, Dallas, Texas.*)

COP IN ACTION

Making Sure Community Policing Initiatives Work

The best way to determine if a department's community policing efforts are effective is to ask the people how they are being impacted by the program. Motivation for evaluation of a community program can be for several reasons:

1. Evaluation will bring forth opinions of residents
2. Information will modify existing policing efforts
3. Input will inform other agencies of success of program
4. Decisions will operationalize community policing
5. Results will be made public through the media

Evaluation results will educate administrators on how well the programs are being implemented. They should ask, "Are we steering the ship on the right course, or do we need to make additional adjustments to get on course?" Results can help in planning for the future in regards to budgeting, personnel allocation, reorganization, and proper use of various resources available to the department.

The evaluation form can be complex or simple, depending on the needs of the department. To get a better response the questionnaire must be short and simple to fill out. Questions should be short and objective, requiring yes or no answers.

> Example:
> How safe is it for you/your family to walk alone in the neighborhood during the day?
> (very safe) (somewhat safe) (not safe) (no opinion)
> In the past year, have you or any member of your household been the victim of a crime?
> YES   NO

> If subjective questions are necessary, keep them at a minimum and as general as possible.

> Example:
> Do you have any comments or suggestions on how this department can improve its services?

Such a survey can be developed easily by any department. There are many resources to develop a good survey. Contacting other departments that have evaluated their community initiatives through surveys and finding out what they did is a practical way of developing a survey. There is no reason to pay for a survey when there are so many available just for the asking.

Distribute a rough draft of the survey to various influential people in the community and employees in the department in order to solicit opinions on how to improve it. Through objective feedback and review of the survey, the evaluation results will be more meaningful to everyone involved.

In order that the results be credible, an outside resource might coordinate the evaluation process. This can be a paid consultant; however this can be expensive, depending on the time and effort involved. An option used frequently is to contact a local university's graduate program for assistance. Students who have independent study projects welcome coordinating a community policing evaluation as part of their academic curriculum. This option is at no cost to the department, and at the same time, the department gets expert advice from a professor who oversees the efforts of the student. This academic source gives credibility to the evaluation and a professional viewpoint when suggestions are made to the police administrators and the community.

The Richmond Police Department (Texas) contacted the University of Houston School of Social Graduate Studies and was able to get the cooperation of the professor and four graduate students to coordinate the evaluation effort. The students took the project for their graduate studies and were supervised by their professor. They were given three months to complete the project for a grade.

Once it has been decided where to conduct the survey, how the instrument should be designed, and who should coordinate the survey, the question remains on whom to survey. It is easy to distribute the survey to people who support the department; however, the results would not reflect an honest report. The best distribution method is randomly. This can be done by fly-picking block captains throughout the city. Picking the block captain can be done through a lottery method, or selecting those who are active with the beat officers.

The number of surveys to be distributed can vary depending on the time and resources available to a department. In Richmond, which has a population of 10,000 residents, the department and graduate student coordinators agreed that 800 surveys would be sufficient. According to a professor, there is at least a 20% return of completed surveys from a surveyed public. The proper distribution and return of the survesy is the key ingredient to successfully measuring opinions.

Beat officers are an important component in the distribution of the surveys. They give the surveys to the randomly picked block captain with a written letter of instructions. The block captains are instructed not to participate in the survey—only to distribute it to their neighbors, or to every third house (randomly determined), business, or apartment on their block.

In Richmond, out of 100 block captains, 40 block captains were picked randomly throughout the city. There were more block captains represented in some beats than others due to the law of random selection. Each beat officer was given 20 surveys to be given to the selected block captains in their beat. Instructions were given to the block captains both verbally and in writing by the beat officer. Also available were surveys printed in Spanish because some beats had a predominant Spanish speaking population.

The collection of the completed survey forms is very simple; residents can either mail them (postage paid by them), return them to the block captain, return them to the beat officer, or drop them off at the police department.

To ensure confidentiality, each person received a blank envelope with the survey and was directed to place the completed survey into the envelope and seal it. Surveys were to be returned within seven days of receipt.

The local media should be used in encouraging citizens to take the time to return the surveys. Newspaper editorials, press releases, and stories on local cable should stress the importance of citizen participation in helping to achieve a greater response.

Historically, 20 percent of distributed surveys are returned and this percentage is acceptable to validate an evaluation. In Richmond, 800 surveys were distributed and of the 283 returned 269 were suitable for extracting data.

Who should interpret the data? The department could hire a professional, but this may be too expensive and the purpose is to get good results for a minimum amount of money. The other option is that someone in the department can go through the data and present it; however many departments do not have analysts, and without a trained evaluator the results may be perceived as not being very credible. Another option is to have graduate students who are taking courses in evaluation methods at a local university interpret the data. This will add credibility to the findings and help the students complete their requirements for their course of study. The work is supervised by a professor at no cost to the department.

In order to get the most information out of the survey it is necessary to gather responses from various demographic data that the survey provides. The survey can be analyzed and interpreted by sex, age, income, ethnicity, and beat. The data can be analyzed by single or multiple categories.

With the accumulated data the department will know how residents like the activities of the department and beat officer, as well as how effective the policing initiatives have been. Data should produce the following:

- Problems that citizens feel are most troubling
- Feeling of safety in the beats
- Respondent's feeling of safety
- Common actions to reduce the chances of being a crime victim
- Satisfaction with the police and beat officer
- Awareness of the Beat Officer–Block Captain program

An ongoing evaluation of the department's initiatives will serve to improve the quality of a community by informing the department where police service is lacking. The evaluation also gives the citizens a voice in their government. With the beat officers being involved in the survey it improves morale and increases ownership of the beat officers towards their beat. It is with good evaluation methods that a department can know if their community policing programs are effective.

Source: Reprinted with permission from George Paruch, "Making Sure Community Policing Initiatives Work," *Law and Order,* October 1998, pp. 81–84.

This chapter will look to the three eras of police evaluations—the traditional, the transitional, and the community-oriented—to determine how police departments have utilized evaluation methods over time and to detail past criticisms of both the use and methods employed. We will describe the traditional methods of evaluating police and how the overall effectiveness of traditional policing has been considered to have limiting effects on crime. We will then analyze the evaluations utilized during the transitional period, moving evaluations from the traditional to the community-oriented. Because the focus for evaluations has changed under the community-oriented policing approach, those key criteria for evaluating the systemic approach will be detailed. The actual methods that have been utilized for assessing community-oriented policing will then be described and reviewed for how evaluations should be conducted and utilized by police practitioners during the implementation process of the systemic approach to policing.

EVALUATION OF TRADITIONAL POLICING

In most police departments, specifically under the traditional style of policing, the bottom-line assessment for determining the overall capabilities of the police has been through the use of crime statistics. The Uniform Crime Reports, started in 1930 by the Federal Bureau of Investigation, requested city, county, and state law enforcement agencies to voluntarily submit their jurisdictions' crime statistics for specific crimes (Dempsey 1994). The statistics became the main emphasis for evaluating the effectiveness and efficiency of individual police departments throughout much of the twentieth century. If crime rates went up, the police were failing in their mission; if crime rates went down, the police were said to be doing their job. Even Sir Robert Peel, in 1829, believed this was the case when, in the publication of Peel's Principles, he stated, "the absence of crime will best prove the efficiency of police" (Sullivan 1977, 11). However, law enforcement is only one aspect of policing; crime rates may reveal very little about the police officer's ability to handle and suppress order maintenance problems.

Another method of determining the effectiveness of the police in many traditional police departments has been through the use of quotas. Although most police departments will deny the utilization of quotas for their police officers and call them various names such as "workload evaluations" or "daily activity reports," they are still a collection of the number of arrests made, calls for service taken, and number of citations issued. Although they speak dramatically about what type of police work officers are performing during their shift, it speaks little to the interaction with the public, ways officers deal with order maintenance issues, and the overall effectiveness of the officers in delivering police services. Additional indicators that have traditionally been utilized by police departments are time spent at work, percentage of arrests that lead to convictions, and citizen complaints against officers (Peak 1995). Although these indicators may represent individual officer performance, they show very little correlation with the effectiveness of the police in dealing with the underlying causes of crime, disorder, and essential quality-of-life issues within the communities they police.

The drawback to evaluating the police in any of these manners is they only make statements about local crime statistics or about the police themselves. They do very little to address the true problems in a neighborhood and do even less to show causation. A correlation does not necessarily equal a causation. If the number of police arrests drops and the number of crimes reported rises, the independent variable of arrest rates does not necessarily correlate with the dependent variable of crimes reported, the independent variable being the cause and the dependent variables being the various effects. It is equally possible that multiple independent variables (such as an increase in the teenage population, the prevalence of drug dealing and prostitution, or environmental factors such as poor street lighting, the presence of graffiti, and "broken windows" in a neighborhood) are influencing the dependent variable. In sum, it is possible that no matter how hard the police work under the traditional methods, crime rates may continue to rise.

The first true evaluation, and in this case a quasi experiment, of police practices was in Kansas City in the early 1970s. The experiment was known as the Kansas City Preventive Patrol Experiment, and it set out to evaluate the effectiveness of the preventive patrol methods. It was conducted by designating that certain areas of Kansas City were to have no proactive patrols, with police responding only when summoned; others were to have enhanced proactive patrols by doubling or tripling police presence; and, finally, certain areas were designated as control areas, where traditional police practices remained unchanged (Kelling et al. 1974, 1975). The researchers evaluated in a pretest/posttest method, with a time lapse of one year, by collecting data on the number of crimes reported, arrest rates, traffic accident rates, police response time, and both citizen attitudes and victimization rates (Kelling et al. 1974, 1975). The evaluation findings revealed that preventive patrols were not effective in altering crime, citizen fear of crime, community attitudes toward the police, police response time, or traffic accidents (Kelling et al. 1974). The Kansas City Preventive Patrol Experiment, with the release of these results, received a vast amount of criticism because it negated basic assumptions about police work. In many cases, the results of the experiment necessitated words of caution (Wilson 1975), whereas in other cases, critics challenged the experimental design itself, stating that the methods utilized were flawed (Larson 1975). It also created a profusion of similar studies in various jurisdictions across the country with largely similar results (see Lewis, Greene, and Edwards 1977; Schnelle et al. 1975; Wagner 1978). As a result of the Kansas City Preventive Patrol Experiment, past practices and assumptions about evaluating the police changed dramatically.

TRANSITIONAL EVALUATIONS

The Kansas City Preventive Patrol Experiment eventually led to multiple evaluations of police departments and their standard beliefs and practices to determine if traditional policing tactics were in fact viable methods of policing. The research from the 1970s and into the 1980s revealed significant limitations in traditional police practices and procedures. Kansas City returned to the specific issue of rapid police response and its effectiveness in dealing with crime (Kansas City Police Department 1980), which was also followed by multiple evaluations (Scott 1981; Spelman and Brown 1984), demonstrating little effectiveness on faster police responses. Additional studies in the area of criminal investigations also revealed little effectiveness, regardless of the traditional methods utilized (Eck 1982; Greenwood and Petersilia 1975; Greenwood, Petersilia, and Chaiken 1977). As Dennis P. Rosenbaum (1988, 371) concluded, "considerable time and effort have been expended to improve police management and efficiency, but the fundamental approach to policing has remained the same: namely, responding to and investigating individual citizen calls for service in a reactive fashion (rather than seeking to identify and address community problems) and treating local citizens as passive recipients of police services (rather than as co-producers of public safety)." As the evolution of policing moved from police–community relations to community-oriented policing, so, too, would the use of evaluation methods.

As community-oriented policing was born in the early 1980s and implemented in a wide variety of formats during most of the 1980s, evaluations were adopted by many police departments to assess the viability and capabilities of this new concept. The majority of evaluations conducted during this time frame were a result of various grants from research institutions such as the National Institute of Justice, the Police Executive Research Forum, the Vera Institute of Justice, and the Police Foundation. These evaluations provided a vast amount of literature on the up-and-coming concept of community-oriented policing and presented many of the advantages and disadvantages of programs, methods, and practices under this new umbrella term.

In 1988, Jack Greene and Ralph Taylor (1988) presented a review of the key studies that had been conducted to that date, including those in Flint, Michigan; Newark, New Jersey; Oakland, California; San Diego, California; Houston, Texas; Boston, Massachusetts; and Baltimore, Maryland. Their findings presented a list of salient shortcomings with the evaluations that are still key concerns today for improving the evaluation process. The first issue raised was the "inadequate operationalization of 'community,'" which was discussed in this book in Chapter 9 (Greene and Taylor 1988, 216). In no study is the term *community* ever defined with clarity or is there any "attempt to use ecologically valid neighborhood units" (Greene and Taylor 1988, 217), despite all of the researchers utilizing the term to definitively describe how the programs impacted the community and how the community responded in kind.

A second shortcoming, largely a result of the first shortcoming, consisted of "confusion about the appropriate level of analysis" (Greene and Taylor 1988, 217). When attempting to evaluate community-oriented policing, the focus has been placed on the community and how the community, as the customer, has responded to the change in police services. The authors criticize the evaluations conducted during this transitional period for not evaluating that which they set out to evaluate. In many cases, researchers analyzed and interpreted at the community level but surveyed individuals. The satisfaction on the part of individuals versus the community as a whole can present two varying viewpoints. It is then important for researchers to analyze at the level they are evaluating and interpret their findings as such.

The third shortcoming Greene and Taylor (1988) described revolved around poor evaluation design, specifically in the area of weak quasi-experimental designs and the lack of control groups. The use of quasi experiments and the methods employed will be detailed later in this chapter; however, the authors distinctly point out the lack of control groups in many of the experiments. In many cases, during the initial stages of implementation, control groups can be designated in neighborhoods that have not been integrated into the community-oriented policing concept. However, once the systemic approach begins to see full implementation citywide, the control groups will have to be redefined based on types of services, programs, or methods employed.

The fourth shortcoming Greene and Taylor (1988) found at the time was a problem with the implementation of community-oriented policing. They found that, in many cases, either very few officers or very few citizens were actually involved in the systemic approach, and so contact between the police and community was minimal. This small-scale involvement caused difficulties in assessing the success or failure of community-oriented policing because so few people had been exposed to the programs and services. This problem reiterates the importance of effective implementation strategies, as described in Chapter 11, prior to the police department moving to evaluate.

Durham Police Department establishing an active Neighborhood Watch program in one of Durham's predominately Hispanic neighborhoods. (*Courtesy of the City of Durham Police Department, Durham, North Carolina.*)

A fifth shortcoming Greene and Taylor (1988, 218) cited was "defining the treatment" or determining exactly what actions the police were taking that should be evaluated as being community-oriented policing. In many cases, multiple programs and methods of delivering police services were being evaluated, whereas in other cases, it was unclear what policing services were actually being performed under the guise of community-oriented policing. It is important that the services or programs the police are providing are identified and specifically evaluated for their individual merit rather than evaluating a host of services; otherwise, the evaluation results will be unclear as to what can be deemed successful and what can be considered a failure.

The final shortcoming Greene and Taylor (1988, 218) delineated consisted of "outcome specification," or understanding what the desired outcome under community-oriented policing should be and how it should be measured. Although it may be a long-term goal to reduce crime under community-oriented policing as a result of community involvement, initially crime rates may not decrease. If the intent of community-oriented policing is to increase the quality of life in a community, evaluating whether crime rates rise or fall is an inadequate method of measuring this outcome. Therefore, consideration must be given to what the desired outcome is from the implementation of a program, how it will be measured, and how it will be interpreted to be a success or a failure. If the program is oriented to enhancing the relationship between the police and the public, then the outcome specification should focus on citizen satisfaction with the police and police satisfaction with the community, not the rise and fall of crime rates.

Two additional shortcomings consist of one the authors touched on, the specific target of the evaluation, and one they did not address, the need for long-term studies. The specific need to determine what the evaluation will target is important in two distinct ways. First, the evaluation must identify which program or service is being targeted, and secondly it must determine who is being targeted for study. In many cases, community-oriented policing is a packaged program that may consist of multiple methods to address a community's concern—it is, after all, a systemic approach. The police may utilize all three components at the same time, thus creating a blend of programs and services. When it comes time to evaluate the benefit of those things implemented, it is important that the evaluation process be tailored specifically to what is being targeted. If it is the benefit of foot patrols in a community, the evaluation must be careful to avoid the influence of a police substation or saturation patrol in the process. It is equally important that the target of the evaluation be identified and the evaluation directed toward these individuals. In a police department engaged in micro-community-oriented policing, unless divided into an experimental group and control group, it makes little sense to evaluate all officers in the department on community-oriented policing because only a limited number are actually participating in the program.

The second shortcoming is the lack of long-term studies. Although the systemic approach to policing is relatively new, the possibility still exists for long-term studies to be conducted for evaluation purposes. The majority of studies are solely focused on short periods of time, ranging from several months to as long as a year. However, because implementation of community-oriented policing is a long-term process, evaluation should also be a long-term process. Studies are needed that evaluate the systemic approach for multiple years rather than multiple months. In a similar vein, it is also critical that the evaluation process remain a long-term and ongoing process. Too many police departments evaluate at the micro-community-oriented policing stage, make adjustments, and move forward without any additional evaluations. Such an approach does not provide current and up-to-date information, nor does it allow for any incremental changes to be made based on these assessments. The evaluation process must be part of an ongoing process to assess the current status of police services, customer satisfaction, and the advantages and disadvantages of community-oriented policing.

As the evaluation process moved into the community-oriented policing stage, many police departments recognized the importance of the evaluation process and have begun utilizing it as a tool to ensure quality policing. In wake of many of the shortcomings during the 1980s, there has been a movement to adopt certain criteria for articulating the basis of evaluation under the systemic approach. The criteria necessary for this basis have had to encompass not only the qualitative and subjective standards that are desired but also a revision of the quantitative and objective standards necessary to assess the success of community-oriented policing. A positive stance has been taken to ensure that the criteria reflect all of the values and goals inherent in this approach, and the literature is replete with descriptions of effectiveness, efficiency, and equity as being the primary foundation (Bureau of Justice Assistance 1994a, 1994b; Eck and Rosenbaum 1994; Goldstein 1990; Miller and Hess 1994; Skogan 1994). However, equally important are two additional criteria that make up this foundation: accountability and authority.

 ## COP IN ACTION

Community Policing: How Do We Know If It's Working?

Community policing is the new direction for law enforcement. Courses and books on how to implement it proliferate, and a federal grant program is established to pay for it, but there is little guidance available on how to determine its effectiveness.

The technique law enforcement traditionally has used to measure the success of programs centers on administrative crime analysis and cost-effectiveness. These measures, however, do not take into account the public's perceptions, thereby rendering them inadequate to evaluate community policing.

The community's perceptions about changes in crime patterns are just as important as the actual crime statistic in community policing. How secure people feel in their homes and whether they believe it is safe to go out at night are just two concerns that are important to citizens and that should be important to the law enforcement agency serving them.

Measuring public perception is not difficult. The difficulty lies in determining what questions to ask and to whom you should ask them. Ideally, an agency should have two groups to evaluate. The first, or experimental, group should consist of residents who are directly affected by a community policing program. The second, or control, group should be demographically similar to the experimental group but should not receive community policing services.

It is essential to conduct a baseline survey before implementing any community policing programs. A follow-up survey should be administered once a program has been in place for a certain period. This method gives the agency the best chance of accurately measuring perception changes.

When survey results of the experimental and control groups are compared, it can be determined if community policing was responsible for changes in the community's perceptions, or if the changes occurred because of other factors. It is both time- and cost-prohibitive to survey all residents in the experimental and control groups. A more effective technique is to select a random sample of both groups and survey those individuals. The results derived from those sampled can then be extrapolated to apply to the entire population. A program's effectiveness can be measured by comparing the differences between the experimental and control groups' perceptions and actual crime statistics and by measuring the cost-effectiveness of the program over time.

Community policing evaluation is not a short-term undertaking. The results must be monitored over a period of years to allow changes in the neighborhoods to stabilize.

Source: Adapted with permission from Drew Davis, "Community Policing: How Do We Know If It's Working?" *Sheriff Times,* Spring 1996, p. 3.

EVALUATION CRITERIA

The term *effectiveness,* up to this point, has been utilized to discuss past quantitative and objective criteria that the police utilized through various arrest statistics and quotas. The emphasis on effectiveness under the systemic approach is different from that of traditional policing. An effective implementation of community-oriented policing will not increase the number of arrest statistics for an officer or satisfy the quotas of the police department but will reduce crime in the community through a variety of means beyond arrests. It will also reduce the community's fear of crime, and it will enhance the overall quality of life. Because the true mark of effectiveness will concentrate on the delivery of police services and customer satisfaction, those measures of this effectiveness should concentrate on solving community problems, how well the community and police work in partnership, and the level of customers' satisfaction with their police. These are the methods of determining the true effectiveness of the police.

If a community-oriented policing program is implemented and it does not reduce the number of crimes or the number of calls for service, it cannot be called a failure, whereas under the traditional style of policing, that may have been the case. Eck and Spelman (1987), under their development of a problem-oriented policing program for Newport News, Virginia, Police Department in 1987, also defined effectiveness. They established five methods of determining if a problem-solving effort was effective, and we can utilize the same five methods under the larger concept of community-oriented policing (Eck and Spelman 1987). A problem can be solved in five ways: (1) by totally eliminating it, (2) by reducing the number of incidents it creates, (3) by reducing the seriousness of the incidents it creates, (4) by designing methods for better handling the incidents, and (5) by removing it from police consideration (Eck and Spelman 1987).

The ability to totally eliminate a problem via strategic-oriented policing, neighborhood-oriented policing, or problem-oriented policing would certainly be the ultimate goal, but despite all hopes for full elimination, the reality of the matter is very few criminal or order maintenance issues will ever completely disappear. However, the second method of solving the problem is reasonable and more likely to occur. An example may be the use of strategic-oriented policing tactics to drive out the criminal element or at least drive it underground. In either case, the problem will be reduced. The third possibility can also be called effective, especially if we can isolate the problem and make it less of a threat to the general public. An example may be isolating the areas frequented by drug users and keeping the drugs away from the children and the abandoned needles away from the playgrounds. The fourth method may make better sense in evaluating many of the programs under community-oriented policing because the police and community may not be able to change or alter the makeup of the problem, but they can be more effective in the delivery of services, referrals, and costs. Finally, the removal of a problem from police consideration details that the police may not be the best organization to provide the solution or effectively deal with the problem. Another agency may be able to deal more effectively with the problem and hence resolve it in one of the above four manners, freeing the police to deal with those problems they are equipped to handle. However, under community-oriented policing, this option should not equate to pawning the problem off on someone else. The police must continue to monitor the problem, follow the success or failure of a solution, and determine if the issue may eventually have to be returned to police consideration.

Therefore, to accurately gauge the effectiveness of the police, the goals of the community-oriented policing program should be addressed and what is considered an acceptable measure of effectiveness should be determined prior to the implementation process. Planning essentially addresses what has been identified as a past shortcoming of outcome specification. Once these issues are resolved, the method for gauging effectiveness should be introduced. Evaluation may cover assessment of citizens' fear of crime, the number of citizens active in addressing problems in their community, the number of citizens serving on community-oriented policing committees, or citizens' assessment of their quality of life and perhaps a decrease in the calls for criminal activity and an increase in the calls for service.

A second criterion for evaluating community-oriented policing is the efficiency of the police department. Because community-oriented policing entails a decentralization of the organizational structure and the utilization of police resources in a more efficient manner, the ability to gauge this efficiency should be a key method of gauging the success or failure of the systemic approach during the implementation process. The goal of becoming more efficient is closely related to exercising a greater use of the resources the police already have on hand and utilizing the relationship with the community to push for even greater efficiency by garnering community support and assistance.

 ## COP IN ACTION

The Forgotten Customer: Discovering Your Employees' Needs and Perceptions

Law enforcement agencies tend to define customers as members of or visitors to communities. An often overlooked customer, however, is the internal one—the employee. Agencies must seek input from their employees even as they must identify and respond to citizens' needs.

Why is it important to identify employees' needs? First, asking employees for their input demonstrates management's interest in and commitment to them. Second, insights and suggestions from employees—those who are responsible for carrying out agency policy—are valuable when instituting change. Employee assessments can also assist the agency in monitoring the impact of policy changes in the organization. Third, a systemic assessment of employee perspectives assists management in identifying areas that need attention before they become problems. Fourth, a well-designed employee assessment process, in which employee input is taken seriously, instills a sense of ownership in the employees. And finally, asking staff what they think demonstrates a practice they will be expected to use in the community—listening to the customer. The bottom line is that employees will be better able to meet citizens' needs if their own are being met.

The Larimer County Sheriff's Department (LCSD) partnered with the Colorado State University (CSU) Social Work Department and its Human Services Assessment Project (HASAP) to study LCSD's employees' needs and perceptions. This partnership provided the LCSD with experienced research professionals who guided the project and performed the data analysis. In turn, the CSU graduate students gained hands-on experience through implementing the project. The LCSD established several ground rules before beginning the assessment process—the most important being the commitment to keep all survey responses confidential. To obtain valid results, the department needed to receive honest answers, and to get honest answers, employees had to be assured that their confidentiality would be maintained.

The LCSD identified issues to address in the survey by listening to the concerns and ideas of employees and administrators, and by examining the issues facing Larimer's county government.

The issues identified were:

- Job satisfaction;
- Benefit issues;
- On-the-job stress;
- Promotion opportunities;
- Morale, teamwork, and trust;
- Satisfaction with physical working conditions and equipment;
- Administrative policies and supervision;
- Strengths and weaknesses of the department; and
- Establishing the sheriff's first priority.

The LCSD staff constructed questions from the issues identified and provided them to the CSU research class to develop a draft questionnaire. Once completed, the LCSD management team reviewed the draft questionnaire and made modification suggestions. The students revised the instrument and the new version was pretested by the LCSD staff and other law enforcement research professionals. The students used the pretest results to make final adjustments to the survey.

The final instrument was distributed to all of the LCSD's 244 employees. Each survey package included a prepaid envelope for returning the completed survey and was addressed to the Human Services Assessment Project. This process resulted in a response rate of 75.4 percent.

The HASAP staff coded the surveys and analyzed the data. The section of open-ended questions generated a lot of handwritten responses that required considerable time to analyze but produced valuable information. The surveys were administered in March 1996, and the final report was distributed in August.

The sheriff's office management team attended two forums during which the lead researchers presented the survey findings and interpreted the results. Afterward, Larimer County Sheriff Richard E. Shockley sent a letter to every employee along with a copy of the executive summary. Department managers received a full report to share with their staffs, and supervisors met with employees to discuss the findings.

The Larimer County Sheriff's Department benefited immeasurably from the survey findings. Management learned that employees were willing, when given the opportunity, to share their ideas, needs, and perceptions. They also learned that employees hold each other and their supervisors in high regard, and that respect and integrity are intrinsic department values. The findings also showed that most employees felt the department's facilities and equipment met their needs, and its policies and procedures were relevant and applicable.

Most important, though, were those findings that revealed a need for improvement. The department's salary and benefits package, although not listed on the survey, was the most frequently cited issue needing attention. Inadequate internal communication also surfaced as a major concern. A number of employees remarked that the department's off-site detention center inhibited communication between employees stationed there and those who worked at headquarters. The combination of the salary package, communication obstacles, and distance issues resulted in some employees not feeling valued or recognized.

The survey results were critical to management successfully negotiating a significant salary increase for LCSD employees with the Board of County Commissioners. The inadequate communication system and distance issues were resolved by giving every employee access to electronic mail. E-mail permits quick and efficient information dissemination to employees; it also enables employees to stay connected to one another. Additionally, the department began an internal newsletter as an informal way to share information among employees. Future plans include an Intranet Web page to make even more information available.

Management decided to reinforce employee value and recognition by holding quarterly employee recognition activities. The events center around introducing new employees, recognizing those who recently completed field training, and publicly distributing departmental awards. Fellow employees and families are encouraged to attend.

After completing the first Larimer County Sheriff's Department internal survey, Sheriff Shockley was asked about his impression of its benefits. Shockley responded, "Internal surveys offer an agency the opportunity to function in reality and remove the veil of perception. This affords the opportunity to gain legitimate answers."

Source: Adapted with permission from Drew Davis, "The Forgotten Customer: Discovering Your Employees' Needs and Perceptions," *Community Policing Exchange,* May/June 1997, p. 7.

It has largely been the case that the government agencies have not been the most efficient because of a number of factors. The police are essentially no different. James Q. Wilson (1989, 349) points out three key reasons for the inefficiency. The first is that "government executives are less able than their private counterparts to define an efficient course of action" (Wilson 1989, 350). The variety of goals found in policing have prevented the police department from concentrating on specific methods to work more efficiently, and the department has thus been allowed to ignore any defining course of action. A second problem has been that "public executives have weaker incentives than do private executives to find an efficient course of action" (Wilson 1989, 351). The police department has generally had little incentive to make the delivery of its police services more efficient in the past, and therefore little concern has been placed on this initiative. And, finally, "public executives have less authority than private ones to impose an efficient course of action" (Wilson 1989, 352). Police departments, from chiefs to the line officers, in the past had little authority to even attempt to make the delivery of police resources more efficient, and this has created a high degree of wasteful spending of resources, time, and money.

Under the systemic approach to policing, these three shortcomings will be addressed in a variety of ways. The police chief and management should not only be required to make the police department more efficient, but they should also have the authority to impose an efficient course of action, derived from community support. The incentives to make the police department a more efficient one under the systemic approach should be derived from the mission, values, and goals inherent within community-oriented policing. In addition, this efficiency can be obtained from the decentralization process by reducing the layers of bureaucracy and moving the authority further down the chain.

Efficiency is then closely tied with moving the responsibility of policing down to the individual police officer, forming closer ties with the community, obtaining their support, and, through the decentralization process, ridding the department of the bureaucracy that is inherent within any traditional police department (Eck and Rosenbaum 1994). If line police officers can implement methods that are more cost-effective, working smarter not harder, then valuable resources, time, and money can be saved. If close ties to the community can solicit the assistance of volunteers for those functions that were once relegated to the police officer or equipment and services can be obtained through a cooperative effort with the business community, again, valuable resources, time, and money can be saved. And if the layers of bureaucracy in a police department can be reduced, the police department can be more efficient in its delivery of services. Therefore, an assessment over time, as the incremental implementation of community-oriented policing takes place, can assist in the evaluation of the efficiency of the community-oriented police department.

A criterion that some believe has the greatest impact on community-oriented policing is equity (Bureau of Justice Assistance 1994a, 1994b; Guyot 1991). Equity is essentially the belief that all citizens should have a say in how they are governed and specifically in how they are policed. Equity is a central belief of the American people, held definitively in our Constitution, and police officers are sworn to enforce it. The delivery of services to the people must allow for equal access, it must provide equal treatment, and it must be distributed in a fair and nondiscriminatory manner.

The equal access to police services is an extremely important criterion for the implementation of community-oriented policing. Under traditional policing, police officers generally spend 90 percent of their time with 10 percent of the community, often ignoring the 90 percent of citizens who are law-abiding. The reasoning is usually that those citizens are not breaking the law, and therefore, their neighborhoods are not important. Under community-oriented policing, such a perspective must never be allowed. Neighborhoods with low crime rates have their own particular problems. Their crimes may not be as serious, but that does not negate their importance. They are as deserving of a police response to their problems as those citizens who live in high-crime areas. At the same time, certain homogeneous groups, such as recent immigrants who may speak little to no English, are often not provided equal police service because of language and cultural barriers. These groups are equally deserving of a police response and must be factored into the programs of community-oriented policing. Equity is largely the premise of the U.S. Constitution and the equal treatment under the law clause, which should be the foundation of any community-oriented policing program.

Therefore, the method of measuring equity under community-oriented policing is vastly different from any form of measurement under traditional approaches to policing. As Eck and Rosenbaum (1994, 12) state, "the most relevant measures are the perceptions of the various publics served by the police. . . . both the quantity and quality of police–citizen contacts are considered important measures of police performance under many community-policing programs." Through the use of interviews and surveys, the police will be able to gauge the equity of the police under community-oriented policing.

Another key criterion for assessing the success of community-oriented policing is the critical aspect of accountability (Guyot 1991). The police must be held accountable to the community rather than only being accountable to themselves. The key distinction revolving around accountability is that centralized control may be an easier method of managing and overseeing the police organization, but it removes the authority from the line officer who deals with the community on a daily basis. While community-oriented policing decentralizes the structure, hence giving the line officer more authority, it also decentralizes by personnel and geography, thus placing a particular officer in a particular neighborhood for a particular length of time. In turn, that officer becomes more accountable to the citizens of that neighborhood because they should recognize that officer as "their officer," and it allows management to hold that officer more accountable for what occurs on his or her beat. This system can also work with management, by placing mid-level managers in charge of specific geographical areas rather than specific times of the day, thus making them more accountable for what occurs in their geographical area.

The final criterion that must be the basis for evaluating community-oriented policing is authority. The authority of the police under traditional concepts has largely focused on the authority of the position of police officer or on a specialization such as Special Weapons and Tactics (SWAT) teams or homicide investigators. Authority then rested on one's position or specialization, enhanced or reduced through policy, procedures, rules, regulations, or directives on the part of management. The majority of policies generally limited the amount of authority, such as the restriction on the use of force, the use of deadly force, or the use of pursuit. Authority for policing was only created by the public through pressure on the local government and police department, and then it was driven again through these same procedures.

From left to right: Assistant Chief Brian Reuther, Councilwoman Maryann Cernuto, Police Chief C. L. "Chuck" Reynolds, Mayor Robert Minsky, and Councilwoman Paula Lewis of the city of Port St. Lucie inaugurating a neighborhood policing office in District II. *(Courtesy of Port St. Lucie Police Department, Port St. Lucie, Florida.)*

Under community-oriented policing, authority is derived from the community. Although some authority is still derived from traditional means, the customers of policing services must determine what authority they wish to delegate to their police officers. Community groups, problem-solving groups, and community-oriented policing coalitions in a particular community will become the authority-granting institution that determines what they will allow their police to do and not to do. For example, although they cannot override officers' authority to write speeding tickets, it is reasonable to protect the majority of citizens by enforcing speed zone regulations. However, the community can provide additional authority to the police by granting access to information and property that they may not have had otherwise, or the community members can remove the authority of the police if they disagree with methods employed by the police—say, under problem-solving techniques—by refusal or action. As community-oriented policing is implemented, the further along the systemic process moves toward institutionalization, the more authority the community will have and hence the more authority it will have over policing. To control policing, to make the police more effective and accountable, increased authority in the hands of the community through empowerment will be healthy for the sake of the community.

Recognizing these five key terms can assist police departments in determining how to evaluate their implementation of community-oriented policing. By utilizing the tenets of effectiveness, efficiency, equity, accountability, and authority when implementing the various programs under the systemic approach to policing, a variety of evaluation measurements can be developed for a clearer understanding of gauging success and failure. As the incremental implementation process continues, these assessments can assist both the police and the community in focusing on the goals and objectives of community-oriented policing and can help determine what changes must occur throughout the process.

 ## COP IN ACTION

Establishing a Baseline Begins with Research

The Washington State Institute for Community Oriented Policing (WSICOP) was founded to help law enforcement agencies in the Pacific Northwest develop a community policing focus based on the interests of citizens served by those agencies. WSICOP is composed of criminal justice faculty and graduate students from Washington State University–Spokane who work in collaboration with representatives from the Washington Training Commission and the Washington Association of Sheriffs and Chiefs of Police.

WSICOP's research experience suggests that social-scientific methods can help police organizations gather useful information for problem identification and problem solving. This is especially true for law enforcement agencies interested in measuring citizen satisfaction with police services, identifying the priorities that the public attaches to specific crimes, and measuring public support for new police-citizen initiatives.

Studies in Washington demonstrate that evaluation research can remove much of the guesswork about what the public wants and how much of their time and tax dollars they are willing to contribute. WSICOP typically finds that more than 50 percent (and as high as 72 percent) of a city's population is willing to attend police-related meetings or make phone calls on behalf of the police to improve the quality of their community.

What methods can police departments use to learn how to form police-citizen partnerships in their communities? Alpert and Moore (1993) recommend community-wide surveys and focus-group interviews as two key ways to assess citizen attitudes toward police services. Other methods, such as community forums (where all interested citizens are asked to attend a town meeting) and key informant interviews (which rely upon the opinions of a handful of community leaders), are less expensive than these two evaluation techniques and are better suited for gathering initial impressions than for actually setting community priorities (Thurman and Reisig, 1996).

Community-wide surveys (of a representative sample of residents) are a primary tool for establishing baseline measures of public opinion about police services and how citizens' attitudes change over time as police organizations modify old practices and implement new ones. Properly administered, surveys offer the most accurate portrayal of community sentiments toward the police and police programs, the fear of crime, and citizen willingness to participate in police-community partnerships. Furthermore, when combined with focus-group interviews, the analysis of citizen survey data can help police administrators pinpoint subgroups according to their personal characteristics or where they live in a city. In so doing, police agencies can learn which groups are most fearful of crime, most critical or supportive of police practices, and most likely to respond to specific community policing initiatives.

Focus-group interviews with representative members of a specific subgroup such as high school students, business owners, minority residents, police employees, and so on are particularly useful for understanding special interest concerns in a community. Focus-group techniques also allow researchers to collect richer data on particular issues by asking citizens probing questions in a small-group setting.

Subgroups such as businesses or schools are usually selected for focus groups because they receive more intensive police services. Subgroups that have relatively high risk of criminal victimization, such as individuals who are poor, elderly, or living in a high crime area and those who have been targeted to receive special community policing services, are also good choices. Finally, a subgroup may be selected because it has historically suffered from a poor relationship with law enforcement agencies—such as youths, students, and minorities.

Larger police agencies that have their own research staff may be well equipped to take on the additional responsibility of systemically collecting citizen data at appropriate intervals of time. However, for most agencies, conducting evaluative research requires more time and staff than are available. Chiefs and sheriffs might want to ask criminal justice departments at nearby universities and colleges for help with these types of evaluations.

Source: Adapted with permission from Quint C. Thurman, "Establishing a Baseline Begins with Research," *Community Policing Exchange,* May/June 1996, pp. 2–6.

EVALUATION RESEARCH

To accurately assess the success and failure of various applications of community-oriented policing, it is important that the police department conduct evaluation research. The evaluation research should not be limited to a particular time of studying, such as during micro-community-oriented policing, but should be utilized at all stages of implementation. It should also attempt to incorporate not only evaluation of various programs themselves but also evaluation of police and community response to these programs (Policing Research Institute 1997). Because the majority of community-oriented policing action will come in the form of programs, the purpose of the research should fall under the broad category of program evaluation.

Program evaluation is not necessarily a type of research but instead is a focus on the purpose of certain research. As programs such as foot patrols or community substations are implemented, it is important to assess how well these programs have been implemented and the impact they have had on their intended target. Program evaluations are therefore focused on answering two questions: (1) Are policies being implemented as planned? and (2) Are policies achieving their intended goals? (see Maxfield and Babbie 1995, 304). To answer these two questions, there are two types of corresponding program evaluations: process evaluation and impact assessment (Maxfield and Babbie 1995). Process evaluation is a method that seeks to determine whether the original policy was implemented in accordance with the original plan. In the case of community-oriented policing, this may consist of the strategic plan or a plan of action determined by the community to address a local problem. The focus of the study is generally on program outputs and the methods utilized in the implementation. If the police and community have implemented a plan of foot patrols to reduce the prevalence of drug dealing in their neighborhood, the process evaluation will focus on the number of officer-hours on foot patrol in that area as well as what the officers spend the majority of their time doing during these foot patrols. If officers spend the majority of their time interacting with the community and dealing with the problem, the process evaluation would state that the plan was implemented accordingly. If the number of hours on foot patrol has not increased or the officers' time is not spent communicating with the community and addressing the problem, the process evaluation would conclude that the implementation of the plan was poor.

Impact assessment is a program evaluation method that seeks to determine if the program implemented has had any impact on its intended target. If the program had a well-developed plan and was implemented accordingly, then the researchers have the

"Community–Neighborhood Improvement through Community Policing" is a quarterly newsletter, published by volunteer Al Forman, that provides feedback to the community on such things as community-oriented policing evaluations. (*Courtesy of the Port St. Lucie Police Department, Port St. Lucie, Florida.*)

capability of determining what impact this action had on the intended target. In the case of the foot patrols in a high-drug area, the impact assessment may look at the reduction of drug dealers and drug arrests in the area, the impact on overall crime rates, or simply the community's perception of the effectiveness of the foot patrols.

The program evaluation methods of process evaluation and impact assessment are complementary to the systemic approach and should be utilized as the two key areas of evaluation research. However, to focus on these two areas and utilize the various methods of evaluation available, it is important to recognize many of the questions that must first be answered. The first question that must be answered is, "What is going to be studied?" The difficulty of this question is revealed in the definition of community-oriented policing. If one were to attempt to evaluate community-oriented policing, one would first have to ask how one would operationalize the overall concept of strategic-oriented policing, neighborhood-oriented policing, problem-oriented policing, and decentralization into a workable form. The same would be true if the police department were to focus on its mission statement or values and goals under community-oriented policing. The problem is that "Community policing expressed merely as a nice idea simply cannot be evaluated" (Hornick, Leighton, and Burrows 1993, 62). Therefore, in the same manner that community-oriented policing must be operationalized into various programs, so, too, must it be evaluated in this manner. Therefore, the question of what is to be evaluated must be answered with a specific program. For instance, one program evaluation has focused on a specific domestic violence program in Portland, Oregon, to assess its success under the community-oriented policing framework (Jolin and Moose 1997).

One alternative to evaluating a specific program is to evaluate the perceptions of the police and the community. Although this evaluation may be conducted as part of reviewing a specific program, such as the foot patrol scenario, it can also be conducted independently to determine the overall view of the public and the police. Evaluating the perceptions of the police can be beneficial to understanding what they like and do not like about the concept and, more importantly, what they support and what they do not support. It can also be a yardstick for how their perceptions change over time as the concept is implemented to see what additional needs the officers may have. In the case of evaluating the perceptions of the community, it only makes sense to evaluate how the customer feels about the "product." Determining how the community feels about the systemic approach can provide feedback to the police department as to where it is, where it needs to go, and how it can get to the point of truly being integrated with the community.

The second question that must be answered is "Who is going to conduct the study". This question, as a result of the community-oriented policing philosophy, can be answered in multiple ways. If the police department is fortunate enough to have a researcher or research unit on staff, the answer may be readily apparent. If the police department does not have this asset, it may find that it has the untapped asset already existing somewhere in the police department. Police officers who enter the field with college degrees or obtain them while working for the police department may have the capability to conduct evaluation research. This skill can be beneficial both to the department, because of cost, and to the officers, because it maximizes their abilities. However, it can also be nonbeneficial because the officers would not be true noninterested third parties. These considerations must be weighed before selecting someone internally.

If the department chooses to find someone outside the police department, it may always hire a researcher, but this can become costly. If the police have established strong community ties, they may find someone in their own community who is capable of conducting such research for free or who may be able to obtain a grant to conduct such studies. If there is a nearby university or college, the department may be able to obtain the assistance of both college professors and students to perform the study. In any case, utilizing the resources available within the department and community is a primary focus of the community-oriented approach to policing.

Once the police department has determined what will be studied and who will conduct the study, the next things the researcher or researchers must carefully review are the definition and goals of the program, as well as the outcomes desired from its implementation. Every aspect of the process must be defined and the goals predetermined; although it is impossible to predict what will happen after the implementation of the program, the desired outcomes of the program should be clarified. In the foot patrol scenario, the researchers must define what is meant by *foot patrol* so the focus of their study is on this particular variable. Is foot patrol interpreted as officers getting out of their patrol vehicles on occasion and walking the neighborhood, or is it the specific placement of two officers walking a specific geographical area for a specific number of hours? Once these operationalization questions are answered, the focus becomes the desired outcome. Is the desired impact of the foot patrols to reduce crime, reduce public fear, show a visible presence, or all of these?

Once the program, goals, and specific outcomes are defined, the key to program evaluation then comes into play. The researchers must determine whether the focus of the program evaluation will be on the process or impact of a program and specifically how these goals will be measured. If the focus is on evaluating the process, then the methods utilized to implement the program and whether it was implemented as planned become the key goals. These goals may consist of determining the number and types of problems identified for resolution, how many programs are proposed under neighborhood-oriented policing versus how many are actually implemented, the level of community participation, the number of community participants, changes in the number of calls for service, or changes in the type of calls for service. If the focus is on evaluating the impact of the program, then what the specific outcomes were will become the key goals to be analyzed. These goals may consist of reducing crime rates due to strategic-oriented policing tactics, citizen satisfaction with police services, job satisfaction on the part of the police, level of fear on the part of the citizens, or the reduction of specific crimes or neighborhood problems.

Once the type of program evaluation and the specific goals are determined, how the goals will be measured becomes an important aspect of the evaluation process (see Policing Research Institute 1997). The goals must be transformed into specific variables that can be measured to determine whether a program is considered a success or failure. In the case of the foot patrols in a high-crime area, if the goal is to reduce public fear, then this goal must be operationalized to determine what fear is and how it will be measured. Because fear is largely a perception on the part of the community rather than any fact-based data gathering, a method must be employed to assess the public's perception. This issue could be operationalized by simply asking community members what their level of fear is or by observing the amount and type of foot traffic in a community after dark to determine if people are more willing to walk alone at night or even come out at all. The way that the researcher attempts to operationalize the goals to be studied generally determines the methods that will be utilized in the study. However, prior to discussing the actual methods used, two other concerns must be addressed.

The first concern is the other variables that may influence or control the outcome. Although the program may be implemented and the specific outcomes previously identified achieved, it is possible that the outcomes were not a result of the program being implemented but another variable. Therefore, it is important that the researchers spend some time considering other variables that may alter the outcomes. As previously discussed, the program may be the independent variable and the outcomes the dependent variable, but another variable that was introduced may actually have produced the desired outcomes. In the foot patrol example, if the public's fear of crime was the gauge and it was operationalized by the number of neighborhood residents outside during a specific time in the evening, the program may be implemented and the number of residents outside may increase, but it may not be a result of the foot patrols. A possible intervening variable may be daylight saving time, which allows for more light during the specified evening hours, hence causing public fear during this time period to decrease. Although foot patrols were implemented and public fear was reduced, the foot patrols were not the cause. Therefore, it is important to consider all of the possible variables that may influence the evaluation to more accurately determine the effect of the program itself.

The second concern that must be addressed once the operationalization of the goals has been determined consists of analyzing both the population and the sample size to be utilized in the evaluation. The population in the evaluation consists of the total collection of individuals who could be part of the study. In most cases, it is very difficult, time-consuming, and expensive to study and evaluate each individual; therefore, a group of individuals must be selected to represent the entire population, and this is known as a sample. The most common method utilized is a random sample, in which a certain number of individuals will be selected and every individual in the population has an equal chance of being selected. If police officers wish to survey a neighborhood's perceptions of community-oriented policing but there are more than 20,000 residences in that neighborhood, they may obtain all of the addresses through the local government or through local utility services, randomly select 200 of these residences, and send the survey to these randomly selected residences. The survey findings will then be representative of the larger population.

Once all of these steps, from determining what is to be evaluated to determining the population and sample of the study, have been predetermined, then the actual evaluation methods must be selected. Program evaluation under community-oriented policing has generally focused on the use of surveys, but sometimes case studies or multiple variables have also been utilized. The latter have been used when researchers have analyzed specific programs as well as when they have evaluated both the police and the community. In the following section, we review the types of methods employed and explore some recent studies conducted on community-oriented policing programs and police and community perceptions of the systemic approach.

CRIME STATISTICS DON'T TELL THE WHOLE STORY

In cities and towns across America, law enforcement agencies continue to develop innovative policing strategies under the umbrella of community policing. Stressing greater accountability to the community, these programs emphasize the need for a cooperative relationship between law enforcement and the community to address the variety of problems associated with crime and the fear of crime.

Unfortunately, when it comes to program evaluation, most agencies are still using very traditional performance measures to assess what is a nontraditional form of policing. Far too many law enforcement agencies rely on traditional indicators generated solely within the agencies—number of arrests, changes in the number of calls for service, number of incident reports filed—as the only measures for gauging effectiveness. While these are important indicators, they have seldom been sufficient to understand the extent and character of a particular program's impact.

Information beyond Traditional Crime Statistics

If municipalities are to establish more effective approaches to evaluate community policing, it becomes incumbent on them to incorporate community-wide information in the process. Especially important to this process is the use of data collected and maintained by public and private agencies other than law enforcement organizations as well as data from community surveys. Combined with traditional performance measures, this data can provide invaluable insights into the effectiveness of various community policing initiatives. A few examples of these potentially valuable information resources are described here.

Health Care System Data

Data from community health care agencies, particularly data from hospital emergency rooms, may offer significant alternative indicators of community policing's impact. Communities targeting family violence, for example, may find that data on emergency room visits can be a valuable alternative source of information on the extent of abuse in the community. While confidentiality issues may prevent the release of individual identifiers, aggregate statistics can provide an additional dimension for determining the impact of family violence programs. For example, the number of abused women referred by medical personnel to shelters may be a more reliable indicator of a community's level of family violence than the number of domestic violence arrests.

School-Based Data

A second source of alternative information is the community's public schools. Many cases of street violence begin in the schools and become fatal on the streets. School data on truancy, suspensions, and expulsions can serve as an early warning system for youth-related problems. For example, the number of students suspended from school for possession of drugs or alcohol may serve as an additional indicator of the level of substance abuse among youths in a particular community. Schools may also provide measures of program impact sometimes not anticipated initially. In Los Angeles, a gang-suppression program that sought to displace gang activity from a specific neighborhood resulted in increased attendance at a school in the same neighborhood because schoolchildren no longer had to pass gang members to get to school. These unanticipated consequences of public safety programs can only be documented if we look outside normal police statistics to find additional measures of a program's impact.

Housing and Licensing Data

Local public housing authorities are another alternative information source. These authorities often maintain a database of complaints that are investigated internally. This data can be used to identify particular acts of violence that do not come to the attention of local police. In Boston, for example, a review of complaints from the housing authority revealed a set of alleged hate crimes whose victims were too afraid to report them to police.

Similarly, local licensing data may include alternative measures of the quality of life in a community, such as complaints by residents about noise from a particular business establishment or underage drinking at a local bar or tavern. Measures such as median home prices in a neighborhood can also be used as indicators of community vitality. Monitoring the number of available business properties or apartments in a neighborhood can likewise provide an indication of overall community health.

Community Surveys

In addition to traditional arrest and incident data, many law enforcement agencies are beginning to collect additional data directly from the community residents, often in the form of community surveys or customer satisfaction surveys. Community surveys can be most effective because they reach the broadest range of individuals impacted by specific police programs. In addition, the survey can directly ask local community members about the program's impact on them and their families. The downside of citizen surveys is the cost. However, some communities have established a permanent funding line to assess the overall level of satisfaction with governmental services on a regular basis.

A second source of direct community feedback comes from customer satisfaction surveys. In most cases, these surveys involve mailing postcards to a sample of those receiving police assistance in an attempt to measure the satisfaction with the service received. This method, generally much less expensive than citizen surveys, can be expanded to include additional questions about residents' impression of a particular crime problem in their neighborhood. Additionally, the sample could be easily expanded from those who have called the police to those who live in a particular neighborhood where a police operation is being implemented, thus providing input from the very people most directly affected.

How helpful this data can be depends on the level of aggregation. Community-wide data is much less useful than data that can be grouped or aggregated more locally, by neighborhood where possible. With the development of easier-to-use mapping software and more accurate geo-coding programs, more data is available at lower levels of aggregation. In Boston, we have worked with the information sources mentioned above at disaggregated levels that correspond to the city's neighborhoods. This neighborhood-level analysis, drawing from multiple sources of information, provides a much richer and more complete picture of a program's impact.

As many law enforcement agencies move to establish community policing initiatives involving multiple partnerships, their program evaluation tools must keep pace. And program evaluation that more closely corresponds to the broadened community-based view of policing will give you the broadest view of community policing success.

Source: Reprinted with permission from Jack McDevitt and Albert P. Cardarelli, "Crime Statistics Don't Tell the Whole Story," *Community Policing Exchange,* November/December 1999.

METHODS

The primary methods of evaluating the police have been through the use of surveys. Surveying is a relatively easy method for gathering data from the police and community and has proven to be less time-consuming and expensive than other methods. Surveys gather information about the public's attitude toward the police and neighborhood problems, and they can be used to detect and analyze problems in neighborhoods or among special population groups, to evaluate problem-solving efforts and other programs, to control crime and reduce fear of crime (Bureau of Justice Assistance 1993), to assess the police attitude toward the public and neighborhood problems, and to gauge the physical environment.

To understand specifically how surveys can be utilized, it is important to discuss the three types of questions they can answer. Surveys generally assess attitudes and opinions, behavior and experience, and characteristics (Bureau of Justice Assistance 1993). The surveys that attempt to address attitudes and opinions are surveys that seek information on the mental state of individuals by asking about their feelings on a number of things, which may include police performance, fear of crime, future plans and intentions, concerns about specific problems, and possible suggestions for police actions. When gauging behavior and experience, these surveys gather data to determine those things that people have been exposed to in their neighborhoods. Examples may include certain behaviors they have seen or exhibited or, most likely, experiences they have had as victims of crime, with the police, with a specific problem, or as part of a specific program. The final question that may be answered through surveys consists of the characteristics of various groups of people found in a particular neighborhood or community. These characteristics may consist of the lifestyles of individuals, the personal history of offenders, the backgrounds of crime victims, or just simple census information that reveals various social factors.

To answer the questions focusing on the three areas of attitudes and opinions, behavior and experience, or characteristics, three types of basic survey data collection methods can be utilized. These survey methods include mail surveys, telephone surveys, and personal interview surveys. The easiest method of data collection is the delivery of a survey through the mail. It is less time-consuming and expensive than the other two methods, and it is a method of reaching large samples. However, on many occasions people do not return the surveys, which can prove frustrating. Many police departments utilize this method with great success to assess all three of the earlier questions, but some have reported low response rates and have had to implement multiple follow-up survey mailings.

Telephone surveys are a good method for increasing the lack of response to mail surveys, but they can become more expensive because they generally take more time from repeated callbacks and time on the phone to proceed through the questions. However, there are benefits because individuals are more willing to answer questions because of the interpersonal effect. Respondents can also ask for clarification of questions, and such barriers as illiteracy and not speaking the language can be overcome on the phone. Very few police departments themselves have utilized this method; however, external researchers for the community-oriented policing programs have used this method with much success.

The final method of surveying is personal interviews. This method has the highest response rate because the interview is much more personable; however, it is the most time-consuming of the three methods. Many police departments (such as those in Baltimore, Maryland; Newport News, Virginia; Tampa, Florida; and Philadelphia, Pennsylvania), have utilized police officers to conduct these interviews with positive results. In some jurisdictions (such as Tulsa, Oklahoma; Atlanta, Georgia; and Portland, Oregon), the use of nonsworn employees has been very successful, as has the use of volunteers in police departments such as that in San Diego, California. One important aspect of utilizing uniformed police to conduct interviews has been that it provides the individuals being interviewed a chance to address their concerns and speak one-on-one with a police officer. This method has been found to reduce citizen fear and create or enhance a positive attitude toward the police (Pate 1986, 1989; Pate et al. 1986; Uchida, Forst, and Annan 1992). This is a good example of how, even in the use of an evaluation method, largely unintended positive results can be achieved.

Officer K. Gunn passes out coloring books during an open house sponsored by the Montgomery County Police Department. *(Courtesy of Montgomery County Department of Police, Montgomery County, Maryland.)*

Surveys

Surveys have effectively and efficiently been employed in numerous ways to assess both community-oriented policing programs and police and community perceptions of the systemic approach (see Thurman and Reisig 1996). One example of the use of surveys on a community-oriented policing program was in Delray, Florida, where the program commenced in the fall of 1990. The police department utilized a pretest/posttest survey design and showed that despite little to no change in public fear, police–community interactions increased, officer performance increased significantly, and the author concluded "that there has been a rather substantial change in the community behavior and attitudes, and in how the community functions as a result of the community policing program" (Wiatrowski 1995, 69).

The analysis of foot patrol programs, under the concept of community-oriented policing, has relied heavily on the use of surveys for its evaluation methods, which can reveal valuable information about this kind of program under the systemic approach. The results of these studies generally show that citizens recognize the increase of foot patrols in their neighborhood, and, additionally, they distinctly notice the absence of foot patrols when they are removed from the neighborhood (Greene and Taylor 1988; Pate 1989). In some cases, foot patrol programs are reported to increase citizen satisfaction (Brown and Wycoff 1987; Oettmeier and Brown 1988; Williams and Pate 1987; Wycoff

1988), whereas in others no change occurs (Esbenson 1987; Pate 1989). Additionally, fear of crime (Brown and Wycoff 1987; Cordner 1994; Greene and Taylor 1988; Pate 1989; Williams and Pate 1987), effect on order maintenance (Cordner 1994; Greene and Taylor 1988; Pate 1989), effect on calls for service (Bowers and Hirsch 1987; McElroy, Cosgrove, and Sadd 1993; Pate 1989), and effect on reported crime (Bowers and Hirsch 1987; McElroy, Cosgrove, and Sadd 1993; Pate 1989; Wilson 1975) have all been found to have either mixed results or results so statistically insignificant as to not be an indicator, either positive or negative. One additional foot patrol study utilizing a pre- and post-survey design, conducted from January 1991 to January 1992 in a public housing area, found that the supplementary foot patrol program "succeeded in achieving greater police visibility in the public housing site, increased positive police contacts . . . and calls for service in the area declined during the project year, and crime victimization, as measured by global survey items, decreased" (Cordner and Jones 1995, 189). However, it is important to note that the study also found that fear of crime increased over the one-year study and that community attitudes toward the police showed both favorable and unfavorable results (Cordner and Jones 1995).

The findings through program evaluation in regards to a variety of programs implemented under community-oriented policing have shown very mixed results. In some cases, the level of fear was reduced, but satisfaction with police did not go up. In other cases, crime rates, local problems, and calls for service dropped, but citizen fear increased. Although these findings may not sound very promising to the future of the systemic approach, these studies reveal something that should be central to program evaluations, the truth. If the studies do not reveal honest attitudes and opinion, behavior and experiences, or characteristics, then the police do not know and will have no way of knowing what programs need to be altered, enhanced, or abolished. It is only with legitimate, reliable, and valid results through evaluation research that the police and community can address the success or failure of their programs.

The use of surveys to assess police officers' attitudes is also common among community-oriented police departments. Generally these departments utilize a one-time survey to assess police officers' attitudes at a certain point in the implementation process of community-oriented policing. It is important to note that a one-time survey is merely an assessment of perception at the time of the survey and cannot be utilized for broad interpretation. One study on officer perceptions of Chicago's community policing program, known as CAPS, was conducted in 1993 and found "that police officers in Chicago are neither unanimously in favor of community policing nor are they equally disposed toward all elements of such programs" (Lurigio and Skogan 1994, 315). However, as a one-time study, it was conducted prior to the implementation of the program by surveying officers at the beginning of the orientation sessions with no follow-up (Lurigio and Skogan 1994). Therefore, this survey cannot be used to assess officers' attitudes of community-oriented policing after their exposure to the program, only prior to its implementation.

Another one-time survey evaluated two cities and looked at police officers' acceptance of community-oriented policing in Cleveland, Ohio, where a ministation program was started in 1984, and in Cincinnati, Ohio, where community-oriented policing was started in 1991 with thirty-one officers assigned to eleven neighborhoods (Kratcoski and Noonan 1995, 182). The study found that officers in both cities "considered community policing in a positive light." However, some misunderstanding existed on the role of the community-oriented policing programs by other rank-and-file officers who generally were not exposed to the program or educated on what the program entailed. This one-time survey was conducted shortly after the implementation process began and therefore can only be used to assess officers' attitudes, opinions, and concerns at that time.

A more accurate method of determining police officers' perceptions of community-oriented policing is through the use of surveys either in a pretest/posttest design or by surveying multiple times throughout the implementation process to avoid just taking a snapshot of attitudes and instead actually gauging changing perceptions over time. One study conducted in Joliet, Illinois, examined a community policing demonstration project started in 1991. A two-year study of police personnel was conducted to gauge such things as job satisfaction, attitudes toward community policing, and degree management was successful at implementing change (Rosenbaum, Yeh, and Wilkinson 1994). The study involved one pretest prior to implementation, one test conducted ten months after implementation, and one posttest twenty-two months after implementation (Rosenbaum, Yeh, and Wilkinson 1994). Officers involved in the program reported "the most favorable changes in attitudes about community policing, perceived skillfulness in problem solving, and relevant street-level behavior," whereas officers not participating in the program reported "change in areas related to the characteristics of their jobs, especially changes in the nature of their work . . . and their level of job satisfaction" (Rosenbaum, Yeh, and Wilkinson 1994, 349). However, the authors point out that at the end of the two-year study, "the fact remains that the absence of change was the norm rather than the exception" (Rosenbaum, Yeh, and Wilkinson 1994, 349).

These mixed results in studying officers' attitudes seem rather consistent both in the literature (Wilson and Bennett 1994) and when looking at the effect management style has on the officers (Wycoff and Skogan 1994). However, when tracking these studies over time, police attitudes and opinions toward community-oriented policing are generally very negative before any exposure to the program, mixed during the initial phases of the implementation process, and extremely positive once the program is in full implementation. Therefore, one key lesson that can be drawn is that it pays to educate all officers in a police department and solicit their input prior to implementation.

One additional area where surveys have been utilized is in gauging public attitudes and opinions of community-oriented policing (see Thurman and Reisig 1996). A review of the literature by Lurigio and Rosenbaum looked to citizens' perspective in evaluating the success of community-oriented policing through the use of surveys. In their conclusions, from the community's perspective, "officers engaging in community policing are rated as more visible, helpful, polite, and effective on a variety of job activities" (Lurigio and Rosenbaum 1994, 160). Surveys of communities after community-oriented policing has been implemented have revealed generally very consistent findings. If community-oriented policing was actually implemented as a program and not merely in name only, public attitudes and opinions, as well as experiences with the systemic approach, were largely positive.

The use of interviews has also been widely utilized as a survey method to assess the capabilities of the programs under community-oriented policing, as well as police and community perceptions. This methodology is generally utilized in concert with written forms of surveys to provide a stronger method of evaluation (see Thurman and Reisig 1996). Two studies of community-oriented policing that have produced an enormous amount of research in this field are the Newark, New Jersey, and Houston, Texas, projects

(Brown and Wycoff 1987; Oettmeier and Brown 1988; Pate 1986; Pate et al. 1986; Williams and Pate 1987; Wycoff 1988). Both surveys and interviews found that the most successful programs were those that involved direct contact between the police and the community (Brown and Wycoff 1987). A problem-oriented policing study was conducted in Baltimore County, Maryland, under the police department's Citizen-Oriented Police Enforcement (COPE) program, which also utilized both surveys and interviews and found it useful not only for the evaluation of the program but as an "integral part of the COPE strategy" (Cordner 1988a, 222–223). The evaluation of the COPE program was found to be "at least moderately successful at reducing fear, satisfying citizens, and solving neighborhood problems, and may even succeed at displacing or deterring certain crimes" (Cordner 1988b, 151; see also Cordner 1988a). The evaluation methods of surveys and interviews to address attitudes, opinions, behavior's, experiences, and characteristics have been extremely valuable to community-oriented policing. As articulated previously, even the evaluation methods of the programs have some usefulness in reducing fear of crime and improving the relations between the police and community because they open up the lines of communication.

In the evaluation of police officers' and community members' attitudes and opinions toward the systemic approach, again surveys and interviews have also proven to be valuable tools. In one such study, the authors looked to a cross-site analysis in which community-oriented policing was implemented in six cities (Baltimore, Maryland; Oakland, California; Birmingham, Alabama; Madison, Wisconsin; Houston, Texas; and Newark, New Jersey), while other cities were designated as control cities in which no community-oriented policing programs were implemented (Skogan 1994). Through the use of surveys and interviews in a pretest/posttest study design, with a ten-month time lapse, the evaluation revealed mixed results, although fear of crime generally decreased and police service was considered to be increased overall (Skogan 1994). Additionally, one study gauging citizens' responses to community-oriented policing utilized both surveys and interviews and was conducted in Cleveland, Ohio, which has utilized the police ministation program as a vehicle for implementing community-oriented policing. Through a survey mailing, with follow-up interviews, researchers found "a great deal of support for the program, considerable satisfaction with the performance of the officers, and a desire to have the program expanded" (Kratcoski, Dukes, and Gustavson 1995, 210). In general, both the police and the community have favorable responses to community-oriented policing that tend to increase over the lives of the programs.

Case Studies

One other research method that has been utilized to evaluate community-oriented policing programs, as well as police officer and citizen attitudes toward the systemic approach, has been the case study. Case studies are a method of research evaluation that tracks the implementation of a program and the response of people over time by recording the events as they occur and looking for common denominators and indicators of a program's success or failure or, in the case of people's perceptions, favorable or unfavorable attitudes. In one analysis of a problem-oriented policing program implemented in San Diego, California, which utilized Eck and Spelman's SARA model, they tracked sixteen problem-oriented policing cases over a six-month period (Capowich and Roehl 1994). The study found that 69 percent of the cases (eleven out of sixteen) were deemed successful.

The case study format has also been utilized in evaluating police officers' perceptions of community-oriented policing as a policing strategy. One such case study attempted to determine whether community-oriented policing was "here to stay" or "on the way out" and was conducted in the following six cities: Santa Barbara, California; Las Vegas, Nevada; Savannah, Georgia; Newport News, Virginia; Edmonton, Canada; and Philadelphia, Pennsylvania (Weisel and Eck 1994, see also Police Executive Research Forum, 1996). The overall findings of the study, controlling for years of service, educational level, race, and sex, were that the majority of officers believed community-oriented policing was "here to stay" (Weisel and Eck 1994). The advantages of case studies such as these are that they provide much more information than a survey or interview and they are qualitative in nature. According to Scott, Duffee, and Renauer (2003), the case study is also a good tool for measuring police–community coproduction or, rather, the outcome of police–community partnerships. A disadvantage of this type of research is often inconsistent findings due to a variety of perceptions on the part of the researchers.

 # COP IN ACTION

Requirements for Successful Experimentation

First, if experimentation is to be successful in a criminal justice agency, it must be the result of sincere collaboration between agency personnel and researchers. The conception, implementation, and conduct of an experiment is, most often, a time-consuming set of activities that departs from the routine business of an agency. Unless agency personnel are deeply committed to knowing what works, and aware that answering questions requires considerable effort on their behalf, experiments will collapse under the pressures of business as usual.

Second, subjects or areas involved in an experiment should be selected randomly. Random selection eliminates biases in the selection of samples of subjects or areas that may distort the findings of the experiment.

Third, the experimental group that receives the treatment should be compared with a randomly selected control group, which does not receive the treatment. By comparing differences between the two groups at the end of the experimental period, researchers will be able to determine the effects of the treatment.

Fourth, relevant data testing the effect of the treatment should be collected immediately before the initiation of the experiment and immediately after its termination in the experimental and control groups. Collection of data in this way allows for comparison both within the groups and between the groups. Moreover, in social experiments it is generally required that careful observation be made of the program's operation over time. It is often the case that experimental programs either function differently than expected or less efficiently. Under such circumstances the meaning of differences, or lack of them, between experimental and control group may result from improper implementation of the new program rather than from the effects of the experiment.

Finally, evaluators should be independent of program managers. Program managers, often deeply committed to the success of programs, can unintentionally destroy the integrity of experiments. Moreover, the credibility of experiments is enhanced when evaluators are independent of program operations.

Police tactics are being revised on the basis of systemically asking and answering the question "What works?" Police are not alone in this. Experimentation is being used throughout the criminal justice system to improve the quality of criminal justice practice. It is a sign of the growing professionalization of the field.

Source: George L. Kelling, "What Works—Research and the Police." *National Institute of Justice: Crime File Study Guide.* Washington, D.C.: National Institute of Justice, 1988.

Various Other Methods

Expanding beyond the use of surveys and case studies, many studies will utilize other methodologies, as well as multiple methodologies, to verify their findings. One community-oriented policing program known as Operation Cul-De-Sac under a Total Community Policing model in the Los Angeles area, which utilized barriers to create geographic communities, derived its findings from "a variety of official and unofficial data sources (i.e., Part I crime data), CRASH Unit (Community Resources Against Street Hoodlums) gang intelligence information, community surveys, and police officer interviews" (Lasley, Vernon, and Dery 1995, 57). The study found "that imposed community boundaries can serve as a vital point of reference for effective police-community partnerships and the re-generation of lasting informal social control networks" (Lasley, Vernon, and Dery 1995, 67). Another community-oriented policing project known as "Community Opportunities Program for Youth (COPY Kids) was an attempt to reach out to local youths at risk of abusing alcohol or illegal drugs or of joining a criminal gang" in Spokane, Washington, during the summer of 1992 (Thurman, Giacomazzi, and Bogen 1993, 554). The kids performed community work, visited various businesses, and spoke with the police officers on a variety of subjects. Through the use of direct observation, group interviews, and survey research, the study concluded that "program recipients . . . benefited from the community service they performed," that "COPY Kids was held in high regards by the parents or guardians of participating youth," and that "positive effects on COPY kids staff also were noted" (Thurman, Giacomazzi, and Bogen 1993, 561).

In the evaluation of two additional cities, Aurora, Illinois, and Joliet, Illinois, "several field methods were employed, including in-person interviews with key participants, focus group interviews, observations, and a comprehensive review of documents" (Wilkinson and Rosenbaum 1994, 115). The study concluded that a bureaucratic police department will have a difficult time with the implementation process, that it is important to emphasize a department-wide implementation, that participatory management can be successful, that the organization's commitment to bureaucracy is inversely related to the speed of implementing community-oriented policing, and that although there is no right or wrong way to implement community-oriented policing, a change in the style of management and decentralization must occur (Wilkinson and Rosenbaum 1994). (See also Table 11-1.)

Finally, two community-oriented policing programs have received in-depth and extensive analysis by researchers who have utilized nearly all of the possible methods for conducting research. Skogan and Hartnett (1997) conducted a detailed and elaborate analysis of the community-oriented policing program in Chicago, which goes by the acronym CAPS (Chicago Alternative Policing Strategy) and began on April 29, 1993. What is most interesting about their evaluation is that they began their research in December 1992, before the implementation of the CAPS approach, thus allowing them to

TABLE 11-1   *Evaluating the Police*

GOALS	PERFORMANCE INDICATORS
Doing justice, or "treating citizens in an appropriate manner based on their conduct"	Nature and type of patrolling strategy, number of traffic tickets issued, crimes cleared, analysis of who calls the police, quality of investigations, cases released because of police misconduct, citizen complaints, lawsuits filed, and results of dispositions and officer-initiated encounters
Promoting secure communities, or "enabling citizens to enjoy a life without fear of crime or victimization"	Existence of programs and resources allocated to crime prevention programs, time and money dedicated to problem solving, rewards, monitoring of police, degree of public trust in the police, fear of crime, and home and business security checks by the police
Restoring crime victims, by "restoring victims' lives and welfare as much as possible"	Number of contacts with victims after initial call for assistance and types of assistance provided to victims, including information, comfort, transportation, and referrals to other agencies
Promoting noncriminal options, by "developing strong relationships with individuals in the community"	Existence of programs and resources allocated to strengthening relationships between the police and the community, including traditional community relations programs, school programs, storefront operations, and officer contact with citizens

Source: Geoffrey Alpert and Mark H. Moore, "Measuring Police Performance in the New Paradigm of Policing." In *Performance Measures for the Criminal Justice System: Discussion Papers from the BJS-Princeton Project,* ed. John J. Diluilo, Jr., et al. (Washington, D.C.: Bureau of Justice Statistics, October 1993).

track Chicago's change to community-oriented policing from the very beginning. In addition, it is a very good example of research combining both process and outcome evaluations because the researchers managed to conduct both. Their findings also highlight the fundamental reason for Chicago moving to community-oriented policing: politics. This fact has also been highlighted in two other publications that have focused on the politics of community-oriented policing in Seattle, Washington, through a combination of various methodologies that produced two in-depth studies on the systemic approach (see Lyons 1999; Reed 1999).

Finally, another methodology that has recently seen usage in the study of community-oriented policing is systemic social observation (SSO). Researcher Reiss studies the police using SSO, which is a systemic field method for teams of researchers who observe the object of study, such as the police, in its natural setting (Mastrofski et al. 1998). Researchers record events as they see and hear them and do not rely on others to describe or interpret events. The researchers follow well-specified procedures that can be duplicated. This approach makes it possible for many researchers to conduct observations rather than relying on the observation of just one. Furthermore, the observation is conducted independent of the object of observation. The researcher does not rely on the officer's report about whether he or she treated a complainant with respect; the researcher makes that observation and judgment (Mastrofski et al. 1998). This method has recently been employed in Indianapolis, Indiana, and St. Petersburg, Florida.

In sum, while surveys—including mail, telephone, and interview—are the predominant method of choice, followed by case studies, there are other evaluation methods to consider. Program evaluations can be conducted through the use of combining such methods as mail surveys and follow-up interview surveys or through such innovative techniques as group interviews or the direct observation of participants. The use of documents, both official and unofficial, can also enhance the evaluation process, as can surveys of the environment conducted by the police or community members. Because there are multiple types of program evaluation methods available to researchers, it is important that a variety be explored. Police departments should seek out individuals who are adept at performing these types of evaluations and should consult a variety of publications concerned with the evaluation research methods.

CONCLUSION

The use of evaluative research is an integral part of community-oriented policing. Because this systemic approach is largely about reassessing traditional police methods and looking to new and innovative methods of delivering police services, the use of evaluative research to determine what works and what does not should become a common occurrence within community-oriented police departments. Incrementalism ensures the long-term viability of the policy and provides a complementary method for program evaluation findings to be integrated into the various programs. As community-oriented policing continues to evolve, program evaluations allow the police to learn from the past successes and failures of the programs implemented and how well the community and line police officers have been involved in, and responded to, the systemic approach. In addition, continued program evaluation research means past research mistakes will not be repeated and successful research methods will be frequently utilized as part of a continual evaluation process.

All of the evaluation research should be based on the five key criteria that should be the fundamental roots of community-oriented policing: effectiveness, efficiency, equity, accountability, and authority. Community-oriented policing, in whatever form it takes through the various programs implemented in support of the systemic approach, should be based on these five criteria and evaluated on that basis. The programs must be effective in addressing crime and order maintenance problems. The programs must be efficient in their use of police resources. They must be equitable and delivered and available to the entire community and not just a small homogeneous group. They must hold management, line officers, and the community accountable for the programs that they implement. Finally, they must transfer authority into the hands of the proper people, whether they are line officers or community members, to accomplish the goals dictated under the systemic approach.

In assessing the success or failure of community-oriented policing programs, based on these five criteria, program evaluation research methods should be employed. Both process evaluations and impact assessments should be conducted on a continual basis for long periods of time to fully determine whether a program should be considered a success or a failure. These evaluations should attempt to assess not only attitudes and opinions but also behaviors, experiences, and characteristics. Methods such as surveys whether through the mail, by telephone, or through interviews, are helpful tools in making this determination. Additional methods that may be utilized include case studies, group interviews, and use of official and unofficial documents. In addition, it is beneficial to utilize not just one but multiple methods for a more accurate assessment. Police departments that plan to conduct evaluations should seek out assistance from both inside and outside the department. They should also review the wide variety of publications detailing program evaluation research prior to starting.

COP ON THE WORLD WIDE WEB

Criminal Justice Resources, Community Policing

http://www.lib.msu.edu/harris23/crimjust/commpol.htm

Florence, Florida, Police Department

http://www.florencepd.org

IPR Reports, Community Policing Evaluations

http://www.northwestern.edu/ipr/publications/policing.html

Rand Corporation Research

http://www.rand.org/justice_area

What Works in Community Policing?

http://www.usdoj.gov/cops/cp_resources/conf_capsules/what_works/what_works.htm

REVIEW QUESTIONS

1. Describe the three eras of police evaluation methods.
2. What are the five key criteria on which community-oriented policing should be evaluated?
3. What are the methods for evaluating community-oriented policing?

CHAPTER 12

The Federal Role in Community-Oriented Policing

It may be said by some that the larger responsibility for the enforcement of laws against crime rests with State and local authorities and it does not concern the Federal Government. But it does concern the President of the United States, both as a citizen and as the one upon whom rests the primary responsibility of leadership for the establishment of standards of law enforcement in this country.

—Herbert Hoover

CHAPTER OBJECTIVES

- Recognize the Violent Crime Control and Law Enforcement Act (VCCLA) of 1994.
- Recognize the Office of Community Oriented Policing Services (COPS).
- Understand the federal role in community-oriented policing.
- Assess the success of community-oriented policing under the federal initiative.
- Compare and contrast community-oriented policing before and after the VCCLA.
- Compare and contrast community-oriented policing before and after September 11, 2001.

The issue of crime in the United States has largely been relegated to state and local law enforcement for most of American history. It was not until the twentieth century that the federal government began to take an active role in the administration of justice, primarily as a result of an increasing problem with crime during Prohibition. Although President Hoover appointed a crime commission (the Wickersham Commission) to study, evaluate, and publish volumes of key findings and recommendations, no legislative activity came out of the commission's findings due to the problems the country faced with the Depression. It was not until the 1964 election of President Johnson that another crime commission would be formed, but this time the federal role in crime control would greatly expand. (See Table 12-1.)

President Johnson established the President's Crime Commission on Law Enforcement and Administration of Justice in 1965; it "was charged with investigating the causes of crime and proposing recommendations to improve its prevention and control" (Advisory Commission 1977). The commission published a general report entitled *The Challenge of Crime in a Free Society* (1967), making more than 200 recommendations for the federal government to "expand its financial support of the criminal justice system at the state and local level" (Advisory Commission 1977). The U.S. Congress passed and President Johnson signed into law many of these recommendations under the Omnibus Crime Control and Safe Streets Act of 1968. The Safe Streets Act was the most encompassing crime legislation passed by the federal government at that time, and by 1980, through the Law Enforcement Assistance Administration (LEAA), operating under the U.S. Department of Justice, more than $8 billion was delivered to state and local agencies in an effort to address the problems of crime (LEAA 1980).

Although the LEAA was quietly phased out by the Reagan administration, many new agencies, operating under the U.S. Department of Justice, began delivering grants to state and local police agencies, such as the Bureau of Justice Assistance (BJA). However, it was not until the Violent Crime Control and Law Enforcement Act of 1994, passed by a bipartisan Congress, that the level of grant funding to state and local agencies reached an unprecedented level. This act, most often referred to as the Crime Bill of 1994, allocated more than $36 billion to be delivered from 1994 through 2000 to address the problems of crime. And specifically, $8.8 billion would go to fund the addition of 100,000 cops operating under the principles of community-oriented policing at the state

TABLE 12-1   *Respondents Responding That Too Little Has Been Spent on Halting the Rising Crime Rate in the United States (1973–1994)*

YEAR	PERCENTAGE	YEAR	PERCENTAGE
1974	66	1988	72
1975	65	1990	70
1976	65	1991	65
1977	65	1993	71
1978	64	1994	75
1981	69	1996	67
1982	71	1998	61
1983	67	2000	59
1984	68	2002	56
1985	63		
1986	64		
1987	68		

Source: Kathleen Maguire and Ann L. Pastore, *Bureau of Justice Statistics Sourcebook of Criminal Justice Statistics*—2005. Washington, D.C.: Bureau of Justice Statistics, 2006.

and local levels. As of the fall of 1994, the federal government had become actively involved in the nationwide implementation of community-oriented policing.

Recognizing the profound impact that the federal government continues to have on the dynamics of community-oriented policing, in this chapter we take a broad look at the federal government's role in community-oriented policing. We explore this role from several early demonstration projects to the establishment of the Office of Community Oriented Policing Services (COPS) under the Department of Justice. We then describe in detail the COPS Office, which is primarily a grant-making institution, by focusing on the various grant programs, such as the "100,000 cops on the beat" grants. Finally, we provide a preliminary assessment of the impact the federal government has had on community-oriented policing and what role it will play in the future.

FROM DEMONSTRATION PROJECTS TO THE COPS OFFICE

A number of the demonstration projects or test sites, where community-oriented policing was first implemented by a few select cities on a very limited scale, were funded by the federal government through either the National Institute of Justice or the BJA. In many cases, research funding was provided to determine what might or might not be effective under the concepts of community-oriented policing, problem-oriented policing, or the broken windows theory. Some of the early experiments in Houston, Texas, and Newark, New Jersey, were sponsored by the National Institute of Justice, and the research was conducted through a grant to the Police Foundation (see Pate et al. 1986). Another famous demonstration project was the adaptation of Herman Goldstein's problem-oriented policing in Newport News, Virginia, with a grant provided by the National Institute of Justice to the Police Executive Research Forum (see Eck and Spelman 1987). Another community-oriented policing program supported by the Department of Justice ran for approximately fifteen years prior to the passage of the crime bill; it was the weed and seed program, which is a community-based strategy to "weed out" violent crime, gang activity, and drugs and "seed in" neighborhood revitalization. Although these and other programs have contributed greatly to the development of community-oriented policing, several factors must be considered when detailing the federal government's early involvement in community-oriented policing.

First, these programs were generally funded by small-scale and isolated grants. The grants were going to specific agencies to do specific tests on some aspect of policing. Second, they were clearly innovative in nature. The agencies were receiving these grants to implement and conduct research primarily because they were testing new and innovative ideas. Finally, the federal government provided seed money but limited its oversight of the grants. These grants would prove useful in the development of community-oriented policing as a systemic approach to policing and assist in developing and defining the role the federal government would later play in the institutionalization of community-oriented policing.

Despite the government's role in community-oriented policing throughout the 1980s, it was not until 1992, with the presidential campaign under way, that the federal government became actively involved in this institutionalization process. Early in the election, President-Elect Clinton began campaigning on the benefits of community policing. He found, however, that the media was not picking up on the concept as a sound bite. Accordingly, his policy advisers devised the concept of adding 400,000 police officers to America's city streets under the most recognizable community-oriented policing tactic: the beat cop (Brann 1996). Realizing that the number of officers was not practical from an economic stance, it was reduced to adding 100,000 cops on the beat, and the sound bite stuck. The media reported heavily on the 100,000 cops concept, and Clinton utilized it as part of his platform to "get tough on crime." He won the 1992 presidential election and entered the White House in January 1993.

REMARKS BY PRESIDENT CLINTON AT THE SIGNING OF THE CRIME BILL— SEPTEMBER 13, 1994

The American people have been waiting a long time for this day. In the last twenty-five years, half a million Americans have been killed by other Americans. For twenty-five years, crime has been a hot political issue, used too often to divide us while the system makes excuses for not punishing criminals and doing the job, instead of being used to unite us to prevent crime, punish criminals, and restore a sense of safety and security to the American people.

. . . One of the reasons that I sought this office is to get this bill because if the American people do not feel safe on their streets, in their schools, in their homes, in their places of work and worship, then it is difficult to say that the American people are free.

. . . When I sign this crime bill, we together are taking a big step toward bringing the laws of our land back into line with the values of our people, and beginning to restore the line between right and wrong. There must be no doubt about whose side we're on. People who commit crimes should be caught, convicted and punished. This bill puts government on the side of those who abide by the law, not those who break it; on the side of the victims, not their attackers; on the side of the brave men and women who put their lives on the line for us every day, not the criminals or those who would turn away from law enforcement. That's why police and prosecutors and preachers fought so hard for this bill, and why I am so proud to sign it into law today.

. . . In a few weeks I will name the head of our program to put 100,000 new police on the street. And early next month, the Justice Department will award grants to put new police on the street in 150 more cities and towns that applied last year.

. . . Today we remember the thousands of officers who gave their lives to make our nation safer, whose names are inscribed in a stone memorial just a mile away from here. We remember the innocent victims whose lives were lost and whose families were shattered by the scourge of violent crime.

. . . My fellow Americans, this is about freedom. Without responsibility, without order, without lawfulness, there is no freedom. Today, the will of the American people has triumphed over a generation of division and paralysis. We've won a chance to work together. So in that spirit, let us rededicate ourselves today to making this law become the life of our country, to restoring the sense of right and wrong that built our country, and to make it safe not in words, but in fact, in the lifeblood of every child and every citizen of this country who believes in the promise of America. Let us make it real.

Thank you and God bless you all.

Source: White House Web page, http://www.whitehouse.gov, March 1999.

The administration then began to work on the creation of the legislative proposal that would become the Violent Crime Control and Law Enforcement Act of 1994, otherwise known as the Crime Bill of 1994. The centerpiece of this legislation, and one of the largest fiscal allocations, was for the 100,000 cops program, which was announced in the president's State of the Union Address on January 25, 1994. Although there was much debate over the crime bill, most of it centered on other provisions of the law, such as the three strikes legislation and some of the laws targeting firearms. In the end, the Violent Crime Control and Law Enforcement Act of 1994 received bipartisan support, with the House of Representatives voting 235 to 195 to approve the act on August 21, 1994, and the Senate voting 61 to 38 in favor on August 25, 1994. The Crime Bill of 1994 was signed into law by President Clinton on September 13, 1994, in a White House lawn ceremony.

The Violent Crime Control and Law Enforcement Act of 1994 (see Table 12-2) is the largest crime bill in the history of the United States and dedicated more than $36 billion to

TABLE 12-2   *The Crime Bill*

Congressional appropriations for 1996 in the Violent Crime Control and Law Enforcement Act of 1994°

Title 1	Public safety and policing	$1.85 billion
Title 2	Prisons	$1.07 billion
Title 3	Crime prevention	$678 million
Title 4	Violence against women	$274 million
Title 5	Drug courts	$150 million
Title 6	Death penalty	None
Title 7	Three strikes legislation	None
Title 8	Mandatory minimum penalties	None
Title 9	Drug control	None
Title 10	Drunk driving provisions	None
Title 11	Firearms	None
Title 12	Terrorism	None
Title 13	Criminal aliens and immigration	$332 million
Title 14	Youth violence	None
Title 15	Criminal street gangs	$1 million
Title 16	Child pornography	None
Title 17	Crimes against children	None
Title 18	Rural crime	$37 million
Title 19	Federal law enforcement	$145 million
Title 20	Police Corps and law enforcement officers' training and education	$20 million
Title 21	State and local law enforcement	$211 million
Title 22	Motor vehicle theft protection	$1.5 million
Title 23	Victims of crime	None
Title 24	Protection for the elderly	$900,000

TABLE 12-2   *(Continued)*

Title 25	Senior citizens against marketing scams	$2 million
Title 26	Commission membership and appointment	None
Title 27	Presidential summit on violence and national commission on crime prevention and control	$1 million
Title 28	Sentence provisions	None
Title 29	Computer crime	None
Title 30	Protection of privacy of information in state motor vehicle records	None
Title 31	Violent crime reduction trust fund	$4.3 billion
Title 32	Miscellaneous	None
Title 33	Technical corrections	None
Total Appropriations for 1996		$9.07 billion

°*Note:* In the event of no expenditures, it is generally the case that either a new law was created or an old law was modified.

be spent between 1994 and the end of 2000. This crime legislation was sweeping in that it not only provided for the new police officers to be hired under the concepts of community-oriented policing but also added new laws, altered old ones, allocated funds to build new prisons, and dedicated additional funding for the Federal Bureau of Investigation (FBI), Drug Enforcement Administration (DEA), Immigration and Naturalization Service (INS), U.S. attorneys, the federal courts, and the Treasury Department. In addition, it banned the manufacture of nineteen military-style assault weapons, expanded the death penalty to nearly sixty federal offenses, required that violent sexual offenders be registered, and initiated the federal three strikes provision. Moreover, it targeted illegal immigration into the United States along the borders, generated additional research funding for DNA analysis, and allocated grant funding for the establishment of boot camps for violent offenders (see U.S. Department of Justice 1994). It was clearly the most sweeping crime legislation passed to date and would have a profound impact not only on federal laws and law enforcement but also on state and local laws and law enforcement.

As a result of the specific initiative to add 100,000 police officers and because a number of the provisions within the crime bill were related to the concepts of community-oriented policing, U.S. Attorney General Janet Reno created a new office within the Department of Justice to oversee community-oriented policing and related grants. The funding would include the $8.8 billion in community policing grants authorized for 1994 through 2000, the establishment of the Police Corps, and a number of crime prevention grants. On October 9, 1994, Attorney General Reno formally established the Office of Community Oriented Policing Services (COPS), and three days later it delivered its first series of grants to state and local law enforcement agencies. In the meantime, the search for a director was conducted and the chosen candidate was Hayward, California, Police Chief Joseph E. Brann. On December 19, 1994, President Clinton named Brann the director based on his experience with implementing community-oriented policing. The present director, Carl R. Peed, was appointed by Attorney General John Ashcroft.

DIRECTOR OF THE OFFICE OF COMMUNITY ORIENTED POLICING SERVICES: CARL R. PEED

Carl R. Peed was appointed by Attorney General John Ashcroft to head the U.S. Department of Justice's Office of Community Oriented Policing Services (COPS). To date, the COPS Office has invested $7.5 billion for the advancement of community policing in more than 12,400 law enforcement agencies throughout the nation.

Prior to joining the COPS Office, Peed served as director of the Department of Juvenile Justice (DJJ), Commonwealth of Virginia. As the leader of this statewide agency, Director Peed managed 2,700 employees and a $237 million budget. As the director of the DJJ, he was responsible for developing policy and providing administrative oversight for 38 regional offices and 110 facilities.

As the sheriff of Fairfax County from 1990 to 1999, Peed gained national recognition for developing model policies and procedures in criminal justice administration. At the Fairfax County sheriff's office, he led a workforce of 560 employees and managed a budget of $35 million. During his tenure as sheriff, Peed was instrumental in the advancement of new technologies in the criminal justice system.

Prior to appointment as sheriff, Peed served as chief deputy to the Fairfax County sheriff's office. During his twenty-year career on the force, he developed several national award-winning programs and served as a consultant for the National Sheriff's Association, the American Correctional Association, and the U.S. Justice Department.

Director Peed holds a Bachelor's from the University of North Carolina at Pembroke. He has also earned a Certificate of Criminal Justice Administration from the University of Virginia. Director Peed served as a member of the Presidential Honor Guard during his enlistment in the U.S. Army at Fort Meyer, Virginia, from 1970 to 1972. He is married and has three children.

Source: Office of Community Oriented Policing Services (COPS) Web page, http://www.usdoj.gov/cops, June 2002.

McAllen Police Department youth basketball team posing with the officers who take time to coach them. (*Courtesy of the McAllen Police Department, McAllen, Texas.*)

OFFICE OF COMMUNITY ORIENTED POLICING SERVICES (COPS) MISSION STATEMENT

We, the staff of the Office of Community Oriented Policing Services, dedicate ourselves, through partnerships with communities, policing agencies, and other public and private organizations, to significantly improve the quality of life in neighborhoods and communities throughout the country.

We will accomplish this by putting into practice the concepts of community policing in order to reduce levels of disorder, violence, and crime through the application of proven, effective programs and strategies. We will meet the needs of our customers through innovation and responsiveness. We will create a workplace that encourages creativity, open communication, full participation, and problem-solving.

We will carry out these responsibilities through a set of core values that reflect our commitment to the highest standard of excellence and integrity in public service.

Source: Office of Community Oriented Policing Services (COPS) Web page, http://www.usdoj.gov/cops, March 1999.

A Washington, D.C., office was established in the fall of 1994, and the agency began to focus primarily on delivering the grants to state and local agencies that would be hiring the 100,000 new police officers. In addition, it quickly established a series of grants to provide technology and assistance funding for local agencies and funding for specific community-oriented policing programs. Finally, the COPS Office turned its attention more fully toward providing training to agencies that were undergoing the process of implementing community-oriented policing. However, in this area it was assisted by an established agency, the Community Policing Consortium, which eventually fell under the direction of the COPS Office.

The U.S. Department of Justice, under the BJA, created and funded the Community Policing Consortium in 1993. The consortium initially was a combined effort by the International Association of Chiefs of Police (IACP), the National Sheriff's Association (NSA), the Police Executive Research Forum (PERF), and the Police Foundation. These four agencies pooled their resources to provide training and technical assistance to five community-oriented policing demonstration sites, which included St. Petersburg, Florida; Knoxville, Tennessee; Denver, Colorado; Austin, Texas; and Hillsborough County, Florida. The consortium also conducted meetings with community-oriented policing leaders in the field and created a monograph entitled *Understanding Community Policing: A Framework for Action* (BJA 1994), which has been distributed widely among police agencies in the United States. In 1994 the Community Policing Consortium added the National Organization of Black Law Enforcement Executives (NOBLE) to its list of partner organizations and began offering an array of training curricula on community-oriented policing. A vast majority of police agencies received their first training from the Community Policing Consortium between 1993 and 1994, largely because it was the most progressive and accessible training on community-oriented policing available. By the end of 1994 and the beginning of 1995, however, with the establishment of the COPS Office, the Community Policing Consortium moved out from under the BJA and fell under the direction of the COPS Office.

The Community Policing Consortium's primary mission is to deliver community-oriented policing training and technical assistance to police and sheriff's departments that are COPS grantees. The training sessions are generally held at the state and regional levels and use a curriculum designed by the Community Policing Consortium; the curriculum reflects the knowledge the consortium obtained from early work with a number of agencies and police leaders. The Community Policing Consortium presents general community-oriented policing training, as well as more specific types of training focusing on sheriff's departments, problem solving, and community partnerships. In addition, it has created training workshops on cultural diversity training, personnel deployment strategies, and "train the trainer" courses. Moreover, the consortium has, in the name of information sharing, created several publications, including the *Community Policing Exchange*, the *Sheriff Times*, and *Community Links*. These and other publications and resources have contributed greatly to the education and training of police and sheriff's departments across the country.

COPS GRANTS

The most visible aspect of the COPS Office has been the hiring grants that allow state and local agencies to hire additional police officers to assist in their transition to community-oriented policing. The grants have essentially fallen into four categories: (1) hiring grants, (2) technology or assistance grants, (3) special programs, and (4) training grants. Because of the impact that these grants have had on community-oriented policing, it is important to understand the types of grants available, how they are delivered, and how they have been used by agencies across the country.

When Director Brann took over the COPS Office, one of his concerns was that the original intent of the crime bill was to assist in the establishment of community-oriented policing in state and local agencies, not to just hire 100,000 new officers. As he said on a number of occasions, "This is the Office of Community Oriented Policing, not the office of 100,000 cops." He therefore set out to ensure that agencies understood that the grants were to assist in the implementation of community-oriented policing. Brann did not want to make the same mistakes in the delivery of grants made under the old LEAA in providing block grants. According to Brann (1996), "In the past money was fueled through the states via block grants. This created too many layers of bureaucracy. Police wanted this removed to make the implementation more efficient and more effective." In the structuring of the new hiring grants, Brann explained, "This office looks to customer orientation. Community-oriented policing is focused on the customer, the citizens. In our case focusing on the customer means focusing on local law enforcement." The simplicity of the paperwork required to apply for a hiring grant and the fact that all grant applications go directly to the COPS Office have earned high levels of satisfaction from the law enforcement community.

The first hiring grants to be delivered to state and local law enforcement agencies were announced on October 12, 1994, only three days after the formal establishment of the COPS Office and prior to the hiring of the director. They were dubbed COPS: Phase

TABLE 12-3   *Officers Funded and COPS, Grant Totals (through February 1999)*

GRANT TYPE	OFFICERS FUNDED	GRANT TOTALS
PHS	2,003	$148,421,993
Phase I	2,570	$189,027,136
AHEAD	3,976	$282,944,668
FAST	6,049.5	$394,422,013
MORE	35,851.7	$966,924,476
UHP	41,874	$3,027,412,482
Total	92,324.2	$5,009,152,768

Source: U.S. Department of Justice, Office of the Inspector General, *Special Report: Police Hiring and Redeployment Grants,* Report Number 99-14, http://www.usdoj.gov/oig/au9914/9914toc.htm, April 1999.

I grants and consisted of the first $200 million in grants, which were allocated to 392 state, municipal, county, and tribal law enforcement agencies. The grants allowed the hiring of more than 2,700 additional officers in these agencies, and the COPS Office was on its way toward reaching the "100,000 cops on the beat" goal. The COPS Office was able to so quickly fund these agencies because the BJA, in anticipation of the president signing the bill and the funds being available for hiring the officers, solicited applications and granted the Phase I awards. (See Table 12-3.)

The BJA awarded these grants through a very detailed grant process, similar to other BJA grant procedures. As a result, agencies had to complete a detailed application and mail it to the BJA, which then conducted an extensive review of the applications. The agencies had to wait until the BJA approved the final grant award before recruiting, hiring, and training the officers. As a result, the Phase I grant process was slow and departments were disappointed in the grant process (U.S. General Accounting Office 1995). Most of the problems resulted because an older bureaucracy was dealing with the grant awards and hence was utilizing award procedures it had developed over a period of ten years. At that rate, it would take well over ten years to fund all 100,000 officers, time the COPS Office did not technically have. Therefore, a new grant delivery mechanism needed to be employed by the new agency formed to handle the COPS grants.

In response to a suggestion from the U.S. Conference of Mayors to expedite the grant application process for the COPS Accelerated Hiring Education and Deployment (AHEAD) and COPS Funding Accelerated for Smaller Towns (FAST) programs (described later), the COPS Office designed a two-step application process to try to get new officers on the street months earlier than they would be under traditional grant award processes (U.S. General Accounting Office 1995). First, for COPS AHEAD, the COPS Office used a one-page initial application to determine the number of officers jurisdictions could recruit and train. Approved jurisdictions were notified of proposed funding levels and cautioned that the funding was tentative and thus if the subsequent application was not approved, the COPS Office would not be held liable for officers hired (U.S. General Accounting Office 1995). In COPS FAST, grant decisions were made based on one-page applications; agencies were later required to submit additional information and a brief budget.

Once the applications were received for the COPS AHEAD and COPS FAST grants, a panel of consultants reviewed them, and applying agencies were awarded the grants unless they were negligent in completing the applications. A grant would fund 75 percent of an officer's pay and benefits for three years, up to a maximum of $75,000 per officer. The local agency would have to fund the other 25 percent of the grant's match and agree that the officer would be an additional hire and not one previously working for the agency. In other words, supplanting of grants was considered illegal under the grant process. In addition, the agency would have to provide a guarantee that at the end of the three-year period, the additional officer hired would not be fired, even though the agency would then have to fund that officer at 100 percent.

On November 1, 1994, Attorney General Reno announced the next two series of grants that would be funded by the COPS Office (for hiring grants to replace the COPS: Phase I grants) and handled by the COPS Office rather than the BJA. They were COPS AHEAD and COPS FAST grant programs. The grants were identical to the Phase I grants, except that the COPS AHEAD grants were for agencies serving populations of 50,000 and over, and the COPS FAST grants were for agencies serving populations under 50,000. Essentially this change did nothing more than divide the grants into large-city police agencies and small-town and rural agencies. However, because some of the provisions within the Crime Bill of 1994 specified that at least half of the funding go to small-town and rural agencies, the division of the grants allowed for this provision to be monitored more closely.

In June 1995, the COPS AHEAD and COPS FAST grants were superseded by the Universal Hiring Program (UHP), under which any agency could apply for the same three-year 75-percent-funded grant to hire an additional officer. The only difference under the funding provision with the UHP program seemed to be the clause that waivers for the non-federal match requirement could be requested if "extraordinary fiscal hardship" could be demonstrated. This added clause was most likely a result of a number of agencies applying for hiring grants, receiving their award notification from the COPS Office, and later having to withdraw from the grant process because the local jurisdiction could not afford the 25 percent match or would be unable to continue funding the officer at 100 percent after the third year. One study found that approximately 10 percent of all COPS hiring grant applicants had to withdraw from the grant process for these reasons (Oliver 1997).

On December 14, 1994, Attorney General Reno, just prior to the hiring of Director Brann, announced the fourth COPS grant program, known as COPS Making Officer Redeployment Effective (MORE). These grants were again directed toward agencies that were attempting to implement community-oriented policing, but rather than hiring new officers, they were attempting to expand the time current officers had available to work the beat. The MORE grants were based on a simple application that could be completed with relative ease by any law enforcement agency and either mailed, faxed, or sent electronically to the COPS Office. These grants were specifically to purchase new equipment and/or technological advancements, to procure support resources such as civilian personnel, or to provide overtime pay for officers. The reasoning was that streamlining the officer's administrative tasks would allow the officer more time to work the beat and hence interact with citizens and solve problems. For instance, if the use of laptop computers would allow the typical officer to complete a report in one hour rather than the standard two hours, use of the laptop would save one hour of an officer's time.

If the standard number of reports an officer completed was two per day, then the laptop would save two hours a day, five days a week, for a full year, thus yielding what would hypothetically be equivalent to hiring a part-time officer. What was most interesting was that this figure would then be utilized by the COPS Office to reach the goal of adding 100,000 new officers. (See Table 12-4.)

The other requirements of the COPS MORE grants were very similar to those of the hiring grants in that the COPS Office would fund 75 percent while the local agency contributed the other 25 percent, and the grant could not be used to supplant funding already dedicated by the local agency for equipment, civilian personnel, or overtime pay.

TABLE 12-4 *Office of Community Oriented Policing Services (COPS) Grants*

"100,000 Cops"

Phase I: The initial officer hiring grants in the fall of 1994

COPS AHEAD (Accelerated Hiring Education and Deployment): Officer hiring grants for jurisdictions of 50,000 population or more

COPS FAST (Funding Accelerated for Smaller Towns): Officer hiring grants for jurisdictions with less than 50,000 population

Troops to COPS: Grants for local law enforcement agencies to hire military veterans under community policing

UHP (Universal Hiring Program): All officer hiring grants fell under this title in 1996

Technology

COPS MORE (Making Officer Redeployment Effective): Grants to police agencies to purchase equipment or technology, hire civilians, or pay for officer overtime with the goal of placing more officers on the street

Training

Community Policing Consortium: A partnership of five leading policing organizations dedicated to training and technical assistance on community-oriented policing

Regional Community Policing Institutes (RCPIs): Regional training institutes founded on local or state partnerships to deliver community-oriented policing training

311: A grant to establish a nonemergency phone number (311) to alleviate calls to 911

Advanced Community Policing: Grants to allow police departments to further develop an infrastructure to institutionalize and sustain community-oriented policing practices

Anti-Gang Initiative: Grants to allow local police and community to address the problem of youth violence as it relates to gang activity

Community Policing to Combat Domestic Violence: Grants for local law enforcement agencies to address the problems of domestic violence from a community- and problem-oriented approach

Police Corps: Grants modeled after the military's Reserve Officer Training Corps (ROTC) that allow tuition waivers for college students who are willing to commit to a service obligation with a local police department on graduation

Problem Solving Partnerships: Grants for local police and community to address a specific problem such as burglaries, drug dealing, or street-level prostitution

Source: Office of Community Oriented Policing Services (COPS) Web page, http://www.usdoj.gov/cops, March 1999.

These grants have been well received by police agencies across the United States, mainly because of their ease of application and the flexibility in the use of the grants. In many cases, agencies simply preferred to apply for the COPS MORE grants primarily because the matching requirements would not be as high for the local jurisdiction. However, most of the agencies that had applied for some form of hiring grants had also applied for one of the COPS MORE grants. After the first series of COPS MORE grants came out in 1995, the COPS MORE grants were renamed each year with the fiscal year attached to the grant series, such as COPS MORE '98 grants.

The third series of grants that the COPS Office began to offer beyond the hiring grants and equipment and technology grants were in the area of special programs. Although some resembled both of these former types of grants, many of the programmatic grants were oriented toward addressing a specific problem or exploring an innovative solution under the community-oriented policing philosophy. The grant proposal applications requested agencies to submit their specific plan under the guidelines the COPS Office would provide; after a review, the grants would be awarded to specific agencies for specific dollar amounts. Again, agencies implementing community-oriented policing, and especially those that had received a hiring grant, were the most likely to also receive one of the special programmatic grants.

One of the first of these grants was very similar to the hiring grants and was called Troops to COPS. It was announced on May 2, 1995, that the Troops to COPS program would provide an agency up to $50,000 if it hired a qualified military veteran as a law enforcement officer under community-oriented policing. The benefit to the agency was that the grant money could be used to help defray the costs of the new officer's equipment, uniform, or vehicles in the first three years of service and the grant money did not require a matching amount. The benefit to the federal government was primarily that the U.S. military was undergoing some drastic cuts in manpower and this program provided the incentive for an agency to hire someone exiting the military. A number of military personnel were hired under this program.

The next program, announced on September 13, 1995, was the first true programmatic community-oriented policing initiative sponsored by the COPS Office: the Youth Firearms Violence Initiative. The grants were for cities to develop innovative community-oriented policing and enforcement efforts to curb the rise in violence associated with young people and firearms. Agencies could apply for a onetime grant of up to $1 million under this initiative. The awards were made to ten cities, including Baltimore, Maryland; Bridgeport, Connecticut; Richmond, Virginia; and Seattle, Washington. Most of the initiatives centered on strategic-oriented policing tactics with such things as curfew enforcement, civil sanctions against local gangs, and firearm confiscation programs.

On April 3, 1996, the COPS Office announced a similar program called Anti-Gang Initiative. Once again, agencies were encouraged to apply for up to $1 million in funding to address the problems gangs posed to communities through drive-by shootings, graffiti, and threats and intimidation. Fifteen agencies (including Austin, Texas; Indianapolis, Indiana; Miami, Florida; and Salt Lake City, Utah) received these grants. The majority of initiatives centered on a combination of strategic-oriented and neighborhood-oriented policing methods because most were designed to utilize the "hot spots" and targeting methods as well as mobilize the community to strengthen local community efforts to keep children from joining local gangs.

Wildwood, New Jersey, community policing officer, McGruff the Crime Dog, and a local youth on the DARE motorcycle take time out from a National Nite Out event for this photograph. *(Courtesy of the Wildwood Police Department, Wildwood, New Jersey.)*

Another series of programmatic grants was entitled Community Policing to Combat Domestic Violence. These grants were open to agencies to apply for up to $1 million to address domestic violence training under the community-oriented policing philosophy, to create problem-solving and community-based partnerships at the local level, or to assist in changing police organization to make it more responsive to domestic violence situations in the community. Only agencies that had been practicing community-oriented policing for at least two years were eligible, but the benefit was that, like the Youth Firearms Violence and Anti-Gang Initiatives, no local match to the grant was required. On June 20, 1996, 336 communities across the country received more than $46 million under this grant program.

Perhaps one of the most interesting grants coming from the COPS Office was utilized to address the growing problem of officers having to respond to 911 calls or, more specifically, 911 calls that were not emergencies. An innovative concept to create a non-emergency alternative to 911 was created, and the pilot project of 311 was born. Through a COPS grant in cooperation with AT&T, the Baltimore Police Department was granted $350,000 to implement the 311 nonemergency phone number along with an aggressive public education campaign to reduce the number of 911 calls, leaving 911 for its original intent, emergency calls only. The pilot project was apparently highly successful in that it reduced the number of nonemergency calls to 911, while giving community members a phone number they could easily remember for making routine calls to the police department for assistance.

COP IN ACTION

"Mayberry Revisited": North Carolina's Police Corps Program Goes Back to the Roots

The folks of Mayberry probably never realized how good they had life. Low crime rate, low unemployment, no worries over urban sprawl or blight, and an easygoing familiarity with everyone in town, including Sheriff Andy and his bumbling but well-meaning law enforcement assistant, Deputy Barney Fife.

Law enforcement officers have certainly changed a lot since those bygone days that show depicted, when just about anyone could be a sheriff's deputy or a police officer. Strict professional standards, formalized certification, and rigorous in-service training have turned our officers into professionals worthy of the name.

But there's one thing the sheriff's office in Mayberry had a good handle on—community policing. It's ironic that a television program thirty years old accurately captured what police experts have been preaching for the past decade—that for community policing to work, police must understand both the community and the needs of the people who live there.

Arguably, the recruitment and selection process is the key to making community policing programs work. It's always been a maxim of successful organizations to "hire the best qualified for the right position." Law enforcement recruitment and selection carries that one step further: Hire those who have a stake in the community.

For the past three years, some of North Carolina's brightest young men and women have been selected to receive fully funded college educations in return for their agreement to serve as law enforcement officers in communities throughout the state.

One might think the recipients of these scholarships would choose the state's major urban centers for their employment. After all, these are young college-educated adults with marketable skills. Why would they want to stay "down on the farm," so to speak? But that is precisely what is happening in many instances.

Yes, North Carolina Police Corps scholarship recipients do sign up for the larger departments located in Durham, Raleigh and Greenville. But what many observers find surprising is that they also sign up for Chowan County, Kinston and Statesville. These young folks, contrary to what we've heard about "slackers" and "Gen-X'ers," actually want to make their world a better place to live.

Sure, these men and women could earn higher pay at the state's larger departments, but sometimes it's not about money. Sometimes it's about making a difference in your own little piece of the world. They recognize police work is a calling, and they feel that calling the strongest in their hometowns.

The Police Corps program provides highly motivated, college-educated law enforcement officers at a pivotal time in the state's history. The state needs well-educated law enforcement officers prepared to meet the challenges of police work in an everchanging society.

The evolving face of the state's citizenry requires law enforcement officers who are sensitive to cross-cultural issues, schooled in the latest police technologies and appreciative of law enforcement's legal complexities.

U.S. Department of Justice law enforcement standards have been responsible for a quantum increase in the professionalism of police officers nationwide. The Police Corps Scholarship Program builds on that by putting police officers with degrees and training on the streets of our state's communities.

Previously a heavily rural state, North Carolina has evolved into an internationally recognized center for entrepreneurship in the fields of technology, manufacturing, medicine and education.

Against this backdrop of progress remains the state's rural heritage. Tobacco fields coexist with cutting-edge computer and pharmaceutical research and development. Transplants to North Carolina span the spectrum from highly educated employees of major companies to members of different ethnic and racial groups seeking better opportunities.

The larger departments of the state have the cachet of being well funded, well equipped, and better paying than the state's smaller departments. But, the reality is that two-thirds of the more than 550 law enforcement agencies in North Carolina have fewer than twenty-five sworn officers.

The hundreds of communities that rely on these smaller departments need professional officers just as do the larger locales. Police Corps helps make that a reality by introducing well-educated and trained entry-level officers into forces that sometimes have as few as three sworn officers.

Scholarship applicants are told up front that the selection process is rigorous, and only the most qualified will receive a scholarship. The typical applicant is a high school senior or college underclassman who has heard about the scholarship through a law enforcement source, such as a school resource officer.

Officers who steer a student in this direction have a vested interest in recommending only the best: They may end up partnering with a Police Corps graduate at some point.

In addition to the obligatory medical screen, applicants must also undergo psychological and physical fitness testing. Communication skills are tested with both prepared and impromptu essay writing. A selection panel made up of seasoned law enforcement officers and allied professionals carefully scrutinizes each candidate. Background checks are conducted prior to board appearances.

How is this program received in North Carolina? The best testimony comes from a town that's benefited from it. Concord Police Chief Robert Cansler says, "The Police Corps Scholarship Program is the epitome of community policing because it assists people from the community, who otherwise may not have the resources, and gives them an opportunity to give back to the community."

Detractors may say the Police Corps program creates a "two-tiered hierarchy" within a department—those who are college-educated and those who are not. However, it has been our experience that these college-educated officers are fully accepted by their colleagues, who are willing to impart to the new officers the knowledge they learned in college—the "College of Experience."

Source: Reprinted with permission from Perry F. Stewart, " 'Mayberry Revisited': North Carolina's Police Corps Program Goes Back to the Roots," *Community Policing Exchange,* March/April 1999, p. 2.

One key provision under the Violent Crime Control and Law Enforcement Act of 1994 was the creation of the Police Corps, modeled after the military's Reserve Officer Training Corp (ROTC). The concept was to utilize grant money to defray the cost of a college education; college students could apply for the scholarships, which could be used toward the cost of tuition, fees, books, supplies, transportation, room, board, and other miscellaneous expenses. In turn, the student, on graduation, would agree to serve at least four years with a state or local police agency. The first grant was awarded in the fall of 1996 to Brian Shane Maynor, who was the son of an officer killed in the line of duty and was enrolled at the University of North Carolina–Chapel Hill. He was granted $7,500 for each year of college. In the first two years of the Police Corps scholarship program, Congress appropriated over $30 million toward this program.

There have been a number of additional COPS grant programs, including a series of grants known as Problem-Solving Partnerships. These partnerships were to be innovative community-oriented policing programs that would bring together police and community members to focus on a specific crime or disorder problem in the neighborhood, such as auto theft, street-level drug dealing, or prostitution, and to develop innovative solutions to address these types of problems. Another grant program was known as Advanced Community Policing; 117 agencies received grants to further develop their organizational infrastructures to allow for the implementation of community-oriented policing. Another programmatic grant series, announced in 1998, was the School-Based Partnership Grants, which were focused on utilizing the methods of community-oriented policing within local schools, essentially treating each school as a neighborhood. Finally, another grant initiative was entitled the COPS Methamphetamine Initiative; grants were awarded to six cities to develop community-oriented policing strategies to deal with the production and use of methamphetamine, especially among youth.

Officer Sandy Minor, the first female motorcycle officer of the St. Petersburg Police Department, with her nephew. *(Courtesy of the St. Petersburg Police Department, St. Petersburg, Florida.)*

TEXAS REGIONAL COMMUNITY POLICING INSTITUTE (TRCPI)

Through a cooperative agreement with the Office of Community Oriented Policing Services (COPS), Training and Technical Assistance Division, in Washington, D.C., the Texas Regional Community Policing Institute was established to serve as a resource for Texas law enforcement agencies by providing information, training materials, and other support for law enforcement professionals who seek to adopt more of a community orientation in their policing activities. Additionally, the TRCPI provides technical assistance to a number of organizations, agencies, community groups, and other Regional Community Policing Institutes.

The Institute's affiliation with Sam Houston State University's College of Criminal Justice and the Law Enforcement Management Institute (LEMIT) of Texas provides an ideal environment within which it can flourish. In addition, the Texas Regional Community Policing Institute (TRCPI) maintains partnerships with several agencies and groups across Texas. A tiered-partnership approach is used with one law enforcement agency and one community group as the Institute's primary partners and several other groups as secondary partners subsumed under the primary partners. Community groups also collaborate with the Institute, providing invaluable input and resources. These partners include the Bill Blackwood Law Enforcement Management Institute of Texas, which operates to provide education, training, research, and service to the Texas law enforcement community in order to inspire excellence in leadership and enhance the effective delivery of law enforcement services.

The Texas Regional Community Policing Institute has provided a wide-variety of programs to include (1) The Executive Leadership Series: Designed for chiefs and top management, this seminar focuses on evolving community policing philosophy and implementation issues; (2) Community-Oriented Policing and Problem Solving (COPPS), aimed at line officers and mid-managers, these workshops provide an introduction to community- and problem-oriented policing, as well as a comparison of traditional models of policing. Participants are involved in practical problem-solving exercises; (3) Executive Issues Seminar Series, offered to agency heads/top command staff and addressed emerging issues in policing; (4) Bulletin Series, conducted in concert with the Texas Law Enforcement Management and Administrative Statistics Program (TELEMASP), the TRCPI produced Bulletins on specific community policing issues; (5) Putting the Community in Community Policing Series, conducted in conjunction with the Crime Prevention Resource Center (CPRC), this series focused on ways to engage the community in community policing; (6) Ethics and Integrity, designed for line officers, this course provided an innovative approach based on the reality of law enforcement and used the actual experiences of participants; and (7) Supervising in a Community Policing Environment, a course designed to prepare first-line supervisory personnel to meet the challenges of managing the community-oriented police officer.

The current director of the TRCPI is Dr. Phillip Lyons, who received his Ph.D., J.D., and M.A. from the University of Nebraska and his B.S. from the University of Houston. Prior to graduate school, he spent several years as a peace officer in the Houston area. Dr. Lyons' duties for the Institute include overseeing the Institute's day-to-day operations, facilitating compliance with reporting requirements, and instructing in various programs.

Source: Texas RCPI online at http://www.shsu.edu/cjcenter/trcpi/trcpi.htm.

The final area of grants created by the COPS Office was for training and technical assistance. (See Table 12-5.) Although the COPS Office took control of the Community Policing Consortium, which continued to provide a variety of training curricula to police

TABLE 12-5 *Office of Community Oriented Policing Services (COPS) Total Grant Awards by State (Other) and Estimated Number of Officers Hired (September 1994 through May 2002)*

STATE	NUMBER OF COPS HIRED*	TOTAL AWARDS ($)
Alabama	1,687.1	114,829,082
Alaska	322.0	40,651,126
Arizona	2,726.1	211,948,846
Arkansas	1,256.5	76,778,276
California	15,106.6	1,076,571,197
Colorado	1,239.6	82,014,409
Connecticut	1,290.0	81,026,361
Delaware	444.2	23,487,567
Florida	7,121.8	459,622,027
Georgia	2,407.7	144,334,286
Hawaii	512.6	20,175,418
Idaho	359.5	25,755,745
Illinois	5,703.5	387,048,240
Indiana	1,534.6	97,995,365
Iowa	706.9	52,771,510
Kansas	833.4	62,113,275
Kentucky	1,343.2	89,892,248
Louisiana	2,044.4	107,759,796
Maine	356.1	29,284,831
Maryland	2,466.1	171,843,845
Massachusetts	2,995.5	198,106,011
Michigan	3,460.1	197,777,167
Minnesota	1,382.2	100,984,881
Mississippi	1,678.1	101,424,320
Missouri	2,232.3	143,684,258
Montana	354.7	36,903,800
Nebraska	628.6	43,765,751
Nevada	388.9	36,130,433
New Hampshire	485.1	45,408,062
New Jersey	4,559.2	298,325,721
New Mexico	717.0	55,760,177
New York	11,877.1	803,115,420
North Carolina	2,925.2	157,392,869
North Dakota	231.6	17,016,495

TABLE 12-5   *(Continued)*

Ohio	3,647.7	233,075,636
Oklahoma	985.1	67,492,225
Oregon	1,006.5	84,450,736
Pennsylvania	3,507.2	207,025,872
Rhode Island	371.3	22,024,524
South Carolina	1,047.2	76,235,245
South Dakota	328.1	38,621,348
Tennessee	2,247.1	145,840,338
Texas	5,779.7	391,604,576
Utah	983.0	86,686,927
Vermont	220.1	23,361,642
Virginia	2,216.9	192,067,630
Washington	1,947.3	148,641,970
West Virginia	662.0	36,895,800
Wisconsin	1,340.9	96,266,558
Wyoming	119.4	7,453,368

Other

JURISDICTION	NUMBER OF COPS HIRED	TOTAL AWARD ($)
America Samoa	40.0	1,280,538
Guam	80.0	6,120,617
North Mariana Islands	65.0	3,979,315
Puerto Rico	3,440.0	140,845,003
Virgin Islands	131.6	11,967,318
Washington, D.C.	799.2	66,306,160

Source: Office of Community Oriented Policing Services home page, Freedom of Information Act, Grantee Report, http://www.usdoj.gov/cops/, June 2002.

°The estimated number of officers hired is based on actual grants to hire new police officers and other grants, such as for technology or secretarial support, that free officers from administrative duties to work the street, thus counting as an officer hired.

agencies across the country, the COPS Office turned to another mechanism for delivering community-oriented policing training. The newest grant series was established in the fall of 1996 for collaborative efforts among police, community, government, and academic institutions to come together to form Regional Community Policing Institutes (RCPIs). These RCPIs were created to establish a more lasting legacy of the COPS Office, which, based on its original mandate, was to disband at the end of 2000. Technically that would also mean the end of the Community Policing Consortium, leaving no means for agencies to receive training and technical assistance. The RCPIs were created to fulfill this need and, in the words of Director Brann, "create a legacy of the COPS Office." The RCPIs would accomplish this goal through a one-year grant of up to $1 million, followed by up to two more years of funding, at which point they would be required to seek other sources of funding to stay in existence. (See Table 12-6.)

TABLE 12-6   *Regional Community Policing Institutes (RCPIs)*

STATE	RCPI GRANT RECIPIENT	RCPI SPECIALTY
Arizona	Arizona Peace Office Standards and Training	Partnership building
	Navajo Department of Law Enforcement	Problem solving
California	Los Angeles County Sheriff's Department	Violence prevention
	Sacramento Police Department	Neighborhood revitalization
	San Diego Police Department	Problem solving
Colorado	Department of Public Safety	Partnership building
Connecticut	New Haven Police Department	Partnership building
Florida	Gainesville Police Department	Problem solving
	St. Petersburg Junior College	Executive training
Georgia	Kennesaw State University	Technology
Illinois	Illinois State Police	Organizational change
	University of Illinois–Chicago	Partnership building
Indiana	Ft. Wayne Police Department	Strategic implementation
Kansas	Wichita State University	Rural community policing
Kentucky	Eastern Kentucky University	Rural community policing
Louisiana	Louisiana State University	Partnership building
Maine	University of Maine	Rural community policing
Maryland	Johns Hopkins University	Ethics and integrity
Massachusetts	Boston Police Department	Ethics and integrity
Michigan	Michigan State University	Organizational change
Minnesota	League of Minnesota Cities	Organizational change
Missouri	Missouri Western State College	Training
New Jersey	John Jay College of Criminal Justice	Problem solving
North Carolina	Charlotte-Mecklenburg Police Department	Crime mapping
Ohio	Great Oaks Institute	Partnership building
Oklahoma	Association of Chiefs of Police	Management and leadership
Oregon	Board of Public Safety Standards/Training	Community team training
Pennsylvania	Pennsylvania State University	Partnership building
Tennessee	Knoxville Police Department	Organizational change
Texas	Sam Houston State University	Partnership building
	University of Texas–Austin	Problem solving
Virginia	Department of Criminal Justice Services	Community Policing Through Environmental Design (CPTED)
Washington	Washington State University	Organizational change
West Virginia	Department of Criminal Justice Services	Statewide implementation.

The RCPIs were created to provide comprehensive and innovative education, training, and technical assistance to COPS grantees and other policing agencies throughout a designated region. Some of the regions included cities and their surrounding areas (e.g., Los Angeles), others consisted of entire states (e.g., West Virginia), and still others encompassed multiple states (e.g., the Minnesota Community Policing Institute). The institutes would draw on their collaborative partnerships to bring to a collective table all of the resources and support of the partner organizations. They would have the latitude to experiment with new ideas, to expand the traditional training curricula, and to develop curricula that support community-oriented policing within a specific region. The RCPIs were also created with the intent that each would conduct research on community-oriented policing in its region as well as evaluate internally the success of its training curricula. Finally, each RCPI was required to create a specialty training area that it could become the expert on, develop curriculum for, and share the training with its regional agencies and the other RCPIs.

COPS DIRECTOR SAYS TRAINING IS INTEGRAL TO ORGANIZATIONAL CHANGE

Joseph E. Brann was sworn in as director of the Office of Community Oriented Policing Services (COPS) on December 19, 1994. Brann formerly served as police chief in Hayward, California, a community of 125,000 people, located in the San Francisco Bay area. During his tenure in Hayward, Brann implemented a nationally respected community policing program that has been used as a model by police departments across the country. He has also lectured and written on community policing.

Before becoming chief of the Hayward Police Department, Brann served in the Santa Ana, California, Police Department from 1969 to 1990. While in Santa Ana, a community of 300,000, Brann designed, developed, and managed a wide array of community policing and crime prevention programs that have been recognized as national models.

Brann received a bachelor's degree in criminal justice from California State University at Fullerton in 1975, followed by a master's degree in public administration from the University of Southern California in 1979. During the Vietnam Conflict, Brann served in Korea as a member of the U.S. Army. Brann is also a graduate of the Federal Bureau of Investigation National Academy.

Q1. How should community policing training affect a department's organizational structure?

A1. A police agency must go through an organizational and cultural transition if it is to move successfully into community policing. It requires chief executives, top administrators, middle managers, and others to challenge and set aside some of their prior beliefs and management techniques. It is not an easy process. But I have seen this happen successfully numerous times, and training assistance helps.

Training and education are also helpful in encouraging traditional, rule-driven organizations to adopt new models of organizational management and have proven to be more effective in both the corporate and public sectors.

Q2. How is this transition process achieved through training?

A2. You start with the basics. Community policing is value-oriented, not rule-driven, and establishing that foundation steers the process. Historically, police training focused on teaching technical skills and adherence to the "right" procedures. Those aspects are still important. But the transition to community policing requires an emphasis on outcomes and expectations, which is why a mission statement or "a sense of purpose" is essential. Once that's established, the process is underway.

The next step in training is to work with strategies and methods that move a department's personnel into activities through their awareness of established values, goals, and the department's mission. Every aspect of the organization should be evaluated, and if necessary, strategies and methods should be refined or improved through the training. Remember, a key element of this philosophy is its adaptability. As long as values and objectives are kept in sight, the right kind of activities will occur.

Q3. Do you feel that organizational change can effectively occur without community policing training, or is the training integral to change taking place?

A3. I think training is essential. A very simple example relates to the delegation skills and discretion exercised by chief executives, middle managers, and supervisory personnel. If they have been engaged in the same type of command activities for many years, it's often very hard for them to give up some of their authority. But decentralization in a department, where and when it's possible, is a positive goal. Decentralizing decision-making to ensure that appropriate decision-making and discretion are exercised at the lowest possible level leads to enhanced effectiveness of officers on the street, and their success benefits the entire organization and the community.

Training is helpful and often necessary in luring police executives away from traditional methods that are comfortable, even though they might not always be effective. It is important for executives to build upon the training and information that have been established. But I don't think it is advisable for a department to try to establish a community policing operation without the training tools that are now available.

Q4. What are your plans for COPS-sponsored training and technical assistance?

A4. In our first year the COPS office focused on awarding hiring grants, and with more than 25,000 additional officers now funded, it paid off. During that time, we began to use the Community Policing Consortium to assist with our training and technical assistance efforts.

In the near future, additional COPS-funded community policing training will be provided to complement the Consortium. We're still busy evaluating the best techniques, methods, and subject areas, and we're eager to hear what people want from us in training and how they want it delivered.

We will be funding regional community policing training centers in different areas of the United States. We're also looking at going beyond traditional classroom lectures that seem to predominate in police training. Perhaps problem-solving exercises in the field that include interaction with key community agencies and community groups are more effective. In remote areas where trainee-trainer interactions are difficult, we'll be looking at things like interactive computers, CD-ROMs, teleconferencing, and satellite networks to bring people together. It's important to remember that there is no one way to do this.

Source: Reprinted with permission from "COPS Director Says Training Is Integral to Organizational Change," *Community Policing Exchange,* March/April 1996, p. 2.

On May 30, 1997, the COPS Office announced that thirty-five RCPIs would be established across the country, funded at nearly $1 million each. A conference was held in Washington, D.C., in August 1997, bringing representatives from all of the RCPIs together to lay the foundation for the RCPI grant process, to share information and ideas, and to allow RCPI members from the police, community, and academia the chance to network. There was little doubt that the RCPIs would have a significant impact on training, information, and research related to community-oriented policing.

ASSESSMENT OF COPS

There is a great need for multiple assessments to be conducted on the COPS Office because this office will have what is likely to be the single greatest impact on policing in the United States to date. More importantly, it will have a definitive impact on the concepts and philosophy of community-oriented policing because all of the grant money, programs, equipment, technology, and resources have been focused on community-oriented policing. Although the early innovations and the fast diffusion of community-oriented policing across the country throughout the 1980s and early 1990s promulgated community-oriented policing, the COPS Office has provided the infrastructure to institutionalize community-oriented policing within state and local agencies across the country. However, the criteria one uses to assess the COPS Office affect the perceptions of how the office is doing. Hence, truly understanding the impact this office has had on community-oriented policing will most likely take years. (See Table 12-7.)

To understand this problem with assessment, one could evaluate the COPS Office as a grant-making institution in much the same manner as the U.S. Department of Justice counterpart, the BJA. In this assessment, one would look at the efficiency of the COPS Office to deliver the grants to state and local law enforcement agencies. In most assessments, it would be

TABLE 12-7 *Authorization and Appropriations for COPS Grant Program (Fiscal Years 1995–1999)*

FISCAL YEAR	AMOUNT AUTHORIZED (BILLIONS)	AMOUNT APPROPRIATED (BILLIONS)
1995	$1.3	$1.3
1996	$1.9	$1.4
1997	$2.0	$1.4
1998	$1.6	$1.4
1999	$1.4	—
Total	$8.2	$5.5

Source: U.S. General Accounting Office (1997) and COPS Office data.

TABLE 12-8   *Reasons Law Enforcement Agencies Have Not Applied for a COPS Grant*

REASON	NUMBER OF AGENCIES	PERCENTAGE
Cost-related factors	4,215	62.5
Could not ensure continued funding	2,745	40.5
Could not meet 25 percent match	1,198	17.7
Other cost reason	272	4.0
Regulations for use of funds too restrictive	576	8.5
Lack of information or deadline	572	8.4
Did not need additional officers	501	7.4
Other reasons	265	3.9
Political or city decisions	206	3.0
Paperwork requirements too burdensome	153	2.3
All reasons equally important	25	0.4
Do not know	267	4.0

Source: General Accounting Office (1995) telephone survey results.

fairly accurate to say that it has done an outstanding job. It responded to the needs and requests of local law enforcement agencies to expedite the grants and make the application forms easy to complete. By allowing for a two-part grant process, in which the first part was a one-page application that would allow for preliminary grant acceptance, agencies could begin the process of hiring the officer; the second part required a slightly more detailed form to be completed by the date money was to be transferred, and the COPS Office was thus able to truly expedite the grant process in an age when most bureaucracies are not able to respond that promptly. It also responded to the local agencies' desire to bypass state review and control over the grants, hence ensuring that the grant process would remain streamlined. In addition, local agencies had to be pleased with the level of grant authorization: 92 percent of the jurisdictions that applied for a grant received initial approval in the first series of COPS AHEAD and COPS FAST grants (U.S. General Accounting Office 1995). Finally, in relation to the goal of adding 100,000 police officers to America's police and sheriff's departments by the end of 2000, as of early 1999, the COPS Office had funded more than 92,000 officers, demonstrating that the COPS Office would meet its goal. Therefore, the office was highly successful as a grant-making institution. (See Table 12-8.)

A REPORT CARD ON COPS

President Clinton announced on January 25, 1994, a plan to put 100,000 new police officers on the street by the year 2000. He averred that those officers would have a major impact on serious crime in the United States. Well, the six years are almost up, and has the highly touted COPS program lived up to the hype? We surveyed law enforcement administrators to find out what they think of the program.

We polled a randomly selected group of administrators throughout the United States to solicit their feelings about the COPS program and whether the actual results agree with the president's predictions and the gushing hype from Washington. Here is what we found.

Of the departments polled, 83 percent have taken advantage of some facet of the program. Most of them, 46 percent, applied for the Universal Hiring Program (UHP) grants. The second most popular part of the program was COPS MORE (Making Officer Redeployment Effective), which accounted for 32 percent of the grants. There was a sharp drop-off after that, e.g., Training and Technical Assistance (2 percent), Community Policing to Combat Domestic Violence (5 percent), COPS FAST (2 percent), and COPS Technology Grant for Computer Reporting (2 percent).

In fairness, components of the program such as the COPS Distressed Neighborhoods Pilot Project were introduced well after the original announcement of the program. Clinton did not introduce the distressed neighborhood program until May 29, 1998. Nevertheless, most agencies concentrated solely on the UHP and COPS MORE components.

The numbers of officers hired varied considerably, depending to a great extent on the size of the individual agency and the community it served. For example, the Bessemer, Alabama, Police Department, which serves a population of 34,000, added 24 officers, which is about 20 percent of its total complement of 120 sworn members. Hampton, Virginia, increased its police force by 39 officers, about 15 percent of its 264-member department. Most departments hired more moderate numbers, e.g., Brownsburg, Indiana (1), Geneva, New York (3), and Puyallup, Washington (2).

For most administrators, though, the numbers were less important than the results of expanding their forces. They reported overwhelmingly that they were pleased with the effects of the program.

Some 95 percent of the respondents said that hiring new officers has been beneficial to their departments, so far. Similarly, 93 percent reported that the funding they have received for equipment, technology, training, etc., has improved their departments' effectiveness.

Most departments have been so satisfied, in fact, that they have applied more than once for grants; 80 percent of them reapplied for grants at least a second time. And, 58 percent indicated they would apply for additional grants. With success rates like these, it is hard to conceive of any problems with the program. Yet, some administrators expressed reservations and a bit of skepticism about COPS.

Chief George Dickerson, Fenwick Island, Delaware, expressed a problem echoed by several of his counterparts. "COPS funding is currently viewed as short term at the three years," he said. "I think you will see a number of police officers laid off due to budget constraints."

That concerned Dickerson, who has hired 1 full-time and 1 part-time officer to augment his 8-member force. Dickerson oversees a unique police force. The population of Fenwick Island is only 385 in winter but swells to 10,000 in the summer. That makes staffing difficult, but Dickerson wants to maintain the best-trained, most technologically advanced force he can year-round. His budget does not provide for the continuation of salaries and grants for officers hired under the COPS program beyond the first three years. He is not alone in that position.

While only 11 percent of the departments responding acknowledged that they were in a position similar to Dickerson's, budgeting for new officers beyond three years was a concern. In fact, among the 17 percent of respondents who had not taken advantage of the program, three-quarters said they hadn't because they would be unable to assume the financial burdens in the future. So, many did not even bother going through the application process. The rest reported adequate staffing currently. Future costs, then, are a major concern—and a barrier to 100 percent success for the program.

Chief Richard Barreto, Miami Beach, Florida, whose department has hired 35 new officers under the program, and who has budgeted for them beyond the three years, put the future cost issue in perspective. He noted that "the real problem with accepting these grants is the mandate to retain the additional officers. The three-year partial funding pales in comparison to the cost of retaining individual officers." He does not perceive that as being completely negative, though. "Most departments are reluctant to increase their staffing beyond what they need," Barreto said. "The grant program has made getting what you need more economical."

Barreto's comments raised two other issues connected with the COPS program. One is total cost; the other is overstaffing, which, conceivably, could lead to layoffs. Some critics of the program fear that agencies might run their own version of a "Rent-a-Cop" program, i.e., hire additional personnel only for the three years covered by the grants and then let them go once the funds dry up. That is not unrealistic, when the total cost of hiring and maintaining a police officer is taken into consideration.

The Sunnyvale, California, Police Department's experience with COPS demonstrated that the costs involved with hiring new officers can be misleading. The city of 121,000 applied for 6 new officers several years ago. However, according to a memo produced by the city manager, the federal grant would support only 5 percent of the total budgetary effect of the new programs during the next ten years. The city would have to support the remainder. That simply did not jibe with Sunnyvale's budget.

COPS pays only 75 percent of an officer's salary the first year, 50 percent the second, and 25 percent in the third, up to a maximum of $75,000 per officer for three years. That may sound good at first, until it is weighed against the true cost per year per officer. For instance, in California, it costs approximately $100,000 a year to maintain an officer's salary, including benefits, training, vehicle, and equipment. Simple math dictates that hiring 6 new officers at a total cost of $600,000 per year ($1.8 million for three years) far outweighs the maximum $450,000 the COPS program would pick up for 6 officers for three years. So, over the three-year period, the city would have to pick up an additional $1.2 million in costs. Figures like that give some administrators pause when it comes to capitalizing on COPS grants—especially when they do not really need the additional resources, as some do not.

Chief Alan West, Moab, Utah, is one of the administrators who has not taken advantage of the COPS program. West, who heads a 13-member department serving a population of 5,500 people, said simply, "We did not need an officer for community policing." Besides, he commented, "I don't think that a grant program of this nature should dictate the manner by which the manpower is utilized."

That, too, was a common complaint among administrators, several of whom noted they were aware of agencies hiring new officers but do not use them for community policing programs. That explains in part why some administrators look very closely at their true need for additional resources and their ability to pay for them several years down the road.

Certainly, there have been cases in which police administrators or their civilian counterparts have stepped back and taken a second look at COPS grants. Chief Steve McCann, Livingston, Montana, fell into that category. "We applied for a grant under UHP and received it," he reported. "However, the City Council then refused to accept it. Go figure." The "figure" part may be exactly why the council chose not to accept the grant. A similar case obtained in East Windsor, Connecticut, in early 1998.

Connecticut congressional representative Jim Maloney announced on January 13, 1998, that rural East Windsor had been awarded $150,000 in COPS grants for two officers. That pleased Chief Thomas Laufer, but he was not positive the town even wanted the money. East

Windsor had accepted funding for 2 officers two years earlier, but Laufer was not sure he needed to increase his staff of 20 sworn officers. He acknowledged that if he did hire the new officers, they would not be used entirely for community policing.

That was a dilemma common among administrators mulling whether to accept COPS grants. After all, what sense is there in hiring officers who may or may not be used for the purposes intended in the COPS program—and for whom there may not be money available anyway when the grants expire? No wonder Dickerson predicted that "I think you will see a number of officers laid off due to budget restraints. I am afraid numerous officers hired under the COPS program will not be retained after the federal funds dry up." Some of his counterparts hope that the funds will not dry up at all—but that may be wishful thinking.

Roughly one-third of the respondents said they would prefer to see the program extended beyond the originally announced six-year limit. The bulk of them, 55 percent, assess the program as a good start toward reducing crime rates, but not a panacea. They simply cannot see any direct connection between the goals of the program and the actual effects on crime rates. Indeed, only 26 percent of the respondents said they can correlate the alleged drops in crime rates to the effects of the program.

More to the point, only 16 percent attributed a decrease in crime in their communities directly to the COPS program. In those cases, the rate was considerably smaller than program directors or politicians would like people to think.

On December 18, 1997, two Democrat senators from Louisiana, John Breaux and Mary Landrieu, announced more than $1.8 million in new federal grants for ten Louisiana law enforcement agencies. The money would put 40 new cops on state streets. Breaux touted the drop in crime rates due to the COPS program. He cited a 22 percent drop in violent crime in New Orleans alone as a result of the program. That figure seemed a bit high to some critics of the program.

Breaux's statement pointed to two more drawbacks to the program mentioned by some skeptics—and supporters as well: the inability to determine exact (or reasonably close) statistical benefits of the program and the fact that COPS has become a vehicle to make politicians look good to their constituents.

It is significant that only 14 percent of the respondents said the results of the COPS program can be measured accurately. A solid 43 percent said emphatically that they cannot be. The remaining 43 percent were not sure. Significantly, only 16% of the respondents said the crime rate has dropped in their communities as the result of the COPS program; 21 percent said it had not. The rest were not sure. Nevertheless, some administrators have been able to determine to some extent what impact the COPS program has had on their communities.

Chief Hines G. Smith, Bellevue, Nebraska, pointed to a 4 percent decrease in crime in his community, which he attributed to the COPS program. He admitted that the program alone will not cause any significant drop in crime rates, though. "The COPS program, while not being the only answer to crime and crime control, is a beneficial and much needed addition to law enforcement," Smith emphasized. Frank Pane, his counterpart in Geneva, New York, concurred.

Pane reported, "In New York State, a combination of tougher sentencing laws for crime committed with guns, fixed sentences rather than determinate sentences for violent criminals, the abolishment of parole for violent felons, and the increased number of officers assigned to street duty has played a major part in reducing crime in our state." As he suggested, the COPS program was but one weapon in a total arsenal that is useful against crime.

Smith added one more benefit to the COPS program. The true value, in his estimation, is the strengthening of relationships between police and citizens. "The redeployment of officers back into the neighborhoods through the hiring of civilian employees has significantly en-hanced our police/community partnership," he explained. Ironically, the hiring of civilians to permit sworn officers to be redeployed is one of the least used features of the program. Only 7% of the respondents said they used it.

The Wicomico County, Maryland, Sheriff's Department noted a slightly higher decrease in crime attributed directly to new hires: 7%. The county hired 18 new officers over the past four years, which composes 24% of the total staff. But, departments that can pinpoint exactly how crime has decreased in their jurisdictions due to the COPS program are few and far be-tween.

That does not stop politicians from touting it in their jurisdictions, though, which rankles some law enforcement administrators. Sixteen percent of the respondents view the program as more of a political vehicle than a realistic attempt to address a real solution to the nation's crime rates. Their perception may be based in part on the fact that so many politicians, from the president on down, use grants as forums to show their constituents they are tough on crime.

It seems to some administrators that no grant can be awarded without a media circus. Witness the previous references to Maloney in Connecticut and Breaux and Landrieu in Louisiana. Other examples abound. On April 1, 1997, Congressman McHale of Pennsylvania announced a $150,000 UHP grant to the Whitehall Township Police Department. McHale took the opportunity to say that "In 1994, I supported the Violent Crime and Law Enforce-ment Act, which authorized the establishment of the COPS programs. . . . Police departments throughout the Lehigh Valley have been awarded more than $2.35 million in funding for 33 police officers under the various grants of the COPS program." The announcements keep coming.

On April 14, 1998, U.S. Senator Fritz Hollings and Representative Jim Clyburn announced a $238,963 COPS grant to several communities in South Carolina. Hollings noted that "Every South Carolinian should be able to walk down the street free from the fear of crime. . . . These new officers will help us increase community safety and step up our war on crime." Clyburn added, "I am pleased that the federal government realizes the need for investment in fighting criminal activities in rural areas like Calhoun County (which received $169,260 to hire 3 ad-ditional deputies) as well as in urban centers of South Carolina and the rest of the nation."

Clyburn's comments supported one of the outcomes of the poll: that law enforcement agencies of all sizes have equal opportunities to receive COPS grants. Only 22 percent said they thought the program is designed more to benefit larger departments than smaller ones, while 65 percent reported that any size department has an opportunity to take advantage of the program. That was one of the goals of the program.

In November 1994, the COPS office announced two new programs: COPS AHEAD (Ac-celerated Hiring Education and Deployment), an expedited hiring grant program for munici-palities with populations of 50,000 and above, and COPS FAST (Funding Accelerated for Smaller Towns), an expedited hiring grant program for jurisdictions with populations below 50,000. Both were superseded on June 19, 1995, by the Universal Hiring Program.

Size of towns aside, 83% of the respondents said that the process is "simple enough" for any department. There was one caveat to the application process in general, though. Chief Lockheed Reader, Puyallup, Washington, who has added 2 officers to his 50-member force, noted that the application is easy. "Getting the money in the bank is more difficult," he said. And, he concluded, "The reporting quarterly is cumbersome." Reservations aside, he is satisfied with the program, which he said is "a good way to get departments to com-mit to COPS."

It is apparent based on the results of our poll that many departments are taking advantage of the COPS program. Its growth rate has been phenomenal. Vice President Gore announced at a December 14, 1998, press conference that $93 million in grants was being released to assist agencies in 531 jurisdictions in upgrading their technology and putting more police on the streets. Three days later he assembled another group of politicians, government officials, and law enforcement administrators to announce an additional $16.5 million in UHP grants to 114 communities in 36 states and Puerto Rico to fund the hiring of 248 new community policing officers.

As of that date, December 17, 1998, there were a reported 92,000 new cops funded. Critics disputed that figure, pointing out that many of the officers counted as "new" under COPS grants were simply sworn personnel being reassigned to street duty. There might be some truth to that idea. After all, it might be as difficult for COPS administrators to get an exact count of new officers as it is for law enforcement administrators to determine the exact rate of crime decrease as a result of COPS grants.

Critics and criticisms aside, the program seems to be having a positive effect on law enforcement and crime rates. The question is whether it will continue.

Perhaps Chief Dickerson best summed up the results of the poll and law enforcement administrators' feelings about the COPS program in his closing comments. "I feel the program has had a major part to play in the reduction of crime," he said. "Think about it: more uniforms on the street is most obvious. The feds need to think long-term funding for these programs." The question now is whether COPS will continue to play a role in the long term.

Source: Reprinted with permission from Arthur Sharp, "A Report Card on COPS," *Law and Order,* February 1999, pp. 76–80.

Rockland County Sheriff's Department Law Enforcement Explorers learn first aid and safety. (*Courtesy of the Rockland County Sheriff's Department, Rockland County, New York.*)

However, delivering the grants and monitoring the grants are two different things. A General Accounting Office report on the ability of the COPS Office to monitor the grants that were awarded so fast in the fall of 1994 and all of 1995 found that the COPS Office was adept at administering the grants but was less skilled at monitoring and evaluating the financial and programmatic impact of the grants (U.S. General Accounting Office 1995, 1997). Although the grantees are required to submit progress and accounting reports on a periodic basis, these are simple budgetary forms that do not reveal much in way of the true use of the grant awards. In fact, it was found that the COPS Office occasionally made contacts by telephone but conducted few on-site visits. Further, those agencies receiving grants under the COPS FAST program were most likely to receive only phone contacts because many agencies were involved and only a few officers were hired. The COPS AHEAD grant recipients were more likely to have an on-site visit because few agencies were involved and many officers were hired.

The primary reason cited by the COPS Office for failure to monitor the agencies receiving the awards was that the agency was limited in personnel and was concentrating more fully on the process of making grant awards than on following up on the grant awards made (U.S. General Accounting Office 1995, 1997). The COPS Office began with fewer than 100 personnel to support its large operation, but by 1997 it was up to approximately 180 personnel and by 1999 had exceeded 200 personnel. Although there was always an intent to monitor the grants and that was part of the original mandate for the COPS Office, clearly the hiring of the 100,000 cops took precedent.

U.S. DEPARTMENT OF JUSTICE, OFFICE OF THE INSPECTOR GENERAL—SPECIAL REPORT: POLICE HIRING AND REDEPLOYMENT GRANTS (COPS)

The following is a summary of the results of the U.S. Department of Justice's Office of Inspector General grant audits of 149 grants to various agencies throughout the country:

For the 149 grant audits, we identified about $52 million in questionable costs and about $71 million in funds that could be better used. Our dollar-related findings amount to 24 percent of the total funds awarded to the 149 grantees. The following are examples of when we would question costs or recommend funds to better use.

- Costs incurred are unallowable according to statutory or regulatory provisions.
- Costs incurred are not supported by documentation.
- Funds were improperly or incorrectly accounted for.
- Funds remain unspent after a reasonable amount of time.
- Essential grant requirements were not met.

The following weaknesses appear to cut across all types of grantees that we audited regardless of size or location.

- 20 of 145 grantees (14 percent) overestimated salaries and/or benefits in their grant application.
- 74 of 146 grantees (51 percent) included unallowable costs in their claims for reimbursement.

- 52 of 67 grantees receiving MORE grants (78 percent) either could not demonstrate that they redeployed officers or could not demonstrate that they had a system in place to track the redeployment of officers into community policing.
- 60 of 147 grantees (41 percent) showed indicators of using federal funds to supplant local funding instead of using grant funds to supplement local funding.
- 83 of 144 grantees (58 percent) either did not develop a good faith plan to retain officer positions or said they would not retain the officer positions at the conclusion of the grant.
- 106 of 140 grantees (76 percent) either failed to submit COPS initial reports, annual reports, or officer progress reports or submitted these reports late.
- 137 of 146 grantees (94 percent) did not submit all required Financial Status Reports to OJP or submitted them late.
- 33 of 146 grantees (23 percent) had weaknesses in their community policing program or were unable to adequately distinguish COPS activities from their pre-grant mode of operations.

Source: U.S. Department of Justice, Office of the Inspector General, Special Report: Police Hiring and Redeployment Grants, Report Number 99-14, http://www.usdoj.gov/oig/au9914/9914toc.htm, April 1999.

This limited amount of monitoring is important for a number of reasons, but two are perhaps most significant: agencies maintaining the grant after receiving the award and supplanting of the grant. In the first, because the grants are only an award for up to three years at 75 percent of an officer's pay, at the end of the three-year period there is a question of the disposition of the officers. Will they be retained by the police agency, or will they be fired or laid off? This question has surfaced with the COPS Office, which has noted that the agencies are required to maintain the officer after the end of the three-year grant because it is part of the agreement to receiving the grant. However, Director Brann has also noted that the statute needs to be further defined and that communities could not be expected to maintain hiring levels indefinitely but that a reasonable period for retaining the officers funded by the COPS Office had not been determined (U.S. General Accounting Office 1997). It also appeared that in the fall of 1998, the question would be raised once again because it would be the first time many of the grants would begin to expire. In anticipation of this event, a number of grants were extended or new grants were given to agencies that had officers whose grants were about to expire, thus delaying the inevitable. In one report, there was at least anecdotal evidence that several agencies had essentially laid off the officer, while in others, the simple accounting figures demonstrated that at some time in the future a police department would not be able to maintain the multiple officers it had hired (National Public Radio 1998). For instance, the Los Angeles Police Department announced that it would hire an additional 710 officers through COPS grants, at a staggered rate of hiring for 1998, 1999, and 2000. However, at the end of the three-year period for all of the grants, it was estimated that it would cost the city of Los Angeles over $70 million a year to maintain these officers. Even in the best of times, such an amount could greatly affect any budget (National Public Radio 1998).

The other major problem with failing to monitor the grants relates to the issue of agencies supplanting their grant money. When agencies agree to the COPS grants, they also acknowledge that they will not supplant the funds they receive. In other words, the grant awards are to be used above and beyond the normal operating budget of the police or sheriff's department and cannot be used to pay for an already hired or employed police officer or sheriff's deputy. However, especially with a limited amount of monitoring, agencies could simply utilize the grant money to pay for a previously hired officer by adjusting the budget or reducing the number of officers the city is required to employ and then hiring the difference through a COPS grant. Although the U.S. General Accounting Office (1997) acknowledged that supplanting was probably occurring, it concluded that "it is difficult to establish with certainty that supplanting has not occurred because of the lack of evidence to determine what would have occurred in the absence of a grant." Having spoken under condition of anonymity with several agency and city accountants in regards to supplanting, one city accountant explained that the city had a mandate to employ five full-time officers. To obtain one of the grants and help defray city costs, officials simply reduced the number of required full-time officers to four when an officer quit and then utilized a grant to hire a fifth "additional" officer. Although this is only one case, one must question how often it occurs.

Another problem that has often been cited is the means by which the COPS Office calculates the number of officers hired to meet the goal of 100,000 officers. During the 1992 presidential campaign, President-Elect Clinton continually called for an addition of 100,000 police officers to the streets of America. Again in the 1996 presidential campaign, both President Clinton and Vice President Gore continued this call and touted the advantages of hiring these 100,000 police officers. In the vice presidential debate, Al Gore stated, "Clinton promised to pass a plan that would put 100,000 new police officers on the streets. It is law." No one would think at the time that this statement meant anything other than adding 100,000 bodies, but the Violent Crime Control and Law Enforcement Act of 1994 was actually very clear that the use of equipment could count for the "hiring" of a new officer. Hence the use of a COPS MORE grant to add laptop computers to the department's equipment could actually count as having hired three new officers. Although the original law authorized the COPS Office to utilize this type of budget "trickery," it leaves one with a less than positive assessment of the goal of hiring of 100,000 police officers.

Finally, several researchers and studies have noted a problem with the method by which grants have been delivered. The primary reason for adding police officers to state and local agencies through the grant process was to help reduce the problem of crime in cities and towns across the United States. However, although agencies with higher crime rates were in fact more likely to apply for COPS grants, there is little relationship between crime rates and whether an applicant jurisdiction was awarded the grant (U.S. General Accounting Office 1995). In addition, several reports have found that some cities, such as Oklahoma City with a 1994 violent crime rate nearly twice the national average, had not applied for any of the COPS grants because they were not able to afford the local match ("Finding Promised Cops," 1996; Sharp 1999). Moreover, several authors have made the argument that because the grants are not awarded on the basis of official crime rates and because they are not a zero-sum game—one recipient's allocation is not dependent on what another recipient receives—these grants are more a distributive form of policy than a regulatory type of policy, as most crime policy tends to be categorized (Leyden, Oliver, and Kilwein 1999). In other words, they are grants that allow politicians to advertise how many officers have been hired in their jurisdiction and how they are responsible for helping the local police and sheriff's departments, thus helping the politicians win votes on the crime issue.

One very important and significant study in the field of criminal justice that was a result of a mandate by Congress to assess what works in the area of crime control policy was published in 1997 under the title *Preventing Crime: What Works, What Doesn't, What's Promising*. This study, conducted at the University of Maryland under Lawrence Sherman as the lead researcher, found that "in general, the evidence suggests that federal appropriations to prevent crime through additional policing is most effective when allocated on the basis of serious crime rather than on the basis of population size" (Sherman et al. 1997, 33). Sherman et al. (1997) state that the grants relate primarily to population size because jurisdictions with higher populations tended to apply for more grants. In addition, they explain the implications that can be drawn from this scientific conclusion:

> One is the "promising" finding that across all large cities, more police produced less serious crime. A second is the finding that each additional police officer assigned to a big city prevents six times as many serious crimes each year as an officer assigned by population (Marvell and Moody 1996). A third conclusion is the finding that directed patrol in crime hot spots "works" to prevent crime in those hot spots, the greatest micro-level concentrations of crime. A fourth conclusion is the "promising" finding that police can reduce gun crime by intensified enforcement of the laws against carrying concealed weapons (Sherman et al. 1997, 34).

As a result of this national assessment of what works in the area of policing, this report to Congress recommended that Congress "consider revising the statutory allocation formula based not only on city-level violent crime, but beat-level and block-level crime as well. Such a revision would be more effective in directing federal funds as precisely as possible for maximum crime prevention" (Sherman et al. 1997, 34). Finally, Sherman et al. also focus their conclusions on the fact that the COPS grants are intended to be applied toward the implementation of community-oriented policing; according to them, "while COPS language has stressed a community policing approach, there is no evidence that community policing *per se* reduces crime without a clear focus on a crime risk factor objective" (Sherman et al. 1997, 35). Thus they conclude that although the "scientific evidence indicates the COPS program is effective, it also suggests it could be more effective if its funding was more focused upon police programs of proven effectiveness" such as directed patrols toward hot spots and problem-oriented policing on a beat-level and targeted basis (Sherman et al. 1997, 35).

In 1998, the COPS Office undertook a major evaluation of its own by conducting what is known as a process evaluation, which looks to see how successfully the COPS program was implemented, not the impact the program had. The report was published by the National Institute of Justice in August of 2000 and was titled the *National Evaluation of the COPS Program—Title 1 of the 1994 Crime Act* (Roth and Ryan 2000).

Sacramento Police Department Management serve as Salvation Army bell ringers in the malls every holiday season.(*Courtesy of the Sacramento Police Department, Sacramento, California.*)

The report explained that the COPS program had four specific goals: (1) to increase the number of officers deployed in American communities; (2) to foster problem solving and interaction with communities by police officers; (3) to encourage innovation in policing; and (4) to develop new technologies for assisting officers in reducing crime and its consequences (see Roth and Ryan 2000, 1). It then detailed the various initiatives under the COPS program (e.g., hiring grants) in order to provide some background on the program. The evaluation, it explained, was funded by the National Institute of Justice and was conducted by the Urban Institute as an independent review of the COPS program. In order to conduct the evaluation, the Urban Institute researchers attempted to address seven specific questions: (1) How did local agencies respond to the exchange offered by the COPS program? (2) What distribution of COPS funds resulted from localities' application decisions through the end of 1997? (3) How did COPS hiring grantees accomplish their hiring and deployment objectives through mid-1998, and how did they expect to retain the COPS-funded officers? (4) How did COPS MORE grantees succeed in acquiring and implementing technology, hiring civilians, and achieving the projected redeployment targets through mid-1998? (5) What increases in policing levels were projected and achieved by local agencies using COPS resources? (6) To what extent had the COPS program succeeded by mid-1998 in encouraging grantees to build partnerships with communities, adopt problem-solving strategies, and participate in prevention programs? and (7) To what extent did grantees' organizations change through 1998 to support and sustain community policing? (see Roth and Ryan 2000, 4–5).

The findings of the process evaluation were mostly positive but held a number of qualifications. In terms of how local agencies responded, the COPS Office found that while 19,175 agencies were eligible for grants, only 10,537 (55 percent) applied and 761 (7 percent) had withdrawn from the application process. The problem, as previously cited, was the financial constraints of many localities for the matching grants. In terms of the distribution, it found that, for the most part, the funds went to jurisdictions with no particular bias, and it highlighted that agencies with the highest murder rates received the majority of funds in an attempt to link murder with crime in order to show that, like the Sherman report cited earlier, COPS programs encouraged funds to go where the most crime occurs. In terms of hiring, the evaluation found that agencies were mostly successful and that police were deployed in community policing activities, but that whether there was retention after the grants expired, it was too soon to tell. The report also highlighted the MORE grants as having been successful and popular with local police agencies and that every $100,000 spent on technology equated to 6.12 full-time equivalent (FTE) officers. In other words, for every $100,000 spent on technology, the COPS grants essentially gained 6 "officers" that counted toward the 100,000 total. As for question 5, the evaluation found that, through 1997, 41,000 grants had been awarded and 39,000 officers had been hired. It projected that, by 2001, there would be 57,200 officers hired but that the number would stabilize at 55,400 by 2003. The rest of the "100,000 cops" would be derived from the MORE technology grants. Finally, in terms of questions 6 and 7 of the evaluation, the researchers reported that the COPS program did help advance community policing in the United States, but they were also quick to point out that community policing has many different meanings for different agencies.

The *National Evaluation of the COPS Program* gives one the impression that the program was very successful, but it should be noted that it is primarily from a process evaluation analysis. In other words, if one asked if the cops Office did give out grants to local agencies like it said it would, the answer is a resounding yes. There is little doubt that the COPS Office achieved the goal of funneling money and adding cops, but there are often questions as to the methods employed. Although the Crime Bill of 1994 allowed for the counting of technology grants to equate to an FTE of a police officer, that part of the money did not put another body on the street like most people believed it would. And in fact, questions have been raised as to whether the COPS program's count of officers or even the *National Evaluation's* count is correct. A Heritage Foundation study found that, by 1998, only 39,617 officers had been hired and that the way the COPS Office counted officers was suspicious (Muhlhausen 2001a). Muhlhausen gives the example that "COPS officials claim that the Spokane Police Department had hired 56 new officers based on three COPS grants worth $4.2 million, but the Spokane Police Department said that it had hired only 25 officers. Nevertheless, COPS officials counted the 31 'missing' officers in the total number of additional officers it supposedly put on the streets" (Muhlhausen 2001a, 1). In addition, another study by Muhlhausen (2001b) looked at the impact that the hiring grants had on crime and found no statistically measurable effect on violent crime and that most of the declining crime was attributed to social changes in minority communities and prison expansion. The greatest effect of the COPS program was found in the COPS funding that targeted specific problems in specific locations, such as gangs, juvenile youth crime, and domestic violence (Muhlhausen 2002b). Muhlhausen concluded that "there are two possible explanations for the ineffectiveness of the COPS hiring and redeployment grants: (1) the actual number of officers 'added' to the street by these grants may be substantially less than the funding indicates, and (2) merely paying for the operational expenses of law enforcement agencies without a clear crime-fighting objective is likely to be ineffective in reducing violent crime" (Muhlhausen 2002, 7).

Research that has more of an independent investigatory perspective and less of a political angle to it was conducted by Jihong "Solomon" Zhao and a number of associates

NATIONAL EVALUATION OF THE COPS PROGRAM

Effect on Level of Policing

Our best estimate at this time is that, by 2003, the COPS program will have raised the level of policing on the street by the equivalent of 62,700 to 83,900 full-time officers. This estimate contains two elements: 39,000–55,000 hired officers (net of attrition and cross-hiring between agencies) and 23,800–28,500 full-time equivalents (FTEs) of officer time created by productivity gains due to technology and civilians acquired with COPS MORE funds. To those who considered the level of policing in 1994 inadequate, this constitutes success, even though it falls well short of the announced target of "100,000 new cops on the beat."

Effect on Transition to Community Policing

It seems clear that the COPS program accelerated transition to locally defined versions of community policing in at least three ways. First, by stimulating a national conversation about community policing and providing training and technical assistance, the COPS program made it difficult for a chief executive seeking professional recognition to avoid considering adopting some approach that could plausibly be labeled "community policing." Second, the COPS hiring funds and innovative policing grants allowed chief executives who were so inclined to add new community policing programs without immediately cutting back other programs, increasing response time, or suffering other adverse consequences. Third, the COPS funds created an incentive for agency executives to adopt community policing.

Effect on Organizational and Technological Innovation

In agencies whose chief executives were inclined toward innovation, the COPS program facilitated their efforts in several ways. First, the broad semantic umbrella offered by the term *community policing* creates latitude for experimentation with new policing tactics and organizational structures. Second, the application required specification of a community policing strategy, thereby offering an occasion for engaging broad segments of the agency and community in planning that strategy. Third, COPS resources allowed departments the opportunity to add new modes of policing without drawing resources away from existing priorities. Fourth, although achieving the projected productivity increased from MORE-funded mobile computers required telecommunications and other technology that were unavailable at the outset of COPS, the MORE funds fueled a large enough market to attract vendors' interest and to stimulate their efforts to satisfy the new demand.

Source: Jeffrey A. Roth and Joseph F. Ryan, *National Evaluation of the COPS Program—Title 1 of the 1994 Crime Act.* Washington, D.C.: National Institute of Justice, 2000.

(He, Zhao, and Lovrich 2005; Worrall and Zhao 2003; Zhao, Scheider, and Thurman 2003). Zhao analyzed the COPS office and the relationship of the grants with a number of macro variables. One study (Zhao, Scheider, and Thurman 2003) found that the COPS hiring grants were associated with more police arrests for drugs and social disorder–related crimes, and that the COPS MORE grants were associated with increased police arrests for social disorder–related crimes. The study's authors concluded that the COPS MORE grants have had the most significant impact on police arrests and that both grants have freed officers' time so officers could engage in community-oriented policing activities, including the targeting of social disorder problems. In another study (Worrall and Zhao 2003), the authors found that COPS funding was strongly associated with community-oriented policing. They did not propose to explain this with any finality, but they suggested that agencies may simply be chasing federal government money. In particularly, they found that the hiring grants were associated with community-oriented policing, more so than other innovative grant dollars, but the hiring grants were more widely available and easier to apply for. They also found that those agencies with multiple grants were more likely to be doing community-oriented policing than those with only a single grant. Finally, in another study (He, Zhao, and Lovrich 2005), the researchers found that cities with a council–city manager style of government were more likely to adopt community-oriented policing than other traditional mayor–council forms of government, and that the COPS grants had a significant impact on the adoption of community-oriented policing. In sum, regardless of why agencies sought out the COPS grants and all of the problems associated with the grants, it would appear that this federal initiative has had an enormous impact on the adoption of community-oriented policing across the nation.

WHAT HAPPENS WHEN COPS GRANTS DWINDLE?

Worrall and Zhao (2003), in the their analysis of the COPS office asked a very important question regarding the COPS grants, "What happens when the well runs dry" (p. 81)? A number of people have asked this same question, ranging from academic scholars to the news media, including National Public Radio and *USA Today* (2003). The original reason for asking this question had more to do with the nature of the grants themselves. The COPS hiring grants were for three years at 80 percent of an officer's pay and benefits. At the end of the three years, the police department became fully responsible for the officer over the rest of his or her career (4–20/25/30 years). Here the well of federal funding was intentionally planned to run dry.

The COPS office, however, found a number of ways to "stay alive" despite the fact it was intended to originally sunset in the year 2000. Additional appropriations by the Clinton Administration assured the COPS office longevity. Yet, as Worrall and Zhao intended in their question, what happens when the COPS office runs out of money as all good federal programs eventually do? At the time of their writing, it was still just that—a question. Now it is becoming reality, and a number of factors have caused the COPS grants to wither.

Whenever there is a change in the executive branch, there is always a desire for the new president to put his mark on government. Continuing the policies of one's predecessor does not give the new executive the credit needed and desired in the political world. This is further exacerbated by a change in political party, as in 2000, when Clinton, a Democrat, was replaced by Bush, a Republican. Although Bush did not outwardly eliminate the COPS office, his intent was to put his own mark on the agency, by shifting the emphasis from community-oriented policing to school resource officers. This allowed the agency to stay alive and continue operating, but it allowed the Bush Administration to put its own mark on the policies of that office. Then September 11, 2001 occurred.

The tragic events of September 11, 2001, had profound impacts on the federal government, many of them highly obvious. The passage of the Homeland Security Act of 2002 and the creation of the Department of Homeland Security are the most evident. However, many programs throughout the various departments in the federal government were impacted, and the COPS office was no different. The emphasis of the COPS budget shifted quickly away from school resource officers and the old hiring grants to the concept of "Homeland Security through Community Policing." The COPS office made the argument that the tenets of community-oriented policing would help to secure the homeland (see Chapter 15 for a further discussion of this argument). As a result, funds were shifted toward homeland security initiatives. However, the Department of Homeland Security needed a budget to match its magnitude in both concept and structure. A number of programs ended up on the side of budget cuts, and the COPS office was clearly one of these agencies.

Starting in 2002, for the 2003 fiscal year budget, the COPS office has continued to see its budget slashed. While the calls by the Administration for budget cuts tend to run much deeper than the actual cuts made, it is evident that the COPS office is being phased out through the budgetary process. For instance, in 2004, the Bush Administration requested that the then $499 million dollar budget be cut to $22 million. The final budget was not quite $350 million. Again, in 2005, the budget cuts were to bring down the COPS office to around $20 million, while the actual appropriations were a little over $221 million. However, moving from its peak of nearly one billion dollars, to half a billion, to $221 million is a considerable slide toward being no longer functional. More recently, as the President releases his plan for funding domestic discretionary programs over the next three years, the proposal is to lower the COPS office to $98 million by fiscal year 2009, cutting its budget by 75 percent in the three-year period (Center on Budget and Policy Priorities 2006). It is evident that the Bush Administration is phasing out the COPS office without an outright elimination of the program. This is done for political purposes because an outright elimination creates more of a crisis in the media than does a continual reduction of funding.

Is the withering of the COPS office the right thing to do? That is a question typically based on one's perspective. Many, such as Muhlhausen, have argued that the COPS office and its grants have not reduced crime, therefore they are wasted government expenditures. Others, such as Zhao and associates, have argued that the COPS grants have led police closer to community-oriented policing, which enhances police–community relations, reduces social disorder and fear of crime, and improves the quality of life. If you think that the police are solely about crime reduction and the record on community-oriented policing reducing crime is spotty at best, it would make sense to eliminate the COPS program. If you think that community-oriented policing provides benefits other than crime reduction that have equal merit, then the phasing out of the COPS office is a tragedy in the making. Regardless of one's viewpoints, however, it would appear that the office will wither on the vine, raising the question about the future of community-oriented policing (see Chapter 15 for further discussion of this issue).

CONCLUSION

Although a complete assessment of the impact that the COPS Office has had on community-oriented policing needs further development, what is clear is that the federal government will undoubtedly have the single biggest impact on the community-oriented policing movement. To ignore the grants, rhetoric, training, and technical support the U.S. Department of Justice provided to state and local law enforcement agencies in the United States and its territories would be to ignore the greatest movement to institutionalize the philosophy of community-oriented policing. More important perhaps is how the role of the federal government has dynamically changed the development of community-oriented policing from a grassroots initiative that simply saw agencies adopting it for innovative and perhaps altruistic reasons to agencies now adopting it because of the grant money available. Therefore, although it is not fully clear how the COPS grants have changed community-oriented policing in the United States, it is certain that they have changed the movement fundamentally and forever (He, Zhao, and Lovrich 2005; Worrall and Zhao 2003; Zhao, Scheider, and Thurman 2003).

The future of the COPS Office is unclear. Although it was set to disband at the end of the year 2000, like all good bureaucratic agencies, it gained new life. It first gained a reprieve by President Clinton and Vice President Al Gore, who called upon Congress to fund an additional 50,000 cops (Clinton 1999). However, Clinton's designated successor to the presidency and the COPS initiative, Al Gore, lost the 2000 election and George W. Bush became president. The Bush administration quickly moved to put its mark on the COPS program by shifting much of the remaining funds to support the hiring of school resource officers. Then, after the events of September 11, 2001, the COPS Office began aligning itself with the concept of homeland security, touting that community policing and homeland security are compatible, which it highlighted at a July 2002 conference in Washington, D.C., with the theme "Community Policing Keeping America Safe." It is unknown which direction the COPS Office and the COPS grants will now take, but one can most likely rest assured that they will continue to play some role in funding police initiatives for some time. The question is, Will they be related to community-oriented policing?

COP ON THE WORLD WIDE WEB

Community Policing Consortium

http://www.communitypolicing.org

Fighting Crime with COPS and Citizens (4-year study of COPS program)

http://www.ojp.usdoj.gov/nij/cops/index.html

Web site containing the National Institute of Justice report as well as ten case studies of various police departments across the country.

Grants of Office of Community Oriented Policing Services (COPS) by State/Jurisdiction

http://www.usdoj.gov/cops/foia/foia_err.htm

Scroll down to "Cops grants awarded by state" and click on your state in a PDF file. Look through the list of grantees for your hometown police or sheriff's department to see what type of grants it has received.

Office of Community Oriented Policing Services (COPS)

http://www.usdoj.gov/cops

Violent Crime Control and Law Enforcement Act of 1994 (full text)

http://usinfo.state.gov/usa/infousa/laws/majorlaw/h3355_en.htm

REVIEW QUESTIONS

1. Describe the impact that federal role in community-oriented policing has played since the early 1990s.
2. Describe the four types of grants provided by the COPS Office. Use examples of such grants in your answers.
3. Assess the impact of the federalization on community-oriented policing.

CHAPTER 13

Comparative Community-Oriented Policing

The police at all times should maintain a relationship with the public
that gives reality to the historic tradition that the police are the public
and that the public are the police; the police are the only members of
the public who are paid to give full-time attention to duties which are
incumbent on every citizen in the interest of community welfare.

—Sir Robert Peel

CHAPTER OBJECTIVES

- Recognize that community-oriented policing is not limited to the United States.
- Learn how to study public policies from a comparative perspective.
- Define *comparative community-oriented policing*.
- Understand community-oriented policing in Canada.
- Understand community-oriented policing in England.
- Understand community-oriented policing in Japan.
- Briefly review community-oriented policing in other countries.

Although community-oriented policing has fast become the primary method for delivering police services in the United States, it has also become the primary method for many police agencies throughout the industrialized world. Community-oriented policing has become the organizational philosophy of policing in the United States, as well as Australia, Canada, Denmark, England, Finland, Israel, Japan, New Zealand, Northern Ireland, Norway, Singapore, South Africa, and Sweden (Baratta 1994; Bayley 1989, 1991, 1994; Brown and

TABLE 13-1   *Countries with Agencies That Practice Community-Oriented Policing*

Australia	Iceland	Nigeria
Belgium	India	Northern Ireland
Canada	Ireland	Norway
China	Israel	Russia
Denmark	Japan	South Africa
Finland	Mexico	Sweden
Great Britain	Netherlands	United States
Hungary	New Zealand	Yugoslavia

Polk 1996; Friedmann 1992; Harman 1992; Skolnick and Bayley 1988a, b). In some cases, the community-oriented policing practices of other countries have paralleled those of the United States with similar time frames of implementation and practices. In other cases, the implementation of community-oriented policing has been very fragmented and delayed for various reasons. Still other systems are referred to as being community-oriented, but the term is more indicative of their culture than applicable to any real systemic change within their policing organizations. Regardless of the status of implementation, when analyzing other countries' adoptions of this new philosophy of policing, much can be learned about implementation not only in these other countries but in the United States as well. Therefore, in this chapter we look at other countries' adoptions and adaptations of community-oriented policing in comparison to efforts throughout the United States. (See Table 13-1.)

COMPARATIVE COMMUNITY-ORIENTED POLICING

An area of criminal justice that has seen rapid growth in study, research, and analysis is comparative criminal justice systems. According to Ebbe (1996, 1), "to understand criminal justice one must study the criminal law and constitution of a country or state, the agencies of the justice system, and what happens to the accused from the time of his/her arrest to disposal of the case." He goes on to explain that "comparative criminal justice studies build on such knowledge, investigating similarities and operation of the criminal justice agencies of various nations and states." As the research in this area has proliferated (e.g., Ebbe 1996; Fairchild 1993; Reichel 1999), many researchers have begun looking more deeply at specific aspects of the criminal justice system, such as policing, and others have begun to narrow the focus by looking at specific topics, such as the topic at hand, community-oriented policing (Friedmann 1992). Because comparative criminal justice system research has expanded greatly, it is important to understand why it is an important area, especially for comparing various countries' adoptions of community-oriented policing.

Fairchild explains that there are three important reasons for comparing systems of justice cross-nationally: (1) to benefit from the experience of others, (2) to broaden our understanding of different cultures and approaches to problems, and (3) to help us deal with international crime problems such as terrorism and drug smuggling (see Fairchild

1993, 3). As related to community-oriented policing compared cross-nationally, it is perhaps the first reason that is most applicable. Looking at other countries and how they have put into practice the philosophy of community-oriented policing can provide a number of new ideas, concepts, programs, and solutions for addressing many of the implementation problems found in police agencies' adoption of the systemic approach to policing in the United States (Kratcoski, Verma, and Das 2000; Lab and Das 2003). In addition, agencies can, perhaps, learn from the mistakes of others.

The second reason is applicable when considering community-oriented policing, especially in the context of comparing other nations' agencies to American agencies, because it is important to understand the cultures of other countries as well as those cultures as they exist in the United States. Because the United States is a diverse and multicultural country, when considering the relationships between the police and the community, the police must understand the many cultures they find within their community. The police–citizen contact that works with one culture may not work with another culture. For instance, many Asian cultures have a high degree of respect for police and will not disagree with the police or question an officer's authority. This aspect of the culture can obviously pose problems for working and dealing with this specific community because it could easily become highly police-driven. Another culture, the Mexican culture, is highly suspicious of the police because of experiences with a very military-oriented police that wields much authority and power. Hence, in dealing with this specific community, police–community partnerships can pose a problem because of this high level of suspicion.

The third category also applies to the concepts of comparative community-oriented policing and can take on significant importance in certain communities. Many countries, especially those that border other countries, may face crime that has an international association. The problems that the police and community must address in these communities may require an understanding of the international relationship that is involved in these crimes to identify the problem that the police and community will have to work to resolve. One example is the black market for cigarettes along the United States–Canada border. This type of crime has created a local problem for many border cities in both countries, but it stems from the passage of federal laws and regulations that created the black market because Canadian cigarettes became cheaper to purchase in the United States than in Canada (Studlar 1997). Because more than 80 percent of the Canadian population lives along this border, a local crime situation is created that is primarily based on an international situation. Another example is the border of the United States and Mexico, where, on almost any given day or night, hundreds or even thousands of people are attempting to cross the border into the United States.

In conducting comparative criminal justice system analyses, such as in the area of community-oriented policing, three approaches the studies can take are historical, political, and descriptive (Reichel 1999). The first approach focuses on reviewing the historical context of a modern criminal justice system to learn how it developed over time and what knowledge this development can provide for other countries (Fairchild 1993). In the case of community-oriented policing, exploring the evolution of the implementation of this concept provides a vast amount of information on current community-oriented policing practices.

The second approach, the political, is oriented to the political and institutional effects on the criminal justice system of a specific country. The political approach often focuses on the governmental processes of public policy and pays special attention to such

Students in Tasmania who have participated in "Adopt-a-Cop," in which
police are "adopted" by either a school or a particular grade at a school.
(*Courtesy of the Tasmania Police, Hobart, Tasmania, Australia.*)

factors as socioeconomic relationships, cultural values, the public–private sector dichotomy, political parties, interest groups, and other institutions of government and governmental control (Heidenheimer, Heclo, and Adams 1990). Because the criminal justice
system is in fact a governmental institution, this approach would apply to not only comparative criminal justice but also comparative community-oriented policing. From this
standpoint, the approach may ask questions such as, "How do politics affect a nation's
justice system or its implementation of community-oriented policing?" (Reichel 1999).

The final approach, the descriptive, is largely based on just that, providing a background description of a specific country's criminal justice system or community-oriented
policing adaptations, which provides an initial overview. From there, it allows researchers
to compare and contrast several nations and their methods of implementation, providing
for a better understanding of a specific nation (Reichel 1999). As Bayley (1979, 111–112)
has explained, a number of policing duties are important in most cultures:

1. Protecting life and property
2. Enforcing the criminal law
3. Investigating criminal offenses
4. Patrolling public places
5. Advising about crime prevention
6. Conducting prosecutions
7. Sentencing for minor offenses

8. Maintaining order and decorum in public places by directing, interrupting, and warning
9. Guarding persons and facilities
10. Regulating traffic
11. Controlling crowds
12. Regulating and suppressing vice
13. Counseling juveniles
14. Gathering information about political and social life
15. Monitoring elections
16. Conducting counterespionage
17. Issuing ordinances
18. Inspecting premises
19. Issuing permits and licenses
20. Serving summonses
21. Supervising jails
22. Impounding animals and lost property
23. Advising members of the public and referring them to other agencies
24. Caring for the incapacitated
25. Promoting community crime prevention activities
26. Participating in policy councils of government

Because Bayley's extensive list was drawn up prior to the implementation of community-oriented policing around the world, only a few of these cross-cultural comparisons reflect the community-oriented policing movement. In looking at cross-cultural community-oriented policing, it is perhaps too soon to draw up a similar list, but most of the cross-cultural comparisons incorporate some elements of the three components of community-oriented policing: strategic-oriented policing, neighborhood-oriented policing, and problem-oriented policing.

The format to be utilized in this chapter focuses more on the descriptive approach but pays some attention to the historical and political approaches as well. Therefore, each analysis will be a brief review of each nation's government and police system, followed by a brief history of when, how, and why community-oriented policing was adopted. Next, what community-oriented policing entails in each country will be reviewed to understand the practical aspects of adoption, specifically analyzing the adoption of the three components. Finally, where within each country community-oriented policing has been implemented will be explored throughout the comparative review. The nations reviewed here are Canada, Britain, and Japan. These three countries were selected because most Americans are familiar with them, because of the extensive literature and studies conducted in each country, and because they are diverse in their methods of community-oriented policing. Although both Canada and Britain have made the move toward community-oriented policing, Canada did so with support and much success whereas Britain did so with much animosity and resistance. Japan, in a sense, has not adopted community-oriented policing, but, as a direct result of its culture and policing practices, it has developed many of the concepts that we have come to see as community-oriented policing. Finally, in the last section we look at other nations' adoptions in an overview and include the community-oriented policing initiatives of Singapore, Israel, Australia, New Zealand, South Africa, Norway, and Belgium, among others.

COMMUNITY-ORIENTED POLICING: CANADIAN STYLE

Canada is a confederation with a parliamentary democracy divided into ten provinces (Ontario, Quebec, Manitoba, Saskatchewan, British Columbia, Alberta, New Brunswick, Nova Scotia, Newfoundland, and Prince Edward Island) and three territories (Northwest Territories, Yukon, and Northern Territories, which were added in 1999) covering 3,849,000 square miles with a population of over 29 million (Reichel 1999). Canada's form of government is a confederation with a prime minister as the head of government and a parliament. The Constitution Act of 1867 gave the Canadian Parliament the legislative authority to create criminal law, and in 1875 a Canadian Supreme Court was created.

Because Canada is a federalist state, it has a largely decentralized form of police organization, which consists of three levels. The first level is the federal police, known as the Royal Canadian Mounted Police (RCMP). The RCMP was originally known as the Northwest Mounted Police and was founded in 1873. In 1970, the RCMP's name and authority were modified by the Royal Canadian Mounted Police Act. The second level is the provincial police, who are responsible for the ten provinces of Canada. Finally, there are the municipal police, who cover the various cities, towns, villages, and townships in Canada (Reichel 1999). It is important to note, however, that the decentralized police service in Canada allows government jurisdictions to contract for their police services. In most instances, the police services are contracted out to the RCMP; such is the case in eight of the

An Edmonton police officer exchanges hats with a local youth. (*Courtesy of the Edmonton Police Service, Edmonton, Alberta, Canada. Photograph by Stacey Armour.*)

ten provinces, with Ontario and Quebec being the exceptions (Kurian 1989). Approximately 54,722 police officers serving in over 581 police agencies across Canada are supported by an additional 19,000 support personnel. Of these police officers, approximately 27 percent work for the RCMP, 16 percent work for the provincial police, and more than 60 percent work for municipal police agencies (Leighton 1991). Canada's five largest police forces include the RCMP, the Ontario Provincial Police, the Surete de Quebec, the Metro Toronto Police, and the Montreal Police, which account for more than 60 percent of all officers in Canada (Leighton 1994). Finally, the five largest urban police departments in Canada are Toronto, Montreal, Calgary, Edmonton, and Vancouver (Murphy 1988).

COP IN ACTION

A Canadian Police Department Evaluates Services

In 1988, the Edmonton Police Service (EPS) conducted a study of their repeat calls for service. The study showed that 21 "hot spots" accounted for almost sixty percent of the calls received. The department assigned a beat officer trained in problem solving to each of the 21 areas and gave each a mandate to work with the community to identify and solve problems. This Neighborhood Foot Patrol Program (NFPP) tested the concepts of community policing and its success was critical to EPS making an organizational transition to the philosophy.

Dr. J. Hornick et al. (1990) evaluated the NFPP and found that as calls for service went down, police and public satisfaction rose. The results convinced citizens, politicians, and the police that community policing was the way to go. EPS's Executive Officers Team (EOT) committed themselves to leading the organizational change to support community policing.

Move toward Community Policing

In 1991, EPS identified six major components for its "change agenda":

- Workload analysis to ensure appropriate placement of facilities and district structure
- Strategy development to decentralize facilities and increase the community's access to police services
- A new service delivery system whereby citizens request service on-site at a facility to help diminish the amount of police response to service-level calls
- Officer assignment to static districts based on natural neighborhood boundaries to be identified through the workload analysis
- Community policing information and training sessions developed for all employees
- EPS staff involvement—either in an operational or support role—in problem solving and community activities

The department met these objectives by conducting three major reviews:

- A retrospective analysis of crime rates and community needs over the previous 10 years
- A workload analysis identifying police service requirements for Edmonton's 273 communities, which enabled EPS to better service communities on a macro level by establishing community stations
- A five-question analysis of every box, or unit, on the EPS organizational chart

Analysts developed 164 recommendations using EPS's core value statement—"Committed to Community Needs"—as a measuring tool. They identified that between 1969 and 1990, the number of boxes on the organizational chart—that is the number of units—doubled from 60 to 120. EPS had staffed the units in years past by removing officers from the street and placing them into the administrative positions created each time a new unit was formed. Based on the 1991 review, 68 officers were returned to the street and another sixty were reassigned back to operational divisions. EPS cut the administrative budget by almost $2.5 million and moved the funds back into the operational budget to assist with the increasing workload. Of the 164 recommendations identified by the organizational review team, 132 of them were presented to the EOT and resulted in significant change.

A mass effort to educate and train community members and create a new service delivery system also occurred during this time. In January 1992, EPS opened its community stations and encouraged the public to report "service-type" calls at these locations. Today, the stations serve as information "clearinghouses" and are considered the focal point of the newly identified Community Service Areas.

The EOT continues to advance community policing and conducted two organizational reviews since 1991 to keep the department from drifting or backsliding from its goals.

Evaluation Results

In 1995, newly appointed Chief John Lindsay initiated a restructuring that put a strong emphasis on information processing and evaluation. Since 1991, Edmonton's total criminal code occurrences dropped 41 percent. The decline continued even after it was anticipated that the rates would stabilize. In the 1994–1995 reporting year, crimes against persons dropped another 6.2 percent and crimes against property decreased by 9 percent. After four years of community policing, the crime numbers are continuing to decrease. What does all of this mean? Because calls for service have decreased 35 percent and 911 calls more than 30 percent, officers have more time to problem-solve in their communities. And citizens report a 93 percent satisfaction rate with community stations.

In 1996, the Edmonton Police Service identified 12 critical organizational issues that are seen as barriers to getting work done. EPS immediately developed strategies to deal with these issues. The department also created an ideal staffing model that will determine a minimum staffing level required to hit target response times.

Community policing, for EPS, at times moves rapidly. At other times it seems to progress at a more evolutionary pace. One element, however, is static. As a department, Edmonton Police Service will continue to strive to take community policing to the next level.

Source: Reprinted with permission from David Veitch, "A Canadian Police Department Evaluates Services," *Community Policing Exchange,* May/June 1996, p. 8.

The police in Canada, for a variety of historical, political, and cultural reasons (Hagan and Leon 1981; Lipset 1986), are "publicly popular, well-financed, politically autonomous, organizationally stable, and ideologically powerful" (Murphy 1988, p. 177). Policing in Canada has not become a serious political or public problem as it has elsewhere, and the police have therefore had the luxury to implement police practices and innovations and conduct research on which methods work in policing and which methods do not (Bayley and Shearing 1996). Community-oriented policing therefore has not come on the heels of some scandal as the panacea for fixing the problems of policing but rather as a matter of choice on the part of the Canadian police agencies. The reasons cited for this movement toward community-oriented policing in Canada include (1) the traditional police system has not worked, (2) budgets for policing had reached a ceiling and required doing more with less, and (3) community-oriented policing is the only system that can combat fear of crime among both the police and citizens in urban areas (Normandeau 1993).

Despite these three reasons, there has been somewhat of a debate about why Canada has adopted the practices of community-oriented policing, including (1) that police in Canada run the risk of not being current if they do not adopt the methods of community-oriented policing (Murphy 1988), (2) that the Canadian police primarily had a desire to return to the traditional principles that had their roots in the nineteenth century (Leighton 1994), or (3) that the Canadian police were merely imitating "U.S.-tested and proven police innovation" (Friedmann 1992, 99). Although it is difficult to discern which reason or reasons were the motivation behind Canadian police agencies initiating community-oriented policing, there has been a high level of information sharing between the United States and Canada (Leighton 1994). It must be noted, however, that many agencies in Canada began implementing community-oriented policing in the early 1980s, at approximately the same time as many of the agencies in the United States and England, in several of its larger departments, including the Metro Toronto Police Department and the Halifax Police Department, as well as in Edmonton, Montreal, Winnipeg, and Victoria (Murphy 1988). Yet it has also been pointed out that the Canadian agencies were slow to adopt the various assumptions of community-oriented policing throughout the 1980s, and it was not until the RCMP and the national leadership finally stood behind community-oriented policing in the early 1990s that it was formally endorsed (Leighton and Normandeau 1990). (See Table 13-2.)

Because community-oriented policing has been implemented since the early 1980s in Canada, albeit at a slow pace, and formally adopted in 1990 by the Canadian government, one would expect that the assumptions of community-oriented policing would become institutionalized in Canadian police agencies adopting the new paradigm in policing. In turning to what agencies have done under the guise of community-oriented policing in Canada, we find that one of the earliest innovators, the Metro Toronto Police

TABLE 13-2   *Mission Statement of the Royal Canadian Mounted Police (RCMP)*

RCMP Community Policing is . . .

A partnership between the police and the community, sharing in the delivery of police services.

With this valuable community cooperation, the RCMP pledges to . . .

Uphold the principles of the Canadian Charter of Rights and Freedoms.

Provide a professional standard of service.

Ensure all policing services are provided courteously and impartially.

Work with the community and other agencies to prevent or resolve problems that affect the community's safety and quality of life.

Act with the Canadian justice system to address community problems.

Promote a creative and responsible environment to allow all RCMP members to deliver community services.

Source: Solicitor General of Canada. *A Vision of the Future of Policing in Canada: Police-Challenge 2000.* Ottawa: Ministry of the Solicitor General of Canada, 1990.

Department, commenced its community-oriented policing program in 1982 primarily as a result of a history of citizen complaints against the police for abuse and excessive force violations. In 1981, the Metropolitan Police Force Project Act established the Office of the Public Complaints Commissioner, and the Police Complaints Investigation Bureau was created to address these complaints (Lewis, Linden, and Keene 1986). Out of this legislation came the movement to be more responsive to citizens' needs, and the community-oriented policing movement was initiated. The Metro Toronto Police Department has subsequently decentralized into neighborhood districts, opened storefront operations, and created citizen advisory groups (Murphy 1988).

Like the Metro Toronto Police Department, other police agencies in Canada began moving toward community-oriented policing in the early 1980s and have, accordingly, begun adopting the various components of community-oriented policing (see Table 13-3). These agencies include Halifax in 1985 (Clairmont 1990), Montreal in 1986 (Rizkalla et al. 1990), Victoria in 1987 (Walker and Walker 1989, 1991), and Edmonton in 1988 (Hawkins 1996; Hornick et al. 1990; Kratcoski and Dukes 1995). For instance, the implementation of community-oriented policing in Halifax commenced in 1985 when the patrol division was reorganized into three districts with specific zones to promote beat integrity. From there, new policies and procedures emphasized the philosophy of community-oriented policing, and the department adopted many of the practices of community-oriented policing such as

TABLE 13-3   *Twelve Principles of Canadian Policing*

1. The role of police officers is one of peace officers.
2. Community consultation should be encouraged, so that police officers and the public carry on meaningful and continuing dialogues to share concerns about common crime problems.
3. Policing should be proactive rather than reactive.
4. A problem-oriented policing strategy should be invoked that will address crime and order problems and their causes.
5. There should be broader police response to underlying causes of problems.
6. Greater interagency cooperation is encouraged.
7. Managerial personnel in police departments must learn to be information managers and engage in interactive policing on a reciprocal basis with community leaders through formal contacts and informal networks.
8. The fear of being victimized must be reduced by ensuring the protection of groups prone to victimization, such as the young and the elderly.
9. Police officers must become generalists responsible for broader ranges of activities than is currently required.
10. Front-line officers must be given greater discretion, responsibilities, and autonomy through agency decentralization and widespread resource deployment.
11. Organizational structure of police agencies must be changed from the paramilitary model to a flatter profile, in which a broader array of police services might be provided to the public.
12. There must be better mechanisms in place to promote greater police accountability to the public.

Source: Solicitor General of Canada. *A Vision of the Future of Policing in Canada: Police-Challenge 2000.* Ottawa: Ministry of the Solicitor General of Canada, 1990.

surveying and interviewing citizens, more authority being invested in the beat officers, and problem solving being encouraged (Clairmont 1990). Another example is in Victoria, where in the late 1980s the department created five police ministations that served specific neighborhoods' needs pertaining to crime as well as other quality-of-life issues (Walker and Walker 1989). These ministations were primarily based on the use of *kobans* in Japan (detailed later) and have proven to be very popular with citizens. In addition, in 1987 the Victoria police adopted the Citizens' Crime Watch (CCW) program, in which volunteers were trained, divided into teams, and assigned to specific areas of the city. At a fairly low cost, the CCW has been credited with assisting in dozens of arrests, recovering hundreds of stolen autos, and assisting thousands of citizens each year (Harman 1992). Finally, one of the most successful adoptions of community-oriented policing in Canada is in Edmonton, Alberta. There, under the leadership of Chris Braiden, the department has been highly successful in its implementation of community-oriented policing through a complete organizational review, the decentralization of the agency in all manners, and the implementation of the three components of community-oriented policing (Friedmann 1992; Hawkins 1996; *To a Different Beat,* 1997).

It must also be pointed out that the RCMP has taken great strides to implement the philosophy and components of community-oriented policing since 1990 (Laing and Hickman 2003). In the early 1980s it began adopting many of the various programs of community-oriented policing, such as community patrols, Neighborhood Watch, business security checks, youth programs, and public safety programs. In 1990, it began to expand its operational framework of community-oriented policing under the program Clients Acquiring and analyzing information, Partnerships, Response, and Assessment for continuous improvement (CAPRA) (Himelfarb 1997). This program has brought about a more holistic and systemic approach to community-oriented policing with regard to the RCMP by focusing on police–community relations through the reorientation of citizens as clients in a total quality management (TQM) style (clients) and by integrating many of the concepts of neighborhood-oriented policing (partnerships) and problem-oriented policing (acquiring and analyzing information, response, and assessment for continuous improvement) into their methods of delivering police services.

There is plenty of rhetoric about the future of Canadian policing, and it is believed that community-oriented policing is moving toward full implementation nationally (Lindsay 2003). There is a strong belief that to fully implement community-oriented policing, police organizations across Canada must be transformed. It is also believed that they must become more open and less hierarchical, allow for greater autonomy of officers, and be based on the mission of solving problems in partnership with the community (Normandeau and Leighton 1990). The Canadian community-oriented policing movement, to date, has been very successful in creating greater police–community interaction and awareness (Normandeau and Leighton 1990), allowing Canadian citizens to see policing in a more positive light. In turn, the movement toward community-oriented policing has been well received by Canadian police officers, and most experienced officers regard community-oriented policing as the future for Canadian policing (Braiden 1986). In sum, then, it can be said that Canada has been highly successful in its movement toward organizing and delivering police services under the community-oriented policing model (see Chacko and Nancoo 1993 for a fuller treatment of Canadian community-oriented policing).

COMMUNITY-ORIENTED POLICING: BRITISH STYLE

The United Kingdom of Great Britain and Northern Ireland has a constitutional monarchy for its form of government and is divided into England and Wales, which have forty-seven nonmetro counties, six metro counties, and London; Scotland, which has nine regions and three island areas; and Northern Ireland, which has twenty-six districts. The United Kingdom has a population of 58 million citizens and covers an area of over 94,000 square miles (Reichel 1999). Although England has a monarchy, a king and queen, the operating form of government is the parliamentary form with a prime minister. The Parliament consists of the House of Commons, the House of Lords, and the monarch. The 22 members of the House of Lords are appointed by the monarch, and the House of Commons consists of 635 elected members. Parliament passes criminal laws in England and utilizes primarily stare decisis for dealing with both criminal and civil cases.

There are forty-one police forces in England and Wales, consisting of twenty-seven county police forces, eight combined police areas, and six metropolitan forces (Her Majesty's Stationary Office 1993). There are approximately 120,000 police officers in England, and more than 27,000 of these officers serve with the Metropolitan Police of London (Freeman 1987). It is important to note that England does not have a national police force, as found in Canada, although the possibility of one has been debated (Bond 1984). The format for governing police agencies in England is through the establishment of local police authorities, which consist of citizens from the region (similar to counties in the United States). These regions are responsible for funding 49 percent of the police force budget, and the British Home Office funds the other 51 percent (Carter 1996). These police authorities then appoint the local chief constable (similar to a police chief in the United States) for a specific term.

The first police agency in Great Britain came as a result of Sir Robert Peel's famous request of Parliament to pass the Metropolitan Police Act of 1829. This act not only established the Metropolitan Police of London but also became the model for other police agencies throughout the world, including those in the United States and Canada. Although many perceive the fundamental principles of Sir Robert Peel, known as Peel's Principles, to be the basis of community-oriented policing, the assumptions go far beyond any consideration of Peel in the early 1800s.

England, unlike Canada, was not seen as having the autonomy to change based on its own choosing but was essentially forced into moving its police agencies toward community-oriented policing in the early 1980s. The reasons given are numerous and varied, including an erosion of public confidence (Kinsey, Lea, and Young 1986), a need for police accountability (Newing 1987; Pounder 1983), and problems of racial discrimination triggering a need for more community participation in crime prevention and control (Holdaway 1991; Willis 1985).

As a result, England began moving toward the concept of community-oriented policing in the early 1980s, bolstered by the 1982 Report of the Royal Commission on the Police, which created the Home Office Crime Prevention Unit to maintain a central repository for crime prevention information and, in particular, to evaluate new initiatives under the new methods of policing (Weatheritt 1988). Another catalyst for the move to community-oriented policing came on the heels of the Brixton riots in 1984, when the Scarman Report articulated the need for the police to adopt the principles of community-oriented policing (Brewer et al. 1988). The riots occurred largely in the early 1980s in Liverpool, Birmingham, London, and several other cities as a result of tensions between the police and the community, especially among members of minority groups. The riots escalated to such a high level of tension that the police were forced to utilize tear gas for the first time in dealing with the large crowds. Finally, in 1993, a Government White Paper proposed an extensive reorganization of the police in England to strengthen the partnership between the police and the public; in 1994 this legislation was passed by Parliament under the Police and Magistrate's Courts Act. Although it did not make the police a national organization, it has effectively moved police agencies toward the model of community-oriented policing (Home Office 1998; Woollons 1994). This legislation has had a profound impact on policing in England, and the extensive changes that most agencies have undergone are not hard to find.

Community-oriented policing in Britain has undergone substantial change in its organizations and methods for service delivery. Several studies have attempted to analyze the change and the impact the change has had and is perceived to have (Bennett 1994; McConville and Shepherd 1992; Reiner 1991). In addition to the various forms of organizational change previously described, Britain has also enhanced its concentration on sector policing (Bennett and Lupton 1992), enhanced its relationship with the public through community meetings and community contact programs (Bennett 1994), and

Northamptonshire police officer speaking with local citizens at a grocery store.
(*Courtesy of the Northamptonshire Police, Northampton, Great Britain.*)

become more proactive in its policing practices (Bennett and Lupton 1992). Most of these changes have come about as a movement toward adopting the philosophy, tenets, and components of community-oriented policing. (See Table 13-4.)

The Metropolitan Police of London has come to be considered the model agency in England for the implementation of community-oriented policing. However, as Carter (1996) explains, it is "a unique entity" in that the Metropolitan Police of London employs 14,000 civilian staff and 28,000 sworn officers. It covers more than 800 square miles of territory and has been divided into eight districts—each headed by a deputy assistant commissioner; the districts are then divided even further, with commanders in control (Carter 1996). Some are divided even further into subdivisions headed by chief superintendents, but all of the divisions with commanders in control have made the move to creating sectors to develop beat integrity. Although this type of decentralization of officers, known as the unit beat system, has been implemented in support of the Metropolitan Police of London's movement toward community-oriented policing, it has

TABLE 13-4 *Strategic Intentions of the London Metropolitan Police Service*

Our strategic intention has seven principal strands. It is our intention:

I. To remain a visible, predominantly unarmed, approachable police service in order to provide a reassuring presence across London. This, our overriding policing style, has its roots deep in the community.

II. To increase consultation with the public and their representatives; to inform and respond to their views, and their particular and changing needs, as far as we can; and to improve our internal communications. We intend to maintain our place as leaders in policing philosophy and practices.

III. To establish a clear view of the relative importance of policing tasks, and improve our performance in those areas of police activity which are identified for priority attention. It may be necessary deliberately to divert manpower away from some areas of work to address these priorities.

IV. To maintain a range of specialist services which, in support of our general policing style, reflect the changing and dynamic needs of those living and working in London. Such specialism must also encompass those national responsibilities we presently bear.

V. To achieve a sufficiency and disposition of personnel—both police and civilian support staff—to make us more effective in the delivery of our service and to realize the full potential of all individuals within the Service, promoting professionalism together with high standards of personal conduct.

All personnel must be well-trained, led, and managed:

VI. To ensure adequate technical and other appropriate support for our workforce. Investment here must be sustained and have as its twin goals the greater effectiveness of staff and the provision of better working conditions for them.

VII. Finally, to give a high quality service to all our customers, particularly the public, delivered in a way that represents good value for money. This requires exacting self-scrutiny of our performance, against agreed standards, through inspection and review procedures. We will continue to promote good practice and correct errors; if we are wrong and grievances are justified, we will accept our mistakes.

Source: London Metropolitan Police Services, *Strategic Intentions,*
http://www.homeoffice.gov.uk/pstc.htm.

been wrought with problems throughout the implementation process (Friedmann 1992). There has been an extensive amount of resistance on the part of both the beat cops and the mid-level managers, and in some cases the unit beat system had to be reconfigured to address these types of problems.

In another example of the movement toward community-oriented policing by the Metropolitan Police of London, each of the local authorities was required in the early 1980s to create a local Police Consultative Committee (Friedmann 1992). These committees were to include members of the local police, citizens from the area, and representatives from both Parliament and the local bureaucratic agencies. The committees were to hold meetings as a forum for soliciting information about problems in the community, discussing methods by which to address both criminal and quality-of-life issues, and developing plans for addressing these problems. The movement was toward the community-oriented policing philosophy and away from the traditional forms of authority and control that had long typified the Metropolitan Police of London (Morgan 1987). However, it has also been pointed out that the sole purpose may not have been greater citizen participation in local crime issues but rather an additional means by which to hold the police accountable (Friedmann 1992; Morgan 1987). Regardless of which is a more accurate reason for this movement, the benefits are real. In the various research conducted on these committees in the late 1980s and early 1990s, the results were mixed as to their success, but many of the issues raised, such as citizen apathy, lack of training and knowledge on the part of the citizens, and management and beat officer resistance, are not new. As in other countries, many of these types of community-oriented policing concepts appear to be very successful in some neighborhoods and complete failures in others.

Despite the difficulties in decentralizing and implementing many of the components of community-oriented policing, the Metropolitan Police of London has come to embody the philosophy and programs of community-oriented policing more than any other agency in England. It has fully adopted many of the programs and methods of community-oriented policing and come to fully embrace the concepts of problem solving (Hoare, Stewart, and Purcell 1984; Newman 1985). And major jurisdictions, such as the Surrey Police, are following suit; the Surrey Police Department has adopted the systemic approach with marked success (Dodd 1996). (See Table 13-5.)

TABLE 13-5 *Statement of Purpose and Values of the London Metropolitan Police Services*

The purpose of the Metropolitan Police Service is to uphold the law fairly and firmly; to prevent crime; to pursue and bring to justice those who break the law; to keep the Queen's Peace; to protect, help and reassure people in London; and to be seen to do all this with integrity, common sense, and sound judgment.

We must be compassionate, courteous, and patient, acting without fear of favor or prejudice to the rights of others. We need to be professional, calm, and restrained in the face of violence and apply only that force which is necessary to accomplish our lawful duty.

We must strive to reduce the fears of the public and, so far as we can, to reflect their priorities in the action we take. We must respond to well-founded criticism with a willingness to change.

Source: London Metropolitan Police Services, *Strategic Intention,* http://www.homeoffice.gov.uk/pstc.htm.

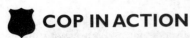

COP IN ACTION

The British Experience of Community-Oriented Policing

A review of current law enforcement professional journals, as well as the popular media, leaves the impression that virtually every police department worldwide is embracing community-oriented policing (COP). Either pushed by government officials to adopt this strategy to stem a rising crime rate, or pulled into it by others anxious to join the bandwagon, COP has become the catchword of contemporary law enforcement.

Consequently, police are adopting a variety of different procedures, labeling each as innovative community policing strategies. While some may be, and others are clearly not, there exists no proven guide to installing COP in an agency.

The British experience in community-oriented policing has provided a popular lead for this program. In fact, the antecedents of a modern community and police partnership can be traced to a proposal first made in Scotland in 1957.

The chief constable responsible for the Gibshill area suggested that it was necessary to "concentrate the attention of the police, the local authority (social) services, the churches, teachers, and others, to produce a better environment," as stated in the book "Community Versus Crime."

In his proposal, the chief envisaged "policing the area rigorously, with specially trained officers who would, I hope, not only protect the property and enforce the law, but attempt to gain the confidence and respect of the majority of the people in the area, and particularly of the children. The officers selected would of necessity be required to show an interest in matters outside the scope of ordinary police work and constant effort would be needed to maintain close liaison between them and parents, churches, and schools serving the district."

Years later, in 1976, the Devon and Cornwall Constabulary embarked on what is considered to be the most extensive commitment to COP in Britain. Beginning with a broad-ranging exploration of ways to reduce crime, the experiment eventually grew to encompass the entire force. This experience and lessons learned from it provide valuable information for those thinking about implementing community-oriented policing in their departments.

Basic to the British model is the requirement to adopt community policing as a force philosophy. Their theory is that COP must permeate the entire organization and not be the exclusive province of one unit.

If it is confined to a select few, officers not assigned will maintain that community policing is not a part of their job and will abdicate responsibility for it to the COP unit. Just as burglaries, homicides, and robberies are assigned to specialized units for follow-up, community issues will likewise be turned over to the COP officers unless the philosophy is internalized by every department member.

Redirecting a department's operative mode to community-oriented policing is a major change, and transforming the organizational culture of any group is a daunting proposition. In a bureaucratic hierarchy such as a police department, this may present a major challenge. It is imperative, therefore, to convince the entire staff, from patrol officer on up, that this is a sincere, long-term commitment to change.

To accomplish this formidable chore, the London Metropolitan Police created an internal marketing department. This unit unabashedly describes its mission as selling community policing to its fellow officers.

With over 28,000 constables, the Met is one of the oldest and largest police departments in the world. Its challenge is to turn around the traditional mindset of an organization which traces its roots to Sir Robert Peel's creation of a professional force in 1829.

Brochures, posters, and their means of advertising have been adopted from the private sector to generate committed internal support for COP. If this task is not accomplished, the Met faces the threat of failure experienced by a sister agency.

This force, which was once the leading proponent of community policing, reverted to its traditional mode of operations after its chief retired. Although the chief had guided the conversion of the agency to COP and effectively led it over the course of years to highly publicized success, he failed to convince all but the true believers. Thus, when he left, his successors, who were not among the converted, repudiated his ideas.

The lesson from this is that all levels of an organization, not only the line officers who actually perform community policing, must be convinced of the benefits of COP. The difficulty of this task is epitomized by the remark of one English constable who surely articulated the thoughts of his colleagues regarding the transition to community policing. As reported in "The Exeter Community Policing Consultative Group," he said, "Chiefs move on. It is not worth changing too much, as the next chief might want a different approach."

The conversion of one's own organization is not the only major obstacle to be overcome. Enlisting the support of peers at the command level in other agencies is also essential.

Law enforcement executives oftentimes provide the necessary clout and resources for change. Alienation of these groups may result in loss of their support, as happened to one British chief who got too far out in front of his colleagues. They resented his exposure in leading the move to COP and may even have felt threatened by this change.

His peers eventually triumphed upon his retirement. They undermined efforts to award him a knighthood, an honor which is ordinarily bestowed on departing chief constables.

A topic of frequent discussion among the British is the uniform worn by their American counterparts. They are bewildered by utility belts festooned with a firearm and holster, ammunition, handcuffs, radio, baton, keys, chemical weapons, and other accouterments. Together with the conspicuous badge, name tag, patches, medals, and additional insignia, the American uniform offers a militaristic image which the British feel erects a barrier between the police and the public, hindering communication.

For their part, the British contend that their uniform presents a soft image. Even with the Roman-style helmet and warrant (ID) numbers worn on their epaulets, they feel their appearance is not intimidating, thereby facilitating interaction with citizens.

A final issue being considered by the British police results from the lessons learned by their European colleagues in dealing with the highly volatile political environment there, combined with the constant threat of soccer violence.

Of utmost concern in community policing is maintenance of the often hard won citizen-officer bond created by this methodology. Confrontations resulting from civil disturbances or mass arrests, though, have the potential of quickly severing this tenuous alliance.

In these situations, the COP officer may have to arrest, perhaps forcefully, the very people with whom he has long worked to create a rapport. The question is whether the COP officer will be able to return to his beat after such conflict and resume his previous relationship with the community, a relationship which may have been painfully disrupted.

The proposed solution being evaluated by the British is the so-called "third force," a unit similar to those already in use on the Continent, whose sole mission is to respond to emergencies. This force would provide an alternative to either COP or traditional policing, to be called out only in situations which could damage the police-community relationship.

Such a unit would, then, bear the brunt of any citizen anger and deflect it from the COP officers. This would allow them to maintain their previously established ties to the community.

The British have a number of objections with this European formula, not least of which is the prospect of having a unit sitting around for lengthy periods of time between emergencies. In an era of tight budget constraints, this proposal isn't an economical use of personnel.

A unique approach to cementing community ties was formulated by the Royal Ulster Constabulary (RUC), which exchanges personnel with area schools. Selected officers are placed on extended detachments to replace teachers who are, in turn, assigned to the RUC. When they return to their regular jobs, they have an insight into the other's profession, which greatly enhances communication between these two vital services.

Children are particular beneficiaries of this program, as they develop a long-term connection with the police which the returning teachers reinforce, creating a ripple effect throughout the student body.

In a similar vein, the Strathclyde Police in Glasgow assigned an Inspector (Lieutenant) to work full-time with a local urban renewal council. His mandate is to provide the law enforcement perspective on a continuing basis to every facet of their redevelopment plans. From housing renovation, building and landscape design, to recreational facilities and schools, this officer ensures that crime prevention is built into every project undertaken.

Historically, rebuilding programs and new construction have been developed in isolation. Only after crime becomes intolerable have police been consulted to fix the problem. The object of this officer's participation is to have a police voice present at the inception of every plan. In this way, it is hoped to eliminate the need to retrofit crime control measures in the future when they are infinitely more expensive, difficult, and, quite likely, less effective.

Rather than reinventing the wheel when embarking on COP, police executives should seriously consider the experience gained by their British counterparts. Many of their methods can be translated directly, saving incalculable time, energy, and money. Other measures, such as creating a specialized riot squad in the uniquely American environment, can merely serve as interesting side lights to this concept.

Over years of practice with community-oriented policing, however, the British have developed and refined a viable model to achieve a better partnership with the citizens we serve, which is well worth emulating.

Source: Reprinted with permission from Eugene Friedman, "The British Experience of Community-Oriented Policing," *Law and Order,* April 1996, pp. 35–37.

As in Canada, then, England has seen a successful adoption of many of the tenets and components of the systemic approach of community-oriented policing (Friedmann 1992; Shapland and Vagg 1988), and it is apparently well received by citizens, government, and the police, at both the beat and constable level (Yates, Pillai, and Humburg 1997). However, it is important to distinguish the approaches of Canada and Britain. In Canada the call for community-oriented policing came from within the policing system, whereas in Britain the call for community-oriented policing has largely come from outside the policing system. For a number of reasons, community-oriented policing has been brought about as a result of demands from the public and action on the part of Parliament. The research on the implementation of community-oriented policing in Britain has also been more prescriptive than descriptive; however, the difference has been that the prescriptive measures have generally come after a realization that the concepts of community-oriented policing have not been completely implemented and many of the police agencies have been found to resist change (Chatterson and Rogers 1989; Weatheritt 1988). So, although many of the agencies are clearly claiming to adopt community-oriented policing, there is apparently a legitimate concern that it is more rhetoric than reality (see Fielding 1995 for a fuller treatment of British community-oriented policing).

COMMUNITY-ORIENTED POLICING: JAPANESE STYLE

Japan is an island country situated off the east coast of Asia. It has a population of more than 125 million citizens living in a country with an area of 145,850 square miles. The population density is very high: 861 citizens for every square mile. Japan has a parliamentary democracy, with the emperor serving as the head of state. The head of government is the prime minister, and the parliament, known as the Diet, is the institution that passes the criminal and civil laws. The current governmental structure in Japan was created in the wake of World War II through the passage of a new constitution on May 3, 1947. This constitution made several profound changes to the pre–World War II Japanese government. It renounced Japan's right to wage war, it forced the emperor to give up his claims to divinity, and it made the Diet the sole lawmaking authority in the country, essentially stripping from the emperor any rights to lawmaking (Farmighetti 1999).

The Japanese, in the post–World War II era, established a system of policing that in many ways is inherently reflective of the community-oriented policing philosophy, despite its implementation prior to the use of the term. The methods of policing were created through a mixture of traditional Japanese culture and the application of an American version of policing. Although Japan maintains a very centralized form of police organization, with the National Police Agency in charge, this agency is overseen by the civilian National Public Safety Commission, and the National Police Agency must work through local prefectures that supervise the local police agency (Fairchild 1993).

One of the keys to Japan's success with policing and driving down crime rates has been the close ties between the police and the community. This connection stems more from the Japanese culture than from any particular method of policing, but it is at the root of the concepts of neighborhood-oriented policing; in this approach it is desired that police have interaction with the community, that they become a known entity in a community, and that they are approachable. The police in Japan go far beyond the role of law enforcers as they reach into many areas of community life by aiding the community to resolve problems that could ultimately lead to disorder (Westermann and Burfeind 1991). One of their methods is the adoption of the *gonin-gumi,* which is a group of five people in a neighborhood who work on solving problems in a specific neighborhood, by working with the police. This program is similar to public safety commissions, problem-solving groups, or citizen review boards in the United States. Although *gonin-gumi,* like its American counterparts, gives local citizens some input into local police practices, the police are still primarily in control (Bayley 1991).

Perhaps the most noted method for providing a form of decentralized service that has seen much in the way of adaptation in the United States, such as in Boston, Massachusetts, is the *koban.* A *koban* is a small booth that sits on the street corners in Japan's larger cities; it is generally staffed by at least three officers but sometimes only one officer. The *koban* often consists of a reception room for personnel, a workroom, and a bathroom. The officers work for twenty-four-hour periods every three days and rotate the staffing of the *koban* while the other officer or officers conduct foot patrols, house and business checks, or investigations (Skolnick and Bayley 1988a, 1988b). The officers are assigned to a specific geographical neighborhood around the *koban*, and they are responsible for all of the households and businesses in that area. The average number of citizens a *koban* is responsible for is around 12,000; hence, in some of the most dense areas of Japanese cities, a *koban* may be situated on nearly every street corner. They cannot be closer together than 0.6 mile, and they generally cover areas under 0.4 square mile. In addition, they are generally placed where more than 320 criminal cases, 45 traffic tickets, and a high level of pedestrian traffic occur within a given year (Bayley 1991). More than 15,000 *kobans* have been placed throughout the city streets of Japan, with "some 6,000 police boxes [being] manned day and night in Japan's towns and in the countryside, the boxes, which double as policemen's homes, number 9,000" ("The Secret of Japan's Safe Streets" 1994, 38).

The *koban*, however, serves as more than a decentralized police station; it also serves as a means for coordinating the quality of life in a community. This lifestyle difference is explained in the observation of a *koban* found in the bar district of Tokyo: "Every few minutes somebody comes in to ask for help. A man dressed exclusively in leather is looking for a certain night club; this is pointed out for him on one of the maps. Another caller wants to report a lost bag; this involves official stamps. Then a grizzled man with a crew-cut enters, bows deeply to the policemen, and hands over ¥200 ($1.95). He is repaying a loan: if you are caught short without money for a bus journey home in Tokyo, the police can be relied upon to help out" ("The Secret of Japan's Safe Streets" 1994, 40). Thus the police in Japan are much more than law enforcers and strive to improve the relationship between the police and community and become a part of the community. This approach is clearly demonstrated in the police bands that give more than 5,000 performances a year, the home visits to the elderly and people of limited mobility, and the expansion of *kobans* in areas that cannot be staffed by having a computer touch-video screen that can answer many questions. However, it should be noted that a number of scholars have recently called into question the notion that the *kobans* are as successful as they are often portrayed and argue that they are often dumping grounds for ineffective officers, that they no longer have the capability of maintaining local contacts in the growing urban environment, and that, at worst, they are nothing more than a means for government surveillance to keep the populace in check (see Brogden and Nijhar 2005).

The biggest difference between Japan and the United States, as well as many other countries, is culture. It is clear that culture plays a role in the success of the police in Japan. Citizens cooperate and have a high level of respect for their officers. They often provide extensive information on illegal activity and people violating the social order of a neighborhood, as well as assisting the local police in the investigation of crimes. As Bayley (1991, 154) has stated, "American police officers fulfill their responsibilities when they bring people into compliance with the law; Japanese police officers seek more than compliance; they seek acceptance of the community's moral values." Therefore, the values of not only the community but the nation as well play a major role in the relationship between the police and the public, making the Japanese culture an important variable in the success of the police.

The crime rate in Japan has decreased for nearly two decades, thus providing a model for adoption of police practices under the rubric of community-oriented policing.

However, some believe that Japanese police practices would find difficult adaptation in the United States not only for cultural reasons but also, as Bayley (1991, 165) explains, because of "the bureaucratic tradition of the [U.S.] police themselves." In most cases, the level of information that the police maintain on citizens in their beat and the oversight (what Americans would call intrusion) into their daily lives would not be well received and would violate the civil rights of American citizens. For instance, suspects may be held for twenty-three days without being charged with a crime and may not have access to a lawyer during this period ("The Secret of Japan's Safe Streets," 1994). According to Fenwick (1996), the Japanese have less freedom of individual choice and expression, and there is an extensive amount of intrusion into their personal lives. Therefore, although the methods of the Japanese police may find some adaptation in the United States under the concept of community-oriented policing, the overall approach could not be transported to the United States. However, as previously stated, many of the concepts of Japanese policing have been transported to the United States; with some adaptation, they have proven to work very well under the framework of community-oriented policing.

OTHER APPROACHES OF COMPARATIVE COMMUNITY-ORIENTED POLICING

Canada, the United Kingdom, and Japan are by no means the only countries that practice community-oriented policing or some variation of the systemic approach to policing. Some countries have adopted many of the concepts, usually foot patrol and *kobans,* and others have made far greater strides in moving toward the institutionalization of community-oriented policing. The following is merely a review of where some other countries currently stand in the process of implementation of community-oriented policing.

Singapore

Singapore has been cited as a model nation in the development of community-oriented policing (Quah and Quah 1987). It has a population of nearly 3.5 million citizens of various backgrounds, including Chinese, Malaysian, and Indian (Fairchild 1993). Because Singapore has only 250 square miles of land, the population density is 13,847 citizens per square mile (Farmighetti 1999). This density in and of itself creates a number of problems in dealing with citizens, crime, and the quality of life. However, despite the high population density, Singapore has maintained very high standards of living, including in health, education, and housing. In 1981, Singapore began an extensive reform of its police agencies, adopting the Japanese methods of policing, specifically the use of *kobans.* The police were encouraged to visit homes and businesses, engage in crime prevention, and increase their foot patrols. The Singapore model has apparently been successful because despite the high population density it has managed to hold crime rates down. However, its very strict laws focused on public order, such as the heavy fines for leaving chewing gum behind and the whipping punishment for spray-painting graffiti, have received much criticism. This approach comes about from a very strict system of punishment coupled with a limited ability for freedom of expression and a police force that intrudes into the personal lives of citizens.

Israel

Israel has also moved toward the adoption of community-oriented policing. It is a small country of nearly 8,000 square miles and a population of 5.5 million citizens situated in the Middle East on the eastern shore of the Mediterranean Sea (Farmighetti 1999). It is a republic with a head of state, a head of government (the prime minister), and a parliament. The police have a very centralized organizational structure and perform most of the standard crime prevention and investigation functions. Israel maintains a police force, but it has also developed a system known as the Civil Guard that operates as a form of neighborhood watch that the police can call on for support (Friedmann 1992). The police themselves have attempted a variety of community-oriented policing initiatives, beginning in 1982, but most of the methods employed by the Israeli police have consisted of small-scale programs. They have incorporated such things as a police day for citizens, the adoption of an add-on unit for police–community relations (PCR), and the adoption of neighborhood police officers (NPOs) assigned to specific neighborhoods (Friedmann 1992). In order to address the larger

Clancy the Koala Cop gives a big hug to one of the young children at the Mater Children's Hospital on Australia Day. (*Courtesy of the Queensland Police Service, Queensland, Australia. Photo by Nadia De Bruyn.*)

concepts of community-oriented policing, in 1995 the police commissioner developed a strategy to move Israeli policing toward the full implementation by the year 2000 (Bensinger 1999; Geva 2003). The plan called for "controlling crime and providing community safety through partnerships with organizations and institutions in the community; working proactively to mobilize community, multiagency, integrated activities for the reduction of crime and fear of crime; emphasizing proactive crime prevention activity in the areas of publicity, education, and training; conducting problem analyses of crimes and quality-of-life problems that the community finds important and most relevant; insisting upon 'real-time' law enforcement functions of the police, especially regarding street crimes that decrease the quality of life in the neighborhood; providing quality police service; and involving the community in the policing activities through the ongoing interactions with the public" (Geva 2003, 104). In order to achieve this end, Israel has established a Community Policing Unit (CPU) to work with the decentralized police stations across the country (Geva 2003). As a result, individual steering committees were established in each of these stations that follow a multiagency model in dealing with crime and disorder (Geva 2003). However, Israel has faced a number of problems with its adoption of community-oriented policing strategies, ranging from citizen apathy and budget constraints to mid-level management resistance and no movement toward decentralization (Friedmann 1992). Although Israel has had some success with its adoption of community-oriented policing, it is clear that it is only beginning to move beyond the preliminary stages of implementation.

Australia

Australia is situated between the Indian and Pacific Oceans and is at the same time the smallest continent and largest island on earth. The population exceeds 19 million citizens, with the majority living along coastal waters, which distorts the population density of 6 per square mile (Farmighetti 1999). The Australian form of government is a democratic federal-state system; the head of state is England's queen, but she has a governor-general as her representative. In addition, Australia has a head of government, the prime minister. This national government oversees six states—New South Wales, Victoria, Queensland, Western Australia, South Australia, and Tasmania—as well as two territories—the Australian Capital Territory (Canberra) and the Northern Territory. Although many of the cities and jurisdictions in Australia have moved toward the concept of community-oriented policing, some of the first changes came about in the early 1980s in Adelaide, South Australia, and in Victoria (Munro 1987). In Adelaide, a comprehensive review was conducted throughout the early 1980s to explore the best ways to reorganize the police to provide the more democratic communal form of policing that was put into place in 1986. It consisted of decentralizing the police into sixteen subdivisions and incorporated the various components of community-oriented policing. The Adelaide experiment, because it was implemented with a systemic approach to policing, has been very successful, whereas the Victoria experiment has not been as successful. In Victoria, the police have essentially implemented several programs—such as Neighborhood Watch and the police–community involvement program—that also attempt to incorporate the components of community-oriented policing, but they did so early on without any larger concept (Munro 1987). Victoria has since improved on its implementation of community-oriented policing, moving beyond the preliminary stages of adoption.

Holroyd Senior Constable Sue Carter conducts a safety audit for Margaret Charteris, a service station manager. *(Courtesy of Mike Combe and the New South Wales Police Service, New South Wales, Australia.)*

New Zealand

A close neighbor to Australia, New Zealand has also begun the process of moving toward community-oriented policing. New Zealand is a much smaller country than Australia, with only 104,000 square miles compared with the nearly 3 million square miles of Australia. New Zealand maintains a population of approximately 3.5 million citizens and has a parliamentary form of government (Farmighetti 1999). The queen of England is also the head of state for New Zealand, and a governor-general serves as her representative. It also has a prime minister, who serves as head of government and the parliament, the governing body. Because the country is so small, the national government oversees ninety-three counties and twelve towns or districts, each of which also has its own local government. In the early 1990s, the New Zealand police began to formulate plans for implementing community-oriented policing and in 1993 published both a corporate plan (a short-term two-year plan) and a vision plan (a long-term five-year plan) for moving the nation's police toward the adoption of community-oriented policing. The implementation consisted of some additional decentralization of the police (additional because the police in New Zealand are already highly decentralized), such as adding more police substations in metropolitan areas and creating community policing centers, and the adoption of the three components of community-oriented policing, including enhanced targeting patrols, community partnerships, and adoption of the SARA model of problem solving.

South Africa

The Republic of South Africa is situated at the southern tip of the continent of Africa; it covers approximately 470,000 square miles and has a population of more than 43 million citizens (Farmighetti 1999). It is a federal republic with a bicameral parliament, and the head of state is the president. South Africa's past is one of government by a white minority, apartheid, and violence. Only in the 1990s did South Africa begin to transform its nation under a democratic constitution and move toward ensuring its citizens the individual rights that Americans so often take for granted. The past is particularly important to South Africa's future, as recognized by Nelson Mandela, who, while president, appointed a "truth commission" to attempt to expose and deal with South Africa's tragic past. The past is important for South Africa's future in regards to policing as well. In the past, the police were often involved in much of the violence and enforced apartheid (Baratta 1994). Political corruption and police brutality were rampant. For the South African Police (SAP) to build a successful future, it must effectively deal with its past, attempt to move toward a community-oriented policing model, and begin to look toward the future. To achieve these goals, the South African government passed the Police Act of 1995, which "provides for the establishment, organization, regulation, and control of the South African Police Service" under the community-oriented policing model and includes community cooperation and civilian oversight (Marks 1997). The goals of the South African Police Services, with foreign assistance, was to create a Basic Training Pilot Program to create community policing officers, to establish the Western Cape Community Policing Project (through the assistance of the United Kingdom) in order to create a collaborative community policing effort between provincial police ministries and nongovernment organizations, and to implement the Community Policing Pilot Project, which, with the assistance of the Belgian Gendarmerie, was to develop community policing at 43 stations across South Africa (Van Der Spuy 2000). All three projects were aimed at entrenching "the philosophy of community policing in police operational practice" (Van Der Spuy 2000, 352). Although it appears that the government is beginning to move policing toward a community-oriented framework and there is evidence that the line officers embrace the concept (Marks 1997), South Africa's past, racial division, and citizen suspicion will prove to be great obstacles to overcome. In a sense, South Africa may be the best test case of community-oriented policing in the world. If the South African Police can successfully implement community-oriented policing under these conditions, then it may be possible to do so in any democratic country in the world.

Recent research by Brogden and Nijhar (2005) has questioned South Africa's ability to implement community-oriented policing successfully. They argue that the community police forums were not structured well, the police were unsure of their role, and citizens were not prepared to take on a co-production role after so many years of having a secret police under apartheid. People feared that the community forums were nothing more than a new means of police intrusion and surveillance into their lives, while conversely many people used these forums as a means of criticizing past police practices. In addition, Brogden and Nijhar (2005) point out that many, including the police, saw community-oriented policing as too soft on crime, and in the wake of a growing crime problem the shift has been to crime fighting. Few people in South Africa, Brogden and Nijhar allege, wish to be involved in helping the police fight crime. Yet they do acknowledge that the changes in policing in South Africa have opened up a once closed institution to public scrutiny, but South Africa's ability for citizen accountability of the police is questionable.

COMMUNITY-ORIENTED POLICING NORTH OF THE 64TH PARALLEL

One of the youngest land formations on earth and the last country to be settled in Europe, Iceland is an island of 40,000 square miles with a population of approximately 275,000. Forty percent of Iceland's surface is made up of glaciers, lava fields, lakes, and rivers. The island nation of Iceland is surrounded by the ring road, Route 1, which is just over 800 miles long. The majority of Iceland's population live in its capitol city of Reykjavik, population 118,000, and the remaining citizens live in other coastal towns.

According to the May 31, 1999, issue of *Barron's Market Week,* a full 70 percent of Iceland's total exports are marine products; further, the inflation rate is a low 1.7 percent, with the unemployment rate at 2.8 percent for 1998. This is due in large part to the country's highly educated labor force, whose members have excellent fluency in English, which enhances opportunities for international trade and investments.

The government of Iceland is a parliamentary republic. The president and the parliament exercise the legislative power. A secret public ballot is held every four years to elect the president and the parliament members. The nation's highest positions of administrative authority are the Ministers of the Government and the Ministry of Justice, one of whose responsibilities is governing the National Police force.

The country of Iceland is protected by a National Police force, supervised by a National Commissioner, who answers to the Ministry of Justice. There are twenty-six police districts and a total of 747 sworn personnel; 128 of these are part-time officers. The capital of Reykjavik has more than 200 sworn law enforcement officers assigned to the following divisions: patrol, crime prevention and research, investigations (subdivided into burglary/theft/robbery, narcotics, violence, and sex crimes units), traffic accidents, and information and surveillance units.

Similar to any large city, Reykjavik has its own unique crime problems. According to Dr. Gunnlavgsson, assistant professor of sociology at the University of Iceland who has studied crime issues extensively, the most pervasive crime problem is substance abuse. Since the beer ban was lifted ten years ago, the Reykjavik police have been very busy controlling and patrolling drinking behavior, especially for the young weekend binge drinkers. As a result, according to Superintendent Armannson of the Criminal Investigative Division in Reykjavik, "Assaults are increasing downtown on weekends." This criminal behavior is the major contributor to Iceland's having a higher ratio of DUI arrests than the United States; Iceland arrests approximately 2,000 citizens each year for drinking and driving offenses. These convicted DUI offenders account for 15 percent of Iceland's total prison population, while an additional 15–20 percent are held on drug-related convictions. Armannson explained that 90 percent of the robbery suspects were young people feeding their drug habits.

Iceland also has strict gun control laws, so restrictive, in fact, that only members of the National Police are permitted to register and own firearms. And although all officers in the National Police are trained in the use of firearms, most carry only pepper mace and small batons. Therefore, in the case of an emergency (such as a suspect being armed), the beat officers call in the services of the Viking Squad, which is a Special Response Team made up of eighteen armed officers.

The National Commissioner of the Icelandic Police also administers the National Police College, or Police Academy. The basic training for the new recruit is four months long, followed by twelve months in the field with a Field Training Officer, or FTO. It is only after four and a half more months of training into a second year that the recruit is considered a certified police officer. The National Police College is also actively involved in in-service training for all members of the National Police Force.

Community policing in the capitol city of Reykjavik is under the control and direction of the Crime Prevention and Research Division. As the police department is aware of the major problem of binge drinking on weekends by the local youth, the community policing efforts are heavily oriented to attempts to curb this problem through several methods, which include the following:

Video patrol: Installation of eight midtown video cameras, which are monitored by police, are used in policing.

Police patrol: In addition to traditional patrol methods, the city also has officers on roller skates and bikes in certain areas. In addition, there are five precincts within Reykjavik that are manned during the day.

Parents shift: A group of volunteers patrol on foot with cellular phones to report juvenile disturbances.

Juvenile officers: Five officers in the Reykjavik district serve as liaisons with public schools and social service.

School programs: Officers give presentations on alcohol and drug abuse.

Youth centers: Eight such centers serve as alcohol-free gathering sites for youth.

Marita anti-drug program: An officer, social service workers, and a former drug offender go into the public schools, usually eighth through tenth grade, to dissuade adolescents from substance abuse. This program was adopted from Norway and introduced in Iceland in 1998.

Follow-up program: An officer visits the cells in police lock-up to check on and talk to detainees, inquiring about why they were arrested and what their specific problems are in order to make appropriate referrals.

Juvenile shelters: A shelter exists to house intoxicated youth brought in by the police.

Crime prevention: Police force works with the organization of shop owners and offers seminars on robbery prevention.

The police in Reykjavik are attempting to address the issues and problems of their city through a number of alternatives. Time and a close examination of these changes in police actions will tell if such concerted efforts will have long-lasting positive results.

Source: Dean Van Bibber, Fairmont State College, Fairmont, West Virginia.

Other Prospects

Other countries practicing some form of community-oriented policing include the Scandinavian countries of Norway, Sweden, Denmark, and Finland (Jackson and Ter Voert 2000; Skolnick and Bayley 1988a, 1988b). Norway has adopted many of the concepts of community-oriented policing, such as the decentralization of the police, interaction with the community, and an emphasis on community crime prevention (Skolnick and Bayley 1988a, 1988b). Sweden has adopted the concept of neighborhood police posts, or *kobans* (Skolnick and Bayley 1988a, 1988b). Denmark has adopted foot patrols, meetings with area residents for problem-solving initiatives, and several neighborhood-oriented policing programs (Skolnick and Bayley 1988a, 1988b). Finland has returned to the concept of the village officer, in which the local police officer lives in the village area he or she polices (Skolnick and Bayley 1988a, 1988b). There are also signs that the Netherlands has begun moving toward community-oriented policing, with some success and many setbacks (Aronowitz 2003; Jackson and Ter Voert 2000). Once again, it should be noted that Brogden and Nijhar (2005) have pointed out that in many Scandinavian countries, community policing has been implemented with a stronger adherence to aggressive tactics (Denmark), it is largely reactive in nature (Sweden), or it is simply a dumping ground for older officers (again Denmark).

A number of other countries are said to have incorporated some aspects of community-oriented policing in their police practices; these countries include India (Raghavan and Sankar 2003), China (Wong 2001), Kenya (Mwangangi 2003), Nigeria (Ebbe 2003), Yugoslavia (Simonovic and Radovanovic 2003), Hungary (Banfi and Sarkozi 2003), Thailand (Puthpongsiriporn and Quang 2005), and Russia (Gilinsky 2003). Finally, in Belgium, the

Reykjavik, Iceland, police officers interacting with citizens during a local parade. (*Courtesy of Professor Dean Van Bibber, Fairmont State College, Fairmont, West Virginia.*)

THE GOOD FRIDAY PEACE ACCORDS: POLICING AND JUSTICE

1. The participants [recognize] that policing is a central issue in any society. They equally recognize that Northern Ireland's history of deep divisions has made it highly emotive, with great hurt suffered and sacrifices made by many individuals and their families, including those in the RUC (Royal Ulster Constabulary) and other public servants. They believe that the agreement provides the opportunity for a new beginning to policing in Northern Ireland with a police service capable of attracting and sustaining support from the community as a whole. They also believe that this agreement offers a unique opportunity to bring about a new political dispensation, which will recognize the full and equal legitimacy and worth of the identities, senses of allegiance, and ethos of all sections of the community in Northern Ireland. They consider that this opportunity should inform and underpin the development of a police service representative in terms of the make-up of the community as a whole and which, in a peaceful environment, should be routinely unarmed.

2. The participants believe it essential that policing structures and arrangements are such that the police service is professional, effective and efficient, fair and impartial, free from partisan political control; accountable, both under the law for its actions and to the community it serves; representative of the society it polices; and operates within a coherent and cooperative criminal justice system, which conforms with human rights norms. The participants also believe that those structures and arrangements must be capable of maintaining law and order, including responding effectively to crime and to any terrorist threat and to public order problems. A police service [that] cannot do so will fail to win public confidence and acceptance. They believe that any such structures and arrangements should be capable of delivering a policing service, in constructive and inclusive partnerships with the community at all levels, and with the maximum delegation of authority and responsibility, consistent with the foregoing principles. These arrangements should be based on principles of protection of human rights and professional integrity and should be unambiguously accepted and actively supported by the entire community.

Source: "The (Belfast) Agreement: Agreement Reached in the Multi-Party Negotiations," April 1998.

city of Antwerp has moved toward a community-oriented policing model and has even gone so far as to add an in-line skate patrol, in which police officers patrol and greet citizens while moving about on in-line skates ("Rollerblades Cops Keep Villains on Straight and Narrow," 1998). Although these countries have far from a full-fledged implementation of the community-oriented policing philosophy, they have put into practice some elements of the concept.

One final adoption of community-oriented policing is under way in Northern Ireland, largely brought about by the Irish Peace Accord. After months of negotiations in 1998, the Belfast/Good Friday Agreement was signed, bringing peace to Northern Ireland after years of fighting between the Protestants and Catholics. The Protestants, the minority in Northern Ireland, favored remaining part of the United Kingdom, whereas the Catholics, the majority in Northern Ireland, favored becoming part of Ireland. The

Belfast/Good Friday Agreement brought about a peaceful settlement, and one issue on the table during the negotiations was the Royal Ulster Constabulary and its policing practices in Northern Ireland. The answer to the dilemma of how policing in Northern Ireland would proceed was the adoption of community-oriented policing. This call for community-oriented policing is very similar to that by the Christopher Commission based on its investigation into the Los Angeles Police Department in the aftermath of the Rodney King beating; although the strained relationships between the police and the citizens are similar, there are many differences between Los Angeles and Northern Ireland. It will be interesting to see how successful Northern Ireland will be with the adoption of community-oriented policing.

ASSESSING COMMUNITY-ORIENTED POLICING INTERNATIONALLY

A flurry of recent research into community-oriented policing around the world is reaching largely the same conclusion, and it is not necessarily a positive one. A good example is the case study of Hong Kong policing. In the 1970s, Hong Kong policing developed along paramilitary lines with strict structures and little public–police interaction. In 1995, the Hong Kong Police launched its "Quality of Service Initiative," essentially its version of community-oriented policing. According to Lau (2004), this initiative has been an utter failure. He argues that this has to do in part with the adherence to the paramilitary tradition and the imposition of the community-oriented policing model on a society that does not share a sense of community. This latter problem was, in part, exacerbated by the return to Chinese sovereignty in 1997. Lau concludes that the greatest issue in terms of the adoption of community-oriented policing is the fact the government took a Western model and attempted to apply it to a city where the local conditions simply are not amenable to Western customs. This has been a growing criticism of the adoption of community-oriented policing in countries, both developed and transitional, across the globe.

Perhaps the most extensive criticism comes from Brogden and Nijhar (2005), in that they explore a number of international models of community-oriented policing in developed, developing, and transitional nations. As they have argued,

> We need to place the development of community policing on a larger canvas—one that perceives it as part of a discredited practice of exporting used goods from the Western supermarkets of policing and other legal institutions to so-called developing and transitional societies. Community policing has been transmitted without the "warts" and without reference to context and to history (p. 229).

Elsewhere, Brogden (2005) has argued that one cannot impose a Western concept on other countries because it does not address their local culture and institutions and is simply "irrelevant" to other societies.

Other researchers have agreed, albeit with a less critical analysis, such as Davis, Henderson, and Merrick (2003) in their analysis of Brazil, Haiti, Uganda, and South Africa. They explain that the implementation of community-oriented policing in Western societies is not always successful and that these societies are typically built on more developed communities and institutions with resources. Many countries to which community-oriented policing is being transported lack stable communities, established institutions, and the resources for implementing this systemic approach to policing. Thus, not taking into consideration the local context and history, which may consist of extreme brutality and corruption by its government (including the police) creates a situation where community-oriented policing is not always be transferrable.

Although community-oriented policing was generally intended to be a grassroots-up adoption of policing methods, in which the local context and history would dictate how it is implemented, what develops out of these programs and policies is not always what was intended. Community-oriented policing, as has been said previously, was not intended as a cookie-cutter model of policing. Rather, it was to consider the local history and context, how well the police and community related, how established and legitimate were the police in the community, the level of resources available, and a number of other factors. Yet as community-oriented policing moved from innovation, through its diffusion generation, to the institutionalization, a number of cookie-cutter programs have come to be seen as "community-oriented policing," and these models have been transported across the United States, Western democracies, and to the developing world. While one hopefully would not disagree with the philosophy that lies behind community-oriented policing, it is acknowledged that what is implemented may not necessarily advance that philosophy. But the alternative is to continue to allow (or advocate) police agencies in developing and transitional countries to carry out state-sponsored violence, brutality, and corruption.

CONCLUSION

Community-oriented policing saw a rapid diffusion across the United States beginning in the 1980s are continuing into the twenty-first century. By 1994, with the passage of the Violent Crime Control and Law Enforcement Act, community-oriented policing had become largely institutionalized across America, due in large part to the grant assistance available from the federal government through the Office of Community Oriented Policing Services (COPS). This movement from innovative demonstration projects to a nationalization of the philosophy has been remarkable but is not exclusive to the United States. When looking at the adoption and implementation of community-oriented policing around the world, there appear to be many similarities to the U.S. experience.

The experiences in Canada and the United Kingdom allow for a strong comparison in that the movements occurred in the early 1980s. Although it has been argued that Canada jumped on the bandwagon in implementing community-oriented policing, the United Kingdom adopted community-oriented policing because of the series of riots that occurred in the early 1980s, and the United States implemented the system because it was trying to find itself, in the end, there are perhaps several primary reasons that underlie the decision to adopt community-oriented policing. Normandeau (1993) cites three plausible reasons: (1) the traditional methods have not worked, (2) budgets for police have reached a ceiling, and (3) community-oriented policing is the only system that can address fear of crime, crime, and quality-of-life issues. All of the countries reviewed have had to deal with changes in not only society but culture as well. The methods of policing that were so

Queensland police constables Jodie Cumner and Andrew Williamson help a lost child outside the Police Beat Shopfront in the Surfers Paradise Mall on Australia's Gold Coast. (*Courtesy of the Queensland Police Service, Queensland, Australia.*)

effectively employed in the past—strict models of discipline and enforcement, top-down hierarchical bureaucracies, and paramilitary organizations—are no longer methods that work well in contemporary society, nor will they function well in the future. The movement toward something else has become the movement toward community-oriented policing.

In looking to the more practical applications of the implementation of community-oriented policing around the world, it is clear that many are adopting the three components of the systemic approach. Many are following the strategic-oriented policing methods by highlighting quality-of-life issues and adopting the broken windows theory. The nations range from Canada to Singapore in the level of adoption, but there are signs of implementation in most of the countries adopting community-oriented policing. The various aspects of neighborhood-oriented policing can be found in countries as diverse as Japan (*kobans*), Belgium (in-line skate cops), and Israel (neighborhood police officers). Finally, the problem-oriented policing methods, especially the use of the SARA model, can be found throughout the world, including most of the countries reviewed in this chapter.

Beyond adoption and implementation of the three components of community-oriented policing, it is apparent that other countries have additional similarities in their implementation, including the decentralization of the department, increased contacts with police and citizens, and the adoption of management techniques such as total quality management. It must also be pointed out, however, that although countries are similar in many of the positive aspects of community-oriented policing, they also face similar problems, such as politics, resistance by line officers and mid-level management, citizen apathy, changes in name only, and fear of police corruption. What is important, then, is that we explore community-oriented policing cross-culturally, that we compare and contrast the U.S. method of adoption with that of other countries, and that we learn from each other's successes and failures in order to move forward with the implementation of community-oriented policing with new ideas and with knowledge to avoid the mistakes of others.

COP ON THE WORLD WIDE WEB

London Metropolitan Police

http://www.met.police.uk

New South Wales Police Department, Australia

http://www.police.nsw.gov.au/main/default.cfm

Northern Ireland Policing Board

http://www.nipolicingboard.org.uk

Royal Canadian Mounted Police

http://www.rcmp-grc.gc.ca/index_e.htm

South African Police Services

http://www.saps.org.za

REVIEW QUESTIONS

1. Define *comparative community-oriented policing*.
2. Compare and contrast the U.S. form of community-oriented policing with that of England, Canada, or Japan.
3. What are the three methods of studying community-oriented policing comparatively?

CHAPTER 14

Caveats

You must first enable the government to control the governed; and in
the next place oblige it to control itself.

—James Madison

CHAPTER OBJECTIVES

- Recognize the various caveats to the systemic approach.
- Analyze past problems and current problems.
- Identify ancillary problems to the implementation process.
- Identify problems with the implementation process.
- Begin to project possible future problems.

It would be rather naive to believe that community-oriented policing, as policy, as philosophy, and in its programmatic format, will be implemented without any difficulty and in such a manner that every police department in the nation will immediately sign on. We live, rather, in a world full of uncertainties, and no individual or group can adequately predict what problems will arise out of a new policy. As policy, community-oriented policing has been debated and discussed for more than fifteen years, and multiple scholars and practitioners have recognized a multitude of problems (see Bayley 1988; Brown 1989; Crank 1994; Goldstein 1987; Joseph 1994; Riechers and Roberg 1990; Rush 1992; Skolnick and Bayley 1988). Some of these predesignated problems have proven to be false rhetoric of institutions resisting change, while others have proven to be well-predicted problems that remain without solutions.

In addition to the predicted and deliberated problems revolving around community-oriented policing, there are also those problems arising out of new policy implementation. New policy creates problems. It is the hope that through reliable and valid evaluation research these problems will be exposed, addressed, and dealt with in a manner tantamount with the original policy. However, as is often the case with public policy, new policy begets more policy. As we learn and identify that which was previously not evident to us and that which could not or simply was not predicted, we must address these problems anew. This fact should not be a problem in and of itself, but the understanding that new policy will create new problems must be accepted for scholars to explore new areas in their research and for practitioners implementing community-oriented policing to effectively and efficiently deal with the new problems as they arise.

Police officers from the Albany Police Department work with local youth to improve their basketball game and jump shots. (*Courtesy of the Albany Police Department, Albany, New York.*)

WALKING THE MINEFIELDS OF COMMUNITY POLICING

Although the arguments put forth by the proponents of the community-oriented approach appear logical and very appealing at a time when the nation faces an alarming growth in violent criminal behavior, police administrators should exercise caution. Given that some hail community-oriented policing as a commonsense answer to rampant crime, there should be an effort to evaluate carefully what this "new" orientation advocates. It appears that the law enforcement community has made a commitment to the ideals encompassed in community-oriented policing. The real question remains: Can the police meet this commitment and make a real difference?

The answer actually will be determined in future evaluations of the efforts of individual departments. However, there exist some realistic implications of the COP philosophy that require immediate consideration. As with crime prevention programs in general, community-oriented policing has a number of potential weaknesses.

The first potential weakness rests in the specific approach adopted. In many agencies that adopt the COP approach to crime, COP becomes an underlying foundation of the law enforcement effort as opposed to merely a strategy that can be applied to real-world situations within the community. But, by making COP an underlying foundation, departments risk subordinating all prevention efforts to a single philosophy—that police organizations are responsible for solving the social problems traditionally linked to crime. Should this philosophy prevail and follow the same path as many previous crime prevention programs, COP could become a program of symbolism instead of substance.

In the past, police administrators often talked very forcefully in support of crime prevention only to fail, for whatever reason, to establish realistic, goal-oriented management practices. These administrators fell short of fully integrating these units into the overall structure of agencies because crime prevention staffs worked outside the agency's operational hierarchy. The results created the perception, especially among operational units, that crime prevention was not "real police work."

Due to the structure of crime prevention operations, officers in those units were seen as a front-line public relations buffer. Accordingly, officers in these units often received assignments that had little to do with crime prevention, such as public or media relations, and other tasks deemed desirable by agency administrators. Left unchecked, this can lead to crime prevention units not being integrated with traditional patrol and investigative activities—in other words, segregated from the department.

The risk is that a community-oriented policing effort could become simply another specialized function within the department—distinct from other agency activities. Such an approach almost undoubtedly would doom an agency's community-oriented policing efforts.

Without question, the greatest potential problem posed by the COP philosophy, like that posed by traditional crime prevention efforts, is the question of evaluation and accountability. What methods and measures will be used to determine success or failure? And, will such strategies be politically motivated or public safety–oriented?

In reality, the issue of methods and measures will take place on two different and distinct levels. The first level is that of the department; the second, that of the individual officer. On the department level, evaluation efforts must be comprehensive. To that end, administrators should obtain citizen and officer perceptions, as well as data, concerning crime rates. Depending on an agency's size and the expertise available for such analysis, administrators may deem it more realistic to assign the responsibility of evaluation to an outside organization rather than to a component within the agency. Generally, outside evaluation lends credibility and standardization to an analysis.

The second level of evaluation, that of officer performance, does not lend itself to the more "packaged" approach possible with departmental analysis. Because COP programs remain somewhat open to empirical question, the issue of how to evaluate officer performance becomes an important consideration. If community-oriented policing is to become the way police officers perform their duties, performance evaluations become crucial to the overall equation and strategy.

Traditionally, officer performance has been evaluated through easily quantifiable measures, such as the number of suspects arrested, tickets and warnings issued, calls handled, and cases cleared, as well as the evaluation of desirable traits. Realistically, such measures no longer may be of value to a department that incorporates the COP approach. An agency that trains and expects officers to perform as community-oriented police officers should develop performance instruments that measure crime prevention activities as well as problem-solving initiatives. Without such measuring systems, merit and rewards become moot.

Two other important issues—training and tactics—must be reviewed with any commitment to a COP philosophy. Obviously, if community-oriented policing is adopted as the way officers perform their duties, proper training becomes a crucial factor to success. Officers must be adequately trained in community policing methods.

In San Diego, California, for example, police officers undergo eight hours of in-service training with reference to the problem-oriented approach. Officers receive instruction on how to identify a problem, analyze it, and, with the assistance of the community, design a solution. While some disagreement exists at this time as to the level of formal and in-service training necessary, the general consensus implies that training should not be shorted.

To this extent, the St. Louis, Missouri, Police Department provides such training on a department-wide basis. Research also strongly supports the idea that agency-wide training may be the most effective, albeit costly, method.

In terms of tactics, proponents of COP may suggest that this approach changes only the practices of law enforcement, not the objectives. Frequently, the debate over the COP design is placed within the context of a conservative versus liberal approach.

As is often the case, new methods of policing may quickly be labeled as "soft on crime." Unfortunately, this has been no less true for COP efforts. Further, because COP focuses on community problems, municipalities risk creating the perception that individuals should not be held accountable for their behavior.

To be an effective strategy, then, community policing must not be presented to citizens as a choice between "hard" or "soft" policing. On the contrary, the severity of current crime problems requires that both types of police tactics coexist. Departments that choose a strong crime prevention orientation will still require traditional and specialized units. Administrators, supervisors, and line officers must clearly understand that community-oriented policing should not be viewed as a substitute for centralized police efforts. COP, at any level, should be viewed only as a means to a goal, not the goal. In the final analysis, the major objectives of police organizations remain those of public safety and security.

Whether community-oriented policing delivers and helps to rebuild the nation's infrastructure of social order remains a question yet unanswered. However, police administrators should remember that enhancing safety and order represents the first responsibility of any law enforcement agency. To promise communities unconditionally that police officers can solve the social problems associated with crime—the very problems that more grandiose and more fully funded programs have failed to resolve—is to mislead citizens in a most serious way.

Source: Adapted from Thomas M. Joseph, "Walking the Minefields of Community Policing," *FBI Law Enforcement Bulletin,* September 1994, pp. 8–12.

It is most difficult to discuss problems that have not yet occurred; thus our focus in this chapter is to discuss and debate those problems that are currently known. Past problems with community-oriented policing are not revealed and detailed to place blame on past participants in the systemic approach or to discourage current and future police departments from implementing community-oriented policing. Rather, they are detailed because they present a sort of caveat emptor to this new paradigm in policing. They are essentially details that articulate that the "buyers" of the systemic approach should beware of what they are attempting to accomplish. Community-oriented policing is a method of policing that holds many benefits in its implementation but also hides many dangers of false hope. Exposing past problems allows police practitioners to be aware of these false hopes and to deal with them effectively as they are exposed to them in a variety of situations.

Many of the key problems have been addressed throughout the previous chapters, but a recapitulation can clarify the problems that community-oriented policing will face during the implementation process. The main areas of focus that can be extracted thus far include the problem with defining what is meant by community-oriented policing. All of the problems are inherent within the changing role of the police, community, management, and organization, as well as many of the problems found within the methods and practices of evaluations. These issues should be of key concern for any police department moving toward the systemic approach because they all revolve around the implementation process. Each of these distinct categories is at some point in the implementation process, and each of these categories can bring with it a host of problems as a result of moving a police department from the traditional to the community-oriented approach.

A broader category of caveats that exists with community-oriented policing may be the result of the implementation process either directly or indirectly, but these caveats can also occur ancillary to the systemic approach. The issues of concern fall into five distinct categories: (1) limited resources and costs, (2) police corruption, (3) politics, (4) pseudo-community-oriented policing programs (look-alikes), and (5) the paradox of the future. The larger discussion will concentrate on the first three categories, the fourth will be debated between this chapter and the next, and the final category will be explored in the next chapter.

IMPLEMENTATION CAVEATS

The process of implementing the systemic approach to policing has focused on many of the obstacles that practitioners will have to face and overcome to achieve the final stage and the ultimate goal: community-oriented policing. Prior to even beginning the process, one difficulty that continues to arise is the lack of a clear definition of community-oriented policing, describing what is meant in both philosophical and practical terms. An organization cannot avoid problems if the organization has no conceptual understanding of what is meant by the term *community-oriented policing*. Additionally, the organization will confront multiple problems if it does not take into account the changing role of the police officer and the new role the community must play in accomplishing all of the tenets of the systemic approach. It is also imperative that the style of management and the organization itself change to complement community-oriented policing, or the implementation process will bear witness to multiple problems that will not derive solutions without these critical changes. And, finally, as previously explored, the use of evaluations must be integrated into the implementation process to ensure that the incremental process proceeds without continuing programs that fail to produce effective, efficient, and equitable results.

The first implementation caveat arises in the lack of an accepted definition. An organization cannot implement a policy without a clear understanding of what the policy entails. The first step in achieving this understanding is through a definition of the concept (Vito, Walsh, and Kunselman 2005). In the case of community-oriented policing, despite many years of scholarly research and practical application, no consensus has been reached as to a standard definition (Bayley 1994; Goldstein 1990; Greene and Mastrofski 1988; Maguire and Mastrofski 2000; Murphy 1988; Oliver 1992; Rosenbaum 1994; Rush 1992). Community-oriented policing means many different things to many different people (Bayley 1994). Much evidence supports this idea, as revealed through the writings of the scholars in the criminal justice/criminology fields, as well as through the various methods police departments have utilized in implementing community-oriented policing. However, despite the vast differences articulated, there are in fact more similarities in both the academic and practical perspectives of community-oriented policing than there are differences. By analyzing the similarities, one can reach a consensus and hence a definition to articulate what is meant by the term *community-oriented policing*. Once this consensus on definition is reached, policy can be articulated and programs implemented with a clearer understanding and, hopefully, with fewer problems.

The second key area of concern when implementing community-oriented policing is the role of the police. The role the police have traditionally played in society is dramatically different under the systemic approach to policing. The change called for in community-oriented policing is not necessarily limited to changing the way police deliver their services but instead includes actually changing the police subculture (Goldstein 1990; Reuss-Iianni and Iianni 1983; Skolnick and Bayley 1988; Vito, Walsh and Kunselman 2005). The police will most likely demonstrate the typical reluctance that accompanies any change, but as a by-product of the police subculture, it is widely believed that there will be an even stronger resistance to change (Anderson 1988; Brown 1989; Dolan 1994; Skolnick and Fyfe 1995; Sparrow 1988). Although some of this resistance to change is thought to originate from the police officers themselves, some believe that there will be organized resistance by way of the police unions (Rush 1992; Skolnick and Bayley 1986, 1988). In either case, police management must take the police subculture and the possibility of a resistance to change into consideration when implementing community-oriented policing to avoid many of the problems inherent in the implementation process.

Another caveat that exists when discussing the police role in community-oriented policing is the ability to fail. The traditional practice of policing leaves little room for the police to attempt new and innovative ideas because there is no freedom to fail. Under community-oriented policing, the police officers must be afforded the opportunity to try different approaches to policing; if a method does not prove effective, they must not be reprimanded or receive a negative evaluation for their failure. Rather, they must be encouraged to continue to address the problem, develop alternative solutions, and implement them until a problem is considered solved or alleviated. Essentially, the police must receive not only the resources but also the support to allow them to accomplish the new objectives under a community-oriented approach to policing (Eck and Spelman 1987; Eck et al. 1987; Meese 1993; Rush 1992; Skolnick and Bayley 1986, 1988). Without this support from the organization and management, the problem that the systemic approach will face is ultimately total failure.

Finally, the changing qualifications for police officers are critically important to the community-oriented policing implementation process. As the police department moves from a traditional style of policing to the community-oriented policing approach, the necessary skills for a police officer to function and perform his or her everyday duties change. The ability to communicate in public, to organize meetings, and to analyze problems and create alternative solutions all become additions to the job requirements. It is therefore imperative that the police department consider a change in the job description for the position of police officer that more closely reflects the community-oriented policing approach and then hire accordingly (Anderson 1988; Dolan 1994; Riechers and Roberg 1990; Roberg 1994). Additionally, the police department must also decide whether to make higher education a requirement for the position (Carter, Sapp, and Stephens 1989; Meese 1993; Radelet and Carter 1994). It is critical that these decisions be addressed early on in the planning stages of community-oriented policing to avoid problems further down the road. At the same time, it is also important for all involved in the implementation of community-oriented policing to recognize that the shift in police officer roles can also create problems for the officers themselves (Buerger, Petrosino, and Petrosino 1999). Officers engaged in community-oriented policing face the potential problems of burnout, tunnel vision, personalization, overidentification with the

Police officers from the Oceanside Police Department are pictured at a local surf event in honor of the community's youth. (*Courtesy of the Oceanside Police Department, Oceanside, California.*)

community, and overcommitment when it comes to the enhanced police–citizen relationship (Buerger, Petrosino, and Petrosino 1999). Care must also be taken in the planning and follow-through to prevent these from occurring.

As with the police and their changing role, there is also a changing role in regards to the community, which is the third area of concern in the implementation process. The community must become involved in community-oriented policing for it to succeed to its greatest potential. There are most assuredly a host of problems associated with the community's role in community-oriented policing. These problems range from police departments leaving the community out of the systemic approach (Goldstein 1987; Mastrofski 1988) and the inability to understand exactly what a community is and how it is defined (Buerger 1994; Grinc 1994; Manning 1988; Riechers and Roberg 1990; Skolnick and Bayley 1988) to the community not understanding its role in community-oriented policing (Eck et al. 1987; Goldstein 1987; Grinc 1994), expecting too much from the programs (Skolnick and Bayley 1988), demonstrating high levels of apathy for both policy and programs (Grinc 1994; Ross 1995), getting the community involved and keeping them involved (Vito, Walsh, and Kunselman 2005); and the police and community having very different belief systems as to what the problems are and how to fix them (O'Shea 2000). All of these problems can be effectively dealt with by including all members of the community in the implementation process, from the preplanning stages to the decision-making processes included within the three components of community-oriented policing. Whether the community is a willing or nonwilling participant in the planning and implementation of community-oriented policing, it must never be excluded from having the opportunity to become involved and must consistently be kept informed of the methods utilized to address both the criminal and order maintenance issues a community faces. The goals of inclusion, communication, and demonstration of the realistic capabilities of the police should alleviate the majority of problems predicted to occur when dealing with the role of the community in community-oriented policing.

CORE CHALLENGES FACING COMMUNITY POLICING

For the past decade, we have witnessed the rhetoric and reality of changes in American law enforcement stemming from the perceived implementation of community policing. Indeed, the philosophy of community policing is value-laden with all the "good" virtues expressed by people governing themselves. The problems with community policing are *not* with the philosophy and mission, but rather with the implementation of change. . . . Hence . . . the core challenges facing community policing are not necessarily with the concept but rather with the definition and implementation process.

Illustratively, we still argue about the definition of community policing. In some cities it is the addition of a bike patrol or extra officers assigned to the DARE program or being the leader in a neighborhood crime watch meeting. The problem, of course, is that community policing has been defined in so many different ways that the evaluation of specific programs has been benign. The result is that "what works" in community policing is relegated to a few initiatives highlighted in a few select cities across the country. The vast bulk of literature on community-oriented policing is anecdotal and more apt to read like propaganda. To date, there is a paucity of methodologically sound empirical research assessing the effectiveness of community-oriented policing.

Do we really see most of the changes once espoused by community policing advocates? How many departments have actually changed the entrance requirements for new officers to reflect changes in the police role? How many have changed recruit training from a military-oriented academy to curriculum more in tune with the new role demanded by community policing? How many departments have flattened their organizational pyramid and placed more decision making in the hands of the officers? How many chiefs have turned the organization "upside down" and have committed to participatory dialogue with officers as a major part of their management style? How many departments have actually changed their organizational culture? How many departments have structurally changed on a citywide basis? Unfortunately, we submit to you only a select few!

Once again, it would be foolhardy to argue against the concept or philosophy of community policing. Who could be against a closer working relationship between the police and the community, against proactive and preventative policing, against information-based and participatory management, against the responsiveness of the government to public demand? Unfortunately, these are only words that have found themselves in mission and value statements, but rarely in meaningful, structural, and long-lasting changes reflected in police departments across the country. To be successful, community policing must confront and hurdle five core challenges in the future.

Challenge 1

There is precious little empirical evidence that supports the idea that community policing has a positive impact on community perception of the police or crime reduction.

Few studies point to successful programs of change. Even the millions of dollars recently spent by the Community-Oriented Policing Office (COPS Office, U.S. Department of Justice) on evaluating community policing focus on specific programs rather than holistic studies of the concept itself. This problem hints at the politicization of the process. But much more importantly, how do we measure prevention of crime? How do we document all that has gone on in the last ten years? How can we be sure that "community" policing ventures were more important in reducing crime compared to more "traditional" tactics such as saturation patrol, directed investigations, zero tolerance, and strong enforcement of curfew and truancy laws? Quite simply, we cannot.

. . . To be successful, we must be able to design empirically strong studies that "test" community policing. Unfortunately, many community policing academics have become more like political zealots than detached, scientific researchers. These studies must evaluate the concept itself holistically and not simply a special program implemented under the rubric of community policing.

Challenge 2

Community policing demands a system change in all of city government.

Community policing requires changes not only in the police but also in the other components of the criminal justice system. Indeed, community policing requires an entire citywide change toward community government. City services must be coordinated, and cooperative ventures between governmental agencies must be developed. The police cannot be an isolated group within a city trying to address major social problems without the combined commitment and resources of the entire city. Police must be able to pass the "baton" to other agencies more appropriately designed to address many social problems, oftentimes first encountered by the police. Contrary to public opinion, the police *cannot* be all things to all people.

They have a very specific set of skills and accompanying training and are well equipped to handle crime-related problems. Broadening the mission of an organization that was having difficulty with a narrow mission to begin with may have not been prudent. Long-term counseling, social work, trash pick-up and inspirational speaking may not be the best fit for the police, and perhaps they should not be. These are most certainly not reflective of the curriculum of current police training academies. Community-oriented policing may have to face the realization that the police will never be able to shake the perception that they are responsible for crime control. As discussed, police still hire the same type of individuals and, for the most part, train them the same way they were trained twenty years ago.

Much more importantly, police organizations continue to promote employees based on the same criteria used under traditional policing methodologies (e.g., civil service examinations and adherence to affirmative action policies). Personnel evaluation systems have not reflected changes in the police role, nor do rewards for police follow community policing standards. Recognition and rewards are still typically based on making arrests and clearing cases. Of course there are exceptions, but these are few and far between. The realities speak the truth—few police departments have actually changed. The organizational culture within policing still reflects a punitive-based, top-down hierarchy that is very cloistered and inflexible. In order to take the next step, city governments must become much more decentralized and responsive to community needs. Teams of city agencies, which include the police, must be managed together in a problem-solving, goal-oriented methodology.

Challenge 3

The implementation of community policing is more "academic" than actual.
Real efforts to involve the community have been mixed at best. Police officials note difficulty in getting good turnouts or participation in their community policing efforts. . . . Whose interest does community policing represent? It would seem on initial inspection that, like other forms of government, interest groups have the ear of the police. What community policing advocates should be asking is "Are we representing the community, or only the most vocal, visible members of it?" The charge that community policing works best in areas that don't need it rings, unfortunately, true. If the principal goal of community policing is to bring order to the community, and if different segments of the community have different views of "order," whose "order" will prevail? What if one segment's preferred "order" compromises the legal rights of some other segment? If community policing is to be successful, it must work in the core ghetto areas of our cities, where crime, poverty, and disorder are most pronounced, and where political factionalization is most apparent.

The programs initiated and evaluated under the rubric of community policing suffer from inconsistent definitions of the concept and the practices. In fact, almost any police intervention being used today that is somewhat "innovative" is labeled community-oriented. In a recent federally funded grant to use community policing to reduce school-related crime in a large eastern city, the final solution adopted by the police and the research team was to use saturation patrol in the areas around the school immediately following dismissal. The authors called the intervention "community-oriented"; however, it was clearly a traditional police tactic. Bike patrol, foot patrol, mounted patrol, and other variations are only community-oriented to the extent that these tactics are done with a community-oriented focus and strategy. Otherwise, they are simply another means to conduct random patrol. Typically, when bike cops are queried about the efficacy of their job, they will only remark at their ability to "sneak up" on the criminals; hence it is difficult to see how this type of patrol is community-oriented.

More visible patrol and a closer working relationship with the community have always been tenets of traditional policing.

Challenge 4

Community policing has been too "politicized."

Unfortunately, community policing has become the buzzword of the last decade. If a department was not involved in community policing, then it was labeled backward, stationary, non-progressive, or worse, Neanderthal. The few scholars and practitioners who questioned the concept were branded "heretics" and unenlightened. In today's world of federal grants and the wake of the [1994] Crime Bill, police chiefs and academicians have too much at stake to criticize community policing. One chief of police recently indicated (on a private basis) that he believed community policing was "bull_____" invented by a few well-meaning individuals to try something new. Unfortunately, he also admitted that he (like many of his colleagues) could not afford to be public about community policing. There simply is too much at stake . . . free officers and free federal money for those involved in community policing. Community policing is now big business, and those individuals managing police departments understand, all too well, the political ramifications of heading a movement against what is deemed as somehow more progressive and better than the status quo.

Unfortunately, the buzzwords of community policing (and there are a thousand acronyms for community policing) have a tendency to infer a short-term fix to a problem—a time-proven political technique designed to address symptoms rather than root causes of major social problems. The buzzwords of community-oriented policing have come to have different meanings in organizations where the line staff was not directly involved in the planning and implementation of community-oriented policing. For example, in Houston the acronym NOP (Neighborhood-Oriented Policing) became Nobody on Patrol in the eyes of many street officers. The concept was never sold or endorsed by the people who needed to believe in it the most, the line officers. Central to any organizational change is the total involvement and commitment of everyone in the organization. Interestingly, community policing has often been a "top-down" decision foisted on the organization; antithetical to the basic concept of community policing's participatory "bottom-up" model. Community policing was never envisioned to be short term. Sadly, few initiatives have been adequately evaluated, and many good efforts implemented under the community policing rubric will eventually go the way of "team policing"—passing quietly into the night—yet another new "movement" begins under a different political posturing. And make no doubt about it . . . community policing is headed on the path of being a political scapegoat just at its predecessor (team policing) did in the late 1970s.

What will happen when federal grants that support community policing cease? High costs in terms of money and people appear to be an indicative feature of community policing, especially if officers are to have a small enough beat to make a difference or if a department is to maintain a high level of response while developing a new strategy for each neighborhood. As federal money becomes much more difficult to obtain and cities start to bear the burden of financing extra officers and programs themselves, community policing will face much more scrutiny and criticism. New political leadership will most assuredly point to the great financial costs of community policing in an attempt to justify their own positions. Community policing will be further politicized as national debate focuses on the search for a new president. What will be the empirical evidence of success? What did we change with a $25 billion Crime Bill? How did we spend all of that money, and what do we have to show for it? Is the Community-Oriented Policing Office (COPS Office) destined to be regarded as the LEAA of the 1990s?

Challenge 5

Community policing is riding the facade of success.

Politically, community policing only can be justified as "successful." Crime is down, violent acts in most major cities are down, unemployment is down, the number of youth between ages fourteen and twenty-one is down, and the general economy is doing well. Unfortunately and most dangerously, some police chiefs and most politicians are taking credit for these statistics. Policing needs to be very careful! What will happen after we have built a public expectation that the police can do all things for all people? What will happen when the wave crests ... when unemployment starts to creep up, the economy shrinks, inflation builds, cutback management highlights the federal agenda, and the new "boom" generation hits the criminal justice system? Will tension further increase between minorities and police and erupt in frustration and riot? During these times, will the police still be able to afford storefront operations, graffiti patrols, crime watch, DARE programs, and other community policing projects? Or, will the police be mandated to respond more effectively to 911 calls?

The issues facing community policing are no different from the issues confronting police in general. Where do we go from here? The answer is quite simple: We continue to press forward in a positive manner, understanding that change is difficult and evolutionary. Police need to refine the concepts of what good policing is and "tweak" their departments to meet existing cultural and organizational demands. We no longer need the buzzwords of community policing, but we desperately need the strong leaders who have taken bold risks in an attempt to find out "what works and what doesn't." We still need those individuals courageous enough to try something new, to bridge a new communication and information age, and to open up a new dialogue with communities of the future. In essence, we need to understand that team policing of the 1970s and community policing of the 1990s represent only the beginning stages of change and that the process has only just begun. Community policing advocates a necessary and important reform. Its recognition of the close relationship of crime to other social problems is a big step in the evolution of American policing. Our immediate job is to safeguard the many worthy efforts of community policing by squarely facing the challenges posed, understanding the inherent nature of police in our society today.

Source: Reprinted with permission from Robert W. Taylor, Eric J. Fritsch, and Tory J. Caeti, "Core Challenges Facing Community Policing: The Emperor *Still* Has No Clothes," *ACJS Today,* May/June 1998, pp. 1–5.

The fourth area of concern lies intrinsically in the organizational structure of the police department and in the related management style (Vito, Walsh, and Kunselman 2005). Although the three components that make up community-oriented policing are necessary for the policy implementation, it is imperative that the police department support these components through the decentralization of the police department. While the programs may thrive for some time without decentralizing the police department, a host of problems will surface because a centralized organizational structure will not support the goals and tenets of community-oriented policing, the line officers, and the initiatives of the community. It is then critical to community-oriented policing that the organizational structure decentralize (Eck and Spelman 1987; Eck et al. 1987; Geller 1991; Goldstein 1987; Greene, Bergman, and McLaughlin 1994; Rosenbaum and Lurigio 1994; Rush 1992; Skogan 1994; Wilkinson and Rosenbaum 1994). It must decentralize not only by structure but by geography and personnel as well to fully implement community-oriented policing and to be completely successful in the endeavor. The police officers, who will bear the brunt of implementing the systemic approach, must be afforded the autonomy and the decision-making ability to handle problems at their level. If the police department retains any centralization, it will constrict the line officers' capabilities in performing their duties under the community-oriented approach, and it will create problems from a lack of support and growing frustration with officers' new role.

Because community-oriented policing is a systemic approach to policing, there must be changes in every facet of the organizational structure. As a police department moves from the traditional style of policing to the community-oriented style, everything from recruiting (Metchik and Winton 1995; Moore 1992; Trojanowicz and Bucqueroux 1990a, 1994) to training (Joseph 1994; Kelling, Wasserman, and Williams 1988; McLaughlin and Donahue 1995; Moore 1992; Worsnop 1993) to performance evaluations (Bureau of Justice Assistance 1994; Eck et al. 1987; Joseph 1994; Kelling, Wasserman, and Williams 1988; Manning 1988; Roberg 1994; Silverman 1995; Skolnick and Bayley 1988) to promotions (Eck et al. 1987; Trojanowicz and Bucqueroux 1994) must change to complement the new philosophy, policy, and programs. No aspect of the police department should remain static during the implementation process, and every facet of the police department must embody the philosophy of community-oriented policing.

Just as important in the process of transforming a traditional police department to a community-oriented police department is the necessity to change not only the organizational structure but the management style as well. None of the previous styles that the police have utilized, ranging from the paramilitary to the bureaucratic model of policing, are conducive to the systemic approach. It is important that police departments move toward a less authoritative and bureaucratic approach to management, moving either toward a corporate strategy (Andrews 1980; Freeman 1984; Moore and Trojanowicz 1988; Radelet and Carter 1994) or toward total quality management (TQM) (Couper 1991; Osborne and Gaebler 1992; Radelet and Carter 1994; Wycoff and Skogan 1994). In both cases, the style of management is conducive to all of the values and goals inherent within community-oriented policing and complements decentralization. Without changing management style, the paramilitary and bureaucratic methods will cause extensive problems with the systemic approach to policing. The line police officers will not have the decision-making capabilities that are necessary at their level; the community will have no input into the process, thus negating the "community" aspects of community-oriented policing; and the decentralization of the organizational structure will not have a management style that is appropriate for its purpose. Lacking any changes in the management style, community-oriented policing will fail to evolve beyond the confines of its programmatic application.

The last caveat with the implementation process resides in the many problems with evaluations. As was detailed in Chapter 11, it is critical that an incremental style of implementation be utilized when moving a police department from the traditional to the community-oriented approach, allowing time for evaluations to be conducted, results obtained and interpreted, and changes made to the various programs. Incremental implementation prevents a multitude of problems from developing when a police department changes too quickly and fails to determine if the programs are effective, efficient, and equitable. Reliable and valid evaluations are critical to the success of community-oriented policing.

It is clear that the majority of problems police practitioners face occur during the implementation process. At every stage of implementing community-oriented policing,

A girl petting a Sacramento Police Department K-9 dog at a Police Department open house. (*Courtesy of the Sacramento Police Department, Sacramento, California.*)

from planning to the full systemic approach, problems occur on a consistent basis. However, if the philosophy of policing embodied in the systemic approach is implemented in an incremental fashion, there should be ample time to make corrections to the various programs and implement changes. Incrementalism is the fail-safe device for bad policy and bad programs. As long as the problems are identified and alternative methods created and implemented, a healthy development of the philosophy, policy, and programs of community-oriented policing should become well entrenched in the daily functioning of the police department.

ANCILLARY CAVEATS

Both scholars and practitioners are concerned with other caveats in the systemic approach to policing. Although these problems are not directly related to the implementation problems discussed previously, they are ancillary issues that can quickly become insurmountable problems. It must not be taken for granted with the implementation of community-oriented policing that these problems will occur but rather that the predicted potential is high. A police chief implementing the systemic approach should thus be aware of these types of problems, give them the consideration they deserve, and watch for them as potential problems that could detract or destroy all of the benefits derived from community-oriented policing. These issues consist of the problems of limited resources and the costs of implementing community-oriented policing, the potential for police corruption, and the negative interference of politics. Additional concerns are pseudo-community-oriented policing police departments and what the future holds for the systemic approach.

The issues of limited resources and excessive costs are often roadblocks to the implementation of community-oriented policing. The literature is filled with debate and concern over this particular issue (see Anderson 1988; Brown 1989; Kelling 1988; Moore 1992; Ross 1995; Sacco and Kennedy 1996; Silverman 1995; Skolnick and Bayley 1986, 1988; Trojanowicz and Bucqueroux 1990a; Worsnop 1993). As Anderson (1988, 151) states, "Done right, community policing consumes significant manpower. Yet a department dare not let it drain resources from responding to emergency calls." However, as Lee P. Brown (1989, 10) argues, "because community policing is an operating style and not a new program, no additional officers are needed." In some cases, the cost of implementing community-oriented policing has been the downfall of the program (Kelling 1988; Trojanowicz 1982; Trojanowicz and Bucqueroux 1990b), while in many cases police departments have become overburdened attempting to hire new officers or attempting to put more officers on the street (Silverman 1995; Worsnop 1993). In these particular cases, community-oriented policing was predominantly considered a program

San Antonio Police Officer Bob Sills fingerprinting a local child at a mall showcase. (*Courtesy of the San Antonio Police Department, San Antonio, Texas.*)

and not the philosophy to which Brown refers. In these cases, community-oriented policing was predestined to fail. A police department must not allow the concepts of limited resources and excessive costs to either prevent the department from implementing the systemic approach to policing or cause the community-oriented approach to fail.

 ## COP IN ACTION

Maximizing Community Resources, Cape Girardeau, Missouri

Community police officers need to be knowledgeable about their communities' resources. This awareness hit me like a ton of bricks when I was given the task of improving the quality of life in my assigned target area. A racially diverse neighborhood, my area is home to residents of a relatively low socioeconomic status and is known as the drug/crime area of the city. I discovered that many of the residents in my jurisdiction had no idea how or where to get help. There are many agencies and programs available to those in need, but it seems that few take advantage of these resources. Why? If Cape Girardeau is like other cities, it's probably because there are little to no outreach programs that get this information to citizens. As an officer, I know that law enforcement agencies are at the top of the list in terms of outreach capabilities. Helping to link those in need with resources should be a natural function of any law enforcement agency.

I have learned that informal neighborhood meetings are one of the most efficient ways to get to the heart of residents' concerns. And frequently, their concerns can be resolved with a simple phone call. For instance, I discovered that many of the residents in my area didn't know to call the parks department to have the neighborhood park mowed, or that the sanitation department will pick up trash left curbside for days, or that it's legitimate to complain to city departments about overgrown weeds and abandoned cars. I developed a resource card that my partner and I now distribute to every new resident we meet. The card lists phone numbers for such resources as shelters, clinics, family support, and food distribution centers. It includes a comprehensive list of city departments. With a quick glance at their card, residents are able to request services, register complaints, or contact their local municipal court, police station, or taxi company. The cards have effectively taught citizens how to utilize city services. The message is that city departments are one of the most valuable and overlooked resources available to police departments and citizens; we just need to help spread the word.

I also found that many of the individuals in my area have not completed their high school education. Fortunately, there is a GED program available through our local vocational-technical school. But unfortunately for the citizens in my target area, the campus is located several miles away and is not on a public transportation line. My partner contacted the coordinator of the GED program and asked if they could hold classes in an area convenient to the people we serve. That call resulted in a collaboration among the Salvation Army, Adult Basic Education, and the police department to hold GED classes in a newly renovated Salvation Army building. This is a perfect example of how we, as officers, can help bring programs to the people who need them.

Another issue we helped our citizens deal with is employment. In our region, the unemployment rate is high, making work particularly difficult to find for those with limited skills and education. My partner and I established a working relationship with the local Private Industry Council (PIC). The PIC has a subsidized job-entry program but has had difficulty locating people eligible for their assistance. We were able to help both the PIC and citizens by identifying qualified persons and making referrals.

Finding people jobs, cleaning up the parks, and seeing that people get educated may not seem like "real" law enforcement to some. I believe, however, that helping citizens gain self-esteem and financial independence is the foundation for rebuilding our communities. For the police department of the '90s [and beyond] to succeed, it will have to be able to identify and maximize its use of community resources. The quest to restore order and quality of life can only be accomplished by first helping our citizens to get their lives together. Like it or not, local police departments must participate in this monumental task. The first step in climbing this mountain is to help others learn how to better their world by using the community's resources.

Source: Adapted with permission from Charles Herbst, "Maximizing Community Resources." In *Community Policing Exchange.* Washington, D.C.: Community Policing Consortium, November/December 1995.

The primary reason that community-oriented policing should not cost any more than traditional policing is that it is not an additional program that will draw on funds and resources but rather is a philosophy and a policy. If the police department implements the systemic approach as a program, it has already determined its outcome in the evaluation process. It will be deemed a failure. If community-oriented policing is implemented as a philosophy, the only changes that will occur lie in the areas of the police perception of their job, ways they perform their function, and integration of the community into their decision making.

A secondary reason that community-oriented policing should not cost more than traditional policing is that police should be utilizing their budget and resources in a more efficient manner. The police must become more efficient in their allocation of resources and begin to look at what programs are considered wasteful of time, resources, and funding and determine how they may be handled more efficiently, reprioritized, or cut. Additionally, community policing becomes more cost-effective for two key reasons, according to Brown (1989, 10): "community participation in the crime-control function expands the amount of available resources, and the solving of problems (rather than responding again and again to the same ones) makes for a more efficient deployment of combined police and community resources." Because one of the goals of community-oriented policing is to develop the relationship between the police and the community, this should make available resources that were previously undiscovered. The assistance of the community can come in many forms, ranging from volunteering for police ministations to providing information and materials that will assist the police in the performance of their duties. And if the police and community work together to address and solve both the criminal and order maintenance problems in a neighborhood, the cost and resources that were repetitively directed at the problem can, in the future, be directed at other problems and concerns.

A third method of dealing with the issues of resources and costs may be to find other sources for them. Community-oriented policing must not be seen as making additional funds and resources necessary to implement the systemic approach; however, this is not to say that additional funding and resources should not be considered. As in traditional policing, if additional funds and resources are available, they can be beneficial to both the police and the community. Since the movement toward community-oriented policing has become a nationally supported endeavor, the federal government has made funds available to support many of the programs that fall under neighborhood-oriented policing, and it has also made more funds available for the hiring of an additional 100,000 police officers (Dilulio, Smith, and Saiger 1995; Marshall and Schram 1993). Additionally, one method of generating new funds for the community-oriented policing philosophy and assisting in the implementation of new programs may be derived through forfeiture dollars, specifically in the area of antidrug initiatives (Trojanowicz and Bucqueroux 1990b). This option should be considered fully before it is implemented because the forfeiture laws may have a negative impact on the police in regards to public opinion. The police do not want to convey the idea that the forfeiture laws exist so the police can confiscate property, sell it, and buy "new toys." And, finally, it is possible that through the cooperation of the community and the local government, a tax increase of some form can assist in the implementation of community-oriented policing in many areas, such as personnel, programs, and training (Moore 1992; Trojanowicz 1982). However, because community-oriented policing is a long-term commitment, it is unknown whether this additional tax increase will have a negative effect on the implementation process at a later date (Silverman 1995). Great care and caution should be exercised whenever a department considers deriving additional funds and resources from outside sources because they can create problems for the concept of community-oriented policing if they are not handled in an equitable manner.

The second ancillary caveat that commands an equivalent amount of attention is the issue of community-oriented policing causing an increase in police corruption. The literature abounds with discussions over whether the systemic approach will cause corruption in the police departments or whether it will actually alleviate concerns about police corruption (Brown 1989; Dombrink 1994; Geller 1991; Goldstein 1987; Kelling 1988; Kelling, Wasserman, and Williams 1988; Oliver 1994; Skolnick and Fyfe 1995; Smith 1994; Wycoff 1988). The discussion focuses to a large degree on the increased power of the line officer and the decentralization of the police, making the argument that police corruption will run rampant through the rank-and-file officers. On the other hand, the response is generally that closer ties to the community and working with a more educated police force, results of the systemic philosophy, will remove those situational factors that create and promote police corruption. As Geller (1991, 269) explained the dilemma, "community policing exposes officers to different opportunities—for success and for corruption."

To answer this dilemma, one must first understand that police corruption is defined as "acts involving the misuse of authority by a police officer in a manner designed to produce personal gain for himself or others" (Goldstein 1975, 3). The explanations for this type of behavior are extracted from a variety of sources including simple exposure to situations that may entice the officer, the authority and subculture of the police, and the style of policing that is employed by the police department (Barker and Carter 1994; Dempsey 1994; Goldstein 1975; Wilson 1968). Although it is apparently hard to determine why police corruption occurs, there is little doubt that it has a negative effect on not only the police department but also the community (Barker and Carter 1994; Dempsey 1994). It is therefore extremely important that the question of police corruption and community-oriented policing be resolved because no police chief will want to move his or her police department from the traditional approach to the systemic if police corruption will be part of the structural environment, fostered by the new approach and allowed to run rampant for the sake of community-oriented policing.

As previously detailed, police corruption has been a problem that police chiefs have had to either face or fear since the inception of the police department, both in the United States and abroad. Because police departments in the United States developed without much management or organization, they were often bastions of corruption. As Kelling (1988, 7) explains, "early policing in the United States had been characterized by financial corruption, failure of police to protect the rights of all citizens, and zealotry. The police chiefs of the day, such as August Vollmer and O. W. Wilson, were placed in charge of organizations that were in poor shape in every aspect of the police department. It was their mission to 'clean them up' and 'straighten them out.' " This was essentially done through a process of centralizing the command of the police department to the charge of the police chief and removing much of the authority from the line police officers (Dempsey 1994; Geller 1991; Goldstein 1990). The ultimate goal at the time was to utilize scientific management theory (Peak 1995) and to professionalize the police (Goldstein 1990) in the hopes of creating a more effective and efficient police department that was less prone to corruption. With curiosity one must now ask, Why move a police department backward in management and organization to the days of rampant corruption? That direct relationship poses the dilemma.

The direct relationship of decentralizing the police department, pushing the authority down the chain of command to the level at which the authority is necessary, and shifting the management style to one that is more participatory is not a movement backward but rather a movement forward. Although the structural concepts appear on the surface to remain the same as the policing structure in the early twentieth century, the environment and quality of personnel are not the same. To equate early-twentieth-century police officers with the rank-and-file officers of the twenty-first century is an exercise in futility. They are not the same. The education level of the police has increased, technology

St. Petersburg Police Department Marine Watch Community Resources Unit boat was bought with drug seizure money. (*Courtesy of the St. Petersburg Police Department, St. Petersburg, Florida.*)

has increased, and (although many line officers would probably disagree) both pay and benefits have increased. Although it may share some of the same principles—foot patrol, decentralization, working with community—policing today is free of many of the elements that hindered policing in its infancy. Why, then, is there so much concern about police corruption if moving a traditional police department to the systemic approach? The answer lies in fear.

The fear of community-oriented policing is largely in the hands of the police chief. It is his or her fear of decentralization, of losing control and authority, and of sharing this power with the community that generates much of the animosity (Brown 1985; Kelling 1988; Kelling, Wasserman, and Williams 1988). Although these may be legitimate concerns, they are not enough to prevent a police department from shifting to community-oriented policing. As Lee P. Brown (1989, 9) stated, "experience has not shown nor even suggested that community policing leads to corruption," and all of the literature from both scholar and practitioner since reflects this fact (Geller 1991; Goldstein 1987; Kelling 1988; Oliver 1994). This is not to say that the potential for corruption does not exist because this potential is also recognized in much of the literature (Goldstein 1987; Kelling 1988; Oliver 1994; Wycoff 1988). Some also feel that community-oriented policing will reduce the occurrence of police corruption because of the organizational values and beliefs inherent within the philosophy that reach far beyond the scope of policy, procedures, rules, and regulations (Kelling 1988; Kelling, Wasserman, and Williams 1988; Skolnick and Fyfe 1995). There is, however, one caveat to this belief.

The caveat is that a previously corrupt police department cannot utilize community-oriented policing as a panacea to its problems. Switching from the traditional to the community-oriented approach is not a cure for police corruption (Dombrink 1994; Geller 1991). The police department will carry with it all of the previous problems it suffered under the traditional approach, but those problems will most likely have an even greater impact on the police department and the community as a result of the change. The community will expect more under community-oriented policing, and if police corruption remains a problem, the community's beliefs in the benefits and all of the values inherent within the systemic approach will be destroyed. Public animosity will only be amplified and community-oriented policing will be deemed a failure.

Although it is apparent that police corruption in community-oriented policing is of great concern to both the scholar and practitioner, no basis in reality indicates that corruption has occurred or will occur because of a shift to community-oriented policing. Some believe that it will actually reduce the occurrence of police corruption, but this opinion, too, is merely subjective in nature. In any event, the potential for police corruption exists in any style of policing and must always be of concern to police management and police chiefs. Various methods of prevention should be utilized, such as an early warning system, and a strong disciplinary model should be maintained in the event of an incident. In any case, the fear of police corruption should not be utilized as an articulable reason for why a police department should not move to the systemic approach.

A third ancillary caveat that can be closely linked to police corruption is the issue of politics and community-oriented policing. Because community-oriented policing necessitates a new role for the police chief in the community, specifically one that ties the two closer together, there is some concern whether this may cause a politically ambitious chief to utilize this role to his or her advantage (Wycoff 1988). There is equal

COP IN ACTION

The Early Warning System

There is a relatively new concept, the "Early Warning System," which is a nondisciplinary management system for identifying potential problem officers. The Early Warning System is a computer database that tracks individual officers based on reportable elements of behavior. Each element in and of itself may not demonstrate any deficiency on the part of an individual officer, but numerous elements over short periods of time may indicate a behavioral problem. If this is the case, then the officer is "flagged."

Reportable elements include, but are not limited to, the following, as described by the International Association of Chiefs of Police (IACP):

- Discharge of a firearm, whether accidental or duty related
- Excessive use-of-force reports
- Any motor vehicle damage
- Any loss of equipment
- "Injured on duty" reports
- Sick leave in excess of five days, or a regular pattern of using one or two sick-leave days over long periods
- All complaints, including supervisory reprimands and other disciplinary action

The committee reviewing the Early Warning System must look into the incidents and attempt to discover the source of the problem. This may be clearly evident based on the information in the database presented before the committee. Analysis should include supervisory evaluations, awards, and commendations. Other considerations may include additional on-duty details, off-duty employment, marital status, number of dependents, extracurricular activities, and participation in fraternal organizations.

The Early Warning System, a proactive nondisciplinary system, is not for the purposes of punishment, in spite of the fact that intervention strategies may resemble punishment for various violations. The system is to intervene in an officer's career to prevent him from becoming a disciplinary problem and facing disciplinary charges and possible termination. This is but one method of assisting police managers in the retention of quality personnel.

The Early Warning System is not in widespread use yet; however, many departments are switching to proactive forms of management with their implementation of community-oriented policing. This system demonstrates a shift in the philosophy of management, moving away from an entrenched reactive mode and moving toward the proactive. If properly implemented, it can dramatically affect a department, decrease the number of complaints, and reduce police corruption.

Source: Adapted with permission from Will Oliver, "The Early Warning System," *Law and Order,* September 1994, pp. 182–183.

concern that although police chiefs may not be politically ambitious, as a result of the role of the chief under community-oriented policing, the chief may become more of a figurehead than the local mayor or city manager, which may create political problems (Brown 1985). And, finally, there are some genuine concerns that as a result of potential political conflicts, police chiefs may lose their ability to implement community-oriented policing or that there will be no political commitment to the systemic approach once a chief is asked to resign, is fired, or chooses to leave on his or her own (Manning 1988; Rush 1992).

In the area of politics and political leaders, there also lies some concern with the implementation of community-oriented policing. Although community-oriented policing is largely a win-win situation for the political leadership (Skolnick and Bayley 1988) because crime, community, and community-oriented policing are all valence issues, the possibility exists that a mayor, city manager, or city council member may turn on the philosophy if any negative publicity is attached to the systemic approach. Additionally, there is the possibility that as a result of the police attempting to deliver a more equitable form of policing, individuals and groups that once enjoyed high levels of police services may see a reduction in service, causing some concerns and political pressure on the community leaders (Trojanowicz and Bucqueroux 1990b). Political pressure can also be derived from multiple-agency collaboration, as some agencies may not be willing or have the organizational capacity to collaborate with the police and local citizens (Giacomazzi and Smithey 2001). This pressure could in turn have a negative effect on the systemic approach because it would not abide by one of the central criteria for community-oriented policing, equity.

The last area of political concern lies with the line officers. As they obtain more authority at their level and they attempt to solve community problems, they may become more politically involved or utilize solutions that move away from political neutrality (Riechers and Roberg 1990). If the police utilize this political power to their personal advantage or the advantage of their fellow officers, then it crosses over into police corruption. If they utilize this authority to solve problems, address community concerns, or set up neighborhood-oriented policing programs, it may result in a violation of their political neutrality, especially if citizens feel coerced into doing what the police officers suggest.

In all of these cases, there must be a political commitment to the systemic approach, just as there must be a line officer commitment, a community commitment, and a government commitment. Once this commitment exists, the values and beliefs of the systemic approach must be adhered to in the political arena as they are on the street. Just as there is potential for political abuses in the traditional police department, there is potential for political abuses in the community-oriented policing department. It is critical that this concern be addressed at every step of the implementation process to ensure that there are no violations or the appearance of any violations. Police chiefs, police officers, and the police department as a whole must do everything in their power to remain politically neutral and continue to serve at the discretion of not only the mayor or city manager but the community as well.

The final ancillary caveat that community-oriented policing may face, and perhaps its most fatal problem, is the possibility of pseudo-community-oriented policing programs, or "look-alikes" (Rush 1992, 50). As community-oriented policing gains popularity and police departments across the country begin to implement the systemic approach, if it is nothing more than a name change, community-oriented policing is destined for failure. Herman Goldstein's explanation of problem-oriented policing can equally be applied to community-oriented policing:

> While the slightest progress toward focusing on substantive matters is commendable, concern about dilution of the concept is justified. Some accounts of claimed implementation of the problem-oriented policing contains very little that reflects any

A Sacramento Police Officer Horse Patrol with local youth at the end of the annual Christmas parade. (*Courtesy of the Sacramento Police Department, Sacramento, California.*)

engagement with substantive problems and little understanding of the overall concept. Among police agencies, some have an uncanny knack for placing new labels on old practices—for claiming change without changing. I have seen elaborate but totally unrealistic schedules for "full implementation" that seem more appropriate to a military exercise than to implementing a complex, necessarily long-term plan for organizational change requiring a radical shift in the way in which employees view their job and carry it out. (Goldstein 1990, 178)

As the systemic approach to policing is evaluated by the media, by the community, by the police, and through reliable and valid evaluative research, if the police department has retained the traditional style of policing but only changed the name, community-oriented policing will be declared a failure and will go the way of so many other attempts at improving the police function.

In similar regards, if community-oriented policing is implemented as a program, it will also see absolute failure. Community-oriented policing is a systemic approach to policing requiring department-wide implementation. All of the components of the concept must be implemented, all of the values and beliefs of the philosophy must be set in place, and every facet of the police department must see a move toward adopting the community-oriented policing philosophy. If the systemic approach is not implemented systematically, it will fail as a philosophy, it will fail as a program, and it will be just one more failed concept that police management attempted to implement. A large part of the success or failure lies in what happens to community-oriented policing in the future, and this issue will be addressed in the next chapter.

CONCLUSION

There is little doubt that community-oriented policing, as a new philosophy, a new policy, or a multitude of new programs, will generate problems for the police practitioner. This chapter has attempted to incorporate the concept of caveat emptor, or buyer beware, into police departments' adoption of the systemic approach. To address many of the potential problems the police department may face, it is important to understand past problems related to the implementation of the systemic approach. Because the majority of these problems will most likely fall into the category of implementation problems, as with the implementation of any new policy, problems will need to be addressed, both prior to and after implementation. The programs that capture much of the community-oriented policing philosophy will generate problems that were previously unseen and unknown. These problems must be addressed every step of the way. The fail-safe device to ensure a police department has not wasted an excessive amount of its budget and resources on a problem program is to implement in an incremental fashion. By implementing in this manner, the police chief, police administration, and line officers will be able to take the corrective action necessary to address the problem in an efficient and effective manner. If the implementation process is not incremental, generally the result will be problems that are too large in scope to change, leaving only two viable options: continue the failed program with the problems or completely shut down the new program. Neither should be seen as a healthy option.

The implementation problems that most likely will occur focus initially on the definition of community-oriented policing. Based on the literature, both practitioners and scholars have difficulty maching consensus on an all-encompassing definition. Therefore it is important to analyze the common themes among most community-oriented policing departments and generate a concrete definition (see Chapter 2). Once this definition is agreed on, there will be a general focus for any traditional police department attempting to implement the systemic approach, and the policy will be understood by both police management and the line officers implementing community-oriented policing. Additionally, defining the roles of the police, community, and police chief is essential to avoiding problems under the systemic approach, as is understanding the changes that will be necessary in management and organizational structures. And, finally, it is important in the implementation process to continually evaluate the various programs implemented and both community and officer attitudes toward community-oriented policing and then make the incremental changes deemed necessary.

Many other problems may occur under the systemic philosophy, just as they may occur under any other style of policing. These are ancillary problems that elicit much concern from both practitioners and scholars, but they are currently unfounded concerns. One of the most prevalent is a concern about additional resources and costs to implement community-oriented policing. However, because it is a philosophical change, it does not entail the expenditure of more resources or more money. More money is not imperative for the systemic approach to work. The police must work within their means as they do in a traditional police department, although as a result of the changes in delivering their services, the police may see some resources and money become available as recurring problems are solved and as community involvement increases in addressing crime and order maintenance issues. The concerns raised in the literature about police corruption and the police losing their political neutrality should not be summarily dismissed. Although there is always potential that these two problems may surface, there is no proof that this is a norm under the systemic philosophy. Finally, look-alikes, traditional police departments changing to community-oriented policing in name only, are a concern for the systemic approach in the long term (Saunders 1999). We analyze the future of community-oriented policing in more depth in the next chapter.

COP ON THE WORLD WIDE WEB

Community Policing versus Policing the Community

http://www.cahro.org/html/policingthecomm.html

Heritage Foundation Report: *Do Community Oriented Policing Services Grants Affect Violent Crime Rates?*

http://www.heritage.org/library/cda/cda01-05.html

This report suggests COPS has not lowered crime rates.

National Evaluation of the COPS Program

http://www.urban.org/pdfs/COPS_fullreport.pdf

This report suggests that COPS has lowered crime rates.

San Antonio, Texas, Police Department

http://www.sanantonio.gov/sapd/COPPS.asp?res=800&ver=true

Wichita, Kansas, Police Department

http://www.wichitapolice.com/cp.htm

REVIEW QUESTIONS

1. Define the term *caveat emptor* and explain why the term *caveat* is used for the title of this chapter.
2. One of the fears of placing police closer to the community is a return to past problems of police corruption. Has this fear been confirmed since community-oriented policing has been widely adopted?
3. Why is the lack of a consensual definition of community-oriented policing a problem in implementing community-oriented policing?

CHAPTER 15

The Future

*To believe in something not yet proved and to underwrite it with our
lives: it is the only way we can leave the future open.*

—Lillian Smith

CHAPTER OBJECTIVES

- Understand the importance of futures research.
- Identify the principles and premises of futures research.
- Identify the methods of conducting futures research.
- Understand the future problems of community-oriented policing.
- Understand the future benefits of community-oriented policing.
- Identify factors that cause future change.
- Assess community-oriented policing in the era of homeland security.

Community-oriented policing is essentially a blending of the traditional principles of policing with the addition of some relatively new concepts. These concepts are what separate community-oriented policing from both the police–community relations era and the traditional methods of policing. Although the core responsibilities of the police changed little throughout the twentieth century, most of society, the environment, and crime changed. It is this change that the systemic approach is attempting to move forward with, and complement, in the United States in the twenty-first century (see Bayley and Shearing 1996).

As stated in Chapter 15, it is very difficult to predict what will occur in the future, and we are often better served discussing what has occurred in the past and analyzing what we currently know. However, this is not to say that looking at the future is not valuable. We can often look to past occurrences and analyze the present to project what may happen in the future. An occasional foray into the future can be beneficial to most disciplines, but it may be especially helpful when it comes to policing and, more importantly, community-oriented policing.

Because the systemic approach to policing is about the future, it is important to know all we can about the problems of the future so the organization can begin to prepare for any conceivable events. It is also important to explore the future benefits that will be derived from change, providing the incentives that may bear on successful implementation of the systemic approach today to achieve the benefits of the future. And, finally, it is important to analyze the future of various factors that may impact or have dramatic effects within the community-oriented policing approach.

A LOOK AT THE PAST, WITH AN EYE TO THE FUTURE: PLANNING FOR THE NEW MILLENNIUM

As we approach the year 2000, we can look back and see that community policing has enjoyed the kind of popularity that one would expect from a philosophy that makes sense. But why is it more successful in some jurisdictions than others, more popular with some law enforcement administrators than others, and more accepted by some communities and business leaders than others? You need only to scratch the surface of the more successful organizations, in both the public and private sector, to find the answers.

People Are Critical to Success

What you will find in each successful case is that the people involved are what makes the difference. In any police organization, officers will have a variety of aspirations. Some want to be detectives, and others field training officers, while others may prefer K-9 units or motorcycle patrol. Those who are more management-minded strive to make sergeant or lieutenant. Not all, unfortunately, will achieve their goal, and of those who do, it will take some longer than it does others. What accounts for the variances? In most cases, it is the path these individuals choose to follow that makes or breaks their success.

Gaining the Correct Perspective

What are your city's goals? Your police department's? Officers who advance quickly in their careers are typically those who view their personal goals in the context of their city's and police department's broader objectives. Look for ways to meet your objectives as you help your department meet its objectives. Let's say one of your department's primary goals is to select and train highly qualified employees. Officers who are on the road to success will seek ways to become involved with recruiting, field training, or becoming role models or mentors. If all you ever wanted to do is ride a motorcycle, be a "narc," or work with a police dog, feel free to pursue those goals and have fun doing that job if you get it, but take your place in line behind those who have decided to proceed in the direction that the department is moving, and watch them spring ahead. The analogy of railroad tracks demonstrates this method well. If the city is moving down one set of tracks, the police department must be operating on a set that at least runs in a parallel direction. In the best circumstances, these two tracks will overlap. If you want to attain professional success, align your tracks with your department's.

Forming Successful Partnerships

Establishing good working partnerships with the community works the same way. Think about how your department can develop solid relationships with private sector companies and their executives. How can you get your people together on a project or program? Can you think of a way to fund such collaborations? How do you ensure success in these kinds of efforts?

Developing a Plan

One of the first steps in establishing your plan is to focus on what you intend to achieve. If you take the time to identify and then later evaluate your initiatives, you will be more likely to succeed. Identify your agency's goals. Do you know of any corporations in your jurisdiction that have similar objectives? Read the paper, and see where the people who influence policy decisions in your community are working. Think about how you can organize your initiatives so that they parallel those of a major company. By doing so, you can almost ensure their interest in supporting your plan.

Next, approach the executive staff of the corporation you've selected. Explain that you would like to call together a meeting of your department's officers and supervisors, and go off-site (away from the department but not necessarily out of town) to do some team building. Tell the company's executives that you believe your staff could learn something from their leadership. Ask if they would be willing to host a meeting in one of their offices so that a few of their executives could join in on a team-building session. Give them an opportunity to address your group and offer your staff the same option. Find out what capabilities they have that may be of benefit to your department. Many corporations, for example, have in-house publishing services or video crews. Maybe your new partner would be willing to help you produce a training video. Many corporations have been known to do such projects at little or no cost just because they want to help. Other corporations are obligated to donate their funds or services each year for tax reasons. Who knows, you might stumble on an organization that is the answer to your funding problems!

Often, establishing these contacts is the first step in building long, meaningful, mutually beneficial relationships among police supervisors and managers and your community's corporate executives. These advocates are powerful resources for your department and should not be overlooked. When grant funds are no longer available, it will be up to you to find the resources your department needs. Plan now for the millennium. How do your railroad tracks align with corporations in your city? If you are not sure, it may pay dividends to find out!

Source: Reprinted with permission from Steve Frew, "A Look at the Past, with an Eye to the Future: Planning for the New Millennium," *Community Policing Exchange,* May/June 1998. p. 4.

FUTURE RESEARCH

The police have traditionally given very little thought to the future of their discipline. The majority of police administrators and police officers are so busy with the details of the day that they often fail to project any further than a year ahead. Some visionary police chiefs exist, but they find they can do little with these visions as they attend to the daily responsibilities of running a bureaucratic organization. In most cases, futures research has been left to the scholar, and usually a special breed of scholar who, until recently, was considered to be exploring a world of fantasy and myth, based on current articulable facts—perhaps little different from the prognosticators of football. However, as the discipline of futures research has developed, it has come to be accepted by many scholars as having some benefit (Tafoya 1991). The purpose or goal of futures research is "to accurately predict trends, incidents, and organizational policy in anticipation of future realities" (Gilbert 1993, 464). Community-oriented policing, as a new evolution in policing in its infancy stage, would benefit from utilizing futures research to assist in the implementation of change. An even greater benefit would be realized if both scholars and practitioners were able to combine their knowledge to derive a more accurate and useful model of what the future may entail for community-oriented policing. It has been said that those who shape the future of law enforcement can utilize, and essentially need, reliable and valid future-oriented data (Campbell 1990; Gilbert 1993). As police chiefs begin the process of implementing community-oriented policing, they are shaping the future. It is therefore only reasonable that they receive this reliable and valid future-oriented data.

FUTURE RESEARCH AND EVALUATION

In 1996, the National Institute of Justice surveyed 2,585 members of the criminal justice system, focusing largely on police chiefs and sheriffs. Those participating in the survey were asked to rank their priorities for future research and evaluation and the following were the top three responses by the police chiefs and sheriffs:

POLICE CHIEFS	SHERIFFS
Community policing	Community policing
Juvenile crime	Drugs
Violent crime	Juvenile crime

Source: Tom McEwen, *National Assessment Program: 1994 Survey Results.* Washington, D.C.: National Institute of Justice, 1996.

The key to understanding how one derives "reliable and valid future-oriented data" must begin with the distinction between a prediction and a forecast. A prediction is simply a guess about the future that something will occur, and it is usually based on more of an instinctual reasoning rather than an educated reasoning (see Joseph 1974; Klofas and Stojkovic 1995; Rothermel 1982; Tafoya 1990). A prediction is attempting to look into a crystal ball and guess what is going to happen. On the other hand, forecasting is considered to be the purest form of futures research (Cornish 1977; Tafoya 1990). In forecasting, the researcher is essentially looking ahead and reasoning the probable future. It is often analogized with the headlights of a car, where we do not see everything that lies ahead but we see enough to allow us to proceed onward toward our destination (Rothermel 1982; Tafoya 1990, 1991). There should be no doubt that this scanning ahead is beneficial to both the police and those in academic fields. Instead of paying attention to what is going on within the confines of our car, we must look out the window and peer as far forward as our headlights will allow us to see.

Many tools are available to allow us this vision. They consist of a variety of methodologies that can provide the valid and reliable information we seek. To ensure these two qualities in futures research, a consensus has evolved regarding certain principles, premises, and priorities to which the futures researcher should adhere (Tafoya 1990). The three principles are (1) the unity of interconnectedness of reality, (2) the crucial importance of time, and (3) the significance of ideas (see Tafoya 1990, 201). The principles adhered to articulate that events do not happen in a random fashion; that since implementation today becomes reality in roughly five years, the projection should be for more than five years; and that when discussing ideas, one must never abide by the status quo.

The three premises of the futurist consist of the consensual understanding that (1) the future is not predetermined, (2) the future is not predictable, and (3) future outcomes can be influenced by individual choices (see Tafoya 1990, 202). Once this understanding

Sacramento police officers preparing refurbished bicycles to be given to needy children at Christmas. *(Courtesy of the Sacramento Police Department, Sacramento, California.)*

is reached, then the three priorities for futures research become clear, and they consist of the goals that futures research should (1) form perceptions of the future (the possible), (2) study likely alternatives (the probable), and (3) make choices to bring about particular events (the preferable) (see Tafoya 1990, 202). In regards to community-oriented policing, the goals are to then look to what is possible with the systemic approach, determine what is most probable for its implementation, and ultimately bring about its full systemic application, which is preferable.

The actual methods of forecasting the future fall into four distinct categories, which include the use of (1) scenarios, (2) qualitative methods, (3) quantitative methods, and (4) the Delphi technique (Tafoya 1990). The scenario method of forecasting is one in which the writing of the future details the hypothetical in a summary format that analyzes the future subject through a factual basis in a multitude of ways (Cole 1995). Although multiple outcomes are possible, they usually describe the best-case scenario, the worst-case scenario, and the most probable scenario, all of which can be extremely beneficial in planning (Cole 1995; Tafoya 1990). The qualitative method is essentially analyzing the future by beginning with a time and place we want to be in the future and working back-ward to understand how this goal can be obtained, a technique extremely beneficial in the planning of community-oriented policing to project the long-term implementation process (Tafoya 1990). The quantitative method consists of a mathematical model that analyzes past trends in order to forecast what the future trends may entail (Tafoya 1990). This method may be beneficial to the systemic approach because much of the information obtained for future numbers of crime and future demographics is generated in this fashion. And, finally, the Delphi technique is perhaps one of the most sophisticated forecasting tools available in futures research. The Delphi technique utilizes a structured group process that moves members from individual responses toward a consensual agreement as to future events that will occur (Tafoya 1987, 1990, 1991). The personnel selected can be scholars in the academic field, scholars in the research field, police practitioners, and police consultants. Essentially any individual with a knowledge base of the subject under consideration can be utilized. The responses are individualistic and obtained through a survey or through the use of computers, compiled together to form a consensus, at which time this consolidated information is provided back to the individual for further consideration. This process may occur several times until a valid and reliable consensus is reached. It is then possible to articulate the consensus information in the form of a forecast of what is most likely to occur and when.

As policing in the United States moves into the twenty-first century, the information provided through futures research can be beneficial to understanding the changes that are occurring. Futures research on community-oriented policing can provide the criminal justice scholar and the police practitioner with an understanding of what future problems may occur under the systemic approach in order to effectively deal with them before they occur. It can provide information on the future benefits of community-oriented policing that may provide the incentives and justification for implementing this evolutionary and systemic approach to policing. And, finally, it can provide the forecast of community-oriented policing so that many of the pieces of the puzzle are put in place, and it can promote thought on those pieces that we have yet to find.

POLICE SUPERVISION IN THE TWENTY-FIRST CENTURY

In the past several years, community-based policing strategies have emerged as the driving force behind most of these changes. Many police agencies—large and small, rural and urban—have incorporated a community-oriented philosophy into their operational approach. While the specific objectives and tactics of this proactive policing strategy may be as numerous and varied as the communities being served, the basic premise remains the same: To promote a partnership with citizens in order to solve problems and improve the quality of life in the community.

The coming changes to and expectations of society will require law enforcement leaders to reexamine many fundamental components of policing. Three that will assume particular importance are agency mission statements, approaches to supervision, and methods of evaluation. The mission statements of the twenty-first century must be redesigned to reflect values. The underlying premise of these mission statements will change from merely enforcing laws to encompass problem solving and the formation of partnerships with the community.

To support these redefined mission statements, supervisors will be expected to promote creativity and broaden the scope of their leadership. They must become leaders with a vision for pulling their organizations forward. In adjusting their command styles, supervisors will find that it makes good sense to allow the line-level personnel who are most familiar with problems in the community to have a say in developing solutions to those problems. In fact, effective community-oriented policing requires input from line-level personnel. As we move toward the next century, the challenges facing communities show every indication of becoming more complex and difficult. To respond adequately to these challenges, police agencies will be required to reexamine their supervision methods. The coming years will bring changes to many long-accepted maxims of police supervision. Police supervisors in the twenty-first century will be required to alter the traditional role of merely seeing that subordinates follow procedures, adhere to manual regulations, and engage in behavior that is consistent with departmental expectations. In their newly emerging roles, supervisors will spend less time commanding and controlling and more time helping officers identify and find solutions to community problems. The supervisors of tomorrow will guide and coach line officers and encourage problem solving, risk taking, and innovation.

As the roles of officers and supervisors change, so too must the methods by which supervisors evaluate their officers. If community policing is to succeed in reducing crime through closer police–community cooperation, simply requiring officers to produce numbers every month will prove to be an inadequate measure of performance. Instead, supervisors of the twenty-first century will evaluate officers primarily on their abilities to assess and solve community problems. Supervisors also will assess officers' effectiveness based on their ability to remain in touch and to communicate with the various groups within their beats.

Community-oriented policing ultimately will change the way that law enforcement agencies provide service to the community. These changes represent philosophical innovations, as well as stylistic ones. Police commanders must remain responsive to the evolution necessary in supervision strategies to ensure the effective implementation of community policing. Today's officers come from a far different ideological plane than officers who entered policing just twenty years ago. Supervisors have an obligation to mold these officers' performance according to the community-based strategies that will be the standard of policing in the next century. To do this, supervisors must inspire these officers to become problem solvers and encourage them to become more entrepreneurial in their jobs.

Despite the many challenges facing society and policing in the coming years, the future looks bright for those in law enforcement. If agency administrators and supervisors embrace change rather than fight it, they stand a much better chance at controlling their own destinies. Now is a good time for law enforcement administrators and supervisors to ask themselves if they are looking toward the future or living in the past.

Source: Adapted from Michael L. Birzer, "Police Supervision in the 21st Century," *FBI Law Enforcement Bulletin*, June 1996, pp. 6–11.

FUTURE PROBLEMS

The majority of problems that can be forecast to occur with the systemic approach to policing have, to some degree, previously been covered. Many of the forecasts detail a difficult implementation process for community-oriented policing and detail many obstacles standing in the way to prevent the systemic approach from truly becoming the next stage in policing. If past is prologue, then the lack of a consensual definition could pose enormous problems for the systemic approach as various agencies are naming a plethora of practices all under the guise of one name. Additional problems that have previously been detailed include the lack of involvement on the part of the police, community, and various government agencies. As Trojanowicz (1994, 262) so distinctly stated, "The future of community policing is in the hands and hearts of more than just the police."

A very definitive forecast for community-oriented policing details much apathy, misunderstandings, and uninterested citizens when it comes to getting involved. We know this from human nature, we know this from many of the theories of collective action, and we know this from personal involvement in our own groups. It is hard to get a majority of people fully committed to any idea.

In returning to the last problem of community-oriented policing in Chapter 14, look–alikes, it is important to understand how they can affect the future of the systemic approach. As previously stated, many police departments have the uncanny ability to implement change without any change. If a police department subscribes to the latest philosophy and transforms to meet the latest standard without any substantive change, it defeats the purpose of ideas oriented to moving the police toward a more productive organization; if evaluated, it destroys the very tool for determining whether the new concept works. Evaluating the look-alikes creates an unreliable and invalid analysis of the systemic approach to policing and may cause irreparable harm to the concept by preventing a true evaluation.

The look-alikes will most likely occur in four forms that are not conducive to the systemic approach that has been detailed in this book. The first look-alike is the police department that changes the name but does not change the department. Community-oriented policing will fail miserably in this setting because the citizens and police officers will see no change, the new approach to policing will be deemed a failure, and none of the potential benefits will be actualized.

The second look-alike is the department that implements community-oriented policing with no clear direction or concept of what the systemic approach entails. In some police departments, this may be the implementation of foot and bike patrols, with no thought to strategic-oriented policing or problem-oriented policing. In other cases, the department may implement all three components but may make no move toward decentralizing. In any of these cases, the forecast is bright for only several years, at which time any benefit derived from the concept will fade.

The third look-alike forecasted to have problems in implementing community-oriented policing is the department that implements the concept overnight. The forecast is predicated on so many other policing programs that the police chiefs have implemented without any concern for the police. Forced down from the top, these programs have failed to take hold because of the resistance by the line officers. Additionally, any program implemented overnight is sure to fail for lack of clarity. Implementing a concept that is at the same time a philosophy, a policy, a new management style, and a host of programs is absolutely sure to fail if there is no clarity.

Finally, the fourth type of look-alike is revealed in the police department that implements community-oriented policing with misconceptions about what it can and cannot do. Perhaps the key forecast within the misconceptions is that many police departments look for a stringent model of structural changes, programs to implement, and goals to achieve without any concern for the ideas behind the systemic approach. No formula exists for implementing community-oriented policing, only guidelines. Every community is different; therefore every community-oriented police department should be different as well. The three components of community-oriented policing and all of the other methods and changes are the clay that is to be molded by way of the consensual movement of the police, community, and various local government agencies.

The final forecasted problem for community-oriented policing lies in the arena of inflated expectations. The inflated expectations may come from anyone but can be divided into three categories: the community, the police, and the government. Regarding the community, community-oriented policing is not a panacea for all of its problems. In many scenarios, community-oriented policing just will not solve or alleviate the problems that the community identifies or demands be addressed. It will also not change many of the core functions of the police that must continue to be implemented even though there will always be community opposition to their application. These functions may be as simple as the continuation of writing traffic citations or responding in riot gear at a civil disturbance. If community members believe these issues will disappear under the systemic approach to policing, then they have been misinformed or have been allowed to develop unrealistic expectations of what community-oriented policing is all about.

 COP IN ACTION

Technology Brings Policing to Higher Level —And Closer to Community Level

In recent years, community policing has meant getting out of central headquarters and into neighborhoods. Police chiefs and sheriffs set up district offices and apportioned their cities and counties into community service areas. Stores offered space for officers to fill out reports and use the telephone. Deputies and police officers were encouraged to get out of the car, walk around, and be involved. Citizens were encouraged to form a Neighborhood Watch or join Citizens on Patrol. Working at the neighborhood level remains one of the best ways to do business and fight crime.

But in this age of the global community, the way we reach people is changing. An example is the way the Seminole County Sheriff's Office is using the Internet to take citizen involvement to the next level.

eLert Links Law Enforcement and Community

The computer screen glows as Webmaster Pete Robinson hovers over his keyboard. A pile of reports, loaded with faces and facts about individuals with felony records, is being loaded into the sheriff's office's Website. Just when Robinson gets the pile almost finished, another pile is dropped on his desk. In this pile are the latest felony offenders released from Florida's prison system. The community wants to know who these people are and where they will live. That's where the eLert system comes in.

eLert is an electronic alert subscriber list. eLert sends information via e-mail to subscribers about sex offenders, sexual predators, or registered felons who have moved into the neighborhood. It offers crime alerts about traveling criminals, people with active warrants, or others about whom the sheriff's office believes the public should be aware. The Website has a search engine that allows users to search by characteristics, words, or phrases. For example, a search for "burglary" will bring up a summary of each posting that refers to a burglary. The search engine then provides a link to that posting.

On the main page of the Seminole County Sheriff's Office's Website (www.seminolesheriff.org) is a listing with the words "E-LERT, Stay Updated by the Sheriff." The user points his or her mouse to a dialog box that says "JOIN." The user clicks, and the eLert questionnaire opens. The user is asked to follow some simple instructions, enter a password, and provide some demographic information, such as a name and zip code. eLert then sends back a message to verify that the user is who he or she says. Then the user becomes a subscriber.

Felon Updates

The computer user at home opens his e-mail. Today's eLert tells of several registered felons and a sex offender or two as well as issues a warning to homeowners that bands of traveling criminals are moving through central Florida. The computer user lives in zip code area 32707. By reading the eLert listing, the computer user sees a registered felon has moved into his neighborhood. If he wants to see what the registered felon looks like, he just points, clicks, and is immediately linked to a site that shows a color photo as well as the individual's criminal record.

"We've actually had subscribers check up on people who do painting or maintenance work," says Robinson. "In some cases, the homeowners have denied registered felons admission to their homes, all because they remembered them from eLert. And I understand that some of the code-enforcement folks use it to see who is living in some of the homes that they must visit so they're forewarned, and hence prepared, if a felon lives there."

To date, the Seminole County Sheriff's Office eLert system, available since March 1998, has close to 850 subscribers. Some 30 new subscribers sign up per month. "The most significant thing we can do about crime is prevent it," says Sheriff Don Eslinger. "It's very important that we communicate efficiently and effectively with members of our community. One way to empower our citizens is with information."

Source: Reprinted with permission from Steve Olson and Pete Robinson, "Technology Brings Policing to Higher Level—And Closer to Community Level," *Community Policing Exchange,* March/April 2000.

Equally possible in forecasting problems is the same inflated expectations on the part of the police officer, who may be led to believe that community-oriented policing is a panacea or that it will be a simplistic approach to policing. It will continue to be as difficult a job as it always has been, and perhaps it will be even more difficult as police officers are required to utilize skills not previously necessary. They will have more authority and more responsibility and will be required to process thought rather than process paperwork.

The inflated expectations can also occur on the part of the local government, which can have an adverse effect on community-oriented policing. The mayor, the city manager, or a city council member may have inflated expectations for community-oriented policing. From their perception, community-oriented policing may well be the panacea for both criminal and order maintenance issues, and without the dramatic changes desired, they may feel the concept has failed. The same may be true of other government agencies, which may believe that the police can accomplish the systemic approach without their assistance, and they may not wish to assist.

Regardless of whether we discuss the community, police, or government when it comes to inflated expectations, it is simply the case that the American mentality is often "We want it now." As in the case of the community-oriented police department that changes overnight, this is clearly a result of what so many want and what so many people

Wichita community-oriented policing officers and local citizens participate in a local cleanup of a neighborhood, specifically in empty lots where excessive dumping has occurred. *(Courtesy of the Wichita Police Department, Wichita, Kansas.)*

expect. If the systemic approach to policing is to work in the long term, the fact that there is an inflated expectation for quick implementation and quick results must be dealt with during every stage of the implementation process. If the inflated expectations of the community, police, and local government are allowed to continue, the forecast shows that community-oriented policing will not be given the ample time it needs to become entrenched and the concept will be deemed a failure before it has time to develop.

FUTURE BENEFITS

In detailing many of the past problems of community-oriented policing to prevent potential problems from occurring, little time has been spent on the benefits of the systemic approach. As we have seen through most of the community-oriented policing evaluations over the past ten years, the response on the part of the community, the police, and the police organization has been somewhat skeptical and cynical at first. After a period of time has passed, those opinions begin to change and everyone involved in the process, and to some degree those who are not, find community-oriented policing to be beneficial. Obviously, if there were not benefits, the concept would never have moved to the position in the literature and in the police departments that it now holds. However, one must ask the question, What are the future long-term benefits of the systemic approach?

Some of the key literature in the area of community-oriented policing has laid the foundation for what benefits are being revealed in our forecasting headlights. The benefits lie in the same areas as the problems and can be broken down by analyzing the benefits to the community, the police, and the police organization (see Table 15-1).

TABLE 15-1   *Benefits of Community-Oriented Policing*

BENEFITS TO THE COMMUNITY

1. The police make a commitment to prevent crime rather than just react to it.
2. Public scrutiny of the police is improved because more citizens know what police do and why.
3. Police officers are accountable for their behavior not only to the department but also to citizens.
4. Police services will be tailored to the needs of each neighborhood.
5. As citizens become more involved in police activities, the community will become more organized and therefore more effective in responding to problems.

BENEFITS TO THE POLICE

1. The police will receive greater community support.
2. The police will be able to share the responsibility for the control of crime and disorder with citizens.
3. Police officers will have greater job satisfaction because they will be able to see the results of their efforts at problem solving.
4. The communication and cooperation among units (e.g., patrol and investigations) in the police department will be enhanced.
5. Police departments will have to reexamine their organizational structure and managerial practices.

Source: Adapted from Lee P. Brown, "Community Policing: A Practical Guide for Police Officials." *Perspectives on Policing.* Washington, D.C.: National Institute of Justice, 1989.

 COP IN ACTION

Enhancing Police Services with Senior Volunteers

The Newark Police Department, like many other police organizations, constantly struggles to enhance services without benefit of additional resources. Leaders are already challenged by managing their departments' existing budgets of tax dollars and city revenue. Our department found that it could enhance services and reduce some of the workload by using senior citizen volunteers to assist with the department's routine activities. In locations where communities are facing fiscal constraints, police volunteers are one of the few mechanisms for improving services without increasing citizens' taxes.

Newark was exposed to the idea of using senior volunteers through Triad. Prompted by information obtained from Triad, we linked up with the local Retired Seniors Volunteer Program (RSVP). RSVP is supported by federal dollars to enhance senior volunteerism in virtually every public service endeavor throughout the community. RSVP provides insurance that covers the volunteers from the time they leave their homes until the time they return and also reimburses them for mileage.

In six years, our program has expanded to fifteen volunteers who work in various divisions of the police department. We have come to value and rely on their services. We are quickly reminded how important their contributions are on those rare occasions when they are unable to work their scheduled hours. The volunteers perform a variety of tasks that assist with daily operations and the delivery of police services to Newark's citizens. Their responsibilities include:

- Preparing a crime information bulletin that is distributed to all personnel twice weekly
- Capsulizing and documenting crime trends
- Assisting with centralized records by servicing citizen requests at the public information window, entering data from crime reports, processing requests for traffic accident reports, and filing reports in the central filing system
- Analyzing all false alarms, preparing follow-up correspondence, obtaining explanations for the false alarms, and ensuring that corrective actions are taken to limit their frequency
- Reviewing 911 calls that are erroneously transferred to our system, and taking action to ensure that future calls are transmitted to the appropriate 911 answering point
- Monitoring party, noise, and disorderly conduct violations related to rental units, and notifying landlords of the violations so that corrective action may be taken in conjunction with the city's ordinance
- Assisting various units with data entry, evidence and property purges, mass mailings, and sorting and filing mug shots

The volunteer program brings the citizens we serve into the police department and creates an environment for ongoing interaction between officers and the senior volunteers. Many of the volunteers say that the appreciation they receive is one of the primary reasons for volunteering with the police department. Officers have an opportunity to interact with caring and supportive citizens and develop a greater sensitivity to senior citizens' concerns.

Advice for Departments Setting Up a Volunteer Program

Employees may be reluctant to allow "outsiders" into the working components of the police agency. They may have a natural fear that volunteers will eliminate or replace their positions. Therefore, it is important to reassure all employees that the volunteers are there to enhance services and to lessen the workload and increase efficiency. Agency personnel must be committed to train the volunteers to perform specific tasks. I have found that once volunteers have been properly screened and trained, they make for a highly professional and very dedicated group of individuals.

Agencies should conduct limited background investigations on the volunteers. It is also wise to get commitments about the frequency and number of hours volunteers are willing to devote.

I can't stress enough how important it is for police agencies to make certain the work given to volunteers is meaningful. Many of the volunteers who come into our department are well-educated, competent individuals who are looking for a challenge and want to know that they are truly contributing to the police operation.

It has been my experience that a volunteer program begins slowly, but if the police department is committed to the concept, it will grow in terms of both the number of volunteers and the complexity of the assignments. As this evolution occurs, the services that volunteers provide will become indispensable; their contributions will benefit both the police agency and the citizens served.

Source: Adapted with permission from Chief William Hogan, "Enhancing Police Services with Senior Volunteers." In *Community Policing Exchange.* Washington, D.C.: Community Policing Consortium, November/December 1995, p. 8.

The benefits to the community include unquestionably the crime prevention techniques the police are implementing that assist not only in preventing crime but also in reducing the public fear of crime (Skolnick and Bayley 1988b; see also Brown 1989; Mastrofski 1988; Skolnick and Bayley 1988a; Wycoff 1988). Rather than maintaining the reactive stance of the traditional style of policing, community-oriented policing attempts to be proactive in nature to prevent crime and order maintenance issues. A second benefit to the community lies in the area of public scrutiny and public accountability (Brown 1989; Mastrofski 1988; Skolnick and Bayley 1988a, 1988b). Under the traditional forms of policing, it was the us versus them mentality, and the idea was that the police would take care of their own by hiding their problems from public view. Under the community-oriented policing approach, the community must not only play a role in the decision-making process for the allocation of police resources but also play a role in what the police do or fail to do. The police then must be accountable to the police organization as well as the public. And, finally, community involvement with the police, with other members of the community, and with community organizations is a positive factor in reestablishing a healthy community (Brown 1989; Skolnick and Bayley 1988a). As people have migrated toward cities for the past 200 years to move closer to other people, they have actually moved further and further apart, as people have become strangers within their own communities. Pulling these people together to address the community's woes, communicate, and work together must assuredly be more beneficial then living as strangers.

The communication and commitment to work together benefit not only the community but the police as well (Brown 1989; Cordner 1988; Skolnick and Bayley 1988a, 1988b; Wycoff 1988). Interaction between the community and the police can increase public knowledge about the role of the police, increase their respect, and most importantly increase their support for the police. The police know the community is behind them and supporting their efforts, thereby creating a healthy environment for the police officer and most likely cultivating a more dedicated officer. Intrinsically tied to this support is the concept of shared responsibility for addressing criminal and order maintenance problems (Brown 1989; Skolnick and Bayley 1988a, 1988b; Wycoff 1988). If police officers see that the community not only supports their role in society but is also willing to work with them toward eradicating the problems in the community, the police will, like the community, come to understand, increase their respect, and develop a more productive and healthy relationship.

Extremely unique to community-oriented policing, and certainly a benefit, is that the systemic approach enhances communication between the public and the police. However, it also enhances the communication from police to police and community to community. As the lines of communication open up between the police and the community, it requires, and sometimes forces, communication among these two groups. For line police officers to implement the various programs, they must communicate with other police officers and seek out their assistance to address problems, develop programs, and work alongside the community. Equally important is the fact that police find themselves communicating up the chain to first-line supervisors and beyond, while police management begins to communicate with line officers in a more dynamic way. Communication becomes a two-way street, and the focus shifts to working together rather than the police officers and police management working against each other.

The Phoenix Police Department's community-oriented policing bike patrol officers in the downtown area stop to say hello to a "little" citizen. *(Courtesy of the Phoenix Police Department, Phoenix, Arizona, and Mr. Bob Rink.)*

In addition to increased communication between the police, there is also greatly enhanced intercommunity communication. As the various programs under community-oriented policing grow and more and more people find themselves involved, relationships between community members tend to grow dramatically. Neighbors who once refused to go next door to meet their neighbors find themselves involved in many situations in which they must work together. Once they are brought together, all pretenses, fears, and beliefs are usually quickly dismissed and a stronger community is forged through open communication. Communities truly begin to develop a sense of community. This sense of community can be advantageous to the police and individual citizens, but, most importantly, it is advantageous to the community at large.

In addition to the benefits from open lines of communication, benefits are realized as the police department begins decentralizing the department's structure, changing the department's management style, and moving toward working together to address the community's needs. As a result of these changes, the police will have a better working environment, one in which they are valued more, and thus greater job satisfaction will become the greatest benefit to the police (Brown 1989; Cordner 1988; Skolnick and Bayley 1988a, 1988b; Wycoff 1988). As a former police officer once explained, "It is sad when you have to quit because the stress of being a police officer comes from within the department rather than from the elements on the street." The benefits to the police officer under community-oriented policing are clear; if the systemic approach is implemented, the forecast holds for a more satisfied police officer and hence a more dedicated employee.

Just as community-oriented policing benefits the community and the line police officer, it also benefits the police organization. The primary benefit to the police organization is increased job satisfaction among the line officers and the increased support derived from the community (Wycoff 1988). There is little doubt that a more satisfied employee will be a more productive worker, take less leave time, and show a stronger attachment and dedication to the organization. Equally, if the community feels its police are doing a good job and it supports their efforts, the increases in resources, legitimacy, and status are all beneficial to the police organization. A second benefit lies in the political arena because community-oriented policing is a win-win situation for the police organization, which may explain why so many police departments are quick to adopt this new philosophy. Because crime is a valence issue—no one supports crime—there can be little doubt that unfolding a new way to fight crime will benefit the police organization politically. Although the police should remain politically neutral, politics cannot always be avoided. In the case of community-oriented policing, there are no bad politics. Finally, little doubt exists that the police practices and procedures under the traditional approach to policing have failed to produce any true effect on crime and order maintenance problems; therefore the mere implementation of the systemic approach may provide the opportunity to become an effective, efficient, equitable, and accountable police department that works with the community, five criteria desired by the public.

The realization of these five criteria is also a key benefit to both the police department and the community. As the police department advances under the systemic approach to policing, these five criteria should be central to the department's philosophy and should be embodied in every policy and program enacted. The police will strive to be more effective in the delivery of their services to the public. They will work to be more efficient in how they utilize their available resources, and they will seek out new ways of delivering their services and tap into new resources available from within the police department, the business sector, and the community as a whole. They will always strive for equity by demonstrating that they are fair in the delivery of services, that they provide equal protection under the law, and that they hold the principles of the Constitution, which they have sworn to defend, as their highest concern. They will be more accountable as police officers, as police managers, and as police chiefs to the public, but, more importantly, they will be more accountable as individuals. Finally, community-oriented policing is the impetus for divesting authority in the police, as well as in the community, for all things related to crime and social disorder. As the police adhere to these five criteria under community-oriented policing, there should be little doubt of the benefits to the community, which includes the police.

THE FUTURE

The future of community-oriented policing is very promising, and the majority of the literature supports this opinion. The advocates, both scholars and practitioners, have identified the systemic approach to policing as being the next stage in policing. Although many agree it is time to begin implementation, most also agree that as a standard in policing, community-oriented policing is still a decade away (see Zhao and Thurman 1997). Although the 1990s was often deemed the decade of community-oriented policing, many believed that the true realities would not come until early in the twenty-first century. A pressing question, and one that must be dealt with, is whether the events of 9/11 and the implementation of homeland security concepts will have an impact on the realities of community-oriented policing. Futures research from the past is actually somewhat enlighting for both the present and the future.

The majority of futures research of the systemic approach is laid out in the foundation of anecdotal evidence and through these advocates of community-oriented policing (Worsnop 1993). In other cases, there is such a vast amount of confidence in the systemic approach that it has been recommended as the answer to many departments' problems. This is especially true in Los Angeles, where the Christopher Commission's investigation in the aftermath of the Rodney King incident called for community-oriented policing as the appropriate model to restore police and community relations (Christopher et al. 1991). And in most cases, the forecasts of the future are positive, such as Bennett's (1989, 331) statement that "the social service functions of police will become more community-oriented." This is not to say, however, that everyone paints a rosy scenario when it comes to community-oriented policing.

Although some scholars either are opposed to community-oriented policing or recommend extreme caution in implementing this style of policing (Bayley 1988; Klockars 1988; Riechers and Roberg 1990; Walker 1984), one futures research forecast (Crank 1995) believes the concept will fail. Crank forecasted that by the year 2000 the majority of police departments in the United States would have implemented community-oriented policing, but by the year 2010, as a result of two unpredictable incidents, the systemic approach will be called into question and eventually be deemed a failure. He also articulates that the "reorientation of patrol" will not work as intended, the costs of rapid response will pose problems, the decentralization and "civilianization" will fail, and "the community-based policing movement failed to take into account historical and institutional features of the broader context in which policing occurred, and that context had profound effects on police organization and activity" (Crank 1995, 116). Although this surely paints a tragic end to the systemic approach, it can provide some information to practitioners and scholars of today.

Because the majority of these problems have previously been addressed, the key concern articulated by Crank is the possibility of a tragic event raising public awareness and public opinion of the community-oriented policing approach. These "historical shocks," as Crank (1995, 123) calls them, could pose potential problems for the systemic approach. The best analogy to one of these shocks and the difficulties community-oriented policing may face can be tied to the riots in the wake of the Rodney King incident. If the police department had previously shifted to the systemic approach and it was either in the implementation process or had seen full systemic implementation, would community-oriented policing have survived in its wake? The first response to this question is that hopefully, under the systemic approach, this incident would never have happened, but that would prove too naive. If an isolated beating occurs, if a citizen is wounded or killed by the police, and if the police have to respond full force in a riot situation, will community-oriented policing be deemed a failure? There are no easy answers to this question, but understanding the potential for its occurrence, police departments implementing the systemic approach should consider the appropriate community-oriented approach to this type of crisis situation.

Although all of these forecasts are beneficial to the literature revolving around community-oriented policing, there is a need for more futures research in this area. The majority of literature is not specifically directed toward the systemic approach except in anecdotal form. To turn to the core of the forecasting research, two key pieces of research provide some in-depth information that can be beneficial to police practitioners. The first source is a Delphi forecast of the future in law enforcement, and the second source details a list of external considerations that may affect community-oriented policing.

The Delphi forecast was conducted by Tafoya (1991) for his doctoral dissertation; he surveyed key scholars, police chiefs, scholar/practitioners, and finally key people in the professional criminal justice, criminology, and law enforcement societies. In three rounds of individual responses on various topics in law enforcement, these researchers reached consensus on many advancements in law enforcement, along with a target date when they would occur (Tafoya 1991). The responses are most interesting for the discussion of community-oriented policing because a variety of advancements are inherent within the systemic approach to policing.

The Delphi forecast, completed in 1986, predicted that, by 1995, "community involvement and self-help in local policing [would become] common practice in more than 70 percent of the nation" (Tafoya 1991, 255). Additionally, Tafoya predicted (1991, 260) that in the same year "University/professionally conducted research [would have] a direct and positive influence on crime reduction strategies." In both of these cases, the forecast has been correct.

Tafoya (1991, 264) had forecasted that by 2005 "more than 50 percent of [all] police agencies [will] have personnel competent to conduct rigorous empirical research." Because the evaluation of the various community-oriented policing programs is critical to determining the effectiveness, efficiency, and equity of these programs, this forecast is of critical importance to the systemic approach. The evaluation process is an integral part of the concept of community-oriented policing, as detailed in Chapter 11, and this forecast is good news in regard to future implementation.

Finally, the Delphi forecast states that by 2025, more than 70 percent of all police departments in the United States will have formal education as a "standard for entry and advancement" (Tafoya 1991, 261) and police executives will "adopt a non-traditional (proactive/goal oriented) leadership style" (Tafoya 1991, 262). Because both of these are integral parts to the police officers' and police chiefs' roles under community-oriented policing (see Chapters 8 and 10), they provide a beneficial description of what is to come in our forecasting headlights. The Delphi forecast clearly articulates many of the fundamentals of community-oriented policing.

The second source of futures research that can provide some forecasting revolves around those forces that are likely to have an impact on the systemic approach but are outside of the police department's and community's capability to control. These four "drivers," as Cole (1995, 13) describes them, consist of (1) demographics, (2) economics, (3) technology, and (4) crime factors. Each of these will have either a direct or indirect impact on the systemic approach to policing, but all four should be taken into consideration when implementing community-oriented policing.

The first concern revolves around the changing demographics of the United States (Cole 1995; Enter 1991). Any shift in the three basic demographic variables of births,

REMARKS BY PRESIDENT BUSH ON PROJECT SAFE NEIGHBORHOODS, MAY 14, 2001, PHILADELPHIA, PENNSYLVANIA

During the last several years, violent crime in America has been decreasing. And all Americans are grateful. Between 1989 and 1999, the violent crime rate dropped 20 percent. And that's a huge accomplishment. It really is. But, unfortunately, American society is still far too violent. The violent crime rate in the United States remains among the highest in the industrialized world.

Nationally, there were 12,658 murders in 1999, two-thirds of which were shooting deaths. And for every fatal shooting, there were roughly three nonfatal shootings. And, folks, this is unacceptable in America. It's just unacceptable. And we're going to do something about it.

Like most major urban centers—cities—in America, Philadelphia suffered from a stunning rise in violent crime. However, Philadelphia, as the Mayor mentioned, has made great progress. For example, in 1990, there were 500 murders; last year there were 319. And the Mayor deserves a lot of credit; so does the Police Commissioner and the policemen and women of Philadelphia. And for that, we're incredibly grateful. And we're grateful for programs such as Operation Sunrise and Safe and Sound and Youth Violence Reduction Project, which, Mr. Mayor, are making your city more safe and more secure for all of the citizens.

But gun violence is still a serious problem. In this city, 3 out of 4 murder victims are shot to death with handguns. Among young victims, that figure rises to almost 9 out of 10. In America today, a teenager is more likely to die from a gunshot than from all natural causes of death combined. These details have caused too many families to bury the next generation. And for all our children's sake, this nation must reclaim our neighborhoods and our streets.

We need a national strategy to ensure that every community is attacking gun violence with focus and intensity. I'm here today to announce a national initiative to help cities like Philadelphia fight gun violence. The program I propose, we call it Project Safe Neighborhoods, will establish a network of law enforcement and community initiatives targeted at gun violence. It will involve an unprecedented partnership between all levels of government. It will increase accountability within our systems. And it will send an unmistakable message: If you use a gun illegally, you will do hard time.

This nation must enforce the gun laws that exist on the books. Project Safe Neighborhoods incorporates and builds upon the success of existing programs. In Richmond, Virginia, for example, during the first year of what's called Project Exile, homicides were reduced by 40 percent; armed robberies were reduced by 30 percent in the first year alone. And thanks to Boston's Operation Cease-Fire, in almost two years, no one under the age of seventeen was shot.

These are tremendous success stories, and ones that are worth duplicating around our nation. My administration is proposing to devote more than $550 million to Project Safe Neighborhoods over the next two years. The funding will be used to hire new federal and state prosecutors, to support investigators, to provide training, and to develop and promote community outreach efforts. All newly appointed U.S. attorneys will be directed to certify to the Attorney General that the new comprehensive gun violence program has been implemented in their districts.

We're going to reduce gun violence in America, and those who commit crimes with guns will find a determined adversary in my administration. Domestic tranquility is a phrase made famous in this city. Project Safe Neighborhoods is one step, and an important step, to making that a reality.

Source: White House Web site, http://www.whitehouse.gov, July 2002.

deaths, and migrations (Farley 1994) could change many of the criminal and order maintenance concerns of the police. Although the birth rates in the United States have decreased, the number of deaths at birth have also decreased, causing a slight increase in the population. Equally important are the advancements in medicine that have prolonged life and advanced the average age of death. And migration to the United States continues to see consistent growth. All of these factors influence the demographics of the United States and will bring with them a host of variables that may impact crime and the police. The potential for an increase in geriatric crimes is already being addressed (Bennett 1989; Kercher 1987; Miller 1991; Steffensmeier 1987), along with an increase in their victimization rates.

The group of most concern in regards to aging is the baby boomers, but an equally interesting trend is the coming of age of their children, the "echo baby boom," which will bring about an increase in juvenile crimes (McNulty 1995; Oliver 1996). The number of teenagers in this generation is projected to reach 11.5 million by 2010, and because most criminologists agree that age is a large factor in crime (Greenberg 1985; Hirschi and Gottfredson 1983), crime is projected to increase. However, what is more disturbing is the increasing number of violent crimes among this age group, which may prove to have the biggest impact (McNulty 1995).

Whether it is the aging of America, the rising numbers of juveniles, the influx of immigrants both legal and illegal, or the projected increases so that minority groups will become the majority by 2050, all of these issues fall under the application of demographics. The growing trends and the forecast of what is to come can provide essential data to understanding today what the police of tomorrow may face. This data is critically important to community-oriented policing because the police of tomorrow will be community-oriented police officers.

The second concern falls in the arena of economics (Cole 1995). The economic viability of the police is of great importance to the future of community-oriented policing. Although the systemic approach can be implemented without the addition of any new funds or resources, cuts in the police department budget would still have detrimental effects on this new approach. Additionally, economic concerns can be applied to the local, state, and national levels because if the economy at any of these levels undergoes a depression or major disruption, regardless of the cause, there is a strong potential for crime rates to increase, the community to break down, and the police to be returned to a position that is reactive in nature. Obviously the economic factors of community-oriented policing should be taken into consideration.

The third concern lies in the area of technology (Cole 1995). As the advancements in technology increase and the applications to the police grow exponentially, a growing concern exists that the police may become more isolated from the public as a result (Radelet and Carter 1994). There is also some genuine concern that the technology will not be utilized in an appropriate manner and may drive a wedge between the public and the police rather than bringing them together. In any event, a role for technology exists in community-oriented policing (Ricucci and McKeehan 1993).

The final concern that will most likely impact community-oriented policing directly is the crime factor (Cole 1995). Recent trends in crime point to different concerns that need to be addressed under community-oriented policing. As previously detailed, there will be a growing trend of geriatric crimes and violent crimes among juveniles. There is also a growing trend of women committing more crime, which may have profound effects on crime and policing (Sileo 1993). In addition, Tafoya's (1987), Delphi forecast of an increase in terrorism by 1995, with the attacks on September 11 a prime example, has the potential of becoming a trend that will prove to be of great concern to policing. There is also the concern of the impact that the future trends of various crime-related issues, such as the legalization of drugs, gun control, euthanasia, capital punishment, domestic violence, the increasing prison population, and pornography, may have on policing in the future (see Monk 1996 for debates on these issues).

As community-oriented policing becomes the chosen method of policing in the United States, many other factors will affect the systemic approach. Although it is relatively easy to understand what will impact the police internally, it is important that both scholars and practitioners understand what will impact the police externally. Comprehending the impact that these four areas of concern will have on community-oriented policing can provide the police with the necessary forecast information, both valid and reliable, that can assist in planning for the future.

A police officer of the Vienna Police Department, Vienna, West Virginia, presents a stuffed lion to a local citizen for wearing her safety belt and having her child in a car seat (left). A stuffed lion is presented to parents whose children utilize their seat belts by the Vienna Police Department, Vienna, West Virginia (right). *(Courtesy of the Parkersburg Newspaper, Parkersburg, West Virginia, and Mr. David Bowie.)*

HOMELAND SECURITY THROUGH COMMUNITY-ORIENTED POLICING

As detailed in Chapter 12, in the wake of the terrorist attacks on September 11, 2001, the federal government's focus has largely been on fighting a war on terrorism abroad and homeland security domestically. As the Office of Homeland Security, followed by the Department of Homeland Security, was established in 2002 and 2003, a shift in funding priorities occurred. Domestic discretionary spending was reduced across a number of federal agencies and departments, while homeland security spending was greatly increased. The Office of Community Oriented Policing Services (COPS) was one of those offices that has seen significant cuts in their budgets.

Shortly after the terrorist attacks on New York City and Arlington County, Virginia, the COPS office implemented a grant program titled, "Homeland Security through Community Policing." The emphasis of the actual grant program was called the "Homeland Security Overtime Program" (HSOP). According to the COPS office, the HSOP was created "to increase the amount of overtime funding available to support community policing and homeland security efforts" (COPS 2003). The office explained that "as state, local, and tribal law enforcement embrace the challenge of securing our homeland, this is now more important than ever" and that the "COPS' HSOP will support programs that increase community safety and security, and reduce public fear" (COPS 2003). The concept was to use the funds to help cities and towns that had their officers on full alert after 9/11, to help protect the homeland, and to adopt the strategies of community-oriented policing to help do this. Yet the COPS office contradicted this concept

Oklahoma City Police Department's Emergency Response Team (ERT) in training for a biohazard response. (*Courtesy of the Oklahoma City Police Department, Oklahoma City, Oklahoma.*)

when it stated that "HSOP grants can be used to pay officer overtime during homeland security training sessions and other law enforcement activities that are designed to help prevent acts of terrorism and other violent or drug-related crimes" (COPS 2003). Unless one takes a very broad interpretation of terrorism, violent crimes such as robberies and rapes and any drug-related crime activity qualified under these grants. Thus the funding was not entirely for homeland security.

These grants were dispersed over the next several years and other mechanisms of the COPS office became involved. The COPS office held training sessions on "Homeland Security through Community Policing," and the Regional Community Policing Institute's, sponsored by the COPS Office, began providing training on anti- and counterterrorism. This concept became widely bandied about and has been the focus of a number of articles discussing the relationship between the two concepts and insinuating that this is the new future for community-oriented policing. But is it?

The argument is that community-oriented policing and homeland security are compatible concepts. The simple viewpoint is that over the past two decades, through community-oriented policing, the police have built up such a strong relationship with the community that they can utilize this to assist in their defense of the homeland and investigation into would-be terrorists. First and foremost, this makes the assumption that community-oriented policing has been that successful. Second, assuming that it has and the police–citizen partnership is strong, it also assumes that the community has the capacity and capability to ferret out would-be terrorists. Recollections of neighbors regarding the 9/11 terrorists included statements that he "seemed nice" or that they were "very quite" people. They did not appear to be terrorists. Which, of course, is simply the point—terrorists want to blend in, not stand out. Thus, there is little the community can look for that would target terrorists.

At a more complex level, the argument for homeland security and community-oriented policing being compatible consists of a number of observations. One is that the organizational change, the flattening of the pyramid (see Chapter 7), contributes to empowered officers who can use their discretion to further their knowledge of the community (Scheider and Chapman 2003). Recent research has demonstrated that although this has been a consistent call for community-oriented policing implementation, it simply has not happened across the board and is still the exception and not the rule (again, see Chapter 7). Additionally, the use of problem-solving skills (see Chapter 5) provides the police with a mechanism by which they can analyze potential targets in their jurisdiction, for identifying targets is the first step in hardening targets (Scheider and Chapman 2003). While it is true that this is a form of problem-solving, risk analysis is a far different problem-solving model than the SARA model, which is the tool most often employed by the local police. Finally, Scheider and Chapman (2003) argue that police and community partnerships are strong and will help in preventing terrorism. While this is true that specific partnering and training in such things as Community Emergency Response Teams (CERT) is important, it is not inherently the same thing as partnering to solve problems of graffiti and other social disorders.

More recently, Doherty and Hibbard (2006) have made the argument that in order for police to collect information regarding potential homeland security threats, they should solicit a number of community information sources such as neighborhood watch programs, religious groups, print shops, fraternities, bars, and schools. They then discuss the ways in which this information can be collected, such as in-person, through neighborhood meetings, and via follow-up calls. What they are advocating is for police to gather information that can be forwarded to a police intelligence unit, an entity that analyzes raw information and attempts to develop actionable intelligence. This can be done and does not necessitate the partnerships of community-oriented policing. Citizens, knowing the importance of this information, are just as likely to provide this regardless of the police–citizen relationship. That said, this type of information collection has the potential to backfire in that it may seem Orwellian in nature and may damage police–community relations if it is perceived as heavy-handed.

Perhaps the most extensive argument for the compatibility of community-oriented policing and homeland security comes from Docobo (2005/2006), whose master's thesis explored this issue. While Docobo argues much of the points already illustrated, he argues that community-oriented policing simply provides the most solid framework upon which to build "homeland-policing." This brings us to the ultimate question dealing with the future of community-oriented policing: Is the movement to homeland security (homeland security through community-oriented policing) simply the next generation of community-oriented policing, or is policing for homeland security an entirely different philosophy, concept, or paradigm?

One could argue that community-oriented policing is the concept that is well entrenched in neighborhoods and police departments across the country and is the proper mechanism to mobilize to prevent terrorism. Yet the person arguing this must look at the concepts behind community-oriented policing and homeland security to determine if they are indeed compatible. To this end, two well-known analyses of the eras of policing and styles of policing can be employed to determine if they are compatible or not. The first, the era of policing (featured in Chapter 1), details how American policing has moved from the political and reform eras and into the community era (Kelling and Moore 1988). It does this by comparing certain elements, such as where does the authorization for the police originate, how are the police organizationally structured, and what is the intended outcome. By adding a fourth category, an era of homeland security, we can compare the concepts behind the two concepts, community-oriented policing and homeland security, to determine if they are compatible (see Table 15-2).

A simple comparison between the community era and what is being called the homeland security era suggests that these two eras are not compatible and hence suggest that we may be moving into a new era of policing. Such a broad interpretation, however, may lose much in the way of details related to these different approaches. What is needed is something more detailed, and this is provided by Greene's (2000) table, which looks more closely at the styles of policing that have developed, specifically traditional policing, community policing, problem-oriented policing, and zero-tolerance policing, all of which have been discussed throughout this book (see Table 15-3.) Adding an additional style of policing, homeland security, allows us to analyze more closely if community-oriented policing and homeland security policing are compatible. Based on such things as focus, forms of intervention, and the locus of decision making, all suggest that the two are vastly different in scope, nature, and style. Therefore, if community-oriented policing and homeland security policing are different, where does that leave the future of community-oriented policing?

TABLE 15-2 *The Four Eras of Policing Based on Organizational Strategy*

ELEMENTS	POLITICAL ERA	REFORM ERA	COMMUNITY ERA	HOMELAND SECURITY ERA
Authorization	Politics and law	Law and professionalism	Community support (political), law, professionalism	National/international threats (intergovermental), professionalism
Function	Broad social services	Crime control	Broad provision of service	Crime control, antiterrorism/ counterterrorism, intelligence gathering
Organizational Design	Decentralized	Centralized, classical	Decentralized, task forces, matrices	Centralized decision making, decentralized execution
Relationship to Environment	Intimate	Professionally remote	Intimate	Professional
Demand	Decentralized, to patrol and politicians	Centralized	Decentralized	Centralized
Tactics and technology	Foot patrol	Preventive patrol and rapid response to calls for service	Foot patrol, problem solving, etc.	Risk assessment, police operations centers, information systems
Outcome	Citizen political satisfaction	Crime control	Quality of life and citizen satisfaction	Citizen safety, crime control, antiterrorism

Adapted by author from G. L. Kelling, and M. H. Moore, "The Evolving Strategy of Policing." *Perspectives on Policing, no. 4.* Washington, D.C.: National Institute of Justice, 1988.

As I have argued elsewhere (Oliver 2004, 2006), I believe that the shift in focus in the wake of 9/11 is toward policing for homeland security. It is my read, based on past changes in public policy, that as a policy reaches the end of its policy life (and they all do), bureaucrats try to adjust known policies to the changes (e.g., community-oriented policing to homeland security through community policing). Eventually the new policy emerges and the previous policy is phased out. I believe this is happening in the field of policing. Money, training, and resources are going to homeland security. Many people, other than myself, for good or bad are discussing the end of community-oriented policing (see, for instance, Table 15-2). It is also evident that the two policies are not compatible as they have

TABLE 15-3 *Comparisons of Social Interactions and Structural Components of Various Forms of Policing, Including Homeland Security*

SOCIAL INTERACTION OR STRUCTURAL DIMENSION	TRADITIONAL POLICING	COMMUNITY POLICING	PROBLEM-ORIENTED POLICING	ZERO-TOLERANCE POLICING	HOMELAND SECURITY POLICING
Focus of policing	Law enforcement	Community building through crime prevention	Law, order, and fear problems	Order problems	Security, antiterrorism, counter terrorism, law and order
Forms of intervention	Reactive, based on criminal law	Proactive, on criminal, and administrative law	Mixed, on criminal and administrative law	Proactive, uses criminal, civil, and administrative law	Proactive, on criminal law and for mitigation and preparedness
Range of police activity	Narrow, crime focused	Broad crime, order, fear and quality of life focused	Narrow to broad—problem focused	Narrow, location and behavior focused	Broad, security, terrorism, crime, fear
Levels of discretion at line level	High and unaccountable	High and accountable to the community and local commanders	High and primarily accountable to the police administration	Low, but primarily accountable to the police administration	High and primarily primarily accountable to the police administration
Focus of police culture	Inward, rejecting community	Outward, building partnerships	Mixed depending on problem, but analysis focused	Inward focused on attacking the target problem	Mixed depending on threat, threat-analysis focused
Locus of decisionmaking	Police directed, minimizes the involvement of others	Community–police coproduction; joint responsibility and assessment	Varied, police identify problems, but with community involvement and interaction	Police directed, some linkage to other agencies where necessary	Police directed with linkage to other agencies
Communication flow	Downward from police to community	Horizontal between police and community	Horizontal between police and community	Downward from from police to community	Downward from police to community
Range of community involvement	Low and passive	High and active	Mixed depending on problem set	Low and passive	Mixed depending on threat

TABLE 15-3 *(Continued)*

SOCIAL INTERACTION OR STRUCTURAL DIMENSION	TRADITIONAL POLICING	COMMUNITY POLICING	PROBLEM-ORIENTED POLICING	ZERO-TOLERANCE POLICING	HOMELAND SECURITY POLICING
Linkage with other agencies	Poor and intermittent	Participative and integrative in the overarching process	Participative and integrative depending on the problem set	Moderate and intermittent	Participative and integrative in the overarching process
Type of organization and command focus	Centralized command and control	Decentralized with community linkage	Decentralized with local command accountability to central administration	Centralized or decentralized but internal focus	Centralized decision making, decentralized exectuion
Implications for organizational change/ development	Few, static organization fending off the environment	Many, dynamic organization focused on the environmental interactions	Varied, focused on problem resolution but with import for organization intelligence and structure	Few, limited interventions focused on target problems, using many traditional methods	Varied, focused on security and threat, but with import for intelli gence and stucture
Measurement of success	Arrest and crime rates, particularly serious Part 1 crimes	Varied, crime, calls for service, fear reduction, use of public places, community linkages and contacts, safer neighborhoods	Varied, problems solved, minimized, displaced	Arrests, field stops, activity location-specific reductions in targeted activity	Arrests, field stops, intelligence gathering, mitiga tion and preparedness

Adapted by author from J. R. Greene, "Community Policing in America: Changing the Nature, Structure, and Function of the Police." In *Criminal Justice 2000: Policies, Processes, and Decisions of the Criminal Justice System*. Vol. 3. Washington, D.C.: U.S. Department of Justice, Office of Justice Programs, 2000.

different goals, means, and ends. Trying to tie the two together is not a solution, but rather an impediment to both community-oriented policing and homeland security.

So, we come to the next logical question if homeland security is replacing community-oriented policing as the prime policy for America's policing: Does this mean that community-oriented policing will go away and hence having studied the tenets and philosophy over the past fifteenth chapters has been a waste of time? The answer is no. The philosophy and tenets of community-oriented policing still hold, and to say that we would abandon the goal of police and community partnerships to deal with the problems of crime and disorder would not be a logical step. Just because homeland security may be replacing community-oriented policing as a policy does not mean that community-oriented policing is no longer valid. It simply means that community-oriented policing must return to its grass-roots efforts and no longer rely on the government bankrolls to fund its initiatives. In addition, one only has to look around at the immense literature and police focus on the concepts of police–community relations to know that even a policy born in 1955 and implemented in the late 1960s still has relevance today; it just no longer has federal government backing. And, maybe, just maybe, that is a good thing.

THE END OF COMMUNITY POLICING: REMEMBERING THE LESSONS LEARNED

We should put to bed the era of community policing and engage, instead, in policing. We should not make the 20-year learning mistake. Let us take the best of what we learned in this business over the last half century and call it policing. What are those things that we have learned?

1. The organization of a police department must exclude the improper influence of politics in promotion, assignment, or the quality of police services provided in the community. At the same time, however, a police organization must remember, understand, and fully accept the role of elected officials and other bodies in setting goals and direction in oversight and review of all of their programs, policies, and actions.
2. Command and control in a hierarchal environment is essential. It must be understood that final accountability stops with the chief, sheriff, or state police director. At the same time, we must remember that the vitality of policing is defined by the work, authority, and decision-making powers of all our personnel.
3. Critical to the success of policing is a philosophy and understanding that in every facet of our work, we inform, discuss with, and value the community. At the same time, however, we must remember that those most impacted by crime and events are busy attempting to make ends meet, and we must understand that they turn to us for our expertise and to do the job that they cannot do.
4. Last, we in law enforcement must admit our mistakes and shortcomings and acknowledge what we either cannot do or do not have the training and background for. We also must recognize and support the role of other providers, those in education and public and mental health.

Source: R. G. Kerlikowske, "The End of Community Policing: Remembering the Lessons Learned." *FBI Law Enforcement Bulletin,* Vol. 73 No. 4 (2004): 6–11.

CONCLUSION

The future of community-oriented policing has arrived. Recent research on the future of community-oriented policing has asserted that much of what has been written about what police departments *should* be doing under community-oriented policing *is* being done and that the future looks promising for further change (Greek et al. 2000; Virginia Community Policing Institute 1999). Bayley and Shearing's (1996, 604) statement that "Community [-Oriented] Policing must become the organizing paradigm of public policing" is beginning to become reality. The future of community-oriented policing is here. As police departments continue to advance in their implementation of this systemic approach to police change, the continued use of forecasting can assist departments in preparing for future changes within this paradigm shift. Forecasting that which lies just around the corner, whether a problem or a benefit, can assist police practitioners and scholars today in both planning and implementation. It is important that this information be reliable and valid, and with the tools of research available, forecasting has become a viable method of understanding what lies ahead in policy implementation. Although forecasting may not have the clarity of hindsight or be as real as the present, futures research can pose questions and provide answers and information about the systemic approach to policing.

Officer T. Pekin of the Montgomery County Police Department has a heart-to-heart talk with a local youth during a DARE event. *(Courtesy of the Montgomery County Department of Police, Montgomery County, Maryland.)*

COP ON THE WORLD WIDE WEB

Community Policing Bibliography

http://www.concentric.net/~dwoods/bib.htm

Future of Community Policing in Florida Report

www.criminology.fsu.edu/faculty/greek/future/futurefinalreport.htm

Future of the COPS Program, U.S. Conference of Mayors

http://www.usmayors.org/uscm/us_mayor_newspaper/documents/06_26_00/cop_article
.html

Justice Technology Information Network

http://www.nlectc.org

Report on the Colloquium on the Future of Community Policing

http://www.vcpi.state.va.us/coll/col.htm

REVIEW QUESTIONS

1. Why is futures research important?
2. What have been the benefits derived from implementing community-oriented policing?
3. Describe the future of community-oriented policing in the era of homeland security.

References

Adams, R. E., W. M. Rohe, and T. A. Arcury. "Awareness of Community-Oriented Policing and Neighborhood Perception in Five Small to Midsize Cities." *Journal of Criminal Justice.* 33, no. 1 (2005): 43–54.

Addesa, Mark. "The Development of Community Policing in Charleston, West Virginia." In *The West Virginia Regional Community Policing Institute (RCPI) West Virginia Community Policing Organizational Assessment,* ed. Willard M. Oliver. Charleston, W. Va.: West Virginia Regional Community Policing Institute, 1998, pp. 73–102.

Allender, David M. "Community Policing Exploring the Philosophy." *FBI Law Enforcement Bulletin* vol. 73, no. 3 (March 2004). Available online at www.fbi.gov

Alpert, Geoffrey P., and Roger G. Dunham. *Policing Urban America,* 2nd ed. Prospect Heights, Ill.: Waveland Press, 1992.

Alpert, Geoffrey P., and Alex R. Piquero. *Community Policing: Contemporary Readings,* 2nd ed. Prospect Heights, Ill.: Waveland Press, 2000.

Anderson, David C. *Crimes of Justice.* New York: Times Books, 1988.

Andrews, Allen H., Jr. "Structuring the Political Independence of the Police Chief." In *Police Leadership in America,* ed. William A. Geller. New York: American Bar Foundation and Praeger, 1985, pp. 5–19.

Andrews, Kenneth R. *The Concept of Corporate Strategy.* Homewood, Ill.: Irwin, 1980.

Aronowitz, Alexis A. "Crime Prevention in the Netherlands: A Community Policing Approach." In *International Perspectives on Community Policing and Crime Prevention,* ed. Steven P. Lab and Dilip K. Das. Upper Saddle River, N.J.: Prentice-Hall, 2003, pp. 58–78.

Austin, Dave, and Jane Bratten. "Turning Lives Around: Portland Youth Find a New PAL." *Police Chief,* May 1991, pp. 36–38.

Austin, David. "Community Policing: The Critical Partnership." *Public Management,* July 1992, pp. 3–9.

Baker, Thomas E., and Loreen Wolfer. "The Crime Triangle: Alcohol, Drug Use, and Vandalism." *Police Practice and Research* vol. 4, no. 1 (2003): 47–61.

Banfi, Ferenc, and Irene Sarkozi. "Crime Prevention in Hungary: A Community Policing Approach." In *International Perspectives on Community Policing and Crime Prevention,* ed. Steven P. Lab and Dilip K. Das. Upper Saddle River, N.J.: Prentice Hall, 2003, pp. 168–179.

Banton, Michael. *The Police in the Community.* New York: Basic Books, 1964.

Barker, Thomas, and David L. Carter, eds. *Police Deviance*, 3rd ed. Cincinnati, Ohio: Anderson, 1994.

Barone, Michael. "Rudy Rules . . . You Got a Problem with That?" *Reader's Digest*, March 1999, pp. 97–101.

Bass, Sandra. "Negotiating Change: Community Organizations and the Politics of Policing." *Urban Affairs Review* 36, no. 2 (2000): 148–177.

Bassett, Adele. "Community-Oriented Gang Control." *Police Chief*, February 1993, pp. 20–23.

Bassett, Nicholas. "Total Quality Management in the Public Sector." Unpublished paper, June 1995.

Bayley, David H. "Community Policing: A Report from the Devil's Advocate." In *Community Policing: Rhetoric or Reality*, ed. Jack R. Greene and Stephen D. Mastrofski. New York: Praeger, 1988, pp. 225–238.

———. *A Model of Community Policing: The Singapore Force Story*. Washington, D.C.: National Institute of Justice, 1989.

———. "International Differences in Community Policing." In *The Challenge of Community Policing: Testing the Promises*, ed. Dennis P. Rosenbaum. Thousand Oaks, Calif.: Sage, 1994, pp. 278–284.

Bennett, Georgette. *Crimewarps: The Future of Crime in America*. New York: Anchor Books, 1989.

———. "Cultural Lag in Law Enforcement: Preparing Police for the Crimewarps of the Future." *American Journal of Police* 9 (1990): 79–86.

Bennett, Trevor. "Community Policing on the Ground." In *The Challenge of Community Policing: Testing the Promises*, ed. Dennis P. Rosenbaum. Thousand Oaks, Calif.: Sage, 1994, pp. 224–248.

Bensinger, Gad J. "The Emulation and Adaptation of American Criminal Justice Concepts in Israel." *International Journal of Comparative and Applied Criminal Justice* 23, no. 1 (1999): 17–23.

Bichler, Gisela, and Larry Gaines. "An Examination of Police Officers' Insights Into Problem Identification and Problem Solving." *Crime & Delinquency*. 51, no. 1 (2005): 53–74.

Bloom, Lynda. "Community Policing Nips Gang Problem in the Bud." *Law and Order*, September 1992, pp. 67–70.

Bohm, Robert M., K. Michael Reynolds, and Stephen T. Holmes. "Perceptions of Neighborhood Problems and Their Solutions: Implications for Community Policing." *Policing: An International Journal of Police Strategies and Management* 23, no. 4 (2000): 439–465.

Bondurant, Elizabeth, "Citizen Response Questionnaire: A Valuable Evaluation Tool." *Police Chief*, November 1991, pp. 74–76.

Booth, Walter S. "Integrating COP into Selection and Promotional Systems." *Police Chief*, March 1995, pp. 19–24.

Bowers, W.J., and J.H. Hirsch. "The Impact of Foot Patrol Staffing on Crime and Disorder in Boston: An Unmet Promise." *American Journal of Police* 6, no. 1 (1987): 17–44.

Boydstun, John E. *San Diego Field Interrogations: Final Report*. Washington, D.C.: Police Foundation, 1975.

Braga, Anthony A., David L. Weisburd, Elin J. Waring, Lorraine Green-Mazerolle, William Spelman, and Francis Gajewski. "Problem-Oriented Policing in Violent Crime Places: A Randomized Controlled Experiment." *Criminology* 37, no. 3 (1999): 541–580.

Braiden, Chris."Enriching Traditional Police Roles." In *Police Management: Issues and Perspectives.* Washington, D.C.: Police Executive Research Forum, 1992.

Brandstatter, A.F., and Louis A. Radelet. *Police and Community Relations: A Sourcebook.* Beverly Hills, Calif.: Glencoe Press, 1968.

Bratton, William J. "William J. Bratton: Police Training for Youth." *Policy Review,* March/April 1996, pp. 26–27.

Breci, Michael, and Timothy E. Erickson. "Community Policing: The Process of Transitional Change." *FBI Law Enforcement Bulletin,* June 1998, pp. 16–22.

Brewster, J., M. Stoloff, and N. Sanders. "Effectiveness of Citizen Police Academies in Changing the Attitudes, Beliefs, and Behaviors of Citizen Participants." *American Journal of Criminal Justice* 30, no. 1 (2005): 21–34.

Brodeur, Jean-Paul. *How to Recognize Good Policing: Problems and Issues.* Thousand Oaks, Calif.: Sage, 1998.

Brogden, M. "'Horses for Courses' And 'Thin Blue Lines': Community Policing in Transitional Society." *Police Quarterly,* 8 no. 1 (2005): 64–98.

Brogden, M., and P. Nijhar. *Community Policing: National and International Models and Approaches.* Cullompton, Devon (UK): Willan Publishing, 2005.

Bromley, Max L., and John K. Cochran. "A Case Study of Community Policing in a Southern Sheriff's Office." *Police Quarterly* 2, no. 1 (1999): 36–56.

Brown, Lee P. "Police-Community Power Sharing." In *Police Leadership in America: Crisis and Opportunity,* ed. William A. Geller. New York: American Bar Foundation and Praeger, 1985, pp. 70–83.

———. "Community Policing: A Practical Guide for Police Officials." *Perspectives on Policing.* Washington, D.C.: National Institute of Justice and the Program in Criminal Justice Policy and Management, September 1989.

———. *Policing New York City in the 1990s: The Strategy for Community Policing.* New York: New York City Police Department, 1991.

———. "Violent Crime and Community Involvement." *FBI Law Enforcement Bulletin,* May 1992, pp. 2–5.

———. "Community Policing: A Partnership with Promise." *Police Chief,* October 1992, pp. 45–48.

Brown, Lee P., and Mary Ann Wycoff. "Policing Houston: Reducing Fear and Improving Service." *Crime and Delinquency* 33, no. 1 (January 1987): 71–89.

Brzeczek, Richard J. "Chief-Mayor Relations: The View from the Chief's Chair." In *Police Leadership in America,* ed. William A. Geller. New York: American Bar Foundation and Praeger, 1985, pp. 48–55.

Bucqueroux, Bonnie. "Community Policing Is Alive and Well." *Community Policing Exchange.* Washington, D.C.: Community Policing Consortium, May/June 1995, pp. 1–2.

Buerger, Michael E. "The Limits of Community." In *The Challenge of Community Policing: Testing the Promises,* ed. Dennis P. Rosenbaum. Thousand Oaks, Calif.: Sage, 1994a, pp. 270–273.

———. "A Tale of Two Targets: Limitations of Community Anticrime Actions." *Crime and Delinquency* 40, no. 3 (July 1994b): 411–436.

Buerger, Michael E., Anthony J. Petrosino, and Carolyn Petrosino. "Extending the Police Role: Implications of Police Mediation as a Problem-Solving Tool." *Police Quarterly* 2, no. 2 (1999): 125–149.

Bumphus, Vic M., Larry K. Gaines, and Curt R. Blakely. "Citizen Police Academies: Observing Goals, Objectives, and Recent Trends." *American Journal of Criminal Justice* 24, no. 1 (1999): 67–79.

Bureau of Justice Assistance. *An Introduction to DARE: Drug Abuse Resistance Education.* Washington, D.C.: U.S. Department of Justice, Bureau of Justice Administration, 1992.

————. *Neighborhood-Oriented Policing in Rural Communities: A Program Planning Guide.* Washington, D.C.: Bureau of Justice Assistance, U.S. Department of Justice, 1994a.

————. *Unleashing Community Policing.* Washington, D.C.: Bureau of Justice Assistance, U.S. Department of Justice, August 1994b.

Bureau of Justice Statistics. *Report to the Nation on Crime and Justice,* 2nd ed. Washington, D.C.: U.S. Department of Justice, 1988.

————. *Drugs, Crime, and the Justice System.* Washington, D.C.: U.S. Department of Justice, 1992.

————. *Summary Findings: Law Enforcement Management and Administrative Statistics, 1999.* Washington, D.C.: Bureau of Justice Statistics, November 2000.

Capezio, P., and D. Morehouse. *A Practical Guide to Total Quality Management.* Hawthorne, N.J.: Career Press, 1993.

Capowich, George E., and Janice A. Roehl. "Problem-Oriented Policing: Actions and Effectiveness in San Diego." In *The Challenge of Community Policing: Testing the Promises,* ed. Dennis P. Rosenbaum. Thousand Oaks, Calif.: Sage, 1994, pp. 127–146.

Cardarelli, Albert P., and Jack McDevitt. "Toward a Conceptual Framework for Evaluating Community Policing." In *Issues in Community Policing,* ed. Peter C. Kratcoski and Duane Dukes. Cincinnati, Ohio: Academy of Criminal Justice Sciences and Anderson, 1995, pp. 229–242.

Cardarelli, Albert P., Jack McDevitt, and Katrina Baum. "The Rhetoric and Reality of Community Policing in Small and Medium-Sized Cities and Towns." *Policing: An International Journal of Police Strategies and Management* 21, no. 3 (1998): 397–415.

Carter, David L. *An Overview of Research in Support of the Community Policing Concept.* Quantico, Va.: FBI National Academy, 1988.

Carter, David L., and Allen D. Sapp. "Making the Grade." *Police Technology and Management,* December 1990, pp. 39–43.

Carter, David L., Allen D. Sapp, and Darrel W. Stephens. *The State of Police Education: Policy Directions for the 21st Century.* Washington, D.C.: Police Executive Research Forum, 1989.

Center on Budget and Policy Priorities. "Proposed Discretionary Caps Would Hit States Hard." July 5, 2006. Available online at http://www.cbpp.org

Chacko, James, and Stephen E. Nancoo. *Community Policing in Canada.* Toronto, Canada: Canadian Scholars' Press, 1993.

Chaiken, Jan M. *Local Police Departments 1993.* Washington, D.C.: U.S. Department of Justice, April 1995.

Chaiken, Marcia R. 2001. *COPS: Innovations in Policing in American Heartlands.* Washington, D.C.: National Institute of Justice.

Champion, Dean J. *Research Methods for Criminal Justice and Criminology.* Englewood Cliffs, N.J.: Prentice Hall, 1993.

Christopher, William, et. al. "Summary Report." *Report of the Independent Commission on the Los Angeles Police Department.* Los Angeles: City of Los Angeles, 1991.

Clark, Jacob R. "Does Community Policing Add Up?" *Law Enforcement News* 20, no. 399 (1994): 1–8.

Clarke, R. V. and Eck, J. E. (2005). *Crime Analysis for Problem Solvers in 60 Small Steps.* Washington, D.C.: Center For Problem-Oriented Policing.

Cochran, John K., Max L. Bromley, and Matthew J. Swando. "Sheriff's Deputes' Receptivity to Organizational Change." *Policing: An International Journal of Police Strategies & Management,* 25, no. 3 (2002): 507–530.

Coffey, Alan, Edward Eldefonso, and Walter Hartinger. *Human Relations: Law Enforcement in a Changing Community,* 3rd ed. Englewood Cliffs, N.J.: Prentice Hall, 1982.

Cohen, Steven, and Ronald Brand. *Total Quality Management in Government.* San Francisco: Jossey-Bass, 1993.

Cohn, Alvin W. *The Future of Policing.* Beverly Hills, Calif.: Sage, 1978.

Cohn, Alvin W., and Emilio C. Viano, eds. *Police Community Relations: Images, Roles, Realities.* Philadelphia: Lippincott, 1976.

Cohn, Ellen G. "The Citizen Police Academy: A Recipe for Improving Police-Community Relations." *Journal of Criminal Justice* 24, no. 3 (1996): 265–271.

Cole, Allen W. "Non-Traditional Problem Solving." *Law and Order,* August 1993a, pp. 59–64.

———. "Better Customer Focus: TQM and Law Enforcement." *Police Chief,* December 1993b, pp. 23–26.

Cole, Allen W., and David Kelley. "Non Traditional Problem Solving: Barricades Eliminate Drug Dealing, Restore Neighborhood." *Law and Order,* August 1993, pp. 59–64.

Cole, George F. *The American System of Criminal Justice,* 7th ed. Belmont, Calif.: Wadsworth, 1995a.

———. "Criminal Justice in the Twenty-First Century: The Role of Futures Research." In *Crime and Justice in the Year 2010,* ed. John Klofas and Stan Stojkovic. Belmont, Calif.: Wadsworth, 1995b.

Communicare. *Community Policing Video Site Visit Series.* Austin, Texas, Police Department. Westerville, Ohio: Communicare Educational Video Productions, 1995a.

———. *Community Policing Video Site Visit Series.* Boca Raton, Florida, Police Department. Westerville, Ohio: Communicare Educational Video Productions, 1995b.

———. *Community Policing Video Site Visit Series.* Fort Worth, Texas, Police Department. Westerville, Ohio: Communicare Educational Video Productions, 1995c.

———. *Community Policing Video Site Visit Series.* Lansing, Michigan, Police Department. Westerville, Ohio: Communicare Educational Video Productions, 1995d.

———. *Community Policing Video Site Visit Series.* Lumberton, North Carolina, Police Department. Westerville, Ohio: Communicare Educational Video Productions, 1995e.

———. *Community Policing Video Site Visit Series.* Portland, Oregon, Police Bureau. Parts I and II. Westerville, Ohio: Communicare Educational Video Productions, 1995f.

———. *Community Policing Video Site Visit Series.* San Diego, California, Police Department. Parts I and II. Westerville, Ohio: Communicare Educational Video Productions, 1995g.

———. *Community Policing Video Site Visit Series.* Sedgwick County, Kansas, Sheriff's Department. Westerville, Ohio: Communicare Educational Video Productions, 1995h.

———. *Community Policing Video Site Visit Series.* St. Petersburg, Florida, Police Department. Parts I and II. Westerville, Ohio: Communicare Educational Video Productions, 1995i.

Community Policing Consortium. *Understanding Community Policing: A Framework for Action.* Washington, D.C.: U.S. Department of Justice, 1994.

COPS. "Fact Sheet: Homeland Security Overtime Program." Washington, D.C.: Office of Community Oriented Policing Services, 2003.

Cordner, Gary W. "The Effects of Directed Patrol: A Natural Quasi-Experiment in Pontiac." In *Contemporary Issues in Law Enforcement,* ed. James J. Fyfe. Beverly Hills, Calif.: Sage, 1981, pp. 242–261.

———. *The Baltimore County Citizen Oriented Police Enforcement (COPE) Project: Final Evaluation.* New York: Florence V. Burden Foundation, 1985.

———. "Fear of Crime and the Police: An Evaluation of a Fear-Reduction Strategy." *Journal of Police Science and Administration* 14, no. 3 (1987): 223–233.

———. "A Problem-Oriented Approach to Community-Oriented Policing." In *Community Policing: Rhetoric or Reality,* ed. Jack R. Greene and Stephen D. Mastrofski. New York: Praeger, 1988, pp. 135–152.

———. "Foot Patrol without Community Policing: Law and Order in Public Housing." In *The Challenge of Community Policing: Testing the Promises,* ed. Dennis P. Rosenbaum. Thousand Oaks, Calif.: Sage, 1994, pp. 182–191.

———. "Community Policing: Elements and Effects." *Police Forum* 5, no. 3 (1995): 1–8.

Cordner, Gary W., and Michael A. Jones. "The Effects of Supplementary Foot Patrol on Fear of Crime and Attitudes toward the Police." In *Issues in Community Policing,* ed. Peter C. Kratcoski and Duane Dukes. Cincinnati, Ohio: Academy of Criminal Justice Sciences and Anderson, 1995, pp. 189–198.

Cordner, Gary W., and Robert C. Trojanowicz. "Patrol." In *What Works in Policing? Operation and Administration Examined,* ed. Gary W. Cordner and Donna C. Hale. Cincinnati, Ohio: Anderson, 1992, pp. 3–18.

Cornett-DeVito, Myrna, and Edward L. McGlone. "Multicultural Communication Training for Law Enforcement Officers: A Case Study." *Criminal Justice Policy Review* 11, no. 3 (2000): 234–253.

Cornish, Edward. *The Study of the Future.* Washington, D.C.: World Future Society, 1977.

Correia, Mark E. "The Conceptual Ambiguity of Community in Community Policing: Filtering the Muddy Waters." *Policing: An International Journal of Police Strategies and Management* 23, no. 2 (2000): 218–232.

Corter, Walter, Richard Whelan, and James J. Lynch. "Solving Problems through Teamwork." *Law and Order,* August 1993, pp. 64–66.

Couper, David C. *Quality Policing: The Madison Experiment.* Washington, D.C.: Police Executive Research Forum, 1991.

Couper, David C., and Sabine H. Lobitz. "The Customer Is Always Right: Applying Vision, Leadership, and Problem-Solving Methods to Community Policing." *Police Chief,* September 1991, pp. 16–23.

Crank, John P. "Watchman and Community: Myth and Institutionalization in Policing." *Law and Society Review* 28, no. 2 (1994): 325–351.

———. "The Community-Policing Movement of the Early Twenty-First Century: What We Learned." In *Crime and Justice in the Year 2010,* ed. John Klofas and Stan Stojkovic. Belmont, Calif.: Wadsworth, 1995, pp. 107–126.

Davis, R. C., N. J. Henderson, and C. Merrick. "Community Policing: Variations on the Western Model in the Developing World." *Police Practice and Research* 4, no. 3 (2003): 285–300.

Davis, Robert C., Pedro Mateu-Gelabert, and Joel Miller. "Can Effective Policing Also Be Respectful? Two Examples in the South Bronx." *Police Quarterly,* 8 no. 2 (2005): 229–247.

Dejong, Christina, Stephen D. Mastrofski, and Roger B. Parks. "Patrol Officers and Problem Solving: An Application of Expectancy Theory." *Justice Quarterly* 18, no. 1 (2001): 31–61.

Deming, W. Edwards. *Quality, Productivity, and Competitive Position.* Cambridge, Mass.: Massachusetts Institute of Technology, Center for Advanced Engineering Study, 1982.
———. *Out of the Crisis.* Cambridge, Mass.: MIT Press, 1986.

Dempsey, John S. *Policing: An Introduction to Law Enforcement.* St. Paul, Minn.: West, 1994.

Denhardt, Robert B. *Theories of Public Organization,* 2nd ed. Belmont, Calif.: Wadsworth, 1993.

———. *Public Administration: An Action Orientation,* 2nd ed. Belmont, Calif.: Wadsworth, 1995.

Dicker, Todd J. "Tension on the Thin Blue Line: Police Officer Resistance to Community-Oriented Policing." *American Journal of Criminal Justice* 23, no. 1 (1998): 59–82.

Dietz, A. Steven. "Evaluating Community Policing: Quality Police Service and Fear of Crime." *Policing: An International Journal of Police Strategies and Management* 20, no. 1 (1997): 83–100.

Dilulio, John J., Jr. "Arresting Ideas." *Policy Review* 74 (Fall 1995): 12–16.

Dilulio, John J., Jr., Steven K. Smith, and Aaron J. Saiger. "The Federal Role in Crime Control." In *Crime,* ed. James Q. Wilson and Joan Petersilia. San Francisco: ICS Press, 1995, pp. 445–462.

Docobo, J. "Community Policing as the Primary Prevention Strategy for Homeland Security at the Local Law Enforcement Level." *Homeland Security Affairs,* 1, no. 1 (2005): Article 4. Available online at *http://www.hsaj.org/hsa/vol1/art4*

Docobo, J. "Community Policing as the Primary Prevention Strategy for Homeland Security at the Local Law Enforcement Level." Naval Postgraduate School Thesis. March (2005). Available online at *http://stinet.dtic.mil/oai/oai?verb=getRecord&metadata Prefix=html&identifier=ADA432340*

Docobo, Jose. "Community Policing as the Primary Prevention Strategy for Homeland Security at the Local Law Enforcement Level." *Homeland Security Affairs* 1, no. 1 (2005): article 4. Available on-line at *http://www.hsaj.org/?article=1.1.4*

Doherty, S., and B. G. Hibbard. "Community Policing and Homeland Security." *The Police Chief,* 73, no. 2 (2006): 15–20.

Doherty, Stephen. "Community Policing and Homeland Security." *The Police Chief* 73, no. 2 (2006).

Dolan, Harry P. "Coping with Internal Backlash." *Police Chief,* March 1994, pp. 28–32.

Dombrink, John. "The Touchables: Vice and Police Corruption in the 1980s." In *Police Deviance,* 3rd ed., ed. Thomas Barker and David L. Carter. Cincinnati, Ohio: Anderson, 1994, pp. 61–100.

Donahue, Michael E. "A Comprehensive Program to Combat Violent Crime: The Savannah Experience." *Police Chief,* September 1993, pp. 12–22.

Donsi, Joseph M. "Police Practices: Ft. Lauderdale's Code Enforcement Team." *FBI Law Enforcement Bulletin,* March 1992, pp. 24–25.

Douthit, Nathan. "August Vollmer." In *Thinking about Police: Contemporary Readings,* 2nd ed., ed. Carl B. Klockars and Stephen D. Mastrofski. New York: McGraw-Hill, 1991, pp. 101–113.

Downs, Anthony. *New Visions for Metropolitan America.* Washington, D.C.: Brookings Institution, 1994.

DuBois, Jill, and Susan M. Harnett. "Making the Community Side of Community Policing Work: What Needs to Be Done." In *Policing and Community Partnership* 1, ed. Dennis J. Stevens. Upper Saddle River, N.J.: Prentice Hall, 2002, pp. 1–15.

Dudley, William, ed. *Police Brutality.* San Diego: Greenhaven Press, 1991.

Duffee, David E., Reginald Fluellen, and Brian C. Renauer. "Community Variables in Community Policing." *Police Quarterly* 2, no. 1 (1999): 5–35.

Dye, Thomas R. *Understanding Public Policy,* 6th ed. Englewood Cliffs, N.J.: Prentice Hall, 1987.

Earle, Howard H. *Police-Community Relations: Crisis in Our Times.* Springfield, Ill.: Charles C. Thomas, 1967.

Ebbe, Obi N.I. "Crime Prevention in Nigeria." In *International Perspectives on Community Policing and Crime Prevention,* ed. Steven P. Lab and Dilip K. Das. Upper Saddle River, N.J.: Prentice-Hall, 2003, pp. 140–150.

Ebenson, F. "Foot Patrol: Of What Value?" *American Journal of Police* 6, no. 1 (1987): 45–66.

Eck, John E. *Solving Crimes: The Investigation of Burglary and Robbery.* Washington, D.C.: Police Executive Research Forum, 1982.

———."Alternative Futures for Policing." In *Police Innovation and Control of the Police,* ed. David Weisburd and C. Uchida. New York: Springer, 1993.

Eck, John, and Ed Maguire. "Have Changes in Policing Reduced Violent Crime? An Assessment of the Evidence." In *The Crime Drop,* ed. A. Blumstein and J. Wallman. Cambridge, United Kingdom: Cambridge University Press, 2000 pp. 207–265.

Eck, John E., and Dennis P. Rosenbaum. "The New Police Order." In *The Challenge of Community Policing: Testing the Promises,* ed. Dennis P. Rosenbaum. Thousand Oaks. Calif.: Sage, 1994, pp. 3–26.

Eck, John E., and William Spelman. *Problem-Solving: Problem-Oriented Policing in Newport News.* Washington, D.C.: Police Executive Research Forum, 1987a.

———."Who Ya Gonna Call? The Police as Problem Busters." *Crime and Delinquency* 33, no. 1 (January 1987b): 31–52.

———."A Problem-Oriented Approach to Police Service Delivery." In *Police and Policing: Contemporary Issues,* ed. Dennis Jay Kenney. New York: Praeger, 1989.

Eck, John E., William Spelman, Diane Hill, Darrel W. Stephens, John R. Stedman, and Gerard R. Murphy. *Problem-Solving: Problem-Oriented Policing in Newport News.* Washington, D.C.: Police Executive Research Forum, 1987.

Eggers, William D., and John O'Leary. "The Beat Generation." *Policy Review* 74 (Fall 1995): 4–11.

Engel, Robin Shepard, and Robert E. Worden. "Police Officers' Attitudes, Behavior, and Supervisory Influences: An Analysis of Problem Solving." *Criminology* 41, no. 1 (2003): 131–166.

Enns, Tracy. "Citizens' Police Academies: The Farmington Experience." *Police Chief,* April 1995, pp. 133–135.

Enter, Jack E. "Police Administration in the Future: Demographic Influences as They Relate to Management of Internal and External Environment." *American Journal of Police* 10, no. 4 (1991): 65–81.

Eve, Raymond A., Daniel G. Rodeheaver, Susan Brown Eve, Maureen Hockenberger, Ramona Perez, Ken Burton, Larry Boyd, Sue Phillips, and Sharon L. Walker. "Community-Oriented Policing in a Multicultural Milieu: The Case of Loitering and Disorderly Conduct in East Arlington, Texas." *International Journal of Police Science and Management* 5, no. 4 (2003): 245–264.

Fairchild, Erika S., and Vincent J. Webb. *The Politics of Crime and Criminal Justice.* Beverly Hills, Calif.: Sage, 1985.

Farley, John E. *Sociology,* 3rd ed. Englewood Cliffs, N.J.: Prentice Hall, 1994.

Farley, William J. "Policing in Tough Budgetary Times: Gaston County Finds New Methods Increase Service." *Law and Order,* August 1993, pp. 53–57.

Farrell, Michael J. "The Development of the Community Patrol Officer Program: Community-Oriented Policing in the New York City Police Department." In *Community Policing: Rhetoric or Reality,* ed. Jack R. Greene and Stephen D. Mastrofski. New York: Praeger, 1988, pp. 73–88.

Feins, J.D. *Partnerships for Neighborhood Crime Prevention.* Washington, D.C.: National Institute of Justice, 1983.

Fielding, Nigel G. "Concepts and Theory in Community Policing." *The Howard Journal* 44, no. 5 (2005): 460–472.

Fleissner, Dan, Nicholas Fedan, David Klinger, and Ezra Stotland. "Community Policing in Seattle: A Model Partnership between Citizens and Police." *National Institute of Justice: Research in Brief.* Washington, D.C.: National Institute of Justice, August 1992.

Fogelson, Robert. *Big-City Police.* Cambridge, Mass.: Harvard University Press, 1977.

Ford, J. Kevin, Daniel A. Weissbein, and Kevin E. Plamondon. "Distinguishing Organizational From Strategy Commitment: Linking Officers' Commitment to Community Policing to Job Behaviors and Satisfaction." *Justice Quarterly* 20, no. 1 (2003): 159–185.

Fosdick, Raymond B. *American Police Systems.* Montclair, N.J.: Patterson Smith, 1969.

Francis, Charles E. "Charleston Tries Voluntary Program." In *Community Policing Exchange.* Washington, D.C.: Community Policing Consortium, January/February 1996.

Frank, James, Steven G. Brandl, Robert E. Worden, and Timothy S. Bynum. "Citizen Involvement in the Coproduction of Police Outputs." *Journal of Crime and Justice* 19, no. 2 (1996): 1–30.

Freeman, Edward R. *Strategic Management: A Stakeholder's Approach.* Marshall, Mass.: Pittman, 1984.

Friedman, Warren. "The Community Role in Community Policing." In *The Challenge of Community Policing: Testing the Promises,* ed. Dennis P. Rosenbaum. Thousand Oaks, Calif.: Sage, 1994, pp. 263–269.

Friedmann, Robert R. "Community Policing: Promises and Challenges." *Journal of Contemporary Criminal Justice* 6 (May 1990): 79–88.

Fung, Archon. "Accountable Autonomy: Toward Empowered Deliberation in Chicago Schools and Policing." *Politics & Society* 29, no. 1 (March 2001): 73–103.

Fyfe, James, J. *Police Practices in the '90's: Key Management Issues.* Washington, D.C.: International City/County Management Association, 1989.

Gaines, Larry. "Community-Oriented Policing: Management Issues, Concerns, and Problems." *Journal of Contemporary Criminal Justice* 10, no. 1 (March 1994): 17–35.

Gaines, Larry K., Victor E. Kappeler, and Joseph B. Vaughn. *Policing in America.* Cincinnati, Ohio: Anderson, 1994.

Gallup, George: *The Gallup Poll: Public Opinion.* Wilmington, Del.: Scholarly Resources, 1964–1994.

Garafalo, James, and Maureen McLeod. "Improving the Use and Effectiveness of Neighborhood Watch Programs." *National Institute of Justice/Research in Action.* Washington, D.C.: National Institute of Justice, April 1988.

Garcia, Venessa. "Constructing the 'Other' within Police Culture: An Analysis of a Deviant Unit within the Police Organization." *Police Practice and Research* 6, no. 1 (2005): 65–80.

Geller, William A., ed. *Police Leadership in America: Crisis and Opportunity.* New York: American Bar Foundation and Praeger, 1985.

———. *Local Government Police Management,* 3rd ed. Washington, D.C.: International City/County Management Association, 1991.

Geller, William A., and Michael S. Scott. *Deadly Force: What We Know.* Washington, D.C.: Police Executive Research Forum, 1992.

Gentile, John R. "Community Policing: A Philosophy—Not a Program." In *Community Policing Exchange.* Washington, D.C.: Community Policing Consortium, November/December 1995, p. 2.

Getz, Ronald J. "A Cops Show of Your Own." *Law and Order,* February 1995, pp. 43–49.

Geva, Ruth. "Crime Prevention: The Community Policing Approach in Israel." In *International Perspectives on Community Policing and Crime Prevention,* ed. Steven P. Lab and Dilip K. Das. Upper Saddle River, N.J.: Prentice-Hall, 2003, pp. 95–112.

Giacomazzi, Andrew L., and David C. Brody. "The Effectiveness of External Assessments in Facilitating Organizational Change in Law Enforcement." *Policing: An International Journal of Police Strategies and Management* 27, no. 1 (2004): 37–55.

Giacomazzi, Andrew L., and Martha Smithey. "Community Policing and Family Violence against Women: Lessons Learned from a Multiagency Collaborative." *Police Quarterly* 4, no. 1 (2001): 99–122.

Giacopassi, David, and David R. Forde. "Broken Windows, Crumpled Fenders, and Crime." *Journal of Criminal Justice* 28 (2000): 397–405.

Gilbert, James N. *Criminal Investigation,* 2nd ed. Columbus, Ohio: Charles E. Merrill, 1986.

———. *Criminal Investigation,* 3rd ed. New York: Macmillan, 1993.

Gilinsky, Yakov. "Crime Prevention: A Community Policing Approach in Russia." In *International Perspectives on Community Policing and Crime Prevention,* ed. Steven P. Lab and Dilip K. Das. Upper Saddle River, N.J.: Prentice-Hall, 2003, pp. 180–191.

Goldstein, Herman. *Police Corruption: A Perspective on Its Nature and Control.* Washington, D.C.: Police Foundation, 1975.

———. *Policing a Free Society.* Cambridge, Mass.: Ballinger, 1977.

———. "Improving Policing: A Problem-Oriented Approach." *Crime and Delinquency* 25, no. 2 (1979): 236–258.

———. "Toward Community-Oriented Policing: Potential, Basic Requirements, and Threshold Questions." *Crime and Delinquency* 33, no. 1 (January 1987): 6–30.

———. *Problem-Oriented Policing.* New York: McGraw-Hill, 1990.

———. Foreword. In *The Challenge of Community Oriented Policing: Testing the Promises,* ed. Dennis P. Rosenbaum. Thousand Oaks, Calif.: Sage, 1994, pp. viii–x.

Goodstein, Laurie. "New Philosophy of Policing." *Washington Post,* December 23, 1991, pp. A1–A7.

Gowri, Aditi. "Community Policing is an Epicycle." *Policing: An International Journal of Police Strategies & Management* 26, no. 4 (2003): 591–611.

Greek, Cecil, Kyubeom Choi, Shun-Yung Wang, and John Higgins. *The Future of Community Policing in Florida: Final Report.* St. Petersburg, Fla.: Florida Regional Community Policing Institute, 2000.

Green, L. *Policing Places with Drug Problems.* Thousand Oaks, Calif.: Sage, 1996.

Greenberg, David. "Age, Crime, and Social Explanations." *American Journal of Sociology* 91 (1985): 1–21.

Greenburg, Reuben, and Arthur Gordon. *Let's Take Back Our Streets!* Chicago: Contemporary Books, 1989.

Greene, Jack R. "Foot Patrol and Community Policing: Past Practices and Future Prospects." *American Journal of Police* 6, no. 1 (1987): 1–15.

———. "Police and Community Relations: Where Have We Been and Where Are We Going?" In *Critical Issues in Policing,* ed. R.G. Dunham and G.P. Alpert. Prospect Heights, Ill.: Waveland Press, 1989, pp. 349–368.

———. "Police Officer Job Satisfaction and Community Perceptions: Implications for Community-Oriented Policing." *Journal of Research in Crime and Delinquency* 26 (1989): 168–184.

Greene, Jack R., and S.H. Decker. "Police and Community Perception of the Community Role in Policing: The Philadelphia Perspective." *Howard Journal* 28 (1989): 105–123.

Greene, Jack R., and Carl B. Klockars. "What Police Do." In *Thinking about Police,* 2nd ed., ed. Carl B. Klockars and Stephen D. Mastrofski. New York: McGraw-Hill, 1991.

Greene, Jack R., and Stephen D. Mastrofski. *Community Policing: Rhetoric or Reality.* New York: Praeger, 1988.

Greene, Jack R., and Ralph B. Taylor. "Community-Based Policing and Foot Patrol: Issues of Theory and Evaluation." In *Community Policing: Rhetoric or Reality,* ed. Jack R. Greene and Stephen D. Mastrofski. New York: Praeger, 1988, pp. 195–224.

Greene, Jack R., William T. Bergman, and Edward J. McLaughlin. "Implementing Community Policing." In *The Challenge of Community Policing: Testing the Promises,* ed. Dennis P. Rosenbaum. Thousand Oaks, Calif.: Sage, 1994, pp. 92–109.

Greene, Jack R., Alex R. Piquero, Patricia Collins, and Robert J. Kane. "Doing Research in Public Housing: Implementation Issues from Philadelphia's 11th Street Corridor Community Policing Program." *Justice Research and Policy* 1, no. 1 (1999): 67–95.

Greene, Jack R., Patricia Collins, and Robert Kane. "Policing Public Housing in Philadelphia: Public Safety Perspectives of the Police and the Community." *Police Practice* 1, no. 3 (2000): 397–434.

Greene, Judith A. "Zero Tolerance: A Case Study of Police Policies and Practices in New York City." *Crime and Delinquency* 45, no. 2 (1999): 171–189.

Green-Mazzerolle, L., C. Kadleck, and J. Roehl. "Controlling Drug and Disorder Problems: The Role of Place Managers." *Justice Quarterly* 36 (1998): 371–403.

Greenwood, Peter W., and Joan Petersilia. *The Criminal Investigation Process, Vol. 1: Summary and Policy Implications.* Santa Monica, Calif.: Rand Corporation, 1975.

Greenwood, Peter W., Joan Petersilia, and J. Chaiken. *The Criminal Investigation Process.* Lexington, Mass.: Heath, 1977.

Griffith, Douglas L. "Citizen Feedback Line." *Law and Order,* December 1993, pp. 37–40.

Grinc, Randolph M. " 'Angles in Marble': Problems in Community Involvement in Community Policing." *Crime and Delinquency* 40, no. 3 (July 1994): 437–468.

Grubb, Robert E., Jr., and Christina M. Terry. "Citizen Police Academies: Benefit or Boondoggle?" Paper presented at the annual meeting of the West Virginia Criminal Justice Educators' Association, Fairmont, West Virginia, April 9, 1999.

Hageman, Mary Jeanette. *Police-Community Relations.* Beverly Hills, Calif.: Sage, 1985.

Hamilton, Sandra. "The Saskatoon Experience." *Law and Order,* December 1993, pp. 20–26.

Harcourt, Bernard E. *Illusion of Order: The False Promise of Broken Windows Policing.* Cambridge, Mass.: Harvard University Press, 2001.

Hawdon, James, and John Ryan. "Police-Resident Interaction and Satisfaction with Police: An Empirical Test of Community Policing Assertions." *Criminal Justice Policy Review* 14, no. 1 (2003): 55–74.

Hawdon, James E., John Ryan, and Sean P. Griffin. "Policing Tactics and Perceptions of Police Legitimacy." *Police Quarterly* 6, no. 4 (2003): 469–491.

Hayeslip, D.W., Jr., and Gary W. Cordner. "The Effects of Community-Oriented Patrol on Police Officer Attitudes." *American Journal of Police* 6, no. 1 (1987): 95–119.

He, N. P., J. S. Zhao, and N. P. Lovrich. "Community Policing: A Preliminary Assessment of Environmental Impact with Panel Data on Program Implementation in U.S. Cities." *Crime & Delinquency* 51, no. 3 (2005): 295–317.

Heininger, Bruce L. "School Resource Officer Program: A Police/School Partnership." Paper presented at the annual meeting of the Academy of Criminal Justice Sciences, March 1997.

Herbst, Charles. "Maximizing Community Resources." In *Community Policing Exchange.* Washington, D.C.: Community Policing Consortium, November/December 1995.

Hersey, Paul, and Kenneth H. Blanchard. *Management of Organizational Behavior,* 6th ed. Englewood Cliffs, N.J.: Prentice Hall, 1993.

Higdon, Richard Kirk, and Phillip G. Huber. *How to Fight Fear: The Citizen Oriented Police Enforcement Program Package.* Washington, D.C.: Police Executive Research Forum, 1987.

Hirschi, Travis. *Causes of Delinquency.* Berkeley and Los Angeles: University of California Press, 1969.

Hirschi, Travis, and Michael Gottfredson. "Age and Explanation of Crime." *American Journal of Sociology* 89 (1983): 552–584.

Hogan, William. "Enhancing Police Services with Senior Volunteers." In *Community Policing Exchange.* Washington, D.C.: Community Policing Consortium, November/December 1995.

Holcomb, Richard L. *The Police and the Public.* Springfield, Ill.: Charles C. Thomas, 1954.

Holden, Richard N. *Modern Police Management.* Englewood Cliffs, N.J.: Prentice Hall, 1986.

Hope, Timothy. "Problem-Oriented Policing and Drug Market Locations: Three Case Studies." *Crime Prevention Studies* 2 (1994): 5–32.

Hornick, Joseph P., Barry N. Leighton, and Barbara A. Burrows. "Evaluating Community Policing: The Edmonton Project." In *Evaluating Justice: Canadian Policies and Programs,* ed. Julian V. Roberts and Joe Hudson. Toronto, Canada: Thompson Educational Publishing, 1993.

Huebner, B. M., J. A. Schafer, and T. S. Bynum. "African American and White Perception of Police Services: Within- and Between-Group Variation." *Journal of Criminal Justice* 32 (2004): 123–135.

Inkster, Norman D. "The Essence of Community Policing." *Police Chief,* March 1992, pp. 28–31.

International City/County Management Association. *Community-Oriented Policing: An Alternative Strategy, Sourcebook.* Washington, D.C.: International City/County Management Association, 1992.

Jackson, J.L., and M.J. Ter Voert. "From the Outside Looking In: A Researcher's View of Current Policing Practices in the Netherlands." *International Journal of Police Science and Management* 2, no. 4 (2000): 360–376.

Jesilow, Paul, Jon'a Meyer, Deborah Parsons, and William Tegler. "Evaluating Problem-Oriented Policing: A Quasi-Experiment." *Policing: An International Journal of Police Strategies and Management* 21, no. 3 (1998): 449–464.

Jiao, Allan. "Community-Oriented Policing and Policing-Oriented Community." Paper presented at the annual meeting of the Academy of Criminal Justice Sciences, Louisville, Kentucky, March 1997.

Johnson, Thomas A., Gordon E. Misner, and Lee P. Brown. *The Police and Society: An Environment for Collaboration and Confrontation.* Englewood Cliffs, N.J.: Prentice Hall, 1981.

Jolin, Annette, and Charles A. Moose. "Evaluating a Domestic Violence Program in a Community Policing Environment: Research Implementation Issues." *Crime and Delinquency* 43, no. 3 (1997): 279–292.

Jordan, W. T. "Citizen Police Academies: Community Policing or Community Politics." *American Journal of Criminal Justice* 25, no. 1 (2000): 93–105.

Joseph, Earl C. "An Introduction to Studying the Future." In *Futurism in Education: Methodologies,* ed. Stephen B. Hencley and James R. Yates. Berkeley, Calif.: McCutchan, 1974.

Joseph, Thomas M. "Walking the Minefields of Community-Oriented Policing." *FBI Law Enforcement Bulletin,* September 1994, pp. 8–12.

Kane, Robert J. "Permanent Beat Assignments in Association with Community Policing: Assessing the Impact on Police Officers' Field Activity." *Justice Quarterly* 17, no. 2 (2000): 259–280.

Kansas City Police Department. *Response Time Analysis: Vol. II, Part I, Crime Analysis.* Washington, D.C.: U.S. Government Printing Office, 1980.

Kappeler, Victor E., Richard D. Sluder, and Geoffrey P. Alpert. *Forces of Deviance.* Prospect Heights, Ill.: Waveland Press, 1994.

Katz, Charles M., Vincent J. Webb, and David R. Schaefer. "An Assessment of the Impact of Quality-of-Life Policing on Crime and Disorder." *Justice Quarterly* 18, no. 4, (2001): 825–878.

Kelling, George L. "Order Maintenance, the Quality of Urban Life, and Police: A Line of Argument." In *Police Leadership in America,* ed. William A. Geller. New York: American Bar Foundation, 1985, pp. 296–308.

———. "Acquiring a Taste for Order: The Community and the Police." *Crime and Delinquency* 33, no. 1 (1987): 90–102.

———. *Foot Patrol.* Washington, D.C.: National Institute of Justice, 1987.

———. "Police and Communities: The Quiet Revolution." *Perspectives on Policing.* Washington, D.C.: U.S. Department of Justice, June 1988.

———. "Measuring What Matters: A New Way of Thinking about Crime and Public Order." *City Journal,* Spring 1992, pp. 21–33.

———. "Crime Control, the Police, and Culture Wars: Broken Windows and Cultural Pluralism." *Perspectives on Crime and Justice: 1997–1998 Lecture Series.* Washington, D.C.: National Institute of Justice, 1998.

Kelling, George L., and William J. Bratton. "Implementing Community Policing: The Administrative Problem." *Perspectives on Policing.* Washington, D.C.: U.S. Department of Justice and the John F. Kennedy School of Government, Harvard University, July 1993.

Kelling, George L., and Catherine M. Coles. *Fixing Broken Windows.* New York: Free Press, 1996.

Kelling, George L., and David Fogel. "Police Patrol—Some Future Directions." In *The Future of Policing,* ed. Alvin W. Cohn. Beverly Hills, Calif.: Sage, 1978.

Kelling, George L., and Mark H. Moore. "From Political to Reform to Community: The Evolving Strategy of Police." In *Community Policing: Rhetoric or Reality,* ed. Jack R. Greene and Stephen D. Mastrofski. New York: Praeger, 1988, pp. 3–26.

Kelling, George L., Tony Pate, Suzane Dieckman, and Charles E. Brown. *The Kansas City Preventive Patrol Experiment: A Summary Report.* Washington, D.C.: Police Foundation, 1974.

———. *The Kansas City Preventive Patrol Experiment: A Technical Report.* Washington, D.C.: Police Foundation, 1975.

Kelling, George, Robert Wasserman, and Hubert Williams. "Police Accountability and Community Policing." In *Perspectives on Policing.* Washington, D.C.: National Institute of Justice and the John F. Kennedy School of Government, Harvard University, 1988.

Kennedy, David M. "The Strategic Management of Police Resources." In *Perspectives on Policing.* Washington, D.C.: National Institute of Justice and the John F. Kennedy School of Government, Harvard University, January 1993.

Kercher, Kyle. "Causes and Correlates of Crime Committed by the Elderly." In *Critical Issues in Aging Policy,* ed. E. Borgatta and R. Montgomery. Beverly Hills, Calif.: Sage, 1987.

Kerley, Kent R. "Perceptions of Community Policing Across Community Sectors: Results from a Regional Survey." In *Policing and Community Partnership,* ed. Dennis J. Stevens. Upper Saddle River, N.J.: Prentice Hall, 2002, pp. 93–110.

Kerstetter, Wayne A. "Who Disciplines the Police? Who Should?" In *Police Leadership in America: Crisis and Opportunity,* ed. William A. Geller. New York: American Bar Foundation, 1985, pp. 149–182.

Kessler, David A. "Integrating Calls for Service with Community- and Problem-Oriented Policing: A Case Study." *Crime and Delinquency* 39, no. 4 (October 1993): 485–508.

———. "The Effects of Community Policing in Complaints against Officers." *Journal of Quantitative Criminology* 15, no. 3 (1999): 333–372.

Kidd, Virginia, and Rick Braziel. *COP Talk: Essential Communication Skills for Community Policing.* San Francisco, Calif.: Acada Books, 1999.

King, William R., and Steven P. Lab. "Crime Prevention, Community Policing, and Training: Old Wine in New Bottles." *Police Practice* 1, no. 2 (2000): 241–252.

Klein, Malcolm W., and Katherine S. Tielmann, eds. *Handbook of Criminal Justice Evaluation.* Beverly Hills, Calif.: Sage, 1980.

Klockars, Carl B. *The Idea of Police.* Beverly Hills, Calif.: Sage, 1985.

———. "Order Maintenance, the Quality of Urban Life, and Police: A Different Line of Argument." In *Police Leadership in America: Crisis and Opportunity,* ed. William A. Geller. New York: Praeger, 1985, pp. 309–321.

———. "The Rhetoric of Community Policing." In *Community Policing: Rhetoric or Reality,* ed. Jack R. Greene and Stephen D. Mastrofski. New York: Praeger, 1988.

Klofas, John, and Stan Stojkovic. *Crime and Justice in the Year 2010.* Belmont, Calif.: Wadsworth, 1995.

Kratcoski, Peter C., and Robert B. Blair. "Dynamics of Community Policing in Small Communities." In *Issues in Community Policing,* ed. Peter C. Kratcoski and Duane Dukes. Cincinnati, Ohio: Academy of Criminal Justice Sciences and Anderson, 1995.

Kratcoski, Peter C. and Duane Dukes, eds. *Issues in Community Policing*, Cincinnati, Ohio: Anderson, 1995b.

———. "Perspectives on Community Policing." In *Issues in Community Policing,* ed. Peter C. Kratcoski and Duane Dukes. Cincinnati, Ohio: Academy of Criminal Justice Sciences and Anderson, 1995c, pp. 5–20.

Kratcoski, Peter C., and Susan B. Noonan. "An Assessment of Police Officers' Acceptance of Community Policing." In *Issues in Community Policing,* ed. Peter C. Kratcoski and Duane Dukes. Cincinnati, Ohio: Academy of Criminal Justice Sciences and Anderson, 1995, pp. 169–186.

Kratcoski, Peter C., Duane Dukes, and Sandra Gustavson. "An Analysis of Citizens' Responses to Community Policing in a Large Midwestern City." In *Issues in Community Policing,* ed. Peter C. Kratcoski and Duane Dukes. Cincinnati, Ohio: Academy of Criminal Justice Sciences and Anderson, 1995, pp. 199–212.

Kratcoski, Peter C., Arvind Verma, and Dilip K. Das. "World Perspective Crime Prevention: A Community Policing Approach." *Police Practice* 1, no. 1 (2000): 105–150.

Krieble, James H. "Community-Oriented Policing: Selection, Training, and Evaluation Ensure Success." *Police Chief* 61, no. 5 (1994): 20–23.

Lacayo, Richard. "Law and Order." *Time,* January 15, 1996, pp. 48–54.

Laing, R. J., and L. T. Hickman, "Community Policing in the Royal Canadian Mounted Police." In *International Perspectives on Community Policing and Crime Prevention,* ed. Steven P. Lab and Dilip K. Das. Upper Saddle River, N.J.: Prentice Hall, 2003, pp. 28–41.

Lardner, James, and Thomas Reppetto. *NYPD: A City and Its Police.* New York: Henry Holt and Company, 2000.

Larson, Richard C. "What Happened to Patrol Operations in Kansas City? A Review of the Kansas City Preventive Patrol Experiment." *Journal of Criminal Justice* 3, no. 4 (1975): 267–297.

Lasley, James R. "The Impact of the Rodney King Incident on Citizen Attitudes toward Police." *Policing and Society* 3 (1993): 20–35.

Lasley, James R., Robert L. Vernon, and George M. Dery III. "Operation Cul-De-Sac: LAPD's 'Total Community' Policing Program." In *Issues in Community Policing,* ed. Peter C. Kratcoski and Duane Dukes. Cincinnati, Ohio: Academy of Criminal Justice Sciences and Anderson, 1995, pp. 51–68.

Lau, R. W. K. "Community Policing in Hong Kong: Transplanting a Questionable Model." *Criminal Justice* 4, no. 1 (2004): 61–80.

Leal, Carolyn V. "Cop Cards." *Law and Order,* October 1992, pp. 63–64.

Lee-Sammons, Lynette. "Beyond Neighborhood Watch: The Role of the Community in Community Policing." In *Community Policing Exchange.* Washington, D.C.: Community Policing Consortium, September/October 1995.

Leighton, Barry N. "Community Policing in Canada: An Overview of Experiences and Evaluations." In *The Challenge of Community Policing: Testing the Promises,* ed. Dennis P. Rosenbaum. Thousands Oaks, Calif.: Sage, 1994.

Lesce, Tony. "Code Enforcement Teams." *Law and Order,* September 1995, pp. 93–95.

Lewis, Dan A., and Greta Salem. "Community Crime Prevention: An Analysis of a Developing Strategy." *Crime and Delinquency* 27 (1988): 405–421.

Lewis, R. G., Jack R. Greene, and Steven M. Edwards. *Special Police Units in Michigan: An Evaluation.* East Lansing, Mich.: Criminal Justice Systems Center, Michigan State University, 1977.

Lindbloom, Charles E. "The Science of Muddling Through." *Public Administration Review* 19 (Spring 1959): 79–88.

Lindsay, John. "The Crime Prevention Continuum: A Community Policing Perspective on Crime Prevention in Canada." In *International Perspectives on Community Policing and Crime Prevention,* ed. Steven P. Lab and Dilip K. Das. Upper Saddle River, N.J.: Prentice-Hall, 2003, pp. 42–57.

Lipsky, Michael. *Street-Level Bureaucracy.* New York: Russell Sage Foundation, 1980.

Lord, Vivian B. "An Impact of Community Policing: Reported Stressors, Social Support, and Strain among Police Officers in a Changing Police Department." *Journal of Criminal Justice* 24, no. 6 (1996): 503–522.

Lumb, Richard C, and Ronald Breazeale. "Police Officer Attitudes and Community Policing Implementation: Developing Strategies for Durable Organizational Change." *Policing and Society* 13, no. 1 (2002): 91–106.

Lurigio, Arthur J., and Dennis P. Rosenbaum. "The Impact of Community Policing on Police Personnel." In *The Challenge of Community Policing: Testing the Promises,* ed. Dennis P. Rosenbaum. Thousand Oaks, Calif.: Sage, 1994, pp. 147–166.

Lurigio, Arthur J., and Wesley G. Skogan. "Winning the Hearts and Minds of Police Officers: An Assessment of Staff Perceptions of Community Policing in Chicago." *Crime and Delinquency* 40, no. 3 (July 1994): 315–330.

Lynch, Ronald G. *Police Manager,* 4th ed. Cincinnati, Ohio: Anderson, 1995.

Lynes, David A. "Cultural Diversity and Social Order: Rethinking the Role of Community Policing." *Journal of Criminal Justice* 24, no. 6 (1996): 491–502.

Lyons, William. *The Politics of Community Policing: Rearranging the Power to Punish.* Ann Arbor: University of Michigan Press, 1999.

Maas, Peter. "What We're Learning from New York City." *Parade,* May 10, 1998, pp. 4–6.

Maguire, Edward R. "Structural Change in Large Municipal Police Organizations during the Community Policing Era." *Justice Quarterly* 14, no. 3 (1997): 547–576.

Maguire, Edward R., and Stephen D. Mastrofski. "Patterns of Community Policing in the United States." *Police Quarterly* 3, no. 1 (2000): 4–45.

Maguire, Edward R., Joseph B. Kuhns, Craig D. Uchida, and Stephen M. Cox. "Patterns of Community Policing in Nonurban America." *Journal of Research in Crime and Delinquency* 34, no. 3 (1997): 368–395.

Maguire, Kathleen, and Ann L. Pastore. *Bureau of Justice Statistics Sourcebook of Criminal Justice Statistics—2000.* Washington, D.C.: Bureau of Justice Statistics, 2001.

Manning, Peter K. "Community Policing." *American Journal of Police* 3 (1984): 205–227.

———. "Community Policing as a Drama of Control." In *Community Policing: Rhetoric or Reality,* ed. Jack R. Greene and Stephen D. Mastrofski. New York: Praeger, 1988, pp. 27–46.

———. "Community-Based Policing." In *Critical Issues in Policing: Contemporary Readings,* ed. Roger G. Dunham and Geoffrey P. Alpert. Prospect, Ill.: Waveland Press, 1989, pp. 432–450.

Marans, Steven, and Miriam Berkman. *Child-Development—Community Policing: Partnership in a Climate of Violence.* Washington, D.C.: Office of Juvenile Justice Programs, March 1997.

Marshall, Will, and Martin Schram. "Safer Streets and Neighborhoods." In *Mandate for Change,* ed. Will Marshall and Martin Schram. New York: Berkeley Books, 1993.

Martin, Susan E. "Policing Career Criminal: An Examination of an Innovative Crime Control Program." *Journal of Criminal Law and Criminology* 77 (Winter 1986): 1159–1182.

Martin, Susan E., and Lawrence W. Sherman. "Selective Apprehension: A Police Strategy for Repeat Offenders." *Criminology* 24 (February 1986): 155–173.

Maslow, Abraham H. *Motivation and Personality,* 2nd ed. New York: Harper & Collins, 1970.

Masterson, Michael F., and Dennis J. Stevens. "The Value of Measuring Community Policing Performance in Madison, Wisconsin." In *Policing and Community Partnership,* ed. Dennis J. Stevens. Upper Saddle River, N.J.: Prentice Hall, 2002, pp. 77–92.

Mastrofski, Stephen D. "Community Policing as Reform: A Cautionary Tale." In *Community Policing: Rhetoric or Reality,* ed. Jack R. Greene and Stephen D. Mastrofski. New York: Praeger, 1988, pp. 47–68.

———. "What Does Community Policing Mean for Daily Police Work?" *National Institute of Justice Journal* no. 225 (August 1992): 23–27.

Mastrofski, Stephen D., and Jack R. Greene. "Community Policing and the Rule of Law." In *The Changing Focus of Police Innovation: Problems of Law, Order, and Community,* ed. David Weisburd and C. Uchida. New York: Praeger, 1991.

Mastrofski, Stephen D., and R. Richard Ritti. "Making Sense of Community Policing: A Theory-Based Analysis." *Police Practice* 1, no. 2 (2000): 183–210.

Mastrofski, Stephen D., Robert E. Worden, and Jeffrey B. Snipes. "Law Enforcement in a Time of Community Policing." *Criminology* 33, no. 4 (1995): 539–563.

Mastrofski, Stephen D., Jeffrey B. Snipes, and Anne E. Supina. "Compliance on Demand: The Public's Response to Specific Police Requests." *Journal of Research in Crime and Delinquency* 33, no. 3 (1996): 269–305.

Mastrofski, Stephen, Roger B. Parks, and Robert E. Worden. "Community Policing in Action: Lessons from an Observational Study." *National Institute of Justice Research Preview.* Washington, D.C.: National Institute of Justice, 1998.

Mastrofski, Stephen D., Roger B. Parks, Albert J. Reiss Jr., Robert E. Worden, Christina DeJong, Jeffrey B. Snipes, and William Terrill. *Systematic Observation of Public Police: Applying Field Research Methods to Policy Issues.* Washington, D.C.: National Institute of Justice, 1998.

Mastrofski, Stephen D., Jeffrey B. Snipes, Roger B. Parks, and Christopher D. Maxwell. "The Helping Hand of the Law: Police Control of Citizens on Request." *Criminology* 38, no. 2 (2000): 307–342.

Mastrofski, Stephen D., James J. Willis, and Jeffrey B. Snipes. "Styles of Patrol in a Community-Policing Context." In *The Move to Community Policing: Making Change Happen,* ed. Merry Morash and J. Kevin Ford. Thousand Oaks, Calif.: Sage, 2002, pp. 81–111.

Matthews, John. "Community Policing: Department-Wide versus 'Task Force' Implementation." *Law and Order,* December 1995, pp. 34–37.

Matthews, Roger. "Developing More Effective Strategies for Curbing Prostitution." *Security Journal* 1 (1990): 182–187.

Maxfield, Michael G., and Earl Babbie. *Research Methods for Criminal Justice and Criminology.* Belmont, Calif.: Wadsworth, 1995.

Mayhall, Pamela D., Thomas Barker, and Ronald D. Hunter. *Police-Community Relations and the Administration of Justice,* 4th ed. Englewood Cliffs, N.J.: Prentice Hall, 1995.

McArdle, Andrea, and Tanya Erzen. *Zero Tolerance: Quality of Life and the New Police Brutality in New York City.* New York: New York University Press, 2001.

McElroy, Jerome E., Colleen A. Cosgrove, and Susan Sadd. *COP: The Research.* New York: Vera Institute of Justice, 1990.

————. *Community Policing: The CPOP in New York.* Newbury Park, Calif.: Sage, 1993.

McEwen, Tom. "National Assessment Program: 1994 Survey Results." *National Institute of Justice Research in Brief.* Washington, D.C.: May 1995.

McLaughlin, Vance, and Michael E. Donahue. "Training for Community-Oriented Policing." In *Issues in Community Policing,* ed. Peter C. Kratcoski and Duane Dukes. Cincinnati, Ohio: Academy of Criminal Justice Sciences and Anderson, 1995, pp. 125–138.

McNulty, Paul J. "Natural Born Killers? Preventing the Coming Explosion of Teenage Crime." *Policy Review* 71 (1995): 84–87.

McPherson, Nancy. "Solution-Driven Partnerships: Just Six Steps Away." In *Community Policing Exchange.* Washington, D.C.: Community Policing Consortium, September/October 1995.

McVety, Bruce. "Community Policing Works." *Law and Order,* February 1994, p. 71.

Meese, Edwin III. "Community Policing and the Police Officer." *Perspectives on Policing.* Washington, D.C.: National Institute of Justice and the John F. Kennedy School of Government, Harvard University, January 1993.

Metchik, Eric, and Ann Winton. "Community Policing and Its Implications for Alternative Models of Police Officer Selection." In *Issues in Community Policing,* ed. Peter C. Kratcoski and Duane Dukes. Cincinnati, Ohio: Academy of Criminal Justice Sciences and Anderson, 1995, pp. 125–138.

Methvin, Eugene. "Where Crime Is on the Run." *Reader's Digest,* June 1998, pp. 101–105.

Miller, Linda S., and Karen M. Hess. *Community Policing: Theory and Practice.* St. Paul, Minn.: West, 1994.

Miller, William D. "The Graying of America: Implications towards Policing." *Law and Order,* October 1991, pp. 96–97.

Monk, Richard C. *Taking Sides: Clashing Views on Controversial Issues in Crime and Criminology,* 4th ed. Guilford, Conn.: Dushkin and Brown & Benchmark, 1996.

Moore, Harry W., and W. Fred Wegner. *Effective Police Supervision,* 2nd ed. Cincinnati, Ohio: Anderson, 1996.

Moore, Mark Harrison. "Problem-Solving and Community Policing." *Criminal Justice: A Review of Research,* vol. 15, ed. Michael Tonry and Norval Morris. Chicago: University of Chicago Press, 1992.

————. "Research Synthesis and Policy Implications." In *The Challenge of Community Policing: Testing the Promises,* ed. Dennis P. Rosenbaum. Thousand Oaks, Calif.: Sage, 1994, pp. 285–299.

Moore, Mark H., and George L. Kelling. "'To Serve and Protect': Learning from Police History." *Public Interest* 70 (Winter 1983): 49–65.

Moore, Mark H., and Darrel Stephens. *Beyond Command and Control: The Strategic Management of Police Departments.* Washington, D.C.: Police Executive Research Forum, 1991.

Moore, Mark H., and Robert C. Trojanowicz. "Policing and the Fear of Crime." *Perspectives on Policing.* Washington, D.C.: National Institute of Justice and the Program in Criminal Justice Policy and Management, June 1988a.

————. "Corporate Strategies for Policing. *Perspectives on Policing.* Washington, D.C.: National Institute of Justice and the Program in Criminal Justice Policy and Management, November 1988b.

Moore, Mark H., Robert C. Trojanowicz, and George L. Kelling. "Crime and Policing." *Perspectives on Policing.* Washington, D.C.: National Institute of Justice, June 1988.

Morash, Merry, and J. Kevin Ford. *The Move to Community Policing: Making Change Happen.* Thousand Oaks, Calif.: Sage, 2002.

Muehleisen, Tom. "Community Problem Solving." *Law and Order,* June 1995, pp. 31–32.

Muhlhausen, David B. "More COPS Funding Will Not Mean More Cops and Less Crime." In *The Heritage Foundation Executive Memorandum,* No. 752. Washington, D.C.: Heritage Foundation, 2001a.

———. "Do Community Oriented Policing Services Grants Affect Violent Crime Rates?" *A Report of the Heritage Center for Data Analysis.* Washington, D.C.: Heritage Foundation, 2001b.

Murphy, Christopher. "Community Problems, Problem Communities, and Community Policing in Toronto." *Journal of Research in Crime and Delinquency* 25 (1988a): 392–410.

———. "The Development, Impact, and Implications of Community Policing in Canada." In *Community Policing: Rhetoric or Reality,* ed. Jack R. Greene and Stephen D. Mastrofski. New York: Praeger, 1988b, pp. 177–190.

Murphy, Patrick. Foreword. In *The State of Police Education: Policy Directions for the 21st Century,* ed. David L. Carter, Allen D. Sapp, and Darrel W. Stephens. Washington, D.C.: Police Executive Research Forum, 1989.

Murphy, Robert A., Robert A. Rosenheck, Steven J. Berkowitz, and Steven R. Marans. "Acute Service Delivery in a Police-Mental Health Program for Children Exposed to Violence and Trauma." *Psychiatric Quarterly* 76, no. 2 (2005): 107–121.

Mwangangi, Mary M. "The Kenyan Perspective on Community Policing and Crime Prevention." In *International Perspectives on Community Policing and Crime Prevention,* ed. Steven P. Lab and Dilip K. Das. Upper Saddle River, N.J.: Prentice Hall, 2003, pp. 127–139.

National Institute of Justice. *Solicitation for an Impact Evaluation of Operation Weed and Seed.* Washington, D.C.: U.S. Department of Justice, April 1995.

———. "Policing Drug Hot Spots." *NIJ Research Preview.* Washington, D.C.: National Institute of Justice, 1996.

Nelligan, Peter J., and Robert W. Taylor. "Ethical Issues in Community Policing." *Journal of Contemporary Criminal Justice* 10, no. 1 (March 1994): 59–66.

Nila, Michael J. "Defining the Police Mission: A Community/Police Perspective." *Police Chief,* October 1990, pp. 43–47.

Nolan, James J. III, Norman Conti, and Jack McDevitt. "Situational Policing: Neighborhood Development and Crime Control." *Policing & Society* 14, no. 2 (2004): 99–117.

Novak, Kenneth J., Leanne Fiftal Alarid, and Wayne L. Lucas. "Exploring Officers' Acceptance of Community Policing: Implications for Policy Implementation." *Journal of Criminal Justice* 31 (2003): 57–71.

Novak, K. J., A. Hartman, A. Holsinger, and M. Turner. "The Effects of Aggressive Policing of Disorder on Serious Crime." *Policing* 22 (1999): 171–190.

O'Brien, John T. "Public Attitudes toward the Police." *Journal of Police Science and Administration* 6, no. 3 (1978): 34–47.

O'Connell, John P. "Community Crime Analysis." *What Can the Federal Government Do to Decrease Crime and Revitalize Communities?* Washington, D.C.: U.S. Department of Justice, 1998, pp. 87–95.

Oettmeier, Timothy, and Lee P. Brown. "Developing a Neighborhood-Oriented Policing Style." In *Community Policing: Rhetoric or Reality,* ed. Jack R. Greene and Stephen D. Mastrofski. New York: Praeger, 1988, pp. 121–134.

Office of Juvenile Justice and Delinquency Prevention. *Promising Strategies: To Reduce Gun Violence.* Washington, D.C.: Office of Juvenile Justice and Delinquency Prevention, 1999.

Oliver, W. *Homeland Security for Policing.* Upper Saddle River, N.J.: Prentice Hall, 2007.

Oliver, W. M. "The Era of Homeland Security: September 11, 2001 to . . ." *Crime & Justice International* 21, no. 85 (2005): 9–17.

Oliver, Willard M. "Community Policing Defined." *Law and Order,* August 1992, pp. 46, 56–58.

———. "The Changing Role of the Police Chief in Community Policing." *Law and Order,* March 1993, pp. 85–86.

———. "The Early Warning System." *Law and Order,* September 1994a, pp. 182–183.

———. "Disciplinary Exceptions to the Rule: Reserve, Auxiliary, and Seasonal Officers." *Police Department Disciplinary Bulletin,* October 1994b, pp. 4–5.

———. "Corruption Potential in Community Oriented Policing." *Police Department Disciplinary Bulletin* 2, no. 12 (December 1994c): 2–5.

———. "Higher Education and Discipline." *Police Department Disciplinary Bulletin,* May 1995, pp. 2–3.

———. "The Juvenile Justice System: A Road Paved with Good Intentions." Unpublished paper, 1996.

———. "The Third Generation of Community Policing: Moving through Innovation, Diffusion, and Institutionalization." *Police Quarterly* 3, no. 4 (2000): 367–388.

———. "Community Policing in Small-Town and Rural Communities: An Organizational Assessment of West Virginia Agencies." *Police Practice* 2, no. 3 (2001): 243–271.

Oliver, Willard M., and James F. Hilgenberg, Jr. *A History of Crime and Criminal Justice in America.* Boston, Mass.: Allyn and Bacon, 2006.

Olson, Mancur. *The Logic of Collective Action.* Cambridge, Mass.: Harvard University Press, 1965.

Osborne, David. *Laboratories of Democracy.* Cambridge, Mass.: Harvard Business School Press, 1990.

Osborne, David, and Ted Gaebler. *Reinventing Government: How the Entrepreneurial Spirit Is Transforming the Public Sector.* Reading, Mass.: Addison-Wesley, 1992.

O'Shaughnessy, Leslie. "Hawaii Innovations." *Law and Order,* September 1994, pp. 50–52.

O'Shea, Timothy C. "Community Policing in Small Town Rural America: A Comparison of Police Officer Attitudes in Chicago and Baldwin County, Alabama." *Policing and Society* 9 (1999): 59–76.

———. "The Political Dimension of Community Policing: Belief Congruence between Police and Citizens." *Police Quarterly* 3, no. 4 (2000): 389–412.

Overman, Richard. "The Case for Community Policing." *Police Chief,* March 1994, pp. 20–23.

Paine, Thomas. *Common Sense,* ed. Issac Kramnick. New York: Penguin Books, 1976.

Painter, Ellen. "The Secrets of Their Success." In *Community Policing Exchange.* Washington, D.C.: Community Policing Consortium, May/June 1995.

———. "Tragedy Sparks Community Policing in Spokane, Washington." In *Community Policing Exchange.* Washington, D.C.: Community Policing Consortium, May/June 1995.

Palmiotto, Michael J., Michael L. Birzer, and N. Prabha Unnithan. "Training in Community Policing: A Suggested Curriculum." *Policing: An International Journal of Police Strategies and Management* 23, no. 1 (2000): 8–21.

Paoline, Eugene A. III. "Shedding Light on Police Culture: An Examination of Officers' Occupational Attitudes." *Police Quarterly* 7, no. 2 (2004): 205–236.

Pate, Antony M. "Experimenting with Foot Patrol: The Newark Experience." In *Community Crime Prevention: Does It Work?* ed. Dennis P. Rosenbaum. Beverly Hills, Calif.: Sage, 1986.

———. "Community-Oriented Policing in Baltimore." In *Police and Policing: Contemporary Issues,* ed. D. J. Kenney. New York: Praeger, 1989.

Pate, Antony M., and Penny Shtull. "Community Policing Grows in Brooklyn: An Inside View of the New York City Police Department's Model Precinct." *Crime and Delinquency* 40, no. 3 (July 1994): 384–410.

Pate, Antony M., Mary Ann Wycoff, Wesley G. Skogan, and Lawrence Sherman. *Reducing Fear of Crime in Houston and Newark: A Summary Report.* Washington, D.C.: Police Foundation, 1986.

Patton, Michael Quinn. *Utilization-Focused Evaluation,* 2nd ed. Beverly Hills, Calif.: Sage, 1986.

———. *How to Use Qualitative Methods in Evaluation.* Newbury Park, Calif.: Sage, 1987.

Peak, Ken, Robert V. Bradshaw, and Ronald W. Glensor. "Improving Citizen Perceptions of the Police: 'Back to the Basics' with a Community Policing Strategy." *Journal of Criminal Justice* 20, no. 1 (1992): 25–40.

Peak, Kenneth. *Justice Administration: Police, Courts, and Corrections Management.* Englewood Cliffs, N.J.: Prentice Hall, 1995.

Peak, Kenneth J., and Ronald W. Glensor. *Community Policing and Problem Solving: Strategies and Practices.* Upper Saddle River, N.J.: Prentice Hall, 1996.

Pegels, C. Carl. *Total Quality Management: A Survey of Its Important Aspects.* Danvers, Mass.: Boyd & Fraser, 1995.

Pelfrey, William V., Jr. "The Inchoate Nature of Community Policing: Differences between Community Policing and Traditional Police Officers." *Justice Quarterly* 21, no. 3 (2004): 579–601.

Perez, Marta Brito. "IACP Offers Training in Community-Oriented Policing." *Police Chief,* May 1993, pp. 39–40.

Perrott, Stephen B., and Donald M. Taylor. "Crime Fighting, Law Enforcement, and Service Provider Role Orientations in Community-Based Police Officers." *American Journal of Police* 14, no. 3/4 (1995): 173–195.

Petersilia, Joan. "The Influence of Research on Policing." In *Critical Issues in Policing: Contemporary Readings,* ed. Roger C. Dunham and Geoffrey P. Alpert. Prospect Heights, Ill.: Waveland Press, 1989, pp. 230–247.

Petersilia, Joan, Allan Abrahamse, and James Q. Wilson. "A Summary of RAND's Research on Police Performance, Community Characteristics, and Case Attrition." *Journal of Police Science and Administration* 17, no. 3 (1990): 219–226.

Podhoretz, Norman. "My New York." *National Review,* June 14, 1999, pp. 35–40.

Police Executive Research Forum. *Themes and Variations in Community Policing: Case Studies in Community Policing.* Washington, D.C.: Police Executive Research Forum, 1996.

Policing Research Institute. "Measuring What Matters: Developing Measures of What the Police Do." *National Institute of Justice Research in Action.* Washington, D.C.: National Institute of Justice, 1997.

Pomrenke, Norman E., ed. *Police Community Relations.* Chapel Hill: University of North Carolina Press, 1966.

Pooley, Eric. "One Good Apple." *Time,* January 15, 1996, pp. 54–56.

Potter, Tom. "How to Plan Strategically for Your Community." In *Community Policing Exchange.* Washington, D.C.: Community Policing Consortium, November/December 1995.

Puthpongsiriporn, S., and T. Quang. "Promoting a Service Culture for Community Policing in Thailand." *Policing: An International Journal of Police Science & Management,* 7, no. 1 (2005): 24–35.

Priest, Thomas B., and Deborah Brown Carter. "Community-Oriented Policing: Assessing a Police Saturation Operation." In *Policing and Community Partnership,* ed. Dennis J. Stevens. Upper Saddle River, N.J.: Prentice Hall, 2002, 111–124.

Quinet, Kenna, Samuel Nunn, and Nikki L. Kincaid. "Training Policing: A Case Study of Differential Impacts of Problem-Oriented Policing Training." *Police Practice and Research* 4, no. 3 (2003): 263–283.

Quinn, James Brian. *Strategies for Change: Logical Incrementalism.* Homewood, Ill.: Irwin, 1980.

———. "Managing Innovation: Controlled Chaos." *Harvard Business Review* 3 (May–June 1985): 73–84.

Radelet, Louis A. *The Police and the Community.* Beverly Hills, Calif.: Glencoe Press, 1973.

Radelet, Louis A., and David L. Carter. *The Police and the Community,* 5th ed. Englewood Cliffs, N.J.: Prentice Hall, 1994.

Raghavan, R. K., and A. Shiva Sankar. "A Community Policing Approach to Crime Prevention: The Case of India." In *International Perspectives on Community Policing and Crime Prevention,* ed. Steven P. Lab and Dilip K. Das. Upper Saddle River, N.J.: Prentice Hall, 2003, pp. 113–126.

Ramsey, Charles H. "Preparing the Community for Community Policing: The Next Step in Advancing Community Policing." In *Policing and Community Partnership,* ed. Dennis J. Stevens. Upper Saddle River, N.J.: Prentice Hall, 2002, pp. 29–44.

Reaves, Brian A., and Timothy C. Hart. *Law Enforcement and Management Statistics, 1999.* Washington, D.C.: Bureau of Justice Statistics, 2000.

Redlinger, Lawrence J. "Community Policing and Changes in the Organizational Structure." *Journal of Contemporary Criminal Justice* 10, no. 1 (March 1994): 36–58.

Reed, Wilson Edward. *The Politics of Community Policing: The Case of Seattle.* New York: Garland, 1999.

Reisig, M. D., and R. B. Parks. "Can Community Policing Help the Truly Disadvantaged?" *Crime & Delinquency* 50, no. 2 (2004): 139–167.

Reisig, Michael D., and Roger B. Parks. "Can Community Policing Help the Truly Disadvantaged?" *Crime & Delinquency* 50, no. 2 (2004): 139–167.

Reiss, Albert J., Jr. "Crime Control and the Quality of Life." *American Behavioral Scientist* 27 (September/October 1983): 43–58.

———. *The Police and the Public.* New Haven, Conn.: Yale University Press, 1985a.

———. "Shaping and Serving the Community: The Role of the Police Chief Executive." In *Police Leadership in America.* New York: American Bar Foundation and Praeger, 1985b, pp. 61–69.

Ren, L., L. Cao, N. Lovrich, and M. Gaffney. "Linking Confidence in the Police with the Performance of the Police: Community Policing Can Make a Difference." *Journal of Criminal Justice* 33, no. 1(2005): 55–66.

Reuss-Iianni, Elizabeth, and Francis A.J. Iianni. "Street Cops and Management Cops: The Two Cultures of Policing." In *Control in the Police Organization,* ed. Maurice Punch. Cambridge, Mass.: MIT Press, 1983.

Ricucci, Ronald A., and Michael W. McKeehan. "The Role of Technology in Community Policing." *Police Chief,* May 1993, pp. 41–42.

Riechers, Lisa M., and Roy R. Roberg. "Community Policing: A Critical Review of Underlying Assumptions." *Journal of Police Science and Administration* 17, no. 2 (1990): 105–114.

Roberg, Roy. "Can Today's Police Organizations Effectively Implement Community Policing?" In *The Challenge of Community Policing: Testing the Promises,* ed. Dennis P. Rosenbaum. Thousand Oaks, Calif.: Sage, 1994, pp. 249–257.

Robinson, Amanda L. "The Impact of Police Social Capital on Officer Performance of Community Policing." *Policing: An International Journal of Police Strategies and Management* 26, no. 4 (2003): 656–689.

Roehl, Jan, Dennis P. Rosenbaum, Sandra K. Costello, James R. "Chip" Coldren, Amie M. Schuck, Laura Kunard, and David R. Forde. *Strategic Approaches to Community Safety Initiatives (SACSI) in 10 U.S. Cities: The Building Blocks for Project Safe Neighborhoods.* Washington, D.C.: U.S. Department of Justice, 2006.

Roh, Sunghoon, and Willard M. Oliver. "Effects of Community Policing Upon Fear of Crime: Understanding the Causal Linkage." *Policing: An International Journal of Police Strategies and Management* 28, no. 4 (2005): 670–683.

Rohe, William M., Richard E. Adams, and Thomas A. Arcury. "Community Policing and Planning." *APA Journal* 67, no. 1 (2001): 78–90.

Rojek, Jeff. "A Decade of Excellence in Problem-Oriented Policing: Characteristics of the Goldstein Award Winners." *Police Quarterly* 6, no. 4 (2003): 492–515.

Roneck, Dennis, and Pamela Maier. "Bars, Blocks, and Crime Revisited: Linking the Theory of Routine Activities to the Empiricism of 'Hot Spots.'" *Criminology* 29 (1991): 725–753.

Rosenbaum, Dennis P. *Community Crime Prevention: Does It Work?* Beverly Hills, Calif.: Sage, 1986.

———. "The Theory and Research behind Neighborhood Watch: Is It a Sound Fear and Crime Reduction Strategy?" *Crime and Delinquency* 33, no. 1 (January 1987): 103–134.

———. "Community Crime Prevention: A Review and Synthesis of the Literature." *Justice Quarterly* 5, no. 3 (September 1988): 323–395.

———. *The Challenge of Community Policing: Testing the Promises,* ed. Dennis P. Rosenbaum. Thousand Oaks, Calif.: Sage, 1994.

Rosenbaum, Dennis P., and Arthur J. Lurigio. "An Inside Look at Community Policing Reform: Definitions, Organizational Changes, and Evaluation Findings." *Crime and Delinquency* 40, no. 3 (July 1994): 299–314.

Rosenbaum, Dennis, Robert Flewelling, Susan Bailey, Chris Ringwalt, and Deanna Wilkinson. "Cops in the Classroom: A Longitudinal Evaluation of Drug Abuse Resistance Education (DARE)." *Journal of Research in Crime and Delinquency* 31 (1994): 3–31.

Rosenbaum, Dennis P., Sandy Yeh, and Deanna L. Wilkinson. "Impact of Community Policing on Police Personnel: A Quasi-Experimental Test." *Crime and Delinquency* 40, no. 3 (July 1994): 331–353.

Ross, Jeffrey Ian. "Confronting Community Policing: Minimizing Community Policing as Public Relations." In *Issues in Community Policing,* ed. Peter C. Kratcoski and Duane Dukes. Cincinnati, Ohio: Academy of Criminal Justice Sciences and Anderson, 1995, pp. 243–260.

Rossiter, Clinton. *The Federalist Papers.* New York: New American Library, 1961.

Roth, Jeffrey A., and Joseph F. Ryan. *National Evaluation of the COPS Program—Title 1 of the 1994 Crime Act.* Washington, D.C.: National Institute of Justice, 2000.

Rothermel, Terry W. "Forecasting Revisited." *Harvard Business Review* 60, no. 2 (March–April 1982): 143–157.

Rush, George E. "Community Policing: Overcoming the Obstacles." *Police Chief,* October 1992, pp. 50–55.

———. *The Dictionary of Criminal Justice,* 4th ed. Guilford, Conn.: Dushkin, 1994.

Russell, Gregory D., and Susan MacLachlan. "Community Policing, Decentralized Decision Making and Employee Satisfaction." *Journal of Crime & Justice* 22, no. 2 (1999): 31–54.

Ryan, Joseph F. "Community Policing: Trends, Policies, Programs and Definitions." In *Critical Issues in Crime and Justice,* ed. Albert R. Roberts. Thousand Oaks, Calif.: Sage, 1994.

Sacco, Vincent F., and Leslie W. Kennedy. *The Criminal Event.* Belmont, Calif.: Wadsworth, 1996.

Sadd, Susan, and Randolph Grinc. *Issues in Community Policing: An Evaluation of Eight Innovative Neighborhood Oriented Policing Projects.* New York: Vera Institute of Justice, 1993.

———. "Innovative Neighborhood Oriented Policing." In *The Challenge of Community Policing: Testing the Promises,* ed. Dennis P. Rosenbaum. Thousand Oaks, Calif.: Sage, 1994, pp. 27–52.

———. "Implementation Challenges in Community Policing." *National Institute of Justice Research in Brief.* Washington, D.C.: National Institute of Justice, February 1996.

Sampson, Robert, and Jacqueline Cohen. "Deterrent Effects of the Police on Crime: A Replication and Theoretical Extension." *Law and Society Review* 22 (1988): 163–191.

Sampson, Robert J., and Stephen W. Raudenbush. "Systematic Social Observation of Public Spaces: A New Look at Disorder in Urban Neighborhoods." *American Journal of Sociology* 105, no. 3 (1999): 603–651.

Sanders, Jerry. "Racial and Ethnic Minorities in San Diego, United States." *Policing and Society* 10 (2000): 131–141.

Sarre, Rick. "Some Thoughts on the Relationship between Crime Prevention and Policing in Contemporary Australia." In *International Perspectives on Community Policing and Crime Prevention,* ed. Steven P. Lab and Dilip K. Das. Upper Saddle River, N.J.: Prentice-Hall, 2003, pp. 79–92.

Saunders, Ralph H. "The Politics and Practice of Community Policing in Boston." *Urban Geography* 20, no. 5 (1999): 461–482.

Scarborough, Kathyrn E., G. Norman Van Tubergen, Larry K. Gaines, and S. Scott Whitlow. "An Examination of Police Officers' Motivation to Participate in the Promotional Process." *Police Quarterly* 2, no. 3 (1999): 302–320.

Schafer, J. A., B. H. Huebner, and T. S. Bynum. "Citizen Perceptions of Police Service: Race, Neighborhood Context, and Community Policing." *Police Quarterly* 6, no. 4 (2003): 440–468.

Schaefer, Richard T., and Robert P. Lamm. *Sociology,* 4th ed. New York: McGraw-Hill, 1992.

Scheider, M. C., T. Rowell, and V. Bezdikian. "The Impact of Citizen Perceptions of Community Policing on Fear of Crime: Findings from Twelve Cities." *Police Quarterly* 6, no. 4 (2003): 363–386.

Scheider, M. C., and R. Chapman. "Community Policing and Terrorism." *Journal of Homeland Security,* April (2003). Available online at http://www.homelandsecurity.org/journal/articles/Scheider-Chapman.html

Scheingold, Stuart A. *Politics of Law and Order.* New York: Longman, 1984.

―――. "Politics, Public Policy, and Street Crime." *Annals of the American Academy of Political and Social Science* 539 (1995): 155–158.

Schmalleger, Frank. *Criminal Justice Today,* 3rd ed. Englewood Cliffs, N.J.: Prentice Hall, 1995.

Schmitt, Sheila. "ROPE: The Resident Officer Program of Elgin." *Law and Order,* May 1995, pp. 52–58.

Schneider, A. et al. 2003. *Community Policing in Action: A Practitioner's Eye View of Organizational Change.* Washington, D.C.: Office of Community-Oriented Policing Services.

Schneider, Stephen R. "Overcoming Barriers to Communication between Police and Socially Disadvantaged Neighborhoods: A Critical Theory of Community Policing." *Crime, Law & Social Change* 30 (1999): 347–377.

Schnelle, John F., Robert E. Kirchner Jr., J.R. Lawler, and M. Patrick McNees. "Social Evaluation Research: The Evaluation of Two Police Patrol Strategies." *Journal of Applied Behavioral Analysis* 8 (1975): 232–240.

Schwab, William A. *The Sociology of Cities.* Englewood Cliffs, N.J.: Prentice Hall, 1992.

Scott, Eric J. *Calls for Service: Citizen Demand and Initial Police Response.* Washington, D.C.: U.S. Government Printing Office, 1981.

Scott, J. D., D. E. Duffee, and B. C. Renauer. "Measuring Police–Community Coproduction: The Utility of Community Policing Case Studies." *Police Quarterly* 6, no. 4 (2003): 410–439.

Scott, Michael S. "The Benefits and Consequences of Police Crackdowns." *Problem-Oriented Guides for Police Response Guides Series.* No. 1. Washington, D.C.: U.S Department of Justice, 2003.

Seagrave, Jayne. "Defining Community Policing." *American Journal of Police* 15, no. 2 (1996): 1–22.

Sharp, Arthur. "Pedaling Not Hard to Peddle." *Law and Order,* July 1995, pp. 35–40.

Sherman, Lawrence W. "Middle Management and Democratization: A Reply to John E. Angell." *Criminology* 12, no. 4 (1975): 363–377.

―――. *Scandal and Reform: Controlling Police Corruption.* Berkeley and Los Angeles: University of California Press, 1978.

―――. "The Police Executive as Statesman." In *Police Leadership in America,* ed. William A. Geller. New York: American Bar Foundation and Praeger, 1985, pp. 459–466.

―――. "Policing Communities: What Works." In *Crime and Justice: A Review of Research,* vol. 8, ed. A.J. Reiss and Michael Tonry. Chicago: University of Chicago Press, 1986, pp. 366–379.

―――. "Police Crackdowns." *National Institute of Justice Reports,* March/April 1990a.

―――. "Police Crackdowns: Initial and Residual Deterrence." In *Crime and Justice: A Review of Research,* 12, ed. Michael Tonry and Norval Morris. Chicago: University of Chicago Press, 1990, pp. 1–48.

―――. "Police and Crime Control." In *Modern Policing,* ed. Michael Tonry and Norval Morris. Chicago: University of Chicago Press, 1992.

―――. "The Police." In *Crime,* ed. James Q. Wilson and Joan Petersilia. San Francisco: ICS Press, 1995.

Sherman, Lawrence W., Catherine H. Milton, and Thomas V. Kelly. *Team Policing: Seven Case Studies.* Washington, D.C.: Police Foundation, 1973.

Siegel, Jeff. "The East Dallas Police Storefront." *Law and Order,* May 1995, pp. 53–55.

Siegel, Larry J. *Criminology,* 5th ed. St. Paul, Minn.: West, 1995.

Sileo, Chi Chi. "Crime Takes on a Feminine Face." *Insight,* December 20, 1993, pp. 16–19.

Silverman, Eli B. "Community Policing: The Implementation Gap." In *Issues in Community Policing*, ed. Peter C. Kratcoski and Duane Dukes. Cincinnati, Ohio: Academy of Criminal Justice Sciences and Anderson, 1995, pp. 35–48.

Simonovic, Branislav, and Miroslav Radovanovic. "Crime Prevention in Yugoslavia." In *International Perspectives on Community Policing and Crime Prevention*, ed. Steven P. Lab and Dilip K. Das. Upper Saddle River, N.J.: Prentice Hall, 2003, pp. 153–167.

Simonsen, Clifford, and Douglas Arnold. "TQM: Is It Right for Law Enforcement?" *Police Chief,* December 1993, pp. 20–22.

Sims, Barbara, Kathryn E. Scarborough, and Janice Ahmad. "The Relationship Between Police Officers' Attitudes Toward Women and Perceptions of Police Models." *Police Quarterly* 6, no. 3 (2003): 278–297.

Skogan, Wesley G. "Fear of Crime and Neighborhood Change." In *Criminal Justice: A Review of Research Communities and Crime*, vol. 8, ed. Albert J. Reiss and Michael Tonry. Chicago: University of Chicago Press, 1986, pp. 203–230.

———. "The Impact of Victimization on Fear." *Crime and Delinquency* 33, no. 1 (January 1987): 135–154.

———. "Communities, Crime, and Neighborhood Organization." *Crime and Delinquency* 35 (1990a): 437–457.

———. *Disorder and Decline: Crime and the Spiral of Decay in American Neighborhoods.* New York: Free Press, 1990b.

———. "The Impact of Community Policing on Neighborhood Residents: A Cross-Site Analysis." In *The Challenges of Community Policing: Testing the Promises,* ed. Dennis P. Rosenbaum. Thousand Oaks, Calif.: Sage, 1994, pp. 167–181.

———. "Community Participation and Community Policing." In *How to Recognize Good Policing: Problems and Issues,* ed. Jean-Paul Brodeur. Thousand Oaks, Calif.: Sage, 1998, pp. 88–106.

Skogan, Wesley G., and Susan M. Hartnett. *Community Policing, Chicago Style.* New York: Oxford University Press, 1997.

Skogan, Wesley G., and M.G. Maxfield. *Coping with Crime: Individual and Neighborhood Reactions.* Beverly Hills, Calif.: Sage, 1981.

Skogan, Wesley G., and Mary Ann Wycoff. "Storefront Police Officers: The Houston Field Test." In *Community Crime Prevention: Does It Work?* ed. Dennis P. Rosenbaum. Beverly Hills, Calif.: Sage, 1986, pp. 179–199.

Skolnick, Jerome H., and David H. Bayley. *The New Blue Line: Police Innovation in Six American Cities.* New York: Free Press, 1986.

———. *Community Policing: Issues and Practices around the World.* Washington, D.C.: National Institute of Justice, 1988a.

———. "Theme and Variation in Community Policing." In *Crime and Justice: A Biannual Review of Research*, 10, ed. Michael Tonry and Norval Morris. Chicago: University of Chicago Press, 1988b.

Skolnick, Jerome H., and James J. Fyfe. *Above the Law: Police and the Excessive Use of Force.* New York: Free Press, 1993.

———. "Community-Oriented Policing Would Prevent Police Brutality." In *Policing the Police.* San Diego: Greenhaven Press, 1995.

Smith, Bruce. *Police Systems in the United States.* New York: Harper & Brothers, 1960.

Smith, Michael R. "Integrating Community Policing and the Use of Force: Public Education, Involvement, and Accountability." *American Journal of Police* 12, no. 4 (1994a): 1–21.

Smith, William J. "Investigation at the Local Level." *Law and Order,* September 1994b, pp. 63–65.

Solar, Patrick J. "The Organizational Context of Effective Policing." *Police Chief,* February 2001, pp. 39–47.

Sparrow, Malcolm K. "Implementing Community Policing." *Perspectives on Policing.* Washington, D.C.: National Institute of Justice and the Program in Criminal Justice Policy and Management, November 1988.

Sparrow, Malcolm K., Mark H. Moore, and David H. Kennedy. *Beyond 911: A New Era for Policing.* New York: Basic Books, 1990.

Spelman, William, and Dale K. Brown. *Calling the Police: Citizen Reporting of Serious Crime.* Washington, D.C.: U.S. Government Printing Office, 1984.

Spelman, William, and John E. Eck. "Newport News Tests Problem-Oriented Policing." *National Institute of Justice: Research in Action.* Washington, D.C.: National Institute of Justice, January/February 1987a.

———. "Problem-Oriented Policing." *National Institute of Justice: Research in Brief.* Washington, D.C.: National Institute of Justice, January 1987b.

———. "The Police and Delivery of Local Government Services: A Problem-Oriented Approach." In *Police Practices in the 90's: Key Management Issues,* ed. James Fyfe. Washington, D.C.: International City/County Management Association, 1989.

Stedman, Robert F. *The Police and the Community.* Baltimore, Md.: Johns Hopkins University Press, 1972.

Steffensmeier, Darrell. "The Invention of the 'New' Senior Citizen Criminal." *Research on Aging* 9 (1987): 281–311.

Stephens, Darrel W. "Policing in the Future." *American Journal of Police* 9 (1990): 151–157.

Stephens, Darrel W., John D. Hartman, and Darryl Herring. "Giving Voice: The Police Chief, Assistant City Manager, and Budget Director Focus on What Works." In *Community Policing Exchange.* Washington, D.C.: Community Policing Consortium, November/December 1995.

Stevens, Dennis J. *Case Studies in Community Policing.* Upper Saddle River, N.J.: Prentice Hall, 2001a.

———. "Community Policing and Managerial Techniques: Total Quality Management Techniques." *Police Journal* 74 (2001b): 26–41.

Stevens, Dennis J. "Community Policing and Police Leadership." In *Policing and Community Partnership,* ed. Dennis J. Stevens. Upper Saddle River, N.J.: Prentice Hall, 2002, pp. 163–176.

Sullivan, John L. *Introduction to Police Science,* 3rd ed. New York: McGraw-Hill, 1977.

Sullivan, William M. *Reconstructing Public Philosophy.* Berkeley and Los Angeles: University of California Press, 1986.

Sweeney, William. "Grant Writing for Technology." *Law and Order,* September 1995, pp. 83–84.

Swiss, James. "Adapting Total Quality Management (TQM) to Government." *Public Administration Review* 52 (1992): 356–362.

Sykes, Gary W. "Accreditation and Community Policing: Passing Fads or Basic Reforms?" *Journal of Contemporary Criminal Justice* 10, no. 1 (March 1994): 1–16.

Tafoya, William L. "Into the Future . . . A Look at the 21st Century." *Law Enforcement Technology,* September/October 1987.

———. "Futures Research: Implication for Criminal Investigations." In *Criminal Investigation: Essays and Cases,* ed. James N. Gilbert. Columbus, Ohio: Merrill, 1990.

————. *A Delphi Forecast of the Future of Law Enforcement.* Ph.D. diss. Ann Arbor, Michigan: University Microfilm International, 1991.

Taft, Philip B., Jr. *Fighting Fear: The Baltimore County C.O.P.E. Project.* Washington, D.C.: Police Executive Research Forum, 1986.

Thayer, Ralph E., and K. Michael Reynolds. "Community-Oriented Policing." *Journal of Planning Literature* 12, no. 1 (1997): 93–106.

Thomas, M. O., and P. F. Burns. "Repairing the Divide: An Investigation of Community Policing and Citizen Attitudes Toward the Police by Race & Ethnicity." *Journal of Ethnicity in Criminal Justice* 3, no. 1–2 (2005): 71–90.

Thurman, Quint C., and Edmund F. McGarrell. *Community Policing in a Rural Setting.* Cincinnati, Ohio: Anderson, 1997.

Thurman, Quint, and Michael D. Reisig. "Community-Oriented Research in an Era of Community-Oriented Policing." *American Behavioral Scientist* 39, no. 5 (1996): 570–587.

Thurman, Quint C., Andrew Giacomazzi, and Phil Bogen. "Research Note: Cops, Kids, and Community Policing—An Assessment of a Community Policing Demonstration Project." *Crime and Delinquency* 39, no. 4 (October 1993): 554–564.

Thurman, Quint, Jihong Zhao, and Andrew L. Giacomazzi. *Community Policing in a Community Era.* Los Angeles, Calif.: Roxbury Publishing Company, 2001.

Tien, James M., and Thomas F. Rich. "The Hartford COMPASS Program: Experiences with a Weed and Seed–Related Program." In *The Challenge of Community Policing: Testing the Promises,* ed. Dennis P. Rosenbaum. Thousand Oaks, Calif.: Sage, 1994, pp. 192–208.

Tien, James M., James W. Simon, and Richard C. Larson. *An Alternative Approach in Police Patrol: The Wilmington Split-Force Experiment.* Cambridge, Mass.: Public Systems Evaluation, 1977.

Toch, Hans. "Research and Reform in Community Policing." *American Journal of Police* 14, no. 1 (1995): 1–10.

Toch, Hans, and J. Douglas Grant. *Police as Problem Solvers.* New York: Plenum Press, 1991.

Trojanowicz, Robert C. *An Evaluation of the Neighborhood Foot Patrol Program in Flint.* East Lansing, Mich.: National Neighborhood Foot Patrol Center, Michigan State University, 1982.

————. "Evaluating a Neighborhood Foot Patrol Program: The Flint Michigan Project." In *Community Crime Prevention: Does It Work?* ed. Dennis P. Rosenbaum. Beverly Hills, Calif.: Sage, 1986, pp. 67–89.

————. "Community-Policing Is Not Police-Community Relations." *FBI Law Enforcement Bulletin,* October 1990, pp. 6–11.

————. "The Future of Community Policing." In *The Challenge of Community Policing: Testing the Promises,* ed. Dennis P. Rosenbaum. Thousand Oaks, Calif.: Sage, 1994, pp. 258–262.

Trojanowicz, Robert C., and Bonnie Bucqueroux. *Community Policing: A Contemporary Perspective.* Cincinnati, Ohio: Anderson, 1989.

————. "The Community Policing Challenge." *PTM: Police Technology and Management* 1, no. 4 (November 1990): 40–51.

————. *Community Policing: How to Get Started.* Cincinnati, Ohio: Anderson, 1994.

Trojanowicz, Robert C., and David Carter. *The Philosophy and Role of Community Policing.* East Lansing: Michigan State University, 1988.

Trojanowicz, Robert C., and Samuel L. Dixon. *Criminal Justice and the Community.* Englewood Cliffs, N.J.: Prentice Hall, 1974.

Trojanowicz, Robert, and Mark Moore. "The Meaning of Community in Community Policing." In *Community Policing Series No. 15.* East Lansing: Michigan State University, National Neighborhood Foot Patrol Center, 1988.

Uchida, Craig D., Brian Forst, and Sampson O. Annan. *Modern Policing and the Control of Illegal Drugs: Testing New Strategies in Two American Cities.* Washington, D.C.: National Institute of Justice and the Police Foundation, May 1992.

U.S. Department of Justice. *Operation Weed and Seed Implementation Manual.* Washington, D.C.: U.S. Department of Justice, 1992a.

U.S. Department of Justice, Office of Justice Programs. *Drugs, Crime, and the Justice System.* Washington, D.C.: U.S. Government Printing Office, December 1992b.

USA Today. "Federal, Local Cuts Pull Cops Off Streets." *USA Today,* December 12, 2003. Available online at http://usatoday.com

Van Der Spuy, Elrena. "Foreign Donor Assistance and Policing Reform in South Africa." *Policing and Society* 10 (2000): 343–366.

Vaughn, Jerald R. "Community Oriented Policing . . . You Can Make It Happen." *Law and Order,* June 1991, pp. 35–39.

Vinzant, Janet, and Lane Crothers. "Street-Level Leadership: The Role of Patrol Officers in Community Policing." *Criminal Justice Review* 19, no. 2 (1994): 189–211.

Virginia Community Policing Institute. *Report on the Colloquium on the Future of Community Policing.* Richmond, Va.: Virginia Community Policing Institute, 1999.

Vito, G., W. F. Walsh, and J. Kunselman. "Community Policing: The Middle Manager's Perspective." *Police Quarterly* 8, no. 4 (2005): 490–511.

Vold, George B., and Thomas J. Bernard. *Theoretical Criminology,* 3rd ed. New York: Oxford University Press, 1986.

Vollmer, August. "Police Progress in the Past Twenty-Five Years." *Journal of Criminal Law and Criminology* 24, no. 1 (1933): 161–175.

Wagner, W. F. *An Evaluation of a Police Patrol Experiment.* Pullman: Washington State University, 1978.

Walinsky, Adam. "The Crisis of Public Order." *Atlantic Monthly,* July 1995, pp. 39–54.

Walker, Samuel. *A Critical History of Police Reform: The Emergence of Professionalism.* Lexington, Mass.: Lexington Books, 1977.

———. *Popular Justice: History of American Criminal Justice.* New York: Oxford University Press, 1980.

———. " 'Broken Windows' and Fractured History: The Use and Misuse of History in Recent Police Patrol Analysis." *Justice Quarterly* 1 (1984): 75–90.

———. *Sense and Nonsense about Crime and Drugs: A Policy Guide,* 3rd ed. Belmont, Calif.: Wadsworth, 1994.

Walsh, William F. "Analysis of the Police Supervisor's Role in Community Policing." In *Issues in Community Policing,* ed. Peter C. Kratcoski and Duane Dukes. Cincinnati, Ohio: Academy of Criminal Justice Sciences and Anderson, 1995, pp. 141–152.

Walsh, William F., Gennaro F. Vito, Richard Tewksbury, and George P. Wilson. "Fighting Back in Bright Leaf: Community Policing and Drug Trafficking in Public Housing." *American Journal of Criminal Justice* 25, no. 1 (2000): 77–92.

Walters, Paul M. "Community-Oriented Policing: A Blend of Strategies." *FBI Law Enforcement Bulletin* 62, no. 11 (1993): 20–23.

Warren, J. W., M. L. Forst, and M. M. Estrella. "Directed Patrol: An Experiment That Worked." *Police Chief,* July 1979, pp. 48–49.

Wasserman, Robert, and Mark H. Moore. "Values in Policing." *Perspectives on Policing.* Washington, D.C.: National Institute of Justice and John F. Kennedy School of Government, Harvard University, 1988.

Watson, Elizabeth M., Alfred R. Stone, and Stuart M. DeLuca. *Strategies for Community Policing.* Upper Saddle River, N.J.: Prentice Hall, 1998.

Watson, Nelson A. *Police-Community Relations.* Washington, D.C.: International Association of Chiefs of Police, 1966.

Weatheritt, Mollie. "Community Policing: Rhetoric or Reality?" In *Community Policing: Rhetoric or Reality,* ed. Jack R. Greene and Stephen D. Mastrofski. New York: Praeger, 1988, pp. 153–176.

Webb, Vincent J., and Charles M. Katz. "Citizen Ratings of the Importance of Community Policing Activities." *Policing: An International Journal of Police Strategies and Management* 20, no. 1 (1997): 7–23.

Webber, Alan M. "Crime and Management: An Interview with New York City Police Commissioner Lee P. Brown." *Harvard Business Review,* May–June 1991, pp. 111–126.

Webster, Barbara, and Edward F. Connors. *Community Policing: Identifying Problems.* Alexandria, Va.: Institute for Law and Justice, March 1991.

———. "Police Methods for Identifying Community Problems." *American Journal of Police* 12, no. 1 (1993): 75–101.

Weisburd, David. "Evaluating Community Policing: Role Tensions between Practitioners and Evaluators." In *The Challenge of Community Policing: Testing the Promises,* ed. Dennis P. Rosenbaum. Thousand Oaks, Calif.: Sage, 1994, pp. 274–276.

Weisburd, David, and Jerome E. McElroy. "Enacting the CPO Role: Findings from the New York City Pilot Program in Community Policing." In *Community Policing: Rhetoric or Reality,* ed. Jack R. Greene and Stephen D. Mastrofski. New York: Praeger, 1988, pp. 89–102.

Weisburd, David, Jerome E. McElroy, and Patricia Hardyman. "Challenges to Supervision in Community Policing: Observations on a Pilot Project." *American Journal of Police* 7, no. 2 (1988): 29–50.

Weisel, Deborah Lamm. "Playing the Home Field: A Problem-Oriented Approach to Drug Control." *American Journal of Police* 9 (1990): 75–95.

Weisel, Deborah Lamm, and John E. Eck. "Toward a Practical Approach to Organizational Change: Community Policing Initiatives in Six Cities." *In The Challenge of Community Policing: Testing the Promises*, ed. Dennis P. Rosenbaum. Thousand Oaks, Calif.: Sage, 1994, pp. 53–74.

Weisheit, Ralph A., L. Edward Wells, and David N. Falcone. "Community Policing in Small Town and Rural America." *Crime and Delinquency* 40, no. 4 (October 1994): 549–567.

West, Marty. "Police and Private Security." *Law and Order,* July 1994, pp. 86–88.

———. "POP in Fresno: Effective Problem-Solving Techniques." *Police Chief,* March 1995, pp. 37–43.

Whisenand, Paul M. 2007. *Supervising Police Personnel: The Fifteen Responsibilities.* Upper Saddle River, N.J.: Prentice Hall.

White, Mervin F., and Ben A. Menke. "A Critical Analysis on Public Opinion toward Police Agencies." *Journal of Police Science and Administration* 6 (1978): 204–218.

Whiteley, Richard C. *The Customer-Driven Company*. Reading, Mass.: Addison-Wesley, 1991.

Whitman, Sylvia. "Police Academies for Citizens." *Law and Order*, June 1993, pp. 66–71.

Wiatrowski, Michael D. "Community Policing in Delray Beach." *In Issues in Community Policing*, ed. Peter C. Kratcoski and Duane Dukes. Cincinnati, Ohio: Academy of Criminal Justice Sciences and Anderson, 1995, pp. 69–84.

Wiauowski, M., and J. Vardalis. "Community Policing and a Model of Crime Prevention in the Community." *Criminal Psychology*, October 1994, pp. 53–57.

Wilkinson, Deanna L., and Dennis P. Rosenbaum. "The Effects of Organizational Structure on Community Policing." *In The Challenge of Community Policing: Testing the Promises*, ed. Dennis P. Rosenbaum. Thousand Oaks, Calif.: Sage, 1994, pp. 110–126.

Williams, Brian N. *Citizen Perspectives on Community Policing*. New York: State University of New York Press, 1998.

Williams, Emma Jean. "Structuring in Community Policing: Institutionalizing Innovative Change." *Police Practice and Research* 4, no. 2 (2003): 119–129.

Williams, Hubert. "Retrenchment, the Constitution, and Policing." *In Police Leadership in America*, ed. William A. Geller. Chicago: American Bar Foundation, 1985, pp. 340–350.

Williams, Hubert, and Antony M. Pate. "Returning to First Principles: Reducing the Fear of Crime in Newark." *Crime and Delinquency*, 33, no. 1 (January 1987): 53–70.

Wilson, Deborah G., and Susan F. Bennett. "Officers' Response to Community Policing: Variations on a Theme." *Crime and Delinquency* 40, no. 3 (July 1994): 354–370.

Wilson, James Q. Varieties of Police Behavior: *The Management of Law and Order in Eight Communities*. Cambridge, Mass.: Harvard University Press, 1968.

———. "What Makes a Better Policeman?" Atlantic Monthly, March 1969.

———. *Thinking about Crime*. New York: Vintage Books, 1975.

———. *Bureaucracy*. New York: Basic Books, 1989.

———. "Just Take Away Their Guns." *New York Times Sunday Magazine*, March 20, 1994.

Wilson, James Q., and Barbara Boland. "The Effect of Police on Crime." *Law and Society Review* 12 (1978): 367–384.

———. *The Effects of Police on Crime*. Washington, D.C.: U.S. Government Printing Office, 1979.

Wilson, James Q., and George L. Kelling. "Broken Windows: The Police and Neighborhood Safety." *Atlantic Monthly*, March 1982, pp. 29–38.

———. "Broken Windows: Making Neighborhoods Safe." *Atlantic Monthly*, February 1989, pp. 46–52.

Wilson, James Q., and Joan Petersilia. *Crime,* ed. James Q. Wilson. San Francisco: ICS Press, 1995.

Wilson, Jeremy M. "Determinants of Community Policing: An Open Systems Model of Implementation." *Rand Infrastructure, Safety and Environment Working Papers*. Washington, D.C.: U.S. Department of Justice, 2005.

Wilson, Laurie J. "Placing Community-Oriented Policing in the Broader Realm of Community Cooperation." *Police Chief,* April 1995, pp. 127–128.

Wilson, O.W. *Municipal Police Administration*. Washington, D.C.: International City Management Association, 1941.

———. *Police Administration*. New York: McGraw-Hill, 1950.

Winfree, L. Thomas, Jr., Gregory M. Bartku, and George Seibel. "Support for Community Policing versus Traditional Policing among Non-Metropolitan Police Officers: A Survey of Four New Mexico Police Departments." *American Journal of Police* 15, no. 2 (1996): 23–50.

Witkin, Gordon. "Police Chiefs at War." *U.S. News & World Report,* June 8, 1992.

Witkin, Gordon, and Dan McGraw. "Beyond 'Just the Facts, Ma'am.' " *U.S. News & World Report,* August 2, 1993, pp. 28–30.

Wong, Kam C. "Community Policing in China: Philosophy, Law and Practice." *International Journal of the Sociology of Law* 29 (2001): 127–147.

Worden, Robert E. "A Badge and a Baccalaureate: Policies, Hypotheses, and Further Evidence." *Justice Quarterly* 7, no. 3 (1990): 565–592.

Worrall, J. L., and J. Zhao. "The Role of the COPS Office in Community Policing." *Policing: An International Journal of Police Strategies & Management* 26, no. 1 (2003): 64–87.

Worrell, Ann. "Officers 'Love Our Kids.' " *Law and Order,* September 1993, pp. 109–110.

———. "Operation Blue: Cops Become Bankers to Aid Elderly Citizens." *Law and Order,* December 1993, pp. 32–35.

———. "Police Museums Offer Opportunities to Teach, Recruit." *Law and Order,* December 1993, pp. 32–35.

Worsnop, Richard L. "Community Policing." *CQ Researcher* 3, no. 5 (February 5, 1993): 97–120.

Wycoff, Mary Ann. *The Role of Municipal Police Research as a Prelude to Changing It.* Washington, D.C.: Police Foundation, 1982.

———. "The Benefits of Community Policing: Evidence and Conjecture." In *Community Policing: Rhetoric or Reality,* ed. Jack R. Greene and Stephen D. Mastrofski. New York: Praeger, 1988, pp. 103–120.

Wycoff, Mary Ann, and Wesley G. Skogan. "The Effect of a Community Policing Management Style on Officers' Attitudes." *Crime and Delinquency* 40, no. 3 (July 1994a): 371–383.

Xu, Yili, Mora L. Fiedler, and Karl H. Flaming. "Discovering the Impact of Community Policing: The Broken Windows Thesis, Collective Efficacy, and Citizens' Judgment." *Journal of Research in Crime and Delinquency* 42, no. 2 (2005): 147–186.

Yates, Donald L., and Vijayan K. Pillai. "Attitudes toward Community Policing: A Causal Analysis." *Social Science Journal* 33, no. 2 (1996): 193–210.

Younce, Thomas C. " 'Broken Window' Stops Drug Sales." *Law and Order,* April 1992, pp. 67–70.

Zhao, J., M. Scheider, and Q. Thurman. "The Effect of Police Presence on Public Fear Reduction and Satisfaction: A Review of the Literature." *The Justice Professional* 15 (2002): 273–299.

Zhao, J. S., M. C. Scheider, and Q. Thurman. "A National Evaluation of the Effect of COPS Grants on Police Productivity (Arrests) 1995–1999." *Police Quarterly* 6, no. 4 (2003): 387–409.

Zhao, Jihong. *Why Police Organizations Change: A Study of Community-Oriented Policing.* Washington, D.C.: Police Executive Research Forum, 1996.

Zhao, Jihong, and Quint Thurman. *The Nature of Community Policing Innovations: Do the Ends Justify the Means?* Washington, D.C.: Police Executive Research Forum, 1996.

———. "Community Policing: Where Are We Now?" *Crime and Delinquency* 43, no. 3 (1997): 345–358.

Zhao, Jihong, Nicholas P. Lovrich, and Kelsey Gray. "Moving toward Community Policing: The Role of Postmaterialist Values in a Changing Police Profession." *American Journal of Police* 14, no. 3/4 (1995): 151–171.

Zhao, Jihong, Nicholas P. Lovrich, and Quint Thurman. "The Status of Community Policing in American Cities: Facilitators and Impediments Revisited." *Policing: An International Journal of Police Strategies and Management* 22, no. 1 (1999): 74–92.

Zhao, Jihong "Solomon," Ni He, and Nicholas P. Lovrich. "Community Policing: Did It Change the Basic Functions of Policing in the 1990s? A National Follow-Up Study." *Justice Quarterly* 20, no. 4 (2003): 697–724.

Zimmer, Lynn. "Proactive Policing against Street-Level Drug Trafficking." *American Journal of Police* 9 (1990): 43–65.

Index